THE FIRST WORLD WAR:
AN AGRARIAN INTERPRETATION

THE
FIRST WORLD WAR
AN AGRARIAN INTERPRETATION

AVNER OFFER

CLARENDON PRESS · OXFORD
1989

Oxford University Press, Walton Street, Oxford OX2 6DP
Oxford New York Toronto
Delhi Bombay Calcutta Madras Karachi
Petaling Jaya Singapore Hong Kong Tokyo
Nairobi Dar es Salaam Cape Town
Melbourne Auckland
and associated companies in
Berlin Ibadan

Oxford is a trade mark of Oxford University Press

Published in the United States
by Oxford University Press, New York

British Library Cataloguing in Publication Data
Offer, Avner
The First World War : an agrarian interpretation.
1. World War I. Economic aspects
I. Title   940.3'1
ISBN 0–19–821946–6

Library of Congress Cataloging in Publication Data
Offer, Avner.
The First World War, an agrarian interpretation / Avner Offer.
p.   cm.
Bibliography: p.   Includes index.
1. World War, 1914–1918—Economic aspects   2. World War,
1914–18—Causes.   3. Agriculture—Economic aspects—Europe—
History—20th century.   I. Title.
D635.038 1989   940.53'113—dc19
89–3190
CIP
ISBN 0–19–821946–6

Typeset by Pentacor Ltd, High Wycombe, Bucks

Printed and Bound in
Great Britain by Biddles Ltd,
Guildford and King's Lynn

For Leah

PREFACE

These pages provide some clues to the origins of the book, but mostly they are a thanks-offering to those who made it possible. Time is the human measure of value. For scholars, it measures the room for research, reflection and writing. I was fortunate in this respect. A research fellowship at the University of Southampton (1981–2) allowed me to make a start. A year at the Department of History, in the good company of Paul Smith and his colleagues, was devoted to Part Three, the book's archival core. It also allowed me to experience the Falklands campaign in a city which served as a port of embarkation for the troops. From 1985 to 1988 I was fortunate to obtain a fellowship at the Department of History, Research School of Social Science, Australian National University. In Canberra I found a combination of scholarly vitality, warm friendship and surroundings of great natural beauty. It gave me a peripheral view of the British Empire to complement the metropolitan one. The generosity of people at these two institutions was vital. I also spent a productive term at Clare Hall, Cambridge, and a few weeks at my old *Mater*, Merton College, Oxford. I am deeply grateful to colleagues in the Department of Economics, University of York, for granting extended periods of leave, and especially to Charles Feinstein, whose trust and support were crucial. Tony Culyer has also been most helpful. In Canberra Oliver MacDonagh and Ken Inglis gave more assistance than I ever hoped for.

Like time, travel is another expensive necessity, and this book required a great deal. I received small grants from the Social Science Research Council and the Hoover Presidential Library Association, and more ample support from the Australian National University. In these straitened times, however, a good deal has had to be self-financed. I would not have gone so far without friends who gave me homes away from home: in Cambridge, Tamy and Jay Winter and Jeremy Levin; in London, Roland Rosner, Meta Zimmeck, Doron and Smadar Lamm, Jeremy Levin, Mike Tintner and Jane Kirwan; in Oxford and Lexington, Ginny and Simon Schama; in Toronto, Julie and Harvey Silver; in San Francisco, Tsofia and Michael Katz; in Munich, Pat and Wolfgang Krieger.

My primary intellectual debt is to historians in five or six different historiographies. Despite much work in many archives this is primarily a work of new synthesis which depends on the labour of predecessors. This was not an arbitrary choice, but was dictated by the nature of the problem. War is often a failure of comprehension. Had the Germans tried harder to transcend their cultural horizons, they might have made better decisions. In consequence, a few parts of the story will be familiar to many readers, who may also notice errors of omission. But other parts are bound to be new and I hope that experts will find something to reflect upon even in their own special fields. I am well aware of the large gaps in my own knowledge.

Several cohorts of economic history students at York helped to shape the ideas in Part Two of the book. I have presented many papers at seminars, conferences and public lectures in Britain, Australia and the United States. The auditors have forced me to clarify my notions and made valuable suggestions and comments. I owe a lot to those who read parts of the book in draft or discussed it with me. If I have forgotten any of them, I hope to be forgiven. They include (in no particular order) A. Imhof, Klaus Loewald, Josh Getzler, Donald Denoon, Ken Inglis, Cameron Hazlehurst, John Eddy, Andrew Frazer, Stephen Wheatcroft, Carole Taylor, Noel Butlin, Kosmas Tshokas, Joy Damousi, John Shannon, Julian Thomas, Flora Gill, Iain McCalman, Shulamit Volkov, F. M. L. Thompson, Morton Rothstein, Doron Lamm, Alan Martin, Lyndal Roper, Amirah Inglis, Mary Mackinnon, Graeme Snooks, Geoffrey Brennan, Chris McGuffie, Jack Goldstone, Philip Pettit and Jonathan Pincus. Special thanks to those who read the whole penultimate draft at short notice. They are Jay Winter, James Walvin, F. B. Smith, Robert Allen and Joanna Bourke. Many of the readers have given a great deal of encouragement in addition to their counsel. Do not blame them for the faults.

Of the many libraries and archives I visited, the staff of the following helped beyond the call of duty: the Morrell Library, University of York, Churchill College, Cambridge, Agriculture Canada and the Public Archives of Canada in Ottawa, the Herbert Hoover Presidential Library at West Branch, Iowa, the Hoover Institution at Stanford and the Food Research Institute at the same University, which made me a gift of invaluable materials. Of great assistance were also the librarians of the Staats-und Universitätsbibliothek, Hamburg, the Staatsbibliothek in Munich, the National Archives in Washington, DC, the Naval Library at the Ministry of Defence, London, the inter-library loan department at the Menzies Library, Australian National University, and the National Library of Australia in Canberra. The Public Record Office in London was very good to work in. If only its hours were longer.

The conception of this book coincided with the birth of an electronic technology of writing. I climbed a ladder of dumb terminals and microcomputers, and learned a new system practically every year. One transition was only managed with the help of Claire Gildener, who copy-typed four chapters which a computer would not read from tape. My daughter Nogah transcribed hundreds of index cards on to floppy disk. Janice Aldridge and Anthea Bundock helped to compile the bibliography. Secretarial staffs at all my universities were unfailingly helpful. Hilary

Walford was an expert editor and adviser. I typed the text myself, with assistance from three American benefactors: Robert Barnaby, the man who wrote *Wordstar*, and Lee Felsenstein and Adam Osborne, idealistic designer and thwarted promoter respectively of the Osborne One computer. My latest marvel, the product of a giant Japanese corporation, does not carry any evidence of individual maternity/paternity.

The great reward in writing this book was the bounty of friendship conferred on me at every turn, especially in Southampton, in Canberra, and while travelling on research. When I set out on this quest, I had no expectation of so much kindness, congeniality and stimulation and it remains a treasured possession.

Gratitude to Leah, my wife, goes even deeper. Without getting involved in the details, she has increasingly influenced my values and judgements. Fortunately, this debt does not need to be communicated in print. Nevertheless, I would like to acknowledge it in the old-fashioned way and dedicate the book to her.

A decade or so spent as a farmer, soldier, public servant and student in Israel in the 1960s and early 1970s prepared me to perceive the agrarian, military and mental patterns of the Edwardian Empire. Those years also exposed me to some of the faces of war.

> Clouds float across my window
> In many towns, on many desks,
> then seasons, years—a decade yet?
> A mound of paper binds me in the net
> of puzzles that research might yet unravel
> and memories that I am ever striving to forget.

July 1988 A.O.

ACKNOWLEDGEMENTS

Ownership of copyright in unpublished documents quoted in this book is acknowledged as follows: Beaverbrook Foundation and Mr A. J. P. Taylor (Lloyd George Papers, House of Lords Records Office), the Controller of HMSO (Papers in Crown Copyright at the Public Record Office), National Maritime Museum (Corbett and Slade Papers), The Hoover Institution, The Hoover Presidential Library Association, The Public Archives of Canada (Mackenzie King, Borden and Lemieux Papers), The United States National Archives (for American official papers), The Master, Fellows and Scholars of Churchill College, Cambridge (Hankey and Fisher papers), Mrs Sheila Sokolov Grant (Grant Duff papers), Viscount Esher (Esher papers), National Library of Australia (Hughes papers). Chapters 15 and 21 incorporate material which first appeared in my article 'The Working Classes, British Naval Plans and the Coming of the Great War', *Past and Present: A Journal of Historical Studies* (May 1985) (World Copyright: The Past and Present Society, 175 Banbury Road, Oxford, England). Chapters 19 and 24 contain material which appeared in articles in the *Journal of Contemporary History*, vol. 23 (Jan. 1988) and in *Australian Economic History Review* vol. 24 (March 1989). I am grateful to the editors for permission to use this material, and to their referees for helpful comments. For permission to use illustrations I am grateful to the BBC Hulton picture library (plates 4–10). Plate no. 1 was kindly provided by Decie Denholm of the University of Adelaide, no. 2 is reprinted from the jacket of S. Roskill, *Hankey: Man of Secrets* (1974), vol. 1, with permission from Collins Harvill, No. 3 is taken from R. MacGregor Dawson, *William Lyon Mackenzie King: A Political Biography* (Toronto 1959), vol. 1, opp. p. 234, with permission from Toronto University Press. Fig. 26.1 is printed with permission from the Hoover Institution. My apologies to any owners of copyright whom I have inadvertently overlooked or have failed to trace.

CONTENTS

PLATES

(Between pp. 236 and 237)

1. Ethel Cooper (centre) in Leipzig, 1913,
   with the composer Sandor Vas (left) and another friend.
2. Captain Maurice Hankey, Royal Marines.
3. William Lyon Mackenzie King in Windsor uniform, 1910.
4. Admiral John Fisher, 1904.
5. Reginald, Second Viscount Esher.
6. Reginald McKenna, First Lord of the Admiralty, 1908–11.
7. Admiral Alfred von Tirpitz.
8. Robert L. Borden, Prime Minister of Canada, 1919.
9. Herbert Hoover.
10. William Morris Hughes,
    Prime Minister of Australia, 1919.

FIGURES

TABLES

ABBREVIATIONS

ADM	Admiralty (British)
Beilagen, Aktenstücke	Verfassunggebende Deutsche Nationalversammlung, *Beilagen zu den Stenographischen Berichten über die öffentlichen Verhandlungen des Untersuchungsausschusses. 2. Unterausschuss. Aktenstücke zur Friedensaktion Wilsons 1916/17* (Berlin 1920), pts. iv, v
ARA	American Relief Administration
CAB	Cabinet Papers, Public Record Office (UK)
CID	Committee of Imperial Defence (UK)
DNI	Director of Naval Intelligence
EP	Reginald, Second Viscount Esher Papers, Churchill College, Cambridge
FG	*Fear God and Dread Nought: The Correspondence of Admiral of the Fleet Lord Fisher of Kilverstone*, ed. A. J. Marder, (1952–9)
FO	Foreign Office (British)
FP	Admiral J. A. Fisher, Papers, Churchill College, Cambridge
Further Reports	Further Reports by British Officers on the Economic Conditions Prevailing in Germany, Mar. and Apr. 1919; PP 1919 Cmd. 208 LIII
GGG	*Grain Growers' Guide* (Winnipeg)
H. C. debs.	House of Commons debates (British)
HIA	Hoover Institution Archives, Stanford University
HP	Maurice Hankey Papers, Churchill College, Cambridge
HPL	Hoover Presidential Library, West Branch, Iowa
JRUSI	*Journal of the Royal United Services Institution*
KAKI	Kriegsausschuss für Konsumenten-Interessen
KD	William Lyon Mackenzie King, Diary of Mission to Great Britain, Mackenzie King Papers, Public Archives of Canada
LG	David Lloyd George Papers, House of Lords Record Office
M&D	B. R. Mitchell and P. Deane, *Abstract of British Historical Statistics* (Cambridge 1971)
MB	Monats-Berichte der Stellvetreter Generalkommandos, Bayerische Hauptstaatsarchiv, Dept. IV. Kriegsarchiv, Munich
NAR	*North American Review*
NID	Naval Intelligence Department (UK)
NLA	National Library of Australia, Canberra
NMM	National Maritime Museum

Officers' Reports	Reports by British Officers on the Economic Conditions Prevailing in Germany, Dec. 1918–Mar. 1919; PP 1919 Cmd. 52 LIII
PAC	Public Archives of Canada, Ottawa
PP	Parliamentary Papers (British)
PRO	Public Record Office (British)
Untersuchung	*Das Werk des Untersuchungsausschusses der Verfassunggebenden Deutschen Nationalversammlung und des Deutschen Reichstages 1919–1930*, 4th ser. (Berlin 1925ff.), 12 vols.
USDA	United States Department of Agriculture
USFA	United States Food Administration
USNA	United States National Archives
USNA, Admiralstab	Germany, Admiralstab der Marine, Akten betreffend Handelskrieg mit U-Booten, microfilm copies at United States National Archives
WO	War Office (British)

INTRODUCTION: ECONOMIC AND SOCIAL INTERPRETATION OF THE FIRST WORLD WAR

I

Summary

Here, in a few pages, is the gist of the book for readers in a hurry, but be warned—only the chapters that follow contain the whole story and every book says more than its author knows. Do not count on this summary alone. The First World War is often depicted as a great industrial war, fought by industrial methods. In fact, given a strong industrial capability on both sides, primary commodities were more decisive: food, industrial raw materials and that most primary of all commodities, people. Germany did not run out of rifles or shells. It suffered badly from shortages of food. Likewise the Allies: their agrarian resources decided the war. So not only a war of steel and gold, but a war of bread and potatoes.

In the late-Victorian period neither Britain nor Germany took their food exclusively from domestic sources. Their large town-dwelling populations specialized in manufacturing and services, and imported much of their staple agrarian requirements. New societies overseas began to specialize in supplying Europe with grain, wheat, timber, wool, cotton, metallic ores, fertilizers and other primary commodities. Diets changed in response. This process of international specialization also affected the strategic balance of power. The economies of both Britain and Germany came to depend on hundreds of merchant ships that entered their ports every month. Overseas resources, the security of the sea lanes and the economics of blockade affected the war plans of the great powers and influenced their decision to embark on war. The transoceanic societies of the United States, Canada and Australia helped to determine the fate of Europe: their role at the start of the war was largely passive but they took an active part in its prosecution and its outcomes.

Economists assume that people behave in a rational way. At first sight a disaster like war, especially on the scale of the First World War, is difficult to square with rationality. Nations may have passions as well as interests. This is not to embrace *irrationality* as an explanation but to consider what kinds of motivation lead to disaster. Economic factors do not declare war by themselves. They have to be perceived and acted upon. So motives are important: the motives of individuals acting in the mass, whether emigrating or enlisting, and also those of individual planners and decision-makers. This study stresses two empirical aspects of rational action. First, the pursuit of goals is affected by a number of regular, recurrent failings which are called, in short, "bounded rationality" and "intuitive reasoning". Second, economic advantage is often traded for social approbation. We may sacrifice our own ends to win the approval of others. These two aspects of rationality help us comprehend actions that might otherwise appear inexplicable.

The book falls into four parts. The first accounts for the defeat of Germany. The second describes the growth of the international agrarian economy before the war and the societies and resources that it created. The third describes how this affected British war plans in the Edwardian period and the British decision for war. The fourth is about German pre-war perceptions and preparations, the decision for war, the origins of the submarine campaign, and the way the war was wound up.

Part One. How was Germany defeated?

Was Germany defeated by blockade or by the land war? German scientists depicted the blockade as a domestic catastrophe but their accounts of famine suffer from serious biases. To understand the problems of food in wartime Germany we need to know about pre-war ideas of food reform and food science. The European diet was rich in fats and proteins. Food reformers asserted that this was excessive, while food scientists debated whether this was the case.

Did Germany really starve? Detailed studies suggest that, on average, food in Germany was sufficient most of the time to meet minimal nutritional requirements, but that consumers had to break the law in order to acquire a good part of what they ate. This, together with psychological deprivation, episodes of real deprivation, changes in diet and shortage of other consumer goods, gave rise to great mental fatigue. Food production and distribution were only established fully on a war footing in the third year of the war. After a serious food crisis in the winter of 1916–17 a combination of rationing and the black market achieved a precarious balance, that was still very stressful to the population. Food played a critical role in Germany's collapse. Civilian morale was deeply depressed and this affected military motivation. The army was also short of food at some important moments. After a military crisis in the summer of 1918, army resistance firmed up again in October, while civilian morale collapsed. When shooting ended, the war was not over and blockade remained in force.

Part Two. The Agrarian Bond: The United States, Canada and Australia

To see how Germany came to be exposed in this way, we need to shift our gaze to Britain. The roots of the wartime blockade go back to the repeal of the Corn Laws in mid-Victorian Britain, and to international specialization in agriculture. England became the workshop of the world, but also an economy whose imports exceeded its exports of goods by a large margin. Most of these imports were taken in food and in other primary commodities.

In order to purchase food overseas, England allowed its own agriculture to run down. The agricultural depression in Britain was not entirely a result of comparative disadvantage; it was also an outcome of social rigidities, a consequence of Britain's unique system of landownership. English farming had to support an excess of both riches and poverty. Britain's overseas agrarian competitors, both in continental Europe and on the grain and cattle frontiers of the new world, had more than economic advantage on their side. The rewards of farming overseas were social as well as material, often *more* social than material. They affected motivation, approbation, status. The same contrast, only more so, applied in Britain's towns. Some 5 per cent of the population left the United Kingdom for good during the Edwardian period. Urban working life in Britain was repressive and materially insecure. In contrast, the overseas economies, although far short of perfection, offered the prospect (often a delusive one) of dignity and comfort.

The economies of Canada, some United States regions, Argentina, New Zealand and Australia developed as suppliers of staple agrarian commodities. Their societies were split between the mercantile centres of population ("the coast") and the regions where staples were extracted or harvested ("the interior"). The interests of the coast tended to overshadow those of the interior and tied these staple-producing societies more closely to Britain. Canadian wheat production in the Edwardian decade created an interior society in response to overseas demand. It was progressive, productive and patriotic, and provided assets in manpower, productive capacity, financial credit and political goodwill for Britain.

The Pacific rim was the furthest away from Britain and yet it also formed strong metropolitan links through capital transfers, emigration, interior development and staple exports. To maintain their British self-identity, the white settlers resolved to exclude Asian migrants. Their motives combined economic protection, working-class aspirations for social equity, and racial animosity. The imperial bond was underpinned by racial exclusion. In the Edwardian period this brought the English-speaking Pacific nations into conflict with Japan, and with emerging nationalism in China and India.

Canada, Australia, the United States and New Zealand felt threatened by Asia. They developed an indigenous nationalism and began to arm. These assertions of independence exposed the weakness of local power and pushed these countries closer to the Empire. Resources mobilized in response to the Yellow Peril stood ready to join the struggle in Europe.

Part Three: The Atlantic Orientation

In Britain the decline of domestic agriculture gave rise to anxiety over the security of food supplies in time of war. Another fear was that shortages might fall short of starvation, but that domestic unrest would hamper the prosecution of war. From examining their own predicament, British planners reached the conclusion that Germany was even less secure and more exposed. It depended on overseas imports for a growing and vital part of its food and industrial raw materials. This inspired a planning effort to examine blockade as a decisive weapon in a coming war with Germany. The Admiralty undertook a series of economic studies of Germany. Evidence about this programme has been suppressed and concealed.

Naval officers perceived the Anglo-German conflict as a commercial struggle which might have to be decided by war. The navy's doctrine of economic warfare was endorsed in 1909 by an inquiry of the Committee of Imperial Defence, which included the Prime Minister, senior ministers, civil servants, naval and military officers. This endorsement formed one of the pillars of British strategy.

The main intellectual force behind the doctrine appears to have been Captain Maurice Hankey, acting in collusion with Admiral John ('Jacky') Fisher, Lord Esher and the First Lord of the Admiralty Reginald Mckenna. The essence of the doctrine was for Britain to face the Atlantic and not the Channel: to rely on overseas assets, to align with the Dominions and the United States, and to avoid a military commitment to Europe. This strategy was founded not only on a calculation of interest, but on a personal bond and a temperamental aversion to war on the part of its champions. Fisher's famous bellicosity was posture and bluff. The four hoped that the prospect of blockade might deter Germany from war. If this failed, they regarded economic warfare as the most effective use of British power.

The blockade raised serious difficulties of morality and international law. The Admiralty helped to negotiate a new law of the sea, with the deliberate intention of disregarding it in wartime. Hankey's blockade plan depended on enlisting the help of the Dominions. Canadian and Australian ministers were given a more detailed account of British strategy than the British cabinet ever received. This was part of a wider quest for Dominion help in resolving Britain's difficulties in the Edwardian period.

Both the Foreign Office and the War Office did not like the blockade plan, and commissioned their own economic studies of Germany. When Fisher left in 1910, the Admiralty abandoned its work on the plans and the focus of economic strategy shifted to the Committee of Imperial Defence. Fisher's successor Admiral Arthur Wilson did not believe in blockade as a decisive weapon, and this was the cause of his downfall in 1911.

As a secretary, then *the* secretary of the Committee of Imperial Defence, Hankey continued the research effort begun by the navy and did his best to promote the blockade strategy. Its substance was confirmed repeatedly by senior members of the cabinet. In August 1914 Britain was not attacked, but made a deliberate decision to enter the war. It was arguably Hankey's naval strategy that Sir Edward Grey presented to cabinet, and the one that the cabinet and the Prime Minister decided to follow. It was a strategy that stressed economic warfare, with a token military effort. It did not involve the mass commitment of manpower. What tilted the balance in favour of a large continental army was the massive enlistment, both in Britain and the Dominions. Pre-war fears about the loyalty of the working classes disappeared and the Dominion response also exceeded expectations. The existence of a colonial outlet for domestic discontents made Britain more plausible as a focus of loyalty.

Part Four. The Other Side of the North Sea

The process of urban and industrial development brought Germany into conflict with Britain in a number of different ways. Tariff protection was one response. The Tirpitz plan of naval construction, although often described as one of the causes of the war, was in many respects an appropriate policy, designed not to bring about war but to avoid it. It was undermined by the impulsive policy of the German government and army.

A number of government bodies and private individuals in Germany studied their country's exposure to blockade. Despite some controversy, the results were remarkably similar to British conclusions and showed a high level of risk. This result impressed the army's leaders, who concluded that a long defensive war was out of the question; it helped to incline them towards a massive attack on France, in the hope of achieving a rapid decision. The prospect of such an attack is what impelled Britain to prepare an expeditionary force.

The decision to start the unrestricted submarine campaign in 1917 was an attempt to turn the tables on the Allied blockade. The problem called for economic reasoning in wartime and involved a "second decision for war", this time with the United States. It turned the tide decisively against Germany and set the seal on its defeat. Although the German Admiralty went through the motions of rational analysis, the conceptual tools it actually applied were not appropriate. This episode forms a classic case of "intuitive reasoning".

The staple producers had an important role at the Versailles peace conference. Canada, although a leading supplier and combatant, did not pursue any particular claims, beyond asking for separate representation. Australia's Prime Minister Billy Hughes was the chief instigator of the massive demands for reparations. His motives had little to do with conditions in Europe and arose almost entirely from Australian considerations. Another important influence on the peace negotiations was Herbert Hoover, the American Food Administrator and Relief Commissioner, whose need to sell American farm surpluses was an important factor in American policy and diplomacy. Both reparations and the war-guilt clause, the most contentious elements of the peace treaty, were influenced by the agrarian interests of Australia and the United States.

The German people thought the armistice signified an end to the blockade. But the blockade continued for another five months and remained the only means of compelling Germany to accept Allied peace demands. The food situation was no worse than the year before. The government retained substantial military food reserves. Drift, lack of purpose and demoralization induced an atmosphere of hedonism and apathy in German society. The blockade also undermined Allied moral pretensions, and made it easier for the Germans to reject the verdict of the war.

To conclude, Britain's late-Victorian policy of free trade led to the Edwardian naval arms race and became a source of insecurity and instability. British naval hegemony, the condition of peace, was no longer tenable in a world of many workshops. Britain faced many challenges in the Edwardian period: from Japan, from the United States, from the Mediterranean. It chose a military approach only to the problem of Germany. The real assets of British security were the bonds and resources of the English-speaking world overseas: economic, social, political, sentimental, forming a complex but effective system of practical kinship. This formidable system failed to deter, because it was not sufficiently visible to Germany, whose view of the world was circumscribed and limited to Europe.

Hankey's and Fisher's "Atlantic orientation" is one of the deepest roots of the North Atlantic alliance, and remains an enduring foundation of British security. It also provided a modern precedent for selecting civilian societies as military targets; this was repeated during the Second World War and remains the basis of nuclear deterrence today.

Although this book gives primacy to economic and social factors, it is also concerned with the moral economy and especially the pursuit of dignity and approbation (two sides of the same coin) as a force in the Edwardian period, acting on immigration and enlistment at the mass level, and on political and military postures at the staff and leadership levels.

I *do not* claim that Britain initiated or started the war. For the war to happen, it was necessary for Germany to begin it. What I want to show is how economic and social conditions predisposed Britain to enter the war. These conditions were also a factor in German decisions.

I *do not* express an opinion on whether Britain was right to join the war. That decision was only the last in a sequence of preparations. Any other policy should have been considered well in advance. If there was failure, it was during those years, from 1906 onwards, and not on 3 August 1914.

There are several issues this book *does not* cover, because space and time are limited. It is primarily about the war between Germany and the English-speaking world and there is nothing about France, Russia, the Balkans or the Middle East. Without Anglo-American participation the war would have remained a European one, and not a world war. In tracing origins of the war I have considered the non-Anglo suppliers only briefly and there is little (apart from statistics and a few remarks) about Argentina, the Danube and Russia. India was a large pre-war grain exporter and its war effort was comparable in scale with that of the Dominions'. There is no space in this book to deal with India's role in the imperial economy, but India is discussed as a source of migrants and as a challenger of the racial monopoly on the Pacific rim. South Africa is also left out. In most respects it played the role of a minor "coast" society, but its domestic complexity was far in excess of its importance for my story. There is little here about the imperial movement in Britain before the war, and especially about tariff reform. Its leading adherents were out of office, and there is a large literature about them. There is not much about the military conduct of the war, or, more narrowly, on the blockade. The emphasis is on causes and effects, origins and outcomes. Finally, this book does not exclude other interpretations. It explores a dimension, a decisive one, which has not received the attention it deserves.

II

Other Writers

This work links with a tradition which seeks the origins of war in economic and social forces. It is a venerable tradition, but not a consistent one. This brief survey touches on some of the main issues, but is not meant to be comprehensive.[1]

---

[1] All books were published in London unless indicated otherwise.

Mercantilism

Mercantilists regarded military power as both a means and as an end of economic activity. Wars may be fought for economic advantage, for colonies and for markets, while economic policy strives (by accumulating population and treasure) to prepare for war. Writing about "power and plenty" as objectives of policy goes back to the seventeenth century and earlier, but the end of the nineteenth century is an adequate point of departure.[2] A new intellectual neo-mercantilism arose in Europe in the 1880s, together with the tariff barriers erected to defend the landowners and peasants against overseas grain. The pace-setters were Germans, whose Empire embraced industrial protection as well. Most German economists supported tariffs as an economic weapon and many of them also fell behind the fleet construction programme around the turn of the century.[3]

At a time when economics in Britain and the United States became more abstract, English-speaking mercantilists were historians rather than economists. In Britain the centre was at the newly-established London School of Economics, which was inspired by the work of academic social reformers (*Kathedersozialisten*) in Germany. The first head of the school, W. A. S. Hewins, was an historian of mercantilism and departed in 1903 to organize the Tariff Commission, a research and propaganda office for the protectionist movement. His successor was another ardent protectionist, the geographer Halford Mackinder, who regarded the Empire as a consequence of British economic power, and as a continuing source of wealth. Prosperity depended on a strong navy. 'A creditor nation cannot afford to be weak,' he wrote.[4]

The relation between power and plenty was more strongly stressed by the American naval officer Alfred Thayer Mahan, whose numerous works on sea-power in history insisted that naval supremacy was a condition of survival and prosperity.[5] Both Mackinder and Mahan were affected by current notions of Social Darwinism that regarded nations and especially races as engaged in a constant struggle in which only the "fittest" would survive.[6]

[2] Mercantilist theorists and their late-Victorian interpreters: J. Viner, 'Power versus Plenty as Objectives of Foreign Policy in the Seventeenth and Eighteenth Centuries', in his *The Long View and the Short* (Glencoe, Illinois 1958).

[3] G. Schmoller, M. Sering and A. Wagner (eds.), *Handels- und Machtpolitik* (Stuttgart 1900), 2 vols. The editors, who were full professors at the University of Berlin, were among the leading economists in Germany.

[4] H. J. Mackinder, *Britain and the British Seas* (Oxford 1906), p. 346; A. Offer, 'Using the Past in Britain: Retrospect and Prospect', *The Public Historian*, vol. 6 (1984), pp. 23–7.

[5] P. A. Crowl, 'Alfred Thayer Mahan: The Naval Historian' in Peter Paret *et al.* (eds.), *Makers of Modern Strategy* (Princeton 1986).

[6] e.g. A. T. Mahan, *The Problem of Asia and its Effect upon International Policies* (1900), pp. 97–9, 110–20; W. F. Parker, *Mackinder: Geography as Statecraft* (Oxford 1982), ch. 3, esp. p. 59.

Other officers writing before the First World War also depicted international relations (and sometimes domestic social relations as well) as a desperate struggle. Economics was a form of warfare. The titles of some of these works convey their urgent tone: *The Future Peace of the Anglo-Saxons*, *The Valor of Ignorance*, *The Struggle for Bread*.[7] Their theme was the need for strenuous social preparation for the struggles to come. A sober and valuable description of the commercial dimension of the Anglo-German conflict was published in 1933, but the theme has not been pursued much further.[8]

Imperialism

Late-Victorian critics of empire resembled the mercantilists in stressing the economic sources of war. Even so strong a moralist as the radical economist J. A. Hobson regarded war, in certain circumstances, as a productive investment:

A necessary or a useful war, economically conducted, might, at any rate from the standpoint of the nation, be regarded as a productive expenditure of capital, and this capital must be considered to survive in forms corresponding to good-will in a private business. Though much of this intangible national capital, consisting in liens upon certain trading advantages or other competitive gains, may be offset in the balance sheets of the world by corresponding losses of other nations, all cannot be written off in this fashion.[9]

The basic anti-imperial model may be found in Adam Smith: as trade and industry develop in the metropolis, wealth accumulates and the rate of interest goes down. In the colonies capital is more scarce and therefore more expensive. The imperial monopoly of colonial trade raises the profits of merchants even more. Capital leaves the metropolis prematurely to look for higher profits in the empire, to the detriment of the home economy.[10] While Smith taught that premature exports of capital were harmful, his disciple Edward Gibbon Wakefield regarded the export of both capital and people as a safety valve that saved metropolitan society from periodic crises of over-production. Karl Marx took up this notion and pointed out that the "overseas" world was already filling up, and that the crisis of capitalism could not be indefinitely postponed by means of emigration.

[7] S. L. Murray, *The Future Peace of the Anglo-Saxons: Addressed to the Working Men and their Representatives* (1905); Homer Lea, *The Valor of Ignorance* (New York 1909); "A Rifleman", *The Struggle for Bread* (1913).

[8] R. J. S. Hoffman, *Great Britain and the German Trade Rivalry, 1875–1914* (Philadelphia 1933); P. M. Kennedy, *The Rise of the Anglo-German Antagonism, 1860–1914* (1980), ch. 15; C. Buchheim, 'Aspects of XIXth Century Anglo-German Trade Rivalry Reconsidered', *Journal of European Economic History*, vol. 10 (1981).

[9] J. A. Hobson, *An Economic Interpretation of Investment* (1911), p. 22.

[10] Adam Smith, *An Inquiry into the Nature and Causes of the Wealth of Nations*, ed. Edwin Cannan (New York 1937), Bk. IV, ch. 3, pt. III, pp. 563–79.

The theme of the competition of capitalists for raw materials overseas as leading to war was developed by J. A. Hobson in his book *Imperialism*, in a response to the South African war at the turn of the century. Property-owners forsook investment at home in pursuit of higher profits in the empire. The competition of empires led to war. Lenin used similar notions to explain the nature of the First World War in his pamphlet *Imperialism, the Highest Stage of Capitalism* (1917). Both these books have had an enormous influence as accounts of imperial expansion in the late-Victorian period, but have carried less conviction as explanations of the First World War. Just *before* the First World War H. N. Brailsford published *The War of Steel and Gold*, which provided a standard "anti-imperial" explanation. He hoped that war in Europe could be avoided, but perceived dangers in the clash over investment opportunities and raw materials in the colonies, and over access to the undersettled and empty tracts of the world. War was an expression of conflicts arising from the process of economic develop-ment and growth, its agents were capitalist entrepreneurs, seeking outlets for investment in primary commodities overseas, or in the manufacture and sale of armaments at home. Investors, bankers, soldiers, diplomats and statesmen acted as agents, in their pursuit of wealth, power and influence. This line was also pursued after the war, with inconclusive results, by P. T. Moon and Eugene Staley.[11]

War does not pay

Both the "mercantilists" and the anti-imperialists accepted that war might be worthwhile for the winners at least, or for overseas investors, the 'economic parasites of imperialism'.[12] Another strand of opinion, which partly overlapped with the anti-imperialists, included writers who regarded war as counter-productive and futile from an economic point of view. Adam Smith condemned imperial wars because he saw them as protecting inefficient monopolies of colonial trade.[13] The doctrine of free trade, which dominated English opinion in the nineteenth century, was posited on peace—although its supporters sometimes also insisted on British naval supremacy.

One book stands out from all the writings on war and economics. It was written by Ivan Bloch, 'one of the leading figures in the world of Russian business and finance',[14] who published it in six volumes as *The War of the*

[11] E. G. Wakefield, *A View of the Art of Colonization* (1849), letters 12–14; K. Marx, *Capital* (Moscow 1954), vol. 1, ch. 33; J. A. Hobson, *Imperialism: A Study* (1902), pt. 1; V. I. Lenin, *Imperialism, the Highest Stage of Capitalism* (1917), English trans. in *Selected Works in Three Volumes* (Moscow 1975), vol. 1; H. N. Brailsford, *The War of Steel and Gold* (1914); P. T. Moon, *Imperialism and World Politics* (New York 1927); E. Staley, *War and the Private Investor* (Chicago 1935).
[12] Hobson, *Imperialism*, ch. 4.
[13] Smith, *Wealth of Nations*, pp. 580–1.
[14] M. Howard, 'Men against Fire: Expectations of War in 1914', *International Security*, vol. 9 (1984).

Future (St Petersburg 1898). Its foresight is astonishing. Bloch argued that rapid, accurate and long-range weapons had given a decisive advantage to the defence. In the war of the future, the deadly accurate fire of infantry and artillery would make it impossible for attackers to come to grips with the defenders. Instead, opposing armies would dig into the ground and become deadlocked in stalemate, not for weeks or months, but for years. All fit men would be sucked into the struggle, all resources mobilized to support them. Once deadlock had set in, war would become a struggle of endurance between civilian populations and a test of economic capacity. But modern economies were no longer self-sufficient. Britain and Germany in particular depended on seaborne food imports. 'In short,' Bloch said, 'I regard the economic factor as the dominant and decisive element in the matter. You cannot fight unless you can eat, and at the present moment you cannot feed your people and wage a great war.'[15]

In a desperate war for survival, civilized warfare would go by the board: 'cruisers and torpedo boats . . . [will] pursue merchant ships, fall on them by night and sink them, with passengers, crews and cargoes, with the object of cutting the communications and paralysing the trade of the enemy.'[16] 'How long do you think your social fabric will remain stable under such circumstances?' asked Bloch. 'The more the ultimate political and social consequences of the modern war are calmly contemplated, the more clearly will it be evident that if war is possible it is only possible . . . at the price of suicide.'[17]

Many themes of the present book are prefigured in Bloch's work, especially that food supply and civilian morale would become decisive in a state of strategic deadlock. It raises some intriguing questions about the role of knowledge and understanding in human affairs. For Bloch to be proved right, his book had to be ignored. There is a fatalistic strain in the book, an acceptance that knowledge *cannot* alter the inevitable course of events. The lesson would have to be learned not from books, but on the battlefields. Bloch even had an inkling of the nuclear impasse when he predicted that, for war to end, it was necessary to have pushbutton weapons of total annihilation.[18]

Bloch was not exactly neglected. His work was quickly translated into French, German and English. In Britain it was promoted by W. T. Stead, one of the most effective journalists of the day. Bloch himself understood why his warning was unlikely to have an impact. It threatened the vested interests of the military profession and, more profoundly, it clashed with a

---

[15] I. S. Bloch, *Is War Now Impossible?*, being an abridgement of *The War of the Future in its Technical, Economic and Political Relationships* (1899), pp. lx–lxi (in an interview with W. T. Stead).
[16] Ibid., p. 109.
[17] Ibid., p. 1.
[18] Ibid., p. xv. He attributed the idea to Rudyard Kipling and Bulwer Lytton.

congenital unwillingness to face unpleasant truths, even at the cost of survival. 'War once being regarded as unavoidable, the rulers shut their eyes to its consequences.' We shall see how this psychological defence is deeply entrenched in policy-making, often with disastrous consequences.[19]

It was difficult for contemporaries to choose from all the apocalypses on offer the one that actually corresponded most closely to the truth.[20] That said, it is intriguing to speculate whether Bloch's vision remained totally without effect. Stead, Bloch's promoter in England, was an intimate friend of Admiral 'Jacky' Fisher, who commanded the British navy between 1904 and 1910. Fisher's plans for economic warfare (which are the subject of Part Three) were in accord with the spirit of Bloch's ideas, but I have not found a document to link the two.

Bloch regarded war, in contemporary conditions, as deeply irrational. This theme was taken up with great effect by a writer best known by his pen-name Norman Angell. Angell's book *The Great Illusion* (1910) quickly became an international best seller. Like Bloch, Angell did not argue that war was impossible, only that it was irrational. Economic activity, he argued, depended on an international web of credit and trade, which would be disrupted by war. Modern war itself was bound to consume resources on a massive scale, and the victors would have no means of realizing their gains and of transferring real wealth from the vanquished. Mercantilist war was an illusion.

Unreason

It is only a short step to the argument that war, and especially the First World War, was a manifestation of *unreason*—whether as a survival of obsolete bellicose social traditions, an expression of psychological disorders or a consequence of plain stupidity.[21] These approaches are often convincing but they largely fall outside the scope of a social and economic study. Nevertheless, they will surface repeatedly in the course of the book.

Social Pre-emption

Joseph Schumpeter's focus on "pre-modern" bellicose traditions in Europe's élites acquired a new life in the 1960s and the 1970s.[22] Fritz Fischer and his followers depicted the war as an outcome of the German Empire's uneven process of social development, in which an élite based on the gentry strove to retain control of a powerful urban economy. The

---

[19] Ibid., p. xlviii; D. Goleman, *Vital Lies, Simple Truths: The Psychology of Self-deception* (New York 1985); N. Dixon, *Our Own Worst Enemy* (1987), chs. 3–4.

[20] I. F. Clarke, *Voices Prophesying War, 1763–1984* (1966), chs. 3–4.

[21] J. Schumpeter, *Imperialism and Social Classes* (New York 1951); C. E. Playne, *The Neuroses of Nations* (New York 1925); B. Tuchman, *The March of Folly* (1984); Dixon, *Our Worst Enemy*.

[22] Schumpeter, *Imperialism*.

construction of Germany's High Seas Fleet, the plans for war and war aims were all designed to pre-empt the necessary social changes and to preserve the landed–bureaucratic–military élites.[23]

Analytical School

The pursuit of causes of war, and especially economic causes, has also taken a more analytical turn. Typically this has involved collecting data on a large number of armed conflicts and identifying regularities. Lewis F. Richardson, a mathematician, collected data about more than three hundred wars between 1820 and 1949, and arrived at a variety of fascinating conclusions. One of them was that, of eighty-three major wars during this period, fifty-eight had at least one direct economic cause.[24]

Richardson's method was to identify variables that were highly correlated with armed conflict, without attempting to work out the causal mechanisms. Similar notions are scattered throughout Quincy Wright's massive *A Study of War*.[25]

Two recent studies demonstrate opposite approaches to the quantitative analysis of war. The first is macroeconomic, regarding war as the unintended consequence of economic change, while the second is microeconomic, taking warriors as economic men who act rationally to achieve the best outcomes. The first may be described as "deterministic", while the second stresses calculation and free choice. Choucri and North have found that domestic growth (i.e. population density and income per head) was a strong predictor of territorial expansion between 1870 and 1914. They explored the correlations between territorial expansion, colonial conflicts, military expenditure, the number of alliances and "violence behaviour". Like the anti-imperialists, they suggest (without pressing the point too strongly) that the mere process of expansion gave rise to war.[26]

A diametrically opposite approach is taken by Bueno de Mesquita.[27] His model posits free will rather than determinism: he regards war as an act of calculating rationality. As proof of this, almost three quarters of the wars in a large sample were "won" by the side that "initiated combat", much more than would be expected if the prospects of victory were random. Bueno de Mesquita harks back to the mercantilists in assuming that war is

---

[23] J. A. Moses, *The Politics of Illusion: The Fischer Controversy in German Historiography* (1975); V. R. Berghahn, *Germany and the Approach of War in 1914* (1973), pp. 211–14; also A. J. Mayer, *The Persistence of the Old Regime: Europe to the Great War* (1981).

[24] L. F. Richardson, *Statistics of Deadly Quarrels* (1960), p. 210.

[25] Q. Wright, *A Study of War* (Chicago 1942), 2 vols. A similarly impressionistic and very acute study based on a large number of wars is G. Blainey, *The Causes of War* (Melbourne 1977).

[26] N. Choucri and R. C. North, *Nations in Conflict: National Growth and International Violence* (San Francisco 1975).

[27] B. Bueno de Mesquita, *The War Trap* (New Haven 1981).

a game worth playing and winning. But the First World War only makes a token appearance in his samples, as a conflict between Austria and Serbia, which Serbia "wins". This neglect of the First World War casts doubts on the sample. There are other difficulties as well. Since Mesquita chose not to apply his model to my war I have not done so either.

Strategy and Politics

Writing on the origins of the First World War is dominated by diplomatic, political and military history of the traditional kind, based on a close reading of documents. It has stressed such factors as national rivalry, arms races, the formation of alliances and calculations of the balance of power. Another strand of historical writing has stressed military preparation, whether through arms races, rigid mobilization plans or the cultivation of an aggressive mentality.[28]

Writers in the strategic–diplomatic tradition also acknowledge the economic dimension. 'The most profound cause [of the Anglo-German rivalry] was *economic*,' writes its leading historian.[29]

My own book is not an overarching theory of war, but an historian's attempt to describe and explain just one war. It is primarily an *economic* explanation, but it is not about trade rivalry, colonies, bankers or the Baghdad Railway. My main contribution is to evoke the elaborate international economic and social systems by which Britain and Germany were provided with food, fats, fibres and other vital primary raw materials and to show how crucial they were for the origins, conduct and outcome of the war.

III

Economic Interpretation of War

War and Rationality

For a person of liberal temperament, the First World War is the origin of our century's woes. Before 1914 each of the great countries of the west was making good progress. For all their deep flaws, the societies of Germany, France, Britain, the United States, Canada and Australia moved towards greater social and political equity. In the Edwardian period, it is true, they were rent by deep divisions. Partly this was an outcome of the rise in food prices, which held down the workers' standard of living. Domestic conflict

---

[28] A recent survey is J. Joll, *The Origins of the First World War* (1984); the militarization of Europe and the cult of the offensive: Howard, 'Men against Fire', and S. Van Evera, 'The Cult of the Offensive and the Origins of the First World War', *International Security*, vol. 9 (1984).

[29] Kennedy, *Anglo-German Antagonism*, p. 464; also his 'The First World War and the International Power System', *International Security*, vol. 9 (1984).

was mostly about a share in the common wealth and a place in the "Commonwealth". Labour movements, women's movements, subordinate nationalities within the European empires, all seemed to be moving towards fuller participation in the national or international community. The First World War fulfilled this agenda of inclusion sooner than anyone had hoped or feared. Women got the vote, Labour entered governments, Ireland, Poland and Bohemia achieved independence, but the cost in destruction, suffering and death made the hopes look hollow.

This confutation of Edwardian hopes is a great turning-point of the twentieth century. Can it be squared with liberal values? These values avow the primacy of reason—and what is more rational than economic theory? "Rationality" has been very influential in the social sciences for about two decades now. In various formulations it is the dominant mindset of our time, in the west at any rate. Can it indicate where the war came from, and why? What is an *economic* interpretation of the First World War? There are two possible approaches. One is to regard the war as a problem of management, to consider the endowment of population, skills, capital, and natural resources, and how it affected the preparations for, the conduct and the outcome of the war. That, in the main, is the road I have followed. Another is to seek for patterns of rationality in the planning, conduct and conclusion of the war. But rationality is a slippery concept. At this point, readers impatient to get on with the story are invited to proceed directly to Chapter 1 and to skip the pages which follow, which consider some of the links between war and rationality. They may wish to come back later.

Rationality does not exclude unfavourable outcomes, but the notion of rationality does at least imply desirable ones. Most of the states that participated in the First World War came out of it much worse than they entered. The war is difficult to reconcile with the benign action of an "invisible hand". Such a costly war was surely not the intent of a kindly providence. On the other hand the assumption of *irrationality* does not take us very far, since it places motives and actions outside the realm of explanation. There are several ways of reconciling reason and war.

To begin with, the initial conditions specified by economic theory for equilibrium (such as perfect competition, perfect knowledge, etc.) are rarely met, so outcomes are less than perfect as well. One way to account for war within the framework of rationality is the game-theory device of "prisoner's dilemma", which shows how two (or many) individuals each pursuing his or her own utility can still arrive at an aggregate outcome that is manifestly bad. This outcome is especially likely when they act purely as individuals, with no trust or collusion.[30] Prisoner's dilemma brings us

[30] R. Axelrod, *The Evolution of Co-operation* (New York 1984).

closer to reality. Rationality does not always deliver the best outcome—it can produce just about *any* outcome. Prisoner's dilemma suggests that unbridled individualism can be self-defeating, and that acceptable outcomes require a supplement to the market. One option is a governance structure to coerce individuals or to "rig" the markets. This is what happens *inside* a corporate firm, a bureaucracy or an army. The other alternative is co-operation and mutual trust.[31]

In practice individuals are constrained by a framework of institutions, by their upbringing, their social position, their limitations as rational beings. A great deal will be said in this book about historical and institutional determinants. The rest of this section will consider individual limitations. However self-defeating human action may be, it is not random. Self-defeating action also has an underlying coherence. Often the means are well chosen, but the ends are inappropriate.

One of the restrictions on rational action may be called "bounded rationality". Even if we do pursue utility with a single mind, that mind is not very well adapted to the pursuit. Our will is not effected by an "invisible hand" but by a "trembling hand". Our mental equipment is not up to the computational requirements of perfect rationality and fails in a number of predictable ways. We may be rational calculators, but very imperfect ones. We are prone to error.

Another aspect of rational action is contained in the concept of "approbation". Individuals value the welfare and the good opinion of others as part of their own well-being. In the words of Adam Smith, 'However selfish soever man may be supposed, there are evidently some principles in his nature, which interest him in the fortunes of others.'[32] In other words, the rational individual is not necessarily egotistical.

Bounded Rationality, Intuitive Reasoning

Economic explanation does not normally consider the behaviour of named individuals, but in war individuals are often crucial. Rationality is efficiency—a choice of the best means to achieve given ends. In order to make rational decisions it is necessary to collect information and choose a course of action. Such a process can be modelled, and, given a goal, sufficient information and a selection of proven methods, it ought to be possible to specify the best course of action. This optimal procedure may be called "formal reasoning". In practice decision-makers often fall short of this ideal, both for good reasons and for bad. Instead they apply a

---

[31] Coercion: G. Brennan and G. Tullock's suggestive 'An Economic Theory of Military Tactics: Methodological Individualism at War', *Journal of Economic Behavior and Organizations*, vol. 3 (1983); co-operation: Axelrod, *Evolution*.

[32] Adam Smith, *A Theory of Moral Sentiments*, ed. D. D. Raphael and A. L. Macfie (Oxford 1976), p. 9.

"bounded rationality" (I shall also use the cognate term "imperfect calculation"). Economists have pointed out some of the reasons why.[33]

1. Most practical projects are simply beyond our capacity to compute. As Herbert Simon puts it, 'For most problems that Man encounters in the real world, no procedure that he can carry out with his information processing equipment will enable him to discover the optimal solution, even when the notion of "optimum" is well defined.'[34]

2. Uncalculating mental states get in the way: emotion, drive, instinct and impulse. Such responses belong to the world of action, even economic action; they are acknowledged by advertising in peacetime and propaganda in war.

3. Knowledge is almost always incomplete. There are not enough data available, and our command of rational procedures is imperfect.

4. People differ in their attitudes to uncertainty and risk. Some seek to avoid risk, others relish it.

5. Delay can alter the nature of problems between the time they are perceived and the time they are tackled.

6. There is uncertainty about the behaviour of others, both allies and opponents.

7. Goals are not always well formulated; indeed there may not be a single unique rational solution to a problem.

A good deal of empirical research in social psychology has shown that there is an "intuitive reasoning" which deviates in a *persistent and predictable* way from "formal reasoning". Such deviations pervade the world of action and form an important reason why things do not turn out the way they are meant to.[35] Here are some of the most pervasive pitfalls of intuitive reasoning, with examples taken from the German submarine campaign against Britain, which also forms the subject of Chapter 24. Similar biases will also be manifest in other episodes described in the book.

1. Availability. The methods chosen are those that happen to be available and familiar, not those most suitable to the task: an economist prefers to apply economic theory, a soldier military force, etc. When you possess a hammer, what you see is nails. One persistent error is to use theories outside their domain of application. Data are also selected from

---

[33] The term "bounded rationality" was introduced by Herbert Simon. I have drawn here on L. Ermini, 'A Survey of Recent Contributions to the Criticism of Classical Rationality' (unpublished paper, University of California at San Diego 1986), H. Simon, *Models of Bounded Rationality* (Cambridge, Mass. 1982), vol. 2, and A. Sen, *On Ethics and Economics* (Oxford 1987). All three works contain extensive bibliographies.

[34] Simon, *Bounded Rationality*, vol. 2, p. 430.

[35] What follows draws mainly upon R. Nisbett and L. Ross, *Human Inference: Strategies and Shortcomings of Social Judgement* (Englewood Cliffs, N. J. 1980).

those that happen to be available: the British Admiralty overestimated the difficulty of convoy because its data did not discriminate between different kinds of traffic in the ports, and greatly magnified the number of seagoing steamers that had to be escorted.

2. Analogy. Objects are assigned to the category they resemble. For example, great events must have great causes; military problems call for military solutions.

3. Vividness. Vivid data are preferred to "boring" ones. 'The death of a single Russian soldier is a tragedy. A million deaths is a statistic'(Stalin).[36] Notorious sinkings like that of the *Lusitania* had an effect which the cumulative damage of merchant ship sinkings did not.

4. Persistence. Once formulated and adopted, theories and beliefs are held tenaciously, even in the face of strong evidence to the contrary. We unconsciously prefer confirming evidence and neglect disconfirming information. The British Admiralty continued to resist the convoy system for merchant shipping, even when it employed it successfully for troop ships.

5. There is a tendency to attribute behaviour to dispositions rather than situations. The German decision for unrestricted submarine warfare is depicted as a symptom of military stupidity, and not as a coherent response to a desperate predicament.

6. There is a whole sequence of failings to make proper inferences from quantitative data and from probabilities. People have a very dim notion of what constitutes a proper sample and how it relates to a population, they find it difficult to identify correlations between variables, and they do not sufficiently recognize that exceptional events will normally be followed by more familiar ones ("regression to the mean").[37]

7. People have misplaced confidence in their own judgement, their own capabilities and their own luck. This is especially common among military leaders. Hence the unreasonable confidence of German naval leaders in the prospects of their submarine strategy.

8. People rarely have a good understanding of their own motives.

Instead of maximizing, people make do. Decision-makers fall back on intuitions and rules of thumb. Outcomes fall well short of the best ones attainable in principle. Instead of collecting data, analysing according to the best statistical procedures, and making an orderly assessment of

---

[36] Nisbett and Ross, *Human Inference*, p. 43.

[37] D. Kahneman, P. Slovik, and A. Tversky (eds.), *Judgement under Uncertainty: Heuristics and Biases* (Cambridge 1982), especially the classic articles by Kahneman and Tversky.

possible action, decision-makers take short cuts. They seek a good alternative rather than the best one; they rely on experience they have accumulated and do not seek new information. Nevertheless, a great deal turns out all right. Not knowing what the best might be, we are satisfied with the good. The adversary is equally hampered. Given the complexity of many problems, intuitive reasoning is economical. My own work is riddled with it. In certain conditions it can be shown to be more efficient, that is more rational, than formal reasoning.[38]

These considerations apply to our story. At every level—the leaders, the planners, the led; the worker, the farmer and the migrant; the admiral and the statesman—all confronted vast problems with imperfect equipment. If things went wrong (as they often did), it is worth considering whether and how failures of reasoning were implicated.

Approbation and Novelty

There are, however, cases where individuals seem to act deliberately against their best interests. Voluntary enlistment in the First World War persisted in Britain and the Dominions into 1916, and in Australia to the end of the war, and into the next world war as well. Now some of the motives for enlistment do fall under bounded rationality or intuitive reasoning. The rewards were magnified, the risks derided. But voluntary self-sacrifice in wartime is common enough, even when the risks are perfectly understood. Likewise the actions of landowners and farmers in Britain and overseas in the late-Victorian period (discussed in Chapters 6–8), which may appear counter-productive, point to a wider conception of utility than the purely material. Adam Smith has cogently expressed the way in which we depend on others: 'What are the advantages which we propose by that great purpose of human life which we call bettering our condition? To be observed, to be attended to, to be taken notice of with sympathy, complacency and approbation, are all the advantages which we can propose to derive from it.'[39]

If self-esteem is our main asset, then the approbation of others is vital. Often in this book, when people appear to act against their interests as individuals, or in ways which interfere with the attainment of their goals, the root of the matter may be something they value more: the good opinion of others. Sometimes this "other" is a voice within, what Smith called 'the impartial spectator'.

Finally, when people act with insufficient regard for the consequences, the motive is sometimes *boredom*. At the individual level, both migration and enlistment, when unaccompanied by any obvious benefit, may be

---

[38] Nisbett and Ross, *Human Inference*, ch. 11.
[39] Smith, *Moral Sentiments*, p. 50.

partly ascribed to the pursuit of stimulation and novelty. At the level of policy and decision-making, some minds cannot tolerate inaction.[40]

Where does that leave an *economic* interpretation of the First World War? Economic factors are important. Land, productive equipment, population, finance, the detail and sum of productive resources, define the possibilities and the opportunities for individuals and statesmen alike. But economic factors require human agency. They do not declare war on their own. The human machine has some regular attributes, but man does not read signals automatically. She or he filters them through preconceptions and needs. How far are those reactions predictable, consistent, rational? Goals are mediated by society and by personality. Economic history is inseparable from social history, and from history in general—the development of institutions and culture. Personality also counts: it affects reasoning and the attitude to risk, which are an expression partly of temperament, partly of social conventions and culture. Economic constraints and social perceptions sometimes leave little room for choice. But each mix of pre-conditions and personalities is unique—and chance, which places particular individuals in particular situations, also has a role to play.

At its best, traditional narrative history understands this already. But every historian still has to rediscover it anew, and find a new way of saying it.[41] The concepts of bounded rationality, intuitive reasoning and approbation are just that—concepts, not a rigorous theory. They can help us to form a realistic conception of how people actually perceived and pursued their interests.

[40] T. Scitovsky, *The Joyless Economy* (New York 1976), passim; Dixon, *Our Worst Enemy*, ch. 13.
[41] e.g. Tuchman, *March of Folly*, ch. 1.

Part One

HOW WAS GERMANY DEFEATED?

1

SOCIETY UNDER SIEGE: GERMANY, 1914–1918

I

Brigadier-General H. C. Rees emerged from the prisoner-of-war camp at
Bad-Colberg, Saxe Meiningen, on 12 December 1918 and reported to
London on his first impressions.

Germany appears to be completely beaten and disorganized; further hostilities on
any appreciable scale are most improbable. The German people are, in my
opinion, fully aware of this fact and accept it as a lesser evil than the continuance of
the war . . . The nation as a whole is on the verge of starvation. . . . Owing to the
lack of raw materials, industry is nearly at a standstill, and the thousands of men
now disbanded will not be able to find work.[1]

Like an invisible net, the problems of food supply entangled German
society and its leadership until the war effort became difficult, then
impossible, to sustain. Germany was not starved into defeat—nor, for that
matter, was it decisively beaten on the battlefield. Its downfall was
ultimately a matter of economic inferiority. The problems of food were
crucial. They affected the course and the climax of the war in a number of
ways and also helped to shape the subsequent peace.

   Why concentrate on food? Germany's economy was one of the most
advanced, the most specialized, the most industrialized and urbanized in
the world, and its total output was second only to that of the United States.
It formed a complex web in which a large variety of inputs produced an
even greater variety of goods and services. Yet the German economy in
wartime was flexible enough to produce the munitions and maintain the
armies in the field. Germany managed to produce most of the industrial
demands of the war but failed to secure a sufficiency of food.

   For a closed economy, food presents a special difficulty, even if the
economy is as flexible and advanced as Germany's was. The demand for
food is not very elastic. One food can replace another, but the human body
must have a minimal level of nutrition in order to function. Consequently,
food supply tied up a great deal of resources which could not be used
elsewhere. Unlike other industries, food production could not be turned
off for the duration but had to go on at full cock. Secondly, food could not
be stockpiled for very long. For most foods the cycle of production was a
year or less, and most food was consumed within one cycle. Only small
stocks were carried over from one year to the next. Most livestock products

[1] Officers' Reports, p. 4.

spoiled quickly if they were not tinned, salted or frozen. Grain also needed careful storage and deteriorated over long periods. The stocks required were physically large and were costly to store and to finance. Fruit and vegetables, as well as potatoes, were very bulky per unit of nutrition and spoiled quickly. All sectors of economy and society (including the military) depended on food. Every single person consumed it every single day. Food was by far the largest outlay of the vast bulk of the population, amounting to more than 50 per cent of expenditure in working-class households.[2] No activity, no individual remained unaffected by the performance of the food sector. Of all commodities, food gave rise to the greatest discontent, and emerged as the war economy's weakest link.

Little is known about the actual quantities of food available in Germany during the war. The first official and semi-official accounts were published soon after the armistice, when the food blockade was still in force. Those who drew up these accounts were still hungry themselves and depicted the food situation in the darkest colours in order to extract concessions from the Allies.[3] British and American observers also reported during the winter of 1918–19. Although somewhat more detached, they relied on German experts and on official data.[4] In the 1920s the Carnegie Endowment for International Peace commissioned several studies and its publications contain a great deal of information.[5] Diaries, letters and memoirs which mentioned food conditions began to appear even before the war was over, and new ones still turn up.[6] Finally, many local and regional studies of civilian experience during the war have appeared in Germany during the last two decades, but they have not seriously altered the picture already formed in the 1920s.[7]

[2] A. V. Desai, *Real Wages in Germany, 1871–1913* (Oxford 1968), p. 22.

[3] 'Schädigung der deutschen Volkskraft durch die völkerrechtswidrige feindliche Handels-blockade', Denkschrift des Reichsgesundheitsamts vom 16. Dez. 1918, *Untersuchung*, 4th ser., vol. 6, pp. 387–442; *The Starving of Germany*, papers read at an Extraordinary Meeting of United Medical Societies held at Headquarters of Berlin Medical Society, 18 Dec. 1918 (Berlin 1919); M. Rubmann (ed.), *Hunger! Wirkungen moderner Kriegsmethoden* (Berlin 1919) (also in English).

[4] A. E. Taylor and V. L. Kellogg, *German Food and Trade Conditions*, ARA Bulletin no. 1 (New York 1919); E. Starling, 'Report on Food Conditions in Germany', PP 1919 Cmd. 280 LIII; E. Starling, 'The Food Supply of Germany during the War', *Journal of the Royal Statistical Society*, vol. 83 (1920); also ch. 26 below.

[5] F. Aereboe, *Der Einfluss des Krieges auf die landwirtschaftliche Produktion in Deutschland* (Stuttgart 1927); F. Bumm (ed.), *Deutschlands Gesundheitsverhältnisse unter dem Einfluss des Weltkrieges* (Stuttgart 1928), 2 vols.; R. Meerwarth, A. Günther and W. Zimmerman, *Die Einwirkung des Krieges auf Bevölkerungsbewegung, Einkommen und Lebenshaltung in Deutschland* (Stuttgart 1932); E. Skalweit, *Die Deutsche Kriegsernährungs-wirtschaft* (Stuttgart 1927).

[6] e.g. Evelyn, Princess Blücher, *An English Wife in Berlin* (1920); C. E. Cooper, *Behind the Lines: One Woman's War, 1914–18*, ed. D. Denholm (1982).

[7] e.g. K.-L. Ay, *Die Entstehung einer Revolution. Die Volksstimmung in Bayern während des Ersten Weltkrieges* (Berlin 1968); G. Mai, *Kriegswirtschaft und Arbeiterbewegung in Württemberg, 1914–1918* (Stuttgart 1983); V. Ullrich, *Kriegsalltag. Hamburg im ersten Weltkrieg* (Cologne 1982); J. P. Bott, 'The German Food Crisis of World War I: The Cases of

II

A group of academic experts and officials (the Eltzbacher commission) began an urgent study of Germany's food situation almost as soon as the guns began to fire. By the time the boffins reported in December 1914 it was clear that nobody would be home for Christmas, and that food might be critical for Germany's success. The commission's task was to determine pre-war consumption levels and the scale of wartime requirements. The study was clouded by statistical, scientific and practical uncertainties. In outline at least the magnitude of the task was clear. About 19 per cent of the calories consumed in Germany came from abroad. For protein the ratio was higher, at 27 per cent, and for fats it was 42 per cent. Under wartime conditions of production, the deficit would be even greater: a quarter of the calories and a third of the protein. Serious as this outlook was, the commission had to put on a brave face. The food available, it said, although far short of peacetime consumption, still stood somewhat above the standard of physiological necessity and pre-war consumption contained a great deal of waste. The problem might be difficult but not desperate. With appropriate measures of economy and substitution, about 90 per cent of the pre-war calories would be available and about 87 per cent of the protein.[8]

The crux of the problem was the balance between arable and livestock production. Animals use grain inefficiently. According to German data, a pound of beef contained only 12–20 per cent of the calories and protein that produced it; for pigs the figure was 15–25 per cent for protein, and 35–45 per cent of the calories. In the United States, at the same time, 1,000 calories in beef cost more than six times as much as the same calories in wheat flour, and protein cost 2.5–3.5 times as much.[9]

After spending the summer of 1916 in Germany, an American physiologist wrote: 'Had the Germans been vegetarians, there would have been no problem. To the people of India, the ratio of grain to population would have constituted luxury. For people accustomed to eating a great deal of meat and animal products, the natural impulse was to cling as closely as possible to established habits.'[10]

Coblenz and Cologne' (University of Missouri Ph.D. thesis, 1981); E. H. Tobin, 'War and the Working Class: The Case of Düsseldorf, 1914–1918', *Central European History*, vol. 28 (1985).

[8] Published in Britain as P. Eltzbacher (ed.), *Germany's Food. Can it Last?* (1915), see esp. pp. 73–5, ch. 5 and pp. 229–32.

[9] [A. E. Taylor?], 'General Considerations Relating to the Importance of the Bread Ration in the Diet of the People, the Conservation of Bread Grains, and Prevention of Waste in the Same' (15 June 1917), fo. 10, Graham Lusk Papers 1/1, HIA; 'Preliminary Study. Comparison of Costs and Efficiency of Various Foods' (n.d. 1917–18?), ibid. 1/4.

[10] A. E. Taylor, 'The Control of Food Supplies in Blockaded Germany' (unpublished typescript, ?Washington DC ?1917), fo. 54; USFA 121/9, HIA.

The Eltzbacher commission recommended a reduction of livestock, to make sure that food found its way directly to the people. In a great *Schweinemord*, about nine million pigs—or about one-third of the herd—were slaughtered up to mid-April 1915.[11]

Grain came under control even earlier. By the beginning of 1915 an Imperial Grain Bureau was in place, with monopoly powers and authority to fix prices for consumers and producers. Bread was rationed, grain was milled to higher percentages, and a "war bread" appeared, adulterated with up to 10 per cent of potato flour. No ration was set for meat and other livestock products and their prices quickly rose.

The Grain Bureau had nowhere to store the grain, which had to remain on the farm until marketing, just as in peacetime.[12] When the *Schweinemord* caused meat and fat prices to rise, farmers diverted food grains and potatoes to their animals. The grain ration had been set at a level of about 65 per cent of total supply, but at the end of the year there was no surplus or carry-over to the next year. Some 3.2 million tons of flour (about one-third of the civilian ration) had "disappeared".[13]

The first two years of war witnessed a succession of piecemeal attempts to organize production and distribution. One after the other fats, sugar, coffee, tea, milk, potatoes and bread fell into short supply and the local authorities (at town and district level) rationed them in an attempt to ensure equitable distribution. A ceiling on prices was the favourite method. Traders quickly adapted. They formed notorious "chains" (*Kettenhandel*) to move supplies to places where prices were high or uncontrolled. Farmers shifted their efforts into those products which were still unaffected by controls. Much of the speculation took place in the open, in the form of newspaper advertisements offering food at inflated prices. An outraged public could not distinguish between profiteering and the legitimate signals of increasing scarcity.[14]

III

Rationing

The war shifted large numbers of people and altered the established patterns of food distribution and consumption. Out of a population of some sixty-seven million about eleven million were serving in the armed

[11] Skalweit, *Kriegsernährungswirtschaft*, p. 97.

[12] O. Böhm, *Die Kornhäuser* (Stuttgart 1898), pp. 74–5; L. Burchardt, *Friedenswirtschaft und Kriegsvorsorge: Deutschlands wirtschaftliche Rüstungsbestrebungen vor 1914* (Boppard am Rhein 1968), p. 193.

[13] Taylor, 'Control of Food', fo. 60.

[14] Ibid., *passim*; Skalweit, *Kriegsernährungswirtshaft*, pp. 115–45. A short account in English: G. Feldman, *Army, Industry and Labour in Germany, 1914–1918* (Princeton 1966), pp. 97–116, 283–91.

forces by 1918, or some 16.4 per cent.[15] Their arduous duties required a rich diet, which became the first call on the country's food. Germany had a large farm sector, with about one-third of the population still in the countryside. Agriculture lost almost 60 per cent of its labour to the army and suffered badly from a shortage of draft animals, fertilizers and imported fodder. But farmers had access to the food they produced and, during the first years of the war at least, could feed themselves before sending anything to the army or the towns.

The towns, especially the large ones, stood at the end of the queue in terms of food supply, but were absolutely crucial to the war effort. Urban populations expanded as men and women thronged to the war industries. Large towns contained less than a quarter of the population but their food problems were acute. More than any other sector, they relied on supplies from a distance and overseas. The bulk of urban population was in the centre and the west and it grew together with the new war industries. Large industrial towns, which had previously supplied themselves from the North Sea ports, now had to draw grain and potatoes from the eastern provinces, a long distance by rail. Cities were the only true markets for food and their richly stratified societies contained great differentials of poverty and wealth, as well as the social, intellectual and political hubs of the federal Empire. Consequently, the German food problem was reduced to a question of how to maintain an adequate supply of food to the towns, especially to the fifty or so *Grosstädten* of more than 100,000 inhabitants.

As the winter of 1915 began, ration cards were issued for fat, sugar, bread and soap. Potatoes began to run out in the spring of 1916. Bread was short. But ration cards did not guarantee food: often it was first come, first served, so queues formed in front of the food shops and people stood long hours in the hope (often frustrated) of buying a few ounces of lard or a few pounds of potatoes. The lines of shivering women on the wintry pavements became known, with wry humour, as the "polonaise" (a Polish dance). Lady Evelyn Blücher, an Englishwoman resident in Berlin, wrote down in her diary in May 1916,

many people kept Easter in the face of an empty larder . . .

. . . The butchers' shops were closed for two to three weeks on set prices being denominated by Government for meat; vegetables were not to be had; butter almost unknown; whilst soap had become so scarce that regulations were enforced forbidding white dresses to be worn in some parts of Germany. Every one is now allowed 1 lb. of soap for washing purposes a month, and 100 grs. of toilet soap extra.

Long processions of women waiting for hours before the butchers', grocers', and

[15] K. Roesler, *Die Finanzpolitik des Deutschen Reiches im Ersten Weltkrieg* (Berlin 1977), table 12, p. 156.

bakers' shops were to be seen everywhere, and gave rise to the name of the "butter-polonaise". These women often got up in the middle of the night, to be first on the scene, and took camp stools with them, working or knitting, and seemed rather to enjoy this opportunity of unlimited gossiping, evil tongues said . . .[16]

High society in Berlin could afford to smile so long as servants danced the "polonaise" for them. Starting in the late autumn of 1915 and rising to a peak in the summer of 1916, the shortages provoked food riots which spread through the large and medium towns. Women looted shops and overturned market stalls.[17] Curiously, we are able to observe these scenes with an Australian eye. In the city of Leipzig there happened to be an Australian woman, Ethel Cooper. She was forty-three when the war broke out, one of those self-reliant Edwardian women who lived on their own and thought for themselves, a student and teacher of music with a bohemian temper, sharp observation and a shrewd mind. For company, she kept a pet crocodile named Cheops, which she sadly sent to the zoo when food ran out. Ethel Cooper wrote weekly letters home to Adelaide and, when she could not post them, stuffed them into the mattress. They give a vivid view of civilian life in Germany during the war. On 18 June 1916 she wrote, 'there is no butter or fat of any sort, and practically no meat, and potatoes have quite given out. There are rows and fights and arrests in the market every day.'[18]

Stocks fell low in the months that preceded the new harvest: June and July were always difficult. The early summer of 1916 was a turning-point. In response to the shortages and riots the imperial government effectively nationalized the food supply system. From being a regulator, it became trader and manager. On 22 May 1916 the government set up a War Food Office (*Kriegsernährungsamt*) with powers to control food at the national level. During the summer of 1916 the food system assumed a form which lasted to the end of the war and beyond. By the onset of winter all the main foodstuffs were rationed. The Food Office published a national ration and attempted to allocate foodstuffs accordingly. Every household registered at neighbourhood shops, where it would get the rationed foodstuffs. That, at any rate, was the plan.

From late 1916 onwards the ration provides a benchmark for the food situation and has been used for this purpose by most writers. But the installation of a new bureaucracy was no solution for a deeply difficult situation. The summer of "polonaizes" and food riots gave way to a winter

---

[16] Blücher, *English Wife*, pp. 135–6.

[17] Ay, *Volksstimmung in Bayern*, p. 84; Ullrich, *Hamburg*, pp. 51–3; Tobin, 'Düsseldorf', p. 279; K.-D. Schwarz, *Weltkrieg und Revolution in Nürnberg* (Stuttgart 1971), pp. 148–51; Cooper, *Behind the Lines*, p. 107. A list of riots in 1916 is given in A. C. Bell, *A History of the Blockade of Germany . . . 1914–1918* (1937), pp. 572–3.

[18] Cooper, *Behind the Lines*; quote from p. 144.

of absolute shortage and real starvation. The harvest of 1916 was a poor one world-wide. In Germany the shortage of transport made it difficult to recover the potatoes from the fields. Potatoes disappeared for long periods and there was little bread. Instead, turnips (*Kohlrüben*) became the staple food for long periods. Ethel Cooper wrote on 4 February 1917,

Coal has run out. The electric light is cut off in most houses (I have gas, thank Heaven!), the trams are not running, or only in the very early morning, all theatres, schools, the opera, Gewandhaus and concerts and cinematographs are closed— neither potatoes nor turnips are to be had—they were our last resource—there is no fish—and Germany has at last ceased to trumpet the fact that it can't be starved out. Added to that the thermometer outside my kitchen window says 24 deg. Fahr. *below zero*. I have never seen that before . . .

Two weeks later she wrote: 'I think that if I were to bray instead of speaking or writing, it is all that could be expected of one, after a month of living on parsnips and turnips.'[19]

The miseries of the "turnip winter" can be followed in the official ration. The crudest and most significant indicator is the heat value of the nation's food, expressed in calories. The Eltzbacher commission proposed 3,000 calories per day as the standard for a healthy, full-grown man. In 1916 the Food Office projected a ration of 1,985 calories; the actual ration it attempted to distribute went down to 1,336; by July 1917 it was down to 1,100 calories. As we shall see, these figures should not be taken literally.[20]

For food, the first half of 1917 was the low point of the war. That, at least, is the message of the official ration, which crept up again to 1,619 calories by November 1918.[21] The turning-point was the potato harvest of 1917, which provided a nutritional cushion throughout the following winter but which petered out in June and July 1918, plunging the country again into an acute food crisis. But national figures are misleading. Farmers and soldiers ate much better than the townsfolk. Every city had a somewhat different ration, depending on such factors as size, proximity to the countryside, municipal competence and regional location. Figs. 1.1 and 1.2 plot the movements of rations in Bonn and Cologne. Bonn was a town of about 90,000 and Cologne had about half a million people. In addition to the bread and potato rations, the numbers of people fed in municipal kitchens is another good indicator of deprivation. Comparable curves are available for other cities, but the one for Bonn is unique in providing a weekly calorie ration. It shows how occasional small windfalls sweetened

---

[19] Ibid., pp. 181–3.
[20] L. Burchardt's invaluable article 'Die Auswirkung der Kriegswirtschaft auf die deutsche Zivilbevölkerung im ersten und im zweiten Weltkrieg', *Militärgeschichtliche Mitteilungen*, no. 1 (1974), relies too much on these traditional sources.
[21] Eltzbacher (ed.), *Germany's Foods*, p. 26; M. Rubner, 'Das Ernährungswesen im Allgemeinen', in Bumm (ed.), *Gesundheitsverhältnisse*, vol. 2, pp. 14–16.

1. Society under Siege

the dismal diet, but these windfalls alternated with weeks of famine even during periods of general improvement. Even 2,000 calories a day (surpassed in Bonn only twice during the war) was still one-third short of the recommended adult male ration.[22]

In addition to the staples of the diet, to bread, potatoes, meat and fat, a large number of household items were in very short supply. Soap was rationed to as little as one small bar of soap a month. Coal was scarce, matches unobtainable, cotton and woollen fabrics no longer manufactured. Much of the warm clothing and many cooking utensils had to be given up later in the war. In the absence of soap and hot water it was hard to keep underclothing and linen clean. Substitutes appeared for these commodities, but few of them gave complete satisfaction. Paper fibres were

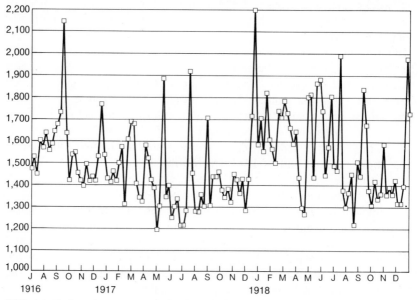

FIG. 1.1. Daily ration in calories per head, Bonn, July 1916–December 1918 (weekly data)

Note: The ration was distributed equally to all adults and most children. For the population structure of Germany in 1910, the nutritional standard per head (comparable to 3,000 calories per adult) was 2,240 calories.

Source: F. W. Bach, *Untersuchungen über die Lebensmittelrationierung im Kriege . . .* (Munich 1919), tables II, VI, X, pp. 148a, 172a, 184a. Each provides maximum and minimum series. The difference is not significant (about 5 per cent). I have used the minimum series, bearing in mind that rations were not always actually distributed, and that there was a certain amount of wastage.

[22] For a potato and bread graph of Düsseldorf, Tobin, 'Düsseldorf', fig. 1, p. 280; a calorie graph for Frankfurt am Main is given in M. Rubner, 'Der Gesundheitszustand im Allgemeinen', in Bumm (ed.), *Gesundheitsverhältnisse*, vol. 1, p. 72. Like much of Rubner's data, it is insufficiently documented.

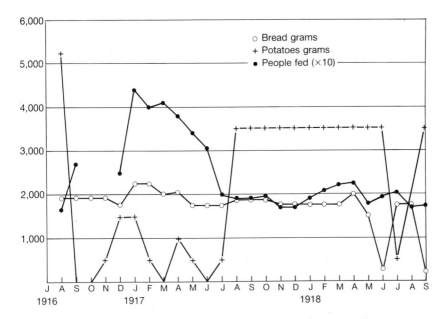

FIG. 1.2. Bread and potato weekly rations and public kitchens, Cologne, July 1916–October 1918 (monthly)

Note: The meat ration remained steady throughout the period at 250 grams but fell to 200 grams (diluted with sausages and other substitutes) and lower (including meatless weeks) from May 1918 onwards.

Source: J. P. Bott, 'The German Food Crisis of World War I: The Cases of Coblenz and Cologne' (University of Missouri Ph.D. thesis, 1981), Appendix B, fos. 217–22.

used for weaving with indifferent success (fig. 1.3). A mock advertisement in a satirical supplement offered stuffings of mattresses as substitutes for tea, tobacco and dried vegetables.[23] All of these shortages affected public health, most of them adversely.

IV

Public Health

If the ration showed a slight improvement after the summer of 1917, other indicators are worse. In the literature of the blockade the evidence of public health occupies a central place.

The first indicator was the *loss of weight*. 'The familiar obesity of the Germans has disappeared,' wrote the American physiologist Alonzo

---

[23] *Ulk* (comic supplement of *Berliner Tageblatt*), 15 May 1918.

'Fabrics made out of paper yarn are not inferior to any other textiles in beauty and durability.'

'They offer a complete substitute for wool, cotton, linen and silk.'

'We owe this to our indefatigable, unique inventive spirit and to our all-conquering enterprise.'

FIG. 1.3. 'The Family Outing', *Simplicissimus*, 4 June 1918

Taylor of what he saw in 1916. In Bonn, the nutritionist R. O. Neumann attempted to live on the official ration exclusively between November 1916 and May 1917, in retrospect the worst time of the war. Neumann lost a quarter of his body weight in seven months, from 76.5 kg. to 57.5 kg. The male inmates of an institution lost one-third of their body weight between mid-1914 and mid-1917, the females one quarter. The inmates of a prison lost 23 per cent of their body weight in the same period. Max Rubner, Germany's leading nutritionist, estimated the gross urban weight loss at 20 per cent of body weight (that is what he lost himself). Extrapolation gave a total weight loss for the civilian population of more than half a million tons of "human mass".[24]

Births and deaths provide another indicator of public health. *Births* had been falling for a generation before the war, but they now declined deeply below the trend. At its lowest, the birth-rate fell almost by half compared to 1914. That was about twice the decline of the birth rate in Britain. But for the war, some three million more Germans might have been born. However, one should be careful not to treat this as a direct measure of comparative deprivation: the age structures and nuptial patterns of the two populations have to be compared, as well as the pace of decline of the birth-rate.[25] One reason for the decline was the absence of men: German husbands left sooner for the front, and more of them died. Married males were only conscripted in Britain in 1916. Food is also implicated. A loss of 10 to 15 per cent below the normal weight for height is sufficient to induce menstrual irregularities. In Germany, during the hungry year of 1917, medical witnesses reported menstrual disorders and a rise in the number of stillbirths. These reports almost ceased when nutrition improved in 1918.[26] Stress also affects reproductive capacity. It is possible to regard the decline in the birth-rate in part as an adaptation to adversity. By reducing the number of new-born babies by half, Germany's women gave themselves more time to dance the "polonaize" in front of the shops and to work in the shell factories. They needed less soap and nappies, hot water and milk, and had more time to look after the babies that remained. In its unborn babies,

[24] Taylor, 'Control of Food', fo. 191; Neumann: J. E. Johanesson, 'The Food Problem in Germany', paper read at the Swedish Medical Society, Stockholm, 28 Jan. 1919, fos. 9–10, ARA papers box 67 [figures from graph, rather than from those in the text], HIA. Rubner places this experiment a year later: 'Ernährungswesen', p. 33; inmates: ibid., p. 21; Rubner's body-weight estimate: ibid., p. 21, and 'Schädigung', pp. 396, 422; prisoners: Rubner, 'Gesundheitszustand', p. 72.

[25] E. E. Roesle, 'Die Geburts- und Sterblichkeitsverhältnisse', in Bumm (ed.), *Gesundheitsverhältnisse*, vol. 1, pp. 10–17.

[26] R. E. Frisch, 'Fatness and Fertility', *Scientific American*, vol. 258 (Mar. 1988), p. 70; H. Sellheim, 'Frauenkrankheiten und Geburtshilfe', in Bumm (ed.), *Gesundheitsverhältnisse*, vol. 1, pp. 295–8; E. Le Roy Ladurie, 'L'Aménorrhée de famine (XVIIe–XXe siècles)', *Annales*, vol. 24 (1969), pp. 1591–4.

Germany had three million fewer mouths to feed. The decline in the birth-rate eased the burden of blockade somewhat.

Death, in its turn, was partly determined by the pattern of births, since infants in the first year of life died at a rate ten times higher than the population average. Just after the war the imperial statistical office calculated the excess of civilian deaths over the pre-war level at a grand total of 762,000, more than a third of battlefield deaths, excluding the victims of the great influenza epidemic of 1918. A more sober estimate a decade later arrived at a number of 424,000 excess civilian deaths (over the age of one), plus 209,000 deaths in the influenza pandemic of 1918, making a total of 633,000 (excluding Alsace-Lorraine). Taken together, the unborn, the war dead (more than two million) and the excess civilian deaths amounted to some 2.7 million adults and more than three million infants by 1918—or about 8 per cent of the population by the end of the war.[27] Altogether, this was a material reduction in the numbers that had to be fed.

In order to isolate the effect of wartime *living conditions* on mortality, it is necessary to remove military casualties. The simplest way to do this is to consider women alone. The trend of mortality confirms the chronology of the food crisis. The increase was only moderate in the first two years. The crisis year was 1917, but 1918 looks worse because of the influenza epidemic (table 1.1). The figures are harsh. At its maximum during 1918 the female death-rate rose more than 50 per cent above the pre-war level. In 1917, which was a more difficult year (apart from the influenza), the excess over 1913 was only 23 per cent, but the excess over Britain was higher, since in Britain female mortality had continued its downward trend. This excess, of about a quarter to a third more than in Britain, seems to give the same rough measure of adversity as the decline in the birth-rate: on these indices of public health, the German experience appears to have been worse, to that extent, than Britain's. The German population suffered from serious food and material shortages, while the population of Britain, on the whole, did not, so the excess over Britain is a better measure of deprivation (with all the previous qualifications) than the excess over peacetime. A higher proportion of men were mobilized in Germany than in Britain and more of them died.[28] Some of my colleagues question whether this placed more stress on the women at home, but I am inclined to think that it did.

The risk of death depended partly on where you lived. If the towns were really so much worse off than the rest of the country, then their mortality

---

[27] 'Schädigung', pp. 398, 401; Roesle, 'Sterblichkeitsverhältnisse', table 5, p. 25. The data were reworked by W. Notestein *et al.*, to arrive at 733,000 excess civilian deaths: *The Future Population of Europe and the Soviet Union* (Geneva 1944), table 3, pp. 75–6.

[28] Mobilization rates: J. M. Winter, *The Great War and the British People* (1985), table 3.4, p. 75.

TABLE 1.1. *Female mortality in Germany and in England and Wales, 1913–1923*

Year	(1) Deaths per 1,000 females		(3) German index as % of English index
	Germany	England	
1913	14.3	12.2	**100**
1914	15.2	12.4	**105**
1915	15.3	13.2	**99**
1916	15.2	11.7	**111**
1917	17.6	11.4	**132**
1918	21.6	14.6	**126**
1919	16.7	11.9	**120**
1920	15.3	10.9	**120**
1921	13.6	10.2	**114**
1922	13.9	10.5	**113**
1923	13.6	9.3	**125**

Source: E. E. Roesle, 'Die Geburts- und Sterblichkeitsverhältnisse' in F. Bumm (ed.), *Deutschlands Gesundheitsverhältnisse unter dem Einfluss des Weltkrieges* (Stuttgart 1928), vol. 1, table 9, p. 40.

Note: The index (col. 3) is calculated as follows: both col. (1) and col. (2) are converted into an index with 1913=100. Col. (3) is the index of col. (1) expressed as a percentage of the index of col. (2).

should also have been worse. Unfortunately sufficient figures are not to hand, but there are a few for the city of Dresden, the fifth most populous in the country, with more than half a million inhabitants. The data are not strictly comparable, in that they cover both males and females (males have higher birth- and death-rates); so I shall compare only the general trends, without attempting to standardize for age (table 1.2).

The significant column is the last (in bold type). In the first three years of the war the mortality trend in Dresden was somewhat better than in Germany as a whole, perhaps because of the lower birth-rate in Dresden, both in peace and in war (since women have a lower death-rate than men, the table actually understates Dresden's advantage). The table suggests that public health conditions in the towns declined more than the average in the last two years of the war, though not *much* more so.

One of the most puzzling features of these war conditions is how little they affected babies. J. M. Winter has written at length about the decline of baby mortality in Britain during the First World War. He approves of an expert who said that 'the infant mortality rate is the most sensitive and subtle index of all measures of social welfare and of sanitary administration, especially under urban conditions'. Accordingly, Winter takes the

TABLE 1.2. *Mortality in Dresden and in Germany, 1913–1918*

Year	(1) Deaths per 1,000 females Germany	(2) Deaths per 1,000 Dresden	(3) Dresden Index as % of German index
1913	14.3	13.0	**100**
1914	14.8	13.3	**99**
1915	14.5	12.2	**93**
1916	14.1	12.3	**96**
1917	15.8	16.2	**113**
1918	19.5	19.1	**108**

Source: Dresden: Dr Dienmann (Official City Physician), 'Dresden' (typescript, n.d. ?1919), table III, in 'Saxony, State of Nutrition and Shortage of Food', American Relief Administration, box 64, Hoover Institution Archives; Germany: Roesle, 'Geburts- und Sterblichkeitsverhältnisse', vol. 1, table 9, p. 40.

Note: The index is calculated in the same way as in table 1.1.

decline of English infant mortality as evidence of an improvement of civilian welfare during the First World War.[29] In Germany, however, this 'most sensitive and subtle index' registered very little movement during the war. While adult mortality rose, the trend of infant mortality was slightly downwards. Indeed, if infant and adult mortality are compared, German

TABLE 1.3. *Infant mortality in Germany and in England and Wales,*
1913–1923

Year	Deaths per 1,000 females aged 0–1		Female infant death-rate index as % of female adult death-rate index	
	Germany	England	Germany	England
1913	137	96	100	100
1914	148	93	102	95
1915	135	96	92	92
1916	128	80	88	87
1917	136	85	81	95
1918	143	86	69	75
1919	131	78	82	83
1920	118	69	81	80
1921	120	72	92	90
1922	116	66	87	80
1923	119	60	91	82

Source: Roesle, 'Geburts- und Sterblichkeitsverhältnisse', vol. 1, tables 9, 11, pp. 49, 55.

[29] Winter, *The Great War and the British People*, p. 142.

babies were better insulated from adult mortality rates than babies in Britain (table 1.3).

Above the age of one, the largest increase in the death-rate affected children and young adults between the ages of five and twenty-five (fig. 1.4). Children under fourteen often received less than the full adult ration. Young people require proteins for body building, and generous amounts of vitamins. Proteins were in short supply, especially milk, which is important for its calcium, its protein and its vitamins. In peacetime, death-rates for children and young adults were very low (between 2 and 4 per 1,000). But these age groups (children and young adults) were also (at the outbreak of the war) numerically large, so the tragedy of youthful death was a feature of life at home as well as at the front.

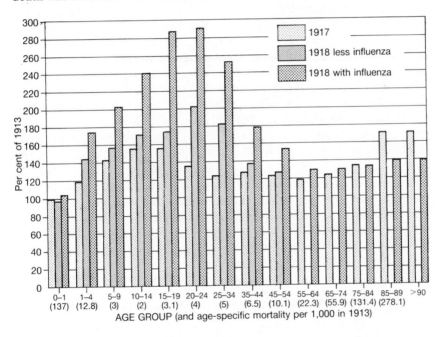

FIG. 1.4. The increase of female mortality by age in Germany, 1917 and 1918

Source: E. E. Roesle, 'Die Geburts- und Sterblichkeitsverhältnisse', in F. Bumm (ed.), *Deutschlands Gesundheitsverhältnisse unter dem Einfluss des Weltkrieges* (Stuttgart 1928), vol. 1, tables 10, 11, pp. 49, 55–6.

The elderly did better than might have been expected, and, although they had high death-rates, they always do. The increase for the more elderly age groups was within the bounds of the national average and often lower. They were especially successful in avoiding the influenza in 1918.

Most additional female deaths in wartime were caused by respiratory illness. Deaths from pneumonia more than doubled; those from tuberculosis almost doubled by 1918.[30] These infectious diseases are sensitive to hunger, cold and insanitary conditions. There was also the murderous influenza pandemic of 1918. "Age infirmity", another major killer, was sometimes a euphemism for hunger and cold, perhaps also for dislocation and stress affecting old people in wartime. On the other hand, with fewer babies being born, there was a corresponding reduction in their fatal disorders.

Non-fatal sickness also increased, but the extent is difficult to judge, as few statistics were kept. Without going into detail, medical publications referred to a new disorder arising from hunger, a swelling, sometimes fatal, known as hunger oedema.

To sum up the evidence of public health: the siege economy did not give rise to famine. People did not, as a rule, drop dead in the streets. Overall mortality increased by up to a third, if we ignore the influenza of 1918. But this understates the problem. Up to twice as many children and young adults died as before the war, and during the influenza year almost three times as many in the young adult age groups. Fortunately, these age groups had low death-rates before the war, so a large relative rise of deaths did not produce overwhelming absolute numbers. The shortfall of births improved mortality figures considerably, since babies were by far the most vulnerable age group. The record of mortality was not catastrophic. Townspeople suffered a little more than country dwellers, while inmates of institutions suffered worst of all. In historical perspective, however, this rise in mortality hardly appears crippling. In the worst year (1918), despite the influenza, the crude death-rate merely reverted to the levels prevailing in the years 1901–5. The war at its worst caused the loss of not much more than a decade of public health progress.[31]

[30] Roesle, 'Sterblichkeitsverhältnisse', p. 58, table 12.
[31] *Statistiches Jahrbuch für das Deutsche Reich*, vol. 35 (Berlin 1914), p. 22.

2

FOOD REFORM AND FOOD SCIENCE

THERE is more to food than calories. The family breakfast, the workers' lunch, the formal dinner, a drink at the pub, an evening at the restaurant— all these different occasions suggest how food is bound up with the customs, habits and daily rituals that provide the framework of personal and social relations. Food conventions and habits distinguish cultures and nations, insiders and outsiders, age and sex, poor and rich. We are what we eat in more senses than one. Food is rich in codes of communication, memory and emotion. A forcible alteration of food habits goes to the very heart of tradition, expectations and identity.

On the supply side, the forms of food production, distribution and storage, the variety of foods produced and their modes of delivery are all tuned to the social, cultural and regional subtleties of their markets. Food is perceived and classified in different ways. The basic scientific categories are carbohydrates, proteins and fats; but other classifications also have a function. The central distinction is between vegetable and animal foods and their sub-categories of cereals, vegetables, fruit, dairy products, meat and fish. Anthropologists point out the different cultural significations of cooked and raw, sweet and salty, masculine and feminine foods. Eating is full of connotations and for government to control food is a daunting social task, especially under conditions of scarcity. Both the cultural superstructure of food and its productive and distributive bases are founded on certain bodily requirements. In order to judge the German food effort in the First World War we have to consider the first principles of nutrition as they were understood in the preceding decade.

In the second half of the nineteenth century the food habits of Europe and the United States changed under the impact of technology and transport. New foodstuffs became staples of the urban diet: white granular sugar, fine wheaten flour, margarine, coffee, cigarettes and chocolate. These staples were processed by machines and transported over long distances, often over the seas, and distributed in large regional or even national markets. Sugar consumption, for example, rose more than fourfold during the century in Britain, up to some 36 kg. per head before the war (79.3 lb.) and to 21 kg. in Germany (46.3 lb.). White wheaten flour was roller-ground out of hard wheat in the big mills of Minneapolis, Buffalo, New York and the port cities of Europe from the 1880s onwards. Margarine displaced butter and lard from the 1870s, while soap, a household commodity that also came out of animal or vegetable fat, was likewise produced for a national market and sold under well-advertised brands and trade marks, sometimes by the same firms that made the margarine. Tinned, chilled and frozen meat came packed or refrigerated from the mechanized abattoirs of Chicago and La Plata. Tea became a daily necessity in Britain, coffee in Germany, while cocoa and dried fruit also became staples. The later nineteenth century brought fresh liquid milk to every city street and tinned milk on to corner-shop shelves. The price of food declined in relation to incomes especially during the last quarter of the century.

This abundance of cheaper energy was not matched by harder work. Hours of work became shorter, while numbers in middle-class and white-collar occupations grew, as machines took over a growing share of mechanical labour in the factories and on the farms. At the same time, eating habits did not adjust to the lighter load of work. On the contrary, as incomes increased, households consumed a richer diet and shifted their preferences from potatoes and grain to dairy products and meat.[1]

'It is one of the axioms of physiology,' wrote the leading American authority in 1904, 'that the majority of the diseases of mankind are due to, or are connected with, perversions of nutrition.'[2] There is a venerable (but fugitive) tradition in medicine of prevention and cure by means of restraint in diet.[3] The modern food-reform movement has its roots in religion and ethics as much as in rationalism. In Victorian Britain the vegetarian society evolved out of the Bible Christian Church, while the origins of food reform in the United States are tied up with the Seventh Day Adventists. Their leader Ellen White stressed the virtues of an abstemious and vegetarian diet, which her followers practised in their communities and gatherings. In the 1870s an Adventist doctor, John Harvey Kellogg, took over and developed a health retreat in Battle Creek, Michigan. He called it, with idiosyncratic spelling, the "Sanitarium". Kellogg was a medical innovator with a genius for publicity and his methods of dieting, exercise and hydrotherapy brought relief to the victims of digestive and general disorders who flocked to his institution. By the turn of the century the Sanitarium accommodated more than a thousand patients at a time, including many of the rich and fashionable. Kellogg also invented many of the health foods that we know today, but the famous cornflakes were created by the marketing genius of his brother William. John Kellogg was one of a number of outstanding American advocates of restraint in diet,

---

[1] The literature of food is too extensive to cite, but many of these themes are discussed later in the book. Germany in particular: H. J. Teuteberg and G. Wiegelmann, *Der Wandel der Nahrungsgewohnheiten unter dem Einfluss der Industrialisierung* (Göttingen 1972); international comparisons: F. Eulenberg, 'Bedeutung der Lebensmittelpreise für die Ernährung', *Handbuch der Hygiene* (2nd edn. Leipzig 1913), vol. 3, pt. 1.

[2] R. H. Chittenden, *Physiological Economy in Nutrition* (New York 1904), p. 455.

[3] J. M. Peebles, *Death Defeated or the Psychic Secret of How to Keep Young* (Battle Creek, Michigan 1908), *passim*.

whose common-sense, pragmatic and intuitive approach had undertones of personal and social salvation, and whose followers included many faddists.[4]

The second part of the nineteenth century was also the time of the emergence of modern nutritional science. Between the 1880s and the First World War physiological chemists established the roles of carbohydrates, proteins and fats and began to understand the importance of vitamins. They also set up dietary norms and published standard daily requirements of calories and protein. The German physiologist Carl Voit proposed 3,000 calories as a daily standard for an adult male in moderate work and recommended 118 grams of protein a day. Excellent publicity for the new standards was provided by W. O. Atwater and his colleagues at the United States Department of Agriculture, on the basis of their own extensive research. In Britain this new understanding found a rapid application by Seebohm Rowntree and his followers, who established that about a third of the urban working class fell below the nutritional minimum and placed this "poverty line" near the top of the national agenda of social reform.[5]

Scientific nutrition before the First World War took two distinct approaches to food norms. Atwater, like Voit before him, surveyed the actual quantities of food consumed by persons of different age, sex and occupation, and treated his observations as scientific dietary norms. As a British writer put it, 'theoretical diet scales reflect the prevailing conditions of the country in which they originate'.[6]

The other approach was critical. Its advocates regarded existing diets as less than ideal if not actually harmful, and sought for better ones by means of controlled experiments. Their aims were similar to those of the food reformers, and were often influenced by the latters' views. A case in point was Horace Fletcher, a wealthy American resident in London, who invented "Fletcherism". This came down to chewing very thoroughly before swallowing. A physiologist at Cambridge examined Fletcher and confirmed that he managed to reduce the craving for food and its intake while maintaining full bodily vigour. Fletcher's example also made an impression in the United States.

Russell Henry Chittenden was Professor of Physiological Chemistry at

[4] J. Twigg, 'The Vegetarian Movement in England, 1847–1981: With Particular Reference to its Ideology' (London University Ph.D. thesis, 1982), fos. 68–87; G. Carson, *Cornflake Crusade* (1959); R. W. Scwartz, *John Harvey Kellogg, M. D.* (Nashville, Tennessee 1970).

[5] C. von Voit, *Physiologie des allgemeinen Stoffwechsels und der Ernährung*; (L. Herman (ed.), Handbuch der Physiologie, vol. 6; Leipzig 1881); W. O. Atwater, *Principles of Nutrition and Nutritive Value of Food*, USDA Farmers' Bulletin no. 147 (Washington DC 1902); C. F. Langworthy, *Food Customs and Diet in American Homes*, USDA Office of Experimental Stations, Circular 110 (Washington DC 1911); B. S. Rowntree, *Poverty. A Study of Town Life* (4th edn. 1902), ch. 4; A. L. Bowley and A. R. Burnett-Hurst, *Livelihood and Poverty* (1913).

[6] Viscount Dunluce and M. Greenwood, *An Inquiry into the Composition of Dietaries, with Special Reference to the Dietaries of Munitions Workers* (1918), p. 24.

Yale University and head of its Sheffield Scientific School. He read about the Cambridge experiment and got Fletcher to stay at his home for a few months in 1902–3. Chittenden observed that Fletcher maintained body weight and remained in prime physical condition despite living on a diet of only about one-half the conventional standard. 'Is it not possible', Chittenden asked himself, 'that the accepted dietary standards are altogether too high?' He raised private and government money and arranged to put this proposition to the test. First he experimented on himself, observing a diet about two-thirds the Voit standard for half a year. His weight fell by 11 per cent and then stabilized, and he found himself in a better physical condition. A rheumatic knee condition disappeared, together with headaches and bilious attacks. Next he tested a low-protein low-calorie regime on three groups for periods of four and five months: his colleagues, a squad of soldiers and some Yale University athletes.

His account of the experiment is both meticulous and engaging. As a rule members of all groups lost some weight, then stabilized. They suffered few withdrawal symptoms and adjusted quickly to lower diets, and especially to the reduction of protein; and they manifested more strength, endurance and vigour, as measured by tests in the Yale Gymnasium.[7]

Chittenden set the minimum requirement of protein at one half or so of the 118 grams per day recommended by Voit. Any excess, he argued, was harmful, even poisonous. He also recommended a much lower intake of calories and attributed many adult medical disorders to overeating. For thoroughness and scale Chittenden's experiments had no precedent and provided food reformers with solid scientific support for a dietary shift from meat and dairy products into grains, fruit and vegetables. These ideas, much more familiar nowadays, also had an impact overseas.[8]

One of Chittenden's colleagues at Yale, the eminent economist Irving Fisher, became converted to food reform after a bout of tuberculosis and the experience of several periods at Battle Creek sanitoria. Fisher was ferociously prolific and worked hard to establish and publicize the link between ill health and overeating. An unquenchable Yankee gadgeteer, pamphleteer and busybody, Fisher undertook his own physiological experiments in diet and endurance and established a nation-wide Committee of 100 scientists and public figures to advocate a Ministry of Health. One of his many business ventures was a Life Extension Institute which contracted with insurance companies to provide medical check-ups

[7] My main sources on Chittenden were his papers at the Yale University Library, including an autobiography, 'Sixty Years in the Service of Science' (typescript, 1936, Yale University Library); H. B. Vickery, 'Biographical Memoir of Russell Henry Chittenden, 1856–1943', *National Academy of Science Biographical Memoirs*, vol. 24, 2nd memoir (Washington DC 1944), pp. 55–104; and two of Chittenden's books, *Physiological Economy*, and *The Nutrition of Man* (New York 1907).

[8] In particular the work of M. Hindhede in Denmark, e.g. *What to Eat and Why* (1914).

and dietary advice to policy-holders. The advice prolonged the customers' lives and provided a return of 200 per cent on the companies' investment. Fisher's watchword was "Health pays!" In the 1920s he became a pillar of prohibition.[9]

Chittenden's work set off the central controversy in nutrition during the Edwardian decade, between the advocates of low- and high-protein diets. Tradition and custom had regarded proteins, and especially meat, as the body-building and strength-giving food; in this, scientific nutritionists merely confirmed the public's preferences. Needless to say, the US Department of Agriculture and its scientists remained firmly committed to meat and milk.[10]

In Germany the weightiest defender of the high-protein diet was the country's leading authority on nutrition, Professor and Privy Counsellor Max Rubner of Berlin. Rubner conceded Chittenden's case for a low physiological requirement of protein in adults; but he continued to insist on the high Voit standard of protein intake, relying mainly on two arguments. First, that a minimum was not an optimum, and that a good padding of protein was needed for "security". Second, he argued from actual dietaries that popular practice was wiser than science, and that universal food preferences should not be lightly disregarded.[11]

Professor Rubner is a key figure in our story. His professional standing in Germany was formidable. He contributed to the Eltzbacher Report in 1914 and wrote another report on the nutrition of towns in 1917. The substance of this report reappeared in the most important official and semi-official post-war documents as well as in the Carnegie histories a decade later. His attitude and approach are stamped on subsequent accounts of the blockade. There is a striking discrepancy between Rubner's eminent status and the quality of many of his publications. He produced a long series of essays (some collected in books) in semi-popular form, with almost no footnotes or references to other published work. He used statistics cavalierly, and came under attack more than once for failings of analysis and fact.[12] The style is dogmatic and the assertions almost

[9] I. N. Fisher, *My Father Irving Fisher* (New York 1956), ch. 7 and pp. 161–3; Fisher published many pamphlets and several books, including the best-selling *How to Live* with E. L. Fiske (New York 1916). His views are set out in I. Fisher, 'National Vitality', *Report of the National Conservation Commission*, US 60 Congress, 2 Sess. 1909 Sen. doc. 676, vol. 3.

[10] Langworthy, *Food Customs and Diet*, pp. 15–19; the protein controversy: Chittenden, 'Sixty Years', fos. 105–6, 163–6, and Sir James Crichton-Browne, *Parcimony in Nutrition* (1909) (an attack on Chittenden).

[11] M. Rubner, *Volksernährungsfragen* (Leipzig 1908); *Wandlungen in der Volksernährung* (Leipzig 1913); 'Über Moderne Ernährungsreformen', *Archiv für Hygiene*, vol. 81 (1913).

[12] M. Beninde and M. Rubner, 'Welchen Einfluss hat die Kreigsernährung auf die Volksgesundheit ausgeübt und übt sie noch aus?', Gutachten der Wissenschaftlichen Deputation für das Medizinalwesen vom 18 Juli 1917, in M. Beninde, *Hungerblockade und*

impossible to follow up and test. This style of argument was well suited for post-war polemics. His essays on the principles of nutrition, both pre- and post-war, contain a robust defence of the traditional diet, high on proteins and calories, and defend the popular association of meat with vigour and health.[13]

Which is not to imply that Rubner was entirely wrong to criticize Chittenden and the low-protein school. The evidence points both ways. Irving Fisher's Life Extension Institute collected statistics on mortality of 745,000 life insurance policy-holders for the period 1885–1908 and found that overweight was highly correlated with premature death, especially from the mid-forties onwards. Similar results (on much smaller samples) had already been noted in Germany.[14] For Fisher this was a strong argument for dietary reform. But the data also showed that, when weight fell below the average, the extension of life was not large, especially in middle age.

In other words, an average or below-average weight already gave as much life expectation as weight control could be expected to provide. What is more, of the numbers in the sample, more than 70 per cent were "underweight". So both Chittenden and Rubner were right. The ordinary diet, or perhaps a somewhat excessive one, shortened the life of a large minority. But for the majority, the average diet did not affect the chances of life. Overeating and overweight might be problems, but they only affected a minority. (What the data do not make clear is whether average or below-average weight persons did not already exercise some restraint in their diet.) This result underscored a point which it is well to remember, and which was made by Chittenden: 'On the matter of diet every man should be a law unto himself, using judgement and knowledge to the best of his ability, reinforced by his own personal experiences.'[15]

Volksgesundheit, Veröffentlichungen aus dem Gebiete der Medizinalverwaltung, vol. 10, pt. 3 (Berlin 1920). Rubner contributed to the 'Schädigung' essay (1918); to Rubmann (ed.), *Hunger!* (1919), and to the 'Main Report of the Free Scientific Commission for the Study of the Present Food Conditions in Germany' (printed, 27 Dec. 1918), ARA 64, HIA (German version as well). For a strong critique of Rubner: R. E. May, *Die deutsche Volksernährung. Gemessen am tatsächlichen Konsum grosser Konsumentenkreise*, offprint from *Schmollers Jahrbücher*, vol. 41, nos. 1 and 2 (Munich and Leipzig 1917), e.g. p. 154 ff.

[13] e.g. Rubner, *Wandlungen*, ch. 8; M. Rubner, *Deutschlands Volksernährung. Zeitgemässe Betrachtungen* (Berlin 1930), pp. 15–35.
[14] I. Fisher and E. L. Fiske, *How to Live: Rules for Healthful Living Based on Modern Science* (15th edn. New York 1919), ch. 2; E. Hirschfeld, 'Die Ernährung in ihrem Einfluss auf Krankheit und Sterblichkeit', in M. Mosse and G. Tugendreich (eds.), *Krankheit und Soziale Lage* (Munich 1913), pp. 142–6.
[15] Chittenden, *Physiological Economy*, p. 470.

3

DID GERMANY REALLY STARVE?

NOT all nutritionists in Germany accepted Rubner's authority, but his influence kept discord out of the post-war histories and official statements. The dissenting nutritionists revealed a reality more complex than the simplicities of patriotic scientists.

When the Eltzbacher commission considered food requirements in 1914, it estimated that pre-war production and imports exceeded physiological needs by about 50 per cent. That ample margin was the source of the commission's optimism. Its members failed to note that physiological need had been deduced from consumption estimates in the first place. This should have alerted the scientists to defects in their data. Perhaps the figures were dressed up a bit, since the group included Carl Ballod, the foremost critic of Germany's food statistics. When he later published his own data, he showed that the margin was only about 15 per cent above the ration recommended by pre-war nutritionists. Take away imports and the surplus disappeared altogether. Furthermore, production figures took no account of wastage in transport, storage and food preparation. A study of household budgets in Hamburg before the war placed the actual pre-war consumption levels at just above the recommended levels, confirming that the loss of imports opened up a big deficit.[1]

Early in 1915 a survey in Munich found a calorie intake still at the pre-war level. One year later, after the first winter of shortages and scarcities, two additional surveys were undertaken throughout Germany by the War Committee for Consumer Interests (KAKI). These surveys (in April and July 1916) covered 1,004 families in fifty-five towns. Calorie intake had fallen by more than a fifth in comparison with pre-war Hamburg (the social composition was similar), but was still quite close to the recommended standards.[2] When KAKI carried out another survey in April 1917, the results were apparently not considered safe enough to publish; by this time calories had fallen almost 40 per cent below the Hamburg pre-war level, and almost a quarter below the standard—but not, it should be clear, to

[1] The Eltzbacher Report is criticized in C. Ballod, 'Die Volksernährung in Krieg und Frieden', *Schmollers Jahrbücher*, vol. 39 (1915), pp. 77–99; the household survey: May, *Deutsche Volksernährung*, pp. 93–105.

[2] G. Welker, *Die Münchener Erhebung über den Lebensmittelverbrauch im Februar 1915* (Munich, Berlin and Leipzig 1915); A. Loewy, 'Über Kriegskost', *Deutsche Medizinische Wochenschrift*, vol. 43 (8 Feb. and 15 Feb. 1917); also W. Zimmermann, 'Die Veränderungen der Einkommens- und Lebensverhältnisse der deutschen Arbeiter durch den Krieg', in Meerwarth *et al.*, *Einwirkung* , pp. 431–56. The KAKI surveys were published in the Imperial Statistical Office's *Reichs-Arbeitsblatt*, vol. 15 (1917), and in its Supplements (*Sonderhefte*), nos. 17 (1917) and 21 (1919).

one-third of the standard, as Rubner and his colleagues implied after the war.[3]

From February 1917 onwards a new source provides much better detail. Two professors at Leipzig, W. Kruse and K. Hintze, began a systematic survey of nutrition in their city. They got fifty-nine families (and three individuals) to record their food consumption daily and to weigh in at monthly intervals. Thirty-three of the families persevered to the end of the war, and most of those were also observed a few times in 1919 and 1920. The sample spanned the classes, from proprietors to manual labourers, with an emphasis on skilled labour and the lower middle class. Saxony's food provision was below average, and Leipzig's food supply was typical of large towns in the state. Kruse's and Hintze's observations make it possible to follow the German food economy in its most critical period from month to month.[4]

Their findings were potentially controversial and they took a great deal of trouble to anticipate criticism. What they did not prepare for was total neglect. The book was published in Dresden in 1922. Its findings were not congenial and the country was in the throes of economic and political turbulence. The publisher was inexperienced and the book made little or no impact. It is not in the American National Union or the British Library catalogues. Rubner passed it over entirely in his chapters in the Carnegie histories and I have not seen it mentioned in more recent literature.

Kruse's and Hintze's point of departure was that food requirements fall as body weight declines. When body weight fell from 70 to 60 kg. (14.3 per cent), the food requirement fell by 12.5 per cent.[5] Losing weight was a good adaptation to food shortage. The Leipzig professors adjusted their data for body weight and also for family size and work performed. Their method was sensible, their procedure thorough, and I have retained it. Tables 3.1–3.3 contain the essence of their findings. The first (3.1) is a comparison of the different food surveys during and after the war, reduced to a single scale.

In this table Kruse and Hintze took a conventional pre-war food norm, derived from Voit, Rubner and Cammerer, of 3,000 calories a day for an adult male and 2,240 per person. They went on to compare it with actual household surveys. Before the war (and up to 1915) the surveys suggested that lower-middle-class families and skilled hard-working labourers normally consumed about a fifth to a quarter more than the nutritional norm,

[3] W. Kruse and K. Hintze, *Sparsame Ernährung. Nach Erhebungen im Krieg und Frieden* (Dresden 1922), p. 88.

[4] Ibid., pp. 11–12; table 'Food Distributed in Nine of the Principal Cities of Saxony per Inhabitant in 1918', in 'Saxony, State of Nutrition and Shortage of Food', ARA 64, HIA; 'Report . . . on a visit to Leipzig, 12–15 Jan. 1919', Officers' Reports, p. 10.

[5] Kruse and Hintze, *Sparsame Ernährung*, table 4, p. 20.

TABLE 3.1. *Food consumption norms and survey data in Germany,*
1885–1920

	Mean food consumption per head and per day, standardized for age structure, for body-weight and for work performed			
	(1) Calories	(2) Protein (grams)	(3) Fat (grams)	
Recommended standards				
a. Per head, standardized for population structure in 1910	2,240	92	44	
b. Adult male (70 kg., medium work)	3,000	123	59	
Surveys	%	%	%	Persons in sample
1. As *a* above.	100	100	100	
2. Zittau handweavers 1885 (Rechenberg)	96	57	83	116
3. 179 Hamburg households, 1907 (May)				
4. Poor Hamburg households, 1907 (May)	99	57	147	16
5. Well-off Hamburg households, May 1907	130	85	192	16
6. 320 metalworker families, 1909	119	80	156	1,300
7. Munich families of moderate means, 1915 (Welker)	118	83	153	10,550
8. Urban survey, April 1916 (KAKI)	97	66	77	4,079
9. Urban survey, July 1916 (KAKI)	96	64	72	644
10. Urban survey, April 1917 (KAKI)	77	59	62	1,597
11. Ditto, standardized for body-weight and work	86	64	67	
12. Leipzig, 1917–18 (Kruse and Hintze)	99	61	55	96
13. Leipzig, Nov. 1919 (Kruse and Hintze)	105	62	86	102
14. Leipzig, Nov. 1920 (Kruse and Hintze)	106	62	110	92
15. Leipzig family no. 99, 1917–19	103	57	37	6

Source: W. Kruse and K. Hintze, *Sparsame Ernährung. Nach Erhebungen im Krieg und Frieden* (Dresden 1922), table 88, pp. 88–9.

Note: Surveys 8–10 not controlled for body-weight and work. This has the effect of depressing the data somewhat.

say about 3,700 calories for an adult male, but the low-earning segment, represented by the Zittau handloom weavers and the Hamburg poor, lived at or very close to the norm.

In 1916 calorie consumption descended to the level of Rubner's recommended nutritional norm. It fell further, almost a quarter below this standard, by April 1917, but if weight loss is taken into account the decline is to a level of about 85 per cent of the norm. Thereafter consumption rose and stabilized at or around the 3,000 calorie norm. In other words, except for the period of the "turnip winter" and for the summer of 1918, the levels of civilian food consumption in Germany (taking weight loss into account) approximated to pre-war norms. Little sign here of the nutritional catastrophe so graphically described by Rubner and his collaborators.

The published Leipzig survey is a rich source. It contains the raw data as well as notes on the occupation and health of every single participant. In its random evocation of individual circumstances it conveys, in a dry sort of way, a sense of the diversity of experiences in a wartime community. For our purpose a good summary of the findings is contained in the tables on weight movements and energy intake (tables 3.2, 3.3). As before, and due to the small number of men in these wartime households, women alone were sampled.

When the survey began most of the weight loss had already occurred. By using the ratios between height and weight and comparing them with pre-war ratios in Saxony, the authors estimated a 9 per cent decline of weight below peacetime for men and 7 per cent for women, or considerably less than half of Rubner's estimate. Another study, of 570 adults in a small town in Bavaria (Weiden) in 1917, showed that the middle and upper classes had lost much more weight than the lower classes, and that lower-class men lost 7.7 per cent and women 4.9 per cent, an echo of the Leipzig findings.[6]

After reaching this low the women's weight stabilized, and then went up again. Over the period as a whole, from February 1917 to November 1918, they gained about 7.5 per cent (on trend), and the result is statistically robust (significant at the 0.01 level). If two cases of exceptional weight gain are excluded, the rate is still 6.3 per cent. This is important. It shows that the balance of food and female work was sufficient to maintain body weight *after the middle of 1917*, and then to increase it gradually.

The data for calorie intake are more precise, and are summarized in

---

[6] Kruse and Hintze, *Sparsame Ernährung*, pp. 26–7; Bavaria: A. Loewy, 'Unternährung', *Realencyklopädie der gesamten Heilkunde* (A. Eulenberg (ed.), Ergebnisse der gesamten Medizin, vol. 2; Berlin and Vienna 1922), p. 47.

TABLE 3.2. *Leipzig female weights, 1917–1918 (kg)*

Year	Month	Mean	Standard Deviation	Persons in sample
1917	2	51.6	7.7	7
	3	51.1	7.2	15
	4	48.9	5.7	9
	5	50.7	7.2	15
	6	50.8	7.4	20
	7	50.5	6.9	24
	8	50.6	6.9	23
	9	50.9	6.8	28
	10	52.1	6.7	29
	11	52.2	6.8	33
	12	52.8	6.4	32
1918	1	53.3	6.4	31
	2	53.5	6.7	31
	3	53.1	6.7	34
	4	53.4	6.7	34
	5	53.5	6.8	32
	6	53.3	6.9	33
	7	53.4	6.7	32
	8	53.7	6.5	31
	9	54.1	6.5	29
	10	53.3	6.3	30
	11	54.1	6.3	27

Source: Data in Kruse and Hintze, *Sparsame Ernährung,* pp. 149–252.

Table 3.3. Column (4) shows the energy available as a percentage of the recommended pre-war norm (2,240 calories per person, or 3,000 calories for an adult male). This column should be compared with col. (1) in table 3.1. In March 1917, in the depth of the turnip winter, the calorie level consumed in Leipzig corresponded quite closely to the level found in KAKI's survey of April 1917, and provides a link with it. Thereafter the level rose. It touched the pre-war norm in June, and then declined again towards the end of the harvest year, in July and August 1917. The post-harvest peak in September increased the standardized calorie intake about 10 per cent above the pre-war scientific norm. From November 1917 to June 1918 the intake fluctuated around the norm, and then fell sharply towards the end of the harvest year. In August 1918 it declined to turnip winter levels. The recovery in September was short-lived. Apart from the stable period between November 1917 and May 1918, the fluctuations are

TABLE 3.3. *Calories per head, per day, Leipzig, 1917–1918*

Year	(1) Month	(2) Households	(3) Standardized mean	(4) % of norm	(5) Actual mean	(6) Standard deviation
1917	3	12	1,812	**80.9**	1,743	256
	4	8	2,116	**94.4**	1,868	188
	5	13	2,196	**98.0**	1,894	239
	6	18	2,241	**100.0**	1,953	221
	7	21	2,148	**95.9**	1,890	254
	8	20	2,192	**97.9**	1,855	200
	9	24	2,494	**111.4**	2,086	403
	10	27	2,469	**110.2**	2,102	505
	11	29	2,265	**101.1**	1,915	324
	12	28	2,279	**101.7**	1,923	275
1918	1	28	2,302	**102.8**	1,953	291
	2	28	2,211	**98.7**	1,889	221
	3	30	2,187	**97.6**	1,898	213
	4	30	2,230	**99.6**	1,941	280
	5	29	2,163	**96.5**	1,895	297
	6	29	2,280	**101.8**	1,985	297
	7	27	2,088	**93.2**	1,832	275
	8	27	1,989	**88.8**	1,759	254
	9	25	2,286	**102.0**	2,000	328
	10	26	2,165	**96.6**	1,917	312
	11	24	2,149	**95.9**	1,868	270

Note: Col. (3) shows the calorie intake of the surveyed households, standardized for age, sex, family size and weight and (for heavy-labour workers) for the work performed, according to the structure of population in Germany in 1910.

Source: Kruse and Hintze, *Sparsame Ernährung,* pp. 149–241.

statistically significant (at the 0.5 per cent level). Calorie intakes correlated poorly with weights, probably for two reasons. Weights were measured once a month, while calorie data were averaged from daily food purchases. Secondly, calorie intake was measured for the whole household, and not for individual women. After the turnip winter this household calorie intake did not fall below 95 per cent of the norm for the rest of the war (except for July and August 1918). The scientific norm, however, was lower than actual consumption levels in pre-war Hamburg, and in Munich during the early days of the war.

Kruse and Hintze claimed that the wartime diet was adequate. While critical of Chittenden, they were nevertheless sympathetic to his idea of the parsimonious diet. They argued that in calories the wartime diet was comparable to some common peacetime nutrition levels. It was higher than the food available to the handloom weavers at Zittau in the 1890s, whose health was satisfactory. According to May's calculations, almost two-thirds of the German population before the war had a nutritional standard comparable to that of his "poor" families (table 3.1, row 4), and to some British pre-war working-class diets, as disclosed by Rowntree and Bowley. For most of the time the level matched Rubner's pre-war calorie norm. Kruse and Hintze actually criticized Chittenden for excessive claims. They argued that his failure to take account of the lower food requirement at lower weights led him to exaggerate the economies achieved by his subjects.[7]

On the face of it, there is a lot of sense in Kruse's and Hintze's argument. In one of his post-war essays Rubner calculated how long it would take to starve to death on the rations officially provided during 1917. He implied that death had been averted, but only by a narrow margin.[8] Now that was manifestly false. German miners, for example, dug more coal in 1918 than in 1914 and only 15 per cent less iron ore.[9] Food was sufficient to sustain these efforts.

Kruse and Hintze showed that (for people in moderate work) the *energy* in the food sufficed. It was the *composition* of the diet that mattered. In comparison with pre-war diets the food was low in meat (animal protein) and even more so in fat. Rubner was a champion of protein and meat, and his recommended diet contained more than twice as much protein as fat. In reality, all the pre-war diets showed protein consumption well below his recommended level, and fat consumption well above it, almost twice as much in pre-war Hamburg. Germans had acquired a taste for meat before the war, but not as much as Rubner supposed; on the other hand, the urban population came to rely on large amounts of cheap fat for their energy in the form of margarine and lard.

In wartime the vast bulk of energy and protein requirements came from vegetable food, from grain and potatoes, and fat consumption fell, not perhaps as low as the ration tables suggested, but to one-half or two-thirds of pre-war consumption. It was the shortage of meat and fat, and not lack of energy as such, that was the most keenly felt. A recent analysis of the KAKI surveys (carried out without reference to the Leipzig study) also shows a strong continuity with peacetime diets.[10] Wartime writers on nutrition said that the absence of fat in the diet was the chief source of the

[7] Kruse and Hintze, *Sparsame Ernährung*, pp. 67–74.

[8] Rubner, 'Ernährungswesen', pp. 22–30.

[9] F. Friedensburg, *Kohl und Eisen im Weltkriege und in den Friedensschlüssen* (Munich and Berlin 1934), pp. 129, 135.

[10] A. Triebel, 'Variations in Patterns of consumption in Germany in the Period of the First

feeling of hunger. Fat takes longer to digest than other foods, and delays the onset of hunger. Without it, even a sufficient intake of energy did not prevent a constant rumbling of the stomach.[11]

It was difficult to cook without fat. Ethel Cooper wrote, 'one feels so dried up often, that I wonder one doesn't creak for want of oiling'.[12] Her letters from Leipzig echo the observations of the two professors. Her circumstances were similar to those of many of the women covered by their survey. After 1916 her letters are obsessed with food. Her body responded in the way described by Kruse and Hintze. In May 1916 she wrote, 'If I look thin, you must not think that I am anything but perfectly well. I never felt better in my life. . . .' In September 1918,

Most people complain of being under-nourished—probably the average German, accustomed to very fatty food and much beer, feels the change more than I do . . . it is deadly monotonous, but I can't say that I feel under-fed—I am certainly always hungry, but I never felt better or fitter in my life, and I can't understand why so few people seem able to adapt themselves to the same regime.[13]

Kruse's and Hintze's medical comments on the women in Leipzig show very few life-threatening disorders. Neumann, the Bonn nutritionist, stated that his working strength suffered no decrease after his weight declined from 70 to 57 kg.[14]

Rubner justified his use of the ration as the measure of food intake because, according to the KAKI survey of 1916, 86–90 per cent of the food was derived from the ration. By 1917 and 1918 even Rubner had to admit that this was no longer the case.[15] The Leipzig survey provides a measure of the scale of black-market and other illicit supplies. In 1918 the average ration of calories per head per day in Leipzig was 1,280.[16] The calories consumed in our sample of households in the same year averaged 1,900.[17] In other words, the calories consumed even by these skilled working- and lower-middle-class families exceeded the basic ration by between 40 and 50 per cent. For another test, take the monthly ration figures for Bonn and compare them with consumption figures for Leipzig. As a town in the Rhineland, Bonn was likely to be better off than Leipzig, a large city in Saxony. Furthermore, the official ration was not always available and should be regarded as a maximum. Between February 1917 and November

World War', in R. Wall and J. M. Winter (eds.), *The Upheaval of War* (forthcoming), table 5.
[11] E. H. Starling, 'The Significance of Fats in the Diet', *British Medical Journal* (3 Aug. 1918), pp. 105–7.
[12] Cooper, *Behind the Lines*, 21 Apr. 1918, p. 252.
[13] Ibid., 28 May 1916, p. 141; 15 Sept. 1918, p. 276.
[14] Johanesson, 'The Food Problem', fo. 10.
[15] Rubner, 'Ernährungswesen', pp. 19–20.
[16] Calculated from 'Food Distributed in Nine of the Principal Cities of Saxony per Inhabitant in 1918', ARA 64, HIA (n. 4 above).
[17] Table 3.3, mean of col. (5) for 1918.

1918 the actual food consumption in Leipzig exceeded the Bonn ration by 29 per cent. The excess was cyclical, higher in the summer and lower in the winter.[18]

These figures place a different construction on the food problem in wartime Germany. Apart from the trauma of the turnip winter of 1916–17 and of the summer of 1918, the problem was not so much an absolute shortfall of food. Although less food was available per head, a smaller ration still answered the basic energy needs once people had lost sufficient weight and limited their exertions somewhat. According to Chittenden, loss of energy and vigour should not have followed loss of weight. That, of course, is not so clear.

It would be wrong to infer from these data that Germans suffered no hunger. After all these were only *averages*. Evened out, the food was sufficient, more or less, to maintain weight. But rations fluctuated a great deal from week to week. If the average just matched the food norm, then it is likely that half the time the people ate less than the norm. Many people ate less *all* the time. Vital staples like bread, meat and potatoes were not to be had for weeks at a time. And there must have been a great deal of hunger from week to week, from one day to another, from one meal to another. The German people were often cold and hungry. But, whatever their complaints, Germany did not starve.

[18] Leipzig: table 3.3, col. (5); Bonn: F. W. Bach, *Untersuchungen über die Lebensmittel-rationierung im Kriege und ihre physiologisch-hygienische Bedeutung* (Munich 1919), tables 2, 4, 10, pp. 148a, 172a.

4

FOOD AND THE GERMAN STATE

I

In wartime Germany rations fell too low to maintain body weight for long periods of time and getting hold of sufficient food became a matter of survival. A large fraction, one-fifth to one-third of the food, could only be obtained through illegal channels.[1]

Food rationing brings out the most far-reaching form of "war socialism"—the principle of distribution according to need. Both Germany and Britain attempted to distribute food equally during the First World War, though they used different approaches. It is curious that societies so deeply committed to inequality should revert to egalitarian principles in wartime. Apparently this answered to a need for equity: 'We are all Germans now,' the Kaiser declared, and the myth of solidarity is one of the strongest bonds in wartime. But levelling strains the fabric of society, and inequality returns through the back door. Indeed, if one assumes that inequality serves an economic function, then the communist principle of distribution is counter-productive unless everyone accepts communal principles of motivation. Equality of consumption did not extend to the military. As we shall see, the principle of hierarchy was stronger there. At home the black market restored the differentials that rationing removed.

Rationing in Germany was mechanical. Not only did it fail to acknowledge inequality of wealth, it took very little account of physical inequalities. Men, women and children received the same basic rations. Children sometimes received less of particular articles and more of others; the sick and nursing mothers received certain additions, while workers engaged in hard physical labour received a small supplement.

Even if the diet actually met the energy requirements of Leipzig townspeople, their food fell short on many other counts. A monthly mean conceals sharp weekly fluctuations, and a week is a long time to go hungry. War food quality was poor and calorie counts should only be taken as maxima. Flour was diluted with potato and turnip, the beer had little alcohol. Ethel Cooper suspected that sausages contained rat; her friend responded, 'Oh, I don't mind *rat* . . . but I have a real horror of rat *substitute*!'[2]

Urban life lost a great deal of its amenity. Electric trams seldom arrived

---

[1] Ch. 3, pp. 52–3, above.
[2] Cooper, *Behind the Lines*, 25 Mar. 1917, p. 189.

or vanished altogether, coal was short and baths were a luxury, public buildings remained unheated, clothes became threadbare and the sheer effort of collecting the ration and searching for illegal food, of queuing in the cold and tramping around town and into the countryside placed an additional drain on calories. Town dwellers fell into a poverty that many, perhaps most, had never experienced before.

A constant refrain in Ethel Cooper's letters is that although she can manage somehow, 'what the poor are doing passes my understanding.'[3] War threw income relativities into disarray. In the towns the well-off could supplement the ration through the black market. But even the wealthy lost a lot of body weight.[4] Among the working classes, experiences diverged sharply. Armament workers did best and, if they were skilled, managed to keep abreast and even ahead of official prices; but the unskilled and those in non-war industries fell badly behind.[5] Local studies confirm the national surveys.

Wage rates of the best-paid workers in the Düsseldorf munitions industries increased 2.3 times during the war, while those of unskilled workers in the same industries rose merely 0.4 times. In Stuttgart the pattern also corresponded to the national one. War industry wages lagged behind the rise in official food prices for some periods and kept up with it in others. Unskilled wages and wages in non-war industries fell very badly behind the rise even of rationed food prices.[6] Longer hours and working wives sometimes added to family earnings, but workers in low-priority sectors had only limited access to unrationed food. Impressions of hardship abound. Richard Stumpf, a sailor on the High Seas Fleet, described how dockworkers came aboard his battleship to beg for scraps of food, which they tried to smuggle off. 'The misery and suffering of these hard-working men was written on their faces.' A returned British civilian gave his impression of a German labourer working on repairs at Ruhleben internment camp. 'He was only just strong enough to walk about, and quite unfitted really for anything like hard work. Semi-starvation had made him pitifully slow and uncertain in all he did; and I remember that it took him three weeks to lay down quite a small piece of concrete.'[7] From a higher base than manual workers, white-collar clerks and minor officials saw their incomes erode as badly as those of the worse-paid labourers. The war brought them into a broad equality of misery with the working

---

[3] Ibid. 6 Feb. 1916, p. 126; and see pp. 107, 109,132, 182.

[4] Blücher, *English Wife*, p. 158; Cooper, *Behind the Lines*, pp. 141, 165, 202.

[5] J. Kocka, *Facing Total War: German Society, 1914–1918* (Leamington Spa 1984), pp. 16–26.

[6] Tobin, 'Düsseldorf', pp. 268–75; Mai, *Kriegswirtschaft*, pp. 393–406.

[7] R. Stumpf, *The Private War of Richard Stumpf*, ed. D. Horn (1969), pp. 259–60, 294–5; E. L. Pyke, *Desperate Germany* (1918), p. 33.

classes.[8] Nevertheless, that is less than the whole story, for this population formed the focus of the KAKI and the Leipzig surveys, which showed an acceptable level of nutrition, apart from the "turnip winter" (and the summer of 1918—which KAKI did not cover). With more than one household member at work, family earnings determined the standard of living more than nominal wage rates.[9] Rationing per head actually favoured large households and those in which women predominated.

When goods are rationed, there is not much point in measuring the movement of so-called "real" wages: the goods that make up the index are not to be had, and those that are purchased illegally carry a heavy premium.[10] To make up an adequate energy ration, food had to be obtained on the black market, often at exorbitant cost. An expert observer estimated that in Berlin in 1918, one-eighth to one-seventh of the bread and potatoes, one-quarter to one-third of milk, butter and cheese and one-third to one-half of eggs and meat were obtained on the black market at prices up to ten times higher than in peacetime. My own data suggest up to one-third of the total, and this conforms to an English estimate made soon after the war, probably after a meeting with the German expert.[11] Other consumer goods were almost unobtainable: soap, fabrics, clothing and footwear—all were scarce, expensive and shoddy. The German man— 'started his weary day with a twenty-minute struggle to shave without soap, during which he has probably cut himself in several places, and has no soothing ointment of any kind to rub on his chin,' wrote a returned internee; an American journalist reported an 'increase of shop-lifting among the better classes . . . because it is the only way to circumvent the food and clothing regulations!' [12] Money gave access to the black market, but illicit goods were not bought by money alone. Ethel Cooper relied on the black market, but she also received illicit goods as presents, treats, in barter, by foraging and even stealing. Some of her friends ran smuggling and trading rings, while others illegally consumed the products of their own estates. Of the Leipzig families, two received food consignments from the Front, which made a considerable difference.[13] Money wages alone did not determine the standard of living, especially in a country so recently urbanized as Germany, where rural connections were still strong.

[8] Kocka, *Total War*, pp. 84–90.

[9] Zimmermann, 'Veränderungen', in Meerwarth *et al.*, *Einwirkung*, pp. 473–4.

[10] U. Malich, 'Zur Entwicklung des Reallohns im ersten Weltkrieg', *Jahrbuch für Wirtschaftsgeschichte* (1980), pt. 2. Malich's own procedures, however, are dubious.

[11] Zimmermann, 'Veränderungen', p. 441; Starling, 'Food Conditions', pp. 5–7.

[12] Pyke, *Desperate Germany*, p. 16.; MI 6B, *Daily Summary of Information*, no. 565, 8 Mar. 1918, ADM 137/2835.

[13] Cooper, *Behind the Lines*, *passim*; Kruse and Hintze, *Sparsame Ernährung*, pp. 154, 227.

II

In ordinary circumstances the distribution of food creates more value than its production. In the United States, for example, in 1914, the farmer's share of the retail cost of a basket of farm food products was 45 per cent.[14] Rationing and its complementary institution, the black market, imposed a heavy burden on the distribution system, and much of it was simply passed on to the consumer.

It is no exaggeration to say that the *whole* day goes in the search for what is necessary to live on just for that day. You have literally to go *three* times for every article of food . . . Until one has experienced it I am sure one can form no idea of what a waste of energy goes on, when *every* necessity of life has to be ordered and called for at an appointed and different hour.

Like many other townspeople, Miss Cooper often ventured out on Sundays into the countryside in her search for food. 'Sometimes one has luck and can find a few eggs or potatoes, but as a rule there is nothing to be had.'[15]

Imagine relegating one-third of the food supply to the status of contraband: to a level with narcotic drugs, or with bootleg whiskey in the United States. To supply a quarter or a third of the country's food outside the legal channel placed a large burden on the means of distribution and supply. Not all the excess price of black-market goods was superprofit: much of it covered the real costs of evading regulations, of concealing, transporting and selling goods in contravention of the law, and of making up for confiscations and fines. This parallel system of supply had to use inferior transport, as one official report described:

One abuse which the shortage of food has created is to be found in the daily plundering expeditions by train to the country, where food has been carted off in great quantities either through persuasion or through force. The Greifenhagen district has so far delivered around 36,000 hundredweight of potatoes and estimates that a further 10,000 hundredweight have been taken out of the area in illegal ways. The rural police have been strengthened by thirty-six men, petty officers and sergeants, from the garrison at Stettin. The transport of potatoes is prohibited on the train and river boats, but the illegal trade has still not quite been stamped out. Potatoes and vegetables are carted away in cars and in small boats that come down, not on the River Oder, but on the River Reglitz. At times, complete anarchy reigned on the railways. The railway personnel, consisting chiefly of conductresses, were completely powerless; nor could the military at the railway stations prevail over the masses.[16]

[14] United States Bureau of Census, *The Statistical History of the United States from Colonial Times to the Present* (New York, 1976), ser. K357, p. 489.

[15] Cooper, *Behind the Lines*, 19 Aug. 1917, pp. 215–16; 3 June 1917, p. 199.

[16] 2nd Army Corps [Stettin] report, July 1917, MB 3 Aug. 1917, p. 17, quoted in Kocka, *Total War*, pp. 157–8.

Over and above the scarcities and deprivations already imposed by wartime, the German system of distribution encumbered itself with two other burdens: law enforcement and law evasion. Both of them cost the state and the economy dearly. The scale of the illicit economy and many casual comments suggest that it was widely tolerated. More positive adaptations also took place. Foremost was the system of municipal feeding. Large towns made their own contracts with suppliers, stored food and distributed it. They also ran communal kitchens that catered for up to a tenth of their populations and provided cheap, dull but nourishing food in exchange for ration tickets. Large manufacturing firms bought considerable quantities of food outside the rationing system to sustain their workers.[17]

The effect of the rationing system was paradoxical: many of those who accepted inequality as a law of nature in peacetime became agitated about it in wartime. This sentiment undermined the legitimacy of ordinary business enterprise. Capitalism coexisted uneasily with war communism. On the other hand, this new doctrine of wartime equality was very alien. Ethel Cooper expressed this duality when she wrote, 'this beastly usury with the bare necessities of life sickens me, and one meets it at every turn, and nobody seems to mind taking part in it, or feel any sort of responsibility in doing it . . .'. How thoroughly the war upset the moral economy is shown by her own foraging expeditions, when she happily stole apples and plums and regretted a duck that got away. 'Where *everything* is forbidden, you simply *have* to break the laws if you want to go on living,' she wrote.[18]

Officials along the food chain, especially in transport and the various food agencies, had plenty of opportunities for corruption, and, if they had not taken them, the black market could not have functioned on such a scale. Kocka quotes from another official report in July 1918:

Things are stolen and taken wherever possible. Whole trains are plundered by the [railway] employees, including officials, as a daily occurrence. The sale of government property for private use increases to a horrendous degree. It is impossible to detail sufficient watchmen and sentries to protect property since one finds time and again that the watchmen participate in the thefts.[19]

On the home front, the German state failed twice over. First, in the task of feeding its citizens: that in itself would be sufficient cause for disillusion

---

[17] The role of municipalities: Skalweit, *Kriegsernährungswirtschaft*, pp. 146–162; the British officers and (later) Bott gave the civic authorities high marks for their food administration: e.g. Officers' Reports, pp. 19, 27; Bott, 'German Food Crisis', p. 134.

[18] Cooper, *Behind the Lines*, 29 Apr. 1917, p. 195; 20 Aug. 1916, p. 155; 4 Aug. 1918, p. 270.

[19] 2nd Army Corps (Stettin), June 1918, MB 3 July 1918, p. 22, quoted in Kocka, *Total War*, p. 98.

and forms a running theme of the protests, strikes and demonstrations of 1916–18. It also forced every citizen into breaking the law. Kocka describes how this alienated not only the workers but also the mass ranks of officials and white-collar employees. Moral trauma compounded physical suffering. The middle classes were insufficiently indigent (or excessively proud) to take advantage of the soup kitchens, and the constant recourse to the black market provoked outrage, humiliation and guilt. When the law had to be broken in pursuit of subsistence, this cut across the habits and values of a lifetime. If a middle-class household could not afford black-market food, the illicit enterprise around them rankled even more. Exchanging heirlooms for food made them feel exposed and humiliated. Good clothing, so important for status, had to be sold, wore out, or was surrendered to a government desperately short of textiles. As Kocka writes, 'the more deeply and intensively the State authorities intervened in most peoples' lives, the more they became identified with the increasing hardships and difficulties . . .'.[20]

Children and youth growing up during the war lost their respect for authority. Young people broke into barns and orchards at night in the search for food. They were the first victims of hunger, and suffered from mortality disproportionately, especially after the age of fourteen, when their bodily needs grew. If everyone became a lawbreaker, youth was more daring. The detected youth crime rate doubled, and we can only guess at the extent of petty stealing, digging in the fields at night, black marketeering and other expedients adopted in order to keep alive. All forms of youth crime increased, including crimes of violence. A government that failed to feed its youth could hardly expect to hold on to its loyalty.[21]

III

Food shortages also affected the armed forces more directly. The navy was originally as well provided as the army, with a very rich ration, but during the turnip winter rations fell in line with the rest of the country. They were still better than those available to civilians, but unlike civilians, the sailors had neither the money nor the time to make use of the black market. In this respect, they were a disadvantaged group. Since the battleships rarely went out of port, officers went home to their families many evenings. They

---

[20] Kocka, *Total War*, p. 157.
[21] L. Richter, *Family Life in Germany under the Blockade* (1919), pp. 42–7; R. von Leyen, 'Die englische Hungerblockade in ihren Wirkungen auf die Kriminalität und Verwahrlosung der Jugendlichen', in Rubmann (ed.), *Hunger!*; E. Rosenhaft, 'A World Upside-down: Delinquency, Family and Work in the Lives of German Working-class Youth, 1914–18' (unpublished paper, Liverpool University ?1984).

were much better paid and often dined conspicuously well. Even Richard
Stumpf, a conservative sailor, a monarchist and anti-socialist, felt his blood
boil: his progress from an unreflecting conservative to a rebellious radical
was literally a gut response to hunger and humiliation, and not a process of
intellectual conversion. The food complaint committees on the High Seas
Fleet formed the cores of the mutinies of August 1917.[22] Nor should the
importance of the navy be slighted. It was vital in protecting two German
flanks: the North Sea coast and the Baltic. It released troops from coast
protection and forced the Allies to concentrate their efforts on the western
front and the Mediterranean and to tie up large resources in their own
superior navies. The Baltic provided a vital trading link with neutrals, and
its loss would have made the blockade more onerous. Like the British
navy, the German navy could not win the war but it had the capacity to lose
it.

From 1916 onwards the army suffered a serious shortage of fodder.
Army horse numbers were below strength and the animals were also
physically weak. Between January and April 1918, 70,000 horses became ill
with exhaustion and about 28,000 died from it on the western front alone.[23]
Desperate army attempts to requisition fodder at home exacerbated the
food crisis of early summer 1918.[24]

For its soldiers, the army managed to maintain an energy ration
throughout—but, like civilian food, it was monotonous and bland. Cooks
and commissaries had a constant struggle to juggle components in order to
make up an acceptable ration. Essential ingredients, like potatoes and fat,
often went lacking for weeks. Some articles, like tinned meat, bread,
substitute tobacco, coffee and tea, were of poor quality. By 1918 absolute
shortages were also common. In the spring offensives of 1918, as
Ludendorff complained, 'the troops stopped round captured food supplies,
while individuals stayed behind to search houses and farms for food'. Since
the rusks in their "iron ration" were virtually inedible, they can hardly be
blamed.

By the late spring of 1918 the army was living from hand to mouth, and
resorted to requisition raids on farmsteads in Germany to ensure its
supplies. Reserves of flour were so low that, when the new harvest came in
the army had to short cut its own storage system and rush flour directly
from the mills to the front. Likewise, potatoes for the northern wing of the
western front were no longer moved through civilian channels. By the
autumn of 1918 the military food supply system for the armies on this wing

[22] D. Horn, *The German Naval Mutinies of World War I* (New Brunswick, New Jersey
1969), chs. 2, 4.
[23] K. Schulze and W. Otto, 'Das Militärveterinärwesen', in M. Schwarte (ed.), *Der grosse
Krieg, 1914–1918* (Leipzig 1923), vol. 9, pt. 2, p. 584.
[24] MB June 1918, pp. 3, 26 MKr. 12852.

was on the point of collapse. When Ludendorff was asked in the War Cabinet on 17 October 1918 about the threat of Allied tanks, he replied that some élite units would make a regular game of shooting tanks. 'It is also an attractive sport for practical reasons, since there is always good food in the tanks.'[25]

Occasional shortages became sufficiently critical for Ludendorff to blame the Allied breakthrough of 8 August 1918, "the black day of the German army", on physical infirmity among the troops, arising from shortage of potatoes and from influenza. Another factor was the breakdown of morale, which the generals blamed on "infection" from reinforcements from the rear. In other words, the poor morale caused by food shortages at home spread to the front by means of young recruits, reinforcements and soldiers returning from leave. German troop morale was badly dented during the summer of 1918, and there is general agreement that it was associated with the state of mind at home.[26] Critics of the military pointed out that one of the main reasons for discontent within the army was inequality in the distribution of rations, with the officers enjoying superior food in their messes, while troops in the rear, with access to the black market, to their own gardens and to animals, lived better than troops in the line.[27]

IV

Food supply was bad in the last three years of the war. In the first two years of the war the authorities responded much too slowly to the mounting crisis, but, once a national system was established in 1916, was it a failure? Could anyone do better? German food administrators worked under difficult constraints.

The Allied blockade of Germany was the most important of these constraints. It had taken a long time to tighten and was only perfected after the United States joined the war. By 1918 imports into Germany had fallen to 39 per cent of their 1913 level in gold marks. Since gold depreciated during the war, the level of merchandise imports was probably about

[25] K. Lau, 'Die Heeresverpflegung', in Schwarte (ed.) *Der grosse Krieg*, vol. 9, pt. 2; E. von Ludendorff, *My War Memories, 1914–1918* (2nd edn. 1920), vol. 2, p. 611; Ludendorff, Protocol of Session of the German War Cabinet of 17 October 1918, in R. H. Lutz (ed.), *Documents of the German Revolution: Fall of the German Empire, 1914–1918* (Stanford 1932), vol. 2, p. 490 (trans. follows H. Rudin, *Armistice 1918* (New Haven 1944), p. 150).

[26] Ludendorff, *War Memories*, pp. 586, 611, 683–4; Ludendorff, War Cabinet Protocol, 17 Oct. 1918, in Lutz, *Fall of the German Empire*, vol. 2, p. 473; H. von Stein, *Erlebnisse und Betrachtungen aus der Zeit des Weltkrieges* (Leipzig 1919), pp. 154–5.

[27] Ludendorff, War Cabinet Protocol 17 Oct. 1918, in Lutz, *Fall of the German Empire*, vol. 2, p. 480; Stein, *Erlebnisse*, p. 157; M. Hobohm, 'Soziale Heermissstände als Teilursache des deutschen Zusammenbruchs von 1918', *Untersuchung*, 4th ser., vol. 11, pp. 123–50.

one-fifth of the pre-war level by 1918.[28] Although detailed data are not available, it is safe to assume that the bulk of pre-war food imports was no longer available, although some continued to trickle in from the neutrals, especially during the first two years. Because of the blockade, Germany was unable, as Britain was, to mobilize the resources of other countries to make up for the failings of its own wartime food production. The labour, draft animals and other inputs that had to remain on Germany's farms were not available for its war industries or for the front.

Before the war Germany had an intensive agriculture, with yields among the highest in the world, achieved by large inputs of labour and fertilizers. About two-thirds of the male labour force in agriculture was called up in the course of the war, some 3.3 million men, including the strongest and most efficient workers and also those with the best knowledge and skills. Intensive agriculture, especially livestock management, depends on experienced judgement, and many farms, perhaps even the majority, lost the man who made those decisions before the war. As more than half the pre-war labour force was female, the loss of skills was perhaps even more critical than the loss of labour power.[29]

Government did a great deal to counteract the shortfall of labour. Some 430,000 migrant labourers had already arrived in Germany for the harvest when the war began, and most of those were detained for the duration. Up to 900,000 prisoners of war went to work on the land. Army headquarters troops pitched in to help and large numbers of soldiers went home on harvest leave. Many farm managers were not drafted and others were discharged. Of those who remained on the land, many were asked to manage a number of neighbouring farms. Schoolchildren and volunteers helped with the harvest. For all these stopgaps, the labour force remained short in both energy and knowledge. H. C. von Batocki, the food controller, regarded the supply of draft animals and of fodder to the army as the heaviest burden that agriculture had to bear.[30]

It is difficult to say by how much agricultural production fell during the war. Harvest statistics before the war overstated output by as much as 15–20 per cent. During the war it is reasonable to assume that agricultural statistics underestimated output, and for obvious reasons. There were

[28] Import and export data in G. Hardach, *The First World War, 1914–1918* (1977), table 6, p. 33. A rough measure of the depreciation of gold is the rise of American prices (the dollar remained convertible to gold), which approximately doubled during the war: *Statistical History of the US*, ser. E40–41, p. 200.

[29] A. Skalweit, 'The Maintenance of the Agricultural Labour Supply during the War', *International Review of Agricultural Economics*, vol. 13 (1922), pp. 850–2.

[30] Skalweit, ibid., *passim*; L. Elsner, 'Foreign Workers and Forced Labor in Germany during the First World War' in D. Hoerder (ed.), *Labor Migration in the Atlantic Economies* (Westport, Connecticut 1985); H. C. von Batocki, *Warenpreis und Geldwert im Kriege* (Königsberg 1919), p. 14.

enormous unexplained leakages between harvest and delivery. With such a large fraction of demand satisfied by illicit means, statistics form a very poor guide. Taking the two most significant crops, which were tightly controlled, a recent estimate shows rye declining from 10.4 million tons in 1914 to 6.7 in 1918; potatoes from 45.6 to 24.7.[31]

Most other resources were also in short supply: fertilizer and fodder were the most critical. German farmers had been using three times as much artificial fertilizer per unit of land as their French counterparts. A good deal of the phosphoric and nitrogenous fertilizers came from overseas in various forms and these chemicals were also needed for explosives. The quantity of phosphoric fertilizer available to farmers fell by some 50 per cent during the war, and the amount of pure nitrogen used declined from about 210,000 tons in 1913/14 to an average 81,000 tons in the last three years of the war. Potash was more readily available and was applied in larger amounts, perhaps excessively. Fertilizers were not controlled and were thus more readily available to farmers who supplied the black market. This diverted more food into illicit trading.

About six million tons of fodder, mostly grain, were imported yearly before the war. In fact, the shortfall was even greater, since a good deal of the rye cultivated at home was used as fodder, while bread was baked from three million tons of imported wheat. Once these imports stopped, comparable amounts of rye had to be diverted from animals to breadmaking. Likewise, potatoes and even turnips were taken away from the pigs and fed to people, while sugar beet, another important source of fodder, was run down for the lack of labour and fertilizer. An American scientist calculated that by 1915–16 the value of fodder available had fallen by a third. In their turn, fewer and smaller animals produced less dung.[32] The railway system suffered badly from lack of coal, shortage of locomotives, rolling stock, repair parts and labour.[33] Since Germany was poorly

---

[31] There are estimates of output in R. Berthold, 'Zur Entwicklung der deutschen Agrarproduktion und der Ernährungswirtschaft zwischen 1907 und 1925', *Jahrbuch der Wirtschaftsgeschichte*, vol. 4 (1974); defects of German agricultural statistics: C. Ballod, 'Güterbedarf und Konsumtion', in F. Zahn (ed.), *Die Statistik in Deutschland nach ihrem heutigen Stand* (Munich and Berlin 1911), pp. 610–12 and other articles in the same book; wartime "leakages": [A. E. Taylor], 'German Experiences in Minimum and Maximum Prices for Agricultural Products' (typescript, n.d., n.p. 1917), USFA 121/3, HIA (also in Lusk Papers 1/1, HIA). Statistics cited are from J. Flemming, *Landwirtschaftliche Interessen und Demokratie* (Bonn 1978), p. 84.

[32] J. A. Perkins, 'The Agricultural Revolution in Germany, 1850–1914', *Journal of European Economic History*, vol. 10 (1981), pp. 84–7; Taylor, 'Control of Food Supplies', fos. 78–89, 208–9; Aereboe, *Der Einfluss*, pp. 40–58; R. G. Moeller, 'Dimensions of Social Conflict in the Great War: The View from the German Countryside', *Central European History*, vol. 14 (1981), pp. 154–5.

[33] Feldman, *Army, Industry and Labor*, pp. 254–9; War Trade Intelligence Department, *Daily Notes*, no. 1029, 30 Sept. 1918, ADM 137/2835; H. Henning, 'Die Situation der deutschen Kriegswirtschaft im Sommer 1918 und ihre Beurteilung durch Heeresleitung, Reichsführung und Bevölkerung' (Hamburg University Ph.D. thesis, 1957), fos. 70–2.

equipped with storage facilities, transport was crucial for orderly food supplies, especially for the large towns which drew their food from a distance. This particularly affected potatoes, a bulky crop which spoiled easily.

V

How much was official policy to blame? For one thing, up to June 1916, when the War Food Office was established, there was no single policy but a patchwork of expedients that interfered with each other. Officials in the Food Office had only limited authority and had to contend with states, municipalities and the army.

From the start, official policy set out to protect consumers rather than encourage production. Despite the German tradition of authority and administration and the widespread use of compulsion, neither the state and local authorities nor the Imperial Food Office attempted seriously to plan agricultural production. They were content to operate mostly through prices. For the first two years of the war the prices set were maximum prices, designed to protect urban consumers and to keep food prices within their reach. For the farmers, this was a cruel inversion of pre-war priorities, when tariffs shielded them from the world market. Now the urban workers took precedence. Since prices failed to keep up with costs, farmers attempted to feed their grain and potatoes to livestock, which remained uncontrolled for much of the first two years. When livestock products came under control, the farmers still gave animals preference, as being more convenient for illicit marketing and for their own consumption.[34]

Throughout the war farmers were made to deliver by a combination of administrative and compulsory measures, at prices below what the market would bear. The first head of the War Food Office, Batocki, attempted to approach the problem rationally, and set it for solution to eleven academic experts on agricultural economics. They recommended a shift towards market pricing, with a change in relative pricing to make grain more attractive to producers and to reduce the attraction of meat.[35] One consequence of these measures was a flourishing black market in livestock products in the two last years of the war. The existence of this outlet meant that compulsion could not be relaxed, and during the food crises in the early summers of 1917 and 1918 such measures were especially severe; they

---

[34] Skalweit, *Kreigsernährungswirtschaft*, and Aereboe, *Der Einfluss*, contain accounts of pricing policies; for a recent survey: Flemming, *Landwirtschaftliche Interessen*, pp. 80–105.

[35] Their report is in F. Aereboe and H. Warmbold, *Preisverhältnisse landwirtschaftlicher Erzeugnisse im Kriege*, Beiträge zur Kriegswirtschaft, no. 6 (Berlin 1917), pp. 44–7.

took the form of requisition parties which searched farm buildings and even dwellings.[36]

A free market for food was out of the question, since, in conditions of absolute shortage, part of the population would simply have had nothing to eat. On the other hand, the agrarians frequently argued that price controls went too far and that more incentives would have produced a larger output.[37] Batocki later argued that some combination of compulsion and incentive was inevitable and that the market could not be liberated entirely. Another road which the authorities chose (reluctantly) was to offer higher prices to producers while keeping retail prices within the reach of consumers and subsidising the difference. This was partly done in the later years of the war but, with little for them to buy, it only partly compensated the farmers.[38]

There is another aspect to consider. Controlled prices made it possible to hold wages down and to contain domestic price inflation. In consequence, Germany was able to continue purchasing with its own currency overseas, and to build up a large trade deficit over the war years, most of it in German marks. During the war, the cumulative trade deficit was 11.1 billion gold marks, about the same (in current prices) as all imports in 1913, or, in constant prices, about half a year's imports in peacetime. The mark lost only about a third of its value compared with the US dollar between July 1914 and July 1918, or about the same as the pound sterling. At the end of the war Germany still had about £112 million in gold at the pre-war rate of exchange (say, US$535 million), which supported the currency and facilitated foreign borrowing and imports. After the war, these reserves were used to purchase food supplies. These assets were the harvest of price and wage restraint at home, and have to be balanced against any additional output that more liberal controls might have induced. Furthermore, by holding down wages, prices and inflation, the authorities were able to use war loans to divert resources from civilian to military consumption.[39]

The German tradition of discipline and a regulatory approach to political economy predisposed government towards organization and compulsion and against price incentives as a tool of policy. This is demonstrated in an

[36] Moeller, 'Social Conflict', pp. 156–9.

[37] M. Schumacher, *Land und Politik* (Düsseldorf 1978), pp. 57–9. The rationale of price controls is set out in Batocki, *Warenpreis*, pp. 8–14.

[38] H. C. von Batocki, 'Rationierung der Lebensmittel', in G. Anschütz, *et al.*, *Handbuch der Politik* (3rd edn. Berlin and Leipzig 1920), vol. 2, p. 238; Flemming, *Landwirtschaftliche Interessen*, p. 102; Skalweit, *Kriegsernährungswirtschaft*, pp. 106–9.

[39] Trade balance: Hardach, *First World War*, table 6, p. 33, derived from H. Kleine-Natrop, *Devizenpolitik in Deutschland vor dem Kriege und in der Kriegs- und Nachkriegszeit* (Berlin 1922), p. 11; exchange rates: Roesler, *Finanzpolitik*, table 30, p. 229; German reserves and foreign borrowing: Deutsche Waffenstillstandkommission, *Der Waffenstillstand, 1918–1919* (Berlin 1928), vol. 2, pp. 51–3; war loans: Batocki, *Warenpreis*, p. 15.

important memorandum of a German staff officer in the economic administration, who questioned the effect of price incentives on farm production, arguing that peasants preferred leisure to additional income. It is suggestive of the cast of mind of authority in Germany at the time that such thinking should have earned him influence and favour.[40] He was not entirely out of touch with reality. In the absence of goods to purchase, peasants are indeed likely to restrict their exertions and conceal their product.

The fundamental problem facing agriculture was the product mix. The most critical shortfall was of fats; from the consumer's point of view, however, the greatest deprivation was that of meat and protein products. Rather more was spent on the tiny rations of meat and fat than on the basic energy ration of grain and potatoes. Germany had reached a peak of meat consumption on the eve of the war and the taste for meat and fat was deeply ingrained.[41]

This resolves one part of the paradox—of a relatively sufficient diet, combined with a sense of deep deprivation. Diet is a matter of culture and habit as much as of bodily necessity. It is not immutable, but Germany did very little to alter dietary notions and to bring them into line with dietary resources. For this the dominant nutritional ideology must carry part of the blame.

War calls for drastic changes in habit and life-style. Army reservists and recruits abandoned their homes and submitted to harsh discipline, to extreme discomfort, to injury and death. This was the outcome of a thorough indoctrination. In comparison, the sacrifice of meat and beer is less cataclysmic, but it gave rise to much more resistance and discontent. Is it too much to ask whether Germany would have started a war in the first place if the price had been a conversion to vegetarianism?

Some indoctrination would have helped the adjustment to the deprivations of wartime. One of the sailors on Stumpf's ship on the High Seas Fleet had embraced "Fletcherism", the doctrine that it was possible to reduce food intake by chewing it properly. He was mocked and hounded by his mates, and had to be transferred. When he walked off the gangplank, a hundred voices jeered after him "Chew! Chew!" The point of this story is that a rational approach to food helped at least one serviceman to adjust to food deprivation. One of the Leipzig families was vegetarian (and Fletcherite); its members kept up their morale despite some discomfort owing to the shortage of fats.[42] Nutritional knowledge already

---

[40] R. Merton, 'Denkschrift über die kritische Ernährungslage' (Berlin, Oct. 1916), repr. in Merton, *Erinnernswertes aus meinem Leben* (Frankfurt 1955), pp. 14–15.

[41] War consumption: Zimmermann, 'Veränderungen', pp. 448–50; pre-war meat consumption: Teuteberg and Wiegelmann, *Nahrungsgewohnheiten*, pp. 129–32.

[42] Stumpf, *Private War*, pp. 334–5; Kruse and Hintze, *Sparsame Ernährung*, pp. 158–60.

favoured plant over animal food, and could have been mobilized for popular indoctrination. This was understood by German officials before the war. Batocki himself, in retrospect, regarded this absence of indoctrination as perhaps the key failing of German food administration. Kruse's and Hintze's whole study was devoted to this point, which other post-war writers in Germany echoed.[43] But the German nutritional establishment was deeply hostile to these notions and gave them no support. There was something radical, perhaps even subversive, in the idea of a "rational" diet. Its proponents in Germany were ridiculed or ignored.[44]

Not so in the United States. Food reform scientists formed a committee to advise the Food Administration. Chittenden was a prominent (perhaps the most prominent) member of this group. One or two experts (especially Alonzo Taylor) were cool towards rational food fads, but Chittenden was eager to use the war as a lever for spreading his doctrines and his opinion generally held sway. Nutritional knowledge played an important role in the food economy campaign which the United States Food Administration launched in 1917 and which achieved good results by persuasion rather than compulsion. For a long time there was a large banner in Grand Central Station in New York proclaiming 'Eat less, look better, feel better, help win the war.' The prohibition of alcohol in 1917 was a measure of the seriousness, conviction and influence of the food reformers on American war policy. It also emphasizes the ascetic and moral dimension of their creeds, which were closely related in spirit to the food reformers', some of whom, like Irving Fisher, were ardent prohibitionists.[45] In 1918, when harvest shortfalls and transport difficulties threatened American shipments of food to the Allies in Europe, Chittenden crossed the Atlantic with the task of persuading the Allies to cut down their consumption by a third or so, indeed down to about German levels. He failed to impress the Europeans, but they were compelled to reduce the standard ration by about 10 per cent.[46]

[43] Officials pre-war: ch. 23 below. H. C. von Batocki, 'Umstellung der Landwirtschaft', in G. Anschütz *et al.*, *Handbuch der Politik* (3rd edn. Berlin and Leipzig 1920), vol. 2, pp. 245, 247; Kruse and Hintze, *Sparsame Ernährung*, pp. 147–8; A. Fischer, 'Volksernährung', in L. Elster and W. Weber (eds.), *Handwörterbuch der Staatswissenschaften*, (4th edn. Jena 1929), supplementary volume, p. 889.
[44] M. Rubner, 'Über Nährwert einiger wichtiger Gemüsearten und deren Preiswert', offprint from *Berliner klinische Wochenschrift*, no. 15 (Berlin 1916), pp. 6–8.
[45] Chittenden, 'Sixty Years', fo. 202. The USFA 'Advisory Committee on Alimentation' included Chittenden among its members. See especially the sympathetic survey of the food reform movement in E. V. McCollum, 'A Primer of Nutrition' (typescript, 25 July 1917), and Chittenden's remarks at the conference of 20 Sept. 1917 'To Consider Questions Relating to the Subsistence of the Army' (typescript minutes), fos. 28–9, and the Alimentation Committee's 'Memorandum', 5 Jan. 1918, all in USFA 36, HIA.
[46] For a report: R. Chittenden and G. Lusk to Herbert Hoover, 5 Apr. 1918, Lusk Papers 1/2, HIA; also Chittenden, 'Sixty Years', chs. 10–11.

It is easy to make too much of the difference between food-supply policies of the English-speaking Allies and those of Germany. In the United States and Britain policy-makers reached for incentives rather than controls and set high minimum prices to raise production, with considerable success. But the Germans were not ignorant of incentives, and incorporated them by 1917. Moreover, the black market embodied a free-market sector which met some of the need for incentives for both producers and consumers. The Germans' plight, after all, was much more serious. Even in the United States, when consumer and producer interests came more starkly into conflict (as in the case of milk production), the balance was struck in favour of the consumer.[47] Both the United States and Britain, and especially the latter, had centralized systems of food supply, with ample storage, which could be controlled much more effectively than Germany's multitude of small farms, many of them within easy reach of the towns. It is not at all clear that more far-reaching incentives would have had the desired effect without a heavy cost elsewhere down the line. It is wrong therefore to blame the German food crises on mismanagement alone. Blockade made them almost inevitable.

[47] B. H. Hibbard, *Effects of the Great War upon Agriculture in the United States and Great Britain* (New York 1919), pp. 136–45.

5

COLLAPSE

WHEN food does not suffice, there are three options: one is to lose weight; the second, to cut down on effort; the third, to suffer in health. Having lost weight already by 1916, the workers could only preserve their health if they reduced their efforts. As the "turnip winter" progressed, the workers in Düsseldorf, failing to get either better food or sufficient wage increases, complained of long shifts and downed tools for the day several times to press for shorter hours. Medical insurance societies reported in June 1918 that the numbers absent from work owing to sickness had risen to 3.48 per cent, almost double the figures for the autumn of 1914. Doctors reported a considerable loss of efficiency, which one of them (dubiously) put at 40 per cent.[1] Two nation-wide strike waves affected the country, in the spring and early summer of 1917 and in January 1918. The first erupted when the bread ration was reduced, at one of the lowest points of the food-supply curve, when the country had still not emerged from the turnip winter. Trade union leaders blamed the inequities of food distribution and in particular the inability of workers to afford black-market prices. The labour unrest in Düsseldorf in June–July 1917 was associated with food shortages. The food question did not dominate the strikes of 1918 in the same way. Rations rose in the winter of 1918, possibly in anticipation of supplies from the Ukraine. Nevertheless, food led the list of the Berlin strikers' *domestic* grievances. In Hamburg shipyard workers restricted their demands to food and working conditions. In the more amply fed Bavaria, however, food came last on the list of peace, constitutional and economic demands.[2]

Soon after the Peace of Brest–Litovsk, *Simplicissimus* published a cartoon entitled 'How a Münchener visualizes the Ukraine' (fig. 5.1). It showed a fat bürger slumbering in a field of yellow grain, with roast chickens flying about, a mound of hams, and with salamis, meat joints and pretzels hanging from clothes lines. But, unlike Romania in 1916, the Ukraine disappointed Germany. The reports of the military governors

---

[1] Tobin, 'Düsseldorf', p. 277; medical insurance: 'Memorandum re Foreign Statistical Intelligence . . . Food Situation, Germany' (based on French intelligence sources, 2nd Nov. 1918), USFA 120/2, HIA; 'Schädigung', pp. 413–14; demands for shorter hours: MB Sept. 1918, p. 31.

[2] Documents in Lutz, *Fall of the German Empire*, vol. 2, pp. 228–9, 231, 243–4; Tobin, 'Düsseldorf', p. 297; 'Niederschrift über die Besprechung der Zentralbehörden im preussi schen Kriegsministerium über die Ursachen der Streikbewegung . . .' 18 Feb. 1918, in W. Deist (ed.), *Militär und Innenpolitik im Weltkrieg 1914–1918* (Düsseldorf 1970), vol. 2, doc. 444, p. 1177.

contain an implausible (but logically sound) proposal for trading Dresden china against Ukrainian food. Although vigorous efforts were made, it proved impossible to extract any useful amounts of food out of that country—the transport capacity was insufficient and Germany had little to give the peasants in return.[3]

FIG. 5.1. 'How a Münchener visualizes the Ukraine', *Simplicissimus*, 2 Apr. 1918

Larger rations in the winter of 1918 merely postponed the crisis into the spring. From May 1918 onwards, and especially during the months before the harvest, there was a serious food crisis. Once again potatoes disappeared from the shops and the bread ration was cut, not only for town dwellers but also for farmers. Official rations and actual food intakes descended back to turnip winter levels. Fodder was short already and the army took emergency measures. In April the War Ministry decreed the forced requisition of oats and of legumes. Squads of soldiers went into the countryside and requisitioned grain and potatoes from the farmers. The peasants bitterly resented this attack; it was not calculated to stimulate the broken-down agrarian economy.[4]

[3] P. Borowsky, *Deutsche Ukrainepolitik, 1918* (Lübeck and Hamburg 1970), pp. 190–200; MB June 1918, p. 67, MKr. 12852.
[4] Food requisitions, MB June 1918, pp. 26–30; July, pp. 28–30, MKr. 12852–3.

The military governors' report covering July 1918 stated that 'economic conditions, and primarily the food situation, were decisive for the general state of mind'. The bread ration had been cut, potato storehouses were empty and meatless weeks and the fat shortage underlined the absence of any substitutes. Public morale, disheartened by the setbacks on the western front, was falling.[5] A number of Allied intelligence agencies kept a close watch on the German economy by scanning the press and interrogating returned prisoners, travellers and departing residents. They were aware of a serious crisis at hand. One report, from 1 August 1918, summed up:

Germany's difficulties, however, do not end with the feeding of the front line. The problem for her is how to maintain the strength of the underfed munitions workers, to bolster up the morale of a dissatisfied nation, and to renew every year the struggle against falling production and depreciating quality of food and materials. The strain is working havoc among the civilian population; it will reach the army in time, and it will be surprising if its signs do not become evident before the spring of next year is far advanced.[6]

The Allies collected a great deal of information on Germany, mainly by monitoring the press, which was remarkably open. Raw data on Germany were circulated daily and weekly in great abundance, but it is difficult to use this material. American army intelligence tried to distil it into a graph, which can serve as a point of departure for discussing the effect of food supply on public morale.[7] I have not reproduced this graph in order to avoid a misleading impression of precision, but it does help to bring the main factors into focus. The American analysts plotted five variables on a single scale: the military position, domestic political unity, the food situation in North Germany, the condition of Austria–Hungary and U-Boat sinkings. A sixth curve, representing morale, was derived from all the rest. After rising euphorically during the first phase of the spring offensive, this curve broke at the end of March, and, after stabilizing in May, continued on its steep decline until the end of the war. Two components went into decline in March: the food supply and Austria–Hungary.

In April the German western offensive met with its first serious reverses and its renewal in June could not prevent a collapse of morale. From March onwards the food situation deteriorated. In July and August 1918 it matched the previous low points of the winter and spring of 1917. It rose only briefly for the harvest in September, and declined again. Austria was in a terminal decline. On 17 June Vienna cut the bread ration by half, to

[5] MB Aug. 1918, p. 1, MKr. 12853.
[6] 'Food Supplies of the Central Empires in 1918', Supplement to MI 6B, *Daily Summary of Information* (1 Aug. 1918), p. 5, ADM 137/2835, Trade Division Papers.
[7] US Army, 'Graph to Indicate Variations in German Morale' [?Oct. 1918], World War One Subject Collection 19, HIA.

630 grams per head a week, and sent telegraphic appeals for bread to Budapest, Munich and Berlin. The ration had fallen to about 760 calories per head, and people were dying of starvation.[8]

In June the German bread ration fell from 200 to 160 grams a day and Foreign Secretary von Kühlmann declared in the Reichstag that the war could not be ended by military means. It was a clear expression of political disunity, of the collapse of support for Ludendorff's war aims. In July Germany's last offensive was halted and reversed, and from August onwards the German armies on the western front were under constant threat of a rout. The prospect of victory, which was the last prop of domestic morale, was taken away.

How was Germany beaten? Was she defeated on the battlefield, or was she crushed by war weariness and the collapse of her war economy? It is idle to argue whether Germany fell because of the battering it received at the front, or owing to the exhaustion of manpower, or to the poor state of supply and broken morale at home. The Allied offensive was the hammer, the home front provided the anvil. German war industry was on its last legs. It lacked the resources to build a German tank to meet the Allied armour. By October a quarter of the machines at Krupp were reported as standing idle due to the lack of the special steel for machine tool bits. Similar bottlenecks stifled the rest of manufacturing industry and transport.[9] As American reinforcements continued to flow into France, and as Germany's Allies collapsed, her defeat became a matter of time. What counts is not why the war came to an end, but *how*. From August onwards very few in Germany continued to expect victory, and the question among both civilian and military leaders was how to snatch something out of the jaws of defeat. The way in which the war ended determined the shape of the peace. Here it is possible to be more precise about the relative roles of army and home.

On 8 August 1918 Germany suffered a major military setback near Amiens. Ludendorff was shattered and lost much of his confidence in the troops. He no longer saw any prospect of victory, and sought for a way to end the war. During August and September he became depressed.[10] The collapse of morale was no retrospective invention. It was also noted on

[8] 'Review of the Situation in Enemy Countries during June 1918', General Staff, War Office, *Daily Review of the Foreign Press*, vol. 1, no. 2, p. 22, ADM 137/2835; W. Böhm, 'Sanitary Statistics and Mortality of the Population of Vienna during the War, 1914–1918' (Mar. 1919), HIA; G. Gratz and R. Schüller, *Der wirtschaftliche Zusammenbruch Österreich-Ungarns* (Vienna 1930), pp. 74–81.

[9] *Untersuchung*, 4th ser., vol. 6, Beilagen 1–2; MI 6B, 'Supplies of Iron and Steel and Condition of Railways in Germany', *Daily Summary of Information* (6 Nov. 1918), ADM 137/2835; also Henning, 'Die Situation der deutschen Kriegswirtschaft', ch. 3.

[10] 'Statement by Baron von dem Bussche . . .' (2 Oct. 1918), in Lutz, *Fall of the German Empire*, vol. 2, p. 461; Ludendorff, *War Memories*, vol. 2, p. 684; R. Parkinson, *Tormented Warrior: Ludendorff and the Supreme Command* (1978), pp. 176–80.

the other side. On 10 September Haig wrote in his diary, 'The German prisoners now taken will not obey their officers or N.C.O.s. The same story of indiscipline is told me of the prisoners from our hospitals. The discipline of the German Army is quickly going, and the German Officer is no longer what he was. *It seems to me the beginning of the end.*'[11]

Ludendorff's morale rose and fell inversely with Haig's. On 29 September (three days after Bulgaria's capitulation) he approached the government and demanded an immediate armistice: 'the line might be broken at any moment . . . he felt like a gambler, and that a division might fail him anywhere at any time.'[12] When the General Staff explained this to the party leaders of the Reichstag, it cited three factors overall: the collapse of Bulgaria, the tanks, which German industry had no means to counter, and the exhaustion of manpower reserves. This urgent plea led to a change of government, and to the dispatch of the first peace note to President Wilson on 3 October.

Ludendorff's intention, as far as it can be fathomed, was not to surrender, but to earn a short respite for his troops. Colonel Heye, head of the Operations Branch of the General Staff, put it clearly to the Chancellor on 9 October:

We *may* be able to hold out until spring. But a turn for the worse may come any day. Yesterday the question of a break through our lines hung on a thread.

Earnestly beg that you do not talk about nervousness. Move for peace is absolutely necessary, still more one for an armistice. The troops no longer get any rest. It is impossible to foresee whether the troops will hold out or not. There are new surprises every day. I do not fear a catastrophe, but I want to save the Army, so that we can use it as a means of pressure during the peace negotiations.

The Army needs rest. If it gets it and receives fresh recruits, it will be able to show fresh achievements.[13]

Wilson's second note, which arrived at Berlin on 16 October, made it clear that such a comfortable outcome was not to be had. His note implied disarmament and a thorough constitutional change. In response, Ludendorff changed his position. German resistance on the western front had firmed up again, and the High Command regained its confidence. From now on Ludendorff strove to break off the negotiations. He demanded new reinforcements, and expressed confidence in the possibility of fighting for several more months, and in a successful national defence.[14]

Winter was only a few weeks off, and with it a relaxation of the military

---

[11] Earl Haig, War Diaries, 10 Sept. 1918, WO 256/34. I am grateful to Robin Prior and Alan Gilbert for a loan of their transcript.
[12] Imperial Counselor of Legation Grünau to the Foreign Office, 1 Oct. 1918, in Lutz, *Fall of the German Empire*, vol. 2, p. 459.
[13] Rudin, *Armistice*, pp. 112–13.
[14] Ibid., ch. 6.

pressure. Ludendorff's assessment was again echoed precisely on the Allied side. On 10 October Haig was still confident that the enemy was beaten, and his plan was to go on hitting him 'as hard as we possibly can, till he begs for mercy'. On the 19th his mood became darker. His attack of 17 October had encountered considerable resistance, and the enemy was not ready for unconditional surrender. 'In that case there would be no armistice, and the war would continue for another year!' The German army, he told the War Cabinet, was capable of retiring to its own frontier, and holding that line if there should be any attempt to touch the *honour* of the German people. Allied armies were worn out. He therefore asked for lenient terms of armistice, and continued in this vein almost until the start of the armistice negotiations.[15] Ludendorff was dismissed on 26 October, but the front did not collapse and the High Command did not repudiate his views. 'The enemy is fighting a very good rear-guard action,' wrote Haig on 31 October, 'and *all are agreed* that from a military standpoint, *the enemy has not yet been sufficiently beaten as to cause him to accept an ignomini-ous peace.*' When the German armistice delegates crossed the lines on 7 November, the guns were firing on both sides.[16]

This is not to say that resistance was anything but futile in the long run. In the short run, however, what made it futile were events *at home*, not at the front. In October and November 1918 the home front was decisive. Once a Wilsonian peace had come out of the bottle, there was no pushing it back in again. The nation could not be spurred to fight to the finish in defence of the Kaiser. The issue was finally decided by the other armed service, the navy. The sailors had not come under the Allied attacks—but were deeply affected by the shortages at home. When they mutinied on 29 October, further resistance was doomed.

During August influenza swept through the towns of Prussia and the embattled formations at the front. From July onwards German society was in the grip of a slow fever. Slow malnutrition numbs the sensibilities. The military governors' report for July 1918 states that 'Early success had raised hopes of an early end for the war during this year. The outlook of a further winter has introduced in many people a certain dullness and apathy [indifference] and pushed economic concerns into the foreground.'[17] On the whole, the governors thought that support for the war still held up. But optimism about the front led to pessimism about domestic prospects.

In August the political situation began to alter rapidly. The Turks were turned out of Damascus, Bulgaria was too weak to be considered an asset, Vienna was starving and could take no more, but the collapse of morale

---

[15] Haig, War Diaries. I have also used J. Terraine, *Douglas Haig, The Educated Soldier* (1963), and *The Private Papers of Douglas Haig, 1914–1919*, ed. R. Blake (1952).

[16] Haig, War Diaries; Rudin, *Armistice*, pp. 332–3.

[17] MB Aug. 1918, p. 1 HKr. 12853 (this report, dated 3 Aug., covers July).

was determined equally if not more by domestic strains. The August reports of the military governors were deeply pessimistic. Morale had been falling for the previous two months and had now sunk to its lowest point since the beginning of the war. In many places the source of this depression was economic, in others the military-political situation, and on the whole it lay in the totality of the current situation.[18] The food supply data show no relief. Leipzig reached a low point in August 1918, and so did Bonn, Cologne and Düsseldorf.[19]

What the reports convey is the unmistakable collapse of resistance and will. In previous months the military governors' reports had been circulated in 232 copies to various organs of government. So bad was the impression they now conveyed that on 28 August the Prussian War Ministry cut out more than 90 per cent of the recipients and restricted circulation to twenty-one. Silencing the bearer of bad news brought no improvements. Only two of the restricted reports were to appear.

Of these, the very last one is of the greatest interest. It conveys the state of opinion and the economic situation in September, before the Ludendorff armistice initiative. It captures the staff officers of the regional commands in a reflective mood, trying to make sense of the new reality around them. One can visualize these writers, mostly perhaps civilians in uniform, unfit officers of the reserve, attempting to describe an entirely new situation. The harvest had not brought the expected relief, and the coming winter gave rise to earnest concern. Writing in from all parts of the country, they had little doubt that the breakdown was final. The prime concern was the collapse of Bulgaria and the weakening of Austria and Turkey, but the bad economic situation took up a fair amount of space in the reports, and it showed little improvement. The governor of the Kassel district predicted renewed unrest, as the only means which labour had to improve its food.[20] Labour had always been more aware of the poor economic situation, and more pessimistic about it than officials, soldiers and bourgeois politicians. This was only to be expected: labour had less to lose from an end to the war.[21] According to the Leipzig survey, while September brought a respite, food supplies deteriorated again in October and November.

At the War Cabinet of 17 October 1918 the interdependence of morale at the front and the rear came out in an exchange between the Social-Democrat Scheidemann and General Ludendorff. Ludendorff urged a last

---

[18] MB Sept. 1918, p. 1 MKr. 12853; Kocka, *Total War*, pp. 155–60; Feldman, *Army, Industry and Labor*, wrote that morale at home was ultimately determined by the military situation, but he was under the impression that 'the food situation had improved' (p. 506).
[19] Figs. 1.1, 1.2, table 3.3 above, and Tobin, 'Düsseldorf', fig. 1, p. 280.
[20] MB Oct. 1918, p. 14 ff.
[21] Henning, 'Die Situation der deutschen Kriegswirtschaft', fos. 214–16.

desperate draft of manpower for a fight to the finish. Scheidemann, the majority socialist, insisted that the war was already lost:

I am willing to believe that we can mobilize hundreds of thousands of men for the Army; but we deceive ourselves if we think that these hundreds of thousands would improve the morale of the Army. The opposite is my firm conviction. The lengthy war has already broken the spirit of the people, and to that [add] their disillusionment. They have been disillusioned by the submarine war, by the technical superiority of our opponent, by the defection of our allies or, at any rate, by their complete bankruptcy, and, in addition, by the increasing distress at home. Now the reaction is coming. Men on leave come from the Army with unpleasant stories; and they return to the Army bringing unpleasant news from home. This traffic in ideas depresses the morale. We should be deceiving ourselves if we tried to gloss it over. Workers are coming nearer and nearer to the point of view, 'An end with horror is better than horror without end.'

LUDENDORFF: Could your Excellency not succeed in raising the morale of the masses?

SCHEIDEMANN: That is a question of potatoes. We have no more meat. Potatoes cannot be delivered because we are short four thousand cars every day. We have absolutely no fats left. The distress is so great that one stands before a perfect puzzle when one asks: How does North Berlin live and how does East Berlin live? As long as this puzzle cannot be solved, it is impossible to improve morale.[22]

A generation of British historians denounced the futility of the western front. In the last two decades the pendulum has swung the other way, with military historians insisting on the primacy of the western front and the secondary role of the naval blockade.[23] But is it really possible to separate the pressures on the home and military fronts?

With access to overseas supplies, Germany might have fielded more men, and held out longer. It might have avoided submarine warfare. However, it is difficult to see how Germany could have purchased overseas on the scale required. Britain's much more ample resources were exhausted by the end of 1916; thereafter, she depended on American goodwill. Whether starved of foreign goods by an actual blockade, or by the inability to buy them, the German economy was simply too weak to take on the combined power of the *entente* and the United States. On the other hand, the German economy held up much better than British blockade planners supposed. Without a series of futile offensives to drain her manpower, food and industrial resources, Germany might have held out much longer. Blockade alone was not sufficient to defeat her.

[22] War Cabinet Protocol, 17 Oct. 1918, in Lutz, *Fall of the German Empire*, vol. 2, p. 481 (trans. follows Rudin, *Armistice*, p. 144).
[23] J. Terraine, *The Western Front, 1914–1918* (1970), p. 57; the theme recurs in his other books; P. M. Kennedy, *The Rise and Fall of British Naval Mastery* (1976), pp. 252, 253, 265.

For the Allies, American intervention was decisive: it saved them from bankruptcy, tightened the blockade and provided sufficient manpower, *matériel* and, most importantly, the food Britain could not produce or buy for herself. The United States had cast its *economic* lot with the Allies almost from the start. With military reinforcement from America, it was only a matter of time before Allied superiority would overwhelm Germany. It is well to remember, however, that American presence on the battlefield was an outcome of Germany's unrestricted U-Boat campaign, launched at the time of Germany's worst food crisis, a scheme to starve Britain before Germany itself was starved out. For the Allies, the western front was not merely a matter of military willpower; it enabled them to draw upon their enormous economic and manpower assets overseas. The decisive offensives in August and September were largely the work of Australian and Canadian troops. British and French armies were weary and the United States' divisions formed the only reserve of fresh troops.[24] The arrival and supply of overseas (and indeed of British) troops at the western front depended on naval supremacy.

The blockade forced the Germans to apportion their scarce food, *matériel* and manpower between the domestic economy and the front lines. The balance was a pretty close one, but the morale at home collapsed first, before that of the army. Once Germany accepted the armistice, civilian disaffection and then the revolution made sure that the war effort could not be resumed. That, however, was not the end of the story.

It is not clear how much fight the German army still had in it in November 1918, maybe enough for another winter. Haig at one point said two years. It is also clear that civilian exhaustion and the naval mutiny made it impossible to go on fighting. But the conflict was not finished yet. Clausewitz has written, 'In War the result is never final. The defeated state often considers the outcome merely as a transitory evil, for which a remedy may still be found in political conditions at some later date.'[25] After the armistice, once the Allies began to demobilize their armies, the food weapon remained the only one available to them, and became decisive in shaping the peace treaty that Germany signed at Versailles.

The end of the shooting was not an end of the war. The German people embraced the armistice in the hope of relief from the blockade. But the armistice left the blockade intact. The Allies were not prepared to occupy Germany and dismantle its sovereignty, so they were left with only one weapon, and that was the food blockade. In the final months before the armistice, the blockade operated indirectly as an important, some would say critical factor in bringing about the German collapse, and especially in

[24] Ch. 25 below.
[25] Carl von Clausewitz, *On War*, ed. and trans. M. Howard and P. Paret (Princeton 1976), p. 80.

determining what form it would take. After the armistice the blockade became decisive. In the diplomatic struggle that followed the armistice, the food blockade is what finally forced Germany to surrender and to sign the Treaty of Versailles in June 1919.

Part Two

THE AGRARIAN BOND: THE UNITED STATES, CANADA AND AUSTRALIA

6

LATE-VICTORIAN BRITAIN: AN IMPORT ECONOMY

THE distant causes of Germany's collapse in 1918 may be found on the new frontiers of farming which opened up during the last third of the nineteenth century. In the 1870s the United States emerged as a great food power. Its grain fields and stockyards threatened to overwhelm European rural economies. In response, Britain replaced home-grown calories with imported ones and ran down farming to build up trade. That adjustment forms the subject of the next three chapters: first, the consequences of becoming the world's largest entrepôt for food; second, the reasons why British farming was battered so badly by competition from abroad; third, what sort of economies developed to provide Britain with agrarian staples.

I

In contrast with previous decades, the prime imports of the nineteenth century were no longer luxuries, but bread and meat, the necessities of daily existence. Sugar and tea, tobacco and coffee and cocoa, the imported luxuries of the past, had also now become addictive necessities.

Going abroad for the bulk of these commodities was Britain's great economic innovation of the late-Victorian period. On the eve of the First World War more than two-thirds of Britain's imports came out of fields and forests overseas; more than half the food (by value) arrived by ship, and some 58 per cent of the calories. For the rest, domestic farming relied on imported fodders and fertilizers. Sixty per cent of iron ores came over the water, mostly from Spain, while the Bank of England replenished its vaults with gold from Australia, Alaska and the Transvaal.[1] Only coal was found locally in plenty, but even coal required imported timber to support the tunnels, and grain to feed the miners. Britain had an economy unlike any other. As the world's greatest importer of food, Britain fashioned new affinities and alliances and began to perceive new dangers. This food-import economy, with its political and strategic ramifications, was the foundation of British prosperity and it influenced reactions to the German challenge.

[1] Years are 1909–13. M&D, pp. 130, 139. Food values: R. H. Rew, 'The Nation's Food Supply', *Journal of the Royal Statistical Society*, vol. 76, pt. 1 (Dec. 1912), p. 104; calories: Rew, *Food Supplies in Peace and War* (1920), pp. 25–7; fodder and fertilizer: F. M. L. Thompson, 'The Second Agricultural Revolution, 1815–1880', *Economic History Review*, vol. 21 (1968).

TABLE 6.1. *Principal agrarian imports to the United Kingdom, 1875–1913 (£m., current prices)*

	1. Grains and flour	2. Meat and animals	3. Other foods: cheese, fish eggs, fruit, etc.	4. Oils and fats	5. Sweets, stimulants, sedatives	6. Raw fibres: cotton, wool, flax, jute, etc.	7. Other primary products	Total	% of all imports
1875	56.1	16.4	15.1	26.9	59.3	92.0	24.3	290.1	77
1895	51.7	33.3	16.4	31.9	45.0	83.1	26.6	288.0	69
1913	84.5	56.7	44.4	80.5	58.6	139.3	54.7	518.7	67

Note: (1) Includes rice, but not sago, starch, etc. (4) Includes butter, margarine, lard, oil, oilseeds, gum tallow, etc. (5) Dutiable in the Edwardian period, and so presumably sinful: sugar, tea, coffee, tobacco, wine, beer, spirits, confectionary, sweetened condensed milk, some dried fruit. (7) Timber, hides, skins and furs, papermaking materials.

Source: Statistical Abstract for the United Kingdom, and M&D, pp. 283–4, 298–300.

Together, food, fodder and fats made up the largest categories of imports, followed by fibres for the textile industries (table 6.1). This table actually understates the value of agricultural imports, since large amounts of grain and meat were carried into Britain across St George's Channel from Ireland.

Exports were never large enough to pay for all these imports and left a deficit ranging between one-third (in the 1890s) to more than one-sixth in 1913. This deficit of goods was made possible by a surplus on two items: firstly, on services to trade—running almost half the world's ships, providing insurance, and lending money to the merchants; second, on overseas investment—the profits, dividends, interest coupons and windfalls of investment and enterprise in other lands. A good part of this investment was sunk in railways, docks and other facilities for extracting and carrying the primary commodities that filled the holds of British ships. Income from investments was larger than the outflow after 1870. Much was reinvested and helped to build up a fat portfolio of assets for Britain in the mines, railways and towns of its suppliers overseas. The payments surplus also made it very easy to import agrarian products.

To judge by its large excess of imports, Britain was an "import economy" more than it was an "export economy". By the end of the nineteenth century imports made up more than a quarter of the Gross Domestic Product.[2] Although a few small countries have exceeded this figure, it can hardly go much higher in a large mature economy.[3] A good deal of output has no competition from abroad: houses and other buildings, public works and utilities, domestic transport, retail trading, and the services of everyone from charladies to judges. None of these enter international trade. Much of their output, however, supports overseas trading, or comes out of it indirectly.

A strategic commodity is an article of trade whose denial can affect the well-being or even the survival of a great power. It does not have to dominate the balance of trade. Like petroleum today, it only has to form a link in the cycle of production and to have no adequate substitutes. During the nineteenth century the outstanding strategic commodity was cotton, which was the mainstay of Lancashire industry and of British manufacturing exports. By the end of the nineteenth century another commodity had achieved that status. This commodity was grain.

Wheat, rye, barley, maize, millet and oats formed the basis of the food

[2] As estimated by R. C. O. Matthews, C. H. Feinstein and J. C. Odling-Smee, *British Economic Growth, 1856–1973* (Oxford 1982), table 14.2, p. 432: higher estimates can be derived from M&D, pp. 283–4, and C. H. Feinstein, *National Income, Expenditure and Output of the United Kingdom, 1855–1965* (Cambridge 1972), table 4, p. T12.
[3] W. S. and E. S. Woytinsky, *World Commerce and Governments: Trends and Outlook* (New York 1955), pp. 65–8.

economies of Europe and North America. Wheat and rye were the main bread cereals, while beer, beef and bacon came out of barley and maize. Bread, meat, milk and fat were all based on grain, although roots and grass also entered into the production of livestock. Statistics of the grain trade underestimate its share of world commerce, since much of it travelled as pork bellies or chilled beef. More wheat was traded internationally than all other grains combined (if rice is excluded) and lack of data will sometimes force us to use it as a proxy for all grain.[4]

Outside the Orient, wheat dominates the other grains. It replaces other foods as a source of energy and protein, while other foods are not adequate substitutes for wheat. A grain of wheat consists of about two-thirds starch and 10–15 per cent protein. It also contains a number of vitamins and trace elements and will support life and health with minor additions, more or less indefinitely. No other food is so suited to be "the staff of life". Cheese, meat and butter cost three to five times more per calorie than grain, which reflects the energy lost in converting vegetable into animal.[5] Animal products make a palatable source of protein, but even in wealthy societies they complement and do not replace cereals in the diet. Growing children may require milk. Fats have a vital place in the diet but a small one. Potatoes are cheaper than grain and a good source of energy but they contain little protein and no fat; they are very bulky to move, and spoil easily.

Two pounds of bread a day, or half the Victorian loaf, provide enough energy to support a hard day's work. Rye, maize, millet and rice have all served as the main staple food, but Europeans chose wheat bread as soon as they could afford it. Alone among grains (which all have a similar food value) wheat yeast rises to become an aerated, smooth, tasty, light-coloured bread with a crusty exterior. As buns or bagels, croissants or crumpet, pasta or pancakes, wheat is very palatable. In late-Victorian Europe wheat was still what economists call a "superior good", whose consumption increases in pace with income. Today, the more affluent consumers in Africa and Asia prefer wheat over maize, millet and rice. Wheat gained ground over rye in Kaiser Wilhelm's Germany, and its consumption levelled off only in the last decade before the war. In Britain consumption per head no longer grew after the 1870s, but, as population continued to grow, so did the total consumed.[6]

Because a grain of wheat is such a concentrated little package, it travels

---

[4] Wheat and flour, $854 million; other cereals $680 million; rice $250 million; all in 1913: P. L. Yates, *Forty Years of Foreign Trade* (1959), p. 224.

[5] R. F. Peterson, *Wheat: Botany, Cultivation and Utilization* (1965), ch. 15; relative costs approximated for Britain in 1912, on the basis of R. H. Rew, 'Nation's Food Supply' and *Food Supplies*.

[6] Consumption trends: M. K. Bennett, 'Per Capita Wheat Consumption in Western Europe; I. Measurements, from 1885–86', *Wheat Studies*, vol. 11 (1935), p. 303.

far at low cost. With steam-powered transport, a bushel of wheat that sold at 80 cents at the farm gate in Kansas only required another 20 cents for the journey to Liverpool.[7] With distance no object, vast tracts of land entered the competition for British markets, since wheat can grow on soils and climates that range from the sub-arctic to the subtropical.

Grain production reflects the wider problems of overseas supply. The land and labour it employs can be used for feed grains, root crops or pasture, and these substitutes link grain prices with livestock markets. On the eve of the First World War grain exceeded every other primary commodity in international trade in terms of value and was second only to coal and iron ore in weight. Grain was one of the bulkiest items imported into Britain, accounting for well over half the weight of imported food and fodder.[8]

Grain was one of the pillars of the British merchant marine. It accounted for more than 17 per cent of the cargoes landed by weight, but this understated its importance to British shipping. Grain travelled very long distances, and required more than the average tonnage per unit of cargo landed; and, because British ships dominated the long-haul ocean routes and had a smaller share of the short European and Mediterranean voyages, much more than 17 per cent of the British merchant marine depended on the carriage of grain.[9] In the season of 1880–1 more than six hundred ships sailed laden with grain and flour for Britain from San Francisco and Oregon alone.[10] Shipbuilding, perhaps the most successful of Britain's industries before the First World War, owed a good deal of its prosperity to the trade in corn.

The significance of wheat and other primary imports goes well beyond their share of national income and their direct linkages with other industries. If Britain was going to derive a tangible benefit from its exports and foreign investments, this had to take the form of material goods. Foods were the single largest counterflow to investment and exports from Britain. British exports of galvanized iron for Australian roofs and locomotives for India's railways were paid for directly or indirectly in grain. Britain's large food deficit acted as a pump for the world's commerce. British investments

[7] C. K. Harley, 'Transportation, the World Wheat Trade, and the Kuznets Cycle, 1850–1913', *Explorations in Economic History*, vol. 17 (1980), pp. 221–3. F. Andrews, 'Freight Costs and Market Values', USDA *Yearbook 1906* (Washington, DC 1906), p. 382, gives a farm value of 69c and 27c as shipping cost. In Minnesota in 1900 the figures were 67c and 22c: H. M. Larson, *The Wheat Market and the Farmer in Minnesota 1858–1900* (New York 1926), p. 251.

[8] Yates, *Foreign Trade*, pp. 70, 128, 150, 224; Rew, *Food Supplies*, p. 26, which, however, does not include fodder grains (about 70 per cent of wheat imports).

[9] This is based on an estimate of 58 million tons of imports in 1912: S. G. Sturmey, *British Shipping and World Competition* (1962), pp. 21–5; grain landed: M&D, p. 99.

[10] R. W. Paul, 'The Wheat Trade between California and the United Kingdom', *Mississippi Valley Historical Review*, vol. 45 (1958–9), p. 403.

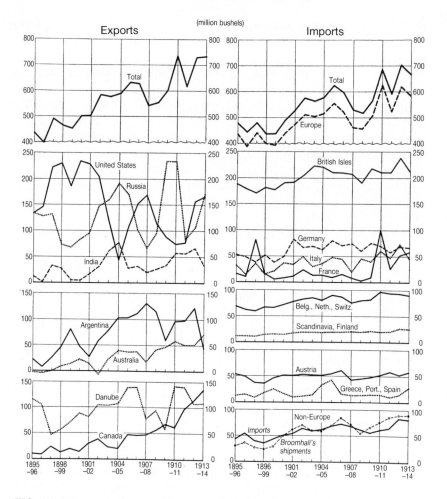

FIG. 6.1. Wheat net exports and imports, principal trading countries, 1895/6–1913/14 (crop years, million bushels)

Source: H. C. Farnsworth, 'Wheat in the Post-surplus period, 1900–1909, with Recent Analogies and Contrasts', *Wheat Studies*, vol. 17 (1941), p. 348.

abroad, which created the capacity for moving staple exports, required that Britain buy these staples for investments to pay off.

Britain did not travel alone on this route to wealth. The Low Countries had been there before and, in the late-Victorian period, Germany began to follow. The Low Countries, Britain and Germany made up the chief wheat-deficit region of the world (fig. 6.1). This region also provided the main setting for the Anglo-German war of 1914.

The other great wheat-deficit region was the industrial and urban north-east in the United States, whose imports amounted to some 118 million bushels in 1910–14. The American south, whose cotton states also relied on the British market, made up the last important wheat-importing region. Total regional deficits in the United States came to 222 million bushels, or approximately the same as all British imports.[11] For grain growers in the west, these were export markets as much as Liverpool or London.

In the 1880s and the early 1890s the grain trade was driven by supply, as ever-larger quantities came to market at ever-lower prices. But from the mid–1890s onwards the tide began to turn. Demand pulled a little ahead of supply. More wheat was exported, while prices held up and even rose. Farmers no longer found empty lands to colonize in the United States, and pushed on to new frontiers, in Canada, Argentina, Australia and India; and Russia took over from the United States as the largest exporter of all (fig. 6.1).

II

After the mid-1890s the North Atlantic cities required as much wheat as the world's farmers could produce, and a little more. Grain poured into Liverpool and the North Sea from the four corners of the earth. The main exporting regions fell into two distinct categories of "farmer" or "peasant", which differed in terms of endowments and assets (fig. 6.1). On the plains of North America and its Pacific slope, in the Pampas of Argentina and the Mallee soils of Australia, farmers had sufficient land, draft animals and machinery, cheap credit, literacy, enterprise, education and scientific support. Peasant growers in Russia, India and the Danube basin suffered from land shortage and high rents, a surfeit of mouths to feed, taxation, usury, political oppression, poor communications, illiteracy and apathy.

For farmers of the northern and southern hemispheres, wheat was literally a cash crop, paid for in dollar, peso or pound at the country railway station. Farmers were "price takers", who committed their land, labour and capital every year with only a rough guess as to their prospective return. Every ploughing and seeding was a speculation on the weather, both at home and abroad, and on future prices in distant exchanges. Peasants also grew the wheat for cash, to pay taxes, rent and interest on their debts. In Russia and the Danube they subsisted largely on rye or maize; in India they only produced an export surplus every once in a while.

[11] The average wheat deficit of the south and west (1910–14) was 88 million bushels (with another 17 million in the mid-west): C. R. Ball *et al.*, 'Wheat Production and Marketing', *USDA Yearbook 1921* (Washington DC 1922), calculated from fig. 50, p. 130.

The grain-deficit countries were large producers in their own right. France, the third-largest wheat grower in the world and a country of discriminating bread-eaters, entered the grain market only infrequently, to make good a harvest shortfall. Britain and the Low Countries purchased most of their grain and Germany's imports fell in between these two extremes. Why did some countries produce less than their needs, and others more?

The decision to grow wheat depends on the world price, but only in the long run. When the harvest is in hand, farmers no longer have much choice and must take the prices offered. They respond to price changes, but sluggishly. Often there is no other crop more profitable than wheat. Even when the farmer loses, he cannot easily shift his dwelling and his capital, which are both anchored to the ground. Slumps are a bad time to pull out, so farmers persist, despite market signals. In the longer term they continue to plant wheat if there is nothing better for them to do, and often there is not.

The ability to compete in the world market comes down to the two questions of cost: first, the cost of production, and, second, the "opportunity cost" of forgoing a more attractive calling. In principle we ought to explain fluctuations in supply by reference to costs. In practice the costs of production interact in exceedingly complex ways. Farm outlays "spill over" from arable to livestock and vice versa, and from one year to the next. Farms vary a lot in performance, and are not consistent from year to year. Some of the principal costs are not independent variables but residues which depend on the price. Land, and the farmer's labour, two of the main elements, do not enter the price, but respond to it. What the farmer can get for his labour (and for his capital), and what the owner can get for his land, depend on the price of the crop. As Ricardo put it, corn is not high because rent is high, rent is high because corn is high. In theory the landowner only gets what is left over; in practice this is more usually the farmer's lot. A large measure of uncertainty is contributed by the weather. All these difficulties appear to place a global model of supply and demand beyond the current reach of economic science.[12] But farmers, merchants and migrants decide from the knowledge available, and historians must follow their lead. Price remains the best cue.

Given a world market price, the indicators that capture conditions of production best are those that reflect the farmer's endowment of land, its productivity and its tenure. In most countries wheat was grown by family units, with only seasonal outside labour. Hence, with a few exceptions,

---

[12] M. K. Bennett, *Farm Cost Studies in the United States* (Stanford 1928), chs. 4–5; G. C. Rausser, 'New Conceptual Developments and Measurements for Modeling the US Agricultural Sector', in G. C. Rausser (ed.), *New Directions in Econometric Modeling and Forecasting in US Agriculture* (New York 1982), p. 5.

land endowment also suggests the labour supply in a particular regime of production. The North American homestead of 160 acres was designed as a household unit. Capital took the form of draft animals and machinery, and the amount of land available suggests the scale of capital on the holding. Finally, the size of the holding multiplied by the yield gives a good idea of labour productivity (or rather, of output per household) in the majority of countries.

Table 6.2 gives a broad indication of conditions of production in the main export and import countries. This table lumps together apples and oranges: statistics from different countries are not strictly comparable, and come out of a range of different samples and proxies. Soils, rotations and climates, currencies and cultures all differ from region to region. Moreover, the data are static, and come from the end of the period, when the pressures of American competition abated somewhat (but earlier data are harder to come by). What the table shows reliably are orders of magnitude—signals strong enough for the farmer, migrant and settler to recognize. This table says something about the reasons for the global distribution of the wheat economy, and of the pressures building up inside it.

Producers in this table fall into three distinct groups. Farmers in North and South America and Australia farmed extensively for low to middling yields but with more than ten times as much land as the average peasant. There are differences within the group. Canada's attractions were manifest: low land prices and high yields. The United States' maturity was reflected in higher land prices, more tenancy and smaller holdings. Australia suffered from drought and poor soils, Argentina from its class of landowners. English-speakers overseas tended to own their land (though often subject to a mortgage) while the Argentinian share-cropper or tenant worked a generous tract. At the metropolitan end, Britain, France and Germany each had its own distinctive form of land endowment, with a smaller holding than overseas, farmed much more intensively to produce a higher yield, and with much higher land values. European holdings produced the same order of output as American ones, but with less land and a higher outlay. German and French cultivators owned their land more often than not, while the English, who were mostly tenants, shared their harvest with landowners and labourers. In Russia and India, peasants hungered for land. Their plots were small, their yields low, they paid high rents and were deeply in debt. Village land values matched those on the prairies but the output per holding was more than ten times lower. In terms of income, land was an order of magnitude more expensive than in the New World. Progress and poverty coexisted inside the peasant countries. Russia, and even India, had their modern sectors in which hired labour worked on medium and large farms using modern machinery. In Russia in particular this sector, although it only accounted for some 10 per cent of the crops, was responsible for most of the exports.[13] Its combination of up-to-date methods and cheap labour made it a formidable competitor, vying with the United States as the leading exporter after the turn of the century. But the peasant producer still grew most of the grain, and his problems dominated rural society.

Britain's agricultural deficit created purchasing power overseas for its industrial exports, while cheap food kept wages down at home. The deficit became a prop of Britain's stagnant export economy in the late-Victorian period. It also created a profitable field for investment abroad. In order for this to happen, imports had to displace domestic agriculture. In the first half of the nineteenth century British agriculture led the whole of Europe (if not the world) in productivity and innovation. Why did it falter in the second half? That is the subject of the next chapter.

[13] G. Pavlovsky, *Agricultural Russia on the Eve of the Revolution* (1930), pp. 190–221.

TABLE 6.2. *Farmers' land endowment, c.1911*

	(1) Size of holding (acres) mean or median	(2) Wheat yield per acre*	(3) Land value (US$ per acre)	(4) Tenant holdings (number as % of total)†
USA	210 (139)[a]	13.9	45 (41)[b]	19[c]
Canada	289 (115)[d]	17.8	3–11 (23–32)[e]	5[f]
Australia	252 (446)[g]	8.5	20–(34)[h]	0–20[i]
Argentina	192 (406)[j]	10.2	7–17[k]	67[l]
England	115[m]	32.5	128[n]	87[o]
Germany	73[p]	25.2	154[q]	6[p]
France	60 (100)[r]	20.2	288[s]	25[t]
Russia	11 (13–27) [19] {178}[u]	9.5	22[v]	High[w]
India	7–8 (13–15) [12.7][x]	10.6	40[y]	62[z]

Notes and Sources:

* Mean, 1895–1909. H. C. Farnsworth, 'Wheat in the Post-surplus Period, 1900–1909, with Recent Analogies and Contrasts', *Wheat Studies*, vol. 17 (1941), p. 381.

† Excluding part-owners.

[a] Mean farm acreage, 1910, West North Central States: Minnesota, Iowa, Missouri, N. & S. Dakota, Nebraska, Kansas (and national average). *Statistical History of the US*, pt. 1 ser. K37, p. 461.

[b] Mean value of farm and buildings per acre, 1910, West North Central States: Minnesota, Iowa, Missouri, N. & S. Dakota, Nebraska, Kansas (and national average). Ibid., ser. K37, pp. 460, 463.

[c] Weighted mean, four spring-wheat states, 1910. M. K. Bennett, 'Average Pre-war and Post-war Farm Costs of Wheat Production in the North American Spring-Wheat Belt', *Wheat Studies*, vol. 1 (1925), p. 206. For white-owned farms in 1910 in the whole of the United States, the proportion of tenants was 31% (excluding part-tenants): *Statistical History of the US*, pt. 1, ser. K114–18, p. 465.

^d Unimproved (improved) holding size, Manitoba, Saskatchewan, Alberta, 1911. F. H. Leacy (ed.) *Historical Statistics of Canada* (2nd edn. Ottawa 1983), ser. M12, 19–21, 23, 30–2, 34, 41–3.

^e Unimproved land, sales by railways and Hudson's Bay Company, average price per acre, 1900–1909. Canada, *Annual Report of the Department of the Interior* 1909, Sessional Paper no. 25 (1909) p. xxiii. (Improved land value per acre, Alberta, Saskatchewan, Manitoba, 1911. Canada, *Census and Statistics Monthly* (Mar, 1912), p. 56.) Canadian dollars.

^f Weighted mean, Manitoba, Saskatchewan, Alberta, 1911. Bennett, 'Average Costs', p. 206.

^g Mean size of closer settlement allotments to 1912, NSW (and Victoria) (1.4m. acres) *Official Year Book of NSW 1911–12*, pp. 611–15, and *Victoria Year-Book, 1911–12*, pp. 626–7. The mean alienated landholding over 50 acres in NSW in 1910 was 1,036 acres, of which 58 acres were under cultivation; this represents 96% of alienated lands, which comprised about one-third of all land: NSW *Year Book, 1909–10*, pp. 490–1. The average area under wheat per holding in 1910–11 was 113 acres (Victoria) and 118 acres (NSW): E. Dunsdorfs, *The Australian Wheat Growing Industry, 1788–1948* (Melbourne 1956), pp. 253–4.

^h Closer settlement estates, up to 1912, NSW (and Victoria). *Official Year Book of NSW, 1911–12*, pp. 611–15, and *Victoria Year-Book, 1911–12*, pp. 626–7.

ⁱ 20.4% sharecropping in New South Wales, 1910–11; negligible in other states. Dunsdorfs, *Australian Wheat Growing Industry*, pp. 246–7, 252.

^j First figure: area sown to wheat per holding; Argentine cereal belt; acreage, 1910–11. J. R. Scobie, *Revolution on the Pampas: A Social History of Argentine Wheat, 1860–1910* (Austin, Texas 1964), table 5, p. 172. Second figure no. of holdings, 1912–13, and acreage under cereals and flax, 1915–16. C. E. Solberg, 'Land Tenure and Land Settlement: Policy and Patterns in the Canadian Prairies and the Argentine Pampas, 1880–1930', in D. C. M. Platt and G. di Tella (eds.), *Argentina, Australia and Canada: Studies in Comparative Development, 1870–1965* (1985), table 3.1, p. 56.

^k Argentine land values, 1911. Scobie, *Revolution on the Pampas*, table 4, p. 171.

^l Percentage of tenants and sharecroppers in 1912–13. Solberg, 'Land Tenure'.

^m England and Wales, mean size of all holdings over 20 acres (96% of all cultivated land), in 1914. Acreage and Livestock Returns for England and Wales, PP 1914–16 Cd. 7926 LXXIX, table 12, pp. 90–3. The mean for all holdings over 5 acres was 78 acres, and for holdings in the arable counties 202 acres: ch. 8 no. 1 below.

ⁿ Mean value per acre, England and Wales, 1910–11. Annual rental of "lands" (includes farmhouses and tithes) multiplied by death duty mean valuation (19.63 years-purchase), divided by agricultural acreage in England (at 27.2m. acres). Rental: J. Stamp, *British Incomes and Property* (1916), table A3, p. 36; acreage: Ministry of Agriculture, Fisheries and Food, *A Century of Agricultural Statistics: Great Britain, 1866–1966* (1968), table 11, p. 25. Death duty valuations; Inland Revenue Annual Report, Great Britain, PP 1914. The lower rental per acre suggested by A. H. Rhee would give a value of $99, but I have used the higher one, as the Inland Revenue was likely to use its own rental estimate to calculate values: H. A. Rhee, *The Rent of Agricultural Land in England and Wales, 1870–1946* (Oxford 1949), table 2, pp. 44–5.

^o Percentage of holdings rented or mainly rented, 1911, in England and Wales. *A Century of Agricultural Statistics*, table 10, p. 24.

^p Farms over 5 acres (94% of all land), 1907. Calculated from *Statistisches Jahrbuch für das Deutsche Reich*, vol. 33 (Berlin 1912), table III/1b, p. 34.

^q Seven Prussian provinces, 1895–1906, mean of means of large estates (over 1,250 acres) and small farms (12.5–50 acres); standard deviation 103. Calculated from T. H. Middleton 'The Recent Development of German Agriculture', PP 1916 Cd. 8305 IV, p. 21.

^r Median farm by size in 1892. C. P. Kindleberger, *Economic Growth in France and Britain, 1851–1950* (Cambridge, Mass. 1964), p. 216. (Farms larger than 40 ha. utilized 47% of all agricultural land in 1892: F. Caron, *An Economic History of Modern France* (1979), p. 131.)

^s Mean value of ordinary arable land sold, 1908–12. France, *Annuaire statistique*, vol. 33 (Paris 1913), 'Propriétés et Revenus', tableau IV, p. 97. The mean value of all non-building land was $240.

[t] 1892. Caron, *Economic History*, p. 131.

[u] Average holding per male peasant in European Russia, 1896. I. M. Rubinow, *Russia's Wheat Surplus: The Conditions under which it is Produced*, USDA Bureau of Statistics, Bulletin no. 42 (Washington DC 1906), p. 53;. (Median holding by no. of households in European Russia, 1905.) [Average of category covering 80% of peasantry, estimated by Lenin, 1905. T. Shanin, *The Awkward Class* (Oxford 1972), pp. 48, 59.] {Estimate for large farms. G. Pavlovsky, *Agricultural Russia on the Eve of the Revolution* (1930), p. 210.}

[v] Average land prices in 50 provinces of Russia from Peasant Land Bank sales, 1911. D. A. Baturinskii, *Agrarnaya politika Tsarskogo pravitel'stva i Krest'yanskii pozemel'nyi bank* (Moscow 1925), pp. 41, 111. The data were kindly provided by Stephen Wheatcroft.

[w] Although peasants owned two-thirds of the arable land, they rented some of the private estate land, and up to 1905 also had large redemption payments to make to the state, which approximated to their pre-emancipation obligations. Rubinow, *Russia's Wheat Surplus*, pp. 44–5.

[x] Land revenue figures indicate an average area of 7–8 acres, but this conceals a difference between irrigated holdings of 4 acres, and much larger ones of the dry-farming areas; for the almost 88% of owners of less than 18 acres, the estimate is of 10–12 acres. H. Calvert, *The Wealth and Welfare of the Punjab being Some Studies in Punjab Rural Economics* (Lahore 1922), pp. 74–5. (Acres per plough and per pair of bullocks, Punjab, 1919–20 [average acreage per holding, Bombay Presidency 1919–22] C. P. Wright and J. S. Davis, 'India as a Producer and Exporter of Wheat', *Wheat Studies*, vol. 3 (July 1927), pp. 337–8.)

[y] Average price of cultivated land in the Punjab 124 rupees in 1910–11. Calvert, *Wealth and Welfare*, p. 108.

[z] Tenancy in the Punjab, 1911 census. Calvert, *Wealth and Welfare*, p. 86.

7

CAUSES OF THE AGRICULTURAL DEPRESSION, 1870–1914

THE depression of British agriculture during the last quarter of the nineteenth century loosened the grip of British landowners on society and politics, it impelled the Irish to revolt, and it helped to split the Liberal party down the middle and to keep it out of power for a generation. As we shall see, it was also one of the distant causes of the First World War. Now what exactly do we mean by agricultural depression? The first symptom that meets the eye is the collapse of prices, followed by the decline of production and finally by the contraction of landed incomes and wealth, of rents and of land values. Hundreds of thousands of labourers left the countryside. The price of wheat fell from 46 shillings a quarter in 1870 to 22 shillings in 1894. The price of meat and wool also declined. Land under grain contracted by some two-thirds in thirty years, most of which reverted to rough pasture. By 1913 Britain imported some four-fifths of its wheat and flour.

Why did British agriculture surrender its markets? Why did it give way? To narrow the question somewhat, did British wheat simply drown in the rising flood of world supplies, a victim of forces beyond its control, or was the failure "endogenous", brought on by the qualities and circumstances of British economy and society?

One traditional answer is that there was no decline to speak of, and therefore nothing to explain. Those who concede a problem invoke such factors as the absence of tariff protection, steam power, soil and climate, consumer tastes, labour productivity and land values. I shall examine the answers one by one as they apply to grain farming. This will cast a light on other sectors as well.

In 1870 wheat acreage still hovered near its historical peak but by 1875 the trend was down. From 3.68 million acres in 1870 wheat acreage came down almost two-thirds to 1.37 million acres in 1904.[1] Alone among the world's larger grain producers, Britain almost halved its production of wheat (Denmark and Belgium, both small, open economies, also cut

---

[1] S. Fairlie placed the peak in the 1840s, but her data indicate that 1869–70 was still within the upper range of historical wheat production: 'The Corn Laws and British Wheat Production, 1829–76', *Economic History Review*, vol. 22 (1969), esp. pp. 95–113; M&D, pp. 78–9; Rew, *Food Supplies*, p. 26; R. J. P. Kain and H. C. Prince, *The Tithe Surveys of England and Wales* (Cambridge 1985), pp. 173–4.

down, but only by 6 per cent and 17 per cent respectively). No major producer has deliberately followed this course, nor was it preordained. Today Britain is once again a net exporter of grain, as it had been in the eighteenth century.

The decline of wheat production is not necessarily evidence of failure or even of depression. This is a view that held the field for two decades, ever since T. W. Fletcher's articles of the early 1960s. In brief, Fletcher argued that the decline in arable production was made up by an expansion of animal products (especially liquid milk), and that the loud agrarian complaints about depression expressed the special interests of a grain grower minority in the south-east.[2]

"Failure" is an emotive term. Objectively it means that agriculture did not make proper use of its land and labour and failed to take advantage of economic opportunities. On the first test, Fletcher's own evidence is damning. His data suggest an overall decline of output (in current prices) of between 10 and 17 per cent from the 1870s to the 1890s. C. H. Feinstein's work suggests that in constant prices output fell by a tenth or so in this period. More milk, butter and meat did not make up for the loss of grain. At the same time population grew almost by half and Gross Domestic Product more than doubled. All the aggregate growth of demand for more than forty years was met by foreign producers, while British farmers rapidly retreated into fresh milk, meat and vegetables, a market segment that foreigners could not enter. By the eve of the First World War foreign producers had more than half the British food market. Another consequence was that agriculture held back British economic growth during the sluggish late-Victorian years. Despite its natural monopolies on fresh milk, meat, butter, fruit and vegetables, British agriculture lost more than half of high-value markets like those for butter, bacon and eggs. If Ireland is regarded as an overseas supplier (which it was, both literally and from a strategic point of view), then the failure is even more pronounced.[3]

On the positive side of the balance, UK agriculture released about a quarter of its work-force, its numbers falling from about 3 million in 1870 to 2.3 million in 1911. So, in spite of a decline in gross output, there was an increase in overall productivity (Total Factor Productivity) of some 0.3–0.4 per cent a year. This was a little less than the increase in the economy overall, but only a third to one-half of productivity increases in the United States before 1900. Low productivity in agriculture held back the growth of

[2] T. W. Fletcher, 'The Great Depression of British Agriculture, 1873–1896', *Economic History Review*, vol. 13 (1960–61) and 'Lancashire Livestock Farming during the Great Depression', *Agricultural History Review*, vol. 9 (1961).
[3] E. J. T. Collins, 'Agriculture in a Free Trade Economy: Great Britain, 1870–1930', in P. Villani (ed.), *Trasformazioni delle società rurali nei paesi dell'Europa occidentale e mediterranea* (Naples, 1986).

the economy as a whole.[4] If labour was more productive, the other factor, land, was not. American farming productivity appears to have stagnated between 1900 and 1920. This suggests the possibility that, with its high yields, British farming had bumped against a technological ceiling. But the accounts of dereliction and neglect, and the evidence of slow mechanization, both point otherwise. In the absence of a sustained effort of agricultural research (except for some small-scale private work), the suggestion is not compelling. The agricultural depression, then, was no figment of the contemporary imagination. Agriculture in Britain led the vanguard of economic retardation and decline, the first great industry to lose the bulk of its domestic market to overseas.

The wheel has taken another turn since Fletcher has written and the late-Victorian depression is no longer seriously in question among economic historians. What still needs to be explained is the reason why.

The flow of wheat ran ahead of demand from the 1870s onwards, and prices began to fall. Wheat came from Kansas and Minnesota, from South Australia, from the Punjab, from Odessa and the Danube. It challenged established growers everywhere, not only in Britain. Other regions coped with new conditions and adapted to them one way or another. Only Britain retrenched so completely.

On the Continent, Germany and France imposed tariffs that rose from nominal levels in the 1880s to some 30 per cent of the British price in the 1890s in Germany, and 40 per cent in France.[5] In Britain this was never an option. The import economy of the south which generated so much of the mercantile, financial, rentier and professional incomes shared a free trade outlook with the textile, metal and machinery export industries of the north, with the shipowners of the great ports and the shipbuilders of the Tyne, the Mersey and the Clyde. Large imperial, military and naval interests relied indirectly on free trade, and investments in primary production and transport overseas were the mainstay of the late-Victorian stock exchange. Working-class electors stood firm against any attempt to exclude foreign grain. Even Joseph Chamberlain's bid for protection held out little hope for agriculture. Chamberlain tempted the colonies with privileged access to the home market. During the tariff reform campaign decade (1903–14) the Empire taken as a whole (Canada, India, Australia)

---

[4] Fletcher, 'The Great Depression', p. 432; estimates of output: Feinstein, *National Income*, table 54, p. T118; also C. O'Grada, 'Agricultural Decline, 1860–1914', in R. Floud and D. McCloskey (eds.), *The Economic History of Britain since 1700* (Cambridge 1981), vol. 2, table 8.3, p. 180; labour force, Feinstein, *National Income*, table 60, p. T131; productivity: O'Grada, 'Agricultural Decline', pp. 178–9; Matthews, Feinstein and Odling-Smee, *British Economic Growth*, pp. 227–33, 462; J. W. Kendrick, *Productivity Trends in the United States* (Princeton 1961), pp. 135–6, 362–4.

[5] Average of tariff as percentage of British wheat prices, 1890–1900: calculated from H. C. Farnsworth, 'Decline and Recovery of Wheat Prices in the "Nineties"', *Wheat Studies*, vol. 10 (1934), tables II, VII, pp. 347, 350.

emerged as the largest and most dynamic wheat exporter and built up sufficient capacity to supply Britain entirely on its own (fig 6.1).

Andrew Bonar Law, who led the Conservative opposition after 1911, dropped agricultural protection entirely from the tariff platform in January 1913. In 1912 he told a colleague that he was willing to let Canada provide all of Britain's wheat requirement, 'thus rendering its cultivation in Great Britain quite unnecessary'.[6] Apart from farmers and landowners, few even among ardent protectionists supported a tariff for grain.

Britain was not the only open economy. Belgium, Holland and Denmark allowed grain free entry, but did not stop growing it themselves. The three countries reduced their production moderately, but more than compensated by a large growth of their livestock sectors. Denmark in particular won a share of the British market for cheese, butter, bacon and eggs, while the Belgians expanded livestock production for home consumption. Of much greater significance were the old North American wheat-growing regions east of the Mississippi. In those states farmers reduced their acreage of wheat in response to the long-term decline of wheat at one-third or so of the British rate. In the corn-belt states of Ohio, Iowa, Indiana, Illinois, Michigan and Wisconsin the reduction was faster, at a little over one-half in most states. In technical terms, the supply elasticity east of the Mississippi hovered around 0.5, whereas in Britain it was larger than 1.6 in the depression period, and more than 1.9 during the revival. And when the corn belt reduced its wheat output, it had a very attractive alternative in the form of maize, which expanded by leaps and bounds. Some of this maize found its way to British markets by way of the meat packers of Chicago. Perhaps the most impressive transformation took place in California, which up to the 1890s was the second largest wheat-growing state, and which kept up its acreage despite the depression of prices as one of Britain's chief suppliers. It dropped out of wheat very rapidly around the end of the century in favour of fruit, vegetable and dairy products for the home market, but only *after* the revival of wheat prices.[7] In the Yankee

---

[6] Charles Bathurst to Christopher Turnor, 6 Aug. 1912, C. Turnor Papers, 4 Turnor 3/5. I owe this reference to Dr Matthew Fforde.

[7] British supply elasticities for wheat in the period of falling prices seem to have been larger than 1.6 on a 7-year trend, while American ones in the corn belt (on 47-year observations) were marginally higher than one, but not in Missouri, Illinois and Indiana. The estimates are not strictly comparable, but reinforce the impression that British farmers responded much more readily to falling prices by decreasing output than their American counterparts. For America east of the Mississippi, elasticities were about 0.5; the respective sources are M. Olson, Jr. and C. C. Harris, Jr., 'Free Trade in "Corn": A Statistical Study of the Prices and Production of Wheat in Great Britain from 1873 to 1914', *Quarterly Journal of Economics*, vol. 73 (1959), and F. M. Fisher and P. Temin, 'Regional Specialization and the Supply of Wheat in the United States, 1867–1914', *Review of Economics and Statistics*, vol. 52 (1970). The corn belt: A. G. Bogue, *From Prairie to Corn Belt* (Chicago 1963); wheat production by region: L. B. Schmidt, 'The Westward Movement of Wheat', in L. B. Schmidt and E. D. Ross

north-east, which most resembled Britain, wheat output fell rather less than in Britain and self-sufficiency remained higher.[8] In short, although not all of the open economies and regions actually increased their production of wheat during these years, none of them retrenched as drastically as Britain, and by combining domestic and imported grain they effected a shift to higher-value outputs, the transformation which eluded British producers.

After tariffs, the second factor most often invoked to explain the decline of British arable is steam power. Now, other things being equal, why should growers thousands of miles away be able to compete with British wheat farmers? The journey to Liverpool still added about a quarter to the price of Kansas wheat. It is true that railways penetrated deep into the prairies, and steamships carried grain over the great lakes and across the Atlantic. By the end of the century the price differential between Chicago and Liverpool almost disappeared. But not all of this can be explained by the fall of freight costs. American prices actually rose *above* the British ones several times after 1900. As domestic markets came to dominate American grain production, prices came to be led by American demand and not by British prices. Exports could only be shipped at a discount. This rise in domestic demand, and the shift out of grain, helps to explain the American withdrawal from European markets, especially in years of short domestic harvest.[9]

It is true that wheat could now pay for a voyage half-way round the globe. But not necessarily under steam. A large proportion of British grain imports travelled under sail for most of its journey. In the 1880s and the 1890s California, Washington and Oregon supplied up to one-half of British imports from the United States. Pacific coast crops had to be manhandled in eighty-pound sacks onto sailing ships which might take four

(eds.), *Readings in the Economic History of American Agriculture* (New York 1925), table II, p. 375. Data by state is available in USDA, *Wheat. Acreage, Yield and Production, by States, 1866–1943*, Agricultural Marketing Service, Bulletin no. 158 (Washington, DC 1955). On California, see Paul, 'Wheat Trade', p. 411.

[8] Production in the American north-east declined by 11 per cent between 1875–9 and 1910–13, compared with 30 per cent in Britain, according to C. K. Harley, 'Western Settlement and the Price of Wheat, 1872–1913', *Journal of Economic History*, vol. 38 (Dec. 1978), table 1, p. 866. His figures for self-sufficiency are close to those of Britain (27 and 23 per cent, respectively) but that is misleading: (1) the first period includes the disastrous British harvest of 1879, and depresses the British benchmark; (2) Harley's estimate of imports is based on an inference from population size. But official data for 1910–15 suggest that self-sufficiency was higher in the American north-east at about 32 per cent, compared with his estimate of 27 per cent: Ball *et al.*, 'Wheat Production', p. 130. Furthermore, population in the American north-east grew much faster than in Britain during the period.

[9] The most recent treatment of the relation between prices and transport is C. K. Harley, 'Transportation, The World Wheat Trade, and the Kuznets Cycle, 1850–1913', *Explorations in Economic History*, vol. 17 (1980).

or five months to cover the 14,000 miles around Cape Horn.[10] Australian wheat came on similar vessels on a journey almost as long. Indian and Russian wheat shipments suffered the handicap of poor transport in the interior, much of it by wagon and barge, and from the absence of cleaning, grading and bulking facilities at the ports. Compared to their foreign competitors, British farmers harvested their crop almost in sight of the mills. It may well be that it cost as much to carry a carload of grain from Lincolnshire to Birmingham as it did from New York to Liverpool. But that was still much cheaper than the cost from Karachi or Port Adelaide, and was not due to a disadvantage of British farming, but to the shortcomings of British railways.[11]

Soil and climate are sometimes invoked to explain the decline of wheat farming in Britain. Ancient English soils had to be manured, fertilized and carefully tilled, while the prairie farmer worked a virgin land. 'It is the unexhausted natural fertility of his soil which gives the advantage to the prairie farmer of the north-west,' wrote James Caird, the agrarian guru, in 1880.[12] But yields in Britain were more than twice as high as on the prairies. British farmers applied a great deal of manure and inorganic fertilizer, not in order to bring their land up to prairie standards, but to give it a boost over and above that level. The suggestion that British soil was inferior to the prairies was tested implicitly in two scientific experiments. For more than fifty years two scientists conducted a study of soil fertility at Rothamsted in Hertfordshire. J. B. Lawes and J. H. Gilbert compared the yield of different doses of fertilizer with that of an unfertilized field, continuously cropped to wheat. The Broadbalk field, subject of this experiment, 'cannot be described as more than fair average wheat land'. Plot no. 3, which remained unfertilized throughout, produced an average yield of 13.1 bushels per acre over fifty years of continuous cropping, and about 12.5 bushels per acre in the last forty years of the century. This was close to the world average, comparable with crop levels in the United States, and higher than Argentina and Australia, India and Russia. A companion experiment on sandy soil in Woburn in Bedfordshire achieved a similar result, with the yield declining from 17 to 13 bushels in twenty years and stabilizing at 9–10 bushels, well within the range of a few large producers overseas. Like the virgin prairies, British soils also

[10] Paul, 'Wheat Trade'. Admittedly the sailing ship continued to improve under the spur of competition from steam.
[11] H. R. Rathbone, 'The Wheat Supplies of the British Isles', in A. P. Newton (ed.), *The Staple Trades of the Empire* (1917), p. 150. From a large contemporary literature, see, e.g. W. R. Lawson, *British Railways: A Financial and Commercial Survey* (New York 1914), chs. 17, 22. In the United States the first stage of transport was also the most expensive and about half the cost of carrying wheat was incurred in the first 200 miles: Larson, *Minnesota*, p. 252.
[12] J. Caird, *The Landed Interest and the Supply of Food* (4th edn. 1880), p. 162.

contained a large store of unexhausted fertility, which took a long time to run down.[13]

The first of the two Royal Commissions which took evidence about the depression blamed it, in part, on "poor seasons". Britain suffered a succession of wet summers at the end of the 1870s, lost half the crop in 1879, and went dry for several summers in the 1880s. But instability is inherent to agriculture, and the British climate was *more* and not less stable than in competing lands. Table 7.1 shows the fluctuation of wheat yields over thirty years in the main export and import countries. The amplitude of the yield is given by col. (2), which gives the mean deviation from the trend. Yields in Canada varied more than twice as much from one year to another as in Britain, in Argentina three times, in Australia four. Even the United States, with its long-established wheat regions, had larger fluctuations than Britain. The table also highlights another advantage to British consumers of buying their grain from many sources. The world variance of yields was much lower than for any single country.

TABLE 7.1. *Wheat yield fluctuations, 1885–1914*

	(1) Yield (mean bushels per acre)	(2) Fluctuations (from a mean of 100 on a uniform scale)
USA	13.5	9.6
Canada	16.2	19.2
Australia	8.6	32.6
Argentina	10.6	24.9
British Isles	31.8	7.6
Germany	27.0	6.9
France	19.1	10.3
Russia	9.2	18.1
India	10.4	9.5
World	13.0	5.4

Note: Col. (2) shows the standard error of least square regression of index of yield (100 = mean) against time. *This provides an average of fluctuations from the trend line on the same scale for all countries.*

Source: M. K. Bennett, 'World Wheat Crops, 1885–1932: New Series, with Areas and Yields, by Countries', *Wheat Studies*, vol. 9 (1933), appendix B.

In the 1880s the wheat-grower's plough moved into lands of greater marginality in which either drought or frost or both caused successive seasons of very heavy loss. In the winter-wheat areas of South Australia

---

[13] A. D. Hall, *The Book of the Rothamsted Experiments* (1905), pp. 32, 35–9; compare with J. A. Voelcker, 'The Woburn Experimental Farm and its Work (1876–1921)', *Journal of the Royal Society of Agriculture*. vol. 84 (1923), p. 116.

and Kansas, and in the spring-wheat regions of Dakota, Minnesota and the Canadian West, growers encountered recurring drought, frost or both, as well as pests and crop diseases which were almost unknown in Britain. Settlers in the new lands, often total newcomers to farming, had little experience of local conditions and often no long-term commitment to their occupation and region. Slowly they found appropriate cultivation methods, tools and seed varieties. Driven by speculative enthusiasm, they embraced unproven doctrines of "dry farming", consisting of extensive fallowing, special tillage tools and routines, and wheat varieties resistant to drought, disease and frost. But these adaptations were slow and incomplete, and only matured after the turn of the century.[14]

Another factor is consumer tastes. It is true that consumers and millers both came to prefer imported wheat and flour. A foreign wheat, Manitoba hard no.1, served as the quality standard at Liverpool, and North American wheat sold at a premium there. Flour millers changed over from stone milling to roller-equipped mills in the 1880s. British wheat varieties are "soft", i.e. low on proteins. Rollers could grind the "hard" winter and spring wheats of North America and Russia. These hard wheats have a high protein (or "gluten") content, and produce a bread that retains moisture and hence its freshness for a longer period. Roller-milled flour also keeps much longer, and made possible, for the first time, a considerable international trade in flour. Hard-wheat flours produced light, porous loaves with a fine grain and texture, which remained fresh on the shelf. Miller, baker and housewife all preferred it. Large roller mills went up in the seaports, where they loaded wheat straight out of the hull, while the British grower lost his country mill, and had to send his crop long-distance by rail.

Roller milling was more efficient but its success is not a clear case of the good driving out the bad. High-gluten bread is the ancestor of the sliced, white, spongy loaves in supermarkets today. Customers quickly came to prefer it, and it is heresy to suggest that customers may be wrong. But the change of tastes was driven primarily by the convenience of millers and bakers. Indeed it is arguable that it was a lack of discrimination in British consumers that facilitated the change. Tastes are fickle and malleable. Economies of scale in food production can be bought at the expense of quality. They can actually be detrimental to public health, like many staples of the late-Victorian mass-foods industry.[15] Roller-milled white

---

[14] M. W. M. Hargreaves, 'The Dry Farming Movement in Retrospect', in T. R. Wessel (ed.), *Agriculture in the Great Plains, 1897–1936, Agricultural History*, vol. 51 (1977); G. Fite, *The Farmers' Frontier, 1865–1900* (New York 1966), chs. 6–7.

[15] The unhealthy effect of refined carbohydrates in British diets in the late-Victorian period: F. B. Smith, 'Health', in J. Benson (ed.), *The Working Class in England, 1875–1914* (1985), pp. 50–4.

bread contained less fibre and fewer vitamins than stone-milled bread. Centuries of stone mills and self-sufficiency left no record of discontent with the English loaf. Across the Channel in France families remained loyal to the soft domestic wheats and the local miller. They baked their own loaves or sent to the baker for his appetizing bread. Since it went stale quickly, they visited the bakery several times a day.

Scientific research might have made British grain more attractive to the miller, but government was not interested. In Canada, the United States and Australia governments supported massive programmes of plant search, import and selection in which tens of thousands of specimens were tested on a network of experimental farms. Eventually these efforts (together with those of amateur and commercial breeders) produced varieties much better adapted to local environments and milling demands, and set in train one of the most economically productive of scientific enterprises. Agricultural research in Britain was undertaken on a tiny scale by amateurs or, in the case of Lawes and Gilbert, by an enlightened entrepreneur. Reflecting the bias of British farming and the business interests of Lawes, most research concentrated on fertilizers and their effect. The baking qualities of British wheat were first taken up after the turn of the century, by chemists and not by botanists. R. H. Biffen began to breed wheat varieties at Cambridge only after 1904. His work was sound but its scale was puny in comparison with overseas efforts, and it failed to deliver a solution. It ought to be added that subsequent work in plant breeding has not sufficiently improved the hardness of British wheat, which is used for biscuits and for blending but not, on its own, for the mass-market loaf.[16]

British farmers took more slowly than their American counterparts to machinery, and especially to the reaper, the most important mechanical innovation of nineteenth-century agriculture and (together with other tools and implements) the most important source of rising productivity in North American grain farming. One reason for their slowness was the abundance of labour in rural England. When labour was cheap, it made sense to avoid the reaper. When wages rose (in real terms) in the 1880s, reapers duly appeared.[17] Another purported reason was the irregular shape and surface of English grain fields and their small size, which denied the reaper the best conditions. Like the labour surplus, these were the heritage of a previous round of innovation in agriculture, the enclosure movement that ended in the 1840s. Paul David has argued that rearrangement of the fields to take the reaper was too costly for landowners and farmers to undertake.[18] But

[16] E. J. Russell, *A History of Agricultural Science in Great Britain* (1966), pp. 207–13.
[17] E. J. T. Collins, 'The Rationality of "Surplus" Agricultural Labour: Mechanization in English Agriculture in the Nineteenth Century', *Agricultural History Review*, vol. 35 (1987).
[18] Productivity in agriculture: W. N. Parker, 'Productivity Growth in American Grain

the making of American fields was not costless either. The sod had to be broken, trees cleared, stones removed, fences and farmsteads erected. British landowners invested heavily and unprofitably in drainage during the "golden age" of 1850–70; it was likewise in their power to arrange the fields to suit the reaper. These machines diffused slowly in the good years and only took over during the decades of secular depression, so perhaps lack of capital was not the main constraint.[19]

The last of our factors is land. Prairie land was cheap, British land was dear. So much is clear from table 6.2. British farming bore a heavy burden of rent, and the opening of free or cheap land posed the greatest challenge to British production. From a theoretical point of view, that is the most persuasive explanation. When prices fell by more than half, British wheat growers could no longer afford to pay the market rate for land and it reverted to alternative uses. This explanation presupposes that British land *had* alternative uses, which could pay more for the land than grain or livestock. But livestock production failed to make up for the decline of grain, and was concentrated in different areas. In the absence of alternative uses, we would expect land values to decline.

Rent and land values fell, but very slowly. Agricultural rents in England and Wales stood at about £40 million in 1842, rising to a peak of £52 million in 1876. By 1882 they had already started their prolonged decline which was still unbroken when it reached £37 million in 1910.[20] Prices at the start and end of the period are comparable, so these data suggest that in the aggregate there was no strong competitor with agriculture for the land in question, although in many particular localities rents held up or rose in response to opportunities for milk production, market gardening or suburban development. Rents declined by more than a quarter between the 1870s and the First World War. Capital values took more of a beating and fell about twice as much. They stood at about thirty-five times the annual rent in the 1870s, falling to seventeen times in the 1890s, rising up

Farming: An Analysis of its Nineteenth Century Sources', in R. W. Fogel and S. L. Engerman (eds.), *The Reinterpretation of American Economic History* (New York 1971); the reaper and its effects: P. David, 'The Landscape and the Machine', in his *Technical Choice, Innovation and Economic Growth* (Cambridge 1975).

[19] J. Atack, 'Farm and Farm-making Costs Revisited', *Agricultural History*, vol. 56 (1982), p. 563; F. M. L. Thompson, *English Landed Society in the Nineteenth Century* (1963), p. 251; A. Mutch, 'The Mechanization of the Harvest in South-west Lancashire, 1850–1914', *Agricultural History Review*, vol. 29 (1981).

[20] J. Stamp, *British Incomes and Property* (1916), p. 36. Ireland and Scotland are left out because of difficulties in their tenurial and rental statistics. This series, based on the income tax Schedule A "lands" assessment, is lacking in some refinements of subsequent analyses, but utilizes their prime source in its most robust form. H. A. Rhee, *The Rent of Agricultural Land in England and Wales, 1870–1946* (Oxford 1949), table 2, pp. 44–5, suggests a decline of rents of about 30 per cent between 1875 and 1910.

again to twenty times (of a depleted rent) by 1910.[21] This suggests a decline of land values of up to 60 per cent between 1875 and 1910. But even at these depressed levels, land values in Britain were three times as high as in the United States and in the 1880s and 1890s the differential must have been much larger. Rents and land values fell, but did they fall fast and far enough?

If high land prices were the problem, why did they fail to fall even more? For one thing, American grain prices provided a floor, which kept British land values from declining even further. After the mid-1890s grain prices started to rise again, though British rents continued to decline. For all the decline in transport costs, they still accounted for some 20 per cent of the price of grain in Liverpool, and that element entered British land values. For the rest, if we imagine British agriculture as a smoothly adjusting system, then perhaps output stabilized at a level permitted by rents, which were governed by factors only loosely related to the price of grain.

---

[21] Capital values: Norton, Trist & Gilbert [a firm of land agents], 'A Century of Land Values', *Journal of the Royal Statistical Society*, vol. 54 (1891), pp. 528–32, reported an average of 35 years-purchase for 106,538 acres sold during the 1870s; R. Giffen estimated 30 years-purchase in 1875 (Agricultural Depression. Royal Commission Final Report, PP 1897 C. 8540 XV, p. 23); Inland Revenue valuations for death duties placed values at 17 years-purchase in 1896, rising to 20 in 1910 and 22 in 1913 (Inland Revenue Annual Reports in the PP), e.g., for 1914, table 28, p. 32.

8

THE SOD HOUSE AGAINST THE MANOR HOUSE

NONE of the common explanations for the decline of British wheat production is sufficient on its own. Tariffs, steam power, soil, climate, consumer tastes, land values, labour productivity all had an effect, but they only tell half a story. They did not disable any other large producer. Natural conditions were benign. The question remains: why was British adaptation so poor?

I

Some of the causes may be found in the social forms of wheat production which had developed in Britain before 1870. England's arable regions stretched in a belt which swung from Devon and Hampshire in the south, through Wiltshire, the south midlands and the home counties, to East Anglia, Lincolnshire, the East Riding of Yorkshire and Northumberland. Farms in the grain counties were much larger than the average. The fourteen counties with the largest ratio of grain to other crops (and with half the land in England) had a mean farm size of 202 acres, well above the other seventeen counties, whose average was 159.[1] In the heart of this region, in Berkshire, Buckinghamshire and Oxfordshire, the average farmer employed about ten labourers, with a bailiff or overseer to supervise them. For every farmer (including relatives and foremen) there were four to six labourers in the grain counties and less than three in the rest of the country.[2]

Most grain farms carried livestock as well. Grain cultivation calls for two or three months of intense labour in two peaks: during the harvest, and when seedbeds are prepared. Livestock provided additional work in turnip and hay fields. Farmers in the east and south of the country maintained a

[1] For farms over 50 acres, which contained 84 per cent of the land in England, and 89 per cent in the corn counties. Spearman's rank correlation coefficient of percentage of land under grain and mean farm size is .715 (the correlation coefficient r = .423). The counties (in order of percentage of land under grain) were: Cambridge, Essex, Suffolk, Huntingdon, Bedford, Hertfordshire, Norfolk, Lincoln, East Riding of Yorkshire, Berkshire, Oxford, Hampshire, Nottingham, Buckingham; percentages of grainland ranged from 54.1 to 34 within this group; calculated from Agricultural Returns for Great Britain, PP 1875 LXXIX, table 3, pp. 46–51; 1880 LXXVI, table 8, pp. 54–7.

[2] Labourers per farm: D. H. Morgan, *Harvesters and Harvesting, 1840–1900* (1982), table 3.7, p. 45; Labourer/farmer ratios in Hampshire and Surrey, the home counties, eastern Counties and south midlands were 6.3, 6.1, 4.7 and 4.6 respectively; well above the English average of 2.8 in 1871: A. L. Bowley, 'Rural Population in England and Wales: A Study of Changes of Density, Occupations and Ages', *Journal of the Royal Statistical Society*, vol. 77 (May 1914), table 6, p. 609.

pool of resident workers to gather the harvest without depending too much on seasonal migrants. For the rest of the year, this reserve army subsisted in semi-idleness and under-nutrition in tumbledown cottages, supported by charity and the Poor Law. Faced with a choice of employing labour very cheaply, or supporting it by means of the poor rates, farmers preferred to use it lavishly to keep their fields and farms in good trim, and also to keep their own hands free of grime.[3]

Wheat growing is a fairly simple matter of ploughing, seeding and harvesting on time. In Britain the job was highly subdivided in order to sustain a three-class society: landowners and their attendant panoply of parsons, attorneys, agents, purveyors and servants; tenant farmers; and farm labourers.

In England's arable counties, in the south and east of the country, most manual work was done by the bottom class of rural society, the agricultural labourers. The south-east had a surplus of labour before the 1870s. In consequence wages were very low, often too low to provide sufficient energy. The south-east labourer had the reputation of a listless, half-witted creature, small in stature, slow in gait; 'two men at low wages were kept to do the work of one well-paid labourer.' Since the workload was so seasonal, a lot of make-work was contrived during the winter months. Farmers paid high rates to the Poor Law unions, which kept many of their seasonal workers alive to gather the harvest. Rural rates came to 13 per cent of the wage bill in the UK in the 1870s, and probably higher in the south-east. High poor rates and the poverty that they underpinned pointed to the social cost of being able to gather the harvest in the short time available. Arable farming with its cycle of exertion and idleness generated a good deal of friction between masters and men; it gave rise to recurrent riot, arson, mutilation and poaching from 1816 to the 1840s. Unrest persisted after the Poor Law reform of 1834 and erupted again in the "Revolts of the Field" of frustrated unionism in the early 1870s.[4]

The decline in grain prices during the depression acted to increase real incomes. Women and children no longer trooped to the fields for a pittance. Most villages acquired primary schools and young labourers

---

[3] A. W. Fox , 'Wages and Earnings of Agricultural Labourers in the United Kingdom. Report', PP 1900 Cd. 346 LXXXII, pp. 8–11, 19. Successive editions of H. Stephens's, *Book of the Farm* describe best practice. C. S. Orwin and E. Whetham, *History of British Agriculture 1846–1914* (1964), chs. 4–5, describe farming developments.

[4] Caird, *Landed Interest*, pp. 62–3; E. Hunt, 'Labour Productivity in English Agriculture, 1850–1914', *Economic History Review*, vol. 20 (1967), p. 282; E. J. Hobsbawm and G. Rudé, *Captain Swing* (1969), ch. 1.; A. Digby, *Pauper Palaces* (1978), chs. 5–6; Morgan, *Harvesters*, ch. 3 and conclusion; J. P. D. Dunbabin, *Rural Discontent in Nineteenth-century Britain* (1974), chs. 4–5; W. A. Armstrong, 'The Workfolk', in G. Mingay (ed.), *The Victorian Countryside* (1981), vol. 2; R. H. Rew, 'Report on the Decline in the Agricultural Population of Great Britain, 1881–1906', PP 1906 Cd. 3273 XCVI. Agricultural rates estimated at £8 million: E. M. Ojala, *Agriculture and Economic Progress* (1952), table XIX, p. 213; agricultural wages: Feinstein, *National Income*, table 23, p. T60.

could read. Hundreds of thousands of them left the land, to be replaced in part by machines, in part by livestock. But even towards the end of the period most of the villagers who remained had neither the energy nor the motivation, nor the intelligence and often not the skill to undertake their work efficiently. A century of labour surplus had taught them the advantage of slowness and their poor diets built up no reserves of energy. After four decades of improvement, Seebohm Rowntree found that farmworkers had enough to eat only in five northern pasture counties in England.[5] On the other hand, farmworkers lived in a cleaner environment and ate simpler food; they seem to have been less prone to infectious and degenerative diseases, and perhaps to have lived longer, although the evidence is ambiguous.[6]

As a rule, wheat farmers who employed labour did not work with their own hands. They allocated jobs, supervised the bailiff and joined in squire's foxhunting and shooting during the season. Cornelius Stovin farmed some 600 acres in Lincolnshire in the 1870s, employed seven men in the summer and six in winter, with two lads and three boys. He paid a bailiff to oversee them. A. G. Street, a farmer's son, remembered that 'there was such a crowd about the place'. His father employed twenty-three men all year round on 630 acres in Wiltshire around the turn of the century. Street's father liked to linger in bed until nine in the morning (this was sufficiently odd for the neighbours to notice, but the son admired his father's knack for business). Stovin 'spent a good part of his own time at the numerous markets and fairs in the district, assessing prices and comparing yields, if not buying or selling himself'. As a Methodist lay preacher he was absent even more than usual. Street's father enjoyed his shooting. Part of his income, like that of other farmers, was taken in leisure.[7]

In the farmer, British wheat farming was meant to support a full-time capitalist-cum-manager; but was the enterprise so complicated as to require the services of such a specialist? Ten workers obviously require a manager, but most holdings did not. Scores of thousands of farmers worked hard on smaller holdings. But the largest category of farms over 50 acres, those between 100 and 300 acres, was intermediate in character.

    [5] W. C. Little, 'The Agricultural Labourer: Review of the Inquiry . . .' Labour. Royal Commission. Fifth and Final Report. Pt. 1, PP 1894 C. 7421 XXXV, pp. 195–234; Liberal Land Enquiry, *The Land* (1913), vol. 1, ch. 1; H. Rider Haggard, *Rural England: Being an Account of Agricultural and Social Researches Carried Out in the Years 1901 & 1902* (new edn. 1906), pp. 239–40, 245; B. S. Rowntree and M. Kendall, *How the Labourer Lives: A Study of the Rural Labour Problem* (1913, repr. 1918), ch.1 and p. 304.

    [6] The question calls for additional research. Some clues are given in Bowley, 'Rural Population', pp. 618–22; B. S. Rowntree, *Land and Labour: Lessons from Belgium* (1910), p. 516; G. M. Howe, *Man, Environment and Disease in Britain* (1972), pp. 202–5.

    [7] C. Stovin, *Journals of a Methodist Farmer*, ed. J. Stovin (1982); quote from editor's introduction, p. 11; A. G. Street, *Farmer's Glory* (1932), pp. 13, 18–19.

'England has too many farms too big for men prepared to use their hands and too small for men prepared to use their heads,' is how one expert put it.[8] A few farmers operated on a much larger scale, with a thousand acres or more, approaching landowners in their social status if not in their economic role.[9]

In the 1870s landowners took more than a third of the net output in rent, even excluding farmhouses; rates and tithe took the total up to 44 per cent (table 8.1). Most rural localities in England also raised a voluntary rate in support of church schools. Altogether in England, not much less than half of the net product was handed over to the squire, the parson and the parish in rent, rates and tithes on the eve of the depression.

TABLE 8.1. *Rent, rates and tithe as a percentage of net farm output, United Kingdom, 1870–9 and 1900–9 (current £m)*

	1870–9		1900–9	
	£m.	%	£m.	%
Rent[a]	56	36	42	31
Rates[b]	8	5	4	3
Tithe[c]	4	3		
Net output[d]	156	100	134	100

Notes and Sources:

[a] Excluding dwelling rents. C. H. Feinstein, *National Income, Expenditure and Output of the United Kingdom, 1855–1965* (Cambridge 1972), table 23, p.T60.

[b] E. M. Ojala, *Agriculture and Economic Progress* (Oxford 1952), table XIX, p. 213. Feinstein *(National Income)* assumes incorrectly that rates were paid by the landowner.

[c] Tithe rent charge was payable by farmers up to 1891, and by landowners thereafter. J. R. Bellerby and F. D. W. Taylor, 'Aggregate Tithe Rentcharge on Farm Land in the United Kingdom, 1867–1938', *Journal of Arrgicultural Economics*, vol. 11 (1955), table 1, p. 201.

[d] Net of external inputs but not labour. Feinstein, *National Income*, table 23, p.T60.

English land tenure was unique. Only 12 per cent of the land was owned by its farmers and 88 per cent of the holdings were farmed by tenants. Contemporary experts often asserted that tenancy was a blessing to farming. It relieved the farmer from the cost of buying land and allowed him to apply his capital entirely to business. High cash rents induced good practice and gave rise to the best agriculture in the world, or at least the highest yields. In depression, it was said, the landlord absorbed the loss.

[8] Middleton, 'German Agriculture', p. 13.

[9] There were 463 farms of more than 1,000 acres in England in 1875, with more than 30 each in Hampshire, Wiltshire (over 90), Norfolk, Lincoln, and Northumberland: Agricultural Returns, 1880; also R. J. Olney, *Lincolnshire Politics, 1832–1885* (Oxford 1973), p. 39; E. G. Strutt, 'Presidential Address', *Transactions of the Surveyors' Institution*, vol. 45 (1912–13), p. 7 ff.; C. S. Orwin, 'III. A Specialist in Arable Farming', *Progress in English Farming Systems* (Oxford 1930).

The most unfortunate farmers were those who owned their land and carried heavy mortgages.[10]

Land prices in Britain were indeed high, higher than in France and Germany in the 1870s although only about half the European level by the eve of the war.[11] High land prices elsewhere did not prevent agricultural success; on the contrary, they were evidence of success. Although French and German land values were supported by tariffs and sugar subsidies, this alone is not sufficient to explain their level. In Belgium, with only moderate tariffs on oats and meat, land values were twice as high as in Britain.[12]

Land values in Britain were high in relation to the surplus produced by the land, typically at thirty or thirty-five times the rent in the 1870s. This suggested a gross return of about 3 per cent, or about the same as the best government bonds. The net rent, deducting capital investments, repairs, insurance and management, placed the return on land well below even the most solid securities.

There is a paradox about these high land prices. Farming is one of the most uncertain of occupations, but farmland was priced like a gilt-edged investment. Granted, before the slump there was a prospect of capital gains, but harvests and prices fluctuate enormously from year to year, and grain prices had fallen on trend for decades at a time. For Britain the paradox can be resolved.

A landowner's position was worth more than his rents. Whether taken in status, power or sport, the rewards of landed property raised its price well above the value of its material outputs. Farmers, who were not in business for status or sport, did not have to pay for the privilege of ownership; but if rents were low in relation to value, they were still high absolutely.[13] For the cost of renting an acre in Britain for one year, you could buy it outright in Canada.

Ricardo and Henry George had considered rent as a pure surplus which does not enter the cost of production. It is more illuminating to follow current economic convention and regard it as a payment for services and goods. Landowners provided farm buildings and fences, which they also kept in good repair; they managed their estates by choosing tenants and prescribing rotations. Some gave their tenants and neighbours a lead in

[10] Caird, *Landed Interest*, pp. 67–70; Agricultural Depression. Royal Commission. Final Report, PP 1897 C. 8540 XV, pp. 31–3.

[11] See Table 6.2. France in the 1880s: *Annuaire statistique* (Paris 1913), table 4, p. 97 (starred); Germany: W. G. Hoffmann, *Das Wachstum der deutschen Wirtschaft seit der Mitte des 19. Jahrhunderts* (Berlin 1965), table 139, col. 7, p. 569.

[12] Rowntree, *Belgium*, pp. 151–7.

[13] I am aware that R. C. Allen, 'The Price of Freehold Land and the Interest Rate in the Seventeenth and Eighteenth Centuries', *Economic History Review*, vol. 41 (1988), attributes high land values to rational calculation, and I intend to publish my reservations elsewhere.

model farming and estate upkeep. The Duke of Bedford financed an experimental station at Woburn, a task reserved for governments in other countries. Large estates might be considered better than small ones, since the overhead of supporting a great family fell on a large acreage, and more was left over for building, drainage and maintenance.

Landowners also assumed a set of voluntary burdens. This outlay was called "charity". It upheld their paternal position and sustained the social fabric in support for education, old age, indigence, disease and poverty. Especially in the close parishes where landowner control was much tighter, charity was a substantial obligation. The Duke of Bedford claimed that his annual outlay on charities came close to his net income.[14]

The owners of large estates filled many other functions of government and administration. In the counties, they acted as magistrates and social leaders, as patrons of the church, of education, sport, art and music. On the national stage, they produced cohorts of unpaid members of Parliament, of army and navy officers, lawyers, judges and civil servants. Rents underpinned the London "season", the court and the crown. Agriculture paid for Britain to have a governing class *de luxe*.

Was landownership value for money? Did rents provide a good social return? One part of the landowner's income is a return for fixed capital and the cost of keeping buildings and fences in good repair. The most recent research has placed capital formation at 10–13 per cent of the annual rent during our period.[15] Some of this, however, was undertaken by farmers. It is difficult to generalize about repairs, since the data are sparse and suspect. In the arable estates during the depression the expenditures, both capital and current, clustered towards the lower end, at 5–15 per cent of the rent. Twenty-five per cent of the rent for both investment and repairs, the figure suggested in a well-known study, may be too high.[16] The effort was often misguided. Specific investments (e.g. in drainage) showed a very low return, if any.[17] Farmers might have acted with a greater sense of the risks involved. As for controlling tenants and tillage, economists might likewise argue that such decisions are best left to the farmers themselves. In fact, landowners normally delegated this function to agents. Annual

---

[14] Duke of Bedford, *A Great Agricultural Estate* (1897), ch. 5, esp. p. 106; Thompson, *Landed Society*, pp. 205–11.

[15] C. H. Feinstein, 'Agriculture', in C. H. Feinstein and S. Pollard (eds.), *Studies in Capital Formation in the United Kingdom, 1750–1920* (Oxford 1988), esp. p. 269.

[16] The study is R. J. Thompson, 'An Inquiry into the Rent of Agricultural Land in England and Wales during the Nineteenth Century', *Journal of the Royal Statistical Society*, vol. 70 (1907), pp. 602–5; also R. Perren, 'The Landlord and Agricultural Transformation, 1870–1900', in P. J. Perry (ed.), *British Agriculture, 1875–1914* (1973), tables 2–3, pp. 116–17; A. Offer, 'Ricardo's Paradox and the Movement of Rents in Britain, *c.* 1870–1910', *Economic History Review*, vol. 30 (1980), p. 242, notes 2–3.

[17] C. O'Grada, 'The Landlord and Agricultural Transformation, 1870–1900: A Comment on Richard Perren's Hypothesis', *Agricultural History Review*, vol. 27 (1979), pp. 40–2.

tenancy did not encourage a lasting commitment to the soil. The research that the Duke of Bedford paid for did not seek to increase productivity, but merely to resolve disputes about the compensation owing to farmers for improvements in fertility. Landlords' hunting and shooting, which enhanced the value of land, gave a great deal of trouble to arable farmers. On the face of it, then, landownership was no bargain, at least during the depression years.

Leaving questions of equity and democracy to one side, the efficiency of paying for government out of rent is a matter not only of its direct cost, but also of the incentive effect on the farmers, of depriving them of some of the positional rewards of ownership. In simpler terms, the domination of society by landowners, quite apart from its high cost, made the farmer a lesser person (yes, some 10 per cent were women). For all their political savvy the landowners failed as agrarian lobbyists, whereas farmers in other countries acting on their own have often succeeded.

A similar redundancy affected rural religion. Tithe had acquired such a bad name by the 1830s that the government had to act, and the impost was commuted to a rent charge and indexed to the price of grain. It remained a significant burden, at about 3 per cent of net output, but at least it moved down together with prices. Farmers and labourers viewed the clergy as part of the landowning establishment. Despite earnest efforts, most of the rural population were cool to the established church. To satisfy their spiritual cravings, labourers and farmers often resorted to self-help. They combined to build their own chapels, and those with a vocation, like farmer Stovin, went on the preaching circuit.[18]

II

In the division of labour, Adam Smith identified one of the sources of modern economic growth. But the division of labour is not always more efficient. In Britain, labour, capital and land were nicely separated, in line with the factors of classical theory. Overseas, on prairie farms, the factors were jumbled up in a single package. The farming family united in their persons the categories of labourer, manager and owner. The worker responded to the incentives of the manager and the landowner. The farmer–manager possessed that intimate knowledge of soil, machinery and animals that is only acquired in a hard day's work. If he or she got any help, it was likely to be from other family members, typically from a wife and children. For every hired hand in American agriculture, there were three

---

[18] R. Jefferies, *Hodge and his Masters* (1880), chs. 14–15; J. Obelkevich, *Religion and Rural Society: South Lindsey, 1825–1875* (1976); A. D. Gilbert, 'The Land and the Church', in Mingay (ed.), *Victorian Countryside*, vol. 1.

farmers and family workers.[19] For many farmers in the west, however, it was their role as landowner that provided the prime incentive. The prospect of rising land values was often their only reward beyond a hard subsistence. On the farm, then, labour was much less divided than it was in the old country. No country mansion broke the sweep of the American prairie, no manor house or rectory. After a generation, farmhouses could be large and barns spacious, but many homesteaders lived for years in timber and tarpaper shanties, or in houses run up quickly with bricks of prairie sod; once papered over inside, these sod houses could be comfortable between torrential rains. Although some farmers came with adequate capital, for many it was a frugal life, a long struggle to accumulate, with very little cash or comforts. Agricultural seasons were short and often it was only the statutory residence required to prove a homestead that kept the farmer on his land at all—often in the most makeshift of shelters, and only for part of the year. In some areas of "suitcase farming" and large-scale "bonanza farming" the land sustained no permanent society. In enterprise and education the prairie farmer was superior to the English farmer. He was much more of a risk-taker, much more restless as well, ready to move into the unknown in pursuit of improvement. Literate farming diaries and memoirs are very few and far between in England, and more plentiful, it seems, on the English-speaking grain frontiers.

A. G. Street's memoir straddles the two genres, and describes a farmer's son in Wiltshire who goes out to break the sod in Manitoba. He finds that Canadians work much harder. At home in Wiltshire the pace had been measured if not actually slow, and the young Street, although he assisted the foreman and attempted most farm jobs, 'did not do much labourious work'. As a hired hand in a Canadian threshing crew, he worked from six in the morning till noontime without a break. 'I thought of the orderly harvest at home. It was almost stately compared to this feverish thing.'[20]

The comparative advantage of prairie agriculture did not arise from cheap land and good technology alone. It was also based on self-exploitation. As J. K. Galbraith explains, self-exploitation arose from the nature of small-scale production. In the large organization, work is broken into standard segments, and people work in accordance with prescribed rules. 'A minimum expenditure of effort is enforced throughout the working day.' On the farm, as in other small enterprises, there is no such minimum, but also no maximum. Unlike the large firm, the farmer is not a price-maker; he competes by working harder and longer than his

---

[19] In 1910: *Statistical History of the US*, pt. 1, ser. K 174–6, p. 468.

[20] The literature on the frontier is very large: a good study is G. C. Fite, *The Farmer's Frontier, 1865–1900* (New York 1966); Canada: H. Robertson's evocative *Salt of the Earth* (Toronto 1974), p. 28 ff.(documents and pictures); Street, *Farmer's Glory*, pp. 26–8, 79.

counterpart in the large organization. He is free to exploit his own labour, and that of his family. Exploitation, in this Galbraithian sense, means 'a situation in which the individual is induced, by his relative lack of economic power, to work for less return than the economy generally pays for such effort'.[21] Self-exploitation is evident in the comparison of town and country incomes. In 1910, after a decade of prosperity, American farmers still earned less than half of non-farm incomes (about 40 per cent on one calculation) and about half of industrial labour earnings—rather less, at that date, and in relative terms, than their UK counterparts, who denied themselves the full benefits of economic masochism.[22] The larger English farmer lived too leisurely a life, and was too far removed from manual toil to push himself hard enough. Nor could he get the same effort out of his men as the homesteader did by personal example. So much is clear in Street's and other memoirs.[23]

Agriculture had no great economies of scale to offer. No grain-growing corporations emerged to challenge the railroads. "Bonanza farms" that appeared in Dakota, Minnesota and California in the 1870s and 1880s were not large by corporate standards, nor did they last. Oliver Dalrymple, the largest of the bonanza farmers, owned about 100,000 acres at one stage but his holdings were divided for cultivation into farmsteads of about 2,000 acres each, and were broken up after a generation. Likewise, the gigantic grain enterprise of Thomas B. Campbell during the First World War did not survive the end of guaranteed prices.[24]

The optimal grain unit was not a land unit but a social unit, and until recently family farming held its own. The land a family farms has grown about tenfold since 1914. In 1973 the technically optimal unit with the lowest production costs in small grains was still the one-man farm, albeit fully mechanized and extending to some 2,000 acres.[25]

In North America, the division of labour began *outside* the farm gate. Once the grain arrived at the local grain elevator, it was taken over by a large company, shipped in bulk and sold in a national market, where fractions of a cent meant the difference between loss and profit. With large national markets for most of the farmer's inputs and outputs, there was much less scope for large mark-ups than in the English market town.

[21] J. K. Galbraith, *Economics and the Public Purpose* (paperback edn. 1975), pp. 87–9.

[22] J. R. Bellerby, *Agriculture and Industry Relative Income* (1956), table 33, p. 201.

[23] e.g. W. de Gelder, *A Dutch Homesteader on the Prairies*, intr. and trans. H. Ganzevoort (Toronto 1973), p. 4.

[24] F. A. Shannon, *The Farmer's Last Frontier: Agriculture, 1860–1897* (New York 1945), pp. 154–61; H. M. Drache, *The Day of the Bonanza: A History of Bonanza Farming in the Red River Valley of the North* (Fargo, N. Dakota 1964), chs. 8–9; H. M. Drache, 'Thomas D. Campbell—The Plower of the Plains', in Wessel, *Great Plains, Agricultural History*, vol. 51 (1977).

[25] H. M. Drache, 'Midwest Agriculture: Changing With Technology', *Agricultural History*, vol. 50 (Jan. 1976), p. 290.

Although farmers felt oppressed by impersonal forces, in fact competition (at least in the grain trade) drove margins down to very low levels.[26] When farmers in Canada set up their own marketing co-operatives, they were not notably more successful than private grain firms.[27] Local merchants were disciplined by the mail order catalogues of Montgomery Ward, Sears and Eaton. In Minnedosa, Manitoba, in the late 1880s, then a town of 600, all of the agricultural implement dealers (6), mortgage and loan companies (5), insurance companies (8) and real estate companies (3) were local franchises of provincial, national or international operations.[28] The saloons of Saskatchewan may have held out the same attraction as the pubs of Lincolnshire, but small-town traders played a less vital and less costly role in the marketing chain. In a one-crop economy there was much less of the buying and selling of stock and supplies than an English mixed farm required.

In Europe across the Channel as well, farmers found their economies of scale only outside the farm gate. Apart from East German estates (which tended to be managed by their Junker owners and were more troubled economically than the peasantry) the dominant pattern was of less division of labour on the farm, more of it outside, than was the case in England. Livestock farming did not offer any great economies of scale. The family farm was quite efficient. The farmer needed help only to process and market his produce. If twenty-five dairy cows formed an efficient unit of production, a creamery might require a thousand. All over the peasant countryside of Western Europe, in Germany, France, Holland, Denmark, even in Ireland, peasants combined together for processing and marketing. Co-operative creameries, dairies, feed-mills, marketing associations spread the risk, handled the output and recycled by-products and profits back to the farms. Capital investment in processing and marketing was secured by the equity of peasants in their own land. Equity in land also underpinned mutual credit associations, which secured a cheap flow of circulating capital.[29]

[26] J. C. Bowen, *Wheat and Flour Prices from Farmer to Consumer*, United States Department of Labor, Bureau of Labor Statistics, Bulletin no. 130 (Washington DC 1913); 'The Wheat Situation', USDA *Agriculture Yearbook 1923* (Washington, DC 1924), fig. 20, p. 127.
[27] V. C. Fowke, *The National Policy and the Wheat Economy* (Toronto 1957), pt. II.
[28] G. Friesen, *The Canadian Prairies: A History* (Toronto 1984), p. 325.
[29] Of the large literature on these topics, see, e.g., C. R. Fay, *Co-Operation at Home and Abroad* (5th edn. 1948); M. T. Herrick, *Preliminary Report on Land and Agricultural Credit in Europe*, US 62 Congress, 3 Sess. sen. doc. 967, ser. 6364 (Washington DC 1912–13); H. Rider Haggard, *Rural Denmark and its Lessons* (1911); Rowntree, *Belgium*; H. L. Westergaard, *Economic Development in Denmark before and during the World War* (1922); C. O'Grada, 'The Beginnings of the Irish Creamery System, 1880–1914', *Economic History Review*, vol. 30 (1977); F. Dovring, *Land and Labour in Europe, 1900–1950* (1956); H. Hertel, *Co-operation in Danish Agriculture* (1918); E. A. Pratt, *The Transition in Agriculture* (1906); M. Tracy, *Agriculture in Western Europe: Crisis and Adaptation since 1880* (2nd edn. 1982).

These social adaptations gave Danish farmers a market power that British farmers found hard to match even on their own ground. Unlike continental counterparts, British farmers had no equity in land as a basis for credit. It required decades for English farmers to win compensation for improvements at the end of a tenancy, and they had no expectation from a rise in value, except a higher rent. Moreover, the absence of legal security exposed them to pressure whenever they tried to assert their interests. A tenant movement for rent reductions in Lancashire in the 1890s (a pasture county supposedly immune to the depression) was quickly quenched by the landowners, who did not hesitate to evict the leaders. Unlike farmers in virtually all other countries, English farmers had no presence in politics; agrarian lobbying was almost entirely in the hands of the landowners, who expected tenants to conform with their party allegiance.[30]

English agriculture suffered from an excess of social classes, and its adaptive reaction was to try and eliminate one or two. Agricultural income in Britain traditionally fell into "three rents", with roughly one-third each for the landowner, farmer and labourer. Economic theory suggests that the first sacrifice ought to fall on rent, and some rent was in fact squeezed out of the system. Money rents fell 30 per cent or so, and the Duke of Bedford, for example, claimed in 1897 that 'Low prices, bad seasons, and a crushing weight of taxation have entirely caused rent, as understood by the political economists, to disappear from the Thorney Estate.'[31] A more detached observer might point out that rents in the aggregate held up rather well. They declined no more than grain prices. Our data suggest that the landowner's share of the net output, an average 36 per cent in the 1870s, declined to about 31 per cent by 1900–9.[32] Rent did not disappear: landowners as a body only lost about one-seventh of their slice of the cake. Nor did the squeeze affect the pure surplus alone, as the Duke of Bedford seemed to suggest. Investment and maintenance also fell.

One successful enterprise showed how it was possible to dispense with the landowner's presence entirely. George Baylis, a tenant farmer's son, purchased a 400-acre farm in Berkshire in 1875 with £17,500 of borrowed money. Lawes's and Gilbert's experiments had shown him that soil fertility did not depend on livestock. He concentrated on arable farming with artificial manures. Baylis made money consistently during years of deep depression and bought in more land, until his holdings extended to some

[30] A. H. H. Matthews, *Fifty Years of Agricultural Politics, being the History of the Central Chamber of Agriculture* (1915); F. J. Fisher, 'Public Opinion and Agriculture, 1875–1900' (Hull University Ph.D. thesis, 1972); A. Mutch, 'Farmers' Organizations and Agricultural Depression in Lancashire, 1890–1900', *Agricultural History Review*, vol. 31 (1983); Street, *Farmer's Glory*, p. 56.

[31] Duke of Bedford, *Great Agricultural Estate*, p. 48; also Haggard, *Rural England*, vol. 2, p. 543.

[32] Calculated from Feinstein, *National Income*, p. T60.

eighteen separate farms totalling 9,600 acres in 1914. Apart from his very first venture, Baylis got his farms clear of the deadweight of landowner-ship. He took them over when there were no other takers, and paid a low price. His method was closer to bonanza farming than to sod-house settlement, but it was a clear departure from the English three-class system.[33] Nor was he entirely alone. The number of farms larger than 1,000 acres in England increased by 13 per cent from 1875 to 1895; of this class of very large farms, one-third was fully owned, and another 10 per cent partly owned, by their occupiers in 1895.[34]

At the other end, there is evidence of another adaptation: to dispense with the idle farmer and unmotivated labourer, and embrace a sod-house or peasant adaptation of relying on self and family labour. There were 4.4 labourers per farmer in England in 1871, but only 3.3 in 1911. In the meantime, the number of working relatives on farms increased by some 70 per cent between the census of 1891 and 1911, and came to about one for every two farmers.[35]

Witnesses before the Royal Commission of 1896 disagreed on the relative merits of farm size, and some thought small was better. Small farms were easier to let. According to one witness, 'small farmers did better than the larger ones . . . because they worked with their men and were able to do a good deal themselves'. Another said that tenants of about 50 acres did well, but only where the man had a family and had not to employ labour. Larger tenants fell back on smaller farms, and larger farmers seem to have suffered most.[36] Clare Sewell Read, a leading agrarian, said of the small owner, 'The only way in which he can possibly succeed is this, in doing the work of two agricultural labourers and living at the expense of one.' Survival was purchased by sons and daughters toiling unpaid. Farmers in Wales and Scotland suffered least because they did not hire labour. Small farming, one witness concluded, was little better than British slavery.[37] A character in Constance Holme's Lancashire novel *The Lonely Plough* (1914) 'was over thirty now, and during all the years he had worked for his father he had never had a penny's wage . . .' (p. 4). Strains and resentment within the family came out in the 1890s, as small farmers attempted to wring more unpaid work out of their sons and daughters, who felt cheated of early independence.[38]

[33] Orwin, 'A Specialist'.

[34] Board of Agriculture. Returns as to the Number and Size of Agricultural Holdings in Great Britain in the year 1895, PP 1896 C. 8243 LXVII, tables III, IX, pp. 5, 17; E. G. Strutt also made a profit on 1,000-acre farms: 'Presidential Address', p. 7 ff.

[35] F. W. D. Taylor, 'United Kingdom: Numbers in Agriculture', *The Farm Economist*, vol. 8 (1955), table I, p. 38.

[36] Farms over 300 acres fell from 30 per cent to 24 per cent of agricultural land in England between 1875 and 1914: Agricultural Returns, 1880, 1914.

[37] Agricultural Depression. Royal Commission. Final Report, PP 1897 XV, pp. 34–6.

[38] A. Mutch, 'Rural Society in Lancashire, 1840–1914' (Manchester University Ph.D. thesis, 1980), fos. 163–4.

Welsh and Scots farmers combined the strategies of the prairie and the peasant on the run-down grainlands of East Anglia. While others migrated overseas, they opened up a frontier closer to home: as rents drifted down, these self-exploiting migrants, accustomed to a much harsher regime, took over land abandoned by the farmer–managers of the eastern counties and settled down to dairy farming with family labour, to produce liquid milk, the cash crop of the 1890s.[39]

III

By a process of elimination the clues cluster around the three-class system of tenure. After wages, rent was the largest cash outlay. Both outlays might have been more productive in the farmer's own hands. In the 1870s UK farmers paid about £60 million in wages, £55 million in rent, and about £12 million in rates and tithes to earn a net income of £36 million (fig 8.1). The only "modern" country remotely approaching Britain in the extent of tenancy was Argentina, but land prices there were only a fifth of the British and (except for sharecroppers just starting up the farming ladder) the rent burden was consequently lighter.

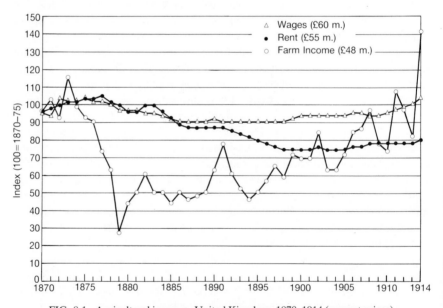

FIG. 8.1. Agricultural incomes, United Kingdom, 1870–1914 (current prices)

Source: C. H. Feinstein, *National Income, Expenditure and Output of the United Kingdom, 1855–1965* (Cambridge 1972), table 23, p. T60

[39] E. L. Smith, *Go East for a Farm: A Study of Rural Migration* (Oxford 1932), provides a retrospective view of this migration.

Fig. 8.1 suggests what went wrong for British agriculture. Take the three classes one by one, labourers first. The stability of wages understates the improving share of labour, since the number of workers fell. Real incomes per head actually rose at a time when farming output stagnated. This suggests that the traditional attitude to labour as an abundant and cheap resource in which quality counted for little was no longer tenable. When Rider Haggard went on his tour of "Rural England" around the turn of the century, the most common complaint he heard from farmers was the poor quality of labour.[40]

Secondly, landowners. Tenancy may have insulated farmers from the full impact of inflated land values but it also withheld the benefits of falling land values. The decline of rent was sluggish and slow. In economic theory, when there is no surplus over cost, rent is supposed to vanish. In fact, the farmer's income vanished, while rents held firm. Social institutions can buck the laws of economics for a long time if someone pays the cost.

Rent levels reflected not the farmers' cost, but the subsistence of landowners. English landed society was founded on agricultural rents. Country houses, the season in London, an expensive education, hunting and shooting, foreign travel and a position in politics were all funded out of the net product of the land. Upper-class consumption costs did not fall together with grain prices. Many owners retrenched or sold, but often too little or too late. As in Russia, the landed interest was a class that agriculture could no longer support, and farmers reacted by restricting production. The machinery of rent collection was too rigid to respond quickly to the disappearance of rent, and continued to extract a surplus which no longer existed. When they found no takers for the land, and sometimes sooner, landowners granted arrears and abatements of the rent, but it took them time.

Now the farmers: in comparison with the other two classes, farmers were the hardest hit, and their troubles filled many volumes of official inquiries in the 1880s and the 1890s. Bellerby calculated that during the depression years 1879–96 the return for effort in farming (the "incentive income") fell down to 38 per cent of the non-farm return.[41] This curve suggests how difficult it was for farmers to move out of agriculture, despite the predominance of annual leases. While the number of labourers fell by more than 600,000, the number of farmers remained roughly constant. It is not sufficiently clear, however, how much retirement and new recruitment there was among the farmers—whether those who farmed at the end of the period were new men, or the descendants of the old ones who had

---

[40] Haggard, *Rural England*, vol. 2, pp. 539–41; S. W. Martins, *A Great Estate at Work* (Cambridge 1980), p. 29.
[41] Bellerby, *Agriculture and Industry*, table 45, p. 233.

soldiered on through the bad times. It may be, indeed seems probable, that there was little else more tempting than farming.

In reality fig. 8.1 understates the farmers' plight quite considerably. Farmers were also liable, almost alone, for the burden of local taxation and tithe. In absolute terms this was not a great deal, no more than about 4 per cent of the net output. But it fell almost exclusively on the farmers, and was not easily shifted. Out of some £48 million net income in the early 1870s, farmers had to bear about £8 million in rates and £4 million in tithe, or a quarter of their net incomes. In 1879 these charges swallowed virtually all the net income. In the 1880s the combined burden approached half the net incomes. Local taxation became the farmers' prime grievance.

Local taxation was a legacy of high farming, which earlier in the nineteenth century left the countryside with an expensive social overhead to maintain. This was made up of tithe rent charge, of church rates for education, and of local taxes, in support of police and law, roads and education. A reserve army of rural labour was also supported in part on the rates, as well as the aged, the sick and the young. An old society, which had lost many of its young adults, was left with a lot of indigence to support.

Slowly the landowners yielded to the laws of political economy. At first they granted abatements and permitted arrears; then they made permanent reductions. Part of the burden of taxation was also lifted off the farmers' shoulders. First, in 1891, landowners accepted liability for tithe rent charge. Then in 1896 the government appeased the farmers with a subsidy equal to one-half the rates on agricultural land. Just as the first half of fig. 8.1 understates the farmers' plight, so the second half understates the strength of their recovery, with the tithe transferred to the landowners, and rates cut in half. Income tax payable by farmers was also reduced.[42] Landowners also paid income tax and from 1894 onwards a much higher rate of death duty.

One of the features of the agrarian frontier was the low social overhead that it carried. Governments in the United States and Canada had allocated land from the public domain to pay for railways, roads and schools. Roads were rudimentary, and welfare almost non-existent. In North America a whole generation passed before the population of a new district settled down and until some sort of social stability built up, until housing, roads and local government began to approach metropolitan standards. The Red River bonanza farms were a social desert. Like their English counterparts, American farmers complained that urban property

---

[42] E. Evans, *The Contentious Tithe* (1976), p. 164; Agricultural Rates Act 1896, see B. Mallet, *British Budgets, 1887–88 to 1912–13* (1913), pp. 108–10; Schedule B reduction, Stamp, *British Incomes*, pp. 88–91; Martins, *Great Estate*, pp. 29 ff. on the impact of the depression on farmers.

escaped its fair share of taxation. But local property taxes were based on land values, and, on the margin of cultivation, they were low. When they rose, valuations lagged behind.[43]

If the Italian tenant on the pampas rented his land, like the British farmer, he did not expect to stay for long, and left no permanent mark on the landscape. He was an agrarian nomad with no roots or community. His children's education was woeful. 'Home was merely a cheap, temporary shelter from the elements,' a mud or adobe hovel. Few tenants planted shade trees or vegetable gardens. Solberg quotes a poem by Jose Padroni:

> No one planted a tree
> And on the farms there were no sheep
> Birds did not sing, the soft murmur
> Of bleating lambs was absent.
> Mothers raised sad children.[44]

Late-Victorian wheat was a "frontier crop". Economists and historians have explained this mainly in terms of location theory. Wheat was more valuable per unit of weight than other grains. It could bear the cost of transport over longer distances and thus colonised cheap land on the thinly settled frontier. When settlement advanced, wheat no longer enjoyed the advantage of transport costs or land prices to the same extent.[45] But wheat was a frontier crop in a more fundamental sense. The chief handicap of the British farmer was the legacy of an old society, which he bore in many forms: in the superstructure of squire and parson, in the small enclosed fields, unsuitable to the easy application of the reaper and the binder, in the impoverished, hungry work-force and the Poor Law; in social attitudes, the class boundaries which inhibited the flow of information, innovation and incentive. The English farmer was shackled by his previous success, by past cycles of innovation, by enclosure and high farming which had formed his fields and farmsteads, which had raised his rents to their high levels. In the past, the agricultural surplus had also borne a good part of regional fixed capital formation, of canals, railways, roads and urban development. England in the 1880s was stuck with an obsolescent agriculture, inherited from a successful past. Landowners (like industrialists who followed the same path later) found it difficult to write off obsolete investments. At the same time, they were unwilling to make new ones. In any case, enterprise

[43] D. A. McQuillan, 'The Mobility of Immigrants and Americans: A comparison of Farmers on the Kansas Frontier', *Agricultural History*, vol. 53 (1979), builds on the work of James Malin. Local taxation: a summary of evidence in the *Report of the Industrial Commission on Agriculture and Agricultural Labor*, US 57 Congress, 1 Sess., house doc. 179, Industrial Commission, vol. 10 (Washington, DC 1901), pp. ccclxxxv–cccxc, esp. the latter.

[44] Solberg, 'Land Tenure', pp. 66–7; Scobie, *Revolution on the Pampas*, ch. 4.

[45] Schmidt, 'Westward Movement', p. 380; Fisher and Temin, 'Regional Specialization', pp. 143–4; Harley, 'Transportation', pp. 227–33.

was required more than investment, and this was inhibited by the deadweight of land values.

Frontier societies typically collected their tax at the customs house, so indirectly the frontier farmer was not entirely immune to taxation. But much of the expenditure supported by the taxes, especially railways and agricultural research, redounded to his benefit. Canada, Australia and the United States kept their defence spending to a minimum during the years of agricultural depression, while Britain deployed a global navy and was always fighting somewhere to uphold the Pax Britannica.[46]

Both the manor house and the sod house are instances in which material values are traded for intangibles; where the driver is not profit but approbation. In the case of the manor house, both before and during the depression, the social structure and its rewards inhibited economic change. The sod-house settler (and the English farmer as well, it seems) accepted a low wage for the privilege of being his or her own master. Since the sod-house settler had no other master, he was able to compete with the British farmer, saddled with the pretensions and cost of the hierarchy above him.

The competition for grain markets was a competition not between soils and climates but between different social orders. It was a conflict between different conceptions of society; between hierarchy and equality; between rentiers and entrepreneurs; between gentlemen and toilers; between subordination and self-sufficiency; between retail and wholesale; between tradition and innovation; habit and systematic research; machinery and hand labour; sod house and manor house. But it would be wrong to regard the depression as a disaster. The crisis of English grain production, and landed society's failure to adapt, took wealth and income away from the landowners and farmers, and gave them to labour, both at home and on the grain frontiers overseas.

[46] L. E. Davis and R. E. Huttenback, *Mammon and Empire* (Cambridge 1986).

9

'LIKE RATS IN A TRAP': BRITISH URBAN SOCIETY AND OVERSEAS OPPORTUNITIES

MANY Britons were unhappy with their country during the Edwardian period. More than 5 per cent of the population left for good between 1900 and 1914.[1] The proportion of young adult single males who emigrated was much higher. The number of net migrants from the United Kingdom to the English-speaking countries was about 2.4 million.[2] More than a million more emigrated and came back again.[3] The previous chapters examined the countryside and showed how status affected motivation and economic performance. This chapter looks at the towns; the next two will examine some of the overseas alternatives.

I

Late-Victorian Britain presents a pattern of economic cycles, the twenty-year "building cycle" overlaid by the shorter-term "Juglar" and "business" cycles. Contemporaries perceived these patterns less clearly, as alternations of "good and bad trade". William Beveridge, in his 1908 book, *Unemployment*, charted them suggestively as 'the pulse of the nation'. For those who lived through these cycles at subsistence level or one step higher, the downbeat spelled a time of anxiety and often indigence.

In many industries intense competition did not leave internal resources sufficient to tide over the downswing and the firm's working men were a cost to be cut, only rarely an asset to be carried. The vaunted flexibility of the market economy often tested its work-force to the limits of endurance. When demand slackened or competitive pressures required a cutback, they were shown the door with an hour's wages. Domestic competition was rife in Edwardian England and there were few barriers to entry of both goods and firms from overseas: an abundance of small firms competed in every sector and, if the large ones were sometimes insulated from competitive pressures, they did not cosset their workers. Intense competition did not produce economic miracles: most of the period was one of stagnation. Dismissal was not only an economic regulator, but also a summary form of discipline. Foremen and managers exercised the power of the sack for

---

[1] M&D, p. 50.
[2] Ibid.
[3] D. Baines, *Migration in a Mature Economy: Emigration and Internal Migration in England and Wales, 1861–1900* (Cambridge 1986), pp. 128–35.

minor infringements or simply on a whim.[4] An intricate system of solidarity, mutual insurance, petty saving and petty credit allowed the wage earner to keep his or her head above water, but incomes were too low to allow most workers ever to save more than a few weeks' wages (very few had even that) and destitution, always only a step away, became a reality in sickness and old age.[5] Disease was rampant: tuberculosis blighted life for the young, the middle-aged, their friends and their kin, while infectious diseases decimated children in particular; one or two out of every ten babies did not live out its first year. It was a grim, dank, sooty, cramping existence, pervaded by the stench of imperfect drains. In mitigation, it offered the addictive pleasures of sugared tea, smoking and beer, and the more wholesome ones of family, conviviality and, occasionally, the countryside.

An added burden to many working-class people in the Edwardian period was the feeling that they were not respected and not required. Insecurity hobbled self-esteem. As Adam Smith has phrased it, 'compared with the contempt of mankind, all other evils are easily supported'.[6] The social and economic intertwined. Because people were plentiful in Britain, and because skill was produced in abundance and cheaply, it was not very highly paid in comparison with North America and Australia. It was more highly paid, to be sure, than unskilled work (which only supported a bare subsistence and was not always available) but not enough to accumulate more than a few pieces of furniture. Workpeople were cheap, so manufacturers relied on their skills as a substitute for specialized and expensive machines. Skill stood in for capital. It was a recurrent rather than a lumpy outlay, and was more easily afforded. A skilled man with general-purpose machinery could turn his hand to a variety of different jobs in quick succession. In many industries this allowed the manufacturer to fabricate his product precisely to users' requirements, as opposed to the mass-production system where users have to accomodate (and indeed are conditioned to accept) the standard output of the production line. The system suited many of Britain's markets, which were fragmented and small. Even such mass-consumption articles as cotton cloth were made in a large variety of qualities and grades. Just as important was the variable quality of the raw materials. In Lancashire's cotton mills, the spinners' skill consisted, it seems, of their ability to produce a specified yarn from variable and often inferior batches of cotton.[7] One reason it did not pay to

[4] W. F. Watson, *Machines and Men: An Autobiography of an Itinerant Mechanic* (1935), pp. 125, 138; A. Williams, *Life in a Railway Factory* (1915), pp. 285, 303.
[5] P. Johnson, *Saving and Spending: The Working-class Economy in Britain, 1870–1939* (Oxford 1985).
[6] Smith, *Moral Sentiments*, p. 61.
[7] C. K. Harley, 'Skilled Labour and the Choice of Technique in Edwardian Industry', *Explorations in Economic History*, vol. 11 (1974); C. More, *Skill and the English Working*

set up specialized machinery operated by specialist (i.e. semi-skilled) labour was that demand could not sustain mass production of many articles. Workers had so little to spend that a mass market for branded goods existed only for margarine, soap, beer, biscuits and cocoa.

Tom Watson described his life as a journeyman engineer before the First World War. He was employed by a succession of small firms to machine small batches of parts on piecework—in one instance every single part of a new four-cylinder motor-cycle engine. On one occasion he was dismissed after three years' work with an envelope containing an hour's pay in lieu; on another on returning from his honeymoon. When business was slack, his lot was 'weary tramping from shop to shop, interviewing foremen and managers; more rebuffs from surly gate-keepers'. When the foreman acted unjustly, he joined in a damaging strike that could have been defused by a single word or even gesture. Watson's evident relish for work was quenched by depressing bouts of unemployment and short-time working. 'What do they care how long you've worked for 'em? They just stick us up on the wall when they don't want us, and take us down again when there's any work to do.'[8] Although skill was the life-blood of industry and the economy, although skilled workers made up its backbone, they were usually regarded by managers and owners as an inert input to be turned on and off as required, and otherwise despised and disregarded.

Like British farmers, most British employers took their workers for granted and treated labour as an abundant resource. Overseas visitors remarked on the bad blood between masters and men. An American wrote in 1904:

Nothing is more frequent than the remark that the workingman does not need more than so many shillings a week . . . This view among employers has prevailed for so long and is so nearly universal that their every effort is to obtain more work for a traditional wage rather than to decrease the cost of production by means which will justify a higher wage. . . . Workingmen have come to accept the view widely too and it is the acceptance of this theory of status which is at the bottom of the deadlock in British industry.

A Manchester journal wrote of the 'stinging reproof that rings through every shop in England—you are paid for working, not for thinking'.[9] When British employers and workmen visited overseas factories, they found that ability and initiative were more highly valued than at home.

Class, 1870–1914 (1980); W. Lazonick, 'Industrial Organization and Technological Change: The Decline of the British Cotton Industry', *Business History Review*, vol. 57 (1983), pp. 195–236.

[8] Watson, *Machines and Men*, pp. 58, 67, 109, 112, 121–5, 132.
[9] Commissioner of Labor, Eleventh Special Report, *Regulation and Restriction of Output* (Washington DC 1904), p. 752; *Mechanical World* (Manchester, Dec. 1900), p. 301; both quoted in S. B. Saul, 'The American Impact upon British Industry', *Business History*, vol. 3 (1960), pp. 27–8.

This theme runs right through the report of a trade union delegation conveyed to the United States by the manufacturer A. Mosely in 1902. Mosely himself wrote of the visit:

One point that has struck me with enormous force, as I believe it has all the delegates, is the close touch and sympathy between master and man, which is carried a step further in the enlistment of the men's good offices to improve factory methods. Suggestions are welcomed (usually a box is provided for their reception), the more so because the American manufacturer has realized that it is not the man sitting in the counting-house or private office who is best able to judge where improvements can be made in machine or method, but he who attends that machine from morning to night. . . . in short, the man feels that the work of his brains will handsomely benefit himself. Is it any wonder, therefore, that American machinery is continually changing and improving, that the evolution of methods is ever and rapidly going on? . . . As a rule the British employer hardly knows his men, seldom leaves his office for the workshop, delegates the bulk of his authority to a foreman whose powers are arbitary, and who, if any of the men under him show particular initiative, immediately becomes jealous and fears he may be supplanted. Hence as a rule a workman making a suggestion to the foreman (the proprietor himself is usually not accessible at all) is met with a snub, asked, 'Are you running this shop or am I?' or told 'If you know the business better than I do you had better put on your coat and go.'

H. Deller, of the National Union of Operative Plasterers, saw the same thing: 'Did a workman make a suggestion to a British employer whereby his business would benefit, or even to his manager or foreman, what would be the result? The man would either be discharged or told abruptly that he was not paid to think, but to work.'[10]

Modern economics regards "learning by doing" and "learning by using" as important sources of productivity growth.[11] The evidence, which could be multiplied tenfold, suggests that the rigid factory regime suppressed the workers' natural creativity. In addition to abusing their dignity, this deprived the economy of an important source of growth. British workers reciprocated by closing ranks in an attitude of sullen alienation. Often, as Watson reports, this went beyond passive resistance and embraced disruption and petty sabotage. Indifference to the goals of the enterprise and a general "bloody mindedness" remain a hallmark of British industrial relations to this day.[12] The Edwardian period was a low point of British productivity growth in peacetime, in comparison with Britain at other times, and other countries at the same time.[13]

[10] Mosely Industrial Commission to the United States of America, Oct.–Dec. 1902, *Reports of the Delegates* (1903); A. Mosely, p. 9; M. Deller, p. 190.

[11] N. Rosenberg, 'Learning by Using', in his *Inside the Black Box* (Cambridge 1982).

[12] Watson, *Machines and Men*, pp. 53, 92; G. Jones and M. Barnes, *Britain on Borrowed Time* (1967); S. J. Prais, *Productivity and Industrial Structure* (Cambridge 1981).

[13] Matthews, Feinstein and Odling-Smee, *British Economic Growth*, table 2.5, p. 31.

This gagging of individuality recurs repeatedly in shopfloor evidence from the Edwardian period, from employers as well as men (with nothing, however, from the foremen, just as very little has come down from farmers). Dudley Docker, a substantial Midlands industrialist, attributed the labour unrest of 1912 to this alienation. It was essentially a reaction against

individual remoteness from the employer, of impotence in the highly organised life of which, as individuals, they form so small a part, and the uncertainty of the future which the trade cycle has bred . . . It will have to be recognised as an elementary business proposition that industrial success is impossible unless the employer studies and trains the sentiments of his workpeople with the same efficiency that he equips his . . . machinery . . .[14]

Alienation and dejection form the central themes of the two evocative working-man classics of the period, Robert Tressell's realistic novel of the life of house-painters in Hastings, and Alfred Williams's vivid and depressing account *Life in a Railway Factory*.[15] The first was about life in a small jobbing firm, the second reported from within a large factory of a giant corporation. Williams deplored the futility of the two decades that he, a gifted self-taught scholar, had to spend in the factory as steam-hammer operator. As the chief stamper he also nursed a wounded craftsmanship. His technical creativity was frustrated by the foremen. 'If a workman proves himself to be possessed of unusual skill and originality, instead of being rewarded for it he is boycotted and held in check.' Managers and foremen were very reluctant to accept ideas from workers, and rewarded them by cutting piecework prices.[16] In his own experience,

The one most appreciated at the works is he who remains silent and slavishly obeys every order, who is willing to cringe and fawn like a dog, to swear black is white and white is black at the bidding of his chief, to fulfil every instruction without ever questioning the wisdom or utility of it, to be, in a word, as clay in the potter's hand, a mere tool and a puppet.[17]

---

[14] *Midland Advertiser*, 17 Aug. 1912, cited in R. P. T. Davenport-Hines, *Dudley Docker: The Life and Times of a Trade Warrior* (Cambridge 1984), p. 76.

[15] R. Tressell, *The Ragged Trousered Philanthropists* (abridged edn. 1915, complete edn. 1955); Williams, *Railway Factory*. P. N. Stearns's highly suggestive book *Lives of Labour: Work in a Maturing Industrial Society* (1975) does not attempt to distinguish the experience of British, German, French and Belgian workers, but probes the common threads of their lives. Inasmuch as continental workers had fewer emigration opportunities, a different workplace culture and different class societies, levels of industrialization and cycles of economic activity, his work provides a good starting-point for testing the hypothesis tentatively put forward in this chapter. Otherwise, the literature on working-class life is simply too large to cite here; S. Meacham, *A Life Apart: The English Working Class, 1890–1914* (1977) provides a good conspectus.

[16] Williams, *Railway Factory*, pp. 300–1.

[17] Ibid., p. 290.

The pressures of competition provide some explanation. Anxiety and fear were the hidden abrasives in the smoothness of market adjustments. Not all (if any) of this dour callousness was functional. Employers depended a great deal on their workers' versatility and skill; to discourage enterprise and suppress self-esteem was literally counter-productive. It penetrated the innermost defences of working-class dignity, since skill allowed workers a consolation for social exclusion in the quality of their workmanship and their control of its mysteries.[18] 'Workmen feel like rats in a trap,' one of them said to Arthur Shadwell, the industrial correspondent of *The Times*. 'It is a strong expression, too strong to be generally applicable,' wrote Shadwell, 'but I understood him very well.'[19] Even if it did them no economic good, some perverse social and inner compulsions made employers stand aloof from their partners in production, and allowed them to condone tyrannical powers and attitudes in their foremen.

Partly, however, the callousness was calculated. Throughout the 1890s and 1900s employers sought a way around their dependence on skill by means of specialized machinery and a tighter work-discipline. That search forms the backdrop of some of the great confrontations of those years, in engineering, shipbuilding and the boot and shoe industries, and the echoes of these efforts to "speed up" and subdivide work resound in the memoirs and testimony literature as an acutely stressful experience.[20] But industry was fettered by its fickle markets and the variety of products they required. The process of deskilling and the transition to new machinery (still short of "mass production") was only partly completed. Instead, it continued to fester. American employers succeeded better in forcing through their new equipment and work practices. In response, British artisans flocked overseas. The proportion of skilled labourers in British overseas emigration rose steadily, to almost one-third of occupied males emigrating between 1903 and 1911, and to more than one-third just before the war.[21]

Individuals can go with the system or buck it. Watson, Tressell, and Williams record instances of generosity and even fraternity between masters and men. Watson encountered a broad-minded liberality in a number of large factories. In small firms, many employers treated their

---

[18] E. J. Hobsbawm, 'Artisan or Labour Aristocrat?', *Economic History Review*, vol. 37 (1984).

[19] [A. Shadwell], special articles on "Labour and Industry", 'VI. Prospects and the Part of the Employers', *The Times*, 28 Feb. 1913, p. 4.

[20] Watson, *Machines and Men*, ch. 10; Williams, *Railway Factory*, e.g. pp. 302, 304.

[21] B. Elbaum and F. Wilkinson, 'Industrial Relations and Uneven Development: A Comparative Study of the American and British Steel Industries', *Cambridge Journal of Economics*, vol. 3 (1979), pp. 275–303; H. F. Gospel and C. R. Littler (eds.), *Managerial Strategies and Industrial Relations* (1983); N. H. Carrier and J. H. Jeffery, *External Migration: A Study of the Available Statistics, 1815–1950* (1953), table N/O (2), p. 115; table N/O (7), p. 124. The first data are for the UK, the second for England and Wales. The second data are for the period 1 Apr. 1912–31 Dec. 1913.

employees decently, 'often regarding them as equals'. We may suspect that this small firm engineering sector worked better. Watson for one thought so. Low overheads and direct contact between manager and worker attracted the more enterprising and capable workers, who chafed under strict discipline. But even in firms like these, proprietors were not immune to an "I'm the king of the castle" mentality, particularly in their attitude to the union.[22]

Another reason for the festering unrest was the upturn of agrarian fortunes at the end of the 1890s, described in the previous chapter. The agricultural depression of the 1880s and 1890s transferred income from the landowner and farmer to the labourer. The price rises of the 1900s turned the tide back to the farmer. For the first time in a generation real wages stagnated and even declined. The contrast between the glitter of Edwardian "society" and the squalour of its slums is familiar. Unskilled and casual unemployment and indigence stood out as the central social problem of Edwardian England. The skilled workers whose dignity was under constant pressure in the Edwardian period organised themselves to exclude the unskilled and prevent any threat to their precarious prosperity.

The great Edwardian migration of 1909–14 coincided with an unprecedented wave of labour unrest—of nation-wide coal, dock and railway strikes which involved a good deal of violence. Some workers chose to fight, others chose flight; some chose "exit", others "voice".[23] Contemporaries agreed that the stagnation of real incomes was at the root of the trouble, although they also perceived other sources of frustration and anger.[24] If the terms of trade between town and country were indeed at the root of the problem, then stoppages and strikes were not a suitable remedy. While real wages overseas also stagnated in many countries during the Edwardian period, at least they stood higher. If the enterprising workman went as far as Vancouver, he could double his wages. British Columbia's population more than doubled in the first decade of the century.[25]

We have few glimpses into the mentality of the Edwardian artisan and even fewer into that of unskilled and casual workers, who still formed the bulk of the work-force. Only the accounts of poverty investigators, almost ethnographic in their style, reveal something of the material culture of the lower classes, whose inner lives remain for the most part obscured.[26]

---

[22] Watson, *Machines and Men*, pp. 186–7, 156–8.

[23] A. O. Hirschmann, *Exit, Voice and Loyalty* (Cambridge, Mass. 1970).

[24] Board of Trade, 'Industrial Unrest', 13 Apr. 1912; 'Labour Unrest', 14 Apr. 1912; CAB 37/110/62–3.

[25] Based on work in progress by R. C. Allen.

[26] But see J. Burnett, D. Vincent and D. Mayall, *The Autobiography of the Working Class: An Annotated, Critical Bibliography* (Brighton, 1984, 1987), 2 vols.

Unskilled labourers were also the largest occupational group among Edwardian migrants. North Atlantic steerage fares were cheap.

II

Several groups above the manual labouring classes also found life stifling in the Edwardian period. There was nothing novel about this. Half a century before Edward Gibbon Wakefield had written that, 'other classes feel more acutely than the common people, the uneasiness and anxiety arising from excessive competition . . .' The Edwardian period added some new twists to 'this competition of capital with capital, of education with education, and of place-hunting with place-hunting'.[27] Women entered office work in large numbers, in competition with male white-collar workers Educated women, however, felt keenly the lack of opportunity and the formal disabilities that kept them down in the professions and in public service. For professionals and educated persons generally, the number of openings was narrowing and the competition very stiff.[28] For unmarried women, 'emigration offered escape from excessive competition, from a steadily narrowing field of suitable employment, and from the require-ments of a rigid code of gentility'. For the emigrant gentlewoman, 'it created a real possibility for redefinition of her social identity'.[29] In the Edwardian period the emigration of professional people from the United Kingdom to the United States rose from its previous level of 1–2 per cent to between 4 and 10 per cent of all migrants between 1904 and 1914. In the twenty months from April 1912, when details of occupation were registered, the proportion of migrants leaving Britain with professional or financial occupations, as well as no occupation at all (i.e. probably 'gentlemen'), was more than 30 per cent of the total.[30]

Economics alone cannot account for the obtuseness that traumatized the life of gifted individuals like Watson, Tressell and Williams, that must have injured the dignity of hundreds of thousands of others. No, there is something peculiar about the class boundaries of Edwardian England which strikes a note of recognition in its residents even today—something deeply ingrained in the society. Its literary culture, at least, seems to be concerned with very little else. Yet we have no convincing historical

---

[27] Wakefield, *Art of Colonization*, pp. 72, 66.

[28] F. Musgrove, 'Middle-class Education and Employment in the Nineteenth Century', *Economic History Review*, vol. 12 (1959), and the response by H. Perkin, 'Middle-Class Education and Employment in the Nineteenth Century: A Critical Note', *Economic History Review*, vol. 14 (1961); A. Offer, *Property and Politics, 1870–1914* (Cambridge 1981), ch. 4 and pp. 103–4; G. Anderson, *Victorian Clerks* (Manchester 1976), pp. 46–7, 130; S. Dohrn, *Die Entstehung weiblicher Büroarbeit in England 1860 bis 1914* (Frankfurt 1986).

[29] A. J. Hammerton, *Emigrant Gentlewomen: Genteel Poverty and Female Emigration, 1830–1914* (1979), p. 187.

[30] B. Thomas, *Migration and Economic Growth* (2nd edn. Cambridge 1973), table 80, p. 382; Carrier and Jeffery, *External Migration*, table N/O (7), p. 124.

account of where this came from. It is one of those elements that are so deeply rubbed into the texture of society that they are almost taken for granted. I have a sense that this stifling propriety hardened in the late-Victorian period and held Edwardian society in a rigid hand. British society was not a staircase but a sequence of social compartments, made up like a set of concentric circles, that seemed impermeable and almost immutable; the rings contained separate, non-competing groups, as thoroughly segregated almost as the races in South Africa in their habitats and life-styles.

Herbert Hoover bought a house and settled in London in 1908 as a wealthy American mining engineer. For him, the 'stratified structure of British society was a constant marvel—and grief'. He held the upper and upper-middle classes in high regard as individuals, and admired their cultivation and integrity. But he resented English condescension. 'America never had such class divisions, such impenetrable stratifications and such misery below. Moreover, America was far in advance in many essential social actions. Free education was universal in the United States long before the "upper class" in England would permit it. To them it was dangerous.'[31]

It required an outsider to perceive the peculiar in what English people regarded as a state of nature. Robert Tressell was such an outsider: less a proletarian than an early Orwell, he came from an Irish middle-class background (possibly illegitimate) and emigrated to South Africa around 1890, where he worked as a journeyman and self-employed decorator in comfortable circumstances. He only arrived in Britain in 1902 or 1903 and died a pauper's death in 1911, before he could carry out his plan to emigrate once again. So *The Ragged Trousered Philanthropists* is not quite an authentic proletarian cry of outrage. It was rather the product of culture shock. The theme of the novel, indeed its very title, expresses Tressell's despair at the acquiesence of his fellow-decorators in their mistreatment and exploitation, at their unreflective acceptance and deference to the values of their superiors. Tressell's large manuscript was not only a testimony, but also a bid (like the parallel book of Alfred Williams) to escape from a trap of poverty and indignity. Tressell died before he found a publisher, but his daughter sold the manuscript for a pittance which she used to pay her fare to Canada, where she married an engineer for Massey-Harris in Saskatchewan. Alfred Williams, who published six books of village lore before *Life in a Railway Factory*, failed in his efforts to get even the most minimal livelihood out of his writing, and died of malnutrition and disease.[32]

[31] H. Hoover, *The Memoirs of Herbert Hoover* (1952), vol. 1, pp. 125, 127.
[32] F. C. Ball, *One of the Damned: The Life and Times of Robert Tressell, Author of the Ragged Trousered Philanthropists* (1973); L. Clark, *Alfred Williams: His Life and Work* (1945, Newton Abbott, 1969).

In England, Hoover wrote, 'the other eighty per cent were reminded once a week in their prayer book that they must respect their betters'.[33] Australians and Canadians felt no such obligation. The Governor-General of Victoria was told in 1903, 'when most of the working classes were doing well . . . [they] considered Jack as good as his master and a bit better'.[34] It would be simplistic to deduce that the flow of emigration responded primarily to the difference in the levels of working-class self-esteem. Its pace was also governed by economic opportunities. This does not rule out the psychological motive; and perhaps it is the economics of labour scarcity that give rise to social dignity. Quantitative studies show that earning differentials alone do not provide a good explanation for migration flows from Britain; it is only when employment opportunites and the prospects for upward social mobility are incorporated in the equation that a good fit emerges.[35]

One symptom of this was the colonial attitude to domestic service. Service was the largest single occupational category in Edwardian Britain, employing more than 2.5 million, of whom some 84 per cent were women. Domestic servants were taken for granted in a middle-class household and some outside help was even used in skilled working-class households. Apart from married women and "spinsters", the proportion of domestic servants among female emigrants from Britain was overwhelming, and their passages were often subsidised.[36] In the Australian boomtime of the 1880s working-class girls were very reluctant to enter service. 'For some inexplicable reason, they turn up their noses at the high wages and comparatively light work offered, and prefer to undertake the veriest drudgery in factories for a miserable pittance,' as a journalist complained. Another journalist stated that 'the idea of degradation [is] attached to the position of "slavey" in the minds of the lower classes . . . .'.

'Ye gentlemen of England,' wrote the author of *Town Life in Australia*, 'who sit at home at ease, how astonished you would be to see your daughter Maud, whose husband is a well-to-do lawyer in considerable practice, setting the table herself because she cannot rely upon her servant doing it properly!'[37] Elizabeth Mitchell, a young Scotswoman, travelled through the Canadian west in 1913–14, at the height of the wheat boom. She tells of how two English maids, recent arrivals in the Canadian west, 'were greatly taken aback when they found that not even the smartest

---

[33] Hoover, *Memoirs*, vol. 1, p. 125.

[34] Lord Sydenham of Combe (George Clarke), *My Working Life* (1927), p. 170.

[35] J. M. Gandar, 'Economic Causation and British Emigration in the Late Nineteenth Century' (University of Missouri Ph.D. thesis, 1982), esp. fos. 175–8.

[36] Carrier and Jeffery, *External Migration*, table N/O (2), p. 115.

[37] R. E. N. Twopeny, *Town Life in Australia* (1883), pp. 56–7; the Melbourne *Argus*, cited ibid., p. 59; pp. 72–3.

woman in town had two servants'. That servant expected to be treated as an equal and to eat with the family. As a result, visitors often helped with the washing-up: 'one makes acquaintance much quicker in the kitchen over a dish-tub or a cake-tin than sitting on a proper chair in a drawing room with folded hands wondering what to say next.'[38] Economics were probably stronger than culture, for in England as well the servant problem became insoluble once other employment for women became widely available after the First World War.

One must beware of taking this argument too far. The percentage of women who were in domestic service in Victoria in 1901 (11.4 per cent of all women) was only a small fraction lower than the percentage in England (12.2 per cent), although the figure in Canada seems to have been only half as large (5.7 per cent); it does not contradict the anecdotal evidence: Australian servants unservile, Canadian ones scarce.[39]

The flood of emigrants in the Edwardian years is all the more remarkable in that there was no crock of gold waiting overseas. What was more important, "push" or "pull"? Economic studies of migration normally stress differences in the "standard of living", i.e. of the quality of (material) life in the home. We are also concerned with the workplace regime, the quality of life at work.

Nominal wage rates were very much higher overseas, but the difference in purchasing power was not so large. Phelps Brown and Browne compared nominal and real wage levels between Britain and the United States in the Edwardian period. When UK wages were taken as 100, American ones were 179. This was for all grades. For skilled craftsmen the average American rate was 230:100. When incomes were reckoned in purchasing power, the American rate was only 118–123. On the other hand, skilled men enjoyed a much larger premium in the United States than in Britain.[40] A similar picture emerged from Shergold's comparison of Pittsburgh with Sheffield and Birmingham. He found that skilled workers earned a good deal more in the United States, but that real wages for the unskilled were much the same in both countries.[41]

A similar picture emerges with regard to workplace regime. The benign environment described by Mosely and his delegates was one of skilled work. For unskilled labourers there is no shortage of evidence for regimes as hard as any to be found in Britain. Many if not most unskilled jobs in industry were taken by recent migrants from continental Europe, whose

[38] E. Mitchell, *In Western Canada before the War* (1915), pp. 57–8.

[39] Calculated from K. Alford and M. McLean, 'Partners or Parasites of Men? Women's Economic Status in Australia, Britain and Canada, 1850–1900', *ANU Working Papers in Economic History*, no. 66 (Apr. 1986), tables 3, 7, pp. 17, 22.

[40] E. H. Phelps Brown and M. H. Browne, *A Century of Pay* (1968), pp. 46–7.

[41] P. R. Shergold, *Working-class Life: The "American Standard" in Comparative Perspective, 1899–1913* (Pittsburgh 1982), pp. 224–6

labour was abundant and cheap. So for skilled workers emigration was very attractive from the point of view of both economics and dignity. For the unskilled the North American towns did not have a great deal to offer, although the outback promised a new start and the prospect of social mobility. It seems that in Australia, at any rate (and in Canada as well), skill differentials were much smaller than in the United States, less even than in Britain. Australia, in contrast with the United States, Canada and Britain, also seems to have had rising real wages in the Edwardian period (only reverting however to the levels of the mid-1890s) and perhaps reflecting the benefit of a shift of the terms of trade in favour of agrarian producers.[42]

In both Canada and Australia there is a school of "colonial pessimists" who depict working-class lives in the darkest colours.[43] Their work indicates that the shadows in the "Workingman's Paradise" were long and deep, but I think they spoil their case by overstatement. To say, as Michael Piva does for Toronto and Terry Copp for Montreal, that all workers experienced a deepening *poverty* in the Edwardian period stretches credibility. There is no doubt a good deal of substance in the pessimist case, with long winters of unemployment, insanitary housing and long hours in "sweated" conditions. This only underlines the importance of "push" in the immigration flows. But even in England, where real wages were indisputably lower, a good part of the working class was living well above the poverty line.

There is other evidence. Owner-occupation of houses in the Dominions was remarkably high: 50 per cent of houses in Australia (only about a third in the large towns), almost 60 per cent in New Zealand (1921).[44] Infant mortality in Australia was considerably lower than in Britain, and New Zealand had the lowest rate in the world.[45] At a time when some 40 per cent of British working-class men were unable to vote, overseas societies had real universal male franchise, and many of their federated states and provinces had a vote for women too. Some intangibles are even less

---

[42] Canadian differentials: work in progress by R. C. Allen; Australian trends: P. G. Macarthy, 'Wages in Australia, 1891 to 1914', *Australian Economic History Review*, vol. 10 (1970), p. 67.

[43] Canada: e.g. T. Copp, *The Anatomy of Poverty: The Conditions of the Working Class in Montreal, 1897–1921* (Toronto 1974); M. J. Piva, *The Condition of the Working Class in Toronto, 1900–1921* (Ottawa 1979); Australia: J. Lee and C. Fahey, 'A Boom for Whom? Some Developments in the Australian Labour Market, 1870–91', *Labour History*, no. 50 (May 1981); S. Fitzpatrick, *Rising Damp: Sydney, 1870–90* (Melbourne 1987).

[44] R. V. Jackson, 'Owner-occupation of Houses in Sydney, 1871 to 1891', *Australian Economic History Review*, vol. 10 (1970), pp. 138–9; J. Phillips, *A Man's Country? The Image of the Pakeha Male: A History* (Auckland 1987), p. 226; work in progress by R. L. Ransom and R. Sutch indicates high levels of home ownership among retiring workers in the United States.

[45] P. Mein Smith, 'Infant Survival in Australia, 1900–1945: Mortality, Rules and Practice' (Australian National University Ph.D. thesis, in progress).

tangible: a warmer climate down under, or, in the absence of any material advantage, a simple desire for novelty and change.

III

The Australian "Workingman's Paradise" was flawed, as the contemporary novel of that title amply demonstrates. But it was still the prevailing perception that between Britain and the daughter economies overseas, especially Canada and Australia, there was a moral gradient. Those who moved along it upwards and outwards usually found themselves endowed with greater self-esteem, unless they came from the very top of British society. In one of D. H. Lawrence's stories a British-born Canadian soldier, on leave in an English town during (or perhaps just after) the first World War, refuses blandishments to stay. 'There's too much difference between the men and the employers over here—too much of that for me.'[46] A greater equality and dignity for everyman was one of the pervasive themes of nascent national cultures overseas, even if it was sometimes belied by a more complex reality.[47]

Elizabeth Mitchell's experience with the washing-up suggests that the free air overseas attracted middle-class and even upper-class migrants. The habit of authority was often tiresome. And the hidden injuries of class are not the only wounds. Families of all classes can inflict injury on their members. The annals of emigration and settlement are full of sons and daughters of well-to-do families setting out on a new start away from home, often with its blessing and support. This class of person, both women and men, figures large in the literature of settlement and gave rise to a much ridiculed category, the "remittance men", to be found in farming, business, the professions and in idleness and dissolution as well, in Canada, in Australia and no doubt also in the United States.[48]

English migrants found it difficult to shed their social stigmata immediately on arrival. Working practices in Britain were defensive, and in cohesive union shops any excess of zeal was frowned upon, even in piecework. Workmen from Britain were consequently unprepared for the pace of work which they encountered. "No English need apply", an apochrypal notice at a Winnipeg building site, became a byword. A manual for British migrants was published under that title. In New Zealand the "new chum" just out from the old country was a stock figure of fun.[49]

---

[46] D. H. Lawrence, 'You Touched Me', *The Complete Short Stories of D. H. Lawrence*, vol. 2 (1955), p. 399. I owe this reference to Susan Edgar.

[47] Australia: R. White, *Inventing Australia* (Sydney 1981), ch. 3, and pp. 76–9, 81; and ch. 13 below.

[48] P. Dunae, *Gentlemen Emigrants: From the British Public Schools to the Canadian Frontier* (Vancouver 1981), ch. 7; p.x shows a contemporary illustration of an Oxfordshire manor house juxtaposed against a frontier log house.

[49] Phillips, *A Man's Country?*, p. 24.

J. S. Woodsworth, a progressive evangelist working with immigrants in Winnipeg, described the new arrivals from the Old Country. The Scotch, Irish and Welsh had done well. The greater number of failures had been among the English. His view was that 'England has sent us largely the failures of the cities. The demand for artisans in our cities is limited.' But his long account of meetings with immigrants (in the depression year of 1908) refers again and again to unemployment and insecurity in the Old Country, to days of tramping in search of work. The unskilled underclass was also numerous among assisted migrants. Woodsworth had a strong dislike, shared by many Canadians, for remittance men: 'Useless at Home, they are worse than useless here.' A contemporary of Woodsworth's told the prospective middle-class migrant, 'remember that you are going to a country where class distinctions are unknown, and where one man is considered as good as another, whether he be a big business manager or the driver of an express wagon.'[50]

The overseas economies held out the prospect of an improved social environment for the working classes, and for a good part of the middle and even upper classes. The absence of gentility is perhaps the most distinctive social aspect of these societies. They were not free of inequality or exploitation, but power and wealth did not rest on the same weight of social convention and rigid exclusion. A similar point was made by Basil Stewart, the electrical engineer who wrote the Canadian migrant manual:

One of the chief obstacles to a complete understanding between Colonials and Englishmen, and vice versa, is the existence of a cultured and leisured class in the old country, whom the Colonial looks down upon with a certain amount of contempt not untinged with envy for the superior culture and refinement which the latter have been able to acquire.[51]

Here is one clue, perhaps, to the arrogance and mutual disdain of British class relations. Such conduct is alien to the code of the gentleman; but so is work of any kind. To toil in business was to admit an incomplete or frustrated gentility. This sense of frustration seems to me to go some way to account for the surliness of class relations in Edwardian England.

For the great majority of British workers, the financial, social and emotional costs of uprooting and migrating across the oceans were simply too high, however attractive the trade-off.

[50] J. S. Woodsworth, *Strangers within our Gates or Coming Canadians* (Toronto 1909, new edn. 1972), ch. 4; B. Stewart, *No English Need Apply, or Canada as a Field for the Emigrant* (1909), *passim*, quote from p. 7.
[51] Stewart, *No English Need Apply*, p. 73.

10

COAST, INTERIOR AND METROPOLIS

I

Economic opportunities facilitated the movement of people from Britain overseas and helped to form new societies. The new communities did not have to reinvent civilization and within one or two generations they had erected urban societies equipped with most of the trappings of provincial Europe. Locked up in the bush or the veldt, these new lands possessed a latent productivity beyond the needs of their small populations. The road to prosperity lay in the transition from pioneering self-sufficiency to exports.

The export of agrarian and mineral staples gave rise to a triangular relationship which linked the settlers' main centre of population, commerce and government, the region of production and the market overseas. Let us call these three zones, "coast", "interior" and "metropolis". "Coast" is used in a metaphorical sense, as the point of contact between the interior and the metropolitan markets overseas. Melbourne, Buenos Aires and New York actually face the sea. Toronto and Chicago are lapped by lakes, and linked to sea routes. Winnipeg is a short distance from a major inland waterway. A small number of urban centres, like Minneapolis and Johannesburg, had, in their exchanges, banks, political influence and processing industries, the attributes of coastal centres. In a few cases, notably British Columbia, the interior actually hugs the coast.

Coast predates the export economy; it was the site of the original settlement which grew to become a centre for trade, finance, industry, government and culture. The interior produced pastoral, arable or mineral staple commodities for export and for consumption on the coast. Metropolis was the staple's end market, a source of capital, migrants and manufactures; of political, social and cultural models; in some societies, the subject of filial sentiments and the seat of sovereignty. For most internationally traded primary commodities, the metropolis was Britain.

The interior staple helped to determine the structure of settler society. Where the staple was range-fed cattle or sheep, as in Texas and Argentina, Australia and mid-Victorian New Zealand, the interior was settled sparsely in large units and dominated by the graziers. Where the staple was timber, the labour force was also (as on the grazing frontier) male, itinerant and seasonal. Where the staple was mineral, as in South Africa's diamond mines and goldfields, settlement took an urban form, labour was proletarian and the interior was dominated (or at least contested) by the mining capitalists. The work required on arable and dairy farms restricted the size of the holding and produced a denser pattern of rural settlement, which developed into a stable society of family farmers. In short, some staples promoted mateship, others promoted matrimony.

Most of the surplus produced in the interior accumulated on the coast. It came there as interest earned on the money lent to farmers, to urban developers and to the railways which carried the grain. It came there in the form of taxes paid (indirectly) by producers in the interior. It came there as the profits of merchants and manufacturers who supplied the interior with its needs, who carried, sold and shipped the staple overseas. Coasts provided the seats of government, banks, the theatres and art galleries, the newspapers, publishers, universities and churches that set the tone and content of public discourse, as well as the law courts and the military commands, where those counted for something. The coast's primary economic role in relation to the interior was to promote, finance and manage public works: the railways, canals and docks that carried the staple and placed it on board ship.

In politics, the coast provided a countervailing power to that of the interior. A good part of the coast economy catered for the needs of its own urban populations, and the concentration of people and economic activity allowed the coast in English-speaking countries to dominate the politics of their societies. The United States, Canada and later Australia developed significant farmer movements, but these were always overshadowed by the political mass of the coast. In Argentina, however, landowner power slowed down the rate of industrial and urban growth. In South Africa the struggle between the Cape mining capitalists and the pastoral Boers of the interior came to a clash of arms.

In the English-speaking coast societies, the overseas metropolis played a number of roles. The pioneers had often been driven out by social and economic pressures in the old society, and the colony's function as an outlet for metropolitan tensions remained important. Along with settlers, Britain provided a language, religions and political models. It no longer aspired to control the life of the settlements, but continued to fill a political role. Britain guaranteed the autonomy of Australia, New Zealand and Canada in a world of expanding empires. It gave their people and their leaders a larger historical stage than their own stature would justify. Britain also underwrote the settlers' own expansion in Canada, Southern Africa and the Pacific.

Britain's free-trade policy and the decline of its agriculture made it the staple producers' largest single market, and thus an important source of their prosperity and growth (continental Europe, however, increased its demand even more than Britain). Britain was able, by selling its textiles and machinery in Europe and the tropical world, to purchase and pay for large quantities of food and raw materials produced in the settlement interiors. In return, Britain enjoyed a consumer's surplus of prices lower than they might otherwise have been. Britain also became a prime source of capital, not only for the crown settlements, but also for the United States and South America, as well as India and South Africa.

Each settler society worked its way through a succession of staples, and staple exports helped to shape its social and political culture. The Caribbean colonies never outgrew their original dependence on plantation sugar but the American south moved from tobacco to cotton; the American west from cattle to wheat and then to corn-fed hogs. Argentina graduated from hides to meat, and then made room for wheat. Australia produced wool, then added mutton and wheat, with periodic mineral booms. New Zealand added meat and dairy products to its wool. Canada was the most prolific of all, with the Newfoundland fisheries followed by the fur trade, then by timber, by King Wheat (from around the turn of the century) and by newsprint. Staple exports went hand in hand with growth and diversification in the coast economy, whose urban development, manufactures and services were so vigorous that both Canadian and Australian historians have disputed at times how much growth really owed to staple exports. As the domestic economy increased its local demand for the staple export commodities, the relation between the coast and the interior came to resemble the earlier one between metropolis and coast.[1]

For the largest exporter of them all, the United States, domestic urban growth and industrial development overshadowed staple exports as a source of growth, but for particular *regions*, and for particular periods, staples were still decisive.[2] The cotton-growing south, the great plains and the Pacific slope all depended on staple exports, whether overseas or to other regions. Wheat was second only to cotton as an American staple export in the 1880s and 1890s, but after 1900 shipments levelled off and then declined. The wheat frontier moved out of the West Central states, and into Canadian prairie provinces, and to Argentina; after the end of the great drought, Australia joined in too. For those three countries, wheat was the great expanding staple of the Edwardian period (fig. 6.1).

---

[1] My approach is influenced by the work of the Canadians W.A Mackintosh and H. A. Innis between the wars. See W. T. Easterbrook and M. H. Watkins (eds.), *Approaches to Canadian Economic History* (Toronto 1967), pt. 1. The recent debate: M. H. Watkins, 'The Staple Theory Revisited', *Journal of Canadian Studies*, vol. 12, no. 5 (winter 1977); R. E. Ankli, 'The Growth of the Canadian Economy, 1876–1920: Export-led and/or Neoclassical Growth', *Explorations in Economic History*, vol. 17 (July 1980). In Australia, despite the continued predominance of primary products in its exports, the domestic interpretation of growth has predominated: R. Pomfret, 'The Staple Theory as an Approach·to Canadian and Australian Economic Development', *Australian Economic History Review*, vol. 21 (1981); N. G. Butlin, 'The Australian Economy Heavily Disguised', *Business Archives and History*, vol. 4 (1964), and his *Investment in Australian Economic Development, 1861–1900* (Cambridge 1964), p. 5. I return to this subject in ch. 11, sec. IV, below.

[2] J. G. Williamson, 'Greasing the Wheels of Spluttering Export Engines: Midwestern Grains and American Growth', *Explorations in Economic History*, vol. 17 (July 1980).

In Britain bankers and financial promoters also cultivated a succession of staples in a sequence of different regions. India received a good deal of railway investment in the 1860s, the United States in the 1870s. In the 1880s Australia and Argentina took in large investments, followed by South Africa in the early 1890s. After a hiatus of overseas investment from the late 1890s until about 1904 it was Canada's turn, as very large sums went out from Britain both as portfolio investment in bonds and shares and as direct investment in land, urban real estate and business enterprises. This capital helped to tool up the Canadian economy for the great outpouring of wheat which began before the First World War. Some of it was lent directly to the settlers, or indirectly through local banks and finance companies. Railways, highways, bridges, canals and harbours formed the largest category of investment, but the bulk was probably spent in urban construction and public works, in the interior, as well as on the coast.[3]

II

Social arrangements were the key to economic success. That is the teaching of economic liberalism, and Adam Smith's explanation of the success of settler economies is hard to improve on. An abundance of land allowed a high output per worker and a high level of wages, with a consequent easy acquisition of property. In the absence of large inequalities based on property, social relations were more genial and generous, the land more productive, the people more prolific.

The colony of a civilized nation which takes possession, either of a waste country, or of one so thinly inhabited, that the natives easily give place to the new settlers, advances more rapidly to wealth and greatness than any other human society.

The colonists carry out with them a knowledge of agriculture and of other useful arts, superior to what can grow up of its own accord in the course of many centuries among savage and barbarous nations. They carry out with them too the habit of subordination, some notion of the regular government which takes place in their own country, of the system of laws which support it, and of a regular administration of justice; and they naturally establish something of the same kind in the new settlement. . . . Every colonist gets more land than he can possibly cultivate. No landlord shares with him its produce, and the share of the sovereign is commonly but a trifle. He has every motive to render as great as possible a produce, which is thus to be almost entirely his own . . . He is eager, therefore, to collect labourers from all quarters, and to reward them with the most liberal wages. But those liberal

---

[3] F. W. Field, *Capital Investments in Canada* (Montreal 1914); D. G. Paterson, *British Direct Investment in Canada, 1890–1914* (Toronto 1976); A. Cairncross, 'Investment in Canada, 1900–13', ch. 3 of *Home and Foreign Investment, 1870–1913: Studies in Capital Accumulation* (1953), pp. 44–6.

wages, joined to the plenty and cheapness of land, soon make those labourers leave him in order to become landlords themselves, and to reward, with equal liberality, other labourers, who soon leave them for the same reason that they left their first master.

   In other countries, rent and profit eat up wages, and the two superior orders of people oppress the inferior one. But in new colonies, the interest of the two superior orders obliges them to treat the inferior one with more generosity and humanity; at least, where that inferior one is not in a state of slavery.[4]

After the natural endowment of land, the chief cause of the settlers' prosperity, according to Smith, lay in the disposition of property. In the French, Portuguese and Spanish colonies, vacant land was engrossed in great estates which passed undivided under a system of entail and primogeniture. The first cause of British success was that

the engrossing of uncultivated land, though it has by no means been prevented altogether, has been more restrained in the English colonies than in any other. The colony law which imposes upon every proprietor the obligation of improving and cultivating, within a limited time, a certain proportion of his lands, and which, in case of failure, declares those neglected lands grantable to any other person; though it has not, perhaps, been very strictly executed, has, however, had some effect.[5]

   Smith accounts here not only for the subsequent differences between North America and Argentina, but also for the difference between the settler societies and the old country. From early on the colonies managed their endowment of arable land so as to establish a society of family farmers. For the coast, the imperative was to people the interior, and arable farming was the most intensive form of occupation. A succession of homestead acts in the United States and Canada, and selection acts in Australia, granted a workable plot of land either free or at a very low price to settlers in return for permanent residence. Large land grants to railways were designed to achieve the same objective. In order to attract traffic the railways sold land at low rates to all comers. It was not as if the land was actually free. Homesteading on the American prairies entailed the costs of travelling out to the holding, of a team of horses or oxen, of dwelling and furnishings, agricultural implements, livestock, tools, fencing materials and cash to survive until the land began to yield. A fully equipped homestead cost a great deal and even a modestly equipped one could cost as much to establish as a lower-middle-class family in Britain earned in a year. But settlers had a range of choices, and could substitute labour and endurance for the capital they lacked; could work for wages in the idle seasons, and live in shanties and sod huts. A homestead was not a lifetime

---

[4] Smith, *Wealth of Nations*, Bk. IV, ch.7, pt. 2, pp. 531–2.
[5] Ibid., p. 539.

commitment. Of the firstcomers, some 50–80 per cent moved on within the first decade. The prize was to see the arrival of genuine homeseekers, of railways and towns and the rise of land values that compensated for the sacrifices.[6] Like most lotteries, the take was probably larger than the sum of the prizes, but the net result was to create an increasingly stable rural society in the interior, supported by a railway system to carry its produce out to the world market and to bring in supplies from the coast. Throughout the 1880s the lure was stronger than the disappointments. As the climate became increasingly marginal, the harvest and grain stocks varied more from year to year. In 1893 and 1894 the good rainfall in the wheat areas combined with a maximum extension of cultivation to return excessively low prices. For all the hardships, for all the disappointments, for all the speculative and tentative nature of western prairie wheat growing, one fact is indisputable: production continued to increase on trend from year to year. Homesteading and dry farming produced an ever-growing surplus of wheat, which became a challenge to the existing social and political order of Europe.

The interiors of extensive grazing economies, whether of cattle in the American west, of the wool economies of Australia or of the hide and meat economy of the pampas, were polarized between the free-spirited proletarian gaucho, cowboy or shearer, and the large graziers; they were too sparsely settled to become democratic societies in any real sense. A similar polarization characterized the share-cropping and small-farmer cotton and tobacco staples of the south, where the black tenant–labourers and poor-white owners remained outside the bounds of civic society.

In contrast, family grain farming gave rise to new and distinctive forms of social and political life. Interior staple economies tended to be one-crop or two-crop economies. Wheat was followed by hogs and cattle, with dairying near the large towns. In the first years the settlers might have little to do with the outside world, relying on their own crop for subsistence and earning cash by occasional wage labour. An established staple farmer found himself at the end of a very long chain. His product had to travel hundreds or even thousands of miles to its ultimate market. And although, the farmer was paid in cash, he did not accumulate it, but took a stream of traded goods approximately equal to the value of his output. Most of these goods came a long way, from the coast, from large-scale producers or distributors. For accumulation the farmer looked to the rising value of his land, and often had to anticipate it with a mortgage. On the whole, however, the American farmer was much less in debt than the owners of land in the old country; mortgage debt came to some 9 per cent of land

[6] Atack, 'Farm-making Costs'; L. E. Decker, 'The Great Speculation: An Interpretation of Mid-continent Pioneering', in D. M. Ellis (ed.), *The Frontier in American Development: Essays in Honor of Paul Wallace Gates* (Ithaca, NY 1969), pp. 375–80.

values in the United States in 1910, compared with 27 per cent in England and 39 per cent in Prussia (in 1896).[7]

While the farmers worked for a deferred reward, their buyers and suppliers received an immediate payment. The interior was much poorer than the coast. In 1910, after a decade of prosperity, American farmers still earned less than half of non-farm incomes, about 40 per cent on one calculation, and about half of what industrial labour earned; rather less, in relative terms, than their UK counterparts.[8] This gap is explained partly by the deferred value of rising land prices and by low incomes in southern agriculture; partly by the approbationary rewards of country life. The settlers settled for a low income in return for a sense of independence and the self-esteem that went with it. But they also reacted with frustration and anger.

III

The grain economy brought two contrasting forms of production into contact and conflict. On one side stood the prairie farmers, archetypes of economic man, producing a uniform product for an impersonal market, and creating property by their own labour. This paragon of possessive individualism depended symbiotically on the opposite form of economic organization, on the large, monopolistic modern corporation, aided and abetted by the economic power of the state. To grow the grain took the efforts of a single household. To bring it to market required a co-ordinated system of many components, with large advantages to size. Prairie grain was purchased in bulk, stored in bulk at several points, carried in bulk thousands of miles by rail and steamship, sold in a fickle market and financed by loans over the whole period. Storage, carriage and sale were done more efficiently on a large scale, in large boxcars, in elevator warehouses, in Great Lake steamers, in big lots on commodity markets, with large tranches of capital. Of all the world's wheat regions, only the American and Canadian prairies operated entirely in bulk and attracted the admiration and envy of competitors world-wide. There is no need to invoke Yankee ingenuity; the traders of the prairies had good economic reasons which did not apply elsewhere. The reason, one of them suggested, was the freezing of the Great Lakes in November, shortly after the end of the harvest. With only a short sailing season before the ice set in, shipping on the Great Lakes had to be loaded with dispatch, and this called for

---

[7] *Statistical History of the US*, pt. 1, ser. K11, K361, pp. 457, 491; Offer, *Property and Politics*, p. 139; A. Meitzen and F. Grossmann, *Der Boden und die landwirtschaftlichen Verhältnisse des preussischen Staates* (Berlin 1906), vol. 6, p. 470; small farmers, however, were much less heavily indebted than owners of large estates.

[8] Bellerby, *Agriculture and Industry*, table 33, p. 201.

handling in bulk further back along the line. In 1901 a lake boat carrying 250,000 bushels could be loaded in two hours. That is why the prairie sprouted elevators, while the harvest elsewhere simply piled up in sacks on railway sidings and docks.[9]

The North American railways of the nineteenth century were the forerunners of the giant modern corporation with their nation-wide activities, tens of thousands of employees, elaborate hierarchy of command, diversified activity and influence on business and government. Grain merchants operated chains of country elevators, and regularly colluded with their competitors to set a price for the farmer. Commission merchants, terminal operators, shippers and banks might be smaller in scale, but still loomed very large on the farmer's horizons. Why did these monolith middlemen, so superior to the farmers in market power, nevertheless operate with such keen efficiency? Farmers often had only one local outlet for their grain. In that case they only had the choice of selling to the local elevator or consigning grain to a commission merchant for sale at the lake terminal town. Railways, grain merchants and warehousemen had to operate efficiently because they competed with other regions for a share of the Liverpool market. Chicago loomed large (but not alone) in the midwest but had to compete with San Francisco, St Louis, Buenos Aires and Odessa. Competition between the regions forced the giants of merchandizing and marketing to operate on tight margins.

The firms which supplied the farmers also waxed on their custom. Often it was the self-same terminal operator who also dealt in coal, groceries, feed and implements. Makers of the machines tended to merge into the large firms, of which a few are still active today and more were active until a few years ago: McCormick (International Harvester) in Chicago; John Deere in Moline, Illinois; Massey-Harris in Brantford, Ontario. Their agents came round to offer ploughs and binders on easy credit, which took many harvests to pay off.

In Canada and Australia, where the coast came to dominate politics, it began a programme of industrial development by means of import substitution and imposed a tariff to protect the infant industries. Farmers resented the tariff. It raised their costs of production and consumption. It also held back international trade and reduced overseas demand for their products. All purchase taxes tend to be regressive and farmers, at the lower end of the income distribution, considered that they suffered more from tariffs than the coast, where protection provided employment and profits. Tariffs became the most persistent source of contention between

[9] R. E. Smith, *Wheat Fields and Markets of the World* (St Louis 1908); interregional competition: Larson, *Minnesota*, pp. 221 ff.; 'two hours' is on p. 223; also M. Rothstein, 'American Wheat and the British Market, 1860–1905' (Cornell University Ph.D. thesis, 1960), chs. 2–3.

coast and interior. In Argentina, where the graziers had a strong influence on politics, a policy of free trade held back industrial development in the towns.

Throughout the 1880s and early 1890s, as settlers encountered harsher conditions on the new frontiers of cultivation, and as export prices slumped, they looked for the root of their troubles overseas. Britain, their main export market, became an object of hostility and resentment, which deepened in the mid-1890s when it rejected the farmers' panacea, a bimetallic currency.[10] After the turn of the century the returns in farming began to grow quite rapidly. Between 1900 and 1910 land prices in the United States almost doubled, and the terms of trade between country and town moved strongly in favour of the farmers. A basket of corn, wheat and cotton bought 54 per cent more manufactured goods in 1909 than in 1899.[11] Demand at home grew and exports declined. The American farmer was inclined to forget his resentment of Britain, and the settlers on the new frontiers in Canada and Australia either felt more favourably disposed towards Britain or became positively deferential.[12]

The interior consisted at different times of one or more generations of settlers, living in a state of relative isolation from each other on largish tracts of land, and working hard to eke a living out of the soil. Every year was a new gamble with the weather and the market. The farmer deeply resented those who carved such a large share (as he saw it) out of his crop: the buyers and carriers, the suppliers and manufacturers, the distant federal government and, even further, the metropolitan manipulators of money and prices. From the mid-1980s, however, the interior's fortunes took a turn for the better. Early settlements stabilized and grew, while rising demand opened up a new frontier. The farmer continued to be at odds with the coast but had the satisfaction of growing revenues and land values. When the new opportunities opened up in Canada after the turn of the century, a great wave of established farmers from the United States pulled up their roots, sold out and moved north into the "last best west", taking with them an established tradition that helped to form the distinctive outlook of the Canadian grain frontier during the Edwardian period.[13]

[10] E. Green, 'Bimetallism' (unpublished paper, 1985); W. A. Williams, *The Roots of the Modern American Empire* (New York 1969), *passim*, e.g. pp. 305–7.
[11] V. Olmstead, 'Annual Report of the Bureau of Statistics for the Fiscal Year 1909–10', *USDA Crop Reporter* (Jan. 1911), p. 7. Land values, *Historical Statistics of the US*, ser. K15.
[12] See the account of the Coronation, *GGG* (Winnipeg), 28 June 1911, p. 22.
[13] P. F. Sharp, *The Agrarian Revolt in Western Canada: A Survey Showing American Parallels* (Minneapolis 1948), ch. 1; K. D. Bicha, 'The Plains Farmer and the Prairie Province Frontier, 1897–1914', *Journal of Economic History*, vol. 25 (1965).

WHEAT AND EMPIRE IN CANADA

I

In England, where there was "ni terre sans maître", every bit of ground was fenced off and grazed, cultivated or hunted. In Canada, the grain frontier was open almost to all: farmers' sons, small tradesmen, skilled artisans, together with many native-born Canadians from the towns and countryside of Ontario, Quebec and the Maritimes and experienced farmers from the United States. Enough capital for a start could even be raised by a few seasons' wage labour.

As an "ideal type", the prairie was the antithesis of the English factory town. Prairie land was divided up into equal squares. Holdings varied from 160 acres (the official homestead allocation) and upwards, but rarely beyond the capacity of a single family. A rough equality prevailed. Some people had more capital, skill, energy and luck. But every settler (with the exception of land grabbers and speculators, whose numbers were large) came there to work with their own hands. A viable holding could only be established by means of self-exploitation; hired labour was too expensive. As in the United States, successful homesteaders often took their gains and started again, or retired to the towns, but the grain frontier was *colonized* by owner-occupiers.

'Surely a person has a chance to get ahead here, as he has nowhere else, but in order to get that chance, he has to say goodbye to an awful lot.' Thus Willem de Gelder, a stoic Dutch homesteader.[1] 'The government bets you ten bucks against a hundred and sixty acres you can't live on the damn place three years without starving to death,' said Billy, the hero of *Army without Banners*, a prairie novel.[2]

There is a moment in homesteading memoirs when all preparations are complete, the long journey is over, a jumble of provisions, timber, farm implements, bedding, trunks and stove is dumped on the open prairie, and the work of construction must begin. It does not last long, this moment of transition, but it sticks in the mind: 'We found the S. W. corner of my land on a Sunday afternoon. . . . I will never forget the completely lost feeling I had as I stood there alongside all my worldly possessions on the bald-headed prairie and watched that team disappear through the hills . . .' Another settler remembered,

---

[1] de Gelder, *Dutch Homesteader*, p. 29.
[2] J. Beames, *Army without Banners* (1931), p. 97.

We reached our homestead at last. I'll never forget the desolate feeling that came over me, when, with the contents of the wagon out on the ground, we sat on a box and looked around, not a sign of any other human habitation or a road leading to one to be seen, nothing but bluff and water and grass. Then I realized that we were at the end of our journey, that this was to be our home, that if we wanted a house to cover us, a stable for our horses, a well for drinking water, it would all have to be the work of our own hands.

Edwardian homesteading happened under the camera's eye, and we can see them in sharp focus, two men, one middle-aged, the other young, sitting on packing cases, leaning against their soddy with a pile of buffalo bones (the first crop) and a sentence inscribed on the bottom of the photograph, 'Sod House The Beginning of Better Things'.[3]

Men often toiled singly for years as hired hands and as bachelor homesteaders, steeling themselves to the loneliness of long winters, seeking an outlet in occasional bouts of drink and paid sex at the railway town. Bachelor homesteading was a tentative business, almost like prospecting for gold. Sooner or later, and often from the very start, marriage and children introduced stability. Unlike Argentinian share-croppers and Australian shearers, Canadian farm families attempted to build a home and a permanent society in the mould of what they had left behind. Two sections of land out of every thirty-six were set aside to pay for schools.

'It was the women who made, and who are still making, farming possible in Canada,' wrote A. G. Street, 'doing dreary, monotonous work, chiefly cooking endless meals for cross, weary men.'[4] Housing was makeshift, fresh food scarce, the water often brackish, the money short. Basic groceries and human company were both a long horse-drawn journey away. Doctors were few and expensive; childbirth and illness fraught with menace. Farm chores came on top of the household ones. For men, breaking the sod or hauling a load of grain into town provided variety, exertion, a sense of achievement and even exhilaration which women had fewer opportunities to share. Isolated on the open prairie, some men and women succumbed to depression, even madness.[5] In Frederick Grove's powerful prairie novel, *Settlers of the Marsh*, a farmer's wife is cruelly mistreated by her husband. Her daughter vows never to marry and rebuffs the hero Niels Lienstadt, a Scandinavian settler. Niels is a reclusive man who builds up a prosperous farm. On an impulse he marries a widow from town, but she rejects the role of prairie wife and withdraws, first from the farm chores, then from household duties, finally into seclusion in her own bedroom. In frustration and desperation, her husband kills her.

---

[3] First memoir, Z. F. Cushing, 1909, Reseray, Saskatchewan; the second, anon. 1904; photograph, E. Brown; all in H. Robertson's evocative *Salt of the Earth*, pp. 28–9, 33.
[4] Street, *Farmer's Glory*, p. 98.   [5] Mitchell, *In Western Canada*, pp. 150–1.

A strong feminist streak runs through the book. Ellen tells Lienstadt that women work harder than men.

'During the first years it is really the woman that makes the living on a pioneer farm. She keeps chickens, cows and pigs. The man makes the land.'
  'But when it is made?' asks Niels.
  'That's where the trouble comes in. Then there are children; and the house takes a fearful amount of time. No one thinks of relieving her of any work. She has always done it. Why can she not do it now?'[6]

That is only one side; prairie women agitated for independence from their husbands, for an equal right in the homestead, in the property created by their work. And they also fought, successfully, for the vote.[7] When frontier societies granted votes for women, this was as much in recognition of their "civilizing" influence as a statement of equality.

FIG. 11.1. 'The Vote Girl', *Grain Growers' Guide*, 8 July 1914

Single women homesteaders were not unheard of. Those who tried soon discovered the realities of prairie existence. Georgina Binnie-Clark, an independent spirit and published writer, came over from England with some capital and the notion that she could set up on the land by employing a labourer. In time she took on more of the fieldwork, but vowed never to touch the chores. Another year, and her resistance crumbled: she was milking and cleaning the troughs with the rest of them. She quarrelled with her hired hand and, when he left, her reflections cast a light on the difference between the old and the new country:

---

[6] F. R. Groves, *Settlers of the Marsh* (Toronto 1925, paperback edn. 1966), pp. 74–5.
[7] L. Rasmussen *et al.* (eds.), *A Harvest Yet to Reap: A History of Prairie Women* (Toronto 1976), pp. 88–9, 148–9.

An extra hand outdoors always increases the indoor work, and no man is kept for nothing. . . . the best system of all for the woman-farmer is to train herself to do all her own chores and hire her field labourer at special seasons by the day even if she has to pay the very highest market price. In Britain we grow up with the idea that kitchens and bedrooms are born clean and remain in that state without labour; none can make clear the labour and energy which women distribute, looking after the personal need of men who never give a thought to the work they are creating, but will spend hours meditating on the work they can evade.[8]

Writers do not usually reflect the average sensibility but no person can create a total fiction. Every person's predicament is unique, but our witnesses have something in common with hundreds and thousands of others: the daily grind was very hard but worth enduring for a sense of dignity that came from casting off subordination and from the prospect of a better existence. Street, de Gelder, Binnie-Clark found a refuge in the open prairie. A. G. Street the farmer's son found that hard labour and rough equality earned him a sense of worth he had not experienced on his father's large farm in Wiltshire. In the Edwardian period, with rising land values and grain prices, the prairies held out a real prospect of success. The settlers did not repudiate their past and did not make a clear break. For them, the margin of cultivation was the road to recognition in a society whose basic values of family and property they aspired to themselves.

John Beames's novel *Army without Banners* is not great literature, but it sets out some of the unspoken assumptions of the genre. Its heroes Billy and Maggie are a poor, young, uneducated couple from rural Ontario, who homestead next to a family of English migrants. Trials and triumphs are described: breaking the sod, the winter snow, destructive hail, the joy of harvests; the beauty and despair of long white winters; the usury of bankers and equipment agents; the tragedy of infant illness and death, the back-breaking labour and the slow rise to prosperity. Billy is good with his hands; Mr Kent, the English neighbour, is not, but learns quickly. He is 'a man of means' with a better sense for business and the two homesteads rise slowly from rude beginnings to a comfortable but still toiling competence. When the First World War breaks out, Mr Kent's son Ted volunteers and eventually goes missing in France, while his other son is wounded. Only then is it revealed that the Englishman's wife is the daughter of a duke, and her husband the younger son of an impoverished peer. But he insists to Billy, 'My name's still Tom . . . a title isn't—ah—compatible with this country. Fact is, I've decided to drop the title.'[9]

Like her American dry-farming counterparts, Georgina Binnie-Clark was at the mercy of a fickle climate. Not until the grain was all in and threshed, with the snow on the ground, was the farmer certain of her yield.

[8] G. Binnie-Clark, *Wheat and Woman* (Toronto 1914, new edn. 1979), p. 227.
[9] Beames, *Army without Banners*, p. 256.

A few years were bountiful, but on average they cancelled out and few of the memoirists made good. A perceptive traveller reported that 'Farming was not, as a fact, generally popular, and many who had tried it spoke of it with a certain horror . . . Various causes were stated, besides the mere attractiveness of town-life, principally the loneliness of the prairie and the impossibility of making farming pay.'[10] But the aggregates leave no doubts in the matter: Canadian grain production rose by leaps and bounds.

Alone and isolated for long periods at a stretch, people of the interior were self-reliant of necessity; they had undergone suffering and hardship. They mastered their tools and their soil. Their basic needs were met: they ate enough or even well. They kept on intimate terms with nature, and their communities were small and simple; social relations, though not always placid, were unceremonious and direct. When homesteaders survived or even succeeded, they achieved the self-respect of those who had won by their own efforts.

Men and women of the prairie felt strongly the contrast between their control over their own domain and their exposure to external forces. In Canada the prairie farmers managed to give their aspirations a strong collective expression.

II

Prairie farmers rarely had the facilities to store grain on the farm, and resented their lack of market control. This frustration became the motive for their movement. Homestead crops were small and rarely uniform; the railway was often a day's haul away, and many farmers simply could not fill a whole boxcar to consign (or "sell on the track") to an agent for sale at the terminal markets in Winnipeg, where they could get the current market price. If a farmer could not muster a whole boxcar, he or she had to sell by the wagonload ("on the street") to an elevator in the locality, which usually belonged to a large company. Where more than one elevator existed, farmers rightly suspected collusion, excessive "dockage" for waste and tampering with the scales. Where only one buyer operated, farmers faced an arbitrary power. When they wanted to "sell on the track", boxcars were often in short supply. Grain piled up at rural stations, and prices fell just when farmers needed money most. Farmers regarded the Dominion officials who graded wheat at the terminal elevator as too severe; elevator operators mixed the grades and sold a higher average grade than they paid for. 'I believe that we lose a grade every time we put our grain into the elevator,' wrote one farmer. Farmers also learned that the milling qualities of different grades did not justify the price differences between them.[11]

[10] Mitchell, *In Western Canada*, p. 148.
[11] Fowke, *National Policy*, ch. 7; 'Mr. Green on the "System"', *GGG*, June 1908, p. 21.

American farmers had trodden this road before, but Canadian farmers acted more effectively. In a few localities they combined to build elevators in competition with the private line. But for real effectiveness the farmers needed to be on the "coast", to partake in the business of buying and selling their grain. A Grain Growers' Grain Company was started in Manitoba in 1905 to buy grain from the farmers and recycle the profits. The grain trade refused it a seat on the Winnipeg Exchange. The farmers prevailed in the end by getting the government to alter the charter by legislation. For many months in 1908 the exchange remained closed. When it reopened the farmers' company had a position on the floor and began to pursue more ambitious goals. Political action had given them a lever against monopoly.[12]

In taking up the fight the Grain Growers realized that they had to capture minds as well as markets, and saw the need to counter the influence of the captive press.[13] The first issue of the *Grain Growers' Guide* appeared in July 1908, and, after a year as a monthly, the paper became weekly, while its circulation and bulk expanded by leaps and bounds. By 1914 it contained some fifty pages a week, densely printed on glossy paper, full of meaty features and regular columns and departments, with many photographs and advertisements, and it had become the leading periodical of the prairies. Thirty-five thousand copies of the *Guide* arriving weekly in remote hamlets and isolated farms, allowed the wheat farmers to form a movement and to discuss their world in considerable detail. It not only reflected the realities of farming but also helped to shape them, by forming the collective aspirations of its subscribers and providing an outlet for their experience.

The opinions of the Grain Growers were not entirely their own creation, but a distinctive form of ideas that became current throughout the English-speaking world, that had its core in the North American wheat and corn belts, but extended a powerful influence into the towns and into Europe as well. It was a special form of populism, a landed populism of the arable frontier, that was related to other populist movements of the Edwardian period.

A central feature of the Grain Growers' ideology may be called *physiocracy*, or the belief in the economic primacy and superior virtue of the countryman. It was *populist*, and celebrated the struggle of common people against large impersonal forces. It was *radical*, and sought for economic and social changes by political means. Each of these elements

---

[12] A near-contemporary source is M. Hopkins [pseud. of H. Joseph], *Deep Furrows* (Toronto 1918); L. A. Wood, *A History of the Farmers' Movement in Canada* (Toronto 1924), chs. 16–17.
[13] 'Making a Farmers' Paper', *GGG*, 13 Apr. 1910.

FIG. 11.2. 'The Same Old Game', *Grain Growers' Guide*, 9 Sept. 1914

linked it into movements larger than itself. Altogether, they made it one of the most distinctive progressive movements of the Edwardian decade.

A recurrent theme in the *Guide* was the prime role of farming in society, and its intrinsic worth. In the words of a farmyard poet,

> But art and science soon would fade
> And commerce dead would fall
> If the farmer ceased to reap and sow
> For the farmer feeds them all.[14]

Farming was a noble occupation, worthy of the best. 'He who has a herd of purebred cattle or other improved farm stock has a chance for exercising all the powers within him, no matter how great,' wrote the *Guide* in 1908. 'It is the cleanest profession outside the ministry,' it wrote in 1911. It featured photographs of workscenes and farmhouses, and aphorisms such as 'although the farm, like history, repeats itself, it is always interesting'.[15]

The *Guide* itself contradicted the image of the rural yokel—a polished and professional weekly magazine, its pages crowded with advertising for

[14] Nina Irving, 'The Farmer Feeds Them All', *GGG*, 23 Feb. 1910, p. 33.
[15] 'The Profession of Farming', *GGG*, June 1908, p. 43; J. R. Messenger, 'Farming as a Profession', *GGG*, 11 Oct. 1911, p. 11; 23 Feb. 1910, p. 9.

the comforts of a consumer society: pianos and gramophones, washing machines, books, motor cars, correspondence courses and the latest in agricultural machinery.

Its physiocracy echoed another movement, which arose in response to the decline of farming and to rural depopulation in the older agricultural regions of the English-speaking world. This movement had an urban perspective, and saw the decline of the countryside as a moral and eugenic danger and which worsened congestion and unemployment in the towns. Its roots went back to the agricultural depression in "metropolitan" and "coast" regions in England and the American north-east. This movement sought to regenerate the countryside. One of its high points was Theodore Roosevelt's Country Life Commission, which took evidence on the decline of farming and recommended a series of measures to rejuvenate the countryside. As Roosevelt said in his special message to Congress,

I warn my countrymen that the great recent progress made in city life is not a full measure of our civilization; for our civilization rests at bottom on the wholesome-ness, prosperity, of life in the country. The men and women on the farms stand for what is fundamentally best and most needed in our American life. Upon the development of country life rests ultimately our ability, by methods of farming requiring the highest intelligence, to continue to feed and clothe the hungry nations; to supply the city with fresh blood, clean bodies, and clear brains that can endure the terrific strain of modern life; we need the development of men in the open country, who will be in the future, as in the past, the stay and strength of the nation in time of war, and its guiding and controlling spirit in time of peace.

In England the Liberal leader David Lloyd George held the same deep belief in the regenerative powers of the countryside. This belief was shared by groups across the political spectrum, even if it left the mass of the population quite cold. "Back to the Land" was also a popular (but ineffective) flag in Ontario and Quebec. The Country Life movement stressed the social value of farming, its intrinsic satisfactions, and looked forward to raising its tone by means of education, a richer social life, moral regeneration, postal and telephone communication and agricultural ex-tension services.[16] It also had romantic undertones: quotations from Thoreau crop up in the *Guide* and the influence of William Morris is evident. The paper was in tune with the mood of urban middle-class progressives in Canada, Britain and the United States. This aesthetic sympathy extended to the paper's title-page, whose design was influenced

[16] 'Special Message from the President . . . Transmitting the Report of the Country Life Commission', US 60 Congress, 2 Sess. 1909, sen. doc. 705, ser. 5408, Country Life Commission, p. 9; H. Plunkett, *The Rural Life Problem in the United States* (New York 1912); L. H. Bailey, *The Country Life Movement* (New York 1911); J. MacDougall, *Rural Life in Canada* (Toronto 1913). England: Offer, *Property and Politics*, chs. 21–2.

by the Arts and Crafts movement in Britain, as well as in some of its advertising.

A cult of the countryside satisfied the aesthetic and spiritual cravings of the progressive mind; social justice had a rural foundation and a setting in the writings of progressive prophets like John Ruskin, William Morris and Walt Whitman. Although somewhat peripheral to the farming movement, which was too close to nature to be taken in by its superficial charms, it did provide a set of values, attitudes and language to share with progressives world-wide.[17]

III

The cover of the first issue of the *Grain Growers' Guide* (fig.11.3) shows a young woman on a pedestal, the scales of justice in one outstretched arm, a wheatsheaf cradled in the other. Her bearing combines the features of classical Greece and of Marianne, the French revolutionary muse. Her equipment includes the scales of justice, but also a pointed scythe. Her face is bright and open, her arms and shoulders bare. In the background is the dark outline of a townscape of belching smokestacks, cranes, a locomotive and a ship. She is Equity, and the inscription elaborates:

> But Crown her Queen
> And Equity shall usher in
> For those who build and those who spin
> And those the grain who garner in
> A Brighter day.

The Society of Equity was one of a number of American agrarian movements whose growth began in parallel with the movement north of the border. Just as Canadian labour unions were often "international", i.e. offshoots of organizations in Michigan and Illinois, so the farmers' movement in Canada absorbed the traditions of the previous generation of American farmers and their movements, the Patrons of Husbandry (Grange), the Patrons of Industry, the Farmers' Alliance and the Populist crusades of the 1890s.[18]

The credo of this movement was a liberal populism: it was the champion of the common man, the producer, against organized parasitical interests. In editorial, cartoon and feature, this theme was hammered home again and again. The journal's full title was *The Grain Growers' Guide and Friend of Labour*. In its first issue the editor explained his ideal:

---

[17] Offer, *Property and Politics*, ch. 20; M. R. Swanson, 'The American Country Life Movement, 1900–1940' (University of Minnesota Ph.D. thesis, 1972).

[18] Sharp, *The Agrarian Revolt*, pp. 32–3.

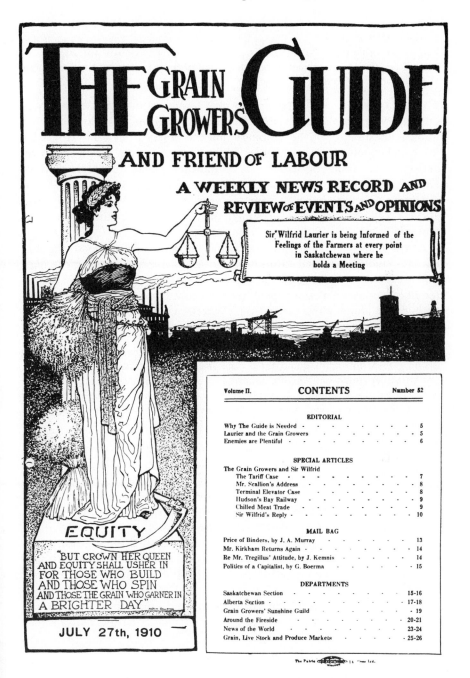

FIG. 11.3. Cover, *Grain Growers' Guide*, 27 July 1910

a great weekly newspaper containing authentic accounts of all matters and movements of importance to the farmers *and other workers*, who are in the same boat as the farmers, so far as being slaves of the capitalist classes who control the natural resources, the means of production and transportation and the mediums and avenues of exchange.[19]

The author was E. A. Partridge, a wheat farmer from Manitoba who was imbued with the lore of late-Victorian Radicalism. Partridge was an uncommon mixture of the visionary and the practical man and it was his drive and imagination that established the Grain Growers' Grain Company and set its high ambitions. He was an ethical socialist from the school of Ruskin, Morris and American Populism. The names and words of American Populist heroes, William Jennings Bryan, William LaFolette and Henry Demarest Lloyd, resonate again and again in the pages of his journal.

David against Goliaths, the weak and virtuous against the strong and wicked—the *Guide* tried to infuse a moral substance into the movement that would carry it beyond mere pressure-group politics. But Partridge (and his successors on the paper) were not content to rely on the justice of their cause alone: they carried their vocation into personal morality as well. As Partridge put it,

This newspaper would help in the work of freeing the people from this slavery by assisting them to organize and get a clear insight into the causes of the present unsatisfactory conditions, and the nature of the remedies, educative, legislative and co-operative, to be applied. It would also try to teach them to escape from the slavery of selfishness, petty greed and the crime of disloyalty in their relations with one another.[20]

Farming was literally "honest toil", quite different from commercial callings. As a writer in the *Guide* wrote, 'Of course there are mean exceptions, but there is not the wholesale dissimulation, misrepresentation, tricking, underhandedness and deception upon which it seems necessary for other trades and professions to thrive. No dollars which go into the farmer's pocket make any other man poorer.'[21] As Partridge put it later, 'Without wishing to adopt a "holier than thou" attitude towards the individual capitalist,—the fact that I never had a chance to be one without deliberately sacrificing my self-respect, probably being the only reason why I'm not one.'[22]

The moralism of the Grain Growers derived much from pietistic and sectarian Protestantism, which was also an element in British radicalism of

---

[19] 'Our Paper', *GGG*, June 1908. Emphasis added.
[20] Ibid.
[21] J. R. Messenger, 'Farming as a Profession', *GGG*, 11 Oct. 1911, p. 11.
[22] E. A. Partridge, *A War on Poverty* (Winnipeg 1925), p. 51.

the period. Outstanding leaders of prairie radicalism from the 1890s onwards, both north and south of the border, came under this influence early in life, and 'exhibited in their public careers an unmistakable evangelical style'.[23]

For economic analysis, the most congenial thinker was Henry George, who was quoted repeatedly in the *Guide*, which printed one of his articles and distributed his books. Henry George, "the Sage of San Francisco", was himself a frontier thinker and first published his ideas in 1879, when California was undergoing its wheat staple boom. His analysis was derived from Ricardo and argued that, with land in fixed supply, landowners took a growing share of the economic surplus and robbed both worker and employer. The remedy was simple: shift all taxes on to the owners of land, especially urban land. Henry George's doctrine, conceived on the wheat frontier (on its "coast" rather than in the "interior"), found an audience back in Europe, where it reinvigorated radicalism and provided both a moral and an analytical lever for its attack on the British land system, both rural and urban.

At first sight his appeal to the wheat farmers of Canada is puzzling. Why should the enemy of the unearned increment appeal to a movement of owner–farmers who pinned their hopes on rising land values? His message fell on willing ears because of its intrinsic radicalism. Prairie farmers did not regard themselves as land monopolists. There was plenty of land for the taking. They resented the speculative holding of land, which drove up its price for working farmers, made it more difficult for them to expand, and, by slowing down settlement, held back development and increased taxes. George's single tax on land speculators was an alternative to the hated tariffs. George was a free trader, and so were the farmers. He provided a text for a populist international of no mean influence. David Lloyd George in Britain shared a good part of the mental world of E. A. Partridge in Canada. He also believed in rural virtue, spoke like a preacher and embraced the tax doctrines of his San Francisco namesake. His "People's Budget" of 1909 was at once a breakthrough in welfare policy, an attack on privilege and a set of land taxes that were founded on the principles of the other George (it was also a budget of naval rearmament). The *Guide* followed the fortunes of English Edwardian Liberals sympathetically and once reprinted a two-page interview with the Welsh statesman.[24]

Grain Grower radicalism was eager to harness politics to bring about change, to use democracy to challenge the interests. This faith in

---

[23] K. D. Bicha, 'Prairie Radicals: A Common Pietism', *Journal of Church and State*, vol. 18 (1976), p. 1.

[24] Lloyd George: Offer, *Property and Politics*, chs. 19–24; *GGG*, 31 July 1912, p. 7, 11, 18.

democracy is shown in the women's pages, which demanded votes and campaigned for equal property rights for women in the homestead. Free-trading prairie radicalism differed from the mercantilist and nativist populism of the coast, which sought to exclude foreign goods and alien races, a populism that took its strongest forms in urban Australia and on Canada's Pacific shores.

It is easy to get carried away by the earnest, good-natured quality of the farmers' radicalism. In reality the movement contained a number of contradictions. For one thing, prairie farming was not a romantic vocation but a hard grind. Its immediate interests were prosaic, material and tangible, not abstract and ideal. So gradually the icons shifted. "The Labourer's Friend" fell from the masthead. Marianne gave way to pictures of horses and tractors, and blunt political cartoons. The Grain Growers faced the inherent difficulty of radicalism, that of keeping the rebel spirit alive. Radicalism is fed by grievances, and success undermines it. Advertisements and features in the *Guide* recorded a rising prosperity. The *Guide* itself, in its glossy format, was a consumer artefact, its cheap price of a dollar a year supported by its hefty advertising.

By the end of the Edwardian period, after half a generation of intensive settlement and development, the wheat-exporting machine of the Canadian interior was in place and ready to work at full capacity. In the process the Canadian interior became a large society, quite stable at its fertile centre, pioneering at its fringes, prosperous, hardy, patriotic. In the Edwardian years the wheat farmer was much more important to Canada than he was to the United States. Perhaps this is why prairie farmers achieved more as a group than their American mentors. Other grain-growing frontiers underwent a similar expansion, but in none of them, in neither Argentina nor Australia, did the wheat farmers acquire such a prominent role in politics, or form such a solid society. By 1910 the farmers felt able to extend their political activities from the provincial to the national level; and this requires an account of the relative position of interior and coast.

IV

Although Canada, Australia, New Zealand and the United States exported primary products to pay for their imports, their wealth in the Edwardian period was already focused on the towns. The staple exporters were also becoming industrial powers. In terms of industrial output per head, Canada, Australia and New Zealand came second only to the United States and Britain, and ahead of Germany and France.[25]

[25] Output of manufactures per head of population in 1913: USA 100, UK 90, Canada 84, Australia 75, Belgium 73, New Zealand 66, Germany 64, France 46, Argentina 23: W. Arthur Lewis, *Growth and Fluctuations, 1870–1913* (1978), table 7.1, p. 163.

The staple interpretation of economic growth regards the prosperity of the coast as a function of the development of the interior. This interpretation came under attack in the 1960s and 1970s during a period of revision in the economic history of North America and Australia. In Canada critics calculated that the wheat boom only accounted for a small proportion of the growth per head during the Edwardian period. In Australia Noel Butlin stressed the central role of urban development and of manufacturing industry, in what was becoming by the 1880s an urban society. Mancur Olson has questioned the importance of exports to overseas development by pointing out that the increase in British demand for wheat only accounted for some 6 per cent of the increased output of the exporting countries between 1895 and 1914.[26]

Olson's procedure, however, is misleading. Only some 15 per cent or so of all wheat entered international trade. The largest wheat exporters (United States, Russia, India) had large domestic populations, and a long-range interior inter-regional trade in wheat. Of the increase in wheat imports to Europe (the largest international export market) Britain accounted for about one-third.[27] Olson's argument also takes no account of the importance of wheat exports for particular countries. In Canada a leading authority recently quoted one of the fathers of the "staples theory" with approval: 'The most fundamental single characteristic of the period [1895–1920] was a high rate of investment induced by improved expectations of profit from the exploitation of natural resources . . . Overwhelmingly most important were the wheat lands of the Prairie Provinces.'[28]

The capital *inflows* into Canada were enormous; between 1910 and 1914 they amounted to almost 15 per cent of the Gross National Product. Exports during these years were correspondingly low, a little more than 15 per cent of GNP. But soon the investment began to pay off. Exports soared during the war years (reaching more than a third of GNP in 1917) and settled down at 22–5 per cent during the 1920s. Wheat exports quadrupled between 1900 and 1910, and quadrupled again between 1910 and 1930.[29] In Australia exports came to about 22 per cent of GNP before the war, of which wool and wheat together accounted for some 50 per cent.[30]

---

[26] Ch. 10 n. 1 above; M. Olson, Jr., 'The United Kingdom and the World Market in Wheat and Other Primary Products, 1870–1914', *Explorations in Economic History*, vol. 11 (1974).

[27] Bennett, 'Per Capita Wheat Consumption', pp. 302–3.

[28] W. A. Mackintosh, *The Economic Background of Dominion—Provincial Relations* (Toronto 1964), p. 41, quoted by M. C. Urquhart, 'New Estimates of Gross National Product, Canada, 1870–1926: Some Implications for Canadian Development', in S. L. Engerman and R. E. Gallman (eds.), *Long-term Factors in American Economic Growth* (Chicago 1986), p. 32.

[29] Urquhart, 'New Estimates', tables 2.11, 2.12, pp. 33–4, 38; Leacy, (ed.), *Historical Statistics of Canada*, ser. M305.

[30] N. G. Butlin, *Bicentennial Diary* (Brisbane 1988), p. 229. The figure provided is for GDP, and I have increased it by 10 per cent to convert to GNP.

There is no question that the coast grew faster than the interior, that the towns increased their population faster than the countryside, although only in Australia did they exceed one-half of the population before 1914. Subsequent research has reinstated the staple. In Canada wheat is once again at the centre. Wheat's contribution to per-capita growth in Canada was high, with estimates of between 20 per cent and more than 50 per cent during the Edwardian boom. What some critics of staple theory miss is the great spurts of *absolute* growth that staple investment booms made possible. The ability to absorb large numbers of migrants in a short period of time while raising incomes all round is the hallmark of the staple economy, or, to be more precise, of its investment phase. About 700,000 migrants remained in Canada between 1901 and 1911 (the population was 5.3 million in 1901). The economy grew at a pace that had few parallels: 7.7 per cent a year between 1901 and 1911, and 9.5 per cent a year in the following decade. The Australian boom of the 1880s was a period of great urban expansion, but this was underpinned by rural investment, railway investment and other public works, which ultimately relied on borrowing from overseas, which only the primary sector could repay.[31] In the process of staple-driven growth, the coast prospered more than the interior, but even the original physiocrats, the French *philosophes* of the eighteenth century, expected the agrarian surplus to end up in the towns.

The primary sector produced a declining proportion—about a third of national income in Australia, and about the same in Canada in 1900–10— and directly employed about the same share of the population.[32] The driving force in Australian, Canadian and New Zealand development was foreign investment. Growth ran ahead when borrowing was high. To pay off external borrowings it was necessary to export, and the primary sector continued to provide the bulk of the exports.

To argue otherwise is to contemplate a colony without a staple export, with little immigration, and with much reduced investment from abroad. Such societies existed in some outlying regions and provide a glimpse of settlement *sans* staples. The French agricultural economy in Quebec and the pastoral Boers in Transvaal both suggest the flavour of such societies, though they are not pure cases as both were touched by past or current staples and had some links with world trade. Staple exports energized and populated coast economies, and the prospect of staple riches generated explosions of growth and attracted the costly investment in public works

[31] W. L. Marr and D. G. Paterson, *Canada: An Economic History* (Toronto 1980), ch. 2, provides an outline of the theoretical considerations. Growth rates, ibid., p. 19. For the most recent overview, with new data, see Urquhart, 'New Estimates', and G. Wright, 'Comment', in Engerman and Gallman (eds.), *Long-term Factors*, pp. 771–8.

[32] N. G. Butlin, 'Australian National Accounts, 1788–1983', *Source Papers in Economic History*, no. 6 (Canberra 1985), table 8; Marr and Paterson, *Canada: An Economic History*, p. 22.

which provided the means of colonizing the interiors. The dependence on staples continues. Primary products still dominate the exports of Canada and Australia today.

V

The trade of the coast economies was not symmetrical. They were keen to export, but from the 1880s onwards protected their new industries against imports. For Canada, with the world's largest industrial power on her doorstep, tariffs appeared vital. Australia was well protected by distance, but most colonies (and New Zealand as well) imposed some kind of protective tariff, and even New South Wales, which had a policy of free trade, used tariffs for revenue.

Tariff policy helped to concentrate population and economic activity on the coast. The societies were young but the towns were dynamic and large. Melbourne, Sydney and Toronto were Victorian cities of the first rank. Between the 1880s and the First World War they shared the formative social and political experiences of urban and industrial growth typical of the times. They struggled with slum housing, cut-throat competition, unemployment and "sweating", the rise of corporate capitalism and its clashes with small business and organized labour. For ambitious young men these were issues that led to greater things. Two future Prime Ministers, Mackenzie King in Canada and Billy Hughes in Australia, made their mark in the crucible of industrial relations. Political leaders were drawn from among lawyers or union activists, from the towns and not the outback.

Economic policy was formed on the coasts. The choices presented themselves in similar fashion everywhere, but the most coherent response was Canada's "National Policy" of 1879. Canada's first priority was population growth and internal colonization, to breathe life and substance into its long, thin body. Its National Policy used industrial tariffs and railroad construction to stimulate the development and growth of a balanced economy.

Some elements of the policy were inimical to the interests of the metropolis and others discriminated against the newly opened interior. It forced development into an east–west orientation that was more costly than the north–south lines of communication. Staple producers had to pay a surcharge on their manufactured inputs. The "Old Country" was shut out of the markets of an important trading partner. Although Britain later got a preferential tariff, this did not improve her position in the Canadian market, to which she provided about one-quarter of the imports. And discrimination against the prairies continued to rankle there. Prairie producers continuously sought to bypass the coast and forge a direct link with their market. In the course of their struggle with the Winnipeg Grain Exchange, the Grain Growers' Company received a helping hand from the Scottish Co-operative Wholesale Society.[33]

Canada did not pluck the National Policy out of the air. The coast was bound to contest its appointed role as economic vassal to Britain, as its agrarian provider and the buyer of its manufactured goods. Theoretical foundations for a policy of industrialization and balanced development were laid down in the United States, the first large coast economy, by Alexander Hamilton in the 1790s and by Matthew Carey in the 1820s. America redoubled its commitment to industrial protection with the McKinley tariff of 1891 and the Dingley tariff of 1898. Julius Vogel's policies in New Zealand in the 1870s followed the same principles, while Victoria, the most dynamic Australian colony in the 1870s and 1880s, took a similar line. New South Wales did not, but did just as well, perhaps even better. The comparison is provocative but not compelling, since New South Wales was better endowed with land and minerals. Although industrial protection figured large in Australian debates, the Australian tariffs appear to have served largely to raise revenues and to make borrowing possible. Government spending on public works (which was very high) was more important as a spur to development than industrial protection.[34] It played an important role in Canada too.

Paradoxically, even as it shut the doors on British exports, the Canadian National Policy reinforced the imperial bond. Canada's separation from the United States was an economic and geographical anomaly that became more apparent as the country prospered. It required a forceful justification, and this was provided by the Union Jack. For Toronto, Ottawa and Montreal, separation was the foundation of their economic, social and political standing. Without the British connection, the Canadian interior might seek another coast and metropolis in the United States. Toronto and Montreal would lose their primacy while Ottawa would vanish entirely. So, even as it shut out British exports, the Canadian coast became more ardently imperialist. For Australia and New Zealand the imperial bond had a different quality. Here the threat was to national security. In the shadow of a rising Japan, the imperial connection was the bulwark of defence. In their oceanic isolation, the colonies of the South Pacific also looked to Britain to prop up their uncertain sense of nationality. For both Australasia and Canada, Britain remained a prime purchaser of their exports and the preferred source of capital and migrants.

[33] *GGG*, Aug. 1908, p. 9; Sept. 1908, p. 41; Wood, *Farmers' Movement*, p. 190.
[34] C. H. Chomley, *Protection in Canada and Australia* (1904); G. D. Patterson, *The Tariff in the Australian Colonies, 1856–1900* (Melbourne 1968), ch. 14; N. G. Butlin, 'Colonial Socialism in Australia, 1860–1900', in H. G. J. Aitken (ed.), *The State and Economic Growth* (New York 1959).

The National Policy succeeded in its aim of establishing an industrial economy in Canada. Between 1870 and 1915 Canadian manufacturing expanded more than sixfold, and, because of the tariff, it came to reflect the American economy, albeit on a much smaller scale. American firms established "branch plants" in Canada in order to get around the tariff. American craft unions also came over the border. All the main sectors of industry were there: iron and steel, engineering, leather, food and drink, transport and clothing, together with the myriad goods and services of a modern urban economy. London, Brantford, Hamilton, Toronto and Oshawa in Ontario became important industrial centres, and another one clustered in Montreal. Canada produced most of her own capital goods and also had a good range of industries to process her timber, grain and non-ferrous metals. Brantford, Ontario, was the centre of the great agricultural implement firm of Massey-Harris, which supplied the west with ploughs and binders and exported all over the world. 'The exploitation of staples set up forces which, in terms of national income, gave rise to a growth of manufacturing. This, in the long run, diminished the importance of the staples themselves.'[35]

In Canada the farmers felt confident enough to venture into national politics. This brought them into collision with the National Policy and with the urban and manufacturing interests of the coast. Their challenge to the policy began with the Prime Minister's tour of the Western Provinces in the summer of 1910. In town after town Sir Wilfrid Laurier heard the same refrain. Farmers rejected the protective aspect of the tariff, 'which compels them to contribute a large percentage of the products of their labour to the privileged and protected classes'.[36] When the harvest was in, the farmers took the message direct to Ottawa. Eight hundred farmers descended on the town on 15 December 1910. On the morning of the next day, they met in front of the Grand Opera House and marched four abreast up Parliament Hill and into the House of Commons, whose members gave it up for the occasion. Special trams conveyed them to a reception at the Governor-General's residence. Laurier, at the head of a decaying government and in search of a platform issue, staked his fortunes on the farmers.

The "Siege of Ottawa" filled the farmers with a sense of their power. 'Although their clothing was not of the latest cut, nor their whiskers trimmed in the most approved style, they realized the part they were playing in the upbuilding of the nation, and their feeling of dignity did not

[35] Marr and Paterson, *Canada: An Economic History*, p. 384.
[36] Memorial of Manitoba Grain Growers' Association to Laurier, Brandon, Manitoba, 18 July 1910, in E. Porritt, *The Revolt in Canada against the New Feudalism* (1911), p. 186.

desert them.'[37] The following year Laurier went to the country on a grain growers' platform.

The Canadian general election of 1911 was a confrontation between coast and interior. It was not the first. The American election of 1896 on the silver question had similarly set the interior against the coast. The issue this time was "reciprocity"—a proposal for mutual tariff reductions between the United States and Canada, on a list of primary products. For the farmers, the attraction was twofold. First, it promised a modest reduction in the cost of agricultural machinery. Farmers compared the prices of ploughs, binders, drills and wagons with much lower ones south of the border. They alleged that Massey-Harris charged them 40 per cent more for binders than it did on those it exported to Britain. A greater attraction was access to the American grain market. In the Edwardian period this had become a leading price-making market, where prices often rose higher than in Britain. What the farmers did not fully consider was that American prices were high *because* of the tariff, and that their entry might well bring them down.

A great deal was at stake for the coast as well. Its privileged access to the interior was in jeopardy, and with it the very foundation of national identity. It did not help the farmers that American senators expressed annexationist sentiments in their own debates on reciprocity. The manufacturers rallied against reciprocity and mobilized the press. The Liberals in Ontario and Quebec split, with large and important groups throwing their weight against reciprocity. Although few manufactured goods fell under the proposed agreement, the manufacturers perceived a threat of the interior attaching itself to another coast. For the railway and shipping industries reciprocity appeared as a dire threat. It seemed that Canada's very existence was called into question.

It is easy to make too much of the economic issues. Other questions were also at stake; the government was stale and a swing of the pendulum was overdue. In any case, it was not very large. A single-member constituency system magnifies shifts in voter preference. Laurier was defeated, but the Liberals only lost 2.8 per cent of their support relative to 1908. The voters' reaction was very diverse. A recent study suggests that the Liberals might have done even worse without reciprocity. On the whole, only farmers seem to have voted with any consistency.[38] Be that as it may, for wrong reasons or right, Canada rejected the farmers' platform and confirmed the hegemony of the coast in settler societies, which was already established in Australia and the United States.

---

[37] [G. F. Chipman], *The Siege of Ottawa* (Winnipeg 1910), pp. 6–10; Porritt, *Revolt in Canada*, ch. 12.

[38] R. Johnston and M. Percy, 'Reciprocity, Imperial Sentiment and Party Politics in the 1911 Election', *Canadian Journal of Political Science*, vol. 13 (1980), p. 712; R. Johnston, M. Percy and K. H. Norrie, 'Reciprocity and the Canadian General Election of 1911', *Explorations in Economic History*, vol. 19 (1982).

FIG. 11.4. 'The Parting of the Ways', *Grain Growers' Guide*, 13 Sept. 1911

ASIAN LABOUR ON THE PACIFIC RIM: THE STRUGGLE FOR EXCLUSION, 1860–1907

AUSTRALIA, New Zealand, British Columbia and California were far away from the North Sea and from the Great Power rivalries of western Europe. Their young economies, however, depended to a greater or lesser extent on European capital and European markets. The Dominion societies looked to Britain for their identities, their institutions and their way of life. To preserve this identity they followed a policy of racial exclusion. The next three chapters consider the costs of racial exclusion and its benefits, how it affected the strategic balance in the North Sea, and how it reinforced the imperial bond in the last years before the First World War.

I

In the late-Victorian period the Pacific rim supported some of the world's wealthiest societies. In contrast, non-white peoples of the Pacific islands and the Asian mainland were poor. The settlers' wealth was concentrated on the coast, in Vancouver, Seattle, San Francisco, Sydney, Melbourne and Auckland, but for the impetus of development and growth they relied on natural resources, on minerals, timber, fish and farming. The Pacific rim has uneven terrains, so it is misleading to compare population densities on its Asian, American and Australian coasts. But the differential of farmland endowment between the poor and wealthy countries (table 6.2) also held roughly true for the natural resources of the Pacific rim. A Japanese statesman pointed out in 1907 that British Columbia alone was twice as large as Japan, possessed boundless resources, but contained only 250,000 people, or a little more than one person for every two square miles.[1]

The bounty of land, in its widest sense, made the settlers wealthy. Not only was their endowment of land perhaps tenfold that of the peasants on the other side of their ocean, but it also allowed them to price their export staples higher than the Asian peasant.

W. A. Lewis argues that prices of "tropical" staples were lower than those of the "temperate" countries of recent settlement. As he puts it, 'If tea had been a temperate instead of a tropical crop, its price would have been perhaps four times as high as it actually was. And if wool had been a

---

[1] As reported by R. Lemieux, *Report of the Minister of Labor of his Mission to Japan on the Subject of the Influx of Oriental Laborers in the Province of British Columbia* (Ottawa, January 1908), p. 10; Lemieux Papers, PAC, MG 27 II D10, fo. 1056.

tropical instead of a temperate crop, it would have been had for perhaps one-fourth of the ruling price.'[2]

In the tropics the peasant can grow either export crops for cash or, alternatively, his own food. To induce peasants into exports, the cash reward must match or exceed the value of the food they can grow for their own consumption. On the world market, tropical staples fetched the value of the food that could have been produced on the same land. Tea, coffee, sugar, jute, rubber and other tropical commodities cost the wages of the labour that produced them. The price of labour in the tropics was low, because each labourer had so little land for his own subsistence, as an alternative to producing for the world market. It was this, the "opportunity cost" of labour, that determined its price. Perhaps this is overstated. In conditions of land hunger, land was unlikely to be costless, so both subsistence land and plantations supported considerable rents. In the temperate zones labourers took a large share of the rent of natural resources. In the tropics it went largely to employers, money-lenders and tax collectors. Most tropical labourers still chose to feed themselves rather than work for export, and could only be forced into export crops or plantation labour by rent, taxes and debt.

Let us carry this argument a step further. Sugar and wheat, two of the main traded commodities, were grown in both temperate and tropical countries. Other things being equal, there was only one price for sugar and wheat, the world market price. When there is only one price, then the difference in income between the Indian ryot, the German Bauer and the Californian farmer comes down to the endowment of factors available to each, and, in the final count, to the amount of land at their disposal.

Land is fixed, but man can move. The shortage of hands on the Pacific rim could easily be made up from Asia. But the labour market was not free, and could not come into equilibrium. Tropical and temperate labour markets were kept strictly apart.

In other words, the wages of labour, the profits of capital and the rent of land in the temperate settlements were not merely a matter of unequal "endowment". Factor endowment is not entirely in the hands of Providence. The exclusion of Asian labour from temperate lands appeared as a necessary condition of individual prosperity in the societies of the Pacific rim. To put it more bluntly, temperate settlement was a land grab. Europeans arrived there first, but it was difficult to entice more of them to come. Apart from periodic gold rushes, British Columbia, California, New Zealand and Australia offered only marginal enticements to Europeans, but were quite attractive to Asians, although distance and cost remained formidable obstacles. Migrants from the Old Country were often in short supply and most of the population growth arose from natural increase.

---

[2] Lewis, *Growth and Fluctuations*, p. 189.

From very early on, the land-grabbing societies, having wrested their territories from aboriginal occupiers, set about to secure their possession from what they perceived to be land-hungry Asians.

Between 1861 and 1901 Canada lost more migrants than it gained, and grew to 5.3 million by natural increase alone. After the 1880s Australia stagnated too. The late 1890s, with the upturn of wheat prices, saw the beginning of a period of extraordinary development in Canada. Immigration was at a low ebb in 1896. Clifford Sifton, the Minister of Interior, set out to get immigrants by fair means or foul and extended his reach well beyond Britain and northern Europe. Sifton established a network of offices in the United States and Britain and his agents ranged widely in Europe. He paid bounties to steamship lines and commissions to agents. Germany and France discouraged emigration and did not permit the agents to tempt their citizens: every soldier and every bayonet counted in the European balance of power. Sifton's agents evaded French law and operated a line in east European migrants through Germany. Sifton's ambition was to people the plains, and he placed economic opportunity ahead of ethnic purity. In a memorable phrase, he declaimed, 'When I speak of quality—on the question of immigration, a stalwart peasant in a sheepskin coat, born on the soil, whose forefathers had been farmers for ten generations, with a stout wife and half a dozen children, is good quality.'[3] Peasants in sheepskin coats came from the eastern marches of the Austro-Hungarian Empire and from Russia. "Other Europeans" made up some 13 per cent of the Canadian population in 1911. In the prairie provinces this rose to about a third. About a tenth of the inhabitants of the prairies in 1911 were Slavs by country of birth.[4] By the time Sifton resigned in 1905 the annual arrivals had swelled more than eightfold; in its peak year of 1913 immigration exceeded 400,000. Some three million arrived in Canada between 1896 and the First World War, helping to boost its population from almost five to eight million.[5]

Australians experienced a similar anxiety about their empty spaces. T. A. Coghlan (the New South Wales official statistician) wrote about Canadian policy with admiration and envy. In a succession of articles and pamphlets around the turn of the century he rang an alarm over the stagnation of Australia's population, with immigration moribund and the birth-rate in decline. New South Wales appointed a Royal Commission on the Decline of the Birth Rate, of which Coghlan was both an instigator and a member. The Commission publicized Australia's population anxieties at home and abroad. Its conclusions stated starkly,

[3] Quoted by J. H. Gray, *Boomtime: Peopleing the Canadian Prairies* (Saskatoon, Saskatchewan 1979), p. 31; Canadian immigration policy: M. F. Timlin, 'Canada's Immigration Policy, 1896–1910', *Canadian Journal of Economics and Political Science*, vol. 26 (1960).

[4] W. B. Hurd, *Racial Origins and Nativity of the Canadian People*, Census Monograph no. 4 (Ottawa 1937), tables 27, 32, pp. 240–1, 250.

[5] Leacy, *Historical Statistics of Canada* , tables A1, A350.

The future of the Commonwealth, and especially the possibility of maintaining a "White Australia", depend on the question whether we shall be able to people the vast areas of the continent which are capable of supporting a large population. This can only be done by restoring and maintaining a high rate of natural increase, or by immigration on a large scale, or by both these means of recruiting posterity.

It quoted Coghlan's words:

Immigration has practically ceased to be an important factor, the maintenance and increase of population depending upon the birth-rate alone, a rate seriously diminished and still diminishing. No people has ever become great under such conditions or, having gained greatness, has remained great for any lengthened period.

But Australia insisted, more strongly than Canada even, on settling only 'desirable immigrants' in her empty lands.[6] Theodore Roosevelt, President of the United States, told a Canadian visitor,

The condition of Australia is really causing me some concern. There is a fine country, the birth rate of which among the white people is decreasing. I look on that as most unfortunate. If the population of the country is not increasing and strengthening, how can it defend itself against the blackbird and the yellowskin? I think it would be better for Australia, seeing that she cannot get the peoples of the northern part of Europe, to take Italians, or do as we are doing in Hawaii, bring in Portuguese, but bring in white races and people the land with them.[7]

For the time being, the United States had fewer compunctions about "suitability". American cities took in many millions of migrants from all parts of Europe, from Italy and Greece, from Russia and Poland, and set them to work on the lowest jobs in their industries. More than five million Americans in 1910 had been born in eastern and southern Europe. Although the migrants met a good deal of opposition locally, business and government were keen to have them.

II

Ships on the Asian side of the Pacific were crammed with migrants, but not, unlike Atlantic migrant ships, with women and children. Their holds were crowded with "coolies", male contract labourers from India and China, bound for work in sugar and rubber plantations, and in mines all over the tropics: the Indians to the Caribbean, Natal, Mauritius, Malaya and Fiji, the Chinese mostly to Malaya. Young men migrated under a

---

[6] T. A. Coghlan, *Report on Immigration with Special Reference to Canada*, Intelligence Dept. New South Wales, Bulletin no. 3 (Sydney 1905); New South Wales, *Decline of the Birth Rate and the Mortality of Infants in New South Wales. Royal Commission Report*, vol. 1 (Sydney 1904), p. 53; N. Hicks, *This Sin and Scandal: Australia's Population Debate, 1891– 1911* (Canberra 1978), pp. 84–92, 139–46.

[7] KD, Washington, 31 Jan. 1908, PAC G 2183, fos. 61–2.

contract of indenture for a period of three or five years, remitted a good part of their wages home to pay their fares and support their families, and finally returned there at the end of their contracts. But many stayed. By 1922 some eight million Chinese lived abroad and the number of Indians exceeded four million. Asian migrant labourers outnumbered the combined populations of Australia and Canada. Almost 16 million Indians emigrated between 1871 and 1915; almost 12 million returned. 'The numbers leaving India and China together, for all destinations, must have exceeded the number emigrating from Europe.' Most of the migration was over relatively short ranges between individual countries in South Asia, but some found its way to the Caribbean, South Africa, South America, Hawaii and the Pacific seaboard of North America. Of the one million Japanese who migrated after the mid-1880s, most went to temperate lands.[8] Most of the tropical exports came out of plantations or mines worked by contract labour. Lewis's theory of the factoral terms of trade has to be modified accordingly. The price of tea was not set by the forgone crop of the peasants' plot, but by the subsistence requirements of the landless labourer, often single, who was the bulwark of plantations, and by the rents and profits of his employers.

Without this supply of labour in bondage, Europe and the United States might have had to pay more for their sugar, and saved themselves a fortune in dentists' bills. Sugar consumption increased more than fourfold in Britain between the 1830s and the 1890s to the amazing level of over 70 lb. per head a year. Tea, coffee, cocoa and sugar accounted for almost a fifth of British food imports before the war. In his addiction to sugared tea and to jam on his bread, the British workman became as bound to the tropical part of his empire as he was to the temperate side for his loaf of bread.[9]

The Atlantic and Asian migrations did not mix. In a few regions the two classes of labour worked side by side, but almost never in direct competition. Where they worked together, whites excluded other workers from the privileges of responsibility and skill (with pay at metropolitan levels and higher). In some cases the duties were similar, the status not. In India, according to a Canadian traveller, trains that carried the mail had Scottish engineers, while ordinary trains were driven by Indians. Station masters were British, as were some of the conductors. Wage differentials reflected, there as elsewhere, not the functional requirements of the job, but the power to exclude.[10] Such parallel labour systems existed on a large scale in South Africa, where "free" white skilled men worked with black

---

[8] Lewis, *Growth and Fluctuations*, pp. 185–91.

[9] M&D, ch. 12, table 6, pp. 356–7; Rew, 'Food Supply', p. 104. A large proportion of British sugar supplies came from Germany.

[10] KD, India, 17 Jan. 1909, G 2215, fo. 194; comparative table of Chinese and Indian railway wages, G 2215, fo. 432.

contract miners for a wage some ten times higher; it existed in Queensland, where Pacific Islanders (Kanakas) worked in the colony's sugar industry. Of the quarter of a million or so seamen employed on British ships in 1905, about a third were foreigners, and about half of these were Asians, mostly Indian Moslems ("lascars"), Goans and Chinese.[11] The two currents of migrants also merged in the American dependency of Hawaii, whose sugar industry was largely worked by Japanese. They arrived as contract labourers in the 1880s and the 1890s and continued to provide the bulk of the labour force. To prevent them from organizing, the planters periodically imported labourers from Portugal and Spain.[12]

The gold rushes of the 1850s attracted tens of thousands of Chinese to California and Australia, and more came to help construct the continental railways in the United States and Canada in the 1870s and early 1880s. Starting as prospectors and contract labourers, they found themselves niches as market gardeners, cooks, laundrymen, domestic servants and furniture-makers. After the 1880s small numbers of Japanese also began to arrive in North America, where they worked as fishermen and labourers. Indians came after the turn of the century, mostly Sikhs from the Punjab. At its highest the total number of Asians in Australasia and North America did not exceed a quarter of a million, the vast majority of whom worked as manual labourers.[13]

The response to their presence was out of all proportion to their numbers and has remained so to the present day. Scores of academic dissertations, articles and books have been written about the Asian attempt to gain a foothold in the temperate zone.[14] The pattern of this reaction was set in its first decade, when the Chinese joined in the rush to

[11] Navigation Conference—Merchant Shipping Legislation—Report of a Conference between Representatives of the UK, Australia and NZ; Australia, Commonwealth PP no. 15, vol. III (1907–8), App. B, p. 171. The figures were:

Merchant seamen	263,686
Foreigners	83,194
Asians	43,483

[12] E. Beechert, 'Labour Relations in the Hawaiian Sugar Industry, 1850–1937', in B. Albert and A. Graves (eds.), *Crisis and Change in the International Sugar Economy, 1860–1914* (Norwich and Edinburgh 1984).

[13] Numbers of Asians on the Pacific Rim.

1.	Australia (1907)	44,075
2.	New Zealand (1901)	3,092
3.	Canada (1911)	43,017
4.	USA (foreign born, 1910)	130,003
	TOTAL	220,187

Sources: (1–2) P. E. Lewin, 'Appendix', in R. Jebb, 'The Imperial Problem of Asiatic Immigration', *Journal of the Royal Society of Arts*, vol. 56 (1908), 'Population Table', p. 604; (3) Hurd, *Origins and Nativity*, table 5, p. 225; (4) *Statistical History of the US*, ser. A108, A115.

[14] C. A. Price, *The Great White Walls Are Built: Restrictive Immigration to North America and Australasia, 1836–1888* (Canberra 1974), is an excellent introduction.

the goldfields of California and Australia. Sometimes the newcomers were treated with curiosity and good humour. But soon the atmosphere darkened. Exclusion leagues formed and agitated, and the authorities, fearful of unrest and mindful of votes, added official and legal sanctions to informal persecution. Not content with economic arguments, working-class orators and leaders sought to justify exclusion and restriction by depicting the Asians and Pacific Islanders as less than fully human, as a source of contamination, a danger to civic and sexual morality, to health and racial integrity. Educated speakers and writers reinforced these notions with the doctrines of struggle and survival derived from social Darwinism, but middle-class opinion ranged more widely and also contained some dissenting voices: on the one hand, those of businessmen and landowners who wanted migrants as cheap labour and an economic stimulant; on the other, those of individuals who felt unease about the morality of racial discrimination.

Australia went through the whole cycle for the first time during the 1850s. Chinese contract labourers had arrived in Victoria even before the gold was discovered and their numbers swelled considerably when the rush began in earnest. By 1857 the 25,400 Chinese in Victoria made up 6.2 per cent of the population, almost 10 per cent of the males, and almost a fifth of the people in the mining districts. First bemused encounters soon made way to systematic harassment and violence, which reached its peak in organized assaults on Chinese mining camps on the Buckland River, Ararat and Lambing Flat (in New South Wales). Juries failed to convict for acts of violence against Chinese. In response to popular demand the government of Victoria restricted Chinese immigration by means of a limit on the number of passengers carried per ton of shipping. Chinese already resident had to pay a high license fee. Those who could not pay lost the protection of the law. Goldfield thugs molested and dispossessed them. In California the reaction was more violent. Chinese miners were expelled from many goldfields and frequently assaulted; scores, if not hundreds, were killed.[15]

In the 1850s the labour movement was undeveloped and the diggers were anything but proletarians. Nevertheless, there is no mistaking the popular, indeed populist character of the anti-Asian agitations—populist, in the sense of common people uniting in the face of a common menace. Labour and progressive movements began to organize and act in the 1870s and from then on they gave the lead in the anti-Asian agitations. For a few brief years in the late 1870s the Irishman Dennis Kearney created a racialist platform for his egalitarian California Workingmen's Party. In

---

[15] K. Cronin, *Colonial Casualties: Chinese in Early Victoria* (Melbourne 1982), ch. 3 and table 3, p. 140; A. Markus, *Fear and Hatred: Purifying Australia and California, 1850–1901* (Sydney 1979), pt. 1.

Australia one of the first serious blows for Trade Unionism was the Seamens' Strike of 1879, which achieved the removal of Asian crewmen from Australian coastal shipping. From then on, the various organs of the labour movement each used its own methods: the trade unions by strikes and boycotts, the political arm by demanding restrictive and exclusionary legislation, journalists and writers by evoking fear and loathing. The pattern became clear: labour was the unbending champion of "White Australia".

By the end of the Civil War almost 60,000 Chinese lived in California, where they made up more than 10 per cent of the population in 1870. They continued to suffer from incidental brutality and casual assault and from occasional murders. San Francisco was the most unionized city in the United States. There, as in Brisbane, Australia, organized labour carried the flag of oriental exclusion. Kearney's Workingmen's Party demanded 'the Chinese must go', and in 1882 the President of the United States signed a Chinese Exclusion Act which brought the immigration to an end. Heavy fines and landing fees achieved the same effect in Australia about the same time. Similar legislation in Canada reduced entries to a trickle.

The most radical of working-class leaders did not flinch from exclusion. Henry George, by far the most influential radical of the 1880s and 1890s, addressed an anti-oriental meeting in 1869, in which he said,

The 60,000 or 100,000 Mongolians on our Western Coast are the thin edge of the wedge which has for its base the 500,000,000 of Eastern Asia . . . the Chinaman can live where stronger than he would starve. Give him fair play and this quality enables him to drive out the stronger races . . . [Unless Chinese immigration is checked] the youngest home of the nations must in its early manhood follow the path and meet the doom of Babylon, Nineveh and Rome . . . Here plain to the eye of him who chooses to see are dragon's teeth [which will] spring up armed men marshalled for civil war.

Victor Berger, leader of the American Socialist Party, insisted that the United States and Canada must be kept 'White Man's Countries' and feared racial contamination. He was willing to fight 'for wife and children' and the party endorsed this racial view. Jack London, the radical California novelist, is quoted as saying, 'I am first of all a white man and only then a socialist.'[16] In Canada, J. S. Woodsworth, one of the leading proponents of "the Social Passion" and later in life leader of North America's only effective socialist party, wrote of oriental immigration with distinct hostility. Apart from the International Workers of the World (a

---

[16] R. Daniels, *The Politics of Prejudice: The Anti-Japanese Movement in California and the Struggle for Japanese Exclusion*, University of California Publications in History, vol. 71 (Berkeley, Calif. 1962), ch. 2 (Henry George, p. 69; Jack London, Victor Berger, p. 30).

small radical group), all Australian socialist parties were uncompromisingly opposed to Asian immigration.[17]

From its very beginning, the Australian Labor Party placed "White Australia" high, if not highest, among its principles. William Lane, editor of the *Boomerang* and the *Worker*, an indefatigable militant socialist, was also 'a fanatical racist'. After the defeat of the Queensland shearers' strike of 1891, Lane led a group of followers to Paraguay to establish "A New Australia" in which to train a millenarian avant-garde. Deep in Paraguay, surrounded by Indians on all sides, the colony's newsletter described its principles as 'a Commonhold of English speaking whites, who accept among their principles Life marriage, Teetotalism and the Color Line. And who believe that Communism is not merely expedient but is right.'[18] During the Edwardian period William Morris Hughes established a strong position in the Australian Labor Party and became its Prime Minister during the war. Hughes had a gift for invective. Of the Kanaka labourers in Queensland he said in the Parliament of New South Wales,

on our northern border we have a breeding ground for coloured Asiatics, where they will soon be eating the heart's blood out of the white population, where they will multiply and pass over our border in a mighty Niagara, sowing seeds of diseases which will never be eradicated, and which will permanently undermine the constitutional vigour of which the Anglo-Saxon race is so proud.[19]

The San Francisco city administration that excluded Japanese students from the primary schools in 1906 was a Union Labor Administration.[20] In British Columbia the federal government's perceived failure to stem the tide of Japanese and Indian immigration provided an opening for socialist candidates and damaged the Liberals severely at both provincial and federal levels.[21]

III

British settlers on the Pacific were haunted by the apparition of an alien ship, loaded with menace, lying off the coasts of their defenceless cities.

---

[17] Woodsworth, *Strangers*, ch. 15; V. Burgmann, 'Revolutionaries and Racists: Australian Socialism and the Problem of Racism, 1887–1917' (Australian National University Ph.D. thesis, 1980), fos. 309–13.

[18] *Cosme Monthly*, Sept. 1896, p. 4, quoted in M. Wilding, 'Introduction' to 'John Miller' (William Lane), *The Workingman's Paradise: An Australian Labour Novel* (repr. Sydney 1980), p. 62; Markus, *Fear and Hatred*, esp. chs. 9, 11, and H. McQueen, *A New Britannia: An Argument Concerning the Social Origin of Australian Radicalism and Nationalism* (1970), ch. 2, esp. pp. 51–2, and ch. 8.

[19] 21 Mar. 1899; quoted in M. Booker, *The Great Professional: A Study of W. M. Hughes* (Sydney 1980), p. 62.

[20] Daniels, *Politics of Prejudice*, p. 31.

[21] K. Adachi, *The Enemy that Never Was: A History of the Japanese Canadians* (Toronto 1976), pp. 78, 84–5; KD, London, 20 Mar. 1908, G 2190, fos. 48–9.

The Victorian concept of "gunboat diplomacy" incorporates this image. The ship in the harbour is also a persistent theme in the history of racial exclusion. From the nineteenth century to the Asian boat people of our own time, crises repeatedly took the form of a shipload of migrants clamouring for entry.

When the steamship *Afghan* arrived in Melbourne in early May 1888, it precipitated such a crisis. The ship carried 268 Chinese passengers, many of them returning residents. In response to mass meetings and demonstrations, the authorities refused to allow any passengers to land and the ship sailed on to Sydney, where it was soon joined in the harbour by two other vessels carrying some 600 people in all. The *Afghan* crisis has the main elements of subsequent ones: a boatload of Asian migrants of uncertain legality, mass meetings at the Town Hall, deputations to the authorities, a crowd of thousands marching down the main avenues. Resident Asians pull down their shutters in fear of violence. Finally a defiant speech by the provincial premier castigates the migrants and denies a landing even to those who were legally entitled to it.[22] In the aftermath of the *Afghan* all the Australian colonies excepting Queensland virtually barred Asiatic entry and this was confirmed by the Federal Parliament in its very first legislation, the Immigration Restriction Act of 1901. The Commonwealth's second statute, the Pacific Island Labourers Act, provided for the gradual deportation of the Pacific Islanders from the sugar fields of Queensland.

By the turn of the century the demand for exclusion was almost five decades old and the principle well and truly established, that Asians were not acceptable. Canada, the United States, New Zealand and Australia had all enacted legislation to restrict or prevent the entry of non-whites, and all of them discriminated against Asiatic residents already in place by denying them some rights, subjecting them to special taxes, denying them some forms of legal protection and preventing male residents from acquiring wives from overseas.[23]

IV

Japanese migrants became the largest body of Asians on the Pacific rim in the first decade of the twentieth century. Between 1901 and 1910 some 127,000 Japanese arrived in California and in 1910 the state's 41,000 Japanese made up about 2.1 per cent of its population. British Columbia

---

[22] A short account of the *Afghan* crisis: D. Johanson, 'History of the White Australia Policy', in K. Rivett (ed.), *Immigration: Control or Colour Bar?* (Melbourne rev. edn. 1962), p. 9; illustrations of Sydney demonstrations in Markus, *Fear and Hatred*, p. 146.

[23] There is a summary list of anti-Asian legislation in Lewin, 'Appendix', in Jebb, 'Asiatic Immigration', pp. 597–605.

had 11,000 in 1908, and, together with the Chinese (16,000) and Punjabi Indians (2,500), they made up almost 15 per cent of the Province's population.[24] A large proportion had come from Hawaii, where the sugar planters had imported almost 80,000 to work the cane from the 1880s and up to 1907.[25]

New troubles began to brew in San Francisco in 1906, when the authorities decided to segregate Japanese pupils in separate schools. This was not merely a snub to the Asian residents of California but a challenge to Japan, by now the greatest naval power in the Pacific. The crisis had not been resolved a year later, when the *Kumeric* dropped anchor off Vancouver with 1,189 Japanese on board. The ship rode in the harbour while its agents foiled the efforts of customs officers to prevent the passengers from landing. Japan had promised to restrict immigration but the *Kumeric* came from Hawaii. Its passengers were labourers locked out during a dispute with the sugar planters. Many migrants had also arrived directly from Japan that summer, together with some 2,000 Sikhs and about 1,300 Chinese. Emotions slowly came to the boil during August and on 7 September a mass demonstration assembled in the streets of Vancouver. Up to 8,000 milled in front of City Hall and listened to inflammatory speeches from self-appointed vigilantes. Afterwards a mob went to the Asian sections of the town and smashed up shops and houses. No lives were lost and injuries were few. As riots go it was not a very serious one, but its reverberations went far and wide and take us into the heart of our story.[26]

A Liberal MP for British Columbia wrote to the Prime Minister in distant Ottawa, warning of the consequences of a Japanese influx for the province and the fortunes of the party.

In a very short time our Province will be Asiatic and I am very much afraid that the trouble which might be averted now by prompt action being taken, will assume gigantic proportions before many years have elapsed. . . . I would very much like to keep this country White and I would also like to keep it Liberal, but it is impossible to keep either one of the two unless the Japs are peremptorily told that they must carry out their understanding with your government.

But exclusion was no longer such a simple option. In a reasoned letter the Prime Minister stated the most important constraint.

[24] Daniels, *Politics of Prejudice*, pp. 1–2; Lewin, Appendix, p. 604.
[25] Beechert, 'Labour Relations', p. 285.
[26] H. N. Sugimoto, 'The Vancouver Riots of 1907: A Canadian Episode', in H. Conroy and T. S. Myakawa (eds.), *East Across the Pacific* (Santa Barbara, California 1972); Adachi, *The Enemy that Never Was*, ch. 3; W. P. Ward, *White Canada Forever: Popular Attitudes and Public Policy Toward Orientals in British Columbia* (Montreal 1978), ch. 4; M. E. Hallett, 'A Governor-General's Views on Oriental Immigration to British Columbia, 1904–1911', *BC Studies*, vol. 14 (summer 1972), p. 60.

conditions, with regard to the Asiatic question, are not exactly the same as they were twenty years or even ten years ago. Up to that time, the Asiatic, when he came to white countries, could be treated with contempt and kicked. This continues to be true yet for all classes of the yellow race, with the exception of the Japanese. The Japanese has adopted European civilization, has shown that he can whip European soldiers, has a navy equal man for man to the best afloat, and will not submit to be kicked and treated with contempt, as his brother from China still meekly submits to.[27]

Japan's emergence as a great power transformed the question for racial exclusion from a domestic one to a sensitive issue of international relations and strategy. It also alerted the Dominions (and the state of California) to the world outside their own borders.

[27] R. G. Macpherson to Sir Wilfrid Laurier, 20 Aug. 1907; Laurier to Macpherson, 27 Aug. 1907; Laurier Papers, PAC MG 26 G, fos. 127979–8.

13

MACKENZIE KING'S ODYSSEY

AFTER the Vancouver riots Laurier sent one of his senior civil servants, the Deputy Minister of Labour William Lyon Mackenzie King, to investigate. King was thirty-three years old at the time, and already rising rapidly in a career that would make him Prime Minister of Canada for a total of twenty-two years between 1921 and 1948. In going to Vancouver he unwittingly embarked upon one of the great adventures of his life, and one that also provides a unique insight into the issue.

King was an exceptional diarist. A bachelor to the end of his life, he was able to spend hours every evening writing up the events of the day. He mixed easily with social equals and superiors, and his diaries make compelling reading and display an exceptional talent for reconstruction and recall.

Soon after his Vancouver inquiry King was invited by President Roosevelt for a personal visit to Washington. There was talk of war with Japan and the President had just ordered the American fleet from the Atlantic to the Pacific. King quickly gained Roosevelt's confidence and the President asked the young Canadian to go to the United Kingdom and communicate American concern about Asian immigration. King visited Washington twice and then spent two months in Britain, where he talked with most of the leading figures in government and opposition. A few months later he set out on another mission, ostensibly to attend an opium control conference, but really to find a way of stopping Asian immigration into Canada. He visited Britain, and went on to India, China and Japan. King's mission was one of a succession of efforts to persuade Asian governments to restrict emigration to Canada and did not lead to any singular achievement. Accounts of King's itinerary and the outcome of his mission may be found in other publications.[1] My purpose is to use the diaries to illuminate attitudes and motives, in the Edwardian period as well as the present.

I

In the Asian labour question of the Edwardian period, what did not happen is of greater import than what did. Like nuclear war in our own

---

[1] R. M. Dawson, *William Lyon Mackenzie King. A Political Biography. 1. 1874–1923* (Toronto 1958), chs. 5, 6; D. Avery and P. Neary, 'Laurier, Borden and a White British Columbia', *Journal of Canadian Studies*, vol. 12 (1977).

times, the Yellow Peril was a non-event that haunted the public mind. There is an imaginary Pacific rim, in which a large Asian emigration was allowed, and we shall refer to that counterfactual region from time to time. But a world that never was is not worth dwelling upon for long, even if the opportunity forgone is an important measure of cost.

The literature on exclusion is largely concerned with the uncomfortable question of racism. For the economic historian, this emphasis comes as a surprise. But it will not go away. We are uneasy about it, King was uneasy about it, and so were most of his protagonists. It is not so very long since the countries in question have shed some of their more blatant racial biases and there is still some way to go. It is tempting to judge King by our own best practice, but that would be a complacent conceit. Rather, the *attractions* of the racist position need to be investigated. Did racism pay off? For whose benefit and at what cost? A balance sheet of exclusion can be derived out of King's diaries, and it reads something like this.

On the *debit* side, exclusion was unsound for the following reasons: (*a*) Moral. Exclusion offended against the ethical and religious principles of humanity and brotherhood, and implied that some peoples, distinguished by pigment and physique, are inferior to others. (*b*) Economic. Exclusion violated the principle of free competition and mobility of factors, and entailed the sacrifice of economic opportunities. Furthermore, it gave rise to the risk of economic reprisals and the loss of markets. (*c*) Political. The denial of the franchise and other rights offended against the liberal principles of democracy and equality before the law. From a socialist point of view, exclusion breached the fraternity of all toilers. (*d*) Imperial. Within the British Empire every one of the King's subjects was entitled to travel and settle freely. Exclusion violated the principle of equality under the crown. (*e*) Defence. By imputing racial inferiority to the citizens of foreign powers, especially Japan and China, exclusion generated international tensions, unsettled the balance of power and endangered world peace.

King regarded other principles (and a few of the preceding ones) as telling *in favour* of exclusion. On the *credit* side he found: (*a*) Morality. Kinsmen came before strangers. Class, national and "race" solidarity came before "the brotherhood of humanity". (*b*) Economics. Economies had thrived under protection. Exclusion prevented unfair labour competition. It also reduced economic inequality within society. (*c*) Race. The "white race" was inherently superior to others. (*d*) Climate. The "white race" was peculiarly adapted to temperate climates, while non-whites were adapted to tropical ones. (*e*) Culture. Uniformity of language and culture had social, economic and emotional benefits. (*f*) Sovereignty entitled nations to exclude whomever they pleased. A variant of this concept was to extend the notion of property and trespass to nations and continents. It was premised on the possession of sufficient force. (*g*) Public Order required restriction, since a large Asian migration was bound to excite domestic unrest. (*i*) Defence. Migrants might pose a threat to national security, especially as spearheads of Japanese expansion.

No one could reconcile these contradictions and any policy would have to sacrifice some principles in order to accommodate the rest.

Here is a new itinerary for Mackenzie King, not the sea routes which carried him across the Atlantic and around the world, but a tour of the main issues of Asian exclusion, as they occur in his diaries.

II

'In speaking of restriction and exclusion of Orientals,' King wrote in his diary in Peking, 'I had asked myself the question as one who believed in Christian teachings and whether a nation which called itself a Christian nation could take a stand on a question of restriction.'[2] As a person of deep religious convictions, King is a good medium for the moral aspects of exclusion. Unlike some practitioners of high policy, King was a "moral realist", who regarded moral obligations as binding. He had a conscience to live with, and his work had to conform with his convictions. King is as morally-minded a statesman as we are likely to find.[3]

If that is really the case then the outlook is discouraging. King's conversations and reflections reveal that moral discourse in high places only attains a superficial quality. His mind was largely made up in advance, his ability invested in squaring ethical convictions with political ones. The moral problem is not faced but is often deflected or evaded by means of casuistical formulas. These formulas had their uses in preserving King's own sense of righteousness and that of his protagonists; less effectively, they also served as bargaining points. It is nevertheless instructive to follow King in his ethical quest. King often leads us to realities that evade the armchair theorist.

King's prime contention was economic. 'So far as the labouring classes were concerned the question was an economic question and not a race question,' he told the British ambassador in Peking. Immigration restriction was not based on race prejudice. 'The economic conditions of which it was the outcome were the standard of living of our people which would be seriously menaced by the competition of persons of a lower standard.'[4]

In these terms, immigration restriction was a form of non-tariff protection. At $500 a head, Chinese migrants to Canada were taxed just

---

[2] KD, Peking, 9 Mar. 1909, G 2215, fo. 784.
[3] King's diaries form the best testimony to his moral life; see also Dawson, *Mackenzie King*, vol. 1, pp. 36–53.
[4] KD, Peking, 6, 9 Mar. 1909, G 2215, fos. 756, 770; London, 29 Mar. 1908, G 2190, fo. 118.

like a box of tea.[5] More narrowly, exclusion could be seen as a trade union restrictive practice, used by a labour aristocracy to protect its turf. In Britain the minority of organized workers, who were marked off from the rest by skill or semi-hereditary privilege, had always striven to exclude majorities of unskilled, casual and female workers. Exclusion was in the bloodstream of the leaders of organized labour in the Pacific, many of whom had emigrated from Britain. Labour leaders in Australia opposed all immigration in the 1890s, and voted against state subsidies to support it. Ethical socialists who stressed class rather than craft solidarity, leaders like James Woodsworth in Canada and Keir Hardie in Britain, naturally stressed economic competition as the root cause of exclusion, while seeking to underplay the element of racial hostility.[6]

By the same token employers, especially those who undertook large capital projects, were often colour-blind, at least as far as immigration was concerned. The Canadian Pacific Railway stood out as a bugbear of British Columbia exclusionists. The CPR relied heavily on Chinese workers to lay its main line down to the coast and continued to rely on Japanese workers to keep it clear. Its ships carried Indian immigrants into Vancouver in defiance of local prejudice. The CPR's fortunes depended on the speed of settlement, and its agents recruited settlers wherever they found them. In 1908 the Railway sold 10,000 acres in Alberta to a Japanese entrepreneur for an irrigated sugar beet colony, to be settled with Japanese farmers. Ten of them actually arrived and began to erect buildings. Their Japanese organizer was well-qualified, 'having passed through a full course in agriculture at the Ontario Agricultural College at Guelph'.[7] The Japanese entrepreneurs who contracted to bring over the migrants of the *Kumeric* to Vancouver were able to show a letter from an executive of the Grand Trunk Pacific Railway, offering work for thousands.[8] Likewise in Australia: for businessmen in the towns, immigration of any kind promised an economic upturn; for sugar planters in Queensland, Kanaka labour was for long the basis of their industry. The vastness of Western Australia and the Northern Territory seemed unattractive to the white man.[9] Fruit farmers in British Columbia cried out for oriental labour. For farmers' wives and for middle-class women in the towns, Chinese and Japanese houseboys

---

[5] As the Chinese governor of Canton told his compatriots in Toronto, KD, Ottawa, 7–13 Dec. 1908, G 2215, fo. 34.

[6] Trade union activity: Australia and California: Markus, *Fear and Hatred*, ch. 9; Hicks, *Sin and Scandal*, pp. 89–90; British Columbia: P. Ward, *White Canada Forever* (Montreal 1978), pp. 48–9, 66–7; New Zealand: W. Belcher and Sir Joseph Ward, in Australia, Navigation Conference (1907), pp. 108–10; Keir Hardie, speech at Nelson, *The Times*, 13 Apr. 1908, p. 7.

[7] Lemieux Papers, July 1908, PAC MG 27 II D10, fos. 961–5.

[8] *Report of W. L. Mackenzie King . . . into the Methods by which Oriental Labourers have been Induced to Come to Canada* (Ottawa 1908), pp. 18–19.

[9] Price, *Great White Walls*, pp. 231–2; Hicks, *Sin and Scandal*, pp. 90–1.

presented a solution to the "servant question". A cabinet minister from British Columbia did not dare to advocate the importation of more Asian labour, although 'he realizes the great want and curses his fate that his gallant wife should have to toast her comely face over the kitchen fire every day because the Chinese head tax makes it impossible for him to get a Chinese cook'.[10] The boldest vision of the counterfactual came from an author in Toronto, who wrote,

if "it is a thing to be desired" that there should be hewers of wood and drawers of water in this great growing country . . . then I would ask, why not induce another human wave, one that would roll across the Pacific from the Far East, where there are millions of human beings packed so closely together that they are constantly facing a state of starvation?[11]

As a good liberal, King professed to abhor protection. 'On purely economic grounds,' he wrote in his diary , 'the greater the area of free trade, the better.'[12] His bluff was called by Liang Yun Ten, President of the Waiwupu and effectively head of government in China, who negotiated with King at Peking. Liang had been educated at Yale. He knew his political economy and threw it back at King. Now that China was going on a gold standard, 'if there was this difference in the standard of living between the peoples of the two countries, would not the best way to remove the difference be to allow the Chinese to enter without restriction, permit free movement everywhere. Wages and prices were gradually rising in China and labour by emigrating freely would gradually bring about one level in all countries.'[13]

Here was a weakness in the economic defence of exclusion. It was not its national well-being that Canada protected, but the well-being of one section of its population, perhaps to the detriment of the rest. This was a position that King, as a liberal and free trader, had already admitted. It was still possible to justify exclusion economically, and King did this several times in his diaries. He thought that, while national income might increase, income per head might decline, owing to Asian competition. As he said to Liang in Peking,

personally considered . . . from the point of view of wealth-production I was one who would welcome the presence of Chinese in much larger numbers. It meant however, that individuals and corporations, or persons who had shares in corporations were the ones who would benefit. They would become wealthier

---

[10] Earl Grey to Sir Wilfrid Laurier, 4 Oct. 1906, Grey Papers, quoted in Hallet, 'Governor-General's Views', p. 54.

[11] R. Larmour, *Canada's Opportunity* (Toronto 1907), pp. 27–8.

[12] KD, Washington, 24 Feb. 1908, G 2183, fo. 237.

[13] W. L. M. King, 'Interview with Acting President of the Waiwupu, March 9th', fo. 3, enclosed with letter to Laurier, 22 Mar. 1909, Laurier Papers, PAC MG 26 G, vol. 567, fo. 153853; Lemieux, *Report of the Minister of Labor*, p. 10.

perhaps. On the other hand large numbers of workingmen would be placed in a less favourable position, and it was the duty of the Government to consider all classes.[14]

The same points recur many times in the diary. A year earlier, he told John Morley, Secretary of State for India,

it was a better thing for the Province of British Columbia that it should develop slowly, that the mass of the white population might become the holders of small properties, than that considerable progress should be made in a few enterprises such as mining and railroading with the result that individuals connected with these corporations might become wealthy, and the mass of men remain wage earners with no stake in the community. That as a matter of fact British Columbia was the only province in which socialism had made much headway. . . . I thought the reason socialism had made the headway it had was because the mass of the people did not hold property and the reason they did not hold property was because in part of the Oriental immigration.[15]

That exclusion entailed an economic sacrifice is a theme that runs through the debate, and was usually made at the polite end of the exclusion argument, in attempts to convince its victims.

In newly federated Australia the issue received a very thorough airing during almost half a year's parliamentary debates on the Immigration Restriction Act of 1901. Alfred Deakin, soon to be Prime Minister, said, 'It is not the bad qualities but the good qualities of these alien races that make them dangerous to us. It is their inexhaustible energy, their power of applying themselves to new tasks, their endurance, and low standard of living that made them such competitors.' On the other side of the House, another future Prime Minister, William Morris Hughes, pronounced,

it is the educated Japanese that we fear . . . There is no conceivable method by which the Japanese, if they once got a fair hold in competition with our own people, could be coped with. There is no social legislation by which we could sufficiently handicap them. We must face this matter while there is yet time . . . the educational test will be swept aside by men who can learn any trade in half the time which it takes a European to acquire it.[16]

With his knowledge of economics, King was able to turn the tables on Liang and depict exclusion as an act of altruism. With dubious logic, he pointed out that, by keeping wages high, Canada was diverting capital to cheap-labour countries, which would benefit from more rapid industrialization. He told Liang,

[14] KD, Peking, 10 Mar. 1909, G 2215, fo. 808.
[15] KD, London, 20 Mar. 1908, G 2190, fos. 48–9; also King's conversation with Sir James Bryce, British ambassador to Washington, KD, Washington, 1 Feb. 1908, G 2183, fo. 71.
[16] Commonwealth Parliamentary Debates, 12 Sept. 1901, quoted by L. F. Fitzhardinge, *That Fiery Particle: A Political Biography of William Morris Hughes, 1. 1862–1914* (Sydney 1964), pp. 134, 136.

the real Yellow Peril was the industrial competition of China, and that as the great laws of nature could not be run counter to at any point without injury being effected in the long run to those who opposed them, or their descendants, so I thought the exclusion of the Chinese was really only helping to make China the greater industrial power of the future.[17]

King made the same points in Japan. Although his purpose was to reconcile the Japanese to a policy of restriction, he was also quite sincere.[18]

Another aspect which concerned King, as well as other Canadians, Australians and Americans, was the prospect of trade with the East. In response to America's exclusion laws, nationalists in China launched a boycott of American goods in 1905, which alarmed the American textile and iron industries. Roosevelt fell back on gunboat diplomacy to persuade the Chinese government to suppress the movement. Laurier, the Canadian Prime Minister, repeatedly insisted that trade with the Orient was not compatible with racial discrimination and perhaps this is one reason why his government followed one of the most moderate policies of restriction.[19]

An obvious refutation of any purely "trade unionist" interpretation of Pacific exclusion is the immigration policy of Clifford Sifton in Canada and the large migrations from eastern and southern Europe to the United States during the same years. Count Okuma, a former Japanese Foreign Minister, pointed out that the European workers who poured in through the Atlantic ports rarely reached the Pacific Coast, and that without oriental labour vast areas would remain uncleared and unimproved.[20] Nativist associations in the Canadian and American interior agitated against the migrants from eastern Europe, who shared neither language, culture, political allegiance nor a common religion with the English-speaking residents. Larmour, the Canadian emigration critic, wrote of the oriental labourer's exclusion that,

it cannot be his color, for we admit the Negro; it cannot be his religion, for we admit the Doukhobour and Mormon; it cannot be his morals, for we have no standard gauge for morality; it cannot be his unthriftfulness; it cannot be his disregard for law and order. If, then, he is sober, industrious, law-abiding, thrifty, what more would we have?[21]

Woodrow Wilson, the Princeton professor and future President, wrote in 1902 that the Chinese 'were more to be desired, as workmen if not as

---

[17] KD, 24 Mar. 1909, G 2215, fo. 864.

[18] KD, 16 Apr. 1909, G 2215, fo. 685.

[19] The Chinese boycott of 1905: H. K. Beale, *Theodore Roosevelt and the Rise of America to World Power* (Baltimore 1956), pp. 212–51. Laurier's attitude: e.g. KD, Ottawa, 28 Jan. 1908, G 2183, fo. 2; American stakes in the Asian market: Williams, *Roots of American Empire*, pp. 437–8.

[20] Lemieux, *Report of the Minister of Labor*, p. 10.

[21] Larmour, *Canada's Opportunity*, p. 28.

citizens, than most of the coarse crew that came crowding in every year at the eastern ports'.[22] King candidly admitted, 'from the point of view of wealth, looking at the strictly economic view of the question', Canada would benefit from a large oriental immigration. However, *'there were considerations other than considerations of mere wealth'.*[23]

In other words, 'considerations of mere wealth' would give rise to a different Canada, or, for that matter, to different Californias, New Zealands and Australias. Other scholars can estimate the wealth forgone. Instead, here is a summary of the main ways in which restriction and exclusion held back the economy.

First, faster population growth. All countries on the Pacific rim actively promoted immigration and took in large numbers during the Edwardian period, while also managing to increase incomes per head. This suggests that existing capital and natural resources could have absorbed even larger numbers of migrants. There is no obvious economic reason for preferring central and eastern European migrants to Asian ones.

Higher population densities would have had an effect on the pattern of development, in providing "external economies" and "economies of scale"—industries and services that require certain thresholds of population and economic density in order to exist.

What effect would Asian migrants have had on wages? The evidence suggests that racial wage discrimination could not be maintained for very long in conditions of labour scarcity, and that migrant Chinese, Japanese and Sikhs attained the prevailing level of income.[24] They made their mark in, and sometimes even dominated, a few sectors such as cabinet making and pearl diving in Australia, market gardening and domestic service everywhere, salmon fishing, sawmill labour and agricultural work in the United States and Canada. Japanese migrants to Canada were, on one account, better endowed with capital than almost any other nationality. Their proposed irrigation settlement in Alberta is an example of the ventures they could have introduced. Successful wheat farmers from the Punjab would have mastered wheat farming on the prairies. If the migrants accepted lower incomes, it was because of legal discrimination, not market competition. The Japanese in particular began to climb the economic ladder if not the social one, and, within the opportunites open to them, made a success of small business and farming. Vancouver's small and recent Hindu community raised large sums of money in support of their

---

[22] Woodrow Wilson, *A History of the American People*, vol. 5 (New York 1902), pp. 213–14, quoted by Daniels, *Politics of Prejudice*, p. 54.
[23] KD, Japan, 16 Apr. 1909, G 2215, fo. 684–5. Italics added.
[24] Yuzo Murayama, 'The Economic History of Japanese Immigration to the Pacific Northwest, 1890–1920' (University of Washington Ph.D. thesis, Seattle 1982), ch. 6.

compatriots on the *Komagata Maru* in Vancouver harbour in 1914, of which more below.[25]

Nor is this all a matter of hindsight. Canada's Trade Commissioner in Japan wrote home to say that the only method of facing labour competition in the East was to acquaint Asian labour with western standards of living and relieve some of Japan's population pressure. Japanese workers were at least the equals of Europeans in quality and, if confined to home, their high motivation and low wages would make them formidable competitors. 'The arrival of a comparatively few Japanese immigrants on a western continent can never endanger western labour interests in comparison to the possible results that may be brought about by discouraging Japanese from going abroad . . .'[26]

The choice, then as now, was not between exclusion and the open door. Migration from Europe was not unregulated, and it was possible, by the same means, to adjust Asian immigration to economic requirements. Indeed, on the Pacific coast it was easier, since Asian migrants arrived by ship, while migrants who came into the region overland could not be controlled.

Australia and New Zealand applied the tightest forms of exclusion. The United States excluded the Chinese but admitted large numbers of Japanese. Canada, the most liberal of all, restricted immigration, but did not stop it altogether until 1913. The number of Chinese entering remained high and reached a figure of almost seven thousand in 1912 despite a heavy landing fee. Their ability to pay a fee of $500 a head suggests a considerable "value-added" in migration from the Far East, for the economy as well as for the migrants.[27]

Cultural cohesion may be important. It also matters what culture it is. Why did Argentina sink into underdevelopment when Australia and Canada managed to escape in the inter-war years? Many factors are involved, but the record of political stability in English-speaking countries compares well with those countries that speak the languages of southern Europe.[28]

---

[25] Capital: the amount of money per capita owned by migrants at ports of entry in 1900. Japanese with $40 were second only to Scots with $42, while at the bottom of the list Lithuanians only had $8: Woodsworth, *Strangers*, p. 183. Accounts of the migrants' economic performance will be found in most of the published monographs cited above.

[26] From a memorandum by Preston, Canadian Trade Commissioner to Japan, predicting the rise of Japan as an industrial power; n.d. (?1907), Lemieux Papers, PAC MG 27 II D10, fo. 832.

[27] P. A. Morris, 'Conditioning Factors Molding Public Opinion in British Columbia Hostile to Japanese Immigration into Canada' (University of Oregon M. A. thesis, 1963), table 2, fo. 5.

[28] Comparative studies: D. Denoon, *Settler Capitalism* (Oxford 1983); Platt and Di Tella, *Argentina, Australia & Canada*; J. Fogarty and T. Duncan, *Australia and Argentina: On Parallel Paths* (Sydney 1984), ch. 1.

Yet another contribution to development and growth that the Pacific rim denied itself was the catalyst of entrepreneurial minorities. Oriental communities of the Pacific rim threw up examples of successful entrepreneurs in commerce, manufacturing and agriculture in spite of prejudice and legal constraints. The American ambassador in London, who admired the Japanese and welcomed them as migrants, told King how he found his Japanese sweep examining books in his library; whereupon King, almost despite himself, recalled the Japanese "boys" at the Hotel Vancouver studying Washington Irving and John Stuart Mill.[29] It is suggestive that Australia, New Zealand and British Columbia, with their ethnic uniformity and lower population densities, have continued to depend for trade on primary staple commodities, while the more open and heterogeneous California has a much more diversified economy, with goods and services based on knowledge as one of its prime resources.

III

Mere racial animosity was not enough. Exclusion had to be justified. In their search for an innocuous doctrine of exclusion, one notion appealed strongly to the statesmen in Ottawa. This was the climatic or "zonal" theory of territorial allocation according to race. The idea is intuitive, but was given a wide currency in *National Life and Character*, published by the Australian historian Charles Pearson in 1893. Like most racialists, Pearson divided humanity into two orders, the "higher" and "lower" races. Whites could only live and labour in the temperate zone, while non-whites belonged in the tropics on the evidence of pigment and physique. It followed that whites had a prescriptive title to the temperate zones.

We are guarding the last part of the world, in which the higher races can live and increase freely, for the higher civilization. We are denying the yellow race nothing but what it can find in the home of its birth, or in countries like the Indian Archipelago, where the white man can never live except as an exotic.

Pearson had to admit exceptions like Texas and Arizona. For the sake of Australia's Northern Territory he held out some hope of acclimatization, but his outlook was fatalistic: 'the lower races are increasing upon the higher, and will some day confine them to a portion of the Temperate Zone.'[30]

For Canadians with their cold climate, the idea held considerable

---

[29] Chinese merchants in Australia: Cronin, *Colonial Casualties*, pp. 26–31; Japanese business success in California: Daniels, *Politics of Prejudice*, pp. 9–10; King and the ambassador (Whitelaw Reid), KD, London, 19 Mar. 1908, G 2190, fos. 11–12.
[30] C. H. Pearson, *National Life and Character: A Forecast* (2nd edn. 1894), pp. 17, 14.

attractions and indeed it seems to have guided Clifford Sifton's immigration policy. He pushed deep into eastern Europe in search of migrants but made no attempt to attract the equally migratory peoples of the Mediterranean.

In his efforts to present exclusion in the best light, Mackenzie King often fell back on the climatic–zonal theory. One of his primary tasks in London was to persuade the India Office to stem the flow of migrants from India. King depicted them to British ministers as persons of poor physique, incapable of hard work, suffering from the cold, to which they were not accustomed. It was in the interests of the East Indians themselves not to come.[31] To maintain this frail fiction King kept himself, deliberately or unconsciously, in a state of ignorance about the origins and character of the migrants. He was repeatedly discomfited to find out that they were strong and healthy, often with a military background, and hailing from the Punjab, where winter could be cold. He was surprised to learn during a conversation in India that most of the migrants were Sikhs.[32] In any case, the climatic argument could hardly apply to Vancouver, 'where roses bloom on xmas day'.[33] It would have carried even less conviction in Peking, where snow fell during King's visit.

Several statesmen attempted to formalize and sanction the zonal theory by treaty. The Monroe doctrine, which placed North and South America off limits to European powers, served as a model. The notion of a "Monroe Doctrine for the Pacific", which would delimit a white or preferably English-speaking sphere of influence in the Islands, had a currency in Australian politics from the 1870s onwards.[34]

The most fanciful idea was thought up by Earl Grey, the British Governor-General of Canada. Grey was a naïve imperialist, full of boyish enthusiasm and impractical schemes, with which he pestered politicians, friends and acquaintances far and wide. He was keen to develop British Columbia, with Asian labour if necessary. But, once he had woken up to the Yellow Peril, he became the Asians' fierce opponent.

In 1908 Earl Grey proposed a convention of the Great Powers, and also Japan and China, to arrive at an understanding 'whereby the areas of the world would be divided into distinct zones, the understanding being that the inhabitants of these particular zones should confine themselves to the areas, and not . . . begin digging in the gardens of their neighbours'.[35] It is

[31] KD, London, 20, 21 Mar. 1908, G 2190, fos. 52–3, 66.

[32] KD, London, 17 Mar. 1908, G 2190, fo. 9; London, 23 Dec. 1908, G 2215, fos. 70–1; Calcutta, 21 Jan. 1909, G 2215, fo. 232.

[33] Earl Grey to Lord Elgin, 25 Dec. 1906, Grey Papers, quoted in Hallett, 'Governor-General's Views', p. 59.

[34] N. Meaney, *The Search for Security in the Pacific, 1901–14* (Sydney 1976), pp. 9, 16, 18–22, 66–7, 92, 142, 171.

[35] KD, Ottawa, 6 Feb. 1908, G 2183, fo. 154. The omitted words attribute the garden metaphor to Root, the American Secretary of State.

likely that this notion came from King. He was an innocent in matters of strategy and international affairs and genuinely failed to see the presumption and arrogance that such a proposal implied. He set down the Governor-General's idea in a memorandum. His own idea, he told Grey, 'was that something in the nature of the Monroe doctrine for the continent of North America in regard to the immigration of peoples from the Orient, was desirable . . .'. Roosevelt and his Foreign Secretary Root were ready to move in that direction.[36]

Laurier was rightly sceptical of the idea that Japan and China would consent to a formal treaty excluding their nationals from North America, but King continued to press it at every opportunity during his travels.

Similar notions recurred in Australia at about the same time. In 1909 the Prime Minister Alfred Deakin sent a proposal to the colonial secretary in London that was similar to Earl Grey's. Deakin did not attempt to justify it on climatic grounds and relied entirely on compulsion and force. His coalition therefore included the impotent Chinese, but not the powerful Japanese or Germans. The mere suggestion of an alignment between Japan and Germany indicates the limits of Deakin's strategic acumen.[37]

At the Imperial Conference of 1911 Sir Joseph Ward, the New Zealand premier, tabled a zonal resolution (which he later withdrew). He told the governments of the British Empire that they should be 'urging upon the various portions of the world that every race should be relegated to its own zone'. He got a deservedly sarcastic and heavy-handed response from the South African representative Malan:

we know that policy in South Africa under the name of the segregation policy of keeping each one segregated in his own area, so the idea is familiar to us. Probably Sir Joseph's first difficulty will be to define the zones and to allocate them. He may be brought into historical investigations which would be rather disconcerting perhaps.[38]

The climate–zonal doctrine provided a legitimation for exclusion, a "title" of sorts. For some, *occupation* was title enough, and they appealed to the simple instincts of possessive individualism. Elihu Root, American Secretary of State, may have planted the idea of zones in King's head. King could not dismiss the ethical aspect:

Of course there was to be considered the doctrine of our common humanity and human brotherhood, but that I thought we might well say that the peace of the family was sometimes best kept and friendly relations promoted by brothers and

---

[36] KD, Ottawa, 7–13 Dec. 1908, G 2215, fo. 35. The 'Memorandum' is in the Laurier Papers, PAC MG 26 G, vol. 764, fos. 217933–5, undated and unsigned. The quote is from KD, Washington, 22 Feb. 1908, G 2183, fo. 208.

[37] Meaney, *Search for Security*, pp. 192–4.

[38] Imperial Conference 1911. Minutes, PP 1911 Cd. 5745 LIV; Ward, pp. 394, 403–4; Malan, p. 410.

their families not sharing the one household. Mr. Root said: 'In regard to brotherhood, because I recognize my neighbour as a brother, I am not thereby obliged to allow him to come into my yard and do what he wishes with my property, to plant his seeds in my garden and take what he can out of my soil.'[39]

This was a labour theory of property with more than a touch of hypocrisy. After all, the dispossession of the previous occupants of the land had been concluded only a few years before.

If King had any illusions about the ethical basis of his position, these were dispelled during his visit to Britain. On 7 April 1908 Richard Jebb, the imperialist writer, read a paper at the Society of Arts on Asian immigration. He had previously consulted King and his paper was informative and competent. Alfred Lyttleton, a previous Conservative colonial secretary, was in the chair. Lyttleton tore right through the pretensions of legitimacy and brought the issue down to its real foundation—naked force.

In effect, the pretension of the Western nations was that they would freely compete through the whole East, upon terms of absolute equality, with the inhabitants of those lands, while the Easterns were to have no access whatever to the West, or to those portions of it where their competition was likely to be formidable. That pretension brought them into a strange and rather serious region of thought. "Free competition in your land; monopoly in ours"—that was the doctrine, and he quite agreed with Mr. Jebb that such a principle could only be maintained and asserted by force.[40]

King found the same candour in Sir Edward Grey, the Liberal foreign secretary. King's sessions with Grey provide a revealing portrait of the British statesman. During one of these interviews, Grey put King's moral delusions very firmly in their place. England, he said, 'had been instructing many Indians in philosophy and the political economy of John Stuart Mill, but it had not been pointed out to them that liberty in the last analysis depended upon force'.[41]

India was one of the main issues in King's two visits to England. The principle in question was no longer humanity in the abstract, but the equality of all subjects before the crown. Indian migrants had only started arriving in Vancouver in 1906, but by 1908 they had formed a sizeable community of about two thousand and some of them were doing well. Like Canada, the Punjab also pushed back the wheat frontier. As the value of their lands increased, enterprising small farmers sold or mortgaged their lands in order to travel to the grain frontiers of Western Canada. In doing

---

[39] KD, Washington, 31 Jan. 1908, G 2183, fos. 36, 37. The argument from the rights of property was made even more explicitly in King's presence by Lord Ampthill, on 7 Apr. 1908, in the discussion which followed Jebb's paper, 'Asiatic Immigration', p. 606.

[40] Lyttleton, in Jebb, 'Asiatic Immigration', p. 605.

[41] KD, Fallodon, 28 Dec. 1908, G 2215, fo. 131.

so they hurled a challenge at Canada's immigration policy. No wonder King found it inconvenient to probe the origins of the migrants, for they were no less (though perhaps no more) suitable migrants than the peasants in the sheepskin coats.[42] The first immigration crisis took place during King's first visit to England, in March 1908. Another migrant ship had lowered anchor in Vancouver. This was the Canadian Pacific steamer *Monteagle*, which had carried a few hundred Sikhs by way of Hong Kong. King, who was in England, learned about the incident from *The Times*.

Canada refused the migrants entry by invoking an order in council, recently issued against the Japanese, that required a "continuous passage" from the country of origin. The paper's correspondent saw the migrants.

Many wore medals won in the Sudan and other campaigns, medals which a certain member of the British Columbian Legislature recently termed "tinpot adornments". A few of the Indians had trachoma, and some others did not possess $25 apiece, but all the rest complied with the regulations. The immigration officer actually declared that they had been admitted, when Ottawa ordered their deportation.

The report continued:

There is now in Vancouver a well-known Indian official who sails by the Empress of Japan tomorrow. He assumes that there will be grave danger of disaffection, even mutiny, among the native troops if these men are deported. I can vouch for the fact that there is intense indignation among the Indians. The order spells tragedy for them. 'We are subjects of the King,' they say. 'This is part of the King's dominions. Why do they keep us out?'[43]

This report captures the Indian, or "imperial" dimension of the exclusion problem. India was in the grip of serious unrest and a campaign of assassination. Congress had taken offence at Canadian exclusion, and the Sikhs were one of the "martial races" which formed the backbone of the army in India. At a time when British rule in India faced its first real challenge since the mutiny, Canadian exclusion exposed the hollowness of Britain's pretensions as a civilizing power. Neither the India Office nor the Viceroy in India would take any action to restrict emigration; they preferred that Canada should take the odium.[44] Canada's policy of exclusion (and Australia's even more so) effectively undermined the notion of equal rights under the crown and consequently this aspect of King's mission did not meet with much sympathy in London.

---

[42] T. G. Fraser, 'Imperial Policy and Indian Minorities Overseas, 1905–23', in A. C. Hepburn (ed.), *Minorities in History* (1978); T. G. Fraser, 'The Sikh Problem in Canada and its Political Consequences, 1905–1921', *Journal of Imperial and Commonwealth History*, vol. 7 (1978), pp. 35–55; Ward, *White Canada Forever*, ch. 5.
[43] *The Times*, 19 Mar. 1908, p. 59.
[44] KD, London, 23 Mar. 1908, G 2190, p. 4.

IV

Asian exclusion also worked to unsettle the global balance of power. That was why the President of the United States lavished so much attention on Mackenzie King, an obscure Canadian civil servant, and that is why he asked him to undertake the first mission to England. With Japan established as a Great Power, the anti-oriental prejudice of the Pacific rim began to generate international tension. In 1900 Japan responded to Canadian complaints by placing a voluntary limit on emigration. Two separate incidents mark the start of a chain of hostility and distrust that culminated some forty years later in the atomic mushroom of Hiroshima. In July 1906 the American authorities on St Paul Island clashed with a party of Japanese sealers. They killed five, wounded two and captured twelve. Japanese poaching methods were cruel, and American sympathy was entirely with the seals; in a fit of ecological zeal and racial hatred, the Pacific coast press applauded this little atrocity, while Roosevelt withdrew American naval ships from the Pacific, in fear of Japanese retaliation.[45] The other incident was the San Francisco school crisis of 1906. Asian male youths with no English had been placed in the same classes as native children much below their age, and this gave rise to a good deal of sexual innuendo. The city administration took advantage of the earthquake to attempt to restrict Asian children to separate schools.

In 1901 Japan had been subjected to an indignity in Australia, when its nationals were excluded as migrants by means of a language test which admitted Europeans. In 1904 the test was amended and Japanese students and visitors were admitted, but this did not mollify Japan.[46]

In dealing with racial matters, one should not rush to ascribe virtue to the victims. China, Japan and India all had and still have their own lists of undesirables and untouchables. They have excluded migrants when it suited their interests and continue to do so. Exclusion and discrimination on the Pacific rim affected none of Japan's vital interests as perceived by her own statesmen. Japan was keen to reap any commercial advantages that might be available. She had built up a merchant marine that dominated the Pacific, and individual entrepreneurs sought openings from Vancouver to Brisbane. But Japan's energies were concentrated on the mainland of Asia, on Korea and Manchuria, which she had occupied in 1905. There, across narrow waters, Japan faced two massive but lethargic powers, Russia and China. Nevertheless, Japan felt its migrants' exclusion keenly; not so much as an insult to the brotherhood of man, with which the

---

[45] R. A. Esthus, *Theodore Roosevelt and Japan* (Seattle 1966), pp. 133–4; KD, Washington, 31 Jan. 1908, G 2183, fo. 54.

[46] Isami Takeda, 'Australia–Japan Relations in the Era of the Anglo-Japanese Alliance, 1896–1911' (Sydney University Ph.D. thesis, 1984), fos. 8–10 and ch. 3.

Japanese held little truck, but in resentment against the inclusion of its nationals in the same category as blacks and other Asians.[47] Whenever possible they tried to limit their migrants voluntarily, rather than have them excluded by the English-speaking countries. A series of "gentlemen's agreements" from 1900 onwards established limits on Japanese immigration to Queensland, Canada, Canada again and the United States.

Theodore Roosevelt had to satisfy the clamour for exclusion in California, as well as maintain good relations with Japan. In 1907 the anti-Japanese sentiment on the Pacific coast rose to a pitch as the Hearst newspapers added their clamour, and the possibility of war between the United States and Japan began to loom. Roosevelt ordered his navy on the long journey from the Atlantic to the Pacific, which later became the first leg of its voyage around the world. Neither of the protagonists was equipped for a proper war—the distances were simply too great. But the crisis was a portent; and Roosevelt called King in from Ottawa in order to give Britain a piece of his mind, and alert it to the gulf opening up between the United States and Japan. He told King of his anxieties. War was not imminent

in the next month or two months, though it may come in that time. We are looking to next year and the years to come. It is hard to say what purpose may not be in the brain of those little yellow men. 'I cannot think,' said the President, 'that [Japan] has a conception of immediate conquest in connection with this country but that she is heading for war appears to be certain.'[48]

King's mission was awkward. Ever since the Anglo-Japanese alliance of 1902, and more so since the Russian naval defeat at Tsushima, Japan had been a cornerstone of British strategy. Japan's presence in the Far East held in check the other European powers in the region, especially Russia and Germany. It made it possible for Britain to withdraw its naval forces to face the German threat. Britain's big trade with China, the security of Hong Kong, India, Ceylon, Malaya and Australia, all came to rest on the understanding with Japan. And while the alliance neutralized the Russian threat to India, the Japanese example stimulated the yearning for independence there. It placed the United States and Britain at odds in the Far East, and gave rise to tensions in India, in Russia, in China and in Australia.

King was so innocent of strategy that, on arrival in Britain in March 1908, he was astonished to discover that there was an Anglo-German naval rivalry, and that many of his informers expected war in the immediate

[47] D. C. S. Sissons, 'The Immigration Question in Australian Diplomatic Relations with Japan' (unpublished paper, Canberra 1971), fos. 13–35; Takeda, 'Australia–Japan Relations', ch. 2; KD, Japan, Apr. 1909, G 2215, fos. 673–78, 688, 690–2, 706–8.

[48] KD, Washington, 25 Feb. 1908, G 2183, fo. 243.

future.[49] He believed that Japan had designs on Canada's Pacific coast and told the Governor-General Earl Grey that he thought many Japanese migrants were spies. In conversation with Roosevelt he cited a scaremonger who called on Britain to guard the narrow defile of the Rockies. Roosevelt confirmed that he had been hearing the same warnings: 'the Japanese will get possession of the passes of the mountains. You will never get them out in a hundred years of fighting. The trouble is,' he concluded, 'the people in England don't hear these things.'[50] This conversation took place a year *before* the publication of General Homer Lea's alarmist book *The Valor of Ignorance*. Lea described a future war, with Japan seizing the Philippine Islands, landing forces on the Pacific Coast and taking Washington, Oregon and California.

Exclusion did not sit well with Britain, whose assets in the Far East now depended on the Japanese alliance. King's task was consequently not easy. In his meetings in Britain King delighted in every statement that this alliance of white and yellow was unnatural. He asked Sir Edward Grey point-blank 'if he did not think the Anglo-Japanese alliance had been a mistake in that it had taught the yellow men to regard themselves as the equal of the white.'[51] From Lord Cromer to John Morley, from Bonar Law to Sir Edward Grey, his informants assured him that the alliance was one of convenience, that, when it came to the crunch, as Sir Edward Grey said to King, 'England could never stand for a struggle of the yellow races as against the white, that these things could not be held by treaty or anything, if there was a race struggle, that the sympathy would be with the white people if there was anything in the way of aggression by Japan'.[52]

Such a racial alliance had momentous implications for Britain. In the Pacific, where Britain had but little naval power and the United States was strong, it required an acceptance of American hegemony. In the Atlantic, it suggested a bond that transcended mere calculation, an attachment that prefigured an alliance. King told Laurier that a common stand on Asian exclusion from North America,

by the people of the United States and the British Empire would amount to a virtual alliance between these two great powers so far as any question arising out of the Oriental immigration was concerned; that it would be a strength to Great Britain against Germany in the present European situation, as it would help to remove the difficulty so far as the orient is concerned and to give England and the United States common cause in this connection.[53]

---

[49] KD, London, 25 Mar. 1908, G 2190, fo. 85.
[50] KD, Ottawa, 27 Feb. 1908, G 2183, fos. 253–4; Washington, 31 Jan. 1908, G 2183, fo. 57; also KD, London, 18 Mar. 1908, G 2190, fos. 18–19.
[51] KD, Fallodon, 28 Dec. 1908, G 2215,fo. 114.
[52] KD, London, 18 Mar. 1908, G 2190, fo. 19.
[53] KD, Ottawa, 7–13 Dec. 1908, G2215, fo. 35.

For Britain to stand off would risk the loss of Canada and Australia. Canada had resisted Roosevelt's pressure to invite the American fleet to Vancouver, but King warned Grey that, if war broke out between the United States and Japan, the residents of Vancouver would not trust a Japanese ship near the coast.[54] They would turn to the United States for protection. Indeed, King suspected that one of Roosevelt's designs in fanning up the tension with Japan was to detach British Columbia and bring it over into the United States. He put this danger continuously before the Colonial and Foreign Offices in London. A war between the United States and Japan, he said to Laurier, would be the beginning of the disruption of the Canadian Dominion.[55]

Evidence of this new strategic reality came from Australia when Deakin, the Prime Minister, bypassed the Colonial Office and invited Roosevelt to send the fleet to Australia on its voyage round the world. Australia, which was deeply anxious about its repeated snubs to Japan, embraced its American protectors and made their arrival into a public festival unequalled in the history of the Federation. The Americans returned the compliment. More than three hundred sailors deserted the fleet in Australia, and 221 eluded capture. It was the Australians who named it, in a deliberate *double entendre*, "The Great White Fleet".[56]

Roosevelt divulged Deakin's invitation to King, and urged him to go on to Australia as well. He offered to send the fleet to British Columbia. Roosevelt was keen to push this common interest, and had long advocated a closer union of the English-speaking peoples in terms of American equality if not primacy. In conjunction with King's mission, he sent a letter to King Edward VII expressing his belief that the interests of Britain and the United States were one alike in the Atlantic and the Pacific, and that Asian labourers should be kept out of English-speaking countries.[57]

Grey's response was to dismiss the reality of the Japanese threat. He pointed out that a war between Japan and the United States was logistically almost impossible and that North America was well beyond the military reach of Japan. Japan had no designs on North America. More positively, the alliance was based on the tacit British understanding that Japan would have a free hand on the Asian mainland, in Korea and Manchuria. In

---

[54] KD, Washington, 28 Jan. 1908, G 2183, fos. 11–13.

[55] Ibid.; and, e.g., in conversation with Lord Elgin, the colonial secretary, KD, London, 17 Mar. 1908, G 2190, fo.9.

[56] R. A. Hart, *The Great White Fleet: Its Voyage around the World, 1907–1909* (Boston 1965), pp. 186–201; Meaney, *Search for Security*, pp. 163–72; Takeda, 'Australia–Japan Relations', fos. 210–29; "Great White Fleet": *Lone Hand* (Sydney, Aug. 1908), p. 351. I owe this reference to Ken Inglis.

[57] KD, Washington, 31 Jan. 1908, G 2183, fo. 48; Washington, 22 Feb. 1908, G 2183, fos. 223–4; Beale, *Roosevelt*, ch. 3; Esthus, *Roosevelt*, p. 222, citing letter from Roosevelt to Edward VII, 12 Feb. 1908, in S. E. Morison (ed.), *The Letters of Theodore Roosevelt* (Cambridge, Mass. 1952), vol. 6, p. 940.

making the alliance the Japanese also indicated the same priorities. It was these priorities more than the agreement itself, that provided security for Australia and for Canada's Pacific coast and commerce. It appears that Roosevelt was also prepared to keep the Japanese occupied on the mainland of Asia. As one eminent scholar writes, Roosevelt was inclined 'to give Japan a wide berth in Manchuria in compensation for the sins of the Californians', in harmony with British interests.[58]

The racial unrest in San Francisco and Vancouver highlighted a new strategic orientation. Britain's alliance with Japan was colour-blind and designed to protect its position in the Orient and its supremacy elsewhere. But in the Far East Britain was no longer a force to contend with. As King realized clearly, the real contest was between Japan and the United States, two rising empires.[59] For Canada and Australia race was a reality. Their policy of exclusion forced them into closer alignment with the United States. This was their first real conflict of interest with London, or rather, in the case of Canada, the first that induced them into a foreign policy of their own and stirred up their independent nationality. Excluding Asians forged a common interest between the overseas settler societies. Britain preferred to maintain the alliance with Japan, but the forces of racial animosity worked against it.

V

Despite his misgivings King put a good deal of conviction into his mission of exclusion. Neither economics nor the arguments from property and force carried much weight with him. As a politician, he believed that exclusion was expedient, even necessary. As an applied moralist, he had to believe that it was right. King's sense of superiority only rarely took the form of physical disdain; it was made up of two elements: religion and culture.

Like most faiths, Christianity brooks no rivals. Whatever accommodations it makes in practice, its doctrines proclaim a unique truth. As a professing Christian, King came to the Orient with a ready-made sense of religious superiority.[60] In this respect he was firmly a Victorian. As a colonial, King had sympathized with Home Rule for Ireland, and even for India. But a visit to the Golden Temple at Benares changed his mind about India. There he saw 'quite the most benighted and wildest spectacle I have ever witnessed. To talk of self-government while any proportion of the

---

[58] Esthus, *Roosevelt*, pp. 306, 308; KD, talk with Bryce, Washington, 1 Feb. 1908, G 2183, fos. 72–3; with Sir Edward Grey, London, 18 Mar. 1908, G 2190, fo. 26; Fallodon, 28 Dec. 1908, G 2215, fos. 113–15.

[59] KD, London, 18 Mar. 1908, G 2190 fo. 27.

[60] KD, Bombay, 16 Jan. 1909, G 2215, fos. 189–90.

nation is given over to idolatry seems the veriest absurdity.' He came to regard England's oppressive rule in India as the necessary part of a civilizing process, 'the chastisement which is necessary before reflection and thought come'.[61]

High intelligence and years of distinction at some of America's best universities did not render him immune to bigotry. Nor did travel and experience of affairs. It is striking how a product of the raw culture of Canada, a mere outpost of European civilization, could regard himself so superior to people whose culture dated back more than two millenia. In King's case, his inability to experience foreign cultures except at the most superficial level was also affected by prudery (perhaps related to that inner reticence that destined his relations with women, so affectionate and promising, always to fizzle out). In Benares he visits the Neepal Temple, 'the obscene frescoes on which mark, perhaps, the lowest depths to which a people in their heathenism can possibly sink. Here is the very antithesis of Christianity. Carnality is made a prime object of religion. We may well thank the providence which has led us out of such a wilderness, and may well recognize the duty which we owe to those who still travel onward.'[62]

He was willing to accept paganism without idolatry. The Temple of Heaven in Peking was more impressive than churches, 'It is curious that in this so-called pagan country one should find the most sublime expression of the underlying belief of all religions worthy of the name.'[63] It is almost as if King's respect for a nation's cultural and religious standing was directly related to its economic, political and military mass. In Japan his appreciation of religion, culture, art and artefacts rose into rapture.[64]

One source of moral strength was not marshalled. Nowhere in his conversations or reflections did King invoke democracy as the hallmark of higher civilization. But King's own instincts were democratic. He repeatedly criticized the English ruling caste in India for their social arrogance, which he regarded as morally wrong and politically mischievous.[65] At the sight of a racially mixed meeting in Calcutta, his religious and democratic convictions converged, and he wrote, 'there must ever be a conflict between Christianity and the kind of barriers which so-called society inevitably erects.'[66]

King's resolution of these contradictions was typical of the man: it was smug and self-deceiving, and was premised on the West's unquestioned superiority not in power and wealth, but in civilization and morality. So

[61] KD, 24 Jan. 1909, G 2215, fo. 373.
[62] KD, Benares, 25 Jan. 1909, G 2215, fo. 376.
[63] KD, Peking, 11 Mar. 1909, G 2215 fo. 571.
[64] KD, Japan, 11 Apr. 1909, G 2215, fos. 654–7.
[65] KD, Calcutta, 19 Jan. 1909, G 2215, fos. 208–9, 219; 21 Jan., fos. 238–9; 28 Jan., fos. 362–3; 25 Jan. fo. 382.
[66] KD, Calcutta, 28 Jan. 1909, G 2215, fo. 363.

was his solution to the dilemma of exclusion. The willingness to share its culture freely with Asia absolved the West from any other obligations, and the duty towards kin overrode the obligation to humanity. King had asked himself in Peking whether a Christian individual and a Christian nation could condone exclusion. Here is the answer:

> were we to restrict with a view of depriving people of one civilization of any benefits which our civilization could give them in the way of light or learning, such an act would be unchristian and selfish in the highest degree, but to say that corporations were not to be allowed to bring men to the Dominion for the sake of exploiting them and lowering and helping to destroy the standards which with great difficulty we were building up for our working classes . . . was not unchristian.[67]

Non-labourers were welcome, but his eagerness to impart the light was not sufficient for King to agree to remit a deposit of $500 that Canada required of every student from China.[68]

After this dose of humbug it comes as no surprise that King was not entirely free of a physical revulsion towards alien races. On leaving India he wrote a racist doggerel verse in his diary, and a few days later, on board ship, he added, 'it is impossible to describe how refreshing it is to be again with people of one's own colour. One becomes very tired of the black races after living among them. It is clear the two were never intended to intermix freely.'[69] Angered at Chinese procrastination, he lost his temper and told the negotiator Liang that 'it was only a few enlightened men who believed in race equality and the like. . . . the popular thing would be to exclude the whole lot of them, students or anybody else . . .'[70] On 21 March 1909 King drafted a cable asking the British government to persuade China not to send a consul who was married to a white woman to Vancouver. It said that 'having a white wife would not be acceptable to Canadians who do not wish to encourage intermarriage'. Later in the day, King had second thoughts; but the British ambassador had already suppressed the cable.[71]

From a political point of view, King was on solid ground. Popular sovereignty was almost unanimous about exclusion and threatened violence if it was not implemented. In the last count King could always shift the blame on to "democracy". On this point Laurier and Roosevelt were in hearty agreement, that, if immigration resumed on any scale, 'the bricks will begin to fly'.[72]

But exclusion did not do away with violence, it merely externalized it;

---

[67] KD, Peking, 9 Mar. 1909, G 2215, fos. 784–5.
[68] KD, Peking, 19 Mar. 1909, G 2215, fos. 837–40; 26 Mar. fo. 876.
[69] KD, Colombo, 29 Jan. 1909, G 2215, fo. 398; at sea, 2 Feb. 1909, G 2215, fo. 406.
[70] KD, Peking, 26 Mar. 1909, G 2215, fo. 876.
[71] KD, Peking, 21 Mar. 1909, G 2215, fo. 855.
[72] KD, Washington, 22 Feb. 1908, G 2183, fo. 203; 24 Feb., fos. 244–6; Imperial Conference 1911. Papers Laid before the Conference, PP 1911 Cd. 5746–1 LIV, Position of British Indians in the Dominions. Memorandum by the India Office, p. 273.

beyond the bounds of Canada perhaps, but still within the British Empire. King was warned several times that exclusion from Canada fuelled unrest in India.[73] He preferred to declare 'India for the Indians and Canada for the Canadians', a doctrine of separate but equal development which he hoped 'would seem to reconcile the teachings of Christianity with the doctrine of exclusion, or, what might be more properly termed, reservation of countries for inhabitants for which it is intended by nature'.[74]

King fancied himself a man of peace, his mission a mission of peace, a cause the furtherance of which was 'the highest mission to which a man can devote his life'.[75] He did not see that, if the poison of racial violence was merely externalized, it was likely to contaminate international relations. King was a beginner in international affairs, and his notion of a peace of exclusion derived from the persuasion of Teddy Roosevelt. The President's peace was not a peace of compromise but a peace of intimidation, or, to use a more polite word, of deterrence. In order to contain domestic unrest, Roosevelt was willing to accept international conflict.

For Britain, for the time being, its interests in Japan and India were more important than racial solidarity with North America and Australia. It had little power to affect Dominion policies, but acted to restrain their tendency towards racial exclusion whenever it could. Its main contribution was to persuade the colonies and Dominions to cast their exclusion policies in the form of a language test, and to avoid direct discrimination on racial grounds. It also resisted Australasian attempts to keep non-white merchant seamen out of their waters.[76] Thus it acted to moderate Australia's exclusion policies, and those of Canada, New Zealand and South Africa.[77]

Roosevelt's purpose (and King's mission) was to detach Britain from Japan and win it over to exclusion. 'You should impress upon the British,' Roosevelt told King, 'that there is a common interest in this matter. If the Japanese understand that there is a common interest there will be peace.'[78] This would not extinguish Japanese (and Asian) resentment, but would simply confront it with an invincible alliance. Japan was not intimidated or overawed, and the thought of its battleships continued to haunt the white nationalists on the Pacific rim.

[73] e.g. Ottawa, 2 Mar. 1908, G 2183, fo. 269; London (interview with John Morley at India Office, 3 Apr. 1908), G 2190, fo. 168; Calcutta, 19 Jan. 1909, G 2215, fo. 211.
[74] KD, Calcutta, 26 Jan. 1909, G 2215, fo. 385.
[75] KD, Washington, 22 Feb. 1908, G 2183, fo. 210.
[76] KD, Ottawa, 28 Jan. 1908, G 2183, fos. 1–2; Washington, 31 Jan. 1908, fos. 37 ff.
[77] Application of the so-called "Natal Act" formula throughout the Empire: R. A. Huttenback, *Racism and Empire: White Settlers and Colored Immigrants in the British Self-governing Colonies, 1830–1910* (Ithaca, NY 1976), esp. ch. 3.
[78] KD, Washington, 24 Feb. 1908, G 2183, fo. 224.

ASIAN LABOUR AND WHITE NATIONALISM, 1907–1914

I

Exclusion was not merely the "dark side" of colonial societies.[1] Rather, racism arose directly out of their virtues of democracy, civic equality and solidarity. It expressed these virtues and often confirmed and reinforced them.

Democracy first. On the Pacific rim, manual workers transformed economic interest and popular prejudice into political action. Democracy elsewhere was still on trial, and in thrall to the middle and upper classes. Exclusion was a harbinger of mass politics. King's political economy was populist in his preference for the smallholder over the large corporation. As an educated easterner he stopped short of the cruder forms of xenophobia, but accepted its democratic legitimacy. The working classes, he said, were far the most numerous, and their interests had to receive full consideration by the Dominion.[2]

The Dominion policy of Asian exclusion opened the sharpest divergence yet experienced between Britain and the settler societies. It forced Australia and Canada into a foreign policy of their own. First Queensland, then the Australian Federation, then Canada, negotiated directly with Japan. King's travels, which greatly extended the scope of independent Canadian diplomacy, were preceded in 1907 by the voyage to Tokyo of Cabinet Minister Rodolphe Lemieux, who negotiated a "gentlemen's agreement" to restrict Japanese immigration.

As the glow of his warm reception in England faded, King began to consider the imperial connection more critically. Asian exclusion had shown the need for Canadian independence. On board ship on the way to China, he wrote in his diary,

I am beginning to see the essential need of Canada shaping her policy from a national view-point. Let her remain a part of the empire for the good of our own people; let her demand a position of equality with that of every other unit. Let her

---

[1] W. D. Rubinstein, 'British Radicalism and the "Dark Side" of Populism', in his *Élites and the Wealthy in Modern British History* (Brighton 1987), contains a suggestive comparison of the anti-Semitic and xenophobic strains in British radicalism and in American and Australian populism.

[2] KD, Peking, 10 Mar. 1909, G 2215, fo. 808.

cease to think in colonial terms and to act in any way as with a colonial status. Let her become a nation or other nations will rob her of this right.[3]

He saw that Canada required its own representatives in the capitals of Asia.[4]

The English governing class, he thought, believed it was born to rule, and had no real conception of self-government.[5] 'What, if the empire ever breaks,' he wrote, 'will be the rock on which it will split, is that the individual soul brooks [no] restraint and loves liberty.'[6] Hence King's sympathy for Ireland, and his anger at English condescension towards educated and wealthy natives in India.[7] King's nationalism does not conform with Ernest Gellner's influential model of European nationalism, except in one respect. That aspect, however, is an important one: local talent resents the alien domination of the best jobs.[8] The governing classes regarded the Empire as a system of employment for their families. As an alternative to independence, King demanded a share of the action: 'As a corrective to a good deal of the talk about Canada contributing cash and dreadnoughts, I think it would be well for someone to ask in the House of Commons how many positions are held in the British navy, army, British consular and diplomatic service and civil service abroad by Canadians.'[9]

While the policy of Asian exclusion brought out a conflict of interests between Britain and its daughter nations, it also underscored their dependence on British power. King wrote down in his diary, 'the Oriental question shows us our position of dependence on the strong arm of Great Britain . . . Heretofore, however, I do not think any obligation of the kind has been apparent.'[10]

Democracy was only the first in a chain of virtues that found their expression in Asian exclusion. On the Pacific rim, on the farthest reaches of British settlement, economic inequalities were smaller and citizenship had a fuller meaning. Fewer people were excluded from the political community; more were able to regard themselves as full-fledged members. Democracy not only amplified popular bias, it also helped to form a popular will. Citizenship was more secure than it was in the class-ridden societies of Europe, and formed the basis of a potential brotherhood embracing both class and nation. This is the subtle process that transformed racism into civic virtue.

---

[3] KD, at sea, 4 Mar. 1909, G 2215, fo. 553; also Peking, 1 Apr. 1909, fo. 626; 9 Mar. 1909, fos. 775, 778–9; Tokyo, 18 Apr. 1909, fo. 701.

[4] e.g. KD, Fallodon, 28 Dec. 1908, G 2215, fo. 119.

[5] KD, London, 3 Apr. 1908, G 2190, fos. 174, 184.   [6] Ibid., fo. 185.

[7] KD, London, 30 Mar. 1908, G 2190, fo. 135; 31 Mar. 1908, fo. 155; British condescension: ch. 13 n. 65.

[8] E. Gellner, 'Nationalism', in his *Thought and Change* (1964), p. 169.

[9] KD, at sea, 24–30 Apr. 1909, G 2215, fo. 714.

[10] KD, London, 17 Mar. 1908, G 2190, fo. 11.

Settler democracy regarded itself as a repository of independence, founded on concepts of equality and social justice. An Australian radical historian described the legacy of values created by this tradition by the turn of the century:

an independence of spirit, the assertion of the worth and dignity of the individual; an egalitarian imperative, the assertion of the equal right of all to material well-being, power, and human respect; an irreverence towards social pretension and authoritarian expression; an ability to accommodate to an unfamiliar or hostile environment, to "make do"; an ironic humour which enabled men to live with adversity and not suffer defeat.[11]

These virtues and values, created in the outback and the bush, suffused into urban society. They were fixed for posterity in the writings of Henry Lawson, Joseph Furphy, Banjo Paterson and Archibald's weekly Sydney *Bulletin*. Likewise in Canada, the traveller found a free-spirited brother-hood in the lumber camps and the distant homesteads.[12] The American ideal stressed rugged independence more than solidarity and mateship. It became one of the nation's prime sustaining myths, but California went far beyond the modest myth-makers of the Sydney *Bulletin*. At Hollywood it transformed the myth of the west into the staple of the world's silver screens.

These myths of the outback had a kernel of reality. They expressed a sort of attenuated solidarity. In Australia and New Zealand the term "mateship" denotes a shared male experience, an unspoken sympathy and comprehension, and a sense of mutual obligation. Frontier solidarity arose out of the work experience and the production process of the dominant staples. The pastoral, mining, timber and land-clearing frontiers of Australia, New Zealand and British Columbia gave rise to a solidarity that was centred on the itinerant, single male worker. The family farms of Alberta, New Zealand and South Australia stressed the solidarity of families and rural communities and their self-images often endowed wives with heroic roles. Hardship and sacrifice also helped to justify the expropriation of aboriginal populations. In the urbanizing and sophistic-ated society of California, and in places like Melbourne, Sydney and Vancouver, the stress was less on community, more on equality of opportunity and a rough equality of esteem, a new society in which an Irishman if not a Chinaman could hold his head as high as any other, where money counted as much as or more than social breeding. This kind of myth is a sustaining force in people's lives; it makes sense of their surroundings and society, and confers a sense of belonging. It is accessible almost to all,

[11] I. Turner, 'Australian Nationalism and Australian History', in his *Room for Manœuvre* (Melbourne 1982), pp. 5–6.

[12] e.g. in J. B. Bickersteth, *The Land of Open Doors, being Letters from Western Canada* (1914). This is mostly about Alberta, where the nativist opposition to eastern European migrants was at its strongest.

whether real drovers and shearers (how many of them read Lawson's stories?) or suburban youngsters in the public schools. Perhaps even, as one historian argues, the bush myth of mateship expressed the aspirations of hard-up Sydney writers. There is no doubting its wide currency. Where both society and nature are harsh at times, the gestures and emotions of brotherhood are doubly cherished.[13]

In the towns, this primitive notion of solidarity was welded into a much longer tradition. The trade union movement took its ethos and leadership in large measure from English craft unionism. In this English tradition solidarity was firmly based on exclusion, on rejecting those outside the fold, whether non-apprenticed tradesmen, women or non-whites. The Australian system of compulsory arbitration of 1904 carried this trade union tradition into partnership with the state. In the same year this partnership was confirmed when the federal government was captured by the first Labor government. In North America Asian exclusion was a regional problem, which did not impinge directly on the national identity. In Australia it affected the nation as a whole.

There was a duality in the colonies' attitude to Britain. England was a caste and class society, while labour meant to build its Pacific "New Britannias" on foundations of equality and harmony. The New Britannia dreamt of a society without alienation—and without aliens. And if it rejected aliens, it could only be British. In this it found a common cause with colonial conservatives. H. H. Stevens, Conservative member of Parliament for Vancouver, stated this clearly in one of his speeches: 'we cannot allow indiscriminate immigration from the Orient and hope to build up a Nation in Canada on the [Anglo-Saxon] foundations upon which we have commenced our national life.'[14]

Brotherhood has to exclude in order to include. It implies a solidarity that goes beyond contract; it is a practical kinship expressed in language, in forms of recreation, in congenial company, in shared but unspoken assumptions that form an invisible bond. The individual derives his self-esteem from the approbation of his fellows and from his own readiness, at least in principle, to stand up for them; their fellowship makes him into something larger than himself, and infuses his own being with meaning and worth. That was the ideal. How much a person could actually fulfil it depended on circumstances and personality. Australian populism, like those of America and Britain, was well equipped with demons: the money

---

[13] The *locus classicus* of this myth is R. Ward's *The Australian Legend* (Melbourne 1958), probably the best-selling Australian academic history monograph, with more than 40,000 copies sold; see H. McQueen's devastating critique in *A New Brittania* (rev. edn. 1976), and the special issue of *Historical Studies*, vol. 18 (1978), devoted to the twentieth anniversary of Ward's book, in which note especially G. Davison, 'Sydney and the Bush: An Urban Context for the Australian Legend'. An excellent treatment of "mateship" (which neglects, however, the family-farm variants of solidarity) is in Phillips, *A Man's Country?*, ch. 1.

[14] 23 June 1914, quoted in Ward, *White Canada Forever*, pp. 91–2.

power, the Jews, the foreigners. Those who are different by habits, language, culture, religion, clothing or tint are the easiest to reject (women were excluded more gently). Surely it is no coincidence that the collectivist creeds of the nineteenth century, the movements of the common man, professed a rancid racism: from socialism, radicalism and populism to that most protean and exclusive of modern mass movements—nationalism.

The populist conception of man in society (it makes but little room for women) has to contend with another. Liberals, as an ideal, regard society as a collection of social atoms whose mutual relations are governed by individual choice, expressed in freely entered contracts. In conditions of freedom, liberalism holds that society tends towards equilibrium and that the interests of capital and labour are in harmony. In theory at least, a liberal does not probe the citizen's beliefs or examine his or her pigment. But neither does he aspire to economic equality or economic justice, and he places a low value on solidarity. This aloof tolerance is at odds with the populist notion of communality, with its high regard for the common man and its disdain for his adversaries.[15] In their actual as opposed to ideal persons, liberals in the colonies were just as likely to hold exclusionist views and to look down on other races (and workers might tolerate and even marry Asians).

Pacific rim societies were not ideal New Britannias, but liberal capitalist societies, in which popular solidarity and its institutions were tenuous, defensive and insecure. Racial solidarity reinforced social solidarity. That is how Asians came to be seen as incapable of assimilation. Their exclusion incorporated everyone else. Even when Asians spoke English, their pronunciation was alien. They could not become "mates". They would not, could not, should not assimilate. In the last count exclusion escapes analysis; like the solidarity it expresses, it arises from instinctual forces, from the desire for approbation, which most individuals crave, and from their need for security. These are legitimate desires and that is their power. But that power can also be malign.[16]

In populist societies, the popular will became an alchemy that transformed xenophobia into virtue, something an upright citizen could affirm. The association with democracy made exclusion respectable even at a distance. King told John Morley, an old-time Radical and Secretary of State for India, that some sober-minded Vancouver citizens had become members of the Asiatic Exclusion League, 'which caused Mr Morley to say that as a sober-minded citizen he would become a member also were he in that part'.[17]

---

[15] Lord Esher's assumptions: ch. 18 below.
[16] This interpretative passage relies on the literature of the Australian and New Zealand bush, the Australian Labor Party, and Asian exclusion, already cited above.
[17] KD, London, 23 Mar. 1908, G 2190, fo. 72.

How virtue can co-reside with its dark side is shown in King's account of an evening spent in London with Miss Violet Markham, a well-off social reformer slightly older than himself. They had met before, but he 'was rather surprised to find that she was a strong liberal in all her sympathies and beliefs . . .'. King found her a delightful companion and exceptionally well informed, with a keen perception and great understanding. She thought England had made a great mistake in the Anglo-Japanese alliance, 'in fact, she deplored Japan ever having defeated Russia, that it was the defeat of a white people by a yellow, and that meant endless trouble in the centuries to come'. On this runway of shared animosities, the evening took off.

During the latter part of the evening we spoke pretty freely in regard to our place in the matter of duty and service to one's country and the object of life. She read me some passages in Browning which I saw for the first time in their full meaning. I was particularly impressed with her fine womanly character and enjoyed the evening exceedingly. It was after midnight when I got back to the Mansions.[18]

II

A Japanese menace of their own creation induced a deep anxiety on the Pacific rim. The English-speaking societies there, isolated by vast distances from the conflicts of Europe, discovered danger on their doorsteps and turned urgently to examine their defences. America sent out the fleet and began arming in earnest. In Canada, Australia and New Zealand the threat created an acute consciousness of exposure and dependence. The three Pacific Dominions agonized about the best investment for their security: whether to build up their own navies or to join forces with Britain. After projecting a naval force of its own and purchasing a few ships, Canada awoke to the size of the challenge and decided to pool its resources with those of Britain. New Zealand never considered going it alone. Australia went further, began compulsory military training for boys and men, and was ahead of any other English-speaking country in preparing its manhood for war.[19] New Zealand was not far behind. Australia also created a substantial fleet unit. The Governor-General wrote to London about the Labor Party: 'It initiated conscription for land and sea service to enforce its exclusion policy against men and goods. As a white aristocracy, it leaves

---

[18] KD, London, 8 Apr. 1908, G 2190, fo. 234; V. Markham, *Return Passage* (1953), pp. 82–3.

[19] A general view: D. C. Gordon, *The Dominion Partnership in Imperial Defence, 1870–1914* (Baltimore 1965). Also R. A. Preston, *Canada and "Imperial Defense": A Study of the Origins of the British Commonwealth's Defense Organization, 1867–1919* (Durham, N. C. 1967); Meaney, *Search for Security*; J. Barrett, *Falling In: Australians and "Boy Conscription", 1911–1915* (Sydney 1979); T. W. Tanner, *Compulsory Citizen Soldiers* (?Sydney 1980).

with indifference half Australia waste, so long as all other races are excluded . . .'[20]

William Morris Hughes, architect of compulsory training in Australia and later the country's leader in the First World War, told the Federal Parliament in 1909 that the Australian position was based on brute force. They had displaced the natives, and now faced 400 million Chinese and 40 million Japanese. 'If the White Australian policy is to be a permanence in this country, there must be behind it a sufficient force of White Australians ready, if necessary, to make good their claim.'[21]

Asian exclusion helped to militarize the Pacific nations, and underscored their dependence, even American dependence, on British support in their conflict with the East. Asia was a danger largely in the mind, not a real threat, and so the capabilities and energies it mobilized stood ready to join the struggle in Europe.

Even if the line from the Yellow Peril to the First World War is not a direct one, the forces that rose to resist Asian immigration suggest how national consciousness was formed, and help to explain how the Dominions responded to the war. The most striking link is how the preservation of "White Australia" became one of the new nation's primary war aims: White Australia came to stand in Australian self-perception for the wholesome qualities of democracy and solidarity that made up that country's idealized self-image. Both opponents and supporters of conscription in 1916 and 1917 invoked White Australia as a prime war aim. For the anti-conscriptionists it was synonymous with the achievements of Australian democracy and the labour movement. As one of them put it during those furious debates, 'if conscription is carried, we may say good bye to all the high ideals for which we have so long fought. White Australia will go in a fortnight. The eight hour day will no longer exist, and unionism will exist in name only.'[22]

Liberalism was suspended in wartime and solidarity had the field to itself. In the ranks of the Australian Imperial Force (like all armies, not a liberal institution) the impulse of solidarity set up a strong resistance to military rank. The men of Anzac (the Australian and New Zealand Army Corps) perceived themselves as 'latter day pioneers, who were as brave and strong and versatile as their forbears and knit together by mateship'.[23]

---

[20] Sir Ronald Munro-Ferguson to Lewis Harcourt, 15 June 1914, Harcourt MSS, no. 6, Dep. 479, Bodleian Library, Oxford, quoted in G. W. Martin, 'Financial and Manpower Aspects of the Dominions' and India's Contribution to Britain's War Effort, 1914–19' (Cambridge University Ph.D. thesis, 1986), fo. 104.

[21] W. M. Hughes, Australian Commonwealth Parliamentary Debates, 7 Oct. 1909, p. 863 *et seq.*; quoted in Booker, *The Great Professional*, p. 118.

[22] E. G. Theodore, Queensland Parliamentary Debates, 22 Nov. 1917, vol. 128, col. 3150; quoted in Fitzhardinge, *Hughes*, vol. 2, p. 290. This point is elaborated by McQueen in an afterword to the third edition of *A New Britannia* (Ringwood, Victoria 1986), pp. 268–70.

[23] Phillips, *A Man's Country?*, p. 149.

Furthermore, the prospect of war, and war itself, ennobled the simple virtues of mateship and raised them beyond good fellowship and into higher realms of virtue. The duality of military values is familiar: the frontier virtues are also required from the soldier, and Australians and Canadians were soon recognized as excellent soldiers. But the soldier also accepts the risk of death and thus attains new heights of selflessness, both in relation to his comrades and in relation to the nation and the state. Self-sacrifice is matched by the beastliness and atrocity that war justifies. Thus does evil arise from virtue, and vice versa. Exclusion enacted the same duality in a milder form. In Australia, at least, the myth of the self-sacrificing digger, grafted on to pre-war populism, created a prime symbol of Australian nationality.

Exclusion not only militarized Dominion Pacific societies. By preserving their ethnic homogeneity, it helped to make their resources more readily available to Britain in wartime. Lacking a clear identity of their own, the white societies of Canada and the South Pacific clung to their British identity and to a fierce (though somewhat ambivalent) loyalty to Britain. Other ethnic groups in the Empire were cooler. In Canada the French did not rush in to join the military effort. The Boers in South Africa remained lukewarm when not actually hostile. For them the primary threat was the subjugated population at home; as they told the other Dominions, 'we have at our door and in our midst a possible enemy which you are happily rid of'.[24] In Australia the Irish were prominent in the resistance to conscription in 1916 and 1917; in Canada, the French. The closer to their British origins the overseas societies, the more cohesive and determined their war effort. In the English-speaking world the war effort of New Zealand and Australia, as measured by war casualties, was only surpassed by Britain itself. Among the men mobilized, casualties were higher than in Britain.[25] To prevent the dilution of kinship was always a declared aim of the exclusionists.[26] In this sense, racial exclusion may be considered to have aided the British war effort. On the other hand, it is doubtful whether a minority of Asians on the Pacific rim would have been found wanting in loyalty to their colony or to Britain. India contributed almost as many men to the war effort as Australia and Canada combined.

For more than a decade before the war Sir Wilfrid Laurier, the Canadian Prime Minister, repeatedly said that Canada could not be counted on to participate in all of Britain's wars. He acknowledged imperial unity but insisted on local autonomy. His country 'was more interested in boxcars

[24] Jan Smuts, 29 July 1909, Proceedings of the Imperial Conference on Naval and Military Defence at the Foreign Office, Whitehall, p. 28, Laurier Papers, PAC MG 26 G, vol. 773, fo. 219695.
[25] Winter, *Great War*, table 3.4, p. 75.
[26] For a typical statement, see the exclusionist petition in the Laurier Papers, n.d. *c.*1910, PAC MG 26 G, vol. 764, fo. 217931.

than in battleships'.[27] But the most he could hope to do was to make sure that British planners did not take his country for granted. He told the British leaders that he thought the nations of Europe had gone mad, but he said that, if Britain was in real danger, 'immediately Canada would step forward, I have no doubt at all of that, to go to the rescue and contribute, not only a small navy, but in every other way in her power'.[28] The Australian Prime Minister Fisher was born in Scotland and less reserved in his support. In 1914 he promised his country's support 'to the last man and the last shilling'. The phrase went back a generation. The Boer War had shown how eager the young nations were to partake in the fate of the Empire. Indeed, it was just that kind of entanglement that Laurier hoped to avoid. But, when war arrived, the colonial response took the form of an emotional surge, beyond any calculation of interest and advantage.

In deploying their troops, colonial statesmen followed the lead of their own volunteers. Whatever calculations they had made beforehand or later, the colonial governments handed over their men to the Empire in a spirit of blind trust. At the outset Australia and New Zealand exercised little more control over the disposition of their troops than the Lancashire County Council claimed for the Lancashire Division, which fought with the Anzacs at Gallipolli.

III

The Pacific Dominions and the United States finally locked Japanese labour out of their territories, but only at much cost to their peace of mind. No longer were boxcars more important than battleships. In 1912 and 1913 California's legislators restricted the rights of Asians to own land, and thereby dragged the United States into another serious Japanese war scare.[29]

Early in 1909 the British cabinet was alarmed by information that Germany was building battleships in secret. On 16 March 1909 the First Sea Lord announced that Britain would speed up her own construction. The colonies reacted swiftly. New Zealand promised to pay the cost of one or even two battleships for the Royal Navy. Australia and Canada followed with generous but less specific promises. At the end of July the Dominion war ministers came to London.

For the Pacific Dominions the issue was not the German menace in the

---

[27] Sir Frederick Borden, Imperial Conference on Naval and Military Defence, 29 July 1909, p. 18; O. D. Skelton, *Life and Letters of Sir Wilfrid Laurier* (Toronto 1921; abridged edn. 1965), vol. 2, p. 114.

[28] Laurier spoke at the Committee of Imperial Defence's 113th Meeting during the Imperial Conference, London, 30 May 1911: the Minutes, pp. 7–8, CAB 2/2/2; also Skelton, *Laurier*, ch. 15.

[29] Daniels, *Politics of Prejudice*, ch. 4.

North Sea but its effect on the Pacific. The heart-warming sight of the daughters rallying to assist the Old Country proves, on closer inspection, to have as its motive the daughters' concern for their own security. The menace was not distant Germany, but Britain's ally Japan.

In Europe Britain had insisted on a two-power standard, on having more battleships than the next two powers combined. For Australia and New Zealand such a standard was a pipe-dream if they refused to consider Japan as an ally. The elegant British solution of an alliance with Japan appeared to the Dominions of the South Pacific like a pact with the devil. Indeed, it had deterred them from taking an active role in imperial defence in the past. Sir Joseph Ward, the New Zealand Premier, declared,

In our country we are just as strong about the maintaining of it for a white race as any portion of the British Empire . . . [If] we were asked to send an expeditionary force to assist in helping the Eastern races, you might just as well ask us to separate ourselves from the British Empire. It would meet a refusal point-blank.[30]

Nothing short of the whole might of the British navy could deter Japan and Ward therefore saw no point in a local or regional naval force. New Zealand's security was bound up with Britain's. So much the better if its gift of a battleship encouraged an occasional visit by a British dreadnought.[31]

Ward realized the futility of a purely Australasian deterrent, and fell back on the might of Britain. He implicitly assumed that Britain would be available to deter Japan and would not be otherwise engaged. Australia, more realistically, assumed the opposite. If the Pacific had a low priority for Britain, then it was imperative for Australia to build some naval power of its own. A small naval unit in Australia was no more appropriate to the scale of the Japanese menace and Asia's "teeming millions" than Ward's dubious British umbrella. But it was a step towards self-reliance.[32]

The Admiralty resolved to use colonial anxieties to get them to build up local forces and take some of the burden off the Royal Navy. It wanted these forces to be substantial: the smallest element of any use, it told the colonials, was a fleet unit to be made up of an armoured cruiser, three unarmoured cruisers, and some destroyers and submarines. Such a force would be self-contained and self-sufficient. One such unit would be manned, commanded, financed by and stationed in Australia. Canada would have another on the Pacific coast. New Zealand and Britain could place a third on the China station and a fourth British fleet would patrol the East India station, partly at India's expense. Together, these units would form a powerful Pacific Fleet, and re-establish a countervailing British power in the Pacific.

---

[30] Proceedings of Imperial Conference on Naval and Military Defence (1909), p. 25.
[31] Ibid., pp. 49–52.   [32] Ibid.; J. F. G. Foxton (Australian representative), pp. 44–7.

Such an order of battle was well beyond the capacity of the British treasury, and could not hope to draw on existing home units. The Admiralty's cardinal point was to get the Dominions to set up their fleet units to relieve the Royal Navy and let it concentrate more fully at home.[33]

It bears repeating. While Britain had her hands full with Germany, the Dominions' problem was Japan. Britain did not ask them for help in the Atlantic, but for relief in the Pacific. Hence the Admiralty's insistence that Canada should base her naval unit on the Pacific.[34]

The security crisis in the Pacific in 1909 was a direct outcome of the Dominion policy of racial exclusion and was not warranted by Japanese intentions. It brought home to the Dominions how much the policy exposed them to the largest naval power in the region. Feeling estranged from the British alliance with Japan, the Dominions fell back on their own resources and adopted some of the trappings of nationhood: a separate diplomacy and foreign policy, and independent navies. At the same time, when faced with the scale of the threat, the only course open to them was to cling closer to the Empire.

The link between racial exclusion and the security of the 'Dominions beyond the seas' (to use Laurier's phrase) was underscored at the next meeting of Prime Ministers, at the Imperial Conference of 1911. The visitors were shown into the inner sanctum of Britain's security, the Committee of Imperial Defence. Sir Edward Grey gave them a survey of Britain's foreign policy, more comprehensive and candid than the British cabinet ever received. But the Dominion dignitaries showed little interest in Germany. As soon as possible, they shifted the conversation to the Far East. Sir Edward Grey wanted to extend the Anglo-Japanese alliance for another ten years, well in advance of its expiry in 1915. This early renewal was required in order to allow Britain to get closer to the United States; more precisely, to conclude an arbitration treaty between the two countries. It was meant to ensure that Britain should never take Japan's side against the United States.

Grey sang the praises of the alliance. The Japanese were model allies. Without the alliance, Japan would become a formidable menace, and 'would at once set to work to build a fleet more powerful than she would have if the alliance did not exist'. Britain would need to establish a two-power standard in the Far East, and that was impossible.

One cloud alone darkened this perfect marriage. It was the Dominion policy of exclusion. But Japan had never made an issue of exclusion in connection with the alliance. If Japan did not challenge exclusion now and the alliance was extended, the matter could rest for another ten years. This

---

[33] Imperial Conference (1909), Reginald McKenna, pp. 63–4.
[34] Ibid., pp. 37–8, 41–2.

was a signal for the Prime Ministers to come out with their anxieties. Laurier, the most urbane and liberal of those assembled, saw the issue in the same light as Sir Edward Grey: the alliance removed the Japanese menace in the Pacific. But the Japanese might contest the immigration restrictions. Laurier blamed the working classes: 'the white worker will not associate with the Asiatic.' He recommended his own policy, which was to reach an informal understanding with Japan. But Canada's policy was much the most liberal. It actually allowed a limited number of migrants, and admitted wives for some of those already settled. Moreover, as far as one can tell, Laurier did not share the racial prejudice of his colleagues.[35]

Pearce, for Australia, was blunt.

The feeling in Australia is certainly very nervous as to the Japanese Treaty and as to any extension of it. I know that when it comes before the public that the Treaty is to be renewed, unless that point is fully made public at the same time, namely, that it does not affect our position as regards immigration, there will be a strong outcry against the renewal of the Treaty, because it has always been immensely unpopular in Australia. There has been this feeling in Australia too—that to a certain extent it degraded the position of the Empire to go into a treaty with an Asiatic country. Perhaps people living in other parts of the Dominions do not quite know the feeling there is in Australia towards the Asiatic peoples and cannot appreciate it.[36]

Fisher, his Prime Minister, was just as blunt, 'We are close to them with a great country and a good country not populated very much, and which we want to keep for people of European descent if we can.' Japan had made serious protests in a diplomatic way.[37]

Exclusion was at once the foundation of national identity in the Dominions and the largest threat to it. That in itself is not a paradox, but one of the constants of national existence. The insistence on ethnic purity has instigated some of the worst bloodshed in the twentieth century. Economic well-being did not depend on maintaining such boundaries. Whether the values at stake, which we have also considered, are worth the cost in suffering and destruction is a question that will appear differently to outsiders and insiders, to ethnic purists and ethnic pluralists. The budding nationalists of the Pacific had no doubts at all.

IV

If the Dominion policy of exclusion threatened to undermine the alliance with Japan, it also posed a threat to British India. Lord Crewe explained

---

[35] Committee of Imperial Defence, Minutes of the 111th Meeting, 26 May 1911, pp. 20–21, 33, 35, CAB 2/2.

[36] Ibid., p. 23.

[37] Ibid., p. 34; also Takeda, 'Australia–Japan Relations', chs. 2–3.

this to the Prime Ministers. He acknowledged a legitimate element of economic protectionism and also the prejudice of "superior people" against racial intermarriage. He reserved his harshest words for an implied attack upon Dominion democracy.

I am disposed to go so far as to say that in most respects the less a white man has individually to be proud of, the prouder he is apt to be of his whiteness, and the more he considers himself entitled to look down upon people of a coloured race . . . there is no man who is more convinced of his superiority to the members of the native races, however cultured or however superior in other respects they may be, than the mere bar-loafer whose mental horizon is habitually clouded by whisky.[38]

His speech was timely, for, as the Japanese menace subsided, the Indian one recurred. Canada found itself in the front line on account of her more liberal immigration policy. In response to the Sikh migration, it recoiled into an attitude of harsh severity. The *Monteagle* migrants of 1908 had been turned back by means of an order in council that required a continuous voyage from the country of origin. Once the Canadian Pacific Corporation declined, on government instructions, to accept passenger bookings from India, this order effectively excluded Indians, visitors as well as migrants. Another order required each migrant to possess $200, well over the sum brought in by the average migrant from Europe, and four times the sum required of the Japanese. In 1910 Canada also empowered the Governor General to exclude immigrants 'belonging to any race deemed unsuited to the climate or requirements of Canada'. This explicitly invoked the climatic–zonal criterion of racial exclusion. Of the three main migrant groups, Indians were now treated the most harshly. Japanese still came in small numbers under the Lemieux agreement; thousands of Chinese paid the $500 landing fee every year. Of the Indians, not only labourers, but merchants, students and tourists were forbidden to land. The Sikh community in Vancouver, no more than four thousand strong, which grew in affluence and confidence, was cut off from compatriots and family, and complained bitterly about it, to the extent of petitioning the Imperial Conference. 'Can there be two definitions for subjects of one and the same Empire?' they asked.[39] But the authorities refused to let them bring wives or brides into the country. Sir Robert Borden, who replaced Laurier as Prime Minister, was much more outspoken in his racialism, and his diaries for 1913 and 1914 suggest that exclusion was one of his three main preoccupations. He deliberately

---

[38] Imperial Conference 1911. Minutes, PP 1911 Cd. 5745 LIV, p. 396.
[39] Petition of the Hindu Friend Society of Victoria, British Columbia, Imperial Conference 1911. Papers Laid before the Conference, PP 1911 Cd. 5746–1 LIV, p. 281.

courted Japanese displeasure and effectively repudiated the "gentlemen's agreement" by closing British Columbia to Asian labourers.[40]

Canada's renunciation of the moderate approach that had served it well in the case of China and Japan set the stage for the last dramatic episode of exclusion prior to the First World War. Sikhs had first been introduced into Canada in 1905 by the Canadian Pacific Railway as labourers, and then as passengers on its steamships from India. Their motives for coming to Canada were not very different from those of the American farmers who migrated north in such large numbers. The wheat frontier had reached its limit in the Punjab as well as in the United States, and land hunger impelled successful farmers to search elsewhere. The rise in the prices of wheat had allowed some accumulation, which was reflected in rising land prices in the province. To judge from the passengers of one ship, most were enterprising peasants who could afford the considerable costs of the voyage as well as the landing fee.[41] As trusted soldiers of the Raj, many of the migrants had acquired some experience of the world beyond their villages, together with confidence and aspirations. They were kulaks rather than coolies.

In their struggle to admit their families, the Vancouver Sikhs exhausted every legitimate approach, but all their appeals to the Imperial Conference and the government in Ottawa and Britain came to naught. The pleas of the Viceroy and the India Office also fell on deaf ears. Canada would not relax the blockade. A few militants exiled by the Indian government had found refuge on the Pacific coast, where they formed the Ghadar, an anti-British underground. Meanwhile, back in India, a group of Sikhs determined to challenge the colour bar and send a ship to run the blockade.

The arrival of their ship in Vancouver on 23 May 1914 created the most dramatic and violent of the "ship in the harbour" episodes. A Japanese vessel, the *Komagata Maru*, was chartered by a Sikh entrepreneur and loaded with more than three hundred migrants. After it arrived, the ship rode at anchor for two months in Vancouver Bay, while the migrants were denied a landing. Canada was not keen to act imperiously against a ship that flew the Japanese flag. The Sikh community in Vancouver rallied to help the migrants with food, lobbying and legal aid. No longer poor coolies shivering in the cold, the popular imagination endowed them with six million dollars worth of property in Vancouver alone.[42] The Sikh display of

[40] Robert Laird Borden diaries, esp. Aug. and Dec. 1913, Jan. 1914, PAC MG 26H, vol. 451.

[41] Fraser, 'Sikh Problem in Canada', p. 37. Complementary accounts of the Hindu migration and of the *Komagata Maru* incidents may be found in Ward, *White Canada Forever*, ch. 5, and H. Johnston, *The Voyage of the Komagata Maru: The Sikh Challenge to Canada's Colour Bar* (Delhi 1979).

[42] A. Laut, *The Canadian Commonwealth* (Indianapolis 1915), pp. 146, 149–50.

cohesion and wealth, acquired in less than a decade, showed that they were as capable as any community in Canada. While negotiations went on twixt ship and shore, the Ghadar underground managed to smuggle arms into the ship. When officials attempted to board, they were met with gunfire, and twenty were injured. Canada's fledgling navy conducted its first operation when the cruiser *Rainbow* stood watch over the hapless ship. Viewed from Canadian documents, the *Komagata Maru*'s arrival appears as a crisis of the first magnitude, a foreshadow of the world crisis of the same summer. In the last days of peace the migrants were persuaded to sail back to Calcutta.

That was not the end of the affair. In the following months Sikh militants assassinated three Canadian police agents, one of them the half-caste spy Hopkinson, who had kept the government informed of Sikh opinion. It was a fate undeserved, since Hopkinson seems to have counselled moderation. On arrival in Calcutta, police handled the returning migrants roughly and a serious riot ensued. More than twenty people, most of them returning passengers, were killed; the others were arrested. Some of the survivors, carrying on the militant tenets of the Ghadar, became active in a violent anti-British underground, which helped to shape Sikh political aspirations and whose activities led indirectly to the massacre of Amritsar in April 1919, and to the breakdown of British–Sikh relations. 'This erosion of a long standing partnership between the British and the Jat Sikhs was due in no small measure to the Canadian experience.'[43]

In the end, the clash with white nationalism in the Pacific encouraged Asian nationalism on the other side of the water. In the process the British Empire was driven into a conflict it could not contain. Agnes Laut, a Canadian bigot who wrote chapter and verse about Hindu (and Chinese) vices, also added,

Hopkinson himself had come from India and was hated and feared owing to his secret knowledge of revolutionary propaganda among the Vancouver Hindus, who were posing as patriots and British subjects. The fact that many thousands of Sikhs and Hindus had just been hurried across Canada in trains with blinds down to fight for the empire in Europe added tragic complexity to an already impossible situation.[44]

The Yellow Peril, *die gelbe Gefahr*, was a term coined by Kaiser Wilhelm the Second. In his juvenile fantasy, the Kaiser failed to comprehend that the "peril" was not a threat to Germany but, if wisely encouraged, a potential source of division among his enemies. In fact, it helped to bring the overseas English-speaking societies closer to Britain, while Germany's inept diplomacy made almost no effort to exploit the

---

[43] Fraser, 'Sikh Problem in Canada', p. 49.
[44] Laut, *Canadian Commonwealth*, p. 143.

racial tensions of the Pacific or to drive a wedge between North America and Asia.[45]

At the Peace Conference after the war, the Dominions, or at least Australia and New Zealand, regarded a racial respite as one of the spoils of victory. But Japan also had some bills to cash. It demanded a statement of racial equality in the League of Nations charter. This demand ran into the stonewall resistance of Billy Hughes, the Australian Prime Minister. It was his strongest and most inglorious stand. Sixty thousand Australian lives had been laid down in the cause of the White Australia, and any acknowledgement even of the principle of racial equality seemed to Hughes to undermine Australia's policy of exclusion. His vociferous, know-nothing stubborn resistance raised an acute discomfort among other delegates, and, after the Japanese had watered down their original proposal, a majority of nations supported them. Even Canada refused to go along with Hughes. But racial equality was premature. President Wilson was not a racist himself, but the United States would not stand for a statement of racial equality enshrined in international law. Despite a majority in favour, Wilson declared the resolution invalid by chairman's prerogative.[46]

The traveller in the countries of the Pacific rim today can see the fantasies and fears of Edwardian racialists thoroughly confounded. On the streets of San Francisco, at the hub of the most thriving and dynamic of Pacific societies, the number of non-whites seems to equal if not exceed the number of whites, and Asians in particular are prominent in enterprise and scholarship, if not yet in society and politics. Official racism is discredited and respectable opinion, at least, has swung the other way. In a visit to Ottawa in 1983 I noted that, of three persons shown on the cover of the telephone directory, two were not white. Australia followed the Canadian lead by seeking non-Anglo migrants in the 1940s and the 1950s, while the colour bar finally fell in the 1970s with the admission of tens of thousands of refugees from Vietnam. But the old fraternal nationalism is not entirely dead, at least not in Australia.[47]

Except for the restricted immigration which effectively came to an end in the Edwardian decade, the counterfactual of open doors, or of a regime of restriction no more harsh than that which prevailed in the Atlantic, belongs

---

[45] For an amateur attempt to sway Roosevelt: KD, Washington, 25 Feb. 1908, G 2183, fo. 243.

[46] Booker, *The Great Professional*, esp. pp. 264–7. Fitzhardinge, *Hughes*, vol. 2, pp. 400–10; W. J. Hudson, *Billy Hughes in Paris: The Birth of Australian Diplomacy* (Melbourne 1978), ch. 5.

[47] G. Blainey, *All for Australia* (Sydney 1984); A. Markus and M. C. Ricklefs (eds.), *Surrender Australia? Essays in the Study and Uses of History. Geoffrey Blainey and Asian Immigration* (Sydney 1985).

to the world of conjecture. For better or worse, the character, the self-identity and the historical fate of the Pacific basin was tied up with the settlers' determination to exclude Asians, and reserve their territories for people of British and European descent. The policy of exclusion, while it perhaps restricted economic development on the Pacific rim, nevertheless helped to maintain its bond with the Empire, and made its resources more readily available to Britain in wartime.

Part Three

THE ATLANTIC ORIENTATION

15

FEAR OF FAMINE IN BRITISH WAR PLANS
1890–1908

'Oh, where are you going to, all you Big Steamers,
    With England's own coal, up and down the salt seas?'
'We are going to fetch you your bread and your butter,
    Your beef, pork and mutton, eggs, apples and cheese!'

'And where will you fetch it from, all you Big Steamers,
    And where shall I write you when you are away?'
'We fetch it from Melbourne, Quebec and Vancouver,
    Address us at Hobart, Hong-Kong and Bombay.'

'But if anything happened to all you Big Steamers,
    And suppose you were wrecked up and down the salt sea?'
'Why, you'd have no coffee or bacon for breakfast,
    And you'd have no muffins or toast for your tea.'

.   .   .   .

'Then what can I do for you, all you Big Steamers,
    Oh what can I do for your comfort and good?'
'Send out your big warships to watch your big waters,
    That no one may stop us from bringing you food.'[1]

Kipling's rhymes capture the gist of Part Two and its implications for national security. The Edwardian economics of blockade are related to economics as this ditty relates to strategy (or, for that matter, poetry). The point is a serious one: international specialization in agriculture affected the balance of power and generated new problems of national security. In so far as these problems were operational and strategic ones, they fell within the province of the Admiralty and the Royal Navy. Naval officers had, however, no training in economics, and showed little aptitude for the subject.

There is an approach to international relations which regards decision-makers as "economic men", who select both the ends and the means of national security with the same perfect rationality that a housewife employs to select a can of beans. Now even the housewife's choice may fall short of the optimal. The strategist even more than the housewife is an intuitive reasoner—making judgements by rule of thumb and falling into recurrent forms of error. Such, however, is the range of variables, so large the realm of uncertainty, that nothing much better than "intuitive

[1] C. R. L. Fletcher and Rudyard Kipling, *A School History of England* (Oxford 1911), pp. 235–6.

reasoning" is available to those who have to plot high policy. The economy cannot determine policy directly, but only through the agency of individuals steeped in the values, assumptions and habits of their environment—some of them gifted with insight and intuition, but even the best of them imperfect calculators. Individuals have to assess the economic circumstances and translate them into initiative and action. This chapter describes how the navy's views of economy and society affected its strategic doctrines, and the chapters that follow suggest how these doctrines influenced the British decision to enter the European war in 1914.[2]

I

When the previous Great War ended in 1815, a landowners' parliament erected a barrier against foreign grain. Malthus the economist and Squire Western defended it: in wartime the nation would have to be fed from domestic resources, and agriculture also had the task of preserving a social balance between the deferential countryside and the restless towns. The purpose of the Corn Laws was not merely to support the gentry, but also to form a bulwark against foreign dangers and domestic discontent.[3]

When the Corn Laws were repealed thirty-one years later, it became even more vital for Britain to dominate the seas. Agricultural protection was sacrificed in 1846 in order to cheapen food, but this carried an obligation to make the oceans safe. Sir Robert Peel defended the Corn Laws as 'a security and insurance against those calamities that would ensue, if we became altogether or in a great part dependent upon foreign countries for our supply'. By the turn of the century the navy had replaced the tariff as the insurance policy. As R. B. Haldane told Parliament in 1902, 'the Commerce of this country was something approaching £1,000,000,000 and the [naval] estimates only amounted to some 3 per cent of that. That was not an extravagant premium of insurance.'[4]

The supply patterns of the late-Victorian economy were an important determinant of the condition of the people. Commodity prices and interest rates began to rise in the mid-1890s after twenty-five years of depression. The upswing indicated a growing international competition for agricultural and mineral products. Grain and animal product prices had fallen during the years of the "Great Depression", providing a boon for British workmen. Prices never regained their 1870 levels before 1914. By that year

[2] Introduction, sec. III, above.

[3] B. Hilton, *Corn, Cash and Commerce* (1977), pts. 1, 2; D. G. Barnes, *A History of the English Corn Laws* (1930), chs. 7–8.

[4] Sir Robert Peel, HC debs. 3 ser., vol. 40 (9 Feb. 1842), col. 232; R. B. Haldane, HC debs. 4 ser., vol. 103 (21 Feb. 1902), col. 814; the latter cited by B. M. Ranft, 'The Naval Defence of British Sea-Borne Trade, 1860–1905' (Oxford University D.Phil. thesis, 1967), fo. 140.

almost 60 per cent of the calorific value of the food consumed in Britain came from overseas, about 40 per cent by crude weight and more than half by value. The upper and middle classes had the first claim on home-produced meat and dairy goods and consumed much more animal food than their relative share of the population. The working classes depended more on cereals. They purchased inferior grades of meat, cheese and butter, and took a lot of sugar in their tea and jam: working-class reliance on seaborne food was higher even than suggested by the market share of imports.[5]

The benefits of free trade must be set against the cost of naval supremacy. How good a bargain did the British consumer strike? For twenty-five years up to 1895 it was a good one. Grain imports increased by 102 per cent (see table 15.1) while their cost only rose some 13 per cent.[6] At the same time the naval estimates, which had settled at a level of about ten million pounds a year after the Crimean War, remained steady for thirty years, and had only crept up to fifteen millions by 1894. During the first two decades of the Great Depression the trade-off between cheap imports and naval spending was strongly positive.

TABLE 15.1. *United Kingdom grain imports and naval expenditure, 1871–1913*

	(1) Grain imports to United Kingdom		(3) Naval expenditure
	---	---	---
	Weight (mil. metric tons)	Cost (£m.)	(£m.)
1871	3.8	42.7	9.0
1894	7.7	48.2	15.5
1913	9.9	80.9	44.4

Sources: Col. (1): M & D, 'Overseas Trade 7' p. 299; col. (2): B. R. Mitchell, *European Historical Statistics, 1750–1970* (abridged edn. 1978), Table C7, pp. 165, 167; col. (3): M & D, Public Finance 4, pp. 397–8.

Note: 1871 was the first year in the statistical series; 1894 was the trough of grain prices, and 1913 was the last full fiscal year before the war. Public Finace 4, pp. 397–8.

The year 1894 was a turning-point. In four years grain prices rose almost 50 per cent before falling back and then resuming their rise. By 1898 there

[5] Import values: Rew, 'Nation's Food Supply', p. 104, and *Food Supplies*, pp. 25–7; more detail in A Committee of the Royal Society, 'The Food Supply of the United Kingdom', PP 1916 Cd. 8421 IX, pp. 241–73; class differences in consumption: J. Burnett, *Plenty and Want* (1979 edn.), pp. 206–39; preponderance of cereals in working-class diets: D. J. Oddy, 'A Nutritional Analysis of Historical Evidence: The Working-class Diet, 1880–1914', in D. Oddy and D. Miller (eds.), *The Making of the Modern British Diet* (1976), esp. pp. 221, 223.

[6] This is not a precise measure of the full benefit of imports, but an indication of their order of magnitude from the top to the bottom of the price cycle.

was a foretaste of possible hazards. The previous harvest was short and Joseph Leiter, the son of one of Chicago's wealthiest merchants, set out to corner the market. In the summer of 1897 he began to speculate on rising prices and purchased very large contracts for future delivery. By December he had overplayed his hand, only to be saved by the Spanish–American war, which broke out in April. Prices rose by more than 60 per cent before the prospect of a good harvest and an end to the war caused the Leiter "corner" to collapse in June. A single speculator had failed narrowly, but a hostile government might yet succeed. In Italy bread riots erupted all over the country between March and May. At their climax on 8 May 1898 more than eighty people were killed in Milan in pitched battles with troops. In September the President of the British Association (a distinguished chemist) declared that wheat-growing land was becoming exhausted all over the world and predicted that a scarcity of wheat was within appreciable distance.[7]

From 1895 onwards the attractions of securing cheap grain at the cost of a fleet contracted almost every year, as table 15.1 indicates. The unit cost of grain imports had fallen almost by half between 1871 and 1894. It rose by 30 per cent between 1894 and 1913, while the cost of naval defence increased by 186 per cent in current prices. Free trade no longer came free. The cost of naval power became a *subsidy* for food not different in principle from the tariffs imposed by continental states during the same period, and similar in its distorting effect on the economy. Like those tariffs, it was a transfer between different sectors—to consumers rather than producers, but also to the merchant marine, the naval service and the shipbuilding, ordnance and armour industries—at the expense of agricultural rents and profits. As far as grain was concerned, the cost of naval power ate deeply into the benefits of free trade. In a world of many workshops, it became difficult to keep ahead in armoured warships. The great mining and industrial export regions along with working-class consumers everywhere became hostages to a weakening naval supremacy.

II

Even a large preponderance of warships could not guarantee the safe

---

[7] Figures on imports, prices and naval expenditure are derived from M&D; the Leiter "corner" and the Spanish–American war: Royal Commission. Supply of Food and Raw Material in Time of War. Minutes of Evidence, PP 1905 , Cd. 2644 XXXIX, *passim*, esp. Q. 696–9, 896–901 (Leiter); 2964–70, 3091–4, 5690–708 (war); M. Rothstein, 'Frank Norris and Popular Perceptions of the Market', *Agricultural History*, vol. 56 (1982), pp. 59–62; the Italian riots: *The Times*, 28 Mar. 1898, p. 6, to 30 May, p. 3, *passim*, esp. 12 May 1898, p. 5. Sir William Crookes' Presidential Address is reprinted in his book *The Wheat Problem* (2nd edn. 1917), pp. 1–41. As a chemist, he promised that the use of artificial fertilizers could postpone the crisis indefinitely.

arrival of cargoes in wartime. British admirals awoke to this problem in the late 1870s, about the same time as foreign grain began to dominate domestic markets. The conundrum is easy to describe but was not easy to solve. In order to bring superior gunpower and armour to bear, fleets had to be concentrated, but the merchant marine was very widely scattered. If naval units patrolled the shipping lanes, they could not challenge an enemy fleet. From the 1870s onwards the Admiralty constructed large numbers of cruisers for trade protection and asked for many more. But this was not a satisfactory solution. On the outbreak of war and possibly for many months afterwards, cargo vessels would be exposed to the menace of enemy cruisers. In time, the marauders would be tracked down and destroyed. Until then there was bound to be an indeterminate "danger period" and merchant ships would trust to luck to avoid capture. What is even worse, they might not dare to sail at all.[8]

The correct tactical solution of convoy was repeatedly rejected because the navy held it as dogma that merchant captains could not steam in formation and that shipowners would not tolerate interference and delay. Another solution arose out of the sheer size of the merchant fleet. With almost half the world's tonnage, there was margin enough for losses.[9] Seafaring was already hazardous. It claimed from two to four thousand lives every year, more than all other British industries combined, and scores of ships foundered every year in the normal course of trade. Some 100,000 lives were lost at sea between 1870 and 1914, of which a large proportion must be debited to free trade.[10] A number of remedies were mooted. A state guarantee for cargoes or ships, and national insurance for war risks, were both the subject of prolonged investigation. Some visionaries advocated an international agreement to confer immunity on private property at sea, while landowners and grain merchants proposed to build up emergency stocks of food.

The navy promised that shipping losses would not be large, while shipowners, merchants and underwriters were more pessimistic. Some risk to seaborne trade in wartime was conceded on all sides, while the remedies remained on paper. Even if actual losses at sea were small, underwriters and shipowners were likely to panic and push up insurance and freights. This was certain to jack up food prices and cripple the export industries,

---

[8] Ranft, 'Naval Defence of Sea-borne Trade', *passim*, partly summarized in his 'The Protection of British Seaborne Trade and the Development of Systematic Planning for War, 1860–1906', in B. Ranft (ed.), *Technical Change and British Naval Policy, 1860–1939* (1977) and 'The Royal Navy and the Mercantile Marine, 1860–1914: Partners in Ignorance', in S. Palmer and G. Williams (eds.), *Charted and Uncharted Waters* (1981). See also A. J. Marder, *British Naval Policy, 1880–1905: The Anatomy of British Sea-power* (1940), ch. 6.

[9] Ranft, 'Naval Defence of Sea-borne Trade', fos. 241–51; Ranft, 'Protection of British Seaborne Trade', pp. 14–15.

[10] G. Patterson, 'Life and Death at Sea, 1850–1900' (paper read at the Social History Society Conference, University of Lancaster, Jan. 1983).

where millions would be thrown out of work. Those who kept their jobs could never afford to pay double or triple prices. It was not the hardship itself that gave cause for concern, or not any more than the poverty already existing. What counted was the *political* threat posed by the working classes. If their misery was prolonged, or if resolve and loyalty weakened, they might force governments to make a compromise peace before the danger period was over. Poverty had become a key issue of strategy and of national survival.

In the minds of those who feared it, the menace combined the traditional violence of the bread riot with the modern one of political revolution. 'Do you imagine, gentlemen,' an army general asked at a meeting of the United Services Institution,

that we in the West End of London, because we happen to have money, that we should be allowed to eat, drink, and enjoy ourselves in time of war when the masses were starving? From the East End of London the masses would march to the West End, would sack our houses, would snatch the bread out of our children's mouths, and say, 'if we are to starve, justice declares we should starve together'.[11]

A more sober prognosis predicted that agitators might be able to take advantage of popular discontent. The secretary of the Working Men's Club and Institute Union explained in 1901 to another gathering at the United Services Institution:

Given a state of semi-starvation consequent on a war, the people would cry out that the war should be stopped, even to the extinction of Britain as a dominant power in the world. This would not be at once, of course. Men would muster to the defence of the country, moved by a patriotism which is largely blind and inherent, not informed and resolved. But, however just the war, or however necessary, you would find men who would see clearly only the side of our opponents. After the first month of starvation, workmen would heed these arguments, and resentment with their terrible lot would grow. The second month the feeling in favour of peace,—peace at any price—would, under the fearful pressure of starvation, finally force the strongest Government to the acceptance of humiliating terms. Of this I am convinced. [12]

Serious discussion took place in naval journals and in parliamentary debates on the naval estimates. In 1897 a group of landowners set up a mock parliamentary inquiry, heard fifty-eight witnesses and proposed a system of national granaries. In Parliament Arthur Balfour admitted the risks of blockade, but dismissed their proposals and refused to grant their request for a Royal Commission. The people would endure hardship and

---

[11] Quoted by Admiral F. A. Close in *Agricultural Committee on National Wheat Stores Report* (1897–8), Q. 5659 , p. 212.
[12] B. T. Hall, speaking in response to Stewart L. Murray, 'Our Food Supply in Time of War and Imperial Defence', *JRUSI*, vol. 45 (1901), p. 722.

support their government, he said; rioting was not likely. He trusted in a strong navy.[13]

The food supply agitation arose as a current of disquiet and dissent among naval officers, insurance underwriters, grain merchants, millers, landowners and farmers, whose profession or business exposed them to the problem. Sectional interest was not always their only guide. Landowners certainly relished 'the strong flavour of protection' (Dilke), but their study of granaries and the corn market showed no clear benefit for the home producer, whose grain was moist and unsuitable for long storage and whose market might be depressed by large stockpiles.[14] Another interest group consisted of doomsday journalists and scaremonger novelists who peddled the thrills of impending catastrophe.[15] By the turn of the century, food supply had joined the many anxieties that agitated the middle classes.[16] The Director of Naval Intelligence wrote to Admiral John Fisher in 1902, 'the panic of the inhabitants of the United Kingdom produced by the dislocation of seaborne trade in the early phases of the war may be sufficient to sweep away any Government bent on seeing the war out'.[17]

III

The balance of economic and naval power shifted too gradually to cause widespread alarm. But alert individuals can often perceive change before it becomes obvious. If they manage to impress a wider public, such persons can sometimes project their own personality on a tide of events that is already flowing. Stewart Lygon Murray (1863–1930) was a man of this kind. In 1900 he was thirty-seven years old and had spent many years rising to the rank of captain in the Gordon Highlanders.

In 1900 Murray began a self-imposed mission to alert the country to the dangers of famine in wartime. In pamphlets and on the platform he depicted the worst possible case, of the fleet destroyed in battle. In two years the fleet could rise again. To secure the time required for rebuilding, it was imperative to stockpile food and encourage its production at home, or else the working classes might not bear the strain. A Ministry of Food

---

[13] *Agricultural Committee on National Wheat Stores*; food supply motion debate, HC debs. 4 ser., vol. 48 (6 Apr. 1897), cols. 642–75.

[14] *Agricultural Committee on National Wheat Stores*, pp. xii-xiv.

[15] Clarke, *Voices Prophesying War*, ch. 4.

[16] A. Summers, 'The Character of Edwardian Nationalism: Three Popular Leagues', in P. Kennedy and A. Nicholls (eds.), *Nationalist and Racialist Movements in Britain and Germany before 1914* (1981), pp. 73–5. Samples of contemporary opinion in R. B. Marston, *War, Famine and our Food Supply* (1897), and the debate on the amendment to the address on national food supply, HC debs. 4 ser., vol. 101 (27 Jan. 1902), cols. 1078–83; (28 Jan. 1902), cols.1119–63.

[17] Prince Louis of Battenberg to Admiral John Fisher, 9 Apr. 1902, Battenberg Papers T93, Broadlands, Hampshire.

was needed, to prepare a system of rationing. Murray compiled an impressive collection of statistics and built a formidable case for his principal demand, an official inquiry into food supply.[18]

In 1902 he retired from the army (as a major) in order to run the campaign full-time. After careful preparation, it began in February 1903 with a burst of orchestrated activity. A manifesto was released on 2 February over the names of assorted dukes, admirals, colonels, MPs, businessmen and trades unionists. Two days later, the Duke of Sutherland convened an inaugural meeting of the 'Association to promote an Official Enquiry into our Food Supply in Time of War' at Stafford House. Another five days, and the leaders of the corn trade sent a manifesto to the Press, warning of famine prices in wartime. On the 16th the newspapers printed a resolution passed by 120 Trades Councils, representing 'nearly a unanimous vote of the whole of the organized workers of the Kingdom in favour of the proposed inquiry'. Representatives of finance, shipping, insurance and commerce gathered for a crowded meeting at the Mansion House on 28 February and were joined by delegates from provincial chambers of commerce in a deputation to the Prime Minister on 5 March. Balfour was not keen, but the Royal Commission was granted.[19]

Murray was a strong social-imperialist. From the start of the campaign he stressed the role of the working classes in the struggles to come and enrolled working-class figures into his campaign. In 1905 Murray published a short book which he 'addressed to the Working Men and their Representatives'. Its very first lines declared that 'Organised labour is a force which has come to stay. Political power has passed to the working classes, in whose hands rests the ultimate decision in all national questions.' The fortunes of labour, he continued, were bound up with those of the Empire:

For, if our Empire fall through neglect of proper defence, with it will fall our trade (because, if our rivals be victorious, they will certainly close all the great markets against us) and with our trade will go our wages and our food. And what would then be left to the British working man?

Murray was no mere sloganeer. His research into food supply was painstaking, he was well versed in Clausewitz and his understanding of modern total war was genuine. 'Social reform', he wrote, 'is a very

---

[18] Murray's main publications in 1900–5 included *The Electors of Great Britain and the Defence of the Country* (1900); *Our Food Supply in Time of War* (1900); 'Our Food Supply in Time of War and Imperial Defence', *JRUSI*, vol. 45 (1901), pp. 656–729; *The Future Peace of the Anglo-Saxons: Addressed to the Working Men and their Representatives* (1905).

[19] The agitation was reported extensively in *The Times*, 2 Feb. 1903, p. 8, 5 Feb. p. 5 *et seq.* to 6 Mar., p. 10: see *Palmer's Index to The Times Newspaper* (1903), Winter quarter, 'Food Supply in Time of War'. The quotation is from J. MacDonald, secretary of the London Trades Council, 28 Feb., p. 5.

important part of Anglo-Saxon defence . . . the patriotic efforts of a nation in war-time will be nowadays largely influenced by the degree of content in which the people live. The greater our content, the greater our patriotism.'[20]

The Royal Commission on Food Supply began its hearings in May 1903. Murray's task was to persuade it of the dire *social* consequences of a shortfall in food supplies and his Association put forward two working-man witnesses. Memories of suffering in the cotton famine and even the French wars were still alive. The bitter strikes and lockouts of the preceding decade were more fresh in the memory. In the course of these conflicts, large communities of workers had to forgo wages for months on end.

But Murray's witnesses before the Royal Commission did not prove effective. As moderate and patriotic trades unionists their warnings of turmoil did not carry conviction. The president of a strike committee described how skilled workers contrived to survive a long dispute by crowding into smaller accommodation, pawning valuables, selling furniture, running down savings, eating inferior foods, and generally tightening belts and relying on mutual support. Charles Booth, an expert on both shipping and poverty, told the Commission that the working classes were well trained in the disciplines of deprivation. For those already fighting for survival, wartime would not hold any great new terrors. The evidence bore mainly on the resources of the skilled artisan, not the unskilled and the "submerged third"—but it helped the Commissioners to overrule the alarmists. Their Final Report recommended some form of "national indemnity" or "national insurance" to keep the ships coming. A minority remained unconvinced, but the majority accepted that the navy could provide a defence against economic disaster and class warfare.[21]

IV

In 1889 Britain began a seven-year programme to build ten battleships

[20] His conception of social reform was idiosyncratic: it embodied a notion of a national minimum. But private employers could not always afford to pay a living wage, so the state would substitute benefits in kind, a "social wage" in current terminology. The example he gives is municipal clubhouses, which would partly offset bad housing and add comfort to working-class life far beyond their cost. Finance would come out of the profits of a nationalized drink trade: Murray, *Future Peace*, pp. 7–8, 108–9. This was in the spirit of the Radical Right: G. Searle, 'The "Revolt from the Right" in Edwardian Britain', in Kennedy and Nicholls (eds.), *Nationalist and Racialist Movements*, pp. 30–1.

[21] Murray's witnesses were B. T. Hall and G. D. Kelley. For his own account of their role, see his 'Memorandum regarding the Effect of a Great Maritime War on the Industrial Classes of the United Kingdom' (n.d., *c.*Feb. 1908), CAB 17/26/B.26(4), esp. fos. (not paginated) 3–5, 9–10. The Royal Commission's Final Report is in PP 1905 Cd. 2643 XXXIX, see esp. pp. 39–44. Booth's evidence is in Q. 6179–6353, pp. 208–15. See also 'Statement Communicated by the President of a Strike Committee as to the Effect of a Strike on the Families Concerned', Appendix XXXVI.B, PP 1905 Cd. 5645 XL, p. 306.

larger and more powerful than ever before, a fleet of thirty-eight cruisers and twenty-two smaller vessels. This project, the Naval Defence Act and its successors, stimulated comparable programmes overseas. France, Russia, Italy, Japan and the United States all began to construct fleets of large capital ships during the 1890s. One of the most ambitious and widely debated of those programmes was contained in the German Naval Laws of 1898 and 1900. The navy that Tirpitz began to build soon drew the attention of Britain's naval leaders.[22] Erskine Childers's novel *The Riddle of the Sands* (1903), with its spectre of German fleets poised for invasion in the Frisian estuaries, had a similar impact on public opinion.[23]

During the Morocco crisis of 1905 Germany emerged as a military threat of the first magnitude and the British armed services began to consider responses and to feel their way towards co-operation with each other. In August 1905 the Naval Intelligence Department received an army memorandum entitled 'British Military Plans in Case of a War with Germany'. The army proposed to land an expeditionary force on the coasts of Northern Germany in order to divert German forces from the battle with France. 'Even if the 120,000 British troops merely occupied some limited tract of country in Schleswig or some other German maritime province they would afford immense assistance to our allies—greater assistance probably than they would on the Franco-German frontier.'[24] Amphibious landings of this type were just what the German General Staff expected.[25] These ideas were welcome at the Admiralty. Maybe that is where they came from in the first place.[26]

In addition to assaults on the beaches, the Naval Intelligence Department also considered *economic* warfare. In the event of war with Germany, the writer of one of its papers reasoned, what economic effect would naval action have? First, blockade would cause the disappearance of the German mercantile marine, 'a loss which to a country becoming increasingly dependent upon industrial prosperity would in itself be a serious blow'. Some German trade might be diverted to roundabout routes

---

[22] H. O. Arnold-Forster, 'Notes on a Visit to Kiel and Wilhelmshaven August 1902 and General Remarks on the German Navy and Naval Establishment' (15 Sept. 1902), CAB 37/62/133.

[23] Clarke, *Voices Prophesying War*, pp. 142–3.

[24] 'British Military Action in Case of War with Germany' (n.d. Sept. 1905), ADM 116/1043B/II, fos. 214–16; also preceding correspondence and Maurice Hankey to Prince Louis of Battenberg, 24 July 1914, Battenberg Papers T37/360. Origin of the Anglo-French military arrangements: S. R. Williamson, *The Politics of Grand Strategy: Britain and France Prepare for War, 1904–1914* (Cambridge, Mass. 1969), chs. 2–3; R. F. Mackay, *Fisher of Kilverstone* (Oxford 1973), ch. 8.

[25] G. Ritter, *The Sword and the Scepter* (Coral Gables, Florida 1970), vol. 2, p. 156.

[26] Williamson, *Grand Strategy*, p. 44; see 'Preparations of Plans for Combined Naval and Military Operations in War. Memorandum by DNI with notes by Sir George Clarke' (Aug. 1905), p. 8, ADM 116/866B.

via neutral Dutch and Belgian ports, but that would not undo completely the effects of blockade: 'trade competition is such that a very little difference in the cost of transport makes all the difference between profit and loss.' To carry goods over longer routes, and to pay for the services of Dutch middlemen, would increase the costs of transport and 'would raise prices in Germany at the very time when the financial strain of war was pressing for a reduction'. Blockade, particularly if indirect shipments to Germany could also be seized, 'would doubtless inflict in the end considerable losses on Germany . . . But the effect would take time to produce, and if we were desirous of supporting France more rapid action might be necessary . . .'—hence the proposals for a British landing in Schleswig and the Baltic.[27]

As the autumn deepened sailors continued to exchange papers with soldiers until suddenly on 3 October 1905 the army withdrew its plan for a north German landing. Such a landing, the army now wrote, would not divert a sufficient number of Germans from the decisive front. Instead, the War Office wanted to place the British army *alongside* the French when war broke out.[28] The army remained wedded to this project until its consummation in August 1914.

From this point onwards the two services parted ways. Littoral landings in the north continued to fascinate the navy, but without the army's interest and support this was an idle fantasy. The mind of the navy was mainly on other things: on ships and shoes and sealing wax—on its internal feuds, on new technologies, on the unending work of running the fleets, on promotion and status. But a few minds in the back rooms of naval intelligence continued to ponder the possibilities of blockade.

Admiralty policy archives have only survived in patches. Papers were taken out of sequence and thrown into "case files" in the Secretariat. Others were used by the official historians and never returned or taken by retiring officers for their private papers. The most important planning office, the Naval Intelligence Department, has left no complete sequence of records, and the story that follows was pieced together from documents scattered in public and private archives. Enough survives, however, to follow the emergence of a plan to resist the economic and political expansion of Germany, and to defeat it by means of economic blockade. A small number of naval officers created the plan in the Naval Intelligence Department between 1905 and 1908. It then came up before higher policy bodies, and became a central element in British war preparation. Yet historians have largely ignored it.

A. J. P. Taylor may be partly to blame. In his influential study, *The*

---

[27] [?NID Memorandum (1905)], ADM 116/1043B, fos. 219–20.
[28] Williamson, *Grand Strategy*, pp. 48–51; War Office, 'British Military Action in Case of War with Germany' (30 Oct. 1905), ADM 116/1043B/II, fo. 218.

Struggle for Mastery in Europe, 1848–1918, he curtly dismissed the economic dimension in the Anglo-German conflict. This was done by deprecating R. J. Hoffman's book, *Great Britain and the German Trade Rivalry*, which had been published in 1933, the year of Hitler's rise to power.[29] Although Hoffman inclined towards an economic interpretation of the conflict, he had to admit there was no evidence of a British conspiracy. There is a connection between the date of Hoffman's research and the silence of the sources. Documents do exist. But, apart from a few leaks early in the inter-war years, none were allowed to appear between the wars, and for a good reason.

Article 231 of the Treaty of Versailles placed responsibility for the war on Germany and its Allies. Although the authors of this clause had something quite different in mind, this article was taken by the Germans as saddling them with guilt for the war. In their eyes it became the moral foundation of the international order set up by Versailles. A large German literature contested this onus of guilt and countered it by invoking the "unlawful" British "Hunger Blockade" of the First World War. A secret department of the German Foreign Office specialized in the War Guilt question. Since Britain defended its blockade as a reprisal for German actions, any evidence about pre-war British preparations was damaging. There was another consideration: by the 1930s the same questions of strategy were once again on the agenda and the lessons of the First World War were weapons in this new debate.[30]

British pre-war leaders were caught in a dilemma. On the one hand they wanted credit for making adequate preparations for the war; on the other, they could not openly admit some of the more aggressive plans. Asquith's memoirs (published in 1923) contain a passing reference to these matters, but they are the last documents to be published until 1961.[31] The official series of British Documents on the origins of the war studiously excluded blockade preparation. Two separate accounts of this project were written up between the wars. The first was contained in the memoirs of Maurice Hankey, secretary of the cabinet and of the Committee of Imperial Defence. Hankey wrote a comprehensive memoir which was finished by 1930. In spite of repeated requests, he was not allowed to publish, and a truncated version only appeared in 1961.[32] Another glimpse appears in

---

[29] A. J. P. Taylor, *The Struggle for Mastery in Europe, 1848–1918* (Oxford 1971), p. 599.

[30] F. Dickmann, *Die Kriegsschuldfrage auf der Friedenskonferenz von Paris 1919* (Munich 1964); U. Heinemann, *Die verdrängte Niederlage. Politische Öffentlichkeit und Kriegsschuldfrage in der Weimarer Republik* (Göttingen 1983); I. Geiss, 'Die manipulierte Kriegsschuldfrage', *Militärgeschichtliche Mitteilungen*, no. 2 (1983). On the drafting of the clause, P. M. Burnett (ed.), *Reparation at the Paris Peace Conference from the Standpoint of the American Delegation* (New York 1940), vol. 1, pp. 66–70.

[31] H. H. Asquith, *The Genesis of the War* (1923), pp. 116–18, 129 and more generally, chs. 15–17.

[32] ': . . during the last ten years I have . . . worked through the material and put together a

A. C. Bell's history of the blockade, which was printed in 1937 as a classified volume of the Official History of the War. It was released to the public only in the same year as Hankey's memoir, 1961. The Germans, however, got hold of a copy and published a translation in 1943, with a long scholarly introduction to underline the perfidy of Albion.[33]

Winston Churchill and David Lloyd George kept silent about the blockade plans in their extensive memoirs. Both works were scrutinized by Hankey for breaches of security.[34] Sir Llewellyn Woodward's study of the Anglo-German naval rivalry (which bears the hallmarks of commissioned history) could hardly have adopted the same self-righteous tone had the documents in question been in print. Even Arthur Marder, writing the first volume of his great naval history of the period in the 1950s, was apparently still under the influence of an unspoken interdict.[35] Despite the revelations of Bell and Hankey, subsequent historians have not taken the story up.[36]

V

In the course of their work on commerce protection and food supply, the navy's planners gradually came to realize that Britain's adversaries might not have sufficient naval power to safeguard their own economies from disaster in wartime. The first hint appears in an Admiralty print of 1903:

A rise in the price of bread would inflict more suffering on neutrals than ourselves, both because the average incomes of the working classes in France, Germany, Belgium and the continent generally are lower than in the United Kingdom, and because bread enters more largely into their dietary.

Using American statistics, they showed that British working-class families

---

very rough cast of the complete work.' M. Hankey to D. Lloyd George, 2 Dec. 1930, LG G/8/ 18/15, fo. 6. On the subsequent history of this opus: S. Roskill, *Hankey: Man of Secrets* (1974), vol. 3, pp. 587–8; HP 25; and J. F. Naylor, *A Man and an Institution: Sir Maurice Hankey, the Cabinet Secretariat and the Custody of Cabinet Secrecy* (Cambridge 1984), *passim*.

[33] A. C. Bell, *Die englische Hungerblockade im Weltkrieg, 1914–15*, 'Nach der amtlichen englischen Darstellung Hungerblockade der A. C. Bell, Bearbeitet u. eingeleitet durch Dr. Viktor Böhmert (Kiel)' (Essen 1943). The German edition only takes the story up to 1915.

[34] See the Hankey–Lloyd George correspondence, LG G/8/18, e.g. 11 June 1938, regarding estimates of German capacity for reparations: 'we do not want this figure to be used against us by Germany today for propaganda purposes.' Regarding Churchill, see Churchill to Hankey, 2 Feb. 1923, and to Lloyd George, 28 Feb. 1923, LG G/4/4/4. Also, Naylor, *Cabinet Secrecy*, pp. 118–19.

[35] Woodward was given access to Foreign Office and Admiralty documents for his book *Great Britain and the German Navy* (Oxford 1935), which was a work of scholarship, but also a contemporary polemic. He makes no mention of blockade planning. Marder was likewise given access to Admiralty archives in the 1930s, long before they were opened to the public: Marder, *British Naval Policy*, pp. v–vi.

[36] D. French, *British Economic and Strategic Planning, 1905–1915* (1982), cites many of the documents but is largely concerned with domestic preparation.

spent 20 per cent of their food budgets on bread, flour and meal. German workers spent about one-third, and the Belgians and French even more.[37]

By 1905 the Kaiser's Empire had come firmly into focus as the prospective enemy. It had emerged as a serious economic rival some years before. Urban and industrial development in Germany proceeded at a pace that left agriculture behind and created a growing reliance upon imported raw materials and foodstuffs and a rising commitment to manufactured exports. In 1906 Germany was second as a grain importer only to Britain, and took in 6.5 million metric tons, or some 20 per cent of its annual consumption. Imports of wheat and barley came to more than a quarter of German consumption. Britain imported 8.9 million tons of grain in the same year.[38] These economic changes attracted notice in the Naval Intelligence Department.

Captain Henry Hervey Campbell took charge of the Trade Division of the Department in August 1906. The Division had been created in 1901 to collect data on the flows of British shipping and cargoes and to plan their defence.[39] In addition to routine work on trade protection, Campbell began to study economic blockade as an *offensive* weapon. He collected statistics on German and British trade in the principal oversea markets and presented his findings in a set of tinted diagrams, lovingly drafted in his own hand. They showed an increase in German market penetration all over the world. For Campbell this suggested weakness, not strength. He was taking the measure of Germany's overseas trade as a target for British sea power and not as a commercial competitor. Some of the most striking diagrams show the extent of German dependence on foreign raw materials and foods.[40] With more than two million tons of shipping, the German merchant fleet may have been only one-fifth the size of the British in 1906 but it was already the second largest in the world and more than one thousand seagoing vessels were a hostage to the Royal Navy if ever it came to war.[41] But how vital were its cargoes to the German economy? How

[37] 'Bread Supply in Time of War', Admiralty Confidential Print, p. 11, Apr. 1903. ADM 137/2749. This passage does not appear in previous versions of this document, which was first prepared by the Board of Trade in June 1898, and reprinted by the Admiralty as 'Food Supply in Time of War', 7 May 1901, ADM 1/7734. The quoted passage is supported by a statistical 'Appendix VI. Note on the Relative Expenditure of the Working Classes on Bread and Flour in Different Countries', pp. 36–9.

[38] B. R. Mitchell, *European Historical Statistics, 1750–1970* (abridged edn. 1978), table D10, pp. 341, 342.

[39] For the origins of the division and its work: Captain E. F. Inglefield (first head of the Department) to H. H. Campbell, 14 Nov. 1907, ADM 137/2864.

[40] 'Trade of the United Kingdom and Germany 1897–1904–5—A Comparison' (n.d., each folio signed by H. H. Campbell), ADM 137/2872. See esp. fos. 8 and 9 of first (handwritten) version.

[41] Shipping tonnage in 'The Economic Effect of War on German Trade', Admiralty Memorandum (CID Paper E–4), 12 Dec. 1908, pp. 21–2; printed as Appendix V, 'Report of the Sub-Committee of the Committee of Imperial Defence to Consider the Military Needs of the Empire' (July 1909), CAB 16/5.

would a sea blockade affect Germany's capacity and will to fight? Captain Campbell took two years, from the summer of 1906 to the summer of 1908, to arrive at an answer.

He was familiar with the arguments of Major Murray, the food supply agitator: popular unrest could sway governments and influence the conduct and outcome of the war. There are documents which link the two men directly. In one note Campbell referred to Major Murray's working-class witnesses at the Royal Commission on Food Supply and added that, 'It has always been known and freely acknowledged that we should have to cope with pressure that would be brought by the working classes, and investigations which have been made . . . and are still being pursued, show in a remarkable way the extent to which this pressure must be anticipated.'[42]

Stewart Murray's most elaborate statement about the dangers of working-class unrest arrived on Captain Campbell's desk in February 1908. It warned of explosive forces lurking beneath the surface of modern democracy. Socialism was spreading and extreme groups like the Marxian Social-Democratic Federation waited for their chance. Murray had tried to persuade a 'foremost Social-Democrat' to support the food supply agitation. The man had allegedly refused, saying:

Certainly not; you are asking me to help you try and deprive us of the only opportunity we shall ever get, the hunger of the people. I regard our present state of society as so rotten that any means are justifiable to destroy it. Our only chance will be the hunger of the people during a war. Then perhaps a blow from without accompanied by a blow from within may shatter this thing miscalled civilized society. That is what I look forward to.

There was also a reference to the 'recent bitter controversies at the Stuttgart Socialist Congress as to whether patriotism should or should not be altogether excluded from the socialist creed'.[43]

Captain Campbell covered this memo with dense annotations and amendments in red ink. He was working to discover chinks in the German armour. He now projected Britain's wartime supply problem on to Germany. If the working classes were indeed Britain's weak link, were not the same classes in Germany just as vulnerable and even less reliable? Germany's supply problem was similar to Britain's. Campbell examined it

---

[42] H. H. Campbell, 'Criticism on Report by Committee on National Indemnity' [Report of Treasury Committee on National Guarantee for the War Risks of Shipping; PP 1908 Cd. 4161–2 LVII] (July 1908, typewritten), fos. 2–3, ADM 137/2749.

[43] S. L. Murray, 'Memo regarding the Effect of a great Maritime War on the Industrial Classes of the United Kingdom. Terms of Reference—Desirability of National Indemnity' (carbon, n.d. but covering letter is dated 7 Feb. 1908), fos. 7–8, 9; top copy (marked 'Personal copy. Henry Campbell' with his annotations), ADM 137/2749; carbon, CAB 17/26, marked 'B.26(4)'.

closely. He studied how the German economy had changed since the Franco-Prussian war. He examined export and import statistics and the capacity of overland and oversea supply routes. His methods were crude but his conclusions were confident. In July 1908 Campbell submitted a long study which ended with the following conclusion: if sea carriage of food and raw materials to Germany was prevented, then land transport by rail over land frontiers would be of no avail. A sea blockade of Germany would 'reduce the German workman to a state which he feels to be intolerable; want of employment, high costs of living are the first steps towards financial embarrassment, once this latter is achieved it is believed that no nation can continue to struggle for long'.[44] Vice-Admiral C. L. Ottley had concluded his term as Director of Naval Intelligence earlier that year. He described these conclusions to the incoming First Lord of the Admiralty, Reginald McKenna:

The Intelligence Dept have all these facts at their finger ends, the problem was constantly under investigation during the whole 3 years I was D. N. I., and Admiral Slade tells me he has given particular attention to it since he succeeded me. . . . throughout the whole period that I was D. N. I. the Admiralty claimed that the geographical position of this country and her preponderant sea-power combine to give us a certain and simple means of strangling Germany at sea. They held that (in a protracted war) the mills of our sea-power (though they would grind the German industrial population slowly perhaps) would grind them 'exceedingly small'—grass would sooner or later grow in the streets of Hamburg and wide-spread dearth and ruin would be inflicted.[45]

The blockade plan grew out of deep existential anxieties in the British public mind. So far it only existed as a planning exercise, but it was not a maverick project. It went with the grain of large economic and political realities; it was attuned to the navy's mood and suited its institutional requirements. Before long it emerged from the back rooms and began to exercise a more pervasive influence.

[44] Captain H. H. Campbell, 'German Trade in Time of War—Effect on the Industrial Output of the Country due to a Call to the Colours, and due to a Scarcity of Raw Materials' (n.d. July 1908?), ADM 137/2872.

[45] Sir C. L. Ottley to R. McKenna, 5 Dec. 1908, McKenna Papers, 3/7/1A, Churchill College, Cambridge. This passage is quoted by A. J. Marder in his *From the Dreadnought to Scapa Flow*, 5 vols. (1961–70), vol. 1, p. 379, but his account of Admiralty views on economic warfare is fragmentary and misleading.

16

POWER AND PLENTY: NAVAL
MERCANTILISM, 1905–1908

I

Another strand in British blockade planning was the Anglo-German commercial rivalry, or rather, its perception by naval officers. This has to be stressed: commercial rivalry is not in itself a direct cause of war. It works through perceptions and minds. Naval officers had little direct experience of economic affairs, except as rentiers, in possession of portfolios of stocks and bonds. Likely as not, they acquired their economic ideas from the Press. For a decade, ever since the "Made in Germany" scare of 1896, the Press had regarded the rising economic power of Germany as a threat to British economic well-being. Whatever the finer points of analysis, the reality of the challenge was hard to deny.[1] It was not as if German growth and expansion directly impoverished Britain (although the loss of parts of some markets was undeniable). On the contrary, Germany was a large customer. Rather, the challenge was a positional one: Germany took the lead in many industries, penetrated traditional British markets overseas (and the unprotected market at home), and enjoyed a prolonged period of prosperity and growth while Britain's economy lurched from one short cycle of depression and recovery to another in a setting of unemployment and stagnation. In a world of tariffs, captive markets and imperial competition, professional formation predisposed naval officers to regard the use of force as a legitimate extension of economic competition. As recently in their experience as 1903 the Royal Navy had mounted a blockade of Venezuela (in collaboration with Italy and Germany) in response to a default on its foreign debt.

A mercantilist view may be found in a paper on 'War with Germany' written by Captain Edmond Slade and printed by the Admiralty in September 1906. Slade commanded the War College at Portsmouth: he was one of the few officers with an influence on strategic thinking and in 1907 he became Director of Naval Intelligence. His perception of the rise of Germany was mercantilistic. German aggression was not the outcome, but the *origin* of her economic prosperity and that prosperity in its turn stimulated her expansionary impulse towards Brazil, south-eastern Europe and the Low Countries. Germany, wrote Slade,

[1] Buchheim, 'Aspects of Anglo-German Trade Rivalry'; Hoffmann, *Britain and the German Trade Rivalry*.

has followed the natural law that the stronger and more capable a state is of looking after itself and of enforcing respect in others, the more prosperous and wealthy it becomes. With this increase of prosperity has also come a great increase in numbers, so that she is now beginning to feel the effect of the growth of population tending to outstrip the means of sustenance. The result of this is that further expansion is felt to be necessary and we must be prepared in the future to see efforts made in various directions in order to obtain room for such increase. . . . whether the authors of the policy would like to draw back now or not, they cannot do so. The expansion must go on until it meets a force stronger than itself, or until the policy directing the state ceases to be of a sufficiently virile nature to stimulate growth and encourage prosperity.[2]

But Slade also realized that economic growth could become a strategic disability, which exposed Germany to that same danger from the sea that Britain had long worried about:

The density of population per square mile in Germany is rapidly attaining such proportions that she is becoming more and more dependent on the sea for feeding her people. She is ceasing to be an agricultural nation, and is becoming a vast industrial nation. This means that she must have the raw material with which to keep her industries going, and if the import is stopped financial difficulties will be entailed which will seriously affect her capability of carrying on a great war. Therefore, besides direct action on her flanks, our efforts must be concentrated on the destruction of that trade. The flow of raw material and foodstuffs inwards, as well as manufactured articles outwards, is rapidly becoming almost as much a necessity for her as it is for us . . .

The Admiralty fixed its mind on the prospect of a single great battle that would decide the command of the sea.[3] This preference grew naturally out of the Royal Navy's great preponderance in hulls and gun-barrels over its prospective rivals. It was reinforced by the verdict on commerce-destroying in that sea-officers' bible, Mahan's *The Influence of Sea Power upon History*. 'Such a mode of war', wrote Mahan (of the seventeenth century), 'is inconclusive, worrying but not deadly: it might be said that it causes needless suffering.' Furthermore,

It is doubtless a most important secondary operation of naval war, and is not likely to be abandoned till war itself shall cease; but regarded as a primary and fundamental measure, sufficient in itself to crush an enemy, it is probably a delusion, and a most dangerous delusion, when presented in the fascinating garb of cheapness to the representatives of a people.[4]

---

[2] Capt. E. J. W. Slade, 'War with Germany' (printed, 1 Sept. 1906), p. 1, ADM 116/1036B.

[3] Ranft, 'Protection of Seaborne Trade', p. 15.

[4] A. T. Mahan, *The Influence of Sea Power upon History, 1660–1783* (1890, Sagamore Press edn. New York 1957), pp. 119, 481.

Like Mahan, Slade only allowed commercial blockade a secondary role in a possible war.

In 1905 the most powerful brain in the Naval Intelligence Department was a lieutenant of marines not yet thirty, with responsibility for port defences. Maurice Hankey (1877–1963) was on the verge of an extraordinary career which left a lasting imprint on British defence policy. From the Naval Intelligence Department, Hankey moved to the Committee of Imperial Defence, where he was secretary from 1912 to 1938. He was also cabinet secretary from 1916 to 1938, and finally served, in a diminished role, as cabinet minister. In the winter of 1906–7 Admiral Fisher appointed a committee to work out a strategy for a naval war with Germany. Hankey was its secretary. In addition to the active members (Captain G. A. Ballard, Hankey and two technical specialists) two other officers were also in on the secret: Captain Slade, head of the Naval War College, and Captain Charles Ottley, the Director of Naval Intelligence. 'We worked under Fisher's immediate inspiration' wrote Hankey in his memoirs. Ballard took the lead, but he 'left to me the general scheme of the report, much of the drafting, and many important details'. Hankey revived his German and 'read a great deal in the original . . . much of my work for the next twelve years was carried out under the influence of this intensive study of five months duration'. 'In the end,' wrote Hankey, 'we produced a comprehensive volume of some sixty pages.'[5] Nothing I have seen in the archives actually fits this description. Instead, there is a set of papers and plans of various versions and dates, many of which were printed by the Admiralty in 1907 and 1908 and bound up as a set of war plans, of which an edition has been published by Commander Peter Kemp.[6] All were unsigned. Commander Kemp's edition is made up of the following elements. First comes an historical essay on 'Some Principles of Naval Warfare' written by the civilian historian and lecturer at the war college, Julian Corbett. Then follows a paper entitled 'War Plans—General Remarks on War with Germany—a Preamble for Reflection and Criticism' (hereafter 'Preamble'), which is a revised version of Captain Slade's 1906 essay on 'War with Germany'. Part III consists of a number of plans for a close blockade of the North Sea and Baltic ports of Germany under different assumptions, together with papers on supplementary landings and raids on the German littoral. The set ends with summaries of some war games and a short critical paper by Admiral A. K. Wilson, Admiral Fisher's trusted colleague and his eventual successor as First Sea Lord.

Admiral John Fisher's series of "war plans" of 1907–8 were not intended to serve as a plan of campaign, but as discrete tactical and strategic studies.[7] It

---

[5] Lord Hankey, *The Supreme Command, 1914–1918* (1961), vol. 1, pp. 39–40.
[6] P. Kemp (ed.), *The Fisher Papers*, vol. 2 (1964), Navy Records Society, vol. 106.
[7] 'War Plans', fo. 72, ADM 116/1043B/I.

is likely that they were printed in order to provide Fisher with ammunition in his struggle with Admiral Charles Beresford.[8]

The plans contain at least two separate and incompatible strategies. One group of officers thought that, in case of war, Germany's dependence on overseas trade offered Britain the prospect of victory by means of commercial blockade. Economic warfare was the decisive weapon. I shall call these officers the naval "economists". A second group was agnostic. This difference emerges in a long paper called 'Notes on Attached "War Plans"' which was filed with the war plans, but was not printed. 'Notes' is a tentative statement of the "economist" position, and there is reason to believe that the author was Maurice Hankey.[9]

Hankey had a knack for exercising power from a subordinate position. His method was to brief seniors and win them over by the force of personality, industry and intellect. Someone so junior in status and rank posed no threat to his "frontsmen" and Hankey could often steer them down roads of his own choosing. He got his way 'not by talking at the meeting, but by insinuating my ideas to each member privately . . . and making him think it is his own. Then I support him at the meeting and we get our way . . .'[10]

Hankey had a singular independence of mind, and refused to be awed by authority. As a marine officer, he escaped the powerful conditioning rubbed into naval cadets. His knowledge of languages, wide reading and broad sympathies acquainted him with a world outside the Service. The 'Notes' have that undeferential undertone; they also express the essence of Hankey's endeavour in the years leading up to the war, a project that absorbed his powers of persuasion and intrigue. Hankey adhered to those principles for the next twenty-five years and endeavoured to work them into British strategic thought and action. The paper has a lucidity and grasp that are hallmarks of Hankey's style. By a process of elimination, only Hankey and Ballard could have penned this document, so it is safe to see Hankey's mind behind the blockading plan even at this early stage, if not earlier. He himself claimed as much.[11]

The 'Notes' open with a restatement of Captain Slade's mercantilistic premises: 'That the continued development of the power and resources of the German empire will render further expansion inevitable, that consequently the balance of power will be upset and Germany will become

---

[8] Adm. R. H. Bacon, *The Life of Lord Fisher of Kilverstone* (1929), vol. 2, pp. 34–5.

[9] It is in a folder labelled Ballard Committee. Hankey was the secretary and the moving force of this committee. The document (17fos.) is also in a format favoured by Hankey, i.e. large type, wide right margin and deep indentation.

[10] Maurice to Adeline Hankey, 28 July 1906; quoted in Roskill, *Hankey*, vol. 1, p. 69.

[11] Hankey, *Supreme Command*, vol. 1, pp. 39–40.

1. Ethel Cooper (centre) in Leipzig, 1913,
with the composer Sandor Vas (left) and another friend.

2. Captain Maurice Hankey, Royal Marines.

3. William Lyon Mackenzie King in Windsor uniform, 1910.

4. Admiral John Fisher, 1904.

5. Reginald, Second Viscount Esher.

6. Reginald McKenna, First Lord of the Admiralty, 1908–11.

7. Admiral Alfred von Tirpitz.

8. Robert L. Borden, Prime Minister of Canada, 1919.

9. Herbert Hoover.

10. William Morris Hughes,
Prime Minister of Australia, 1919.

predominant on the Continent unless we are prepared to check her progress.'[12]

Slade had acknowledged the value of economic warfare, but (in keeping with Mahan's dicta) he only allowed it a secondary role. In contrast, the operational war plans which followed his 'Preamble' are founded on the premise that a close commercial blockade, supported by raids and landings on the German littoral, provided an adequate strategy; or, in other words, that a decision could be secured by economic pressure. 'It is clear,' writes Hankey in the 'Notes' (I shall assume his paternity) 'that the authors of the "War Plans" [the Ballard Committee] and the writer of the "Preamble" [Slade] hold very divergent views regarding the power of this country to apply adequate pressure upon Germany by the attack of trade and commerce.' A maritime power and a continental industrial state had never fought a great war in modern conditions. Germany's new dependence on imports and Britain's control of the merchant marine had altered conditions since Mahan wrote.[13] Indeed, Mahan himself had changed his mind long before. In 1894 he made a distinction 'between *guerre de course*, which was inconclusive, and commerce-destroying (or commerce prevention) through strategic control of the sea by powerful navies'. Such a strategy might well be decisive. In 1907 Mahan wrote that,

in the development of her merchant shipping Germany, to use a threadbare phrase, has given a hostage to Fortune. . . . Germany is bound over to keep the peace, unless occasion of national safety—vital interests—or honor drive her, or unless she equip a navy adequate to so great a task as protecting fully the carrying trade which she has laboriously created. The exposure of this trade is . . . a circumstance making for peace.[14]

The prospects of commercial blockade were not only for naval officers to decide, but also for economic experts. Referring to Campbell's work at the Trade Division, Hankey wrote:

It is at least arguable whether a continental country could in the present day hold out against the effects of a blockade such as that maintained by the British fleet against Napoleon. This is a subject on which the opinions of Political Economists would be more valuable than those of Naval Officers. . . . The fundamental question, on which as has been pointed out, authorities are divided, is whether any pressure of this kind which we can apply will be sufficient. This "master problem" is being examined as far as possible by the Trade Division of the NID. But, on a point

[12] 'Notes on attached "War Plans"' (1907), fo. 226, ADM 116/1043B.

[13] Ibid., fo. 228.

[14] A. T. Mahan and Lord Charles Beresford, 'Possibilities of an Anglo-American Reunion', *NAR*, vol. 159 (1894), p. 561; Mahan, *Some Neglected Aspects of War* (1907), p. 181.

of such transcendental import it is considered that the highest financial and commercial experts might well also be called into secret council.[15]

Here were the seeds of a project which Hankey eventually carried out.

If the blockade project was unsound, then Britain could not rely upon the navy alone. In that case a large land army would have to be raised. On the other hand, if economic warfare was the decisive strategy, then a close blockade was imperative, 'with a view to the eventual entry of the Baltic . . . so to bring the utmost pressure on the German nation which it is possible to exert by sea power alone'. Much of the paper deals with the deployment of naval units. It concludes by restating the essential points:

it is an historical fact that no war has hitherto been brought to an end by such means as it is here proposed to employ. But on the other hand it must be remembered that the modern industrial situation is unprecedented and the effect of such a blockade as is here proposed defies calculation. One thing at least is certain, viz. that in Germany such action on our part is undoubtedly greatly feared.[16]

German fears and British "economist" attitudes certainly fed on each other. In July 1905, at the height of the Morocco crisis, Admiral Fisher sent a squadron of battleships on a provocative cruise into the Baltic. He boasted to a friend that, 'With great difficulty I've got our Channel Fleet up the Baltic and cruising in the North Sea. "Our drill ground should be our battle ground." Don't repeat that phrase, but I've taken means to have it whispered in the German Emperor's ear!'[17]

Fears of blockade were a constant refrain in the German Press. After 1905 the diplomatic isolation of Germany and the acceleration of naval construction raised these fears into prominence once again. They were no secret to the Admiralty.[18]

The Admiralty 'War Plans' file contains another "economist" paper from 1907 in the form of comment on a report of the British naval attaché in Berlin, Commander Dumas:

The strategy he advocates consists, in a few words, of starving Germany into submission by destroying her sea-borne trade. He anticipates, from German Manoeuvres, that the Germans believe that England intends to institute a blockade of the German coasts . . . he recommends, as the only method of luring the German Fleets to sea, the attack of their trade which, by driving them to desperation, will, he believes, force them to come out.

    [15] 'Notes', fos. 228, 231, ADM 116/1043B.
    [16] Ibid., fo. 242.
    [17] John Fisher to Julian Corbett, 28 July 1905, in *FG*, vol. 2 (1956), p. 63; Mackay, *Fisher*, p. 364; also 'British Naval Policy and German Aspirations', *Fortnightly Review*, Sept. 1905, repr. Admiralty, pp. 1–2, ADM 116/904B.
    [18] Ch. 23 below. See Vice-Adm. R. Siegel (ret., German Navy), 'Some Reflections on the Necessary Strength of the German Fleet and the Question of Disarmament', esp. pp. 1–2; transl. by the Admiralty from *Deutsche Revue* (Nov. 1908), ADM 116/1070 and 116/940B, with marginal comments.

The author (Hankey again?) affirmed his belief in blockade even more strongly, and summed up with the following considerations:

1. German trade is growing rapidly.
2. The consumption of wheat per head is rising.
3. Germany is becoming more and more dependent on oversea carriage for food and raw materials.
4. There are not sufficient neutral ships to replace British and German ships (trading to Germany) laid up by a war.
5. German trading ports are so placed geographically as to be readily closed by an enemy strong on the sea.
6. A great deal of the money lost to Germany by stoppage of trade would necessarily find its way into England . . .
8. Even supposing Germany obtained wheat etc. by land the prices would be very high.

He continued:

In view of the above, and postulating as we must, a very large fighting superiority for the British Fleet, the weight of argument against any desire on the part of Germany to provoke a war with Britain is very great, and it is difficult to avoid the conclusion that, *in such a war the strangulation of her commerce would be a deadly blow to her.*[19]

II

In the meantime Campbell, at the Trade Division, had begun his study of the impact of the Franco-Prussian war on the German economy. By extrapolating from 1871 on to conditions in 1907, Campbell confirmed the "economist" case, that Germany had become very vulnerable to economic pressure. Campbell assumed that Germany would be fighting Britain only. France and Russia would be neutral but unfriendly to Germany, which would have to mobilize as a precaution. In these circumstances, its economy would work under two constraints, a shortage of labour and of vital imports. Germany had grown enormously dependent upon such imported raw materials as cotton since the previous war and a call-up might be the lesser evil, 'for by this means she can better keep those men in hand, who otherwise will be scattered over the country, in want, dissatisfied and a danger to the community'.[20] Russia might be able to meet German requirements for grain if the harvest was good and other exports cut down. But Germany's imports from eastern Europe mostly travelled from the Black Sea to the North Sea. Campbell doubted whether Russian railways

---

[19] 'M.0171/07', fos. 225, 261, ADM 116/1043B. Emphasis added.
[20] Capt. H. H. Campbell, 'German Trade in Time of War—Effect on the Industrial Output of the Country due to a Call to the Colours, and due to a Scarcity of Raw Materials,' (n.d. July 1908?), ADM 137/2872.

could carry the grain if German ports were closed. If the Dutch and Belgian ports took over part of the strain, that would merely crowd out other vital imports: 'One thing is certain, transference from sea carriage to overland transport must add enormously to the cost for the consumer, it is this additional cost that we must produce and reduce the German workman to a state which he feels intolerable.'

In May 1908 the inquiry was taken further. British consuls in Hamburg, Antwerp, Rotterdam and Frankfurt were asked to report 'how far Germany does depend on overseas supplies, and to what extent these overseas supplies can be deviated from their normal to new channels in time of war . . .'.[21]

It may be argued that the "economist" mentality was mainly defensive; indeed, I shall argue along these lines myself in the next chapter. But that was not how it was presented. Officers like Slade (as we have seen) regarded the conflict as a struggle between rival trading empires. Admiral Fisher took a similar view. As early as August 1902 he wrote to his jingo journalist friend Arnold White with a request to 'sow the seed and foster its growth':

The German Emperor may be devoted to us, but he can no more stem the tide of German commercial hostility to this country of ours than Canute could keep the North Sea from wetting his patent-leather boots! It's inherent. Their interests everywhere clash with ours, and their gratitude for all our astounding beneficence to them is nil! [This, doubtless, a reference to Britain's free trade policy which opened British markets to German goods without reciprocity.] It is a fact that at Hong Kong, a body of German merchants assembled to drink champagne in gratitude for our reverses in the Transvaal; looking thereby to German ascendancy there, through Holland, which they intend to annex. Mind, this in our colony, where we give them every freedom to oust our own merchants and our steamship lines from their former predominant position![22]

Apart from such asides (which recur in Fisher's letters) the militant mercantilist view is not easy to document from official sources. A clear statement from within the Naval Intelligence Department is contained in a paper on 'War with Germany' by Captain Osmond de B. Brock, an assistant DNI, dating from 10 June 1908. It follows the War Plans prints and merits quotation at length.

It is frequently said that this country will never provoke a war with Germany on the grounds that we have nothing to gain and everything to lose. This was true and is so at the present time; in the near future Germany will be a most formidable competitor for the World's trade, her fleet will rival ours and the condition of

---

[21] The questionnaire and the reports are in FO 371/460. Sir Francis Oppenheimer's very significant reply (from Frankfurt): ch. 20, sec. II, below; Bell, *History of the Blockade*, p. 25.
[22] *FG*, vol. 1, pp. 259–60.

affairs will be entirely altered. Whether two great commercial and maritime powers can exist side by side remains to be seen, all that can be said is that such a state of affairs has never existed previously in the world's history and no reasons can be adduced—except the growing dislike to wars on account of their wide-spreading qualities—to show that history is unlikely to repeat itself. If the historical fact that European waters are too small for two maritime nations is accepted, a war between ourselves and Germany appears inevitable. It need hardly be said that our relative superiority in Naval power to Germany is considerable to-day and it is equally true that it will require very great efforts on our part to maintain this superiority, whether these efforts are a greater drain on the country's resources than those which a war would cause must be decided by statesmen; in the present condition of public affairs it may be predicted with certainty that the British Government will never force a war on Germany, however much such a course is desirable from strategical reasons. This is not considered to be the case by continental opinion, which also points to history and shows how England has invariably attacked any power which she considered was becoming too formidable. There is a lot to be said for this view and the contrary opinion held by Engish apologists is largely due to the national hypocrisy which refuses to face facts and seldom cares to analyse motives to their bed-rock foundation . . . Both nations have the same principal object—the cause of many wars—viz: destruction of a commercial competitor. To this in Germany's case may be added the wish for colonies which can only be satisfied by Great Britain. Our object is the same as Germany's, viz 'the removal of a trade rival', and is uncomplicated by any further objects such as territorial enlarge-ment.[23]

This statement of naval mercantilism was typical of views held in Britain on the Radical Right, and expressed in such journals as the *Daily Mail* or Maxse's *National Review*.[24] It is not surprising that such views should also be expressed within the navy, in close conjunction with strategic plans.

But what sort of significance do they carry? Economic factors do not declare wars by themselves. They impinge on policy through the preconceptions and calculations of officials. In this paper, the intelligence officer suggests that the cost of crushing the enemy once and for all might be cheaper than the cost of sustaining the arms race. In other words, an economic justification for preventive war. We shall hear an echo of these calculations once again, in Sir Edward Grey's speech to the House of Commons on 3 August 1914, which carried Britain into the war. For the moment, we can regard them as expressing one kind of understanding of the nature of British preparations for war, and one underlying motivation

---

[23] Capt. O. de B. Brock, 'War with Germany' (10 June 1908), fos. 649–51, ADM 116/1043B/1.
[24] Collections of this material: Twells Brex (ed.), *"Scare Mongerings" from the Daily Mail, 1896–1914* (1914), and J. L. Maxse, *"Germany on the Brain" or, The Obsession of "A Crank": Gleanings from the National Review, 1899–1914* (1915); the Radical Right: A. J. A. Morris, *The Scaremongers: The Advocacy of War and Rearmament, 1896–1914* (1984).

for planning and for action. The timing is also significant, for in the summer and autumn of 1908 British naval strategy entered a new phase.

<h1 style="text-align:center">III</h1>

These mercantilist meditations, and Campbell's more practical investigations, might be dismissed as routine contingency planning. But in the autumn of 1908 they acquired a sudden urgency. The navy had to decide on a definite strategy because the Prime Minister had started an official inquiry into 'the Military Needs of the Empire', by means of a sub-committee of the Committee of Imperial Defence (CID). This sub-committee, which first met on 3 December 1908, was an imposing gathering, chaired by the Prime Minister, and consisting of senior cabinet ministers, civil servants and military chiefs. Rear-Admiral Slade, the Director of Naval Intelligence, presented the navy's strategy at the second meeting. His paper, eight pages of printed text and nine pages of supporting tables, is the basic document of the navy's strategy of economic warfare, and the crown of Campbell's labours. In time of war, it stated, Germany's predicament was analogous to Britain's:

> The cases of Great Britain and Germany are not dissimilar as regards their wealth-producing sources. This country is practically dependent on industrial production, and so to a very great extent is Germany. This condition implies a necessity for raw material, consequently a dependence on the sea. Our need for overseas supplies may be the greater, but our power to obtain those supplies is also greater, largely due to our superior geographical position.[25]

A stoppage of imports or even a mere rise in the prices of raw materials and foodstuffs, in both countries, 'must tend to produce a position which might become intolerable'. The destructive mechanism was ultimately financial. Unable to export, Germany would suffer distress, unemployment and finally bankruptcy. Over and above its naval and geographical advantages, Britain had further resources in the form of a huge merchant fleet and large overseas investments, both providing additional credit in wartime. Without such advantages the German Empire would exhaust its capacity to wage war.

The Committee of Imperial Defence only required a short discussion to accept this strategy. Lord Crewe (whose judgement Asquith later rated highest among his colleagues) put the attractions in a nutshell: 'the general conclusion to be derived from the Director of Naval Intelligence's

---

[25] 'The Economic Effect of War on German Trade', Admiralty Memorandum (CID Paper E–4), 12 Dec. 1908, p. 25; printed as Appendix V, 'Report of the Sub-Committee of the Committee of Imperial Defence to Consider the Military Needs of the Empire' (Additional tables in Appendix VI), (July 1909), CAB 16/5.

Memorandum was that *Germany would suffer much more loss from a war than we should.'* The notion of a cheap war, with economic as well as political attractions, could not be more clearly stated. In its report the committee concluded: 'we are of the opinion that a serious situation would be created in Germany owing to the blockade of her ports, and that the longer the duration of the war the more serious the situation would become.' But economic pressure would work too slowly to save France. So it also extended a qualified and conditional approval to the General Staff's plan of sending an Expeditionary Force of five divisions to reinforce the French.[26]

A few historians have questioned the authority of the Committee of Imperial Defence.[27] It is true that the Committee had no executive powers of its own. It provided an agenda for meetings of the Prime Minister and his inner Cabinet with naval and military commanders, and the top civil servants. But its members were amply endowed with executive power and personal authority in their own right. The assembly of powerful figures around a common table for prolonged consultations is what gave the Committee its great significance.[28] This judgement is confirmed by hindsight. When Britain entered the war in 1914, the outline plans presented to the CID by the navy and the army, and approved more than five years previously, were executed almost to the letter.

In 1910, however, after Fisher's departure, the navy largely abandoned its work on economic warfare. The project was then taken up by Captain Maurice Hankey, at the Committee of Imperial Defence. He was not acting entirely on his own.

[26] 'Report of the Sub-Committee . . . to Consider the Military Needs of the Empire' (July 1909), pp. xviii-x (my italics), CAB 16/5. The form of words used appears to give an implicit priority to naval means, although too much should not be read into this exegesis. The text is: 'in the event of an attack on France by Germany, the expediency of sending a military force abroad, or of relying on naval means only, is a matter of policy which can only be determined when the occasion arises by the Government of the day.' Asquith's rating of Crewe appears in his *Letters to Venetia Stanley*, ed. M. and E. Brock (Oxford 1982), letter 395, 16 Apr. 1915, p. 545.

[27] This critical view of the CID and Hankey originates from J. P. Mackintosh, 'The Role of the Committee of Imperial Defence before 1914', *English Historical Review*, vol. 77 (1962), and has been accepted by a number of historians whose research has centred on Foreign and War Office records, and especially by N. d'Ombrain, *War Machinery and High Policy* (1973). Hankey's account is in his *Supreme Command*, vol. 1, esp. ch. 8. Given his abilities and special knowledge, one has to rate his authority as high or higher than that of his critics.

[28] This is also the opinion of a distinguished Canadian historian, C. P. Stacey, *Canada and the Age of Conflict* (Toronto 1977), p. 163.

17

THE ATLANTIC ORIENTATION: HANKEY, FISHER AND ESHER

I

Between 1910 and 1914 the doctrine that inspired the blockade project was this: the key to Britain's security was not the balance of power on the continent, but the resources of English-speaking societies overseas. Not a "continental commitment" but an "Atlantic orientation". The German challenge offered Britain a range of possible responses, from complete inactivity to massive intervention. The choice was partly a matter of judgement, partly a matter of values, partly a matter of temperament, if the three can be separated. As a serious strategic option, the Atlantic orientation was largely the creation of three unorthodox individuals: a junior staff officer, a retired Admiral and a gentleman of leisuré. The three were Captain Maurice Hankey, Admiral Jacky Fisher and the second Viscount Esher. There was a fourth man, the First Lord of the Admiralty Reginald McKenna—he will make his appearance later.

Fisher commanded the Royal Navy between 1904 and 1910. He had marked the young Hankey for preferment as early as 1900 and continued to regard him as a protégé. He helped to install Hankey at the Committee of Imperial Defence (CID) and endowed him with the full measure of his generosity and friendship. Fisher's rapport with Esher was also of long standing. It was cemented when the two served together on the War Office Reconstitution Committee in 1903, and began the process of modernizing the British land forces. Their collaboration on the "economist" project appears to have started in 1908. Each of the three was a distinctive and original Edwardian personality, standing far above the common run.

All three derived their authority from irregular sources and all three exercised an influence that far exceeded their formal authority. Take Fisher first. He wielded charismatic authority at the top of a powerful bureaucracy. Between 1904 and 1909 he completely overshadowed the ministers who were his nominal superiors. No one remembers Cawdor or Tweedmouth, and McKenna only came out of the shadow after Fisher's departure. Neither his predecessors nor his successors ever achieved such an ascendancy. Fisher rode over the constitutional and conventional limits of his office by sheer force of personality. Eventually this proved his undoing, when he ran ahead of his resources. After his retirement Fisher continued to act like a monarch-in-exile and to meddle in naval affairs. It is easy to dismiss him as a cantankerous pensioner during those years, except that his pretensions were justified, and he was reappointed First Sea Lord soon after the war broke out.

Hankey's authority was exercised differently, and lower down the ladder of office. Staff officers sometimes acquire powers well in excess of their rank. Henry Wilson in England and Ludendorff in Germany both had a decisive influence before they arrived at the top. Indeed, Ludendorff always kept the pretence of inferior rank. In Germany this vesting of authority in subordinates was almost a rule. But Hankey's case was unique. As a captain of marines, a mere three rungs up the ladder, he already aspired to steer the British Empire. Influential supporters helped him to become secretary of the CID, a position that was well beyond a captain's expectations. The position was his own creation. His two predecessors Clarke and Ottley had restricted themselves to a technical function. Even before he became the secretary, Hankey made a bid for real power. Like Fisher, his authority ultimately rested on exceptional gifts of personality.

Esher's authority drew on a more archaic model. He was a courtier. As head of the Office of Works towards the end of Victoria's reign, he administered the Royal Palaces and stage-managed jubilees, funerals, coronations, the pomp and circumstance that sustained the monarchy. He gained the confidence of Queen Victoria, and King Edward VII came to depend on him for trivial and crucial arrangements alike. This position at the court was one of the keys to the confidence of Balfour, and his performance on two commissions after the South African war earned him a personal membership of the CID, of which, at first, he was one of only two permanent members. Esher, like his two other friends, excelled at using other people. Fisher and Esher, the King's Secretary wrote, 'both preferred to come in at the back door instead of the front'.[1] Esher, like Fisher, manipulated the Press, cultivated friends in both parties, and was able to fall back on the King. While he relished power as much as Hankey and Fisher, he shrank from formal responsibility. Twice he was offered the War Office, and once the Viceroyalty of India; thrice he refused, saying that he preferred the substance of power to its trappings; also, he might have added, to its inevitable exposures and punishments.

After 1908 relations between the three went beyond a unity of purpose and ripened into a warm and intimate friendship. Their bond spanned the generations. Hankey was thirty-three in 1910, Fisher was sixty-nine, Esher fifty-eight. After 1910 both Fisher and Esher lived away from London much of the time and relied on Hankey to keep them informed. A large number of letters attest to the quality of the friendship. It was free of the rancour so common among colleagues. They came together to promote a cause, not to protect a position, and they had a positive delight in each other's attention.

---

[1] Sir Frederick Ponsonby, quoted by J. Lees-Milne, *The Enigmatic Edwardian: The Life of Reginald, 2nd Viscount Esher* (1986), p. 181.

Subordinates exercise power at the sufferance of their superiors. None of the three had security of tenure, and after 1910 only Hankey had an official appointment (though both Fisher and Esher were members of the CID). Yet they managed to push policy a fair distance their way. By defining the options for action, and prescribing a programme, Hankey was able to influence the terms of strategic debate. His very weakness was a source of strength. Why should men of power delegate it downwards? In bureaucracies knowledge is power and the person with titular authority often has no time to study the choices that have to be made. The power to promote some choices and exclude others is a substantial one. Power has to be delegated; and sovereign statesmen prefer to share it with subordinates rather than yield it to their equals. If a subordinate is competent there is less inhibition in delegating authority the more junior he or she is. Hankey drew his power from such unconscious or deliberate delegation of power. But he was only able to do so on account of his ability and sense of purpose. His promotion of the "economist" strategy was driven by springs in his personality and values. To a lesser but still important extent this was also true of his friends.

II

Hankey

Hankey left Rugby School at eighteen for a career as an officer in the marines. He was an exceptional kind of soldier: inquisitive, well-read, imaginative, artistic; he continued for a time to practise the violin aboard ship.[2] During his service with the Mediterranean fleet he studied French, Italian and Greek, and he felt embarrassed at his compatriots' condescension to Maltese and Greeks. Hankey devised innovative landing exercises for his marine detachment. On board ship he undertook unofficial intelligence work and wrote on tactical matters. As a junior officer he won distinction in two of Fisher's tactical essay competitions, and typed one on his own typewriter, another sign of the innovative temperament. In 1900 he began to consolidate his military thinking, and subsequently completed a number of chapters on 'Warfare on the Littoral'.[3] His official and private papers, as well as his memoirs, are written with fluency, penetration and skill. As another instance of non-conformity, he preferred a diet of wholemeal bread, raw vegetables, fresh fruit, eggs and nuts, and complained when he could not get it on board ship.[4]

---

[2] Roskill, *Hankey*, vol. 1, pp. 40–1.   [3] Ibid., pp. 58, 52.
[4] G. Mallaby, 'Maurice Hankey', *The Dictionary of National Biography, 1961–1970* (Oxford 1981); Maurice to Adeline Hankey, 25 July 1906, HP 3/14; also Maurice Hankey to Lord Esher, 3 Aug. 1912, EP 5/41.

In letters to his wife Hankey comes out as a romantic sentimentalist whose ideas and values were out of step with those of the average naval officer. Thrown together with a group of naval and military officers on a long cruise in 1906, he wrote to his wife, 'I fear I am not a great success socially . . . I hold contrary views to the others on almost every subject— generally so fundamentally contrary that it seems useless to air them.'[5]

Hankey was an intellectual in uniform. As a thinking man, the problem he had to face was how to reconcile rationality and violence. War can be a conflict of minds; it is always a conflict of will: the will to win regardless of destruction, dismemberment and death. There is no way around this brutal reality. As a tactical dilemma it became more evident (though perhaps not evident enough) to Hankey's generation of officers. Both infantry and artillery firepower had increased manyfold since the American civil war, while mobility on the battlefield slowed down to the pace of an infantryman's slog. An enemy front could only be taken by smothering a wall of fire with a tide of people, at a tremendous cost in injury and lives.[6]

This was a personal dilemma as well as a strategic one. No cunning, it seemed, could eliminate the fearful odds of actual combat. Reason rebels against this conclusion, for it posits the risk of self-destruction as the price of success. This dilemma has to be faced by those who choose military careers. Bloch found a deep pessimism among European officers about their chances of survival.[7] Partly, however, it was a matter of tempera- ment. Faced with a challenge, some were more inclined to fight, others towards flight. Career officers were not always imaginative. Or they could gamble on seniority and a safe billet before the slaughter began. Hankey pondered this problem. As a young officer, he had revelled in the physical and mental exuberance of tactical exercises. A few years later, as a married man and a more reflective person, he wrote candidly to his wife,

The fact is I am a man of peace. I have no desire for war or active service, in fact I strongly deprecate either, and though I should do my duty if sent to the front I could not work up much enthusiasm unless I felt sure that our cause was just, and in 99 cases out of 100 wars appear to me unjust and wrong. Under these circumstances I question whether I am justified in remaining in a service in which I am tolerably well paid in peace in order that the country may exact unquestioning obedience and sacrifice from me in war. To me it seems that I am to some extent a humbug and hypocrite in accepting such a position. But if I give it up what am I to do? The inexorable force of circumstances seems to indicate that I must continue as I have begun. If so I shall seek administrative and organizing posts . . . rather than active

[5] 30 July 1906, HP 3/14.
[6] Howard, 'Men against Fire'; M. Howard, 'The Armed Forces', *New Cambridge Modern History*, vol. 11 (1962), pp. 206–18; S. Bidwell and D. Graham, *Fire-Power: British Army Weapons and Theories of War, 1904–1945* (1982), chs. 2, 3.
[7] Bloch, *War of the Future*, p. xxxv.

billets, in the hope that I may eventually find a stepping stone into some more congenial service.[8]

Hankey was a rational calculator, and had scant regard for the military mystique, with its demand for conformity and ritual aggression as the price of approbation. But he did not have all the courage of his convictions. His career had a streak of venality and self-regard. It is evident in this letter, and it received a more public expression at the end of the First World War, when he accepted a financial reward from Parliament which Lloyd George (with a better moral sense) decided to turn down. Hankey's instinct for self-preservation is a clue to the spirit in which he approached the question of national defence.

Hankey's strategy of national survival was akin to his strategy of personal survival. From this point of view, two elements of economic warfare appealed to Hankey's temperament. As Liddell Hart would later put it, Hankey sought an "indirect approach", a strategy that minimized the necessity for bloodshed, a course of limited commitment and limited liability. Even better, the threat of blockade might deter Germany so effectively that war was avoided altogether.

Another shipboard episode captures the difference in outlook between Hankey and the average military man. It underlines his dislike of violence and his calculating approach to power:

Last night at dinner, in order to divert my thoughts from sea-sickness, I started an argument about arbitration as the proper means of settling differences between civilized nations in lieu of war; they all turned on like one man but I stuck to my guns; the general got particularly annoyed and talked about 'sickly sentimental-ity' . . . It is curious what queer views some people have. Furse, for instance, who is quite a reasonable and in many ways an able man, and is certain to rise to the top of the tree in the Army, seriously believes that the destiny of the British race is to conquer the whole of the world 'vi et armis' and to rule it for ever afterwards. He forgets that numerically we form only a very small proportion of the world population, that compared with many other races our rate of increase is very slow, that the nation will not have conscription at any price, and that we are little if any better at fighting than the other nations of Europe and America, to say nothing of Japan, to whom we are almost certainly inferior in bravery and self-sacrifice.[9]

Like a greyhound among mongrels, Hankey had a sense of his own fitness. From 1902 onwards he was successively on staff positions within the Admiralty and he realized that there ought to be no limit to his ambition; he understood how policy was made and he had the measure of his abilities. After rubbing shoulders with politicians he no longer stood in awe of them. As early as 1906 he canvassed for a position in the CID. Already

[8] Maurice to Adeline Hankey, 14 Oct. 1906, in Roskill, *Hankey*, vol. 1, p. 74.
[9] Maurice to Adeline Hankey, 27 Aug. 1906, HP 3/14.

he had a notion of what he could do with it. Staff work on the Owen Committee on overseas defence, he wrote to his wife,

adds to my reputation in precisely the direction in which we wish it added to—not as a fighting man but as a sound peace administrator. Imagine, for instance, if I could get the billet which Captain Ottley suggested to me! It would get me into personal contact with all the leading men of the day. In such a case any liberal tendencies would make themselves manifest, and liberals are so rare among naval and military men that it might lead to all sorts of possibilities.[10]

In January 1908 Hankey became an assistant secretary at the CID, the launching pad of his ambitions. We shall follow his work there in some detail. Before that, however, how did this reluctant warrior come into concord with the fire-eating Fisher?

III

Fisher

You cannot remain indifferent to Admiral John Arbuthnot Fisher. Many naval colleagues hated his guts and questioned his judgement, but I trust that most readers of his letters, papers and memoirs, even if they are put off by some of the bluster, will warm to his imaginative and extrovert personality. His pen (and his bold, oversized, often underlined handwriting) exudes emotional energy and intelligence; his impish curiosity flits from one topic to another, mixes shop, gossip, politics, endearment and affection. Fisher had a steely sense of purpose and was a dangerous man to cross. He was also a man of exceptional professional competence who inspired confidence in superiors and subordinates. Often he was able to hold his own in committee rooms against the sharpest lawyer-politicians of the day. He understood that public opinion was as vital as intrigue and took care to cultivate journalists and manipulate the Press.

Fisher was entirely a self-made man, with no blue blood, broad acres or money to smooth his way. His temperament was one of uncontained exuberance, gushing forth alike in his letters and in marathon bouts of dancing, which he continued well into retirement. There was also a serious reflective side to his personality, a deep religion and love of literature. Like Hankey, his self-approbation was ample. He had no need for that obtuse arrogance that bolstered the self-esteem of so many officers and flawed their personalities.

Fisher is famous for statements of blood-curdling bellicosity. For three or four years he toyed with a plan to descend on the German fleet without

---

[10] Maurice to Adeline Hankey, ?11 Aug. 1906, Roskill, *Hankey*, vol. 1, p. 74.

warning and sink it in its moorings.[11] He liked to boast about his plan to force the Baltic and land an army 'on a stretch of ten miles of hard sand which is ninety miles from Berlin'.[12] Fisher regarded "humanity in warfare" as humbug. Rather, he said, 'hit your enemy in the belly and kick him when he is down, and boil your prisoners in oil (if you take any!), and torture his women and children, then people will keep clear of you'. His writings are shot through with these notions.[13]

Invariably, however, this was not sabre-rattling for its own sake but firmly associated with an idea of deterrence. 'Don't imagine I'm warlike,' he wrote to Winston Churchill, who definitely was. Fisher simply wanted his signal to Germany to be unambiguous and clear. In another letter he described his reading of Norman Angell's anti-war book *The Great Illusion* as 'heavenly manna': 'So man did eat angel's food,' he wrote.[14] To his intimate friend the radical journalist W. T. Stead he exclaimed, 'I am not for war, I am for peace ! That is why I am for a supreme Navy . . . my sole object is peace. What you call my truculence is all for peace.' In Stead's own judgement Fisher 'had the not uncommon notion . . . that nations are deterred from going to war by a fear of the atrocities which accompany conflict'.[15] Like Hankey, he hoped that preparation for war would act as a deterrent. As he wrote to Esher, 'it is a most serious drawback not making public to the world beforehand what we meant by war! It is astounding how even very great men don't understand WAR!'[16] For a military man to stress so strongly the *horror* of war suggests an exceptional sensibility.

Fisher was a man of strong democratic instincts and a warm humanity. As a lieutenant he thought nothing of blacking his hands and giving a hand when coaling ship; as First Sea Lord, he injured the pride of the executive officers by striving to achieve equality of esteem for engineering officers. He broadened the base of the officer class by abolishing fees at the Naval College; 'brains don't go with money,' he told his political master. Likewise, he encouraged Alfred Yexley, the brave journalist who acted as tribune for the lower deck, and helped to open roads of promotion for seamen and stokers. In a letter to Yexley he wrote, 'I always think

[11] Fisher to Lord Lansdowne, *FG*, vol. 2, p. 55, and p. 168 n. 2; J. Steinberg, 'The Copenhagen Complex', *Journal of Contemporary History*, vol.1 (1966), pp. 38–9; Williamson, *Grand Strategy*, p. 43.

[12] In 1909. Bacon, *Fisher*, vol. 2, pp. 182–3; and Fisher to Esher, 25 Apr. 1912, *FG*, vol. 2, pp. 454–5; also J. A. Fisher, *Records* (1919), pp. 75–6.

[13] W. T. Stead, 'Character Sketch—Admiral Fisher', *Review of Reviews* (Feb. 1910), p. 117; R. H. Bacon, *From 1900 Onwards* (1940), pp. 327–8; Fisher, 'Submarines' (20 Apr. 1904), p. 3, ADM 116/942.

[14] Fisher to Churchill, 5 Mar. 1912, *FG*, vol. 2, p. 436; to G. Fiennes, 19 June 1911, ibid.

[15] Stead, 'Admiral Fisher', p. 117.

[16] 25 Apr. 1912, *FG*, vol. 2, p. 454; also to Churchill, 5 Mar. 1912, ibid., p. 436.

"sympathy" is the greatest word in the world!' He admired Admiral Nelson because 'He never flogged a man.'[17]

Fisher's conception of deterrence was in line with modern thinking, if still rather optimistic: he hoped to deter by a combination of overwhelming superiority and terror.[18] Apart from his letter to Lord Lansdowne I have found one semi-serious suggestion of preventive war in his correspondence, but even that is coupled with a statement (elicited with his arm round the waist of 'the wife of the biggest millionaire in Bremen') that the German mercantile world was in 'blue fright' of war.[19]

Fisher's aversion to war (at least to mass warfare on land) comes out in his opposition to Britain's continental commitment. There is an undertone of anxiety and even horror in Fisher's resistance to the expeditionary force (together with a dash of inter-service rivalry). 'Suicidal idiocy', he called it in 1909.[20] 'I simply tremble at the consequences if the British Redcoats are to be planted on the Vosges frontier,' he wrote to Esher in 1911, and later as well.[21] He would rather sacrifice money than men. 'We have heaps of *money*', he wrote, 'to buy anything we like—whether battleships or Garden Cities. But our shortage is *men*.'[22]

What are we to make then of his daring projects for the Baltic landing? According to Fisher, the idea was actually suggested to him by a German general in a moment of candour at the Hague Peace Conference of 1899, as the strategy that would cause the greatest trouble for Germany.[23] One of the virtues of the plan was that it kept the army out of mischief elsewhere. There is a question whether Fisher ever considered the Baltic plan seriously. As Mackay writes, 'the feasibility of a Baltic expedition or a landing on the German North Sea Coast was never thoroughly and realistically examined at the Admiralty. At the heart of the matter was Fisher's continuing refusal to establish a naval general staff with responsibility for drawing up war plans.'[24]

Fisher had been under real gunfire at least twice, and knew from

[17] Fisher to the Earl of Tweedmouth, 23 Feb. 1907, *FG*, vol. 2, p. 119; Fisher to Esher, 5 Aug. 1907, ibid., p. 334; to John Leyland, 17 Oct. 1911, ibid., pp. 393–4; to Yexley, 8 Dec. 1910, ibid., p. 343. On Nelson: J. A. Fisher, *Memories* (1919), p. 26.

[18] Fisher to King Edward VII, 8 Sept. 1907, *FG*, vol. 2, p. 130.

[19] Letter: n. 11. Fisher to Arnold White, 1 Oct. 1911, *FG*, vol. 2, p. 388. White was a radical right-wing jingo, and Fisher cultivated his goodwill.

[20] Bacon, *Fisher*, vol. 2, p. 183.

[21] 20 Sept. 1911, *FG*, vol. 2, p. 386; 25 Apr. 1912, ibid., p. 454.

[22] Fisher to Hankey, 13 Apr. 1911, HP 5/2A.

[23] Fisher to Esher, 25 Apr. 1912, *FG*, vol. 2, pp. 454–5. German impressions of Fisher's bellicosity: the report of the German naval delegate at the Hague Peace Conference of 1899: J. Lepsius *et al.* (eds.), *Die Grosse Politik der Europäischen Kabinette 1871–1914* (Berlin 1924), vol. 15, doc. 4274, pp. 225–30.

[24] Mackay, *Fisher*, p. 354.

personal experience about the terrors of war. The prospect of war did not fill him with joy: he was a creator, a moulder of men and machines, a man of courage but without a taste for blood. Fisher's refusal to draw up war plans or establish a staff may well have sprung from an unconscious aversion to bloodshed, especially on the grand scale. This speculation is backed by some evidence. Churchill's and Hankey's Dardanelles plan appealed to Fisher's imagination at first; it was certainly more plausible than his own Baltic project and, given better planning and leadership, might have ended in more success. As the landing approached, Fisher developed cold feet, expressed increasing reservations and then resigned. His bellicosity was calculated, with none of the unthinking gung-ho quality of such naval leaders as Roger Keyes. He was too intelligent, too humane, to relish war for its own sake.

Like other naval officers, Fisher's appreciation of the conflict with Germany was vaguely mercantilistic. Although not frequently expressed, he regarded trade as the root of the conflict of the two empires. In 1908 he wrote to King Edward, 'that we have eventually to fight Germany is just as sure as anything human can be, solely because she can't expand commercially without it'. Another insight is given by his statement to Hankey that '*Tariff Reform means certain war with Germany!*'[25] It suggests that he regarded economic ambitions as the motor of Germany's drive.

He regretted the conflict with Germany but thought that Britain's alliances should be governed by the prospect of German expansion, and he pressed the need to cultivate Turkey and Russia. In 1911 he went further to say that he was 'dead against the French "Entente" (*really it is an alliance*).'[26]

Fisher's commitment to economic warfare was another reason for holding international lawyers in contempt. More than a year before the Hague conference of 1907 he worried about its consequences:

All the world will be banded against us. Our great special anti-German weapon of smashing an enemy's commerce will be wrested from us. It's so very peculiar that Providence has arranged England as a sort of huge breakwater against German commerce . . . such is our naval superiority that on the day of war we 'mop up' 800 German merchant steamers. Fancy the 'knock-down' blow to German trade and finance! Worth Paris! These Hague Conferences want trade and commerce and going by train de luxe to Monte Carlo all to go on just as usual, only just the Fleet to fight! ROT![27]

Fisher claimed that liberalism came to him late in the day, as a consequence of his experience as First Sea Lord. Until then his rise was

[25] 14 Mar. 1908, *FG*, vol. 2, p. 169; Fisher to Hankey, 12 Mar. 1913, HP 5/2A.
[26] Fisher to J. A. Spender, 25 Oct. 1911, *FG*, vol. 2, p. 398.
[27] Fisher to Captain Seymour Fortescue, 14 Apr. 1906, *FG*, vol. 2, p. 72.

undisturbed, and his relations with Conservative ministers correct. He had no politics, and had voted in turn for both parties.[28] He may have been a closet Liberal before. In his memoirs he claims to have been a pro-Boer.[29] This would be akin with the commander of Britain's nuclear submarines having an empathy with the Irish Republican Army. Towards the end of the Edwardian period he moved towards an increasingly radical liberalism.[30] Maybe lack of pedigree and property inclined him that way; he certainly found the Liberal ministers McKenna, Lloyd George and Churchill congenial enough. But he also regarded navalism and liberalism as natural allies: as he wrote to Hankey in 1911, '*be perfectly assured* that to begin with Asquith will *never* be permitted by his party to assist in any policy which signifies participation in *continental military operations*'.[31] Public opinion, he wrote, would 'never permit an English soldier to fight on the Continent of Europe in a Franco-German war'.[32]

IV

Fisher's alternative to the "continental commitment" may be called the "Atlantic orientation": a scheme for basing the defence of the United Kingdom on the bonds of culture and commerce of the English-speaking nations, and especially those between England and the United States.[33] On a visit to the United States in 1910 he perceived a deep desire to draw closer to Britain. 'But Ireland blocks the way!' he wrote, 'And Home rule all round is the necessity.' So much for another shibboleth, *the* shibboleth, of British Unionism.[34]

The new orientation came to Fisher late in July 1908. On the 22nd he was still considering naval dispositions against a German–American alliance. On the 25th he 'went off into a long tirade . . . and said that we would never attempt anything against America'.[35] The vision appears in a letter a few weeks later.

one cannot conceive of such German madness as to make war against England, for that Frankfurt merchant is right: it would be the collapse of the German Empire

---

[28] Fisher to J. L. Garvin, 12 Aug. 1907, *FG*, vol. 2, p. 128.

[29] Fisher, *Memories*, p. 263.

[30] Fisher to Esher, 14 Mar. 1910, *FG*, vol. 2, pp. 313–14; also p. 298.

[31] Fisher to Hankey, 13 Apr. 1911, HP 5/2A.

[32] Fisher to Julian S. Corbett, 1 Dec. 1913, *FG*, vol. 2, p. 495.

[33] M. Howard, *The Continental Commitment* (1972).

[34] Fisher to Vaughan Nash [Asquith's private secretary], 30 Dec. 1910, *FG*, vol. 2, p. 347; also to G. Fiennes, 9 Mar. 1911, ibid., pp. 361–2, and to Esher, 27 Mar. 1911, EP 5/39; Fisher to Hankey, 3 Apr. 1911, HP 5/2A, fo. 9.

[35] Slade diary, 22, 25 July 1908, Slade Papers NMM; [J.Fisher], 'War Plans and the Distribution of the Fleet' ('1907 or 1908'), fos. 2–3, ADM 116/1043B/I.

and the forerunner of that great and impending bulwark against both the Yellow man *and the Slav*—'THE FEDERATION OF ALL WHO SPEAK THE ENGLISH TONGUE!'[36]

An American alliance seemed much more valuable to him than sovereignty over Canada. The United States would find a common interest with Britain in resisting German expansion into South America and Morocco, and Japanese expansion in North America, especially Mexico. He scotched any talk of defending Canada against the United States, which the hapless Slade attempted to sell him in 1908, and hoped for American–Canadian tariff reciprocity, a cause of Canadian anti-Empire liberalism.[37]

Fisher was prepared to discard imperial sovereignty and replace it with an Anglo-American federation, with England, Wales, Scotland and Ireland all joining as federated states. In 1910 he visited the United States for his son's marriage to an American heiress, and was fêted widely. The visit left a deep impression. He wrote about it to Esher:

They gave me figures to show their population now nearly 100 millions, and certain *to be 250 millions*! Their language *English*, their literature *English*, their traditions *English & quite unknown to themselves their aspirations English!* We shall be d—d fools if we don't exploit this for the peace of the world and the dominance of our race! All this marvel comes about by their school system which is a wonderful engine of assimilation. . . . Even the German-descended American dreads the coming German aggression and puts his money on England! also they are looking round the corner at Japan and imagine anything possible between Japan & Germany as regards sharing in the spoil of China! What we want is a great organization to run this English Speaking Federation on the lines of the United States Constitution where each state of the Union enjoys true Home Rule! . . . I simply saw miracles in America—all d—d rot about Canada equalling the United States! *They haven't got the climate!*[38]

The United States was not to be counted as a naval rival. Its fleet gave Britain an added margin of superiority. He foresaw 'a great English-speaking Federation—absolute independence of units but a solid whole against the universe'.[39]

The source of these ideas is clear. Fisher attributed them to John Bright and Theodore Roosevelt but they bear the imprint of Andrew Carnegie, the steel baron and philanthropist, who had been preaching the cause of

[36] Fisher to Arnold White, 30 Aug. 1908, *FG*, vol. 2, p. 191.

[37] Fisher to King Edward VII, 4 Oct. 1907, *FG*, vol. 2, p. 143; Slade diary, 9, 10 May 1908, NMM; Fisher to Esher, 27 Mar. 1911, EP 5/39. Reciprocity: ch. 11 above; Fisher to Arnold White, 20 Dec. 1910, *FG*, vol. 2, pp. 346–7; 15 July 1911, p. 379; to A. G. Gardiner, 19 Jan. 1911, ibid., pp. 351–2; to G. Fiennes, 8 Feb. 1912, ibid., p. 430; also to Lionel Yexley, 8 Dec. 1910, ibid., p. 342–3.

[38] Fisher to Esher, 17 Dec. 1910, EP 5/39; a very similar letter to Arnold White, 20 Dec. 1910, *FG*, vol. 2, p. 346.

[39] Fisher to Esher, 5 Aug. 1910, *FG*, vol. 2, pp. 333–4; to Arnold White, 20 Dec. 1910, ibid., p. 346; to G. Fiennes, 9 Mar. 1911, ibid., pp. 361–2.

Anglo-American reunion since the early 1890s. In 1893 he wrote an article which created some commotion in naval circles in Britain and America. Carnegie, who divided his time between Britain and the United States in the 1890s was (in Britain) a political Radical. His vision clearly spelled out the implications of Anglo-American union for England: home rule all round, for Ireland, Scotland, Wales—and for England. India would move towards self-government. Canada and perhaps Australia would also join on a level of equality. England would have to dismantle the monarchy and disestablish the church. Carnegie was a strong republican.[40]

Sir George Clarke, who had been secretary of the Colonial Defence Committee, and would later be the first secretary of the CID, wrote to point out how impracticable such a programme was, and to propose a naval alliance instead. The real foundation of Anglo-American amity, he wrote, was the economic dependence of the United States on Britain, which took three-quarters of American farm exports. 'Upon this vast trade the welfare of agriculture, which acts and reacts upon the whole fabric of national prosperity, must mainly depend . . . there is no possible alternative customer for $461,250,000 worth of farm produce.'[41] Lord Charles Beresford (later Fisher's deadly enemy) wrote that the Empire, the monarchy and the church were insuperable obstacles.

That Fisher was willing to sacrifice the symbols and the substance of British imperialism, both at home and overseas, is testimony to several things. It testifies to his democratic sympathies. The United States fired his imagination. 'I am going there to die!' he wrote to Esher.[42] Like Carnegie, he regarded the integration of the two societies as a gain more than a loss. In 1910 Fisher looked to Carnegie to finance an Anglo-American Federation movement.[43] It also underscores his liberalism, albeit an idiosyncratic one. No real Tory could have swallowed such notions (though Balfour was sympathetic), while some at least were compatible with liberal beliefs. Thirdly, it is a testimony to the gravity with which he viewed the German threat. In assessing it, Fisher was not swayed by hallowed icons and institutions. He approached the necessary measures in an unsentimental and calculating manner (though he left the all-important matters of sentiment out of account). Fourthly, it is a testimony to his strategic intuition. Fisher anticipated the strategic realities of the twentieth century: the hegemony of the United States and the transformation of Britain into a

---

[40] Fisher, *Memories*, p. 23; Andrew Carnegie, 'The Reunion of Britain and America—A Look Ahead', *NAR*, vol. 156 (1893); G. S. Clarke, 'A Naval Union with Great Britain: A Reply to Mr. Andrew Carnegie', *NAR*, vol. 158 (1894); Mahan and Beresford, 'Possibilities of an Anglo-American Reunion'; Sydenham of Combe [G. S. Clarke], *My Working Life*, pp. 121–4; J. F. Wall, *The World of Andrew Carnegie* (New York 1970), chs. 14, 18.

[41] Clarke, 'Naval Union', p. 360.

[42] 17 Dec. 1910, EP 5/39.

[43] Carnegie finance: Fisher to Esher, 17 Dec. 1910, EP 5/39.

partner instead of a leader. He saw the parallel rise of a continental threat, and the economic and demographic power of the United States, and reckoned that security and American partnership were good trade-offs for an untenable world primacy. This strategic logic is what carried Britain through the two world wars, and it remains the bedrock of British security to this day.

Like Fisher, Carnegie believed in an Anglo-American 'Kriegsverein with power so overwhelming that its exercise would never be necessary'. Like Carnegie, Fisher wrote (in 1919), 'Hereditary titles are ludicrously out of date in any modern democracy and the sooner we sweep away all the gimcracks and gegaws of snobbery the better!' He proclaimed himself a republican—because republics were peace-loving.[44] His brain was not going soft—he was merely following through the logic of his Edwardian values and associations.

Other Unionist causes were also inimical to Fisher's vision. Unionists were the party of conscription, and conscription made it possible to fight on the Continent, a prospect that was anathema to Fisher. We have seen already that he regarded the Unionist programme of tariff reform as a guarantee of war. In other words, the Tories were the war party.

In Germany, Tirpitz could not conceive that Britain would withdraw its naval forces from the Empire, but Fisher frustrated his design by pulling in units from the Pacific and North American stations, and concentrating them in home waters. He was just as willing to contemplate a pullback from the Mediterranean.[45]

Fisher's reaction to the challenge of a powerful Germany and to Britain's inevitable relative decline was to create a permanent deterrent in the form of an Atlantic bond. It was a sober, realistic and responsible vision. At the Admiralty he cultivated American naval officers, and especially Commander William S. Sims, the American Inspector of Target Practice, who had the ear of President Roosevelt. Had Fisher been able to read American naval plans, he would have been strongly reassured. The General Board, a committee of senior Admirals, regarded American interests as closely bound with those of Britain. In December 1910 Sims repaid Fisher's attention by proclaiming at a banquet at the Guildhall that 'Britain could count on every man, every ship and every dollar'. Although Sims was reprimanded by President Taft for this speech, eventually he commanded the United States naval forces that came to Britain's aid in 1917.[46]

---

[44] Wall, *Carnegie*, p. 677; Fisher, *Records*, pp. 73–5.

[45] Mediterannean: Fisher to Churchill, 5 Mar. 1912, *FG*, vol. 2, p. 437.

[46] E. E. Morison, *Admiral Sims and the Modern American Navy* (Boston 1942), pp. 172–3, 275–84, 364 ff.; American plans: R. D. Challener, *Admirals, Generals, and American Foreign Policy, 1898–1914* (Princeton 1973), pp. 26–7; General Board: J. W. Coogan, *The End of Neutrality: The United States, Britain and Maritime Rights, 1899–1915* (Ithaca, NY 1981), pp. 59, 66.

Fisher's strategic conception was mainly set down in the form of inspired intuitions. But one of his associates soon gave it a theoretical form. The naval historian Julian Corbett was close to Fisher, and lectured as a civilian at the Naval War College at Greenwich. In 1911 Corbett published a book called *Some Principles of Maritime Strategy*. Despite its title, Corbett's real concern was the employment of Britain's *land* forces. He argued that Britain's isolation from the Continent and its naval supremacy gave it the choice of restricting its commitment and exposure, even when the continental powers threw in everything they had.

What may be called the British or maritime form [of war] is in fact the application of the limited method to the unlimited form [of war], as ancillary to the larger operations of our allies—a method which has usually been open to us because the control of the sea has enabled us to select a theatre in effect truly limited . . . Its value lay in its power of containing a force greater than its own. That is all that can be claimed for it, but it may be all that is required.[47]

There was no virtue in attack for attack's sake, and no need for Britain to stake everything on the struggle. The book is full of historical explications of the principle; the most effective one being the Russo-Japanese war, in which Japan achieved its aims without occupying extensive territory or destroying the bulk of the Russian army. A large part of the book was devoted to purely naval strategy and tactics, some of it sound, some of it less so. Here again Corbett did not regard the naval battle as an end in itself, but rather as a means towards an economic decision:

By closing [the enemy's] commercial ports *we exercise the highest power of injuring him which the command of the sea can give us.* We choke the flow of his national activity afloat in the same way that military occupation of his territory chokes it ashore. He must, therefore, either tamely submit to the worst which a naval defeat can inflict upon him, or he must fight to release himself. He may see fit to choose the one course or the other, but in any case we can do no more by naval means alone to force our will upon him.[48]

V

Esher

Reginald, the Second Viscount Esher, and the third member of the triad, was not an old aristocrat of the blood, but the son of a judge who had risen to the peerage.[49] His ascendancy was even more irregular than that of Fisher and Hankey, who, after all, were paid servants of the state. If Esher

---

[47] J. S. Corbett, *Some Principles of Maritime Strategy* (1911), pp. 63, 64.
[48] Ibid., p. 187. Emphasis added.
[49] This section is based on Esher's Papers, on his published *Journals*, and on the two biographies, P. Fraser, *Lord Esher: A Political Biography* (1973), and Lees-Milne, *Enigmatic Edwardian*.

had money worries, they were carefully concealed: he entered Parliament in 1880 as a Liberal at the age of twenty-eight, acting all the while as Private Secretary to Hartington, the party's second in command. In 1895 a timely turn of patronage made him Permanent Secretary (i.e. official head) of the Office of Works. This ministry was responsible for the upkeep of the Royal Palaces, and it gave Esher his foothold at court.

To inspire confidence was his special gift. The magnetic power of personality, whether at an intimate dinner, in the committee room or on the platform, is the secret of dominance among equals, and yet we know little about it. Esher was a competent administrator (although not sufficiently to prevent unrest among his own house-servants and offspring), very intelligent, and had a gift for lucid writing, but fell well short of the ebullient genius of Fisher or the penetration and independence of Hankey. Perhaps he inspired such confidence because everyone felt he was safe: here was the perfect gentleman, with an urbane manner, widely and well connected, telling everyone what they wanted to hear in exquisitely polite accents. The journals which he kept (with an eye to eventual publication) record merely conventional ideas and sentiments, though they are quite revealing none the less. He was a sentimentalist, a sensualist, a social conformist and a snob, constantly on the move between his house in Scotland ("The Roman Camp"), another house near Windsor Palace ("Orchard Lea"), Buckingham Palace, the bureaux of Whitehall, the Clubs of Pall Mall and the restaurants and theatres of the West End.

Esher did not rely on personal charm alone to open the doors of high places but surrounded himself with the potent halo of royal charisma. In the evolution of British democracy the monarch retained a broad but poorly defined residual authority. Esher cultivated this residual power and used it for his own ends, especially the right of the King to be informed. After his departure from the Office of Works (in 1902) he kept a hand in courtly administration, and retained rooms at St James Palace and Windsor Castle. He was often called upon to advise on the fabric of the palaces and on staff problems; and to stage-manage ceremonial functions. He saw the King almost daily. Just as important was his grip on the Royal Archives. He prepared an edition of Queen Victoria's letters which gave him a good grasp of constitutional precedents. Other persons were excluded. The Viscount acted as a channel of communication between the political and official worlds and the King.

The prestige of royalty enabled Esher to meet any man as an equal. Of the intimacies which this made possible, none was more important than the trust of A. J. Balfour, who inherited the Premiership and leadership of the Unionist party in 1902. Balfour appointed Esher to the War Office Reconstitution Committee in 1903, and offered him the War Office soon after. Just before his resignation in 1905 he made Esher a permanent member of the CID, to maintain, so he thought, a reliable presence there during the period of Liberal government that would follow.[50] Esher remained in favour with Balfour's Liberal successors. He worked closely with Haldane on his army reforms and kept in touch with the development of strategic policy throughout the Edwardian period, without, however, occupying any official position apart from the CID.

One feels sometimes that acceptance had become for him almost an end in itself; he was capable of intimacy with Liberal and Conservative leaders at the same time. The editor of the xenophobic *National Review* wrote to him in terms of fellowship to denounce the treason of the Liberal *Westminster Gazette*, whose editor, J. A. Spender, corresponded with Esher on the same close terms. The slippery courtier published articles in the Liberal *Nation* at the same time as he wrote for the right-wing journal.[51] He also strove to influence events directly. 'Power and place are not often synonymous,' he wrote, and did not restrict himself to any particular sphere of competence: he was just as prepared to influence the appointment of the Professor of English at Cambridge as to stop the army from going to France (failing, as it turned out, in both cases).[52]

During the constitutional crises of 1910–11 and 1914 Esher worked to steer the King away from pitfalls and to uphold the constitutional character of the monarchy. But he was no democrat.[53] His position as 'a man outside the constitution' was, ultimately, parasitical on the crown.[54]

In politics Esher's instincts were conservative. He detested Bonar Law, Carson and F. E. Smith, the diehards and parvenus who deposed his favourite politician, A. J. Balfour. The Liberals, he thought, were more capable statesmen, more likely to contain the social unrest and master the constitutional difficulties.[55]

This pragmatic Liberalism created another bond with Fisher and Hankey. It sat well with Fisher's favourite aphorism that 'the secret of successful administration is the intelligent anticipation of agitation'. Coming from such an astute ingratiator, written evidence is suspect. Even letters always contain an element of calculation. It seems, however, that Esher came under Fisher's spell and never shook it off. Fisher provided Esher with the elements of his strategic outlook. In 1906 Esher still took a continental view of British defence. 'We have ceased to be an island state,'

---

[50] Esher to J. S. Sandars, 2 Dec. 1905, *Journals*, vol. 2, p. 122.

[51] L. J. Maxse to Esher, 2 Sept. 1910; H. W. Massingham to Esher, 19 Sept. 1910, EP 5/39; J. A. Spender to Esher, 6, 8, 28 Aug. 1910, Esher, *Journals*, vol. 3, pp. 12–13, 18.

[52] Quote from Lord Esher, *Cloud-Capp'd Towers* (1927), cited in Fraser, *Esher*, p. 6 [not found on the page cited]; correspondence on English professorship at Cambridge: June–July 1912, EP 5/41.

[53] Esher to Sir Bernard Mallett, 4 Dec. 1913, Esher, *Journals*, vol. 3, p. 146.

[54] This anomalous position was attacked in the Press several times: Fraser, *Esher*, pp. 196, 242–3, 251.

[55] Esher to Fisher, 20 Apr. 1912, *Journals*, vol. 3, p. 88.

he wrote, and advocated compulsory military service. In 1907 he raised funds for Lord Roberts's conscription campaign.[56] From 1908 onwards he fell into line with Fisher and strongly opposed the dispatch of an expeditionary force to France. For the critical "Military Needs of the Empire" committee he wrote a strong paper suggesting that no troops be sent to France.

That the pressure which can be brought to bear upon Germany by the threat— known not to be an idle one—of seizing her mercantile fleet by the closing of the Elbe and the Baltic in war, by the deadly injury to her commerce and the fear of raids, as well as by the freedom of action and moral support afforded to France, *might be held to be a sufficient fulfilment of our share in the partnership between us and the French nation.*

If it was necessary to send a land force for political reasons, then he suggested a symbolic force of six mounted brigades, or some 12,000 men.[57] In 1909 he raised 'a large sum' from the Australian pastoralist and mining magnate W. A. Horn to establish a naval league called "The Islanders". The membership allegedly reached seventy thousand.[58] In 1912 he echoed Fisher in a memorandum for *The Times* in which he took Hankey's and Fisher's line that, as a trading nation, 'we should be mad to entangle ourselves in a continental strife on land'.[59]

Like Fisher, Esher also took a mercantilist view of German economic growth, which was bound to lead to military expansion. In 1907 he wrote in his journal,

Germany is going to contest with us the Command of the Sea, and our commercial position. . . . She must have an outlet for her teeming population, and vast acres where Germans can live, and remain Germans. These acres only exist within the confines of our Empire. Therefore, *l'Ennemi c'est l'Allemagne.*[60]

'International commercial struggle for the open markets of the world . . . was slowly but surely taking the place of the somewhat aimless national rivalries,' he wrote in an article for the *Deutsche Revue* in 1910.[61] 'In the Middle Ages policy was dominated by religion. In modern times by commerce,' was one of his aphorisms.[62]

---

[56] Esher to Lord Knollys, 30 Sept. 1906, *Journals*, vol. 2, pp. 185–6; Fraser, *Esher*, pp. 192–3; correspondence with W. W. Astor, Lord Iveagh *et al.* 30 Sept. 1906 to 7 Mar. 1907, EP 19/6.

[57] Lord Esher, 'The Assistance to be Given by Great Britain to France if She is Attacked by Germany' (14 Dec. 1908), App. VII, Report of the Sub-Committee of the Committee of Imperial Defence (1909), CAB 16/5; Fisher to Esher, 15 Mar. 1909, *FG*, vol. 2, p. 232.

[58] Fraser, *Esher*, pp. 203–4, 206, 245, 252–3.

[59] Ibid., p. 253.

[60] Esher, 3 Dec. 1907, *Journals*, vol. 2, p. 266; also Esher to Lord Knollys, 30 Sept. 1906, *Journals*, vol. 2, p. 186.

[61] Draft article about King Edward VII (1910), EP 4/3.

[62] EP 19/5.

Japan's victory in 1905 drove Esher into a pessimistic world view which saw the teutonic and western peoples approaching an implacable struggle against the Yellow Peril.[63] The clash with Germany was more immediately threatening and just as inevitable, and also gave rise to a deep pessimism. Esher sought to block Germany's mercantilistic expansion with a countervailing Atlantic bulwark. A short note from January 1911 lists his immediate 'OBJECTIVES':

1. the [*sic*] maintain the overwhelming supremacy of the British Imperial Navy.
2. To bring about a Treaty of Arbitration and permanent alliance between Great Britain and the United States.
3. To convert the Triple into a Sextuple European Entente.
4. To provide an organized bulwark against the disruptive and destructive forces of Anarchical Socialism.[64]

The Liberal journalist Spender commented on a letter from Esher in February 1911: 'You do well to look across the Atlantic. The new world *is* some day going to redress the balance of the old & if (1) we can settle the Irish question & (2) manage the Japanese Alliance so that the U.S.A. will consent to it, so English-speaking unity will really come into sight.'[65] In 1913 he wrote that maybe the balance of power in Europe no longer possessed the same importance to Britain that it once had.[66]

For all his concern with defence, Esher's attitude was the very opposite of "bellicist". There was nothing of the militarist in him. The decisive evidence of this was his response to Norman Angell's book *The Great Illusion*, which was published partly at Esher's urging in 1910. Angell argued that (contrary to conventional belief, and indeed to Esher's previous beliefs), commercial rivalry did not lead inevitably to war, and that it was not possible to make economic gains from aggressive war. Here was a formula to avert war, and Esher embraced it. His ability to raise money, which he previously employed for conscription and naval agitation, was harnessed for the new creed. He became the chairman of a foundation devoted to the spread of Angell's teaching and spoke in public in support of his doctrines on several occasions.

VI

Esher, Fisher, Hankey: each of the three contributed a different element to the genesis of the Atlantic orientation. Hankey formulated the idea of economic blockade as decisive weapon and worked to translate a strategic

---

[63] Esher, 28 Nov. 1905, *Journals*, vol. 2, p. 120.
[64] 10 Jan. 1911, EP 4/3.
[65] J. A. Spender to Esher, 3 Feb. 1911, EP 5/36.
[66] Esher to Lord Percy, 27 Oct. 1913, EP 4/4.

conception into a practical plan. Fisher added the American dimension, and stressed the trade-off of primacy against security. Esher contributed his prestige, his contacts and his knowledge of strategic questions.

The three were tied by bonds of friendship. Fisher had a special talent for affection. 'My beloved Hankey', he wrote to his protégé, and showered devotion upon him. He worked strongly behind the scenes to get Hankey into a position of influence.[67] Fisher's bond with Esher was equally strong, and also contained emotional undertones. Esher called their correspondence 'nautical love letters'; they invariably began 'My beloved friend' and would end with 'Yours to a cinder' or 'Yours till hell freezes'.[68] Esher also conducted a close correspondence with Hankey, although one senses a slight tension between the two.

While a psychological dimension is strongly in evidence, it is difficult to pin down. What does it signify? One clue can be derived from the opposite mentality. The records of war are full of obstinate martinets who presided over bloody fiascos and pyrrhic victories. This type of commander has been dissected in a classical study by Norman Dixon. Often the obtuse commander conforms to the qualities of what some psychologists have described as an "authoritarian personality". Such men adhere uncritically to conventional values, and suppress dissent. They oppose the subjective, the imaginative and the tender-minded; they believe in fate and are disposed to think in rigid categories; they have a generalized hostility towards others, and a preoccupation with dominance, power and their own status, coupled with an assertion of maleness, strength and toughness; and are characterized by an exaggerated sexual prurience. They are imbued with status insecurity and rigid views on sex and aggression. The least competent commanders display profound disturbance of the ego, rigidity, dogmatism and are motivated by fear of failure. General Haig, with his stubborn and futile offensives on the western front carried on regardless of cost, typified many of these attributes.[69]

Fisher, Hankey and Esher manifested, on the whole, the opposite mentality. Competent commanders, says Dixon, show the absence of authoritarian psychopathology, enormous self-confidence and general robustness of the ego. In simpler terms, they seek life, not death. Fisher is the epitome of this life-affirming personality, and Hankey, while lacking his exuberance, had the same openness and flexibility of mind. His sympathy towards other ethnic groups is a relevant clue. The letters of both men reveal a warm, caring heterosexuality, and Fisher's flirtations are especially endearing in their good humour and humanity.[70] Esher was

[67] HP 5/2A, e.g. 27 Jan. 1911, fo. 6.
[68] Lees-Milne, *Enigmatic Edwardian*, p. 181.
[69] Norman Dixon, *The Psychology of Military Incompetence* (1976).
[70] e.g. his engaging letter to Mrs Reginald McKenna, 20 Apr. 1912, *FG*, vol. 2, p. 446.

more complicated. He was the most perverse of the three, and was sometimes inclined towards a pessimistic fatalism. Certainly he was above convention, and very far from a bellicist. But he was led by the other two, and especially Fisher. His lavish affections were centred almost entirely on men, and there was a whiff of sensual attraction in his attachment to the other two.

Both Fisher and Esher were impressed by Norman Angell's anti-war book. All three regarded war not as an end, but as an instrument of last resort, to be applied as clinically and briefly as possible, and if possible to be averted altogether by deterrence. From this perspective, the Atlantic orientation appears, at the root, as a temperamental disposition, an aversion to bloodshed and a desire to stave it off or at least to contain it within limits. It was a strategy underpinned by humanity and rationality. As Hankey described it to McKenna, his political master, 'the powerful weapon of economic pressure,—at the same time the most effective and most humane method of compelling our enemy to make peace on our own terms'. He added a quotation from one of Edmund Burke's speeches:

In a state of warfare it must be the wish of every good mind, to disarm the enemy rather by despoiling than by killing them, as well from motives of humanity as personal interest.[71]

Unlike the attitudes of the German General Staff (and those of some officers on the British General Staff),[72] it was the opposite of fatalism: a search for security, not for sacrifice.

[71] M. Hankey, 'Copy of memo sent to Mr. McKenna', 11 May 1911, HP 7/6, fo. 2.

[72] e.g. C. E. Callwell, *Field Marshall Henry Wilson: His Life and Diaries* (1927), vol. 1, pp. 121, 134–5; T. Travers, *The Killing Ground: The British Army, the Western Front and the Emergence of Modern Warfare, 1900–1918* (1987), pp. 45–6.

18

THE DOMINION DIMENSION

THE pressures of international rivalry turned Britain's attention towards the settler societies even before the turn of the century. At the Imperial Conference of 1897 Joseph Chamberlain, the British Colonial Secretary, probed the possiblities of stronger political ties. By the next conference in 1902 he had a more coherent conception. Britain would grant the white colonies favoured access to its markets, in return for stronger military and political bonds. The Empire would become a free-trade zone, with preference for colonial staples in the British market, and protection for British manufactures in colonial markets as well as at home. Under the name of "tariff reform", this project became the central and most divisive issue in British politics before the First World War. With agricultural prices on the rise, it was not a good time to place a tax on food, and Britain's voters rejected it three times, in 1906 and twice in 1910.[1]

The search for imperial support continued under the Liberals. An Imperial Conference met in 1907, another (for defence issues only) in 1909, and another in 1911. Even free trade economists looked to the Dominions (as they came to be called after 1907) in the Edwardian period, and these countries took a growing share of British trade. Canada, Australia, New Zealand and South Africa took 11.4 per cent of Britain's exports in 1902, and 14 per cent in 1913. In that year Australia, New Zealand and South Africa all took about 60 per cent of their imports from Britain. From 1910 onwards the "Round Table" movement revitalized the vision of imperial federation. It was a Conservative group of Oxford-trained intellectuals and civil servants, with offshoots in the Dominion capitals. The Imperial Conference of 1911 decided to investigate the economic resources of the Empire, and a Royal Commission on the Natural Resources and Trade of the Dominions began its work in 1912, looking at ways for mobilizing overseas resources more effectively in the imperial interest.[2] The Atlantic orientation also sought strength in empire, but it was more closely aligned with the Liberals, the party in power.

---

[1] The imperial movement: J. Kendle, *The Colonial and Imperial Conferences, 1887–1911: A Study in Imperial Organization* (1967); tariff reform: A. Sykes, *Tariff Reform in British Politics, 1903–1913* (Oxford 1979) and, most, comprehensively, W. Mock, *Imperiale Herrschaft und nationales Interesse: "Constructive Imperialism" oder Freihandel in Grossbritannien vor dem Ersten Weltkrieg* (Stuttgart 1982).

[2] J. C. Wood, *British Economists and the Empire* (1983), pp. 129, 133, 171–2. The Royal Commission produced a series of comprehensive reports during the First World War, and reported in 1917: Natural Resources, Trade and Legislation of Certain Portions of HM's

To implement the Atlantic orientation, Hankey and Esher followed two lines of action. They aimed to enlist the co-operation of the great agricultural nations within the British Empire, primarily Australia and ˙ Canada. Support from these countries was essential for economic warfare; they provided a significant amount of Germany's raw material and food imports, and were well placed to capture German shipping. Hankey and Esher also strove to make the Committee of Imperial Defence a focus for Dominion integration, and an instrument for prevailing in the strategic debate. Hankey was an exceptionally independent and enterprising assistant secretary at the CID, and both Esher and Fisher were members. The CID was the triad's point of contact with British war policy.

The "naval scare" of 1909 had galvanized the Dominions into a new awareness of strategic realities in Europe, and in the summer of 1909 they rallied to London for an Imperial Defence Conference. While Dominion support was welcome in London, no one there had a very clear idea of Canadian and Australian expectations. The Prime Minister expressed the traditional British desire to shift some of the Empire's defence expenditure on to the Dominions, and to bring their contribution into better alignment with the size of their seaborne trade.[3] The navy and the army both made a bid to place Dominion units under greater British control. The outcome of the conference, however, underlined the real motivation of the new nations on the Pacific rim: Japan was on their mind, not Germany. Their promised capital ships were destined not for the North Sea, but as nuclei for their own fleets, which, together with British units, might form a powerful fleet in the Pacific.[4]

Lord Esher perceived the importance of the Yellow Peril in Dominion perceptions, and how it inclined the Dominions towards the United States. In 1909 an American general depicted a Japanese military invasion of the Pacific coast in a sensational book. Its effect in the United States was picked up by Admiral Fisher during his visit there. Mackenzie King heard similar scaremongering directly from President Roosevelt.[5] Lord Esher singled out the issues raised by the book as an example of the grand strategic questions with which the CID should be concerned. He diagnosed racial attitudes as a bond between the English-speaking nations on the Pacific and foresaw the possibility of war between Japan and the United States over the question of Asian exclusion:

Dominions. Final Report, PP 1917–18 Cd. 8462 X; statistics calculated from Memoranda and Tables. Trade Statistics and Trade of the Self-governing Dominions, PP 1914–16 Cd. 8156 XIV. See also J. Kendle, *The Round Table Movement and Imperial Union* (Toronto 1975).

[3] H. H. Asquith, Proceedings of the Imperial Conference on Naval and Military Defence, 28 July 1909, pp. 2–6, Laurier Papers, PAC MG 26 G, vol. 773.
[4] Ch. 14, sec. III, above.
[5] Lea, *Valor of Ignorance*; KD, Washington DC, 31 Jan. 1908, G 2183, fos. 57–8; Fisher to A. G. Gardiner, 19 Jan. 1911, *FG*, vol. 2, p. 352; also ch. 13, no. 50, above.

The racial quarrel which looms over the heads of these two nations has a very direct interest for us, inasmuch as while we are bound on the one hand by Treaty to Japan, and by the probable sympathy of the people of this country with the view that the Japanese have established a moral right to be treated upon an equality with European races, we are hampered on the other hand by the prejudices of our Colonial fellow-countrymen in Australia and Canada against men of colour. There is very great likelihood that, in the event of war brought on by the insistence of the Japanese that they should be accorded equality of treatment with Europeans in regard to settlements in countries other than their own, the sympathies of the majority of the English people would be on the side of the Japanese, while the sympathies of at least two of our great dominions would be on the side of the United States.[6]

Maurice Hankey was just as closely attuned to Dominion sentiments. His parents were Australian, his wife South African. Hankey's family had investments in Canada and some land in South Australia.[7] To get the Dominions involved in British war plans became one of Hankey's prime objectives. In November 1909 he wrote a document that foreshadowed his whole accomplishment at the CID before the war. It was a proposal to harness the CID to work on the 'War Organization of the British Empire'; in effect, for detailed contingency plans, and for wartime co-ordination between government departments at home and in the Dominions overseas. 'It is an axiom', he wrote, 'that in order to terminate a war effective pressure must be put on our adversaries. The most obvious methods in which such pressure can be asserted by ourselves are by the attack of trade and the attack of colonies.'[8] The Dominions would seize German ships in their ports, or capture German colonies. Other elements of economic warfare that he mentioned were an intelligence service to track German shipping, financial pressure, and the "cornering" of vital commodities. This was in line with the "economist" doctrine of blockade, and the memo contains no mention of any land action in France.[9]

When King Edward VII died, Esher suggested inviting large delegations of Dominion MPs for the Coronation. 'Once such a body has met, informally and on the occasion of an Imperial ceremony, it will be far

---

[6] Lord Esher, 'Functions of Sub-Committees of the Committee of Imperial Defence' (21 Jan. 1910), CID paper 112-B, CAB 4/3/1/112B. Compare the more racist attitudes of Liberal statesmen, ch. 13, secs. III–IV, ch. 14, sec. I.

[7] Canadian investments: Hankey to Fisher, 8 Apr. 1912, FP, 1/11/566, fo. 47; South Australia: Roskill, *Hankey*, vol. 1, p. 28.

[8] (11[?16] Nov. 1909), HP 7/4, fos. 1–7, cited fo. 4; also Hankey, *Supreme Command*, vol. 1, ch. 8.

[9] A similar agenda was contained in an army document of very close date: 'E1.5. Questions Requiring Joint Naval and Military Consideration. Notes Handed by the Director of Military Operations [Brig.-General Henry Wilson] to Secretary C. I. D. 13.12.09', WO 106/45. Perhaps it was a response to Hankey's memo, which had been sent about a month before to the War Office and the Prime Minister.

easier to summon them again merely to discuss business, and we shall thus have the nucleus of what in less than a generation might become a true Parliament of Empire.' In the transition to a true imperial constitution, 'the power of the Crown may be almost incalcauble'.[10]

The opportunity came the following year, when the Dominion Prime Ministers assembled for the Coronation and the Imperial Conference of May 1911. Hankey and Esher determined to use this gathering to tighten the imperial knot by means of a Dominion presence on the Committee of Imperial Defence, and by the same token, to increase the CID's authority and prestige. They also intended to fight the continentalist tendencies in Whitehall and Westminster.[11]

The Dominion Prime Ministers were going to attend a meeting of the CID, for a briefing on British strategy. Since that strategy was still undecided, it was vital for Hankey that the session should take an "economist" and navalist course. He worked hard. In the run-up to the conference, Hankey prepared a long paper for McKenna, the First Lord of the Admiralty, and spent three hours coaching him for his speech. It contained the gist of the "economist" blockade doctrine. He prepared a shorter paper for the Prime Minister.[12] The outcome was gratifying.

The Dominion statesmen assembled three times in the oak-panelled conference room of the CID. Grant Duff, an army staff officer, was disturbed by the plebeian intrusion into that citadel of conspiracy. 'Fisher', he wrote of the Australian Prime Minister, 'is a carpenter from Ayrshire— a labour politician rather than a statesman—Pearce [the Defence Minister]—also curiously enough a carpenter is not Australian born.'[13]

Hankey, humbly taking minutes, had the satisfaction of seeing his ideas declaimed to the delegates by Asquith, Grey and McKenna, and later set up in print and circulated as statements of imperial strategy.

Reginald McKenna, the First Lord of the Admiralty, was effectively a fourth member of the cabal, although his membership is not so thoroughly documented. His relations with Fisher and Hankey were close and warm, and the circle of friendship also included McKenna's wife Pamela, to whom Fisher often wrote in terms of mock flirtation and real endearment.

[10] Esher to Sir A. Bigge [the King's secretary], 11 May 1910 (typed extract), EP 16/12.

[11] 'Note by Lord Esher' (10 Jan. 1911) in 'Report of a Sub-Committee of the Committee of Imperial Defence assembled to formulate Questions . . . to be discussed at the Imperial Defence Conference, 1911' (11 Mar. 1911), p. 10, CAB 5/2/67C.

[12] Hankey to Fisher, 31 May 1911, FP 1/10/526a, fo. 50; M. Hankey, 'Copy of memo sent to Mr McKenna' (11 May 1911); Hankey, 'Imperial Defence Committee—Notes for the Prime Minister's Opening Statement to Representatives of the Dominions attending the Imperial Conference' (23 May 1911), both in HP 7/6; Fisher to Mrs McKenna, 18 May 1911 and to Reginald McKenna, 24 May 1911, *FG*, vol. 2, pp. 371–3.

[13] Diary of Major A. Grant Duff, 30 May 1911, Grant Duff Papers, Churchill College, Cambridge 2/1, fo. 74.

Unfortunately for the three, McKenna was forced to leave the Admiralty in September 1911; but he did not forget his lessons.[14]

McKenna's speech to the Dominion statesmen followed the spirit of Hankey's brief in its stress on the decisive impact of naval supremacy and economic warfare. The enemy, he said,

> would neither be able to transport his forces nor continue his trade, and *the result of the economic pressure of the destruction of overseas trade in almost any modern State would be so serious as I believe to constitute something even more than a crippling blow.* We see in times of bad trade how nations suffer from high prices and want of employment; but such evils as we see in depression of trade could not be compared for a moment to the effect of closing the ports of the enemy against food and raw materials, and I have no doubt that, certainly in the specific cases which I shall come to immediately, the effect upon the enemy of stopping the bulk of his foreign trade would be of the most serious kind.[15]

On the next day Asquith appealed more directly to the Dominions as Britain's staple suppliers, and argued that their export trade had created an interest in naval security. Canada's Sir Wilfrid Laurier had questioned whether it was in Canada's interest to support Britain in all conceivable conflicts. Asquith replied:

> We have witnessed an enormous expansion, and in no case more marked than in the case of Canada, of the overseas commerce in which all the Dominions now participate. I have here the figures for the last completed year 1909, and the total overseas trade of Australia in that year was no less than 116,000,000 pounds of sea-borne trade in which Australia is interested, and the 70,000,000 pounds in which Canada is interested would, as I say, at once be put in peril on the outbreak of war.[16]

Laurier resisted the implication that this committed Canada to *military* adventures. 'I would have a very strong objection that Canada should have to take part in the military operations of Great Britain . . . all the nations of Europe to-day, in my humble estimation have gone, if I may say so, mad.'[17] Grant Duff recorded his impression of the meeting:

> the general upshot was that the Dominion Ministers, including Laurier, were forced to acknowledge that *owing to the extent of their oversea trade* which would be liable to capture, their idea of non-participation in a naval war was no longer tenable. Laurier admitted without reserve *the duty of the Dominions to seize enemy ships* in their harbours on the outbreak of war, and only held out, reasonably I

---

[14] Fisher's correspondence with McKenna was voluminous (*FG*, vol. 2); with Pamela McKenna it was intimate and warm (e.g. 12 Feb. 1910, *FG*, vol. 2, p. 306): Fisher to Hankey, 27 Jan. 1911, HP 5/2A, fo. 6; on the foursome: also Hankey, *Supreme Command*, vol. 1, pp. 145–8.
[15] CID, minutes of 112th meeting, 29 May 1911, p. 5, CAB 2/2 fo. 95. Emphasis added.
[16] Ibid., 113th meeting, 30 May 1911, p. 6.
[17] Ibid., p. 7.

think, for the right to put their naval or military forces at the disposal of the imperial government or not as they choose.[18]

Hankey was overjoyed. In a long and exuberant letter to Fisher he reported the proceedings in detail. 'You would have revelled in Sir Edward Grey's statement, as I did. From beginning to end he laid stress on the fact that *sea power* is the keynote of our foreign policy. . . . not a word of the Army.' McKenna's statement 'was an excellent exposition of the general principles on which we propose to act in time of war both for the protection of our own interests and for damaging the enemy's. Esher says it was quite admirable and created a most favourable impression.' As for Laurier's reservations, Hankey also came out convinced that 'There is no doubt it will be "all right on the day".' The Prime Minister also performed as a good navalist. 'Five years ago he could not have done it, but for five years we have been educating him . . .'. Military matters only occupied 'a beggarly hour'. Hankey concluded his account: 'the whole three days were of enormous value, constituting a death blow almost to the militarists.'[19]

Flushed with ambition, he attempted to build two more bridges between Britain and the Dominions. He persuaded the Prime Minister to provide for representation of the Dominions on the CID, and to establish affiliate CIDs in each of the Dominions. He also began to muse on a plan to go to Australia for five years as secretary of the Defence Committee there, and for his place on the British CID to be taken by an Australian officer. A year later he proposed to go to Canada on a similar errand. From the epicentre of British strategic deliberation, Hankey regarded the Dominion partnership as the most vital element.[20]

But we must not run too far ahead. Time now to see how the other actors reacted to the plans of the three.

---

[18] Grant Duff diary, 30 Mar. 1911, fo. 70, Grant Duff Papers 2/1. Emphasis added.
[19] Hankey to Fisher, 31 May 1911, FP 1/10/526a, fos. 5–51.
[20] Ibid., fo. 51; Hankey to Fisher, 8 Apr. 1912, FP 1/11/566, fo. 47.

19

MORALITY AND ADMIRALTY: 'JACKY' FISHER, ECONOMIC WARFARE, AND INTERNATIONAL LAW

ONE foggy summer night during the naval manœuvres of 1888, a squadron of the Royal Navy crept up the river Mersey and lowered anchors two hours after midnight. Liverpool and Birkenhead lay at its mercy. Admiral Tryon, in command, announced he would spare the two cities for a ransom of one million pounds. Other towns were not so "lucky". 'Greenock is in ashes,' wrote *The Times*, 'Ardrossan has been destroyed, Campbelltown has been punished for some unknown sin—perhaps that of helping to return a Gladstonian at the late election.' Aberdeen was bombarded, the Forth Bridge (in construction) blown up, Filey laid waste. A distinguished jurist wrote a letter of protest to *The Times*. Many officers responded, and one of them wrote, 'the talk about international law is all nonsense. Who can enforce it?' This opinion was held as firmly by other naval men who wrote in (with a single exception).[1] Even if such a dismissive view of the law is granted, the question remains: The law of nations, with its teachers and textbooks, its conventions and treaties, must fulfil some function, otherwise it would not exist. What sort of obstacle did it pose to the blockade plan?

The blockade project took as its target not the German armed forces, but the civilian population. This raised some difficult questions of law and morality. When Imperial Germany planned to violate Belgian neutrality, it did not flinch from violating international law. A similar necessity affected some British war plans. The Royal Navy helped to negotiate, codify and promote a legal code that clashed with some of its own strategic ideas. Two Edwardian Liberal projects came into conflict: the blockade plan as a method of overcoming Germany in a future war, and the reform of maritime law which took place in stages from 1907 onwards. This moral and legal dilemma forms the subject of this chapter.

I

'Jacky' Fisher was no respecter of the laws of war. In this he merely expressed prevailing opinion in the late-Victorian navy. Fisher repeatedly

---

[1] *The Times*, 9 Aug. 1888, p. 7; 10 Aug., pp. 9, 10; 17 Aug., p. 7; 18 Aug., p. 8. The jurist was T. E. Holland, who wrote on the 9th and the 18th. Admiral Tryon defiantly repeated the outrages the following year: Bloch, *War of the Future*, pp. 103–4.

asserted that any talk of restraint in war was dangerous nonsense, and told both friend and foe that might was always right. He had a deep suspicion of international agreements. 'The inevitable result of Conferences and Arbitrations is that we always give up something. It's like a rich man entering into a Conference with a gang of burglars!'[2] Fisher wrote these words in response to Sir Edward Grey's determination to codify the law of the sea, an enterprise that Fisher had to reconcile with his own lawless view of international relations.

During the maritime wars of the eighteenth and early nineteenth centuries the Royal Navy had molested merchant shipping on the high seas with scant regard for the protests of neutrals. In 1812 Britain went to war with the United States to uphold this practice. War had established British naval mastery, and many sailors and writers considered the rights of capture to be the foundation of British naval power.

Some four decades later, at a conference at the end of the Crimean War, Britain came round and renounced her previous position. In the "Declaration of Paris" of 1856 Britain effectively conceded a doctrine that neutral powers had consistently asserted against her during the French wars.[3]

Between the Declaration of Paris and the First World War it was widely assumed in Britain that food for civilian populations could not be treated as contraband of war. Not every country agreed. France declared rice absolute contraband in her war with China in 1885 and Bismarck endorsed the French embargo in the following words: 'The measure in question has for its object the shortening of the war by increasing the difficulties of the enemy, and is a justifiable step in war if impartially enforced against all neutral ships.'[4] Likewise, Russia treated food as contraband during the Russo-Japanese war of 1904–5. But these instances stood out and the principle was not admitted in Britain. For half a century the naval powers complied with the Declaration of Paris, or perhaps they had no clear temptation to defy it; its conventions took firm root in international law.[5]

The main points of the declaration may be summarized briefly as follows:

1. Neutral trade should be immune from belligerent interference in wartime ("Free Ships Make Free Goods").

---

[2] [J. Fisher], 'War Plans and the Distribution of the Fleet' ('1907 or 1908'), ADM 116/1043B/I.

[3] Text of the Declaration in T. G. Bowles, *The Declaration of Paris of 1856* (1900), pp. 122–4.

[4] Bismarck argued that interference would prejudice German commerce in this particular instance. The passage is translated from the *Norddeutsche Allgemeine Zeitung*, 8 Apr. 1885, and was quoted by T. McKinnon Wood, HC debs. 5 ser., vol. 27 (28 June 1911), col. 451.

[5] A short conspectus in Supply of Food. Royal Commission. Report; PP 1905 Cd. 2643 XXXIX, pp. 22–4. The same impression is conveyed by the parliamentary controversy, e.g. HC debs. 5 ser., vol. 27 (28 June 1911), cols. 434–696.

2. Enemy goods carried in neutral ships could not be seized ("The neutral flag covers the enemy's goods").
3. Neutral cargoes could not be captured even when carried in enemy ships. ("Neutral goods . . . are not liable to capture under the enemy's flag.")
4. All these points were subject to a substantial qualification. Neutral immunity did not extend to "contraband of war".

"Contraband of war" was not clearly defined in the Declaration of Paris. Goods in this class fell under two categories. "Absolute contraband" consisted of articles which are useful only in war, like guns, bayonets, uniforms and ammunition. "Conditional contraband" was a category of goods which were useful in peace as well as war. They could only be captured if clearly consigned to an enemy's base of operations or its military authorities. Conditional contraband might include food, but the boundaries were not clear.

The legal immunity of food from capture was rooted in a *moral* convention, in the principle that Geoffrey Best has aptly called 'humanity in warfare'. Civilized warfare strives to avoid unnecessary suffering by making a distinction between combatants and non-combatants.[6] This moral dimension accorded well with British interests, especially in its exclusion of food from contraband of war. When Captain Prince Louis of Battenberg, the Director of Naval Intelligence, gave secret evidence to the Royal Commission on Food Supply, he dwelt on the practical difficulties of imposing a blockade on the British Isles, and then on those arising from international law. He added, 'Then there is the larger question of humanity. You cannot condemn forty millions to starvation on the ground that they assist in defending their country, because you include women and children.'[7] By the late-Edwardian period food imports made up almost two-thirds of consumption and their protection in wartime became increasingly problematic.[8]

British admirals had no relish for trade protection. They prepared for duels of battle fleets, and regarded the protection of widely-scattered merchant ships as an onerous burden. Short of attaching a cruiser to every tramp, there seemed to be no tactical solution to the problem. One source of relief was to rely on neutral carriers and to take advantage of their immunities. From this point of view it was in Britain's interest to reinforce neutral rights. There was no guarantee that the law would be upheld all round, but Britain's most likely neutral supplier, the United States, had a

---

[6] G. Best, *Humanity in Warfare* (1980), chs. III/5–7, IV.

[7] Supply of Food. Royal Commission. Evidence, 5 Nov. 1903 (confidential proof), p. 11, ADM 137/2872.

[8] Report and Proceedings of a Sub-Committee of the Committee of Imperial Defence Appointed to Inquire into Certain Questions of Naval Policy raised by Lord Charles Beresford (12 Aug. 1909, printed Oct. 1909), pp. 285–304, CAB 16/9.

long tradition of standing for its rights, and also had the power to do so.[9]

Britons considered the law of the sea from three different aspects, the neutral, the defensive and the offensive. (*a*) As a neutral in other peoples' wars, and as the world's largest carrier, Britain stood to benefit from neutral immunities and rights. (*b*) As a besieged island Britain gained an additional margin of safety if some of her cargoes travelled in neutral bottoms. (*c*) On the other hand, if Britain wanted to project her naval power in a continental war, then neutral immunities were not compatible with a strategy of maritime blockade.

The traditions of free trade inclined many Liberals to support neutral immunities, to the extent even of proposing to abolish contraband and conferring immunity to all private property at sea. Lord Loreburn, the Liberal Lord Chancellor, advocated this view.[10] On the other hand, there was also a deep suspicion of the Declaration. Lord Charles Beresford described it as a 'false, rotten, misleading and treacherous treaty by which Great Britain voluntarily gave up half her power of protection and offence.' A similar view was propagated by the maverick Liberal MP and journalist Thomas Gibson Bowles. 'Jacky' Fisher also shared it.[11]

When the Royal Commission on Food Supply reported in 1905, it only considered the neutral and defensive viewpoints, and ignored the offensive uses of sea power. One year later the Department of Naval Intelligence began to work on its economic blockade plans, and also to prepare for the International Peace Conference that was going to be held in The Hague in 1907.

Rear Admiral Charles L. Ottley , the head of the Department, was also designated as naval delegate to the Hague conference. Ottley was a man of assurance, intelligence and polish, who specialized in the political and diplomatic aspects of naval staff work. After serving as naval attaché in five capitals and as Director of Naval Intelligence between 1906 and 1908, Ottley became Secretary of the Committee of Imperial Defence until 1912. Clearly a man of some consequence, he was close to the heart of naval policy-making throughout the Edwardian period. Ottley was no Liberal— in 1903 he actually stood for Parliament as a Conservative. But in matters of sea law he was a moderate.

In 1906 a departmental committee was set up to consider British policy

---

[9] Supply of Food. Royal Commission. Report, PP 1905 Cd. 2643 XXXIX, p. 26, section 111. The whole problem was considered in detail in Battenberg's secret evidence, 5th Nov. 1903, ADM 137/2872.

[10] R. T. Reid [later Lord Loreburn], 'Capture of Private Property at Sea', *The Times*, 14 Oct. 1905, p. 4; Lord Loreburn, *Capture at Sea* (1913), *passim*.

[11] Mahan and Beresford, 'Anglo-American Reunion', p. 573; Bowles, *Declaration of Paris*. For a brief survey of the two traditions: 'Right of Capture of Private Property at Sea', Report [of the Departmental Committee in Preparation for the 2nd Hague Conference] (8 Feb. 1907),pp. 4–5, CAB 37/86/14; more comprehensively: B. Semmel, *Liberalism and Naval Strategy: Ideology, Interest, and Sea Power during the Pax Britannica* (Boston 1986), *passim*.

for the Hague conference. Ottley drafted a paper on 'The Value to Great Britain of the Right of Capture of Neutral Vessels'. He wrote that immunity for neutral ships and cargoes was to Britain's advantage, as a means of protecting food supplies in wartime, even if it might rule out naval pressure against an enemy. In looking forward to the coming conference, Ottley regarded the doctrine of 'free ships, free goods' as established. He argued that British interests required as narrow a definition of contraband as possible, restricting it strictly to military equipment:

... conditions have profoundly changed since this country was engaged in European war.

Railways and other ways of communication have been immensely developed. We are no longer in a position to seriously embarrass a European enemy by the always dangerous method of interference with neutral commerce. In the case of war with Germany, for example, we could not hope to prevent that country obtaining any contraband required over her land frontiers.

Contraband for Germany, even if sent oversea from the United States, could always be landed in neutral European ports under the very guns of our cruisers, and the onus of proof as to its ultimate destination would rest with us.

In the course of the American civil war the northern navy had intercepted southern cargoes as far away as the West Indies, invoking a doctrine of "continuous voyage", that allowed the capture of contraband anywhere if its ultimate destination was proven. But for Britain to invoke this doctrine against Germany might bring a clash with the United States, so the right to capture contraband carried by neutrals no longer had its former value for Britain. Economic warfare of this kind was ruled out in conflicts between the Great Powers.[12]

The Committee accepted Ottley's argument. This did not mean the abolition of blockade. Enemy ports would be blockaded and enemy shipping captured, but neutrals would continue to trade freely. Sir George Clarke, the secretary of the CID, argued that the shock to Germany merely from the loss of its own shipping and ports would be severe enough. In a longer war, German trade would recover somewhat by the use of neutral ports. He also thought that German–British trade would actually continue indirectly and that German goods would find their way into British bottoms and ports. The Committee decided to retain blockade, but to limit contraband.[13] The maritime code that Ottley and his colleagues

---

[12] Capt. C. L. Ottley, 'The Value to Great Britain of the Right of Capture of Neutral Vessels' (9 May 1906), pp. 1–2. FP 8/20.

[13] Sir George Clarke, 'The Capture of the Private Propery of Belligerents at Sea', Hague Conference Dept. Cttee (n. 11 above), App. B, p. 16; British preparations for the conference: Coogan, *End of Neutrality*, ch. 4.

negotiated in 1907 and 1908 was consistent with this line of reasoning, and extended neutral trading rights in wartime.

II

The story of Edwardian sea-law reform has been told before.[14] Between 1907 and 1914 the Liberal government made a sustained effort to codify the law of the sea and to place it under the jurisdiction of a recognized international tribunal. This effort began at the second Hague Peace Conference of 1907, and continued at the London Naval Conference of 1908–9, which issued the Declaration of London in February 1909. The Declaration came under intense public and parliamentary scrutiny before it was rejected by the House of Lords in 1911. Despite the failure of Parliament to ratify the Declaration of London, the Admiralty incorporated its substance into British naval manuals and the Foreign Office accepted it as an expression of Britain's legal obligations.

Without a tribunal positive law can hardly be said to exist, since every enactment is open to self-serving interpretations. To judge by his actions, Sir Edward Grey considered maritime law to be largely in harmony with British interests, and he worked to give it some teeth. At the Hague conference in 1907 the British delegation won support for an International Prize Court. Delegates from the main maritime nations assembled in London in December 1908 to devise a code for the new tribunal. They took the current customary law of the sea as their point of departure, and in February 1909 they agreed on a set of principles known as the Declaration of London.[15]

The volume of comment and controversy excited by public issues is not always proportional to their importance. Four principal issues dominated the London naval conference and subsequent public debates, but only one of them is of fundamental importance. Britain could afford to concede a few subsidiary interests in order to achieve its main purpose, and these concessions attracted disproportionate controversy. This is by way of amends for neglecting some aspects of the Declaration, in order to concentrate on the key issue of contraband.

For the first time an international convention specified a list of

---

[14] The best account is in Coogan, *End of Neutrality*, chs. 6,7. My own work, which is partly based on different sources, owes much to his clear exposition. Also of value are C. Parry, 'Foreign Policy and International Law', in F. H. Hinsley (ed.), *British Foreign Policy under Sir Edward Grey* (Cambridge 1977), pp. 89–110; B. Ranft, 'Restraints on War at Sea before 1945', in M. Howard (ed.), *Restraints on War* (Oxford 1979), pp. 39–56; Lord Devlin, *The House of Lords and the Naval Prize Bill, 1911* (1968), and Semmel, *Liberalism and Naval Strategy*, ch. 7.

[15] Text in J. B. Scott (ed.), *The Declaration of London, February 26, 1909* (New York 1919), pp. 112–29.

contraband commodities. Absolute contraband was restricted to a short list of munitions and military supplies. At the insistence of the continental powers the list of articles under conditional contraband was extended to include food (but this category, as we have seen, still excluded food consigned for civilian consumption). This British concession of neutral rights (and its being classed as a concession), together with others, indicates that Britain was striving for greater immunity for neutrals.[16] The most important innovation was a long "free list" of goods, which, as the delegates reported, 'placed it beyond the power of belligerents in future to treat as contraband the raw materials of some of the most important of our national industries.'[17]

The Declaration of London preserved the essence of the Declaration of Paris. It extended neutral rights and immunities by defining contraband, and defining it narrowly, and especially by the introduction of a "free list".

Sir Edward Grey had hoped to ratify the Declaration without reference to Parliament, but after the Naval Panic of 1909, it came under sustained public and political attack. Britain's interests as a neutral, as a besieged island and as an aggressive belligerent were simply not compatible with each other, and Grey found himself under attack from all three angles—the neutral, the defensive and the offensive. An invisible hand stirred up Chambers of Commerce throughout the country to send in petitions and protests and 138 half-pay admirals signed a petition against the declaration. Most of the public criticism came from the neutral-defensive point of view.[18]

It has not been easy for subsequent historians to make sense of the Declaration of London.[19] Grey's policy is not really problematic, if one accepts that his prime consideration was the safety of the merchant marine

---

[16] In another concession neutral ships carrying contraband could be sunk in certain circumstances without being taken into port. Britain also gave up the doctrine of "continuous voyage", consisting of the right to seize contraband in transit between neutral ports. In return, the scope of blockade was extended beyond the coastline, to a "sphere of action" [*rayon d'action*] of 800 miles from the coast.

[17] Report of British delegates to the London Naval Conference, FO 371/794, p. 3, fo. 381. Board of Trade, Admiralty and Foreign Office officials were keen to exclude industrial raw materials from contraband: 'Notes of the Meeting of Interdepartmental Committee on Naval Conference of the 4th January, 1909, respecting contraband', ADM 116/1073.

[18] Eyre Crowe, 'Notes on Mr Gibson Bowles' article on the Declaration of London, in the May number of the "Nineteenth Century"' [n.d. ?May 1909], ADM 116/1079. The central figure in the anti-Declaration movement was the the flamboyant MP, T. G. Bowles: see his *Sea Law and Sea Power* (1909). Letters from shipowners, Chambers of Commerce and Navy League in FO Miscellaneous no. 4 (1910), Correspondence Respecting the Declaration of London; PP 1910 Cd. 5418 LXXIV. Crowe suspected that the agitation was encouraged by Slade's successor at the Department of Naval Intelligence: Crowe to Slade, 3 Jan. 1910, Slade Papers, microfilm reel 3. ADM 116/1236 contains documents relating to the agitation.

[19] Ranft, Parry, Devlin, Coogan and Semmel differ considerably in their interpretations.

and of food supply in time of war.[20] Britain conceded subsidiary matters, in order to secure the vital ones. At worst, British delegates failed to consider all the implications, and in consequence left Britain more exposed than under previous customary law. Edward Grey's behaviour seems to confirm this. He wrote that the Declaration was required on grounds of 'General Policy'.[21] John Coogan also suggests that Grey, together with other "Continentalists", did not mind curtailment of naval capabilities because they did not believe that sea power could be decisive.[22]

It is more difficult to reconcile the Declaration with Admiralty plans to fight Germany to an economic defeat. Rear Admiral Slade (the Director of Naval Intelligence) who presented the blockade plan to the CID, was also the naval delegate to the London conference, which opened one day after his presentation. The other naval delegate was Rear-Admiral Ottley, who had apprised his minister McKenna of the economic warfare plan on the day the conference opened.[23] McKenna was First Lord of the Admiralty between 1908 and 1911. He became an ardent "economist" and worked closely with Fisher and Hankey. In the course of the London conference McKenna more than once attempted to throw a spanner in the works, always arguing against the surrender of belligerent rights. 'In dealing with a formidable opponent such as Germany, every legitimate weapon would have to be used,' he wrote to Grey.[24]

Clearly there are some puzzles here to be resolved. How did Slade and Ottley come to advocate economic pressure in their role as strategic planners, and yet acted to restrict the navy's freedom in their capacity as naval diplomats? What game was the navy playing at the London conference? On Christmas Eve 1908, with the conference already in session, the Foreign Office delegate Eyre Crowe reported to Grey that Admiral Fisher regarded the whole exercise as a farce.

Sir J. Fisher told me personally 3 days ago that in the next big war, our commanders would sink every ship they came across, hostile or neutral, if it happened to suit them. He added, with characteristic vehemence, that we should most certainly violate the Declaration of Paris and every other treaty that might prove inconvenient.[25]

---

[20] '. . . having regard to the enormous commercial interests of this country, as well as to the fact that it must more often be neutral than belligerent . . .'—'Naval Conference Committee, Further Report. 26 Oct. 1908, signed by British delegates', ADM 116/1079.

[21] 'Minute by Sir Edward Grey', 26 Dec. 1908. ADM 116/1079.

[22] Coogan, *End of Neutrality*, p. 121.

[23] Ch. 16, sec. III, above.

[24] 'Naval Conference' [report of meeting of Grey, McKenna and British delegates on 15 Dec. 1908] (typed), fo. 2; subsequent memos indicate that this is a later clarification of McKenna's view.

[25] [Eyre Crowe], minute of 24 Dec. 1908, (a gloss on a report of the meeting of Sir Edward Grey and R. McKenna of 15 Dec.), FO 371/794, fo. 146.

Three years later Fisher wrote in a letter about this very matter,

Perhaps I went a little too far when I said I would boil the prisoners in oil and murder the innocent in cold blood, etc., etc., etc. But it's quite silly not to make war damnable to the whole mass of your enemy's population, which of course is the secret of maintaining the right of capture of private property at sea . . . [26]

Here is the contradiction we have to explain. Coogan's explanation that Fisher's target was the German navy and not the German economy is obviously incorrect.[27] Fisher (though not all his successors) was deeply committed to the concept of economic pressure as the decisive strategy. Both Ottley and Slade, the naval delegates, are on record as exponents, if not actual supporters, of this militant line. But Ottley and Slade also played a constructive and loyal role in the sea-law negotiations, supported the Declaration strongly and stood up for it on every subsequent opportunity. How is this puzzle to be resolved? If Fisher was so adverse to the rule of law at sea, why did he allow his naval delegates to spend two years in the pursuit and conclusion of such compromising agreements?

It is just possible that the naval delegates never received a proper briefing, and were left to construct the naval case according to their own lights. Slade found it difficult to get any guidance from Fisher during the naval conference deliberations.[28] In 1908 Fisher was fully preoccupied by the defence of his reforms, and in his struggle with Lord Charles Beresford, the aristocratic admiral who challenged his leadership and campaigned for his dismissal.[29]

Some parliamentary critics argued that the delegates (and especially the Foreign Office delegates) had simply fallen in love with their own handiwork. Certainly they felt proud of their achievement. Maybe it was partly a matter of muddle and neglect. That is not uncommon in secretive bureaucracies.[30]

Perhaps it was not simply a case of benign neglect. It was not Fisher's way to allow such matters to be settled by default. A more Machiavellian interpretation may be required. Fisher more than once alluded to himself as a Machiavellian.[31] An Admiralty document of 1908 suggests this very interpretation, when it says:

When Great Britain is belligerent, she can be safely trusted to look after her own interests, but the dangerous time for her is when she is neutral and does not wish to

---

[26] Fisher to Esher, 25 Apr. 1912, *FG*, vol. 2, p. 453; Bacon, *1900 Onwards*, pp. 327–8.

[27] Coogan, *End of Neutrality*, pp. 84–5.

[28] Slade diary, 6 May, 7 May, 20 May 1908; Slade Papers, NMM.

[29] Slade diary, 7 May 1908; Bacon, *Fisher*, vol. 2, pp. 45–50.

[30] Prince Louis of Battenberg's evidence to the Royal Commission on Food Supply, 5 Nov. 1903, Q. 250, ADM 137/2872.

[31] Fisher to Arnold White, 12 Oct. 1909; to John Leyland, 7 Nov. 1911, to Mrs Cecil Fisher, 2 Dec. 1911; *FG*, vol. 2, pp. 271, 412, 417.

take such a strong line as to render herself liable to be drawn into war. At such a time, the existence of a well reasoned-out classification of goods will be of enormous advantage, not only to Great Britain, but to all other commercial communities.[32]

The rule of law requires an acceptance of its authority in advance. That was the point of setting up an international tribunal. The Admiralty document just quoted plainly suggests that the law will only be respected if it is to Britain's advantage. It is a Machiavellian acceptance which makes advantage a condition of adherence. Fisher may have allowed Ottley and Slade to get on with the job in the interest of good relations with the Liberal government, and also as a subterfuge which might create false confidence in Germany.

We know that Fisher's confidence in his two delegates was waning in 1908–9. Slade was banished in April 1909 to the East Indies station and Ottley was kept out of Fisher's inner circle, and resented his exclusion from the group which drafted Fisher's so-called 'War Plans'.[33]

Public debate fanned up parliamentary tempers, and the Declaration became a party-political issue by the time it came up for parliamentary approval. A strong resistance began to build up in the Navy, in the Press and in the Unionist Party.

In February 1911 the issue of the Declaration of London came to a head. The Naval Prize Bill was about to come before Parliament. At the CID, Rear Admiral Ottley remained strongly committed to the Declaration that he had negotiated. In addition to political controversy, he had to reckon with a challenge within his own house. It came from his subordinate Hankey, already beginning to flex his muscles as manipulator and wire-puller. Hankey drafted a strong attack on the Declaration of London, and asked Ottley to send it on to the Minister. This amounted almost to mutiny.[34]

In his paper and in two others that followed Hankey forcefully restated the case for economic pressure as the decisive strategy. He argued that blockade could not be effective without the power to stop neutral ships and capture their cargoes.

Ottley's response was defensive and conciliatory. He stressed the political and diplomatic difficulties of total economic war. This would amount to a rejection, not of the Declaration of London, but of the whole

---

[32] 'Notes on Contraband' [typewritten memo, no signature, no date, *c*.1908], ADM 116/ 1073.

[33] Sir C. Ottley, 'Note of a Conversation with Lord Fisher (At the Admiralty—December 1909)', encl. with Ottley to Fisher, 12 Jan. 1912, FP 1/9.

[34] These papers are preserved in three collections: in HP 7/5, CAB 17/87 and ADM 116/ 1236. They are discussed in Hankey, *Supreme Command*, vol. 1, pp. 98–101, Bell, *History of the Blockade*, pp. 20–2, and Coogan, *End of Neutrality*, pp. 137–9.

edifice of maritime law consecrated by the Declaration of Paris. Ottley was right to be uneasy—the notion of a war waged against civilians, although common in the navy, was less palatable to Liberal opinion. Ottley wrote that, 'The relegation of peaceful commodities notoriously intended for the use of the civil population, to the category of absolute contraband, not only violates the Declaration of Paris, but runs counter to the policy to which we have ourselves consistently adhered for the last hundred years . . .'[35] In addition to the moral dimension, Ottley's main rejoinder to Hankey was to invoke the United States, the most powerful neutral, whose attitude formed an obstacle to the economic isolation of Germany.

At this point, however, Ottley took a new tack. Once command of the sea was established, HM Government would have complete freedom of action. Then, but only then, it could safely discard the Declaration, and implement Fisher's doctrine of "cruelty is kindness." Whether he had always held that view (which seems to me unlikely) or whether he had finally realized where the wind was blowing, Ottley now endorsed a Machiavellian interpretation of his cherished Declaration, while still taking care to invoke the interests of civilization.

Ottley and Hankey, the two protagonists, went to lay their cases in person before the First Lord McKenna. A staff officer reported the confrontation in his diary, in the following words:

22 February 1911 . . .

The 'worry' over the 'Declaration of London' still goes on—and Hankey has now turned against it and denounced it as equivalent to tying up our right arm in a war with Germany.

Fisher apparently allowed it to be negotiated with the deliberate intention of tearing it up in the event of war. Characteristic.

24 February.

McKenna's standpoint seems much the same—the Germans are sure to infringe it in the early days of the war, then with great regret we tear it up—If they don't infringe it we must invent an infringement.[36]

Hankey's last exchange with Ottley concludes with the words, 'Salus Civitatis, Suprema Lex—'the safety of the state is the highest law'.[37]

Soon after, Fisher began to intrigue behind the scenes to get Ottley replaced by Hankey as secretary of the CID. Ottley became increasingly remote and withdrew for long periods to his Scottish home, where he remained even during the tense weeks of August–September 1911. He

---

[35] 'Remarks by Sir Charles Ottley on Capt. Hankey's paper' (17 Feb. 1911), fo. 4, ADM 116/1236.

[36] Grant Duff diary, 22, 24 Feb. 1911, fos. 50–1; Grant Duff Papers 2/1.

[37] M. Hankey [last document in exchange with Ottley, no title, 8 Mar. 1911], fo. 10: CAB 17/87.

even failed to attend the crucial meeting of 23 August 1911. Meanwhile, Hankey effectively ran the Committee. Ottley's term was coming to an end, and he asked for security of tenure and a pension before applying for renewal. Neither was forthcoming. Instead, he was suddenly offered a lucrative position as a director of Armstrong's, a large armaments firm. Lord Esher did nothing to discourage him. Ottley continued to beg for his modest demands to be met but in vain. At the very same time a protégé of Winston Churchill (Sir Francis Hopwood) got much better treatment and received the pension rights denied to Ottley. If Ottley was wanted, he was not wanted badly enough. Treasury inflexibility provided a convenient excuse. Ottley left for Newcastle with an aching heart and Hankey took his place. In all the encomiums for Ottley there is not a single phrase of sincere regret.[38]

Fisher and McKenna did not ignore the problem of powerful neutrals. The United States Navy's General Board, in its own preparations for the Hague conference told the secretary of the navy,

The General Board is of the opinion that our interests are now so closely bound up with Great Britain, that we should exert our diplomatic efforts to dissuade Great Britain from giving up the great advantages she holds over Germany, due to her great navy and her excellent strategical position in regard to Germany's commerce. This great advantage would be lost to Great Britain should she join with the United States in its previous mistaken policy of urging an international agreement to exempt private property from seizure in time of war . . .[39]

Fisher's answer to the problem was based on a shrewd intuition of the real inclinations of the United States. In his intuitive way Fisher correctly assessed that in a conflict with Germany, American hostility would not pose a serious risk.[40]

III

The Declaration of London controversy was spirited and inconclusive. The House of Commons spent three days rambling backwards and forwards over the issues. Unionist speakers accused the government of placing British supplies at risk, while at the same time forsaking an offensive weapon and throwing away belligerent rights. McKinnon Wood, for the

[38] Fisher support for Hankey: Fisher to Esher, 9 Nov. 1911, 2 Apr. 1912, *FG*, vol. 2, pp. 414, 442; Grant Duff diary 2/2, 29 Feb., 23 Apr. 1912; Fisher to Hankey, 27 Jan., 25 Oct., 13 Nov. 1911, HP 5/2A, fos. 6, 34, 49. In greatest detail in a series of letters from Ottley and Hankey to Esher, 21 Dec. 1911 to 29 Apr. 1912, EP 5/38 and 5/40. Also R. S. Churchill, *Winston S..Churchill*, vol. 2, Companion vol., pt. 2 (1969), pp. 1363, 1367, 1368. Compare this interpretation with Roskill, *Hankey*, vol. 1, pp. 110–12.
[39] General Board to secretary of the navy, 28 Sept. 1906, quoted in Coogan, *End of Neutrality*, p. 59.
[40] Ch. 17, sec. IV, above.

government, answered, 'To maintain our commerce in time of war and to keep our industrial classes in work is a very high belligerent interest.' The debate took place during the Agadir and the Parliament Bill crises, and was not regarded by Liberal MPs as a suitable opportunity to question Sir Edward Grey's foreign policy.[41]

Another reason for the indecisive quality of this debate was the endemic uncertainty about the meaning of international law. In the absence of an effective sanction, its authority was dubious. Even an international tribunal, which Grey proposed to establish, did not guarantee compliance with its jurisdiction. Britain's interests in wartime were hidden behind the veil of uncertainty. In the absence of solid historical precedents, the political writers and speakers of Edwardian England could not predict the circumstances in which the law would be applied. As one MP admitted, he did not know whether the offensive or defensive contingency was more likely.

International law presents a problem that is similar to the game theory "prisoner's dilemma". In that game each player has the choice of trusting the other player or betraying him. There is no contact between the two. For each player, the outcome depends on the protagonist's choice. If both players choose trust, their joint reward is highest. The highest *individual* prize goes to a player who succeeds in betraying a trusting protagonist. If both players do not cooperate the outcome is intermediate. The worst outcome for a player is for his trust to be betrayed. Betrayal appears to be the rational choice. It offers the highest prize, and avoids the worst punishment. But when both players choose betrayal they both do poorly. To achieve the best joint outcome they must both make a leap of faith and co-operate.

Like prisoner's dilemma international law relies on mutual trust to achieve the best outcome. But individual players always face the temptation to betray, dragging the others down with them. After a breach of trust, normative (or "civilized") expectations are suspended, and replaced by uncertainty and hazard. Once trust has gone, the law can no longer be invoked and the best outcome is no longer within reach.[42] Like the prisoners in the game, the Edwardians could not be certain of the winning formula, and therefore split between trust and treachery—with a good measure of controversy, anxiety and worry. The sea-law negotiations presented an opportunity for Britain to develop some trust with Germany by increasing neutral immunities. Although neutral immunities were in fact fortified, there is not a hint that appeasement was intended.

A new note of uncertainty entered after the end of the Declaration of London controversy. Its initiator was Fisher, and it rose out of his

[41] See HC debs. 5 ser., vol. 27 (28, 29 June, 3rd July 1911). Quote from 28 June, col. 457.
[42] See Axelrod, *Evolution*.

involvement with the Royal Commission on Oil Fuel in 1913. This led Fisher to examine the effect of the submarine, just emerging as a credible weapon, on Britain's defence doctrine. On the one hand, he was reassured. The submarine put paid forever to any thought of invasion. On the other, it placed Britain's food supply in grave danger. Fisher did not regard the Declaration of London as providing any defence. He saw that, if necessity justified drowning thousands of soldiers of an invasion fleet, it would not stop at a few crewmen on a grainship. *'The essence of war is violence and moderation in war is imbecility.* Nor would it be a waste of torpedoes to use them to sink these valuables cargoes of grain and merchandise.'[43] At one point this scared Fisher so much that he proposed to build a channel tunnel, or rather twenty of them! He then changed his mind when he saw that a channel tunnel would strengthen the continental commitment.[44]

In a comprehensive memorandum on the effect of the submarine on economic warfare, Fisher predicted how the new technology was going to change the rules of the game. The submarine had no prize crew to put aboard its captures, and would have to sink them.

All that would be known would be that a certain ship and her crew had disappeared, or that some of her boats would be picked up with a few survivors to tell the tale. Such a tale would fill the world with horror, and is freely acknowledged to be an altogether barbarous method of warfare; but again, if it is done by the Germans, the only thing would be to make reprisals. The essence of war is violence and moderation in war is imbecility.[45]

Julian Corbett responded to this with disbelief: 'Do you really think that any Power now-a-days would incur the odium of sinking merchant ships out of hand? It has never been done without first securing the crews and passengers. This submarines cannot do.'[46]

Fisher printed these words, as well as his answer: 'I shrug my shoulders and reply, "Did anyone say one word when Admiral Togo in cold blood, and before the declaration of war, sunk an English steamer with 2,000 Chinese troops on board, and only picked up the English crew? . . . No— Might is right!"'[47] Winston Churchill responded:

I do not believe this would ever be done by a civilized Power. If there were a nation vile enough to adopt systematically such methods, it would be justifiable, and indeed necessary, to employ the extreme methods of science against them: to spread pestilence, poison the water supply of great cities, and, if convenient

[43] Fisher, 'Battleships and Trade in the Mediterranean' (24 July 1912), *FG*, vol. 2, p. 469.
[44] Fisher, 'Our Food and Oil in War' (printed, n.d. Apr. 1913, p. 2), FP 6/2; Fisher to Corbett, 1 Dec. 1913, *FG*, vol. 2, p. 495.
[45] Fisher, 'The Oil Engine and the Submarine' (printed Dec. 1913), p. 10, HP 5/2.
[46] Corbett to Fisher, n.d. [late Nov. 1913], FP 1/14/752, fos. 54–5.
[47] Fisher, 'Postscript' (Jan. 1914), FP 8/33.

proceed by the assassination of individuals. These are frankly unthinkable propositions and the excellence of your paper is, to some extent, marred by the prominence assigned to them.[48]

The precise nature of the reprisals was not, in fact, discussed in Fisher's paper. It was Churchill who chose to think the unthinkable—while Fisher had a premonition of the horrors to come, and how helpless both law and morality would stand before the perceived necessities of national survival. The appearance of the submarine went far to remove the legal and moral inhibitions that might have held back the blockade project.

[48] Churchill to Fisher, 1 Jan. 1914, FP 1/14/763.

20

BLOCKADE AND ITS ENEMIES, 1909–1912

THE Atlantic Orientation encountered some formidable resistance. A good deal of it came from within the navy itself. Both the Foreign Office and the General Staff pushed for a stronger "Continental commitment".

I

The Navy

The Royal Navy commanded by far the largest national array of warships, but only had a smallish brain relative to its missions. The Board of Admiralty was absorbed in detail. A few planners worked in the intelligence department and the war college, but there was no regular General Staff. Strategic authority was centralized in the person of Admiral John Fisher and he made a principle of never discussing his plans.

In service bureaucracies the alternation of field and staff duties periodically sweeps away the actors. By 1910 the naval stage was swept as clean as the cast in a Shakespeare play. Fisher had to leave in January 1910. Arthur K. Wilson who replaced him was a capable but haughty sea-dog full of studied arrogance. He also had the political ineptness that comes from brooking no contradiction for a great many years. Wilson was primarily a sailor, and tactics interested him more than strategy. Fisher admired his seamanship but other officers regarded his nickname "'ard 'eart" as well-earned. 'He will never consult anyone and is impatient in argument, even to being impossible,' wrote one of them.[1]

Wilson inherited Fisher's absolute authority and used it to discard a good deal of Fisher's legacy. He was a strong anti-"economist" and did not believe in blockade. In 1909 he told the Prime Minister and Sir Edward Grey, 'A war between Germany and ourselves would be a slow process of ruin to both the countries, and neither could bring the other to terms.' It would not be decisive, he said, because Germany could make up her wartime needs from the neighbouring neutrals. In other words, he did not share Fisher's cynical view of international law.[2] Wilson did not get on with

---

[1] Vice-Admiral F. Bridgeman to Fisher, 21 Nov. 1909; Fisher to Arnold White, 10 Nov. 1911; Fisher to Churchill, 16 Jan. 1912, *FG*, vol. 2, pp. 282, 415–16, 427; Fisher to Hankey, n.d. (?Nov. 1911), HP 5/2A.
[2] 'Report and Proceedings of a Sub-Committee of the Committee of Imperial Defence Appointed to Inquire into Certain Questions of Naval Policy raised by Sir Charles Beresford' (12 Aug. 1909), pp. 305, 313, CAB 16/9.

McKenna, his superior and Fisher's ally. Soon after his appointment Wilson knocked out yet another prop of Fisher's strategy, and decided to ignore the Committee of Imperial Defence.[3] Campbell, the blockade planner, went out of favour even before Fisher's departure, and the Trade Division was disbanded.[4]

But the "economist" flame was not extinguished. Hankey kept it burning at the CID. As in 1907, the "master problem" remained the prospects of blockade. This question seemed capable of an objective answer. But national economies are not machines and there is scope for substitution and adaptation. On the other hand, adaptation is not automatic—rigidity or folly could foil it. Not that such intangibles (which counted for so much when war came) greatly concerned the planners. Planning is contingent on a string of probabilities and we may marvel at the confidence of the protagonists in those pre-war inquiries and debates. But that is to misjudge the issues. The probabilities of war were overshadowed by the imperatives of departmental conflict. In wartime, as Clausewitz has stated, even simple actions become very difficult; war is a resistant medium. So is bureaucracy: firmness of purpose and clarity of view are worn down in the frictions of procedures and personalities. More was at stake than objective truths. It may be banal to stress this point, but strategic choices were also existential ones for brass-hats and frocks: choices that determined their roles in elaborate games of status and pride.

By 1910 the seniority of the "senior service" had come to hang on the slender threads of Captain Henry Campbell's economic studies. If they were sound, then the navy was entitled to a leading role in the coming war with Germany and—what was more immediately significant—to primacy in peacetime. It would carry the struggle alone or at the most, use the army 'as a projectile to be fired by the navy' for landings and raids.[5] If the "economic" strategy was unsound, then, as its manifesto warned in 1907, 'it behoves us to set about raising the necessary land forces'.[6] This axiom of naval primacy was a considerable influence within the navy for the "economist" position. However, if blockade was not a decisive but an auxiliary weapon, as Ottley and Slade believed, then it followed that the navy's role should be subordinate to that of the army.[7]

For Fisher, who investigated the army's South African shambles as a

---

[3] Fisher to Ottley, 25 Feb. 1910, *FG*, vol. 2, p. 309.

[4] Marder, *Dreadnought*, vol. 1, pp. 192–3, 202–3.

[5] Fisher to Esher, 19 Nov. 1903, *FG*, vol. 1, p. 291 (quote); 15 Mar. 1909, *FG*, vol. 2, p. 232.

[6] 'Notes on attached "War Plans"' (1907), fos. 230–1, ADM 116/1043B.

[7] Slade left the Naval Intelligence Dept. in 1909, possibly as a penalty for independence and friendship to the army; he certainly saw eye to eye with Crowe: Mackay, *Fisher*, p. 411; Slade's diary, 11 Nov. and 3 Dec. 1908; and Eyre Crowe to Slade, 3 Jan. 1910, Slade Papers, microfilm reel 3, NMM.

member of the Esher committee, subservience to the army was unthinkable. In Germany a military officer had once commanded the fleet. In Britain Fisher thought the reverse was conceivable: the Esher committee's reformed War Office was modelled on the Admiralty, and Fisher went so far as to suggest the subordination of the army to the navy under a single command.[8]

Fisher supported the entente with France, but resisted operational links with political allies. 'As regards sea-fighting they would be a d—d nuisance,' he wrote in 1901.[9] Likewise military co-operation with France would jeopardize the "economist" strategy—or, more precisely, would push it into the background. In his preface to the navy's war plans he wrote, 'The one great drawback is that if France is our ally Germany may get her compensation on land for this slaughter of her commerce. So it is "splendid isolation" that England wants. The geographical position of Germany immensely favours us in a maritime war.'[10]

A military alliance with France would effectively place Britain on a land frontier with Germany. Fisher's distrust of the army came out strongly on 3 December 1908, at the first meeting of the "Military Needs" committee. According to one account he said that 'to dispatch British troops to the front in a Continental war would be an act of suicidal idiocy . . .'[11] Mackay, Fisher's most exhaustive and recent biographer, questions the authenticity of this report. But there is another one by Hankey, who was present. Fisher, he wrote three years later, 'held that to send troops would be a great mistake'. Germany would throw an overwhelming force at the British contingent, defeat it and march the remnant to Berlin; 'to send an army at all would, he [Fisher] maintained, be to put our head into the lions mouth.' The proper form of assistance to France 'was to put such severe economic pressure on Germany that she could not continue the war'. If Germany defeated and occupied France the economic pressure would not be diminished but would even be tightened.[12] Wealth and geography were a substitute for blood.

You see my beloved Hankey [Fisher wrote in 1911] . . . Providence has arranged for us to be an island and all our possessions to be *practically* islands and therefore *130,000* men provide an invincible armada for the unassailable supremacy of the British Empire whereas it takes 4 millions of Germans to do the same for Germany! *This has got to be rubbed in.*[13]

---

[8] Fisher to Viscount Knollys, *c*.28 Feb. 1904, *FG*, vol. 1, pp. 300–3.

[9] Fisher to Arnold White, 18 Nov. 1901, *FG*, vol. 1, pp. 211–12.

[10] [J. Fisher], 'War Plans and the Distribution of the Fleet' ('1907 or 1908'), fo. 9, ADM 116/1043B/I.

[11] Bacon, *Fisher*, vol. 2, pp. 182–3; Marder, *Dreadnought*, vol. 1, p. 387.

[12] Hankey to McKenna, 15 Aug. 1911, fos. 1–2, HP 7/3. Mackay's doubts: his *Fisher*, pp. 404–5.

[13] Fisher to Hankey, 13 Apr. 1911, HP 5/2A.

Fisher's strategic doctrine brought him into collision with the Foreign Office and the General Staff. The opposition was led by Eyre Crowe of the Foreign Office, and by General Henry Wilson of the General Staff. Crowe and Wilson both sponsored economic studies of their own in order to discredit the naval scheme.

II

The Foreign Office: Eyre Crowe and Francis Oppenheimer

At the Foreign Office Edward Grey and Eyre Crowe were upset by the "economist" resistance to their creation, the Declaration of London.[14] To counter the aggressive navalism of Bowles, his MPs and retired admirals, the Foreign Office called on an expert who stood high as an authority on German economy. One of the consuls who received a questionnaire from Campbell's team in May 1908 was Sir Francis Oppenheimer, the British honorary consul in Frankfurt.[15] Oppenheimer belonged to a wealthy German Jewish merchant family and inherited the office from his father, who carried on business in both Britain and Germany. Francis himself was born in London, educated at Balliol and was called to the bar. He was a bachelor, a bohemian and a snob, with a strong craving for acceptance. He carried out the consulate in style at his own expense and entertained royalty, aristocracy and visiting dignitaries. On the business side he also went beyond the call of duty. Oppenheimer's early years in the consulate coincided with the rise of Anglo-German commercial rivalry. From 1900 onwards his annual reports charted the economy with Germanic thoroughness, though with little analysis or flair. Every year they increased in bulk and came to be used in the fiscal and commercial controversies of the Edwardian period. Oppenheimer's social contacts in Germany made him welcome in London, where he was cultivated by Eyre Crowe, the most forthright of the office's Germanophobes. When another report from Frankfurt arrived at the Foreign Office in October 1909, it was just what Crowe needed.

More than a year before Oppenheimer had been sent (by mistake) the Admiralty's questionnaire for consuls on the facilities for importing and transporting food and raw materials into Germany in wartime. His report,

[14] Grey's clashes with McKenna: ch. 19, n. 24 above; 'Naval Conference' (typescript report of conference of Grey and McKenna, 15 Dec. 1908); letter of Sir Grahame Greene (Permament Sec., Admiralty) and Crowe, late Dec. 1908, and other documents, ADM 116/ 1079; Eyre Crowe's altercation with Bowles: FO print no. 18125 (13 May 1909), containing Bowles's letter to Grey, 29 Apr. 1909, and Crowe, 'Notes on Mr. Gibson Bowles' article on the Declaration of London . . .', both in ADM 116/1070. Crowe's anger: his letter to Slade, 3 Jan. 1910, Slade Papers, microfilm reel 3, NMM.
[15] The consuls: ch. 16, n. 21; Oppenheimer: his memoir *Stranger Within: Autobiographical Pages* (1960), and J. McDermott, 'Sir Francis Oppenheimer: "Stranger Within" the Foreign Office', *History*, vol. 66 (June 1981).

which ran to seventeen pages in print, was comparable (in miniature) to the Royal Commission report on food and raw material supplies to Britain. It showed a better grasp of German economic life than the work of Campbell and the naval "economists". Its conclusions, however, were based on the dubious premise that Germany and Britain would be fighting each other alone, without allies on either side.

A naval "economist" reading the body of the paper would have found a great deal of comfort. It revealed that there was an enormous dependence on foodstuffs from abroad, and that imports of the key commodity, wheat, had largely shifted from Russia to Argentina. Oppenheimer believed that both the overseas supply and overland transport capacity were sufficient to provide the necessary food across land frontiers, particularly if food was not treated as contraband. Raw materials were a more difficult proposition. 'As German industry must chiefly rely upon foreign raw materials for its manufacture, any interrupted supply would necessarily result in the closing of numerous factories, and would be little short of a national calamity.' Many vital commodities came from the British Empire or from overseas, and transport was bound to become congested by the rerouting of imports overland. Higher freights and insurance could derange the export industries, and the longer exceptional conditions prevailed, the more rapidly the disastrous effect would grow. Much depended on the effectiveness of the blockade and whether it extended also to the Dutch and Belgian ports, which Oppenheimer considered to be 'quasi-German'. An "economist" would have asked the crucial question of whether Germany's neighbours were themselves likely to be subject to blockade. Oppenheimer assumed they were not. He concluded that imports would come in by roundabout ways, and that 'it is doubtful whether the blockade would in the long run prove really effective'.[16]

For his masters in the Foreign Office this conclusion counted far more than the assumptions that produced it. Eyre Crowe suggested that Oppenheimer's report completely undermined the naval case:

the pressure which could be put on [Germany's] resources as regards imported food supplies and raw material is very slight, and can never amount to a strain sufficient to induce Germany to sue for peace. There will be a certain amount of extra expenditure and a radical diversion of traffic, but these are not sacrifices that a nation will not readily bear in the pursuit of national war.[17]

Oppenheimer's expertise was priceless and he was able to dictate his own terms. Traditions and precedents were waived. Oppenheimer demanded and received a transfer to diplomatic status, a salary and the senior

[16] F. Oppenheimer, 'Information required as to the Nature of German Overseas Trade', FO print 9529 (Oct. 1909) (quoted p. 17), ADM 116/940B.
[17] Eyre Crowe, FO minutes, 6 Oct. 1909, FO 371/673, fo. 150. I owe this reference to McDermott's article.

rank of "Counsellor". Transfers from the "cinderella service" to diplomatic rank were most unusual, and no other Jew had ever gained a position in the diplomatic branch, or a place in the Berlin diplomatic corps.[18] He was now commercial attaché for all of northern and western Europe, but remained in Frankfurt, ignored embassy protocol and communicated with Crowe directly, over the ambassador's head. He continued to dispatch timely and thorough reports, although none so valuable as that of October 1909.

The Atlantic perspective suggests two observations on the Foreign Office's continental commitment. First, that the transoceanic English-speaking world was unfamiliar and even alien to the Foreign Office: more alien than real aliens. Diplomats were steeped in the affairs of the continent of Europe: it provided their basic frame of reference. Take the career of Charles Hardinge, permanent head of the Foreign Office in 1906–10, and one of the architects of the *entente cordiale*. His career began with a prolonged apprenticeship in French and German. The road to the top led mainly through continental Europe: long years spent in Constantinople, Berlin, Bucharest and Sophia, Paris and St Petersburg. There was only one brief period in Washington DC in the 1890s, and another in Teheran.[19]

Australia, Canada and New Zealand were backwaters, and "belonged" to the Colonial Office. The United States was only a legation into the 1890s, and the ambassador from 1907 to 1913 was not a professional diplomat, but James Bryce, an academic, a writer and a Liberal politician. "Intuitive reasoners" give more weight to knowledge that is ready to hand. Paradoxically, the very professionalism of the Foreign Office, its mastery of European affairs, created a blind spot towards the English-speaking world. Professional diplomats felt at ease in upper-class European society, as they never could in plebeian and plutocratic democracies overseas. As Fisher put it, 'My pretty big experience with our diplomats is that their habitual residence abroad and their marriage with foreigners leads to their ceasing being Englishmen. (To put a man like Bryce from the outside is a very rare occurence!)'[20] Arno Mayer has revived Joseph Schumpeter's explanation of the origins of the First World War as a 'remobilization of Europe's *ancien regimes*'.[21] In contrast with old-world diplomats, Fisher was a democrat and "modernizer"; Hankey a man with colonial roots and an open mind. Could it be that a conservative and aristocratic Foreign Office was cool to a strategy that was essentially "commercial"? Oppenheimer certainly thought so.[22]

---

[18] Oppenheimer, *Stranger*, pp. 14, 213.
[19] Lord Hardinge of Penshurst, *Old Diplomacy* (1947).
[20] Fisher to A. G. Gardiner, 5 Oct. 1911, *FG*, vol. 2, p. 390.
[21] Mayer, *Persistence of the Old Regime*, p. 4; Schumpeter, *Imperialism*.
[22] Oppenheimer, *Stranger*, p. 266.

III

The Army

The army was also a repository of pre-commercial values. General Henry Wilson, commandant of the Staff College and then Director of Military Operations, was the opposite of what Hankey and Fisher stood for: an Ulster loyalist, anti-Liberal, a friend of France, and a pessimist with a zest for military life. Unlike Hankey and Fisher, he did not believe in deterrence but in victory. In 1911, for example, he suggested an alliance with Belgium. When asked when the Germans should be told, he answered 'not be disclosed at all if possible. The operation will be doubly effective if it comes as a surprise.' He did not think the knowledge would deter, or perhaps he hoped that it would not.[23] As Esher later wrote about him, 'From the Surrey village where he taught the rudimentary principles of war, his pupils went forth imbued with the sense of its cataclysmic imminence. . . . When others prattled of peace, he prepared their souls for war.'[24] He also did his best to make sure that his pupils would not miss the war when it came.

The army even more than the Foreign Office was keen to discredit the "economist" doctrine. It began to consider it even before the navy. An army memo of 1903 compared a war between Germany and Great Britain to a struggle between an elephant and a whale. Each being supreme in its own element, they would find it difficult to grapple. After looking at the strategic options the author concluded that 'the destruction of German commerce . . . is the only weapon with which we can hope to induce the enemy to sue for peace on terms advantageous to our interests'.[25] Two years later another staff study reached the same conclusion. Economic warfare would be decisive: 'The loss of her trade would be a heavy blow and one which would doubtless, ultimately, bring about an end of hostilities.'[26]

The army changed its mind as soon as it began to contemplate an active role in the Franco-German conflict. In November 1905 the military attaché in Berlin, Lt. Col. Edward Gleichen, completed a paper on 'Possibilities of British Offensive Action v. Germany'. He still assumed a war between Germany and England alone. Not surprisingly, he also anticipated subsequent conclusions based on the same restrictive assumptions. The

[23] 'Reply by General Wilson to Home Office' (30 Nov. 1911), fo. 369, WO 146/47.
[24] Lord Esher, *The Tragedy of Lord Kitchener* (1921), quoted in Callwell, *Wilson*, vol. 1, pp. 73–4.
[25] E. A. Altham (Asst. Quartermaster General), 'Memorandum of the Military Policy to be adopted in a War with Germany' (10 Feb. 1903), in CID print 20A (23 Feb. 1904), p. 9, WO 146/46.
[26] Col. Drake, 'War with Germany' (1905), fo. 23, E 2.1, WO 106/46.

damage to Germany would be serious, he concluded, but not fatal.[27] In 1908 another army study arrived at the same conclusion. It assumed that Great Britain was at war with Germany with Russia neutral, but inclined towards Germany. It then proceeded to show that railway capacity in Russia was equal to moving vital grain imports to Germany overland.[28] The army produced this study even before the "Military Needs of Empire" inquiry. Either they reasoned along the same lines as Captain Campbell in regarding economic warfare as the obvious naval strategy, and therefore worth countering in advance—or they got wind of the work being prepared at the naval Trade Division.

In 1909, after the end of the "Needs" inquiry, the army set about to challenge its findings. It did so in the form of a list of questions sent to the Board of Trade.[29] The Board of Trade complied with a large report of forty pages, a detailed statistical study of German trade flows. William Harbutt Dawson, the best British authority on Germany, was an official of the Board, and it is not too fanciful to imagine that he helped to produce it. The assumptions this time were a war between the triple *entente* and the triple alliance. Once again, the detail underlined how utterly dependent Germany had become on overseas trade. The conclusion was that Rotterdam and Antwerp 'could nevertheless handle a sufficient tonnage to prevent the blockade from effectively stifling the foreign trade of the country'. This was emphasized twice on the margins. As an army officer stressed, neutral supplies were vital.[30]

Hankey managed to obtain this study, which he described to McKenna as an attempt to undermine their strategy. Henry Wilson, he wrote, 'attempted to collect evidence to prove that the power of the Navy to put economic pressure on Germany is non-existent. They addressed a cunningly devised set of questions to the Board of Trade some time ago, which they may attempt to bring up if the Admiralty still maintain that naval means are sufficient.'[31]

There are two points to be made about both the Board of Trade inquiry and the Oppenheimer report (the latter, by the way, also available at the War Office). Neither of these reports (nor any of the previous army ones) differed materially in its findings from the naval investigation, and all

---

[27] fos. 4–5. This was ch. 8 of a typescript on 'Military Resources of Germany'. Gleichen to Frank Lascelles (ambassador in Berlin), 3 Nov. 1905, CAB 17/61.

[28] War Office, 'M. O.-3 (B)' (28 Sept. 1908), fo. 4, ADM 116/1073.

[29] Spencer Ewart (Director of Military Operations) to Winston Churchill, 29 Nov. 1909, in 'W. O. 46/47B (E2/7), "Effect of a Blockade and Information re Germany in England, correspondence with the Board of Trade"' (Nov. 1910) (two versions), WO 106/47; another version, CAB 17/61.

[30] Board of Trade, 'Memorandum for the Army Council' [n.d. 1910], fo. 21, R. St. G. ?Gorton, covering letter [n.d.] WO 106/47. Henry Wilson initialled this note on 28 Nov. 1910, and the War Office revised and edited the memorandum for its own use (ibid., fos. 158–77).

[31] Hankey to McKenna, 15 Aug. 1911, HP 7/3, fo. 5.

showed a high degree of dependence on imports of food and raw materials. The army and the Foreign Office were only able to dismiss the blockade strategy by assuming that imports could go on through neutral neighbours. This suggests why the Declaration of London, with its protection of neutral rights, was vital for Britain's continental strategists, and helps to explain at least the Foreign Office's vehemence in its promotion and defence.

A second point is that both studies affected to apply reason and calculation to policy. Both of them suffered from a failing of "intuitive reasoning", the tailoring of assumptions to fit the desired outcome. To assume that neutral trading with a blockaded country could go on in wartime was at least questionable, but it was not questioned by either the army or the Foreign Office because it ran counter to their own plan of action. Having set their minds on a continental war, neither the army nor the Foreign Office was going to be swayed by inconvenient probabilities.

IV

The CID: Trading with the Enemy and Other Projects

The army's continental adventure was underpinned by detailed plans for mobilization, supply and transport. Hankey decided to establish a comparable foundation for the "economist" option. Far too much of the navy's planning was founded on flimsy generalities. The "master problem" of its adequacy had not been sufficiently studied. Legal, administrative, economic and political implications were unclear and no plan of action existed, except for the deployment of warships—and even that was tentative. Threatened with a loss of momentum, Hankey decided to harness the resources of the Committee of Imperial Defence to the task of laying the groundwork for an economic war against Germany.[32]

From 1910 onwards the CID undertook a series of inquiries that required politicians, civil servants and experts in law, finance, insurance and commerce to assess the implications of economic warfare and to lay down guidelines for action. These inquiries are contained in a series of printed volumes which represented an effort comparable in scope and format with some of the main blue-book (i.e. parliamentary) investigations of the time, and were partly modelled upon them. Historians have neglected these volumes, and, while David French has described a few, he has not placed them in the context of the strategic controversy, and has thus overlooked some of their true significance.[33]

---

[32] Ch. 18, nn. 8, 9 above; Hankey, *Supreme Command*, vol. 1, p. 85.

[33] The main inquiries on policy in time of war (some produced several reports) were: local transportation and distribution of supplies; treatment of enemy and neutral ships; treatment of aliens; press and postal censorship; aerial navigation; wireless stations throughout the

Hankey regarded this project as part of the task of establishing the blockade strategy. In 1911 he invoked the report on the "Military Needs of the Empire" (1909). 'The exertion of economic pressure is an essential feature of the policy,' he wrote. 'The Committee of Imperial Defence has for the past 12 months been engaged mainly in constructing machinery to give effect to this policy, and is still engaged in the same task.'[34]

The elements of Hankey's "economism" are well-documented and easily stated. At the root was a bitter rejection of military intervention on the continent of Europe. Like Fisher, Hankey regarded this as 'not . . . even a gambler's throw . . . a military blunder of the first magnitude. Great risks would be run for the chance of doubtful advantages . . .'.[35] It foreclosed other options by claiming all available manpower. There was method behind the madness, for the continentalists' real motive was to bring about conscription. Once the absurdity of a limited expedition was perceived, they calculated that even a Liberal government would accept an army on continental lines. Having failed to frighten the country into conscription with the invasion scare, the General Staff wanted to gain the same end by means of a continental commitment. So far as inter-service rivalries went, Hankey had gone to the root of the matter. Overall, however, his conception of the problem was economic rather than military.

This dominates his account of the "opportunity cost" of conscription, contained in a later paper. Conscription, or even a less-than-total mobilization, would deprive the economy of labour just at the time when it could generate the greatest advantages. Labour shortages could exacerbate port and transport congestion; but, more important, they could damage the economy in a period of potential buoyancy. Hankey was one of the few to foresee prosperity rather than destitution in wartime. His prescription was to sit tight and let the continentals bleed to death, on the model of the Napoleonic wars. 'Our aim should be to continue our trade, and so to keep the economic conditions of life in this country tolerable, while they are becoming progressively more intolerable to the inhabitants of the enemy's country.'[36] Given that the springs of German ambition were economic, an

---

Empire; submarine cable communications; trading with the enemy; insurance of British shipping; resources and economic position of London; co-ordination of departmental action ("War Books"). For the location of documents and reports, see PRO, *List of the Papers of the Committee of Imperial Defence to 1914* (1964), chronological sequence and App. A, pp. 41–3; see also French, *British Economic Planning*, chs. 2, 4.

[34] Hankey, 'The Declaration of London from the Point of View of War with Germany' (16 Feb. 1911), fos. 1–2, ADM 116/1236.

[35] Hankey, 'The Case against Sending the Expeditionary Force to France' (Nov. 1911), fos. 8, 11, HP 7/3, fos. 19, 22.

[36] Hankey, 'Some New Aspects of the National Service Question', n.d. [French, *British Economic Planning*, p. 38 n. 41, dates another copy 15 Mar. 1913], pp. 4, 5, CAB 17/100.

economic strategy would provide an effective deterrent. This is a point that connects his work of 1911–12 with the early paper of 1907, and with Mahan's ideas of the same year.[37]

The deeper purpose of the economic strategy was not to fight a war but to prevent it. The document of November 1911 is a lucid statement of the idea of economic deterrence, and merits quotation at length:

What, it may be asked, is the real deterrent to Germany from attacking France, when she knows that England is behind the latter country? Is it the fear of four or six divisions of British troops, or is it the consciousness that the commercial prosperity which Germany has built up since 1870, and on which she has concentrated every effort, will be shattered? Surely the latter! Germany knows that her mercantile marine will be at the mercy of Great Britain once the war breaks out. Some 900 German merchant ships outside the Straits of Dover, with their cargoes, will be captured or have to lie up in neutral ports. Nearly 20% of her commerce, normally carried on with the British Empire will cease. Her ports will be blockaded and her commerce even with neutrals will be carried on only through the ports and communications of adjacent neutral countries, which will soon be congested if the traffic is considerable. No German ships will be available to carry her trade to and from these neutral ports; British ships will not be permitted to do so; and the remaining portion of the world's shipping will only be sufficient to carry a portion of her trade at exorbitant freights. Handicapped by lack of raw materials, shortage of labour owing to mobilization, the heavy cost of land transport through neutral countries, and high rates of freight, German manufactures will be unable to compete in the world's markets and will have to close down. Prices will rise on all imported articles at the time when many of the breadwinners are absent at the front and employment is bad. In short, the most tremendous economic pressure must be anticipated.

It is the knowledge of this which deters Germany from war, and it is her knowledge of this which renders the "entente cordiale" of enormous value to France. In comparison with this the assistance which we could render by military means is insignificant. Our proper policy is by a study of German commercial and financial conditions to organize ourselves to support the action of the Navy in bringing economic pressure to bear on Germany by every means—a policy which is now being exhaustively worked out by the Committee of Imperial Defence, much progress having already been made in this direction.

It is believed, however, that the true motive of those military officers who have pressed the need for military action so ably, is to bring about conscription in this country. The first attempt in this direction was to raise a scare about Invasion and to frighten the British people into military conscription. This was frustrated.[38]

---

[37] Ch. 16 nn. 14, 15 above.
[38] Hankey, 'The Case against Sending the Expeditionary Force to France' (Nov. 1911), fos. 8–10, HP 7/3, fos. 20–22; Admiral Reginald Bacon explained his retirement from the navy in 1911 with the belief that naval deterrence would prevent war: Bacon, *1900 Onwards*, p. 182.

V

Hankey had a clear vision of the blockade strategy, and of his role in promoting it. But using the CID for these ends was an uphill struggle. Hankey was at his most effective on the sub-committees and "technical" investigations where policy options were determined in detail. Fisher continued to coach him from afar:

So long as this government is in power *(until January 1916 for certain)* you need have no fear whatever of the military party getting on top—nevertheless it is expedient of course in the proceedings of the CID *(which are printed)* that all possible should be eliminated which gives any ground for any other text than "The Navy *first* and *all*"![39]

Fisher's successor in office Admiral A. K. Wilson failed to grasp that "economism" was the precondition of naval primacy; by making conscription unnecessary, it brought Liberalism and the navy into an alliance. As we have seen, Wilson was sceptical about economic warfare. His political judgement was poor, and he failed to appreciate how much his own personal position depended on the predominance of the "economist" strategy. Fisher saw the matter more clearly: as he wrote to Hankey in April 1911, 'A. K. Wilson's private opinion is that conscription wouldn't be a bad thing, he also favours an increased Regular Army—he doesn't see that both these things play the devil with the Navy and *you won't convince him!*'[40] Fisher also realized that Wilson's weakness posed a threat to his ally McKenna.

The proof came on 23 August 1911, at a special meeting of the CID to determine a military policy in the Morocco crisis of that summer. This oft-told story bears some re-examination. The session was set up by the military faction. "Economists" were carefully excluded. Fisher was not invited, nor was Esher, who in any event was ill. Hankey alerted McKenna a week in advance, but the naval case foundered on Admiral Wilson's presentation. Wilson's very first sentence, when he began his disastrous testimony after lunch, was: 'The policy of the Admiralty on the outbreak of war with Germany would be to blockade the whole of the German North Sea coast.' Having proclaimed blockade as the main naval effort, Wilson then made a gross error. Instead of attempting to show how it could decide the outcome of the conflict, he launched into the technical detail of a close blockade and described a fantastic series of raids and landings. The politicians were apparently bemused by this gung-ho performance, which entirely missed the point of the meeting. As Grey said 'So far as he could judge, the combined operations outlined were not essential to naval

[39] Fisher to Hankey, 13 Apr. 1911, HP 5/2A.
[40] Ibid.

success, and the struggle on land would be the decisive one.'[41] Wilson's performance was to be his downfall and also swept away McKenna, whose fault was to have appointed the elderly admiral (on Fisher's advice). The economist strategy failed by default. But Asquith refused to close his options and to endorse one strategy at the expense of the other. Lost ground could still be regained.

VI

Nothing had prepared me for the magnitude of the staff effort made at the CID under Hankey between 1910 and 1914. The centrepiece was the Trading with the Enemy inquiry of 1911–12. Its report is a bulky folio volume of 475 pages. It contains the record of careful deliberation and preparation for an economic war on Germany. The terms of reference concerned the legal problem of whether and how much commercial intercourse with the enemy should be tolerated in wartime. In fact it became another forum in which blockade strategy was deliberated and developed.

Hankey himself contributed a substantial historical study. With his aptitude for languages his time might have been better spent on a closer study of the German economy. In the final report Hankey reprinted the naval economic analysis of 1908, one of Francis Oppenheimer's reports, and several additional papers by the Board of Trade, but it did not take up the question of German economic capacity with the gravity it deserved. Hankey's own power to control the inquiry was limited. He was only the secretary, and not an official member, and there were a number of counter-currents to fight. Some members insisted on sticking rigidly to the terms of reference. Large British financial interests stood to lose from war with Germany; the acceptance houses in the City who discounted foreign bills, and the insurance industry, with a large portfolio of German shipping risks, might come under serious pressure in case of war. Likewise, the Yorkshire woollen industry was a large exporter to Germany and sugar supplies came to Britain mostly from that country and her ally Austro-Hungary. In the spirit of the Declaration of London, Professor L. Oppenheim (no kin), the Committee's legal adviser, wrote that all trade except contraband should continue, while the Board of Trade, in a similar vein of "business as usual", stressed the possible damage to British interests and recommended that many kinds of commerce should be allowed to go on.[42]

Such a half-hearted approach to economic warfare was not consistent

[41] CID, minutes of 114th meeting, 23 Aug. 1911, pp. 11–13, CAB 2/2/2.
[42] Report and Proceedings of the Standing Sub-Committee of the Committee of Imperial Defence on Trading with the Enemy 1912 (10 Sept. 1912), *passim*, CAB 16/18A.

with the original motive for the inquiry, and the task of steering it back on course fell to Lord Esher. In February 1912 Esher wrote what was perhaps the most powerful and succinct statement of the "economist" position. Germany's exposure to blockade was comparable to Britain's, he wrote, except that in a war against the *entente* she was hemmed in from all sides. Her plan, he accurately stated, was to invade France and to make peace, 'possibly in a few weeks, certainly in a few months'. To prevent this rapid overthrow, Antwerp and Rotterdam should be blockaded, 'whatever the political costs'. There was no room for half measures. As he stressed in another memo for the inquiry, 'all trade with Germany would automatically cease, not only trade between Germany and Great Britain'. Public opinion would not tolerate business as usual. He concluded the first memo by stressing the *deterrent* effect of the mere threat of economic warfare:

> If [Great Britain] is engaged in a war against Germany, and if she possesses the alliance of France and Russia, she undoubtedly possesses the means of exercising such enormous and fatal pressure upon Germany, by putting every obstacle in the way of commercial intercourse, either direct or indirect, between the British and German peoples that Germany would be forced to make peace. So fatal would the pressure be, that I for my part can hardly conceive that Germany, except by an act of madness, would embark upon a war under such conditions.[43]

Esher's vision of "total war" was at odds with the spirit of the Declaration of London and, before submitting it to the committee, he sought reassurance from Fisher.[44] Fisher answered immediately, and in no uncertain terms: 'As you say, it must now be proclaimed in the most public and authoritative manner that direct and indirect trade between Great Britain, *including every part of the British Empire*, and Germany must cease in time of war.'[45]

In the end, and not without a struggle, this was also the conclusion that the Committee arrived at. Unlike the War Office and Oppenheimer inquiries, it assumed a war of the *entente* against the Triple Alliance and it stressed the vital role of economic blockade.[46] This conclusion was worked by Hankey into his 'War Book', the CID's detailed step-by-step administrative contingency plan for war.[47] It was also communicated to the Dominions.[48] Hankey's work was not in vain. The first shot fired in anger

---

[43] 'Memorandum by Lord Esher' (12 Feb. 1912), ibid., App. XX, pp. 412, 413; also 'Note by Lord Esher', App. 27, p. 428.

[44] Fisher to Esher, 20 Apr. 1912, FP 1/11.

[45] Esher to Fisher, 25 Apr. 1912, *FG*, vol. 2, p. 453.

[46] Trading with the Enemy Report (1912), p. 3, CAB 16/18A.

[47] CID Co-ordination of Departmental Action on the Occurrence of Strained Relations and on the Outbreak of War, War Book 1914 (30 June 1914), p. 7, CAB 15/5.

[48] CID, no. 105-C, 'Trading with the Enemy', Note by the secretary (17 Nov. 1913), CAB 5/3/1.

by British forces in the First World War was from Fort Nepean near Melbourne, Australia, across the bows of the German merchant steamer *Pfalz*. The vessel stopped after the first shot, turned around and returned to port.[49]

[49] E. Scott, *Australia during the War* (Official History of Australia in the War of 1914–1918, vol. 11; Sydney 1936), pp. 36–7.

21

PREPARATION AND ACTION, 1912–1914

I

The CID meeting of 23 August 1911 made it more likely that Britain would send its regular army to help France if Germany attacked. Neither Hankey nor Esher or Fisher considered that this foreclosed the issue. Hankey acknowledged the navy's poor showing, but the fact that no formal decision was taken he regarded as a defeat for the army.[1]

In the autumn the Cabinet, Liberal back-benchers and Liberal newspaper editors all reacted to the prospect of a continental intervention. A majority of cabinet members opposed it. 'The net result was a continuation of the contradiction and confusion that had characterised British grand strategic planning.'[2] The strategic issue remained in suspense.

The "continental commitment" was a coherent response to the threat of German military attack on the Continent. I shall not speculate about the precise motives and perceptions of its supporters. Was the strategy the right one? The answer turns on an assessment of the cost, and on what the alternatives might have been. It helped the soldiers forget their South African fiascos, and, in the "national service" movement, did something to militarize society. Hankey for one regarded the expeditionary force as a product of domestic motives. Conscription was associated with the jingo Press, which was also strongly anti-Liberal, and its sympathizers were mainly Tory. By making conscription necessary, the continental commitment ran squarely against Liberal traditions and was viewed with suspicion by Labour. In his warning to McKenna on the eve of the August meeting, Hankey explained that, after getting a decision for military action, General Wilson would 'seek to show that without conscription we cannot fulfil our obligations'.[3]

There was a hidden link between the two strategies, which the blockade planners were unable to perceive. German statesmen and soldiers understood the threat posed by the sort of blockade that Hankey envisaged. It increased their fear of encirclement. A short, decisive war could be over before any damage was done, and it had other attractions as well. For such a war to be decisive, Germany had to take the offensive, and

---

[1] Hankey to Fisher, 24 Aug. 1911, FP 1/10/530a, fo. 60.
[2] Coogan, *End of Neutrality* (1981), pp. 142–5; Esher's journal, 24 Nov. 1911, EP 2/12.
[3] Hankey to McKenna, 15 Aug. 1911, HP 7/3; conscription: D. French, *British Strategy and War Aims, 1914–1916* (1986), p. 4; R. J. Q. Adams and P. P. Poirier, *The Conscription Controversy in Great Britain, 1900–18* (1987), pp. 20–4.

it could reach a rapid decision only against France. This strategy was known in Britain in broad outline, and perceived as a threat, which called for military intervention. Here was the link between blockade and the expeditionary force. On the British side, it may be recalled, a limited expeditionary force was designed to sustain the allies in the field while the blockade did its slow work.[4]

II

A boost for the Atlantic orientation came from the Conservative election victory in Canada in September 1911. This election was fought over some of the issues close to the core of Hankey's strategy. The main issue was the Liberal proposal for tariff reciprocity between Canada and the United States, designed to bring the two economies closer together. Prairie farmers supported it. They wanted access to the American market and a source of supply in the mid-west as an alternative to Ontario. Financial and business circles in Toronto and Montreal, for domestic reasons, saw their interests as bound up with Britain. The Conservative victory did not imply a break with the United States. On the contrary, Sir Robert Borden, the new leader, went out of his way to state 'the duty of Canada to become more and more of a bond of goodwill and friendship between this Great Republic and our Empire'.[5]

Borden had to contend with French Canadian isolationists among his supporters, but his own outlook was an imperial one. He had none of Laurier's reservations about British militarism, and also rejected Laurier's plans for an independent navy. Instead, he offered three battleships to Britain. In return Borden wanted a voice in British foreign and defence policy. He also hoped to encourage Canadian shipbuilding. In June 1912 Borden sailed to England to discuss his proposals.[6]

The lawyer from Nova Scotia had a high, if sometimes strenuous, time there. At one sumptuous dinner he only had tea and dry toast: 'comparative fasting was my surest safeguard against collapse'. (Laurier had also found British dinners a trial.)[7] He enjoyed the limelight. Borden's diary is disappointing as a substantive source: on the face of it, he took as much interest in the ladies (and they in him) as in affairs of state (the diary falls silent about this topic once he is back in Ottawa).[8]

The red carpet was rolled out. Like the Dominion Prime Ministers a year

[4] German attitudes: ch. 23 below.
[5] Speech in New York, 8 Dec. 1911, R. C. Brown, *Robert Laird Borden: A Biography* (Toronto 1975), vol. 1, pp. 230–1; Stacey, *Age of Conflict*, pp. 150–1; the election: ch. 11, sec. V, above.
[6] Stacey, *Age of Conflict*, ch. 6.
[7] *Robert Laird Borden: His Memoirs*, ed. H. Borden (abridged edn., Toronto 1969), vol. 1, p. 169; Skelton, *Laurier*, vol. 2, p. 29.
[8] Borden's diary, Borden Papers, PAC MG 26 H, vol. 451.

before, Borden was introduced to the CID, which he visited a few times, and attended two formal meetings. He wanted a permanent seat for Canada on the Committee. This was also a favourite idea of Hankey's, who probably put it into Borden's head. Hankey had written to Fisher a few months before, 'I hope in time to add Dominion Representatives and to get a British Empire War Book. I hope to go privately and at my own expense to Canada this summer, ostensibly to look after some family investments . . . but really to sow the seeds of this scheme, which is worked out in some detail.'[9] Hankey was not averse to conducting his own foreign policy. He went to see Borden privately without authority and in secret (not a secret he kept from Esher), and spoke to him 'very plainly indeed. . . . I shall be very disappointed if good does not come out of it.'[10]

Hankey had high hopes of Borden. Fisher offered to go to Canada and persuade Borden to construct a new design of battleship in Quebec.[11] Esher's expectations were even higher, inflated by the Canadian wheat boom which reached its peak that year, and by his ignorance of the Canadian climate and landscape. He wrote during Borden's visit:

Canada, outside the British Islands, is the pivot of the British Empire. Canada is potentially the largest, the wealthiest, and the most thickly peopled of that portion of the earth's surface which in the future appears likely to be the heritage of the Anglo-Saxon. Within a measurable space of time Canada will contain a population in excess of Great Britain, and when finally the centre of the world's gravity has shifted from Europe westward, Canada, with her vast resources, and her central position midway between Europe and the Far East, is bound to be a most serious competitor against the United States for the financial and commercial supremacy of mankind. There appears to be no obstacle to this realization of the Canadian dream, unless it should happen that the Western races fail to maintain their moral and intellectual superiority over the races of the East.[12]

Borden's demand for a voice in British councils received a cool response. A few months later he introduced the Naval Aid Bill and told his Parliament of the expectation of a permanent seat for Canada on the CID. Lewis Harcourt, the British colonial secretary, reacted quickly and stated that the CID was an advisory body and could not become an executive one. Canada was better served by direct access to British ministers. Harcourt's reluctance to give the Dominions access to the CID suggests that the Committee counted for more than its academic detractors have allowed.[13]

    [9] Hankey to Fisher, 8 Apr. 1912, FP 1/11/566, fo. 47.
    [10] Hankey to Esher, 16 July 1912, EP 5/41; another meeting between the two: Hankey to Esher, 31 Aug. 1912, ibid.
    [11] Hankey to Esher, 3 Aug. 1912, EP 5/41; Fisher to Esher, 14 Sept. 1912, *FG*, vol. 2, p. 478.
    [12] Lord Esher, 'The Naval and Military Situation', in his *King Edward VII and Other Essays* (1915), p. 179; first printed in the *Westminster Gazette*, 11 Sept. 1912.
    [13] Stacey, *Age of Conflict*, ch. 6; also Hankey's reports to Esher, 3 and 31 Aug. 1912, EP 5/41.

In retrospect, Borden's visit was the pre-war high point for the Atlantic orientation, but he promised more than he could deliver. The Naval Aid Bill festered for two more years in the Canadian parliament and the three battleships, which figured in British naval calculations, never materialized. A Canadian minister attended the CID only once, on 14 July 1914. Unlike Australia, Canada was left with no naval capacity at all. The navy that Laurier began was neglected, and had only one brief moment in the limelight, when its only operational warship, the old cruiser *Rainbow*, kept vigil over the Asian immigrant ship *Komagata Maru* in Vancouver harbour on the very eve of the First World War.[14]

III

Canada's sudden prominence also highlighted the dangers of the French connection. Hankey went on holiday to Normandy that August and came back with his prejudices confirmed:

They don't strike me as a really sound people. If they put up with bad water, inferior sanitation, slow yet unsafe railways (permanent way and rolling stock badly kept), a wretched press etc. how can we believe that their army is good? . . . I suspect that the Germans could "beat them to a frazzle" any day. If this happens under existing conditions all the blame will be put on "perfide albion". We ought at least to make it clear that we are not going to send our Army in until it suits us.[15]

Esher, for his own part, attempted to bring the strategic debate out of the closet. In two lectures before small audiences he depicted it as a debate between reason and emotion. War was unreasonable. Norman Angell's book *The Great Illusion* showed that there was no prospect of economic gain. Esher told his listeners obliquely about the "Trading with the Enemy" inquiries, and about the apprehension of business and financial witnesses. They had not read the book, he said, 'but by some mysterious process the virus of Norman Angell was working in their minds, for one after the other these magnates of commerce and of finance corroborated by their fears and anticipations the doctrine of the "Great Illusion".' Likewise, he said, the great German commercial and financial houses restrained their government in the crisis of August 1911. This was based on a confidential memorandum by Francis Oppenheimer.[16] A war on the modern scale was an act of folly that would impose heavy sacrifices on the civilian population. But economic motives did not exclusively dominate

[14] G. N. Tucker, *The Naval Service of Canada* (Ottawa 1952), vol. 1, ch. 9 and pp. 148–9; the *Komagata Maru* incident is described above, ch. 14, sec. IV.

[15] Hankey to Esher, 25 Aug. 1912, EP 5/41.

[16] Esher, 'Modern War and Peace', lecture delivered at Cambridge University, 1912 and at Glasgow, 1913, in *King Edward VII*, p. 223; 'Report by Sir Francis Oppenheimer on War Finance in Germany', Trading with the Enemy Report, App. XXVIII, CAB 16/18A.

individuals or nations: 'economic forces, in spite of their predominant results, over a long space of time, do not from day to day and from hour to hour govern the policy of nations, or nullify the effects of sentiment, of passion or of resentment. These are the lions in the path of peace.'[17]

A few months later Esher attempted to reach a wider public still, and wrote a series of articles for the *Westminster Gazette*, a semi-official Liberal organ. He urged that the Prime Minister should publicly renounce a continental commitment.

It might be very bad diplomacy, but it would be high and honest statesmanship, if the Prime Minister of this country were to explain in terms admitting of no doubt that our expeditionary force is a reinforcement, an armed reserve, maintained for the purpose of relieving and strengthening our forces scattered along the frontiers of the Empire, and that it is not organized or equipped for service on European battlefields.[18]

The editor J. A. Spender was at one mind with Esher, but thought that the articles revealed so much about the *de facto* commitment to France that they would encourage militarism there, and he declined to publish.[19]

Esher had a grand design to make the CID into a true Imperial General Staff, a high command for the whole Empire.[20] As a permanent member of the Committee this would give him exceptional power. It amounted almost to a constitutional revolution that would take power out of the ministries and cabinet, and confer it on a new amorphous body—such was the scale of Esher's ambition. With Hankey in charge of the CID Esher hoped to convert it into a sort of peacetime war cabinet: a standing committee of the CID that would be in almost constant session and deal with issues as they arose. Esher also had another brainwave: move the CID into No. 11 Downing Street, next door to the Prime Minister, and make the secretary (i.e. Hankey) his "chef de Bureau".[21]

Hankey had his doubts, but he rose to the bait. The strategy in case of war was still undecided; or rather, the priority of strategies was still uncertain. '*All are wobblers from the Prime Minister downwards!*' wrote Fisher in 1911, and this still remained true in 1912 and 1913.[22] Armed with Esher's concept, Hankey attempted to reopen the question. He drew up a plan for a committee chaired by the Prime Minister to determine the deployment of forces in time of war, and to monitor war preparation in the United Kingdom, India, the Dominions and the colonies.[23] He wanted

---

[17] Esher, 'Modern War and Peace', p. 214.
[18] Published subsequently as 'Naval and Military Situation', *King Edward VII*, p. 192.
[19] See Esher–Spender letters, 10, 14 Mar., 5, 7 May 1913, EP 5/42.
[20] Esher, memo, no title, 10 Jan. 1911, p. 3, EP 4/3.
[21] Hankey to Fisher, 8 Apr. 1912, FP 1/11/566, fo. 46; Esher, 'Notes of Conversation with Lord Haldane, 11 Aug. 1911', p. 4; Esher to Hankey, 5 Aug. 1912, both HP 4/4; d'Ombrain, *War Machinery*, pp. 270–1.
[22] Fisher to Hankey, 13 Apr. 1911, HP 5/2A.
[23] Hankey to Esher, 12 Nov. 1911, EP 5/42.

Dominion representation, and new powers to initiate strategic discussions. He also wished to draft departmental contingency plans on the British model (the 'War Books') for the whole of the Empire. It was a bold attempt to take over strategic management and, with Dominion aid, to steer strategy away from France and towards Britain's transoceanic interests. The Dominions would also be integrated into British blockade preparations. Finally, Hankey broached the question of housing for the CID, and suggested quarters as close as possible to the Prime Minister's residence, maybe even at 10 Downing Street itself.[24] This was Hankey's boldest pre-war attempt to take over the strategic process. It failed because Asquith would not be drawn. Perhaps it was too transparent. This failure indicated the limits of unauthorized power.

In the summer of 1912 Hankey had every reason to be confident that the "economists" were still in the running. Borden had abandoned Laurier's scruples and embraced an active imperial policy. The Trading with the Enemy Committee concluded its sittings with agreement that there was to be no "business as usual" in wartime and that commerce was to be a decisive weapon.[25] Its report provided an opportunity to place the economic strategy before senior members of the cabinet.

On 6 December 1912 the Committee of Imperial Defence devoted a long session to the report, with Asquith in the chair. Lloyd George, Churchill and Harcourt were present. They endorsed the report and agreed that implementation depended on the Dominions, which had to be taken into confidence. Asquith expressed 'some diffidence in laying down a policy the main weight of which would fall upon the Dominions and Colonies and India'. Llewellyn Smith, for the Board of Trade, confirmed that 'the essence of the policy recommended was to cut off the supply of raw material'.

The participants also appreciated that economic warfare was not compatible with Belgian and Dutch neutrality under the Declaration of London. They pondered the implications. 'If [Holland and Belgium] were neutral,' said Lloyd George, 'and accorded the full rights of neutrals, we should be unable to bring any effective economic pressure upon Germany. It was essential that we should be able to do so.' He reaffirmed that 'we could not hurt Germany except through her industries and by cutting off her supplies of corn and meat'. Churchill did not believe that the Low Countries could choose to remain neutral: 'if these countries were friendly to us they would certainly be overrun by the enemy. In other words they would be in the occupation of a belligerent, and could be blockaded on that ground alone.' Asquith was more realistic: while Belgium might be forced to take sides, he was less certain as regards the Netherlands. Lloyd George

---

[24] Hankey, 'Future Work of the Committee of Imperial Defence' (22 Nov. 1912), HP 7/8 ('sent to Prime Minister').

[25] Trading with the Enemy Report, p. 3, CAB 16/18A.

eventually hit on the solution. If the Low Countries remained neutral, their imports should be rationed. It was not essential to treat them as hostile, but they should only be allowed to import enough for their own needs (this device of rationing was the one eventually used during the war). The official conclusion said: 'In order to bring the greatest possible economic pressure upon Germany it is essential that the Netherlands and Belgium should either be entirely friendly to this country, in which case we should limit their oversea trade, or that they should be definitely hostile, in which case we should extend the blockade to their ports.'[26]

In other words, a German violation of Belgian and Dutch neutrality would be a positive benefit to British economic strategy. Indeed, it was almost necessary for British success.[27] Hankey had reason to be satisfied. This was a concrete ministerial endorsement of the "economist" strategy, as good as any that the military plan ever received.

IV

Major Stewart Murray's warnings of social upheaval and disruption of essential supplies materialized during the movement of labour unrest that began in 1911. Troops were called out to ensure the flow of goods. Docks, railways and coal mines were disrupted by industrial action. In August 1911, at the height of the transport strike, *The Times* wrote that, 'At whatever cost the food supplies must be maintained. At present they are fast running out, and . . . a very few days would see a regular famine in some foodstuffs, a serious shortage in others, and a large rise in the price of all.'[28] Murray's nightmares were being rehearsed in peacetime. As Murray had predicted, agitators also made their appearance. In March 1912, after the army had shot strikers on several occasions, the government arrested and prosecuted Tom Mann and four fellow syndicalists. They had published an 'Open Letter to British Soldiers', which called on the troops not to shoot their brothers.[29]

In 1913 Murray read another paper to the United Services Institution, about 'The Internal Condition of Great Britain during a Great War'. On previous occasions he had merely warned of extremists on the left. This time he arranged to have them present. Fred Knee, secretary of the London Trades Council and a veteran member of the Social Democratic Federation, spoke from the floor in moderate terms. It was not the underclass which would rebel, but the well-off artisan who stood to lose

[26] CID, minutes of 120th meeting, 6 Dec. 1912, pp. 6–8, CAB 2/3/1.
[27] The same point had been made by Winston Churchill at the 116th meeting of the CID, minutes, 25 Apr. 1912, p. 9, CAB 2/2/3.
[28] *The Times* leader, 12 Aug. 1911, p. 7.
[29] *Tom Mann's Memoirs* (1923, Fitzroy edn. 1967), pp. 230–62.

decent wages and decent food. He 'will not sit idly down; he will make a row about it'. It was better to plan for rationing and relief before the onset of a crisis. A stronger line was taken by Jack Williams, another member of the SDF and the London Trades Council. Williams asserted the claims of labour to be consulted in wartime and declared that it was a force against war. His argument brought the ideas of the Second International before an audience of notables, officials and officers. Williams's short appearance was designed to confirm those very fears that the Admiralty had long been prone to. A hungry work-force, he said, would not allow a war to continue.

who is to say that a general strike shall not be declared, and that we will refuse to work any goods whatever on behalf of the classes who proclaim war? We have the right to do it, we have the power to do it. . . . in my humble opinion we shall not starve; we shall take what we want. I remember the words of Lord Haldane some years ago who said at the Guildhall, 'It is not danger from without this country has to fear; it is danger from within.' You have got to fear danger from the class which has been neglected so long, and if you think that you can have a war with another nation, whether it be Germany, or Austria, or Russia, or France, or whatever nation it may be, without consulting the working classes, you are very much mistaken on the point. That is my opinion.[30]

In France and Germany the working classes were reconciled to military service. For British workers it held little appeal. But a few shrewd souls had realized long before that war might take some slack out of the labour markets, and that employment might actually increase.[31]

The CID's investigations of supply problems in wartime had shown that labour would be hard-stretched to operate the transport system and to supply continental allies. In 1913 Hankey turned this into an argument against conscription: here was a role more suitable for Britain: to provide cannon, and not the cannon fodder. Both the "continental school of compulsionists" and the "Home Defence school" had set their hearts on armies of half a million to a million. In either case, wrote Hankey in 1913,

the results could be nothing less than disastrous. The transport services would be demolished, the mills, mines and agriculture would all be short of labour at a time when it was specially required. This might result in a general and universal destitution and starvation and the Government would be subjected to heavy pressure to bring the war to an end at all costs . . .

If the war is prolonged as it well may be—we in this country possess a priceless advantage. Being surrounded by sea, we are not compelled, as other countries are, to make these tremendous drains on our labour supply in war. Our aim should be to

---

[30] S. L. Murray, 'The Internal Condition of Great Britain during a Great War', *JRUSI*, vol. 57 (1913), pp. 1603, 1606; Fred Knee: *The Diary of Fred Knee*, ed. D. Englander (Coventry 1977).

[31] Charles Dilke, HC debs. 4 ser., vol. 48 (6 Apr. 1897), col. 658; G. D. Kelley, Supply of Food. Royal Commission Evidence, Q. 8744, p. 313.

continue our trade, and so to keep the economic conditions of life in this country tolerable, while they are becoming progressively more intolerable to the inhabitants of the enemy's country . . .

Alone among the planners, Hankey could see that the war economy might not entail a labour surplus, but a labour shortage.[32]

As war began to loom late in July 1914, the peace party in the cabinet attempted to brandish the bogey of "labour unrest". Lloyd George reported despondency among financiers and businessmen, who predicted 'violence and tumult' when winter came. John Morley warned that 'in the present temper of labour, this tremendous dislocation of industrial life must be fraught with public danger'. But to no avail. 'This first-class and vital element in settling our policy received little of the attention that it well deserved; it vanished in the diplomatic hurry.'[33]

Members of the cabinet were not swayed by the economic dislocation and the labour unrest which they expected. This was a devil they knew, and it now held few terrors. For three years they had faced successive waves of labour, women's and Irish unrest and managed to stay in the saddle. At the Treasury, civil servants contemplated a subsidy to employers to keep the works running for three days a week. Cyclical unemployment was even more familiar, and nothing drastic was done. A government committee to deal with distress was appointed on 5 August, but it did not go beyond the conventional nostrums of local relief works and charity. In this field as in finance, the attitude was "business as usual".[34]

On the last day of July 1914 Hankey wrote to Esher that there was still no decision between the naval and military strategies. 'The great question as to whether we shall do what our War Office friends want or not is, I believe, quite undecided, and it must be settled at the Cabinet and not here.'[35] Nicholas d'Ombrain attributes this statement to smugness, and to Hankey's lack of awareness as to where true strategy was made. It takes great confidence on the part of a scholar to dispute the man on the spot from a distance of sixty years, and moreover a man whose understanding of the defence bureaucracy verged on genius.[36] To assume, like d'Ombrain, that Hankey was misinformed or misguided about where real authority lay, is to assume that supreme authority resided in the War Office and not in

---

[32] [M. Hankey], 'Some New Aspects of the National Service Question' , CAB 17/100, fos. 4–5; French, *Economic and Strategic Planning*, p. 38 n. 41, dates a copy in the Mottistone papers to 15 Mar. 1913.

[33] J. Morley, *Memorandum on Resignation* (1914, publ. 1928), pp. 5–6.

[34] R. G. Hawtrey, 'Memorandum on the Scheme Suggested to the Board of Trade, on August 4th, by Sir Algernon Firth, Bart.' [early Aug. 1914], Hawtrey Papers 1/10, Churchill College, Cambridge; relief works and the Prince of Wales national appeal: G. D. H. Cole, *Labour in Wartime* (1915), pp. 81–96.

[35] Hankey to Esher, 31 July 1914, EP 5/46.

[36] d'Ombrain, *War Machinery*, pp. viii–xi, 273.

the CID. Neither of these organs had unfettered powers of sovereign command. On 1 August the cabinet decided to pursue a *naval* strategy and *not* to send a force to the Continent. Churchill slipped a note to Lloyd George in cabinet, saying that, 'The naval war will be cheap—not more than 25 millions a year.'[37] That was also the notion that Sir Edward Grey presented to the House of Commons two days later.

By most accounts Sir Edward Grey's speech prevented a split in the cabinet, captured the Liberal party and committed the country securely to war. His rhetoric turned on moral and diplomatic issues and then moved on to economic costs and benefits. Tradition projects an apocalyptic backdrop on to that Monday afternoon. But the prospect that Sir Edward Grey described to Parliament was not one of bloody carnage. The sacrifice he predicted was primarily *economic*, and would be incurred whether Britain declared war or remained neutral. To remove any doubt, he made this point not once, but three times in succession (italics added):

For us, with a powerful fleet, which we believe able to protect our commerce, to protect our shores, and to protect our interests, if we are engaged in war, *we shall suffer but little more than we shall suffer even if we stand aside.*

We are going to suffer, I am afraid, terribly in this war, *whether we are in it or whether we stand aside.* Foreign trade is going to stop, not because the trade routes are closed, but because there is no trade at the other end. Continental nations engaged in war . . . cannot carry on the trade with us that they are carrying on in times of peace, *whether we are parties to the war or whether we are not.*[38]

This crucial passage was informed by the plans for limited war and maritime blockade put forward by the navy. Grey was not a member of the "Military Needs of the Empire" committee of 1908–9, but he was well versed in the "economist" plan. He had crossed swords with McKenna about it in December 1908; and he stated its premises cogently to Admiral A. K. Wilson in 1909. Grey's war speech of 3 August 1914 contains distinct echoes of that interview.[39] After Grey's speech to the Dominion statesmen in 1911, Hankey described him to Fisher as a convinced navalist.[40] Asquith, Lloyd George and Churchill had all discussed the plans at meetings of the CID.

Grey was not averse to war as a method of settling disputes. On one occasion his reckless attitude to war was viewed with dismay by CID secretaries Grant Duff and Ottley, both officers and by no means

---

[37] See C. Hazlehurst, *Politicians at War, July 1914 to May 1915* (1971), pp. 87–91.

[38] HC debs. 5 ser. vol. 45 (3 Aug. 1914), col. 1823.

[39] 'Report and Proceedings of a Sub-Committee of the Committee of Imperial Defence Appointed to Inquire into Certain Questions of Naval Policy raised by Sir Charles Beresford' (12 Aug. 1909), evidence of Admiral of the Fleet Sir Arthur Wilson (24 June 1909), pp. 305–7, 312, esp. Q. 2583, p. 312, CAB 16/9.

[40] Hankey to Fisher, 31 May 1911, FP 1/10/526a, fo. 50.

pacifists.[41] Grey had nursed a grudge against the Turks since early in his period in office.[42] At a CID meeting about Turkish activities in the Persian Gulf the Foreign Secretary said that, 'Turkish authority in Arabia was in a precarious condition and we could easily exercise very considerable pressure at this moment. We could stop reinforcements on their way to Yemen with decisive effect. *He recognised that was an act of war, but war must be faced if necessary.*' [43] Just previously the Chief of the Imperial General Staff had said that the Turkish army was large and improving, the climate was abominable, and 'he didn't know why we wished to maintain our position there at all'. That Grey had set his mind and bound his country to intervention in France is not in serious doubt.

Faced with the German aggression he had long foreseen, the Foreign Secretary was prepared with a strategy of limited commitment and maximum gain. The choice between a maritime and a continental strategy did not appear so stark to the politicians as it did to the admirals and generals. At the "Military Needs of the Empire" committee of 1908–9 it was agreed that the one complemented the other, as the two elements of a limited enterprise. What Grey offered the cabinet and Parliament was this strategy of limited liability. Economic warfare had been contemplated for years by ministers and officials. It was an efficient option that made it easy for Britain to opt for war. While Britain had prepared its expeditionary force down to the last detail, it made absolutely no preparations for any larger undertaking.

Hansard does not confirm the alleged power of Grey's speech. What it actually conveys is a different impression. After Grey had finished, the other speakers on that day, both Labour and Liberal, were almost unanimous in deploring the prospect of British entry. Grey's thrice-uttered promise that intervention would cost no more than standing aside was condemned by speaker after speaker as dishonourable, callous and unreal. Radical and Labour MPs spoke of the danger of economic collapse and popular unrest. Josiah Wedgwood said: 'Starvation is coming to this country, and the people are not the docile serfs they were a hundred years ago. They are not going to put up with starvation in this country. When it comes, you will see something far more important than a European War— you will see a revolution.'[44]

After war was declared, the labour movement assumed that the struggle for peace was lost, and largely adopted an attitude of "sane patriotism". Trade union and parliamentary leaders turned to their traditions of self-help. Many of the leaders, when they managed to avoid the recruiting

[41] Grant Duff diary, 2/1, 5 May 1911, fo. 65, 10 June 1911, fo. 75.

[42] Offer, *Property and Politics*, p. 335.

[43] CID, minutes of 110th meeting, 4 May 1911, p. 2, CAB 2/2/2. Emphasis added.

[44] HC debs. 5 ser., vol. 45 (3 Aug. 1914), cols. 1836, 1837, 1839, 1859; Wedgwood, col. 1838.

platforms, spent much effort in relief activities. Everyone had anticipated an economic crisis. Unemployment and short-time working duly appeared, and were loyally borne during the first few months.[45] The passivity of the workers and their capacity for coping with adversity had originally persuaded decision-makers that no serious threat would come from that quarter. For their part, most Labour leaders (MacDonald excepted), took it that, once war had been declared, politics were over and the issue had been decided. What they failed to realize was that the nature of the war still remained to be determined. For years now British participation had never been seriously in question. At stake was the form that participation would take.

Working-class compliance was not merely passive. For a few weeks strategy was indirectly theirs to determine. After war was declared, the decision to send the expeditionary force was delayed for another two days. The final decision was taken in a 'War Council' made up of the Prime Minister, three cabinet ministers, the First Sea Lord and eleven generals. Julian Corbett described it less than two months later in an official paper,

The Staff studies of recent years had all pointed to the probability that our most formidable danger in going to war was an internal danger. Since the Navy could not guarantee the flow of food and raw materials to this country during the first weeks of the war, it was apprehended that our preparations might be paralysed by popular disturbances aroused by the menace of starvation and widespread cessation of employment. Labour, in fact, might be forced by hunger into an attitude of dangerous antagonism and it was from representatives of labour that the opposition came.[46]

This is not strictly true. When the War Office made plans for 'Home Defence' in 1908, it did not make any provision for internal security. Ireland was recognized as a threat and troops were earmarked for keeping the peace there, but none were allocated specifically for this task in England and Wales.[47] The Metropolitan Police, the Home Office and the army repeatedly examined schemes to arm the police (e.g. with 5,000 obsolescent rifles) in order to deal with riot and panic. Nothing came of it before 1914, and the first scheme for 'Suppression of Civil Disturbance in London' was only ready six months into the war.[48] Perhaps that was why

[45] Cole, *Labour in Wartime*, ch. 3; R. Harrison, 'The War Emergency Workers' National Committee, 1914–1920', in A. Briggs and J. Saville (eds.), *Essays in Labour History*, vol. 2 (1971), pp. 211–28; J. M. Winter, *Socialism and the Challenge of War* (1974), pp. 184–99.

[46] [J. S. Corbett], 'Historical Report on the Opening of the War' (printed proof, 10 Oct. 1914), p. 7, Corbett Papers 7, NMM; circumstances of its composition in Sept.–Oct: D. M. Schurman *Julian S. Corbett, 1854–1922* (1981), pp. 156–7. The final (and slightly revised) version is dated 1 Nov. 1914 and bears the imprint of the CID, Historical Section (CAB 17/ 102B).

[47] 'Home Defence: Appreciation of the Situation in the United Kingdom in the Event of Hostilities with a European Maritime Power' (War Office, 1 Sept. 1908), p. 11, WO 33/462.

[48] For details: WO 32/5720. I owe this reference to Dr N. Hiley.

the parliamentary protests of 3 August had such an impact. There was panic in the City and the success of counter-measures (Bank Holiday, moratorium and bank rate increase) could not yet be judged. International credit seemed set to break down even before fighting had seriously begun. Corbett, who had seen the War Council minutes, wrote that

The Commander-in-Chief then again pressed to be given five divisions but to this the Government would not assent. It was not that any force was required to repel oversea attack; it was the internal danger which had always overshadowed our view of what war would bring. Already there was an incipient food panic, and should it spread to the mass of the labouring population serious trouble might result. It was a danger which everyone up to this moment had regarded as one that it was impossible to ignore: the warning note which had been sounded in the House of Commons from amongst the Labour benches emphasized its reality, and the Prime Minister announced that two divisions must be kept back to deal with it.[49]

Hankey understood that a continental commitment could not be restricted, and that escalation was inevitable.[50] As soon as Kitchener went to the War Office, he began to realize this expectation and to form volunteer armies for a war that would last years and not months.[51]

Of the three, it was Esher who had paid the closest attention to this question. When Lord Roberts began his agitation for a mass army of national service, Esher was among his early adherents. It was, as he saw it, both a means to resolve the strategic problems facing the British Empire and also a tool of domestic stabilization. Esher spent much energy in recruiting for the Territorial Army. Disenchantment with universal military service appears to have set in in 1908, together with his attachment to Fisher's and Hankey's economic strategy. At the "Military Needs of the Empire" committee of 1908–9 he first expressed doubts about the use of a mass army for Britain. In 1909 he broke formally with Lord Roberts. As the late-Edwardian boom picked up, recruitment to the Territorials began to fall; they never achieved their establishment strength and this failure drove Esher to doubts over the fibre and patriotic commitment of the masses.[52] From Liberal electoral success he deduced that conscription was

---

[49] Corbett, 'Historical Report on the Opening of the War', p. 10 (slight changes in final version, see n. 46 above). The War Council minutes were only printed in 1916, and indicate that the question of internal security was first mentioned by Kitchener. Otherwise they confirm Corbett's account: ('Secretary's Notes of a War Council Held at 10, Downing Street', 2nd meeting, 6th Aug. 1914, pp. 1–2 (printed Sept. 1916), CAB 22/1). Asquith is reported to have said that 'the domestic situation might be grave'.

[50] Hankey, 'Some New Aspects of the National Service Question' (July 1913), CAB 17/100, fos. 4–5.

[51] French, *Economic and Strategic Planning*, pp. 124–5.

[52] Esher to J. A. Spender, 7 May 1913, EP 5/43; Esher, 'Attack on the British Isles from Oversea. Memorandum by Lord Esher' (proof of CID print no. O. A.–53, 6 Nov. 1913), p. 1, EP 19/7; Esher, 'Naval and Military Situation', *King Edward VII*, p. 203; Fraser, *Esher*, pp. 192–4, 244.

politically impractical and Fisher echoed his views. Esher hoped that rational calculation would prevail, but he worried about the popular passions that war could unleash: 'We must not permit ourselves to forget that in private life the measure, the balance of loss and gain, although telling in the long run, does not by any means always dominate men's actions.'[53] Esher's doubt about a mass army was related to his rejection of the continental commitment—and a hopeful projection of the rationality, moderation and caution which informed himself and his collaborators into the mentality of the masses.

Esher was right about the *politics* of the matter. It took more than two years to overcome *political* resistance to conscription. But the delay was only possible because of the surge of volunteers. His fear of popular passions proved justified. Instead of rioting, the masses rushed forward to don uniform. No one had foreseen this in advance, so the uniforms had not been prepared.[54] Without this tide of enlistment, Kitchener's continental strategy would have required difficult compulsory measures at home. In this sense at least, it was popular support that decided between the naval and military strategies. That was the real death of Liberal England. Hankey had an inkling of the full-employment war economy. But he failed to realize that a national effort that required the *physical* energies of the workers would also capture their *emotions*. It never occurred to him and to Fisher (as it did to Major Murray) to seek a link with working-class leaders. Esher did see that popular bellicism had to be countered, but his medium, the Norman Angell movement, was too highbrow and too far removed from the masses.

Major Stewart Murray would not have been surprised. He believed in the popular appeal of a mass militia. As early as 1900 he wrote that, 'It is almost impossible to tell what will, and what will not, appeal to the excitable town masses of to-day, and work them up to fever heat, till they even clamour for war to enforce their opinions.' In 1913 he predicted that 'Popular passion is the firebrand which may at any time fire the European powder magazine.'[55]

V

When the war broke out, hundreds and thousands of individuals voluntarily subsumed their individual fates into that of the nation. The approbationary motive dominated the individual one. The theme of national unity, of the abolition of social differences in wartime, was

[53] Esher, 'Modern War and Peace', *King Edward VII*, p. 214.
[54] Asquith, *Letters to Venetia Stanley*, letter 143, 3 Sept. 1914, p. 217.
[55] Murray, *Electors of Great Britain*, p. 8; 'The Internal Condition of Great Britain', p. 1564.

widespread in Europe in August 1914, and it had its effect in Britain as well, although the army reproduced and even emphasized the social distinctions of civilian life.[56] 'The Board of Trade estimated that roughly 750,000 men, or a little over ten per cent of the industrial work force, joined up during the first two months of the war. . . . the deluge of working-class recruits surprised even the most patriotic observers.' Almost 1.2 million men enlisted between August and the end of December 1914.[57] Resistance to militarism was one of the first defensive mechanisms that workers dismantled. The naval planners miscalculated the impact of labour. In the crucial first few months there was no active resistance.

A tide of enlistment also rose in the colonies. In Australia, 'when the recruiting depots opened they received an embarrassment of riches. Though complete unanimity is not attained among millions of people, the response of Australians at the beginning of August 1914 was close to it.' A Canadian remembered, 'Everybody just jumped up and wanted to go to war. They had this terrific propaganda, and there were recruiting officers on every corner.'[58] Throughout the British Empire, as in Britain itself, enlistment was both enthusiastic and voluntary. Campaigns for conscription had failed in both Britain and the Empire, although Australia and New Zealand had moved towards it with compulsory military training, and Canada had stepped up the training of its militia. The people who rushed to volunteer did so for a variety (and often a mixture) of motives. One was economic. The international staple economy had entered one of its cyclical slumps. In Canada the wheat boom broke in 1913, and the summer of 1914 saw large numbers of workers laid off, both in the west and in the big cities of the centre. Unemployment was an effective recruiter. In Australia a rural study has also shown that the first volunteers came disproportionately from among the landless and the casual labourers.[59] Others sought an escape from intensely competitive occupations, especially in urban white-collar employment. Yet another reason for enlistment was the pursuit of novelty. For people born in a distant corner of the Empire, enlistment was an opportunity to see the metropolitan world they had heard so much

---

[56] R. N. Stromberg, *Redemption by War: The Intellectuals and 1914* (Lawrence, Kansas 1982), ch. 5; E. J. Leed, *No Man's Land: Combat and Identity in World War I* (Cambridge 1979), ch. 2.

[57] J. M. Winter, 'Britain's "Lost Generation" of the First World War', *Population Studies*, vol. 31 (1977), p. 452; J. W. M. Osborne, 'The Voluntary Recruiting Movement in Britain, 1914–1916' (Stanford University Ph.D. thesis, 1979), fo. 247.

[58] L. L. Robson, *The First A. I. F.: A Study of its Recruitment, 1914–1918* (Melbourne 1970), p. 23; Jack Burton, in D. Read (ed.), *The Great War and Canadian Society: An Oral History* (Toronto 1978), p. 95.

[59] R. T. Naylor, 'The Canadian State, the Accumulation of Capital and the Great War', *Journal of Canadian Studies*, vol. 16 (1981), p. 27; Read (ed.), *Great War*, pp. 100–2; J. McQuilton, 'The Home Front in a Local Government Area: The Case of Yackandandah, 1914–18' (paper presented at the Australian National University, 1987).

about. A Canadian veteran remembered, 'I wasn't at all happy in the confinement of working in a bank, and I jumped at the opportunity to get free of some of the restraints that I had been under as a young person growing up and at the opportunity to see something else of the world, and probably, for lack of a better way of expressing it, I searched for a direction.'[60] For those in comfortable, secure lives, war provided a release, a whiff of excitement. Social psychologists have observed that 'perfect comfort and lack of stimulation are restful at first, but they soon become boring, then disturbing'.[61]

A disproportionate number of the overseas volunteers had been born in Britain—more than a third of those who served in the Canadian forces, and almost a quarter of those who volunteered in Australia during the first eleven months, much more than their share in the general population. There was a big surge of emigration to the Empire in the years 1910–13, the last great pulse of the staple economy, and the migrants were disproportionately males of military age. The Canadian provinces with the highest level of enlistment were Manitoba, Alberta and British Columbia, which also had the highest proportion of British-born. These were prairie and timber provinces, the focus of the pre-war resource boom (curiously, Saskatchewan, the third prairie province, came fairly low down the list).[62]

Migration was an assertion of individual freedom, a search for dignity and worth. The Empire was a repository of hope. The opportunities it offered for self-betterment made it possible to identify with and to fight for. Migration gave people a choice, a measure of control over their own lives. It is ironical that they used this choice to submit to autocratic disciplines and to hardships worse than any they had escaped. The British army, drawing on the ethos of British society, regarded people as expendable. Herein lies one of the tragic and ironic aspects of the war: people freely gave up the freedom they had found in the outlying societies. This difference in values between the metropolis and the Empire was cherished in uniform as well. The Anzac "diggers" had a disdain for military authority, and a self-perceived superiority over the British soldiery in attitude, initiative, physique and even in gait.[63] Australia rejected

---

[60] Robert Swan, in Read (ed.), *Great War*, p. 92; Richard White, work in progress on Australian enlistment; Offer, *Property and Politics*, p. 64.

[61] Scitovsky, *Joyless Economy*, p. 31.

[62] C. A. Sharpe, 'Enlistment in the Canadian Expeditionary Force, 1914–1918: A Regional Analysis', *Journal of Canadian Studies*, vol. 18 (1983–4); L. L. Robson, 'The Origin and Character of the First A. I. F., 1914–18: Some Statistical Evidence', *Historical Studies*, vol. 15 (1975).

[63] This self-perception was also common in New Zealand and to some extent in Canada: Phillips, *A Man's Country*, pp. 163–92; Read (ed.), *Great War*, pp. 116–17, 124–9. C.E.W. Bean, the Australian Official Historian, celebrated the Australian virtues of independence and dignity: C. E. W. Bean, *Anzac to Amiens. A Shorter History of the Australian Fighting Services in the First World War* (Canberra 1948), pp. 6–9, 536–7.

conscription, even the soldiers voted against it, and it gave rise to bitter debates in Canada.

The difference in values found an expression in tangibles as well: in the British approach to capital punishment. The British army executed more than three hundred of its own soldiers during the war—about two companies of infantry. The crimes, apart from nineteen cases of murder, were disciplinary—desertion, cowardice, quitting post, disobedience, striking officer, sleeping on post, etc. As British employers used fear to keep their workers in line, British generals felt the need to terrorize their soldiers. Often the grounds for execution were flimsy, the legal procedures dubious. The Germans only executed forty-eight soldiers, less than one-sixth as many. Australia, with a volunteer army, refused to allow its soldiers to be shot, and those sentenced to capital punishment were often released after short periods of imprisonment. General Haig, and several Australian officers, regarded the introduction of the death penalty 'as a matter of grave urgency' but it would be absurd to suggest that the Australians were inferior to the British as fighting soldiers.[64] The British victories in 1918 depended on Australian divisions.

The surge of emotional patriotism was the approbationary motive for enlistment at its most intense. Wartime breaks down the social barriers and enables individuals to become part of a whole from which they previously felt excluded. It was exhilarating to feel the hearts of others 'beating time with their own'. All across the Empire the outbreak of war was experienced by white men and women as a great tide of communal feeling.[65]

It was a response that tilted the balance, subtly at first, then more decisively. It specified one of the variables hidden from the pre-war planners. Was war tolerable? How willing were the masses to carry its burdens? What was the subjective perception of its costs? The voluntary surge made it possible to begin to contemplate more massive sacrifices later on.

For a short period labour became an active element in British strategy. Navalists had given much thought to the problem of labour obstruction of war. They did not foresee a *craving* for war, and their strategy of economic warfare was cast aside for the time being by the positive response of those very workers whose reactions they had feared. Labour's goodwill gave the upper hand, for the time being, to the generals.

But even this surge of enlistment was not yet a decision for the Somme

---

[64] British executions: A. Babington, *For the Sake of Example* (1983); German executions: M. van Creveld, *Fighting Power* (1983), p. 113; Australian policy: Babington, *For the Sale of Example*, pp. 191–2; A. Ekins, 'Taming the Diggers: The Other Face of the Anzac Legend' (paper presented at the Australian Historical Assoc. Conference, Sydney 1988).
[65] The image is from Smith, *Moral Sentiments*, p. 22.

and Passchendaele. Writing in the 1920s, at the height of his powers, Hankey recalled,

On the night of August 4th–5th, once the War Telegram had been despatched, nothing that I could do could influence the situation. I felt no great anxiety about the ultimate result of the war. Years of saturation in the subject had led to the conviction that in the long run sea-power must bring us victory. My belief in sea-power amounted almost to a religion. The Germans, like Napoleon, might overrun the Continent; this might prolong the war, but could not affect the final issue, which would be determined by economic pressure. Hence, on that eventful night, I went to bed excited but confident.[66]

Hankey was an extreme navalist, but the assumptions of an economic war, with a limited military commitment, continued to influence British strategy well into the war.[67] David French says that in 1914–15 the government still tried to win the war with economic pressure, relying on the Allies to bear the brunt of the war on land. That suited Kitchener. His New Armies 'were not just intended to win the war for the Entente, but to win the peace for Britain'.[68]

---

[66] Hankey, *Supreme Command*, vol. 1, p. 165.
[67] M. G. Fry, *Lloyd George and Foreign Policy* (Montreal 1977), vol. 1, p. 197.
[68] French, *British Strategy*, pp. 23, 25.

Part Four

THE OTHER SIDE OF THE NORTH SEA

22

ECONOMIC DEVELOPMENT AND NATIONAL SECURITY IN WILHELMIAN GERMANY

In the last decade of the nineteenth century the German Empire began to look overseas for markets and raw materials, but it lacked the naval capacity (regarded as vital by Britain) to safeguard its maritime trading routes. This dilemma defines the economic aspect of Germany's security problem before the First World War. It narrowed the range of choices open to German leaders, until, in 1914, they imagined themselves surrounded by a wall, with only a single gate. That gate might soon be locked. They perceived only one choice: to break out, or to remain hemmed in by looming threats.

I

The basic facts of German economic development in the late-Victorian period are familiar. They can be expressed in a few simple numbers. Between 1891 and 1911 the German people increased from 49 million to 65 million and the output per person rose from 457 Marks (£23) to 741 Marks (£37) a year. In Britain during the same years, the output per head increased only about half as much, to £47, and the population was smaller: about 45 million in 1911. In the last years before the war the German Empire disposed of a larger net product than the United Kingdom, and its output per worker, though still lower than Britain's, was growing three times as fast.[1]

Germany's rapid growth took place primarily in the cities, as farm production fell to 23 per cent of the net national product in the last years before the war. Large numbers left the countryside for the towns. Cities of more than one hundred thousand inhabitants expanded their share from 12 per cent of the population in 1890 to 21 per cent in 1910, while towns and villages (under two thousand) fell from 53 to 40 per cent.[2]

Foreign trade grew much faster than the economy as a whole. Between 1890 and 1913 the ratio of imports to the net national product rose from 17 to 20 per cent, and the ratio of exports from 13.1 to 17.5 per cent—about

[1] German population and net national product: Hoffmann, *Das Wachstum*, table 1, pp. 173–4; table 248, pp. 825–6; Britain: Feinstein, *National Income*, tables 17 (p. T42) and 55 (p. T120). The two series are not strictly comparable and, moreover, are given in current prices. Nevertheless they convey the extent to which Germany had overtaken Britain. Output per worker: Matthews, Feinstein and Odling-Smee, *British Economic Growth*, pp. 31–2.
[2] Hoffmann, *Das Wachstum*, table 7, p. 35; table 6, p. 178.

three-quarters of the levels prevailing in Britain (excluding services). Like Britain, Germany entered the international system of specialization. In consequence, its economy became a large consumer of imported primary products, which were paid for, as in Britain, by the export of manufactures, by services, and by income from overseas investment. In industry, the growth of imports ran just a little ahead of output, and even declined somewhat in the last few years before the war. But a few industries became much *more* dependent: textiles, fats, leather and raw iron. German industries looked increasingly abroad for their markets. Their dependence on exports (the ratio of the indices of exports and output) rose from 0.71 at the beginning of the period to 0.95 at its end.

Imports of foodstuffs grew even faster during this period than all imports (4.8 per cent versus 4.1 per cent a year), and much faster than the economy as a whole (which grew about 3.9 per cent a year).[3] In absolute terms the growth of foreign trade was enormous: imports grew 150 per cent from 1890 to 1913, exports 200 per cent. This trade filled the bottoms of the world's second largest merchant fleet, whose tonnage rose from 1.2 million in 1890 to 3.3 million in 1913.[4] Briefly, then, Germany's strong economic growth in the Wilhelmian period was externally oriented.

II

The large expansion of Germany's trade overseas from the 1890s onwards became a bridle on the exercise of continental power. It opened up a new dimension of danger that could no longer be managed by the army alone. The rest of this chapter is about the perception of this threat, and the policies available to meet it.

Germany was now second to none in Europe for industrial power. In terms of manufacturing capacity and technology it was more than a match for any single European power. Industrial power had military implications. As far as infantry and artillery were concerned, this did not seem to matter a great deal. The equipment, although expensive, was a burden that even much weaker economies, such as Russia, Austria and Turkey, were able to carry. The prospect of keeping armies in the field for years, and of feeding the guns with millions of expensive and complicated shells, was still only dimly perceived.

In continental Europe, military might was measured not by economic capacity but primarily by the number of bayonets. In France the population rose hardly at all during these years; migrants entered Germany in considerable numbers (mostly from eastern Europe), while Britain experienced a huge outflow, especially in the last decade before the war.

---

[3] Data in ibid., ch. 3.6.

[4] In current prices. At constant 1913 prices, growth was 120 and 220 per cent respectively: Hoffmann, *Das Wachstum*, pp. 817, 820–1.

Before the war, industrial might appeared to be decisive not for land but for sea power. The challenge was not to construct a battleship but to pay for it. Seven or eight powers could build a modern warship. But investment in fighting ships came in big lumpy instalments. The limits of Germany's sea power were the limits of taxation. The constraints were political. The German economy was as large as Britain's and growing faster, but how much was it willing to pay in taxes?

That depended on the perception of danger. The two continental power blocs, the Franco-Russian alliance on the one side and the German–Austrian on the other, were closely balanced in military terms. This rough equality, instead of creating balance, became a source of instability. Germany achieved a margin of superiority after Russia's defeat by Japan, but German leaders regarded this as a temporary advantage, which might soon fade, and was already overshadowed by the Anglo-French *entente*.

National security inspires strong passions. It is also shrouded in secrecy and technical complexity, which places it beyond the reach of informed debate. The economic dimension of national security was mediated by bureaucracies. Like the blind men describing an elephant, each set of officials groped for solutions in its own sphere of competence. The army, the navy, the civilian administration and the Chancellor, the Foreign Office—each attempted to deal with one aspect of the problem. If the difficulty fell outside its sphere, the inclination was to do nothing. There was no forum comparable to the Committee of Imperial Defence in Britain, where security issues could be considered as a whole. The Chancellor had no power to supervise the army and the navy. The Emperor alone held all the strings. His personality was unbalanced and he fell under the influence of different officials in turn, or acted impetuously on his own shaky judgement. The pervasive militarism of the professional and upper-classes inclined the Emperor and his officials towards war.

At the diplomatic level, the Foreign Office did not have any acute awareness of the impact of economic specialization, and did not single it out as a separate aspect of foreign policy. Domestically urban growth was the prime outcome of economic specialization. The Marxist Social Democratic Party threatened the established ascendancies. It grew primarily in the large industrial towns. Many historians have taken the theme of the challenge of industrialization to the Prussian ascendancy as the central issue of the Wilhelmian period. Eckart Kehr, who pioneered this approach to Wilhelmian history in the 1920s, underlined the intimate link between domestic politics and naval construction.[5] It would be superfluous for me to venture into this field.

[5] E. Kehr, *Battleship Building and Party Politics in Germany, 1894–1901* (1930, ed. and trans. P. R. Anderson and E. N. Anderson, Chicago 1973).

III

Naval Armaments and the Tirpitz Plan

Germany's naval armament under Wilhelm II was a fundamental cause of the Anglo-German war. Almost every aspect of the arms race was affected by the process of economic specialization.

Early in the period the question of blockade was raised but not answered by Caprivi. This Chancellor, who had been a general and also head of the Admiralty, initiated a liberal trading policy designed to encourage the process of specialization. Caprivi, the most "industrial" of German Chancellors, also saw the risks very clearly. In 1891 he told the Reichstag: 'The existence of the State is at stake when it is not in a position to depend on its own sources of supply . . . It is my unshakable conviction that in a future war the feeding of the army and the country may play an absolutely decisive part.' It was a question that continued to preoccupy the Chancellor. Caprivi's answer, however, was to not to arm, but to aim for self-sufficiency in food.[6]

For an industrializing country with bounded agricultural resources, self-sufficiency formed a constraint. In 1895 the Emperor declared that 'the extent of a nation's maritime commerce ought to be the measuring stick of the size of her navy'.[7] This was the view of Germany's dominant naval personality, Admiral von Tirpitz, who had already started his long-term project for raising Germany into the front rank of the world's naval powers. From 1898 onwards, from his position as Minister of the Navy, Tirpitz mobilized political and social forces to push his plan through Parliament. Its purpose was to build, within a generation, a naval force that the Royal Navy could not afford to challenge. Not necessarily as strong as the Royal Navy, but strong enough to establish a local parity or near parity in the North Sea. Until the project was completed, Germany would have to pass through a "danger zone" in which her intentions were obvious, but her capacity to assert them incomplete.[8]

In 1912 Churchill called the German Navy a "luxury fleet", and most English-speaking historians have regarded the policy as a disastrous misconception. In German historiography this has been a recurrent refrain from Eckart Kehr in the 1920s to Berghahn and Deist in the 1970s. Certainly it did not save Germany from the dangers it was designed to meet, and perhaps it even increased these dangers.

---

[6] Caprivi, 10 Dec. 1891, quoted in W. H. Dawson, *The Evolution of Modern Germany* (1908), p. 248; 8 Mar. 1893, see E. Kehr, *Economic Interest, Militarism and Foreign Policy*, ed. G. A. Craig (Berkeley, Calif. 1977), p. 57; Burchardt, *Friedenswirtschaft*, pp. 52–3, 55, 179–82; I. N. Lambi, *The Navy and German Power Politics, 1862–1914* (1984), pp. 34, 59–60.

[7] Paraphrased by Lambi, *The Navy*, p. 34.

[8] The literature on the Anglo-German naval race is enormous. A rounded account can be derived from Woodward, Steinberg, Berghahn, Hubatsch, Hallmann, Herwig, Deist (listed in the bibliography).

My own view is that the project was in some respects inevitable, in some respects appropriate, and that its failure was not a foregone conclusion. Hindsight is not entirely sufficient to evaluate the policy. We should take account of what might have happened, and also ask whether there was a real threat to consider, and how appropriate a response was the Tirpitz plan.[9]

Tirpitz based his naval propaganda squarely on the expansion of German interests, especially its commercial interests, overseas. This had an appeal to broad sections of German society. If the economy was to grow at its current pace, then further industrialization, specialization, exports and imports were inevitable. Tirpitz therefore staked his project on the economically progressive forces of German capitalism.[10] Britain's extensive foreign trade and imperial interests were often invoked to justify its claim for naval dominance. It is hard to dismiss Germany's entitlement to follow the same course. It is no more reprehensible to aspire to become Number One than to aspire to remain there.

Weapons are wicked, but that is not a sufficient argument for withholding them from Germany alone. Tirpitz did not invent long-term naval armament plans. As Admiral Fisher conceded, it was Britain that set the ball rolling, first with its Naval Defence Act of 1889, and then with the "Spencer Plan" of 1894, each of which set out a long-term project of capital ship construction. 'Of all the damnable silly things ever done,' Fisher wrote in 1911, 'the Naval Defence Act beats everything!' The arms race was already in full swing when Germany joined it. To claim that British arms were benign and others wicked, as the British Prime Minister did (in all sincerity) in 1907, was worthy of the derision it received.[11] Churchill, who plotted in secret 'to secure Belgium as a co-belligerent with us against Germany' in order to maintain economic pressure on Germany, told the Canadian Prime Minster sanctimoniously that, while the German navy was a gun pointed at Great Britain, 'nothing we can do on the sea can menace the freedom or security of Germany, nothing that we can do on the sea can make any difference to that which makes life worth living for them. For us the matter is very different.'[12]

The threat to Germany was a real one. That was demonstrated by the wartime blockade. As a German naval diplomat wrote in the *Deutsche*

[9] D. Kaiser, 'Germany and the Origins of the First World War', *Journal of Modern History*, vol. 55 (1983).

[10] [Reichsmarineamt], *Die Seeinteressen des Deutschen Reiches. Zusammmengestellt auf Veranlassung des Reichsmarineamtes* (Berlin 1898); Schmoller et al., *Handels- und Machtpolitik*; Reichsmarineamt, *Die Entwicklung der deutschen Seeinteressen in dem letzten Jahrzehnt* (Berlin 1905).

[11] Fisher to J. A. Spender, 25 Oct. 1911, *FG*, vol. 2, p. 398; H. Campbell-Bannerman, 'The Hague Conference and the Limitation of Armaments', *The Nation*, 2 Mar. 1907.

[12] Belgium: Churchill, CID, minutes of 116th meeting, 25 Apr. 1912, p. 9; denial of threat, Churchill, CID 118th meeting, 11 July 1912, p. 9, both CAB 2/2/3.

Revue in 1908, 'Germany's endeavour therefore must be to possess a fleet which is powerful enough to make blockade of our coasts impossible, even by the most powerful foreign navy, which would at the same time obviate the danger of a harrying of the coastal towns and of a landing in force.' This text was circulated as an Admiralty print in Britain.[13] It is a moot point whether Germany could have fought the war at all without its battle fleet: if it could, it would have been in much harder circumstances, with its North Sea and Baltic coasts open to landings (which Admiral Fisher had always contemplated), its Baltic trade destroyed, its submarines insecure in their bases. And if it is argued that unilateral disarmament would have kept Germany out of war altogether, that is a counsel of perfection that no country, not even a committed neutral like Holland, Switzerland or Sweden, has adopted in modern times.

When the Tirpitz project was prepared and implemented, sea power was being used extensively all over the globe. Diplomacy often became subordinate to naval assertion. Japan won decisive superiority over China in 1894, the Turks were humiliated at Crete, the United States gained an empire in the Caribbean and the Pacific, and a foothold in China, which it went on to punish in company with the European powers, during the Boxer Uprising. Germany was directly involved in some of these episodes. The most impressive demonstration of sea power was the Boer War, in which Britain was able to project its military power six thousand miles. At the end of 1899 the Royal Navy seized the German merchant ship *Bundesrath* and detained it in Durban for a prolonged search. Soon afterwards it intercepted two other ships, the *General* and the *Herzog*, the latter carrying a Red Cross mission sponsored by the Kaiserinn. None of the ships was found to carry any contraband. Public opinion in Germany was inflamed at this blow to national dignity, and at the country's utter naval impotence.[14] In the Edwardian period the demonstrations continued. Germany teamed up with Britain and Italy to blockade Venezuela for non-payment of debts; the Russians held up British shipping in the Red Sea and actually sank one boat before their battle fleet was demolished at Tsushima; in 1906 the border between Egypt and Palestine at Akaba was determined by the visit of a British warship. There was evidence enough of the importance of sea power. If Germany declined to arm, it would place itself at the mercy of other naval powers. The growing size of the economic and imperial interests at stake was a constant theme of the Tirpitz propaganda. And if the threat might appear too remote, it was

[13] Vice-Admiral R. Siegel, 'Some Reflections on the Necessary Strength of the German Fleet and the Question of Disarmament', trans. from *Deutsche Revue* (Nov. 1908) as an Admiralty print, ADM 116/1070, Nov. 1908.
[14] Coogan, *End of Neutrality*, pp. 37–41.

driven home by Admiral Fisher, who sent his warships on a deliberately provocative cruise into the Baltic in July 1905.[15]

Tirpitz's fleet was not merely a bulwark against England: it was also a bulwark against domestic political reform. That has been the burden of the most impressive and detailed scholarship, Kehr's work on the first Naval Law and Berghahn's studies of the Tirpitz plan. The navy was designed to unite urban money and manufacturing power with agrarian political and military interests in an expansionist overseas project that would defuse the tensions between these interests, and would also take some wind out of the socialist pressure for reform.[16] This role of the fleet is in agreement with the main thrust of my interpretation, namely that the adjustment to economic specialization was a root cause of the war. The socialist menace was itself an outcome of rapid industrial development and urban growth. Agricultural protectionism, which created such bitterness between town and country and became a key issue in domestic politics, was a reaction to the rise of overseas grain production. And overseas development of primary producers created export opportunities for German industry. International specialization upset the world distribution of economic power, and also, in consequence, the domestic balance between primary producers and industry.

None of the great powers, and few of the medium ones, were willing to forgo naval construction during the Edwardian period, even if there was no hope of parity with prospective enemies, and with the Royal Navy in particular. Japan, Russia, Italy, France, Austria, the United States all embarked on large projects of naval construction. In the case of the United States, Japan and the Mediterranean countries, the effect was to force Britain to abandon traditional spheres of influence. Britain gave up peripheral interests and concentrated in the North Sea, against the German navy. A lesser German construction effort would also have raised the alarm in Britain: the realignment of British politics towards France began at an early stage of the Tirpitz plan.

The operational role of the German navy was not incoherent. Like their counterparts in Britain, German admirals regarded capital ships as all-purpose decisive weapons which would secure the achievement of all missions, whether trade protection, coastal defence or commerce raiding.[17] In fact, they provided safety for the Baltic and the German coast, and cover for the submarine bases. The battle cruiser *Goeben* was also

---

[15] Ch. 16 n. 17 above.

[16] Kehr, *Economic Interest*, chs. 1–4; V. R. Berghahn, *Der Tirpitz-Plan. Genesis und Verfall einer innenpolitischen Krisenstrategie unter Wilhelm II* (Düsseldorf 1970); more briefly, in Berghahn, *Germany*, chs. 2–3.

[17] See Lambi, *The Navy*, pp. 62–8.

instrumental in blocking the Dardanelles and cutting off Russia. Tirpitz understood that a close blockade of the German North Sea ports was no longer technically feasible. Britain would have to place its pickets on the exits into the Atlantic. This gave the German navy an opportunity. In 1907 Tirpitz set out harassment in the North Sea and commerce destruction as the only feasible strategy for the High Seas Fleet. Both during and after the war he argued that its capital ships should have been much more active in the North Sea. A British First Sea Lord later asked, 'What would not Nelson have done with the German fleet in 1914 and 1915?'[18] The success of the *Goeben*, of the Dogger Bank encounter, and of the battle of Jutland—all suggest that there was some scope for the inferior power to make use of weather, darkness and short steaming ranges to challenge and wear down the British Grand Fleet. The submarines played no part in Tirpitz's original design, but the capacity to build and to operate them depended on the industrial and institutional foundations of Tirpitz's navy.[19] Germany's High Seas Fleet tied up much larger British resources.

The opposite argument also carries some weight: that the loss of the navy or even a substantial part of it would have exposed Germany's flanks. Either way, as a fighting force or as a "fleet in being", the navy was not a useless instrument. The Tirpitz plan, however, if carried through, was not designed primarily to fight and win a war, but to win *without* war. Of course it created a risk of pre-emption. But, despite some fire-eating talk by Fisher, no one seriously planned to raid and destroy the German fleet, nor would this have been an easy task.[20] By the time the war broke out, Germany had narrowed down British superiority to 1.5:1 in capital ships. The German fleet was never "ready" for war. As David Kaiser argues, Tirpitz was (like his counterpart Fisher) a blustering cold warrior. At the famous 1912 conference with the Kaiser, Tirpitz pleaded unreadiness. In July 1914 the fleet was not consulted and was unprepared for war.[21]

Critics of the plan blame Tirpitz for drawing Britain into continental affairs. However, without a German navy, Britain's power to intervene would have been much greater. Would the temptation to do so have been any smaller? A smaller German navy would have released some men for the army, but the coast still had to be watched for an English landing. It is just as possible to argue that Britain's insistence on naval primacy drew it

---

[18] Tirpitz to Chancellor von Bülow, 20 Apr. 1907, quoted in Lepsius *et al.*, *Grosse Politik*, vol. 23, pt. 2, esp. p. 365 (see Ritter, *Sword and Scepter*, vol. 2, pp. 151, 153); A. von Tirpitz, *My Memoirs* (1919), pp. 354–82; A. Müller, *The Kaiser and his Court*, ed. W. Görlitz (1961), p. 19; Admiral of the Fleet Lord Chatfield, *The Navy and Defence* (1942), p. 175.

[19] G. R. Weir, 'Tirpitz, Technology and Building U-Boats, 1897–1916', *International History Review*, vol. 6 (May 1984).

[20] Steinberg, 'The Copenhagen Complex'.

[21] Tirpitz, *Memoirs*, p. 289; J. Röhl, 'Admiral von Müller and the Approach of War, 1911–1914', *Historical Journal*, vol. 12 (1969), pp. 661–3; Kaiser, 'Origins'.

into the continental affray. Another line is that the British naval threat should have dissuaded the German army from executing its aggressive designs. One undertone of the criticism of Tirpitz is that he obstructed the military with Britain's needless antagonism. Perhaps he was not successful enough in provoking the British deterrent. Unlike Fisher, Tirpitz was a genuine reactionary. But it was the army, after all, that pressed for war. All these considerations suggest that the fleet was not an irrational policy, or at least not more so than other armament programmes of the time. What was irrational was the way it was squandered by Germany in the military gamble of August 1914.

The Edwardian period was a time of rapid technical progress at sea, and that made the fleet construction programme even more attractive. The effect of technology was to write off many of the large existing naval assets that Britain and other powers had accumulated, and to create an opening for dynamic newcomers. The launching of the *Dreadnought* in 1906 pulled all the runners in the capital ship race back to the starting line by introducing a new standard of gunnery, armour and speed.

Another destabilizing factor was the submarine. It was only one of a whole series of weapons based on the mine and the torpedo that pitted cheap munitions against costly battleships. That the submarine was capable of upsetting the balance of naval power was clear to naval officers and politicians in Britain, even if it was too novel a prospect to effect a complete reappraisal of doctrine.[22] Although the German Admiralty did not develop a doctrine of submarine economic warfare (which Fisher and Balfour clearly foresaw), it kept up with the technology, and created the skills and the boats to make effective tactical use of this arm during the war.[23]

Other innovations also shifted the balance away from capital to skill, and thus from the strong to the weak. Humble mines, which sunk several British battleships (and Lord Kitchener as well), were among the most effective naval weapons of the war. A torpedo was first dropped from an aeroplane in 1915, and, although aviation did not play an important part in the naval war, it belonged to those innovations that acted to devalue the traditional capital ship and provided openings for wealthy upstarts like Japan and the United States—and, potentially, for Germany as well. A whole range of innovations did not favour the strong or the weak in particular, but rather the innovator. Their effect was to destabilize the

---

[22] J. Fisher, 'Submarines' (20 Apr. 1904), ADM 116/942; A. J. Balfour to Fisher, 15 Oct., 2 Nov. 1910, FP 1/10; Balfour to Fisher, 20 May 1913, *FG*, vol. 2, pp. 485–6; Churchill to Fisher, 30 Aug. 1913, FP 1/13; anon., Memo on submarines, 24 June 1913, FP 1/13; [Fisher], 'The Oil Engine and the Submarine' (13 pp. printed, n.d. 1913), HP 5/2; P. Scott, letter to *The Times*, 4 June 1914, as recounted in his *Fifty Years in the Royal Navy* (1919), pp. 274–5.
[23] Weir, 'Tirpitz'.

balance of power. These belonged to the realm of ship design, armour, ammunition, the calibre of gunnery and its control. Wireless telegraphy (and aerial reconnaissance) were the two innovations that probably worked against the weak, in facilitating the concentration of superior power, and making blockade more effective, thus underlining its threat.[24]

The rise of other naval powers created an opening for Germany. British superiority was no longer axiomatic. In several theatres, some of them vital for safeguarding its imperial interests, Britain had to concede superiority to regional powers: to Japan in the Far East, to the United States in its coastal waters and in the Pacific, to the Mediterranean countries in the Mediterranean. In economic terms, it was no longer in Britain's power to maintain absolute superiority against a determined building campaign by the United States.

The international proliferation of naval power created an opportunity for diplomacy which Germany failed to grasp. No single hand co-ordinated its policies. The navy, the army, the Foreign Office and the Chancellor all pursued their own objectives. It was this that destroyed Germany's bid for world influence—not the construction of a navy. The build-up of the German navy was a reaction to the Royal Navy. In the lawless world of international relations, a desire to challenge the balance of power was not in itself blameworthy. There was nothing sacred about the status quo. Having run down its agriculture and created a dependency on imports, Britain regarded its naval superiority as vital. Germany, following down the same road, was entitled to feel the same way. Until it had achieved parity with Britain, the navy on its own lacked the power or the incentive to start a war. Its role was necessarily subordinate. It fell to the statesmen and the army to begin the war and to sacrifice much, in terms of political capital, that the navy could still achieve.

Naval construction strained the resources of the imperial tax system. That system, like all fiscal systems, was the expression of past and current political forces. The struggle over taxation followed the basic fissures in German politics and society, which in turn reflected the effects of rapid economic growth. After 1909, and even more so after 1912, when the German effort moved away from the navy and back to the army (a fateful shift in the direction of war), it was largely on account of the fiscal pressures of preceding years. This leads directly into the question of economic preparations for war.

---

[24] There is no comprehensive work on technical change during the Edwardian period, but a good feel for the issues can be derived from J. T. Sumida, 'Financial Limitation, Technological Innovation, and British Naval Policy, 1904–1910' (University of Chicago Ph.D. thesis, 1982).

IV

Economic Protection

Tariff protection for agriculture from the 1880s onwards, and especially the high Bülow tariff of 1903, was an important economic preparation for war. But that was a by-product, and not the main purpose, of Germany's agrarian tariffs.

Protection kept in being the infrastructure of agriculture, and high land prices ensured a "high farming" approach: heavy inputs for heavy yields. Behind the tariff wall, German farmers intensified their production by shifting to animal products and root crops, especially sugar beet and potatoes. A British writer summed it up in 1916, 'The German feeds from 70 to 75 persons per 100 acres of cultivated land, the British farmer feeds from 45 to 50.'[25] This productive capacity stood between Germany and starvation in 1917 and 1918, when the blockade was drawn tight.

In 1892 the Chancellor, Caprivi, reduced tariffs all round as part of a more liberal commercial policy. His tariff was due to expire in 1902, and this prospect provided the impulse for a wide-ranging debate on the development options available to Germany. This debate, with its two extremes of "agrarians" and "industrializers", took place largely among economists and historians. As is the wont of academics, it went beyond the immediate issues and explored large questions of principle. Once the new tariffs were decided in 1902, it died down. The debate offered the first serious opportunity since the Corn Law debates in Britain in the first half of the century to reflect on the social and economic consequences of international specialization in agriculture. The theoretical case for free trade and for industrial and export development is familiar. In Germany's concrete conditions, its defenders argued, only industry, urbanization and colonial development offered any hope of absorbing a growing population and raising its standard of living. Germany's place in the international division of labour was as manufacturer and trader.

On the other side, economists and historians with agrarian sympathies highlighted what economists today might call "diseconomies of scale" or over-rapid urbanization: in the large towns, working-class life was alienated, unethical, subversive, democratic, cramped and sickly; in the country, according to the agrarians, it could be organic, hierarchical, traditional and healthy. The free traders denied that the country was a

---

[25] Middleton, 'Recent Development of German Agriculture', p. 41; on intensification also J. A. Perkins, 'The Agricultural Revolution in Germany, 1850–1914', *Journal of European Economic History*, vol. 10 (1981). A recent short survey: M. Rolfes, 'Landwirtschaft, 1850–1914', in H. Aubin and W. Zorn (eds.), *Handbuch der deutschen Wirtschafts- und Sozialgeschichte*, vol. 2 (Stuttgart 1976).

better breeding-ground for soldiers. Although agrarians often mentioned self-sufficiency in wartime as a benefit of protection, it was usually mentioned as a consequence and only rarely as the prime motive for raising tariffs. It is doubtful whether the debate actually swayed any opinions. Support and opposition lined up approximately according to interest groups. But the views of agrarian economists gave the tariffs a legitimacy they might otherwise have lacked.[26]

Like their Canadian populist contemporaries, the Prussian professors expressed their concern about the corrupting embrace of modern capitalism, and their preference for a traditional social order, even at the expense of economic efficiency. One cannot help being struck by the analogy of values, by the way in which social fundamentalism, both feudalist and populist, dressed itself up in green.[27]

In the present context, however, what counts is whether agricultural protection affected Germany's preparedness for war. On this there is little room for doubt. Agricultural output continued to rise after the new tariff was enacted in 1902.[28] It is not easy to show the precise linkages, since so many factors were involved. Education, co-operation, credit and confidence were probably just as important as direct price incentives. As a British official wrote, 'The main value of the tariff policy to German agriculture was the sense of security which it created in the farmer. It was the conviction that he was essential to the community . . . rather than the prospect of receiving an extra two marks per 100 kilos.'[29] Kenneth Barkin has argued the opposite, by showing that some food imports rose, and that the number of animals per head stagnated. This shows that in some sectors (e.g. wheat) production did not keep up with population: for animals, without information on their yields, numbers alone are meaningless. Other statistics show meat production rising from 48 to 52 kg. per head of the population between 1901 and 1911; milk from 329 kg. per head in 1900 to 341 in 1911.[30] But all German pre-war agricultural data are insecure. What has to be asked, is whether production would have been larger with a lower tariff. The example of Britain suggests that it would have been much smaller. Admittedly, the increases shown by Hoffmann are small and subject to error; but even if one accepts, as Barkin argues, that protection

---

[26] K. Barkin, *The Controversy over German Industrialization, 1890–1902* (Chicago 1970), pt. 2; A. Mendel, 'The Debate between Prussian Junkerdom and the Forces of Urban Industry, 1897–1902', *Jahrbuch des Instituts für deutsche Geschichte*, vol. 4 (1975); translations of representative texts, F. W. Taussig (ed.), *Selected Readings in International Trade and Tariff Problems* (Boston 1921); academic influence on the Chancellor: Barkin, *Controversy*, pp. 220–1.

[27] This point has been made by Mendel, 'Debate', p. 337.

[28] Hoffmann, *Das Wachstum*, ch. 8.

[29] Middleton, 'Recent Development of German Agriculture', p. 34.

[30] Hoffmann, *Das Wachstum*, pp. 173–4, 302, 308.

increased the price, and thus reduced the food values available to the working classes, that does not affect our argument that it made available a larger domestic capacity in wartime.

Barkin suggests that bread and potatoes are nutritionally inferior to livestock products—few nutritionists would agree today. There remains the question of price. Barkin paints a gloomy (but imprecise) picture: and no doubt consumers would have been better off before the war without the tariff. But would it be wise for them to spend their surplus on the kind of cheap processed foods the British preferred, the white flour, the refined sugar, the processed fats and frozen meat, the cheap imported staples that have given Britain the worst dietary heritage in Europe?[31]

How much did agricultural protection cost the German economy? S. B. Webb reckons a little more than 1 per cent of national income for grain, a little less than 2 per cent for livestock.[32] Considered as an insurance premium, the subsidy for grain was not unreasonable. The hidden subsidy for livestock might be regarded as excessive. It should, however, be set against those social costs of rapid urban growth (in housing, food and health) that were not incurred because rural depopulation was delayed. What these figures bring out is the importance of protection for German national security. Without protection, imports would have taken a much larger share of the German food market. Would such a dependence on overseas have tempted Germany to build an even larger fleet? Would it have followed the opposite course, and abandoned the idea of war altogether?

As it was, the tariff policy reduced conservative pressures for all-out naval armament. A free trade economy would have entailed either massive naval construction, or a strong peace diplomacy. The British example indicates that battleships were the more likely outcome. In fact, protection fell short of agrarian demands, and short also of establishing complete self-sufficiency.

If tariffs reduced the pressure for naval armament, they increased the likelihood of a continental war in a number of ways. Firstly, they guaranteed sufficient supplies for a short war from domestic sources. Secondly, as Barkin has shown, the high tariffs were forced on Russia during its war with Japan; this hampered the Russian economy and antagonized Russian statesmen.[33] Thirdly, the tariffs increased the domestic tensions between the left and the right. Some contemporaries, and many historians, have sought to explain the war almost entirely as a

[31] Barkin, *Controversy*, pp. 253–70; the British diet: G. Channon, *The Politics of Food* (1987).
[32] S. B. Webb, 'Agricultural Protection in Wilhelmian Germany: Forging an Empire with Pork and Rye', *Journal of Economic History*, vol. 42 (June 1982), pp. 324–5.
[33] Barkin, *Controversy*, pp. 248–9.

pre-emptive strike against the left within Germany.[34] The Social Democrats bitterly opposed the tariff. To the extent that these arguments are valid (and they do seem to carry a good deal of weight) then they add conviction to the view that the Bülow tariffs helped to create a climate conducive to war. Finally, Kehr has argued that the Bülow tariffs also induced a sense of complacency about more direct economic preparations for war.[35] That is the subject of the next chapter.

[34] This source of danger was already known to Fisher (letter to his son, 21 Aug. 1911, *FG*, vol. 2, p. 381) and was conventional wisdom on the left in Germany: e.g. K. Liebknecht, *Militarism and Anti-Militarism* (1906, English trans. Glasgow 1917), p. 18. It is central to the Fischer school's interpretation of the origins of the war: e.g. in Berghahn, *Germany*, ch. 9.

[35] Kehr, *Economic Interest*, pp. 57–61.

23

GERMANY: ECONOMIC PREPARATION AND THE DECISION FOR WAR

I

THE perils of dependence on overseas trade began to attract serious discussion in Germany around the turn of the century, in conjunction with the tariff and naval construction debates. According to the naval office, some 74 per cent of Germany's imports arrived by sea, directly and indirectly.[1]

Was it possible to prepare in advance for the loss of imports and the closure of markets? This was not merely a technical problem. It could not be separated from the large questions of foreign policy and military strategy. What sort of war was in prospect?

Germany's policy in the Morocco crisis of 1905 and even in the second one of 1911 suggested that it would seek to advance the national interest by all means short of war. In 1905 the conditions for attack (with Russia disabled by revolution and war) were better than they later became. But if, as a result of such restraint, Germany found itself attacked, then it faced the menace of a blockade and the prospect of a difficult defensive war.

A different course, which appealed to German generals, was not to draw a firm line between diplomacy and war but rather, in the manner of Clausewitz, to take action if the situation called for it.[2] The General Staff had a strategic plan of pre-emptive attack. This plan, evolved by Count Alfred von Schlieffen during his long tenure as chief of the Great General Staff, called for a rapid flanking advance into northern France, and a holding action against Russia, with the aim of destroying the French army in the space of two months or so. Schlieffen had no quick fix for the Russian front, and conceded that Russia could sustain a long war; but such a war would not be crippling for Germany if fought on the eastern front alone.[3]

A prolonged defensive war on land was a sign that the chosen policy (whether peace or war) had failed. As Germany gradually inclined towards a preventive attack, a static war of defence remained a residual, second-best, undesirable outcome, only tolerable as an alternative to outright defeat. Economic preparations for war reflected these priorities.

---

[1] 'Untersuchung des Reichsmarineamts' (28 Jan. 1907), in Reichsarchiv, *Kriegsrüstung und Kriegswirtschaft* (Berlin 1930), 2 vols., in Reichsarchiv, *Der Weltkrieg, 1914 bis 1918* (Berlin 1925–1942), 14 vols., vol. 2. Anlagen, no. 75, p. 220.

[2] F. von Bernhardi, 'The Duty to Make War', *Germany and the Next War* (1912, English trans. 1914), ch. 2; also F. Fischer, The War of Illusions: German Policies from 1911 to 1914 (1975), chs. 9, 10, 18. [3] Burchardt, *Friedenswirtschaft*, p. 15.

There are two main accounts of this process. The German archives published two volumes in 1930, and their findings were amplified and extended in a study by Lothar Burchardt in 1968. Burchardt's work is exhaustive, exemplary and invaluable, and I have largely followed in his footsteps, though I have arrived at some different conclusions.[4]

The problem of economic preparedness began to occupy the General Staff in the early 1880s, and worried Caprivi in the early 1890s. As in Britain, however, the real turning-point came in 1906. After the Morocco crisis of 1905, the threat of war acquired a new immediacy. This crisis, that motivated Captain Campbell in Britain to examine the German economy for signs of weakness, also inspired many Germans to do the same. Indeed, both Admiralties were aware of the thinking on the other side.[5]

The strongest inclination in Germany, however, was to do nothing. Large interests supported inaction. Conservatives and agrarians argued that subsidies and support for agriculture in peacetime would secure food supplies in war. Active preparations for war would divert government support away from agriculture and undermine one of its main justifications. The Kaiser was one of many who believed that more intensive cultivation, reduction of fallows, higher yields, "internal colonization" of pasture and moorland, and economies of consumption promised an adequate food supply.[6]

From a different point of view, the Naval Office also discouraged economic preparations. Tirpitz's propaganda did a great deal to flesh out the dangers of blockade and to provide statistical ammunition. The Naval Office's answer to the bogey it had created was to build a bigger and better battle fleet. War had no place in Tirpitz's grand design—the whole point was to avoid war during the "risk period" and, arguably, later as well. So the Naval Office regarded practical measures as less than urgent.[7]

For the civil service, war preparation posed theoretical, administrative, political and fiscal difficulties. Germany's conservative bureaucrats were not inclined to intervene in economic affairs, which they regarded as the sphere of private interests. In a federal state, and with no single chain of authority, a policy of intervention was not easy to impose. If legislation was called for, more obstacles appeared. Civil servants were reluctant to face parliamentary and public controversy over issues of war and peace. They had little experience and even less inclination to enter a parliamentary

---

[4] Reichsarchiv, *Kriegsrüstung*; Burchardt, *Friedenswirtschaft*.

[5] See references to Royal Commission on Food Supply in the German Naval Office memo, n. 1 above, p. 223 of the item cited; and the translation of Vice-Admiral Siegel's article from the *Deutsche Revue* (Nov. 1908), ADM 116/1070.

[6] e.g. O. von Moltke, 'Noch ein Wort über Krieg und Volksernährung', *Preussische Jahrbücher*, vol. 155 (1914); Burchardt, *Friedenswirtschaft*, pp. 53, 67–8, 96–8, 113–6, 120–1, 158.

[7] Burchardt, *Friedenswirtschaft*, pp. 20, 55, 60, 72–3, 163–4, 169–70, 184–7.

arena whose legitimacy they did not entirely accept. Such debates could alert foreign powers, increase international tension and even provoke foreign counter-measures. Finally, there was the question of money. The Empire's finances were gravely stretched by the naval programme and Bülow's attempts to extend them by means of death duties failed in the face of agrarian opposition, and created a chronic fiscal crisis. Bethmann Hollweg also attempted to keep his escalating armaments expenditure within the bounds of sound finance. The Imperial Treasury resisted any plan that called for additional spending.[8]

On top of these practical difficulties there were also conceptual ones. Without clear guidance on strategy and foreign policy, it was difficult for officials to choose a policy. Technical, economic and financial difficulties added complication. The temptation to prevaricate, or to do nothing, was strong.

II

Economic preparation involved many issues. Hindsight identifies fodder and food as the critical ones. On the face of it, Germany's dependence on raw materials was much greater than the shortfall of food, although little official attention was given to this deficit before the war. Later, when serious difficulties arose, raw materials did not prove critical to the war effort to the same extent as food.[9]

Official discussions in 1906 established that the grain stored in Germany would only last for nine to ten months if the harvest was poor and the borders and ports were closed.[10] Eight years of additional study and debate did little to change this outlook. But there was no certainty. Planning was bedevilled by the weakness of agricultural statistics. The scale of imports was easy to establish but the level of domestic production and the condition of stocks were unclear. Neither the size of the harvest, nor the stocks carried by farmers, nor the weight and number of animals could be established precisely.

Carl Ballod, a government statistician and Professor at the University of Berlin, undertook a prolonged and single-handed campaign to get the authorities to invest in better information. It only required a modest outlay. After a great deal of official discussion, a landowners' organization was persuaded to undertake an annual stock-taking of grain in 1910. After

[8] P.-C. Witt, 'Reichsfinanzen and Rüstungspolitik, 1898–1914', in H. Schottelius and W. Deist (eds.), *Marine und Marinepolitik im kaiserlichen Deutschland 1871–1914* (Düsseldorf 1972), pp. 156–77; Burchardt, *Friedenswirtschaft*, pp. 74–6, 203, and ch. 6.
[9] Burchardt, *Friedenswirtschaft*, pp. 78–95.
[10] Reichsarchiv, *Kriegsrüstung*, vol. 1, pp. 307 ff. and C. Ballod, 'Gutachten des Preussischen Statistischen Landesamts vom Juni 1906', *Kriegsrüstung*, vol. 2, no. 73, pp. 213–16.

a few more years of extended discussions, the Treasury agreed to grant 200,000 marks, and the Minister of the Interior to pass the legislation for an official survey of year-end stocks. The first of these official surveys took place on 1 July 1914, but its results only became available in December. This was virtually the only practical measure of economic preparation for war undertaken officially in Germany.[11]

III

A number of academics and businessmen wrote and published about economic preparation for war, from 1906 onwards. Burchardt calls these pamphleteers the "warners". Their writings consist of letters to the government, essays in journals, and a few books.[12] I shall concentrate on the proposals relating to food.

Three broad classes of measures found particular favour among the warners. In view of the dominance of Rubner's wartime and post-war nutritional orthodoxy, it comes as a surprise to find that the warners knew about rational nutrition and gave the parsimonious diet a role in their plans. Comments on the need for substitutions already appear in such official documents as the naval memorandum of 1907.[13]

In 1908 W. Behrend published an essay on 'The Potato in Wartime'. Behrend inclined towards the rational dietary approach, and was especially influenced by the Danish nutritionist Hindhede. With its tremendous productivity, the potato offered a solution to the shortfall of imports, and Germany led the world in potato production. Tubers could replace some imported grain and also much of the meat consumed. If the industrial use of potatoes was diminished, stocks would rise sufficiently.[14] This idea had its limitations, in that potatoes are a bulky crop, difficult to transport and to store, and subject to large harvest variations. A shortage of potatoes induced the worst nutrition crisis of the war, the turnip winter of 1916–17. But Behrend's basic insight was sound.

Many warners advocated an "Economic General Staff", to plan the administration of the war economy in advance. Like Stewart Murray in Britain, they anticipated unemployment in some industries and labour shortages in agriculture. Some "General Staff" plans incorporated labour exchanges. The Economic General Staff concept was a far-sighted and

[11] Ballod, 'Güterbedarf und Konsumtion', in Zahn (ed.), *Die Statistik in Deutschland*, pp. 610–12, and other essays in this volume; Ballod's record: Burchardt, *Friedenswirtschaft*, pp. 102–4. The survey issue is discussed extensively by Burchardt.

[12] See Burchardt's bibliography; also A. Blaustein, 'Versuch einer Bibliographie zur Kriegswirtschaftslehre', *Weltwirtschaftliches Archiv*, vol. 3 (1914).

[13] 'Untersuchung des Reichsmarineamts' (28 Jan. 1907), in Reichsarchiv, *Kriegsrüstung*, vol. 2. Anlagen, no. 75, p. 223.

[14] W. Behrend, 'Die Kartoffel im Kriege', *Preussische Jahrbücher*, no. 134 (1908).

shrewd proposal which was also cheap to implement. In peacetime, however, it had two unwelcome implications. It suggested government intervention, and it cut across established lines of authority. These features doomed it to fail. Within days of the outbreak of war, Walther Rathenau set up the Raw Materials Section (*Kriegsrohstoffabteilung*) in the War Ministry. But it took two long and bitter years to set up its equivalent for food, the War Food Office of June 1916.[15]

The third measure was stockpiling. In practice, this amounted to the storage of bread grains, and particularly of wheat, which was the grain in greatest deficit. Apart from sugar, grain was the easiest food commodity to store and was a good substitute for all the rest.[16]

In Germany as in Britain, granary proposals emerged in the 1890s, in connection with agrarian demands for protection and subsidy. Count von Kanitz's bill to nationalize the grain trade was repeatedly before the Reichstag during the 1890s. This proposal, which was the focus of agrarian demands, envisaged government granaries to regulate market price of grain and to provide an emergency store for wartime. [17]

Many of the warners advocated stockpiling. A high point was an essay published by Karl Fröhlich in *Schmollers Jahrbücher* in 1912. Schmoller was the dean of German economists, a nationalist with naval leanings, and he sent a draft of Fröhlich's paper to the Chancellor Bethmann Hollweg. Fröhlich began with the danger of a total blockade; surveying bread grain imports over the previous ten years, he showed that domestic production only covered about ten months. Taking the defective harvest statistics into account, the deficit was larger, two to three months in every year. Much depended on when war broke out: the shortage was much larger towards the end of the harvest year. Behrend's proposal to substitute potatoes for grain was unrealistic, since potatoes did not contain sufficient protein, and the meat supply was not sufficient to provide more than 22 grams of protein per head per day, far short even of half the Voit norm of 118 grams (though close enough to the Chittenden standard, assuming other sources of protein). But 60 per cent of the fodder to produce milk was imported. Furthermore, the potato harvest fluctuated enormously. In order to avert hunger in time of war, it was imperative to provide granaries, and to store two million tons of grain. The annual cost (in interest, assuming the money was borrowed) was modest, and only amounted to 24 million marks a year (including storage). The capital sum, of course, was more frightening— about 600 million marks, or some £30 million.

Delbrück, the Minister of the Interior, reassured the Chancellor.

[15] Burchardt, *Friedenswirtschaft*, pp. 136–45; Feldman, *Army, Industry and Labor*, pp. 45–52.

[16] Ch. 6, sec. I, above.

[17] Barkin, *Controversy*, pp. 91–5; Burchardt, *Friedenswirtschaft*, pp. 116, 183.

Interior ministry officials dismissed Fröhlich as an amateur, while failing to meet all of his points. Subsequent scholars have lamented this myopia, but the official response was actually a mixture of obtuseness and good sense. It was obtuse in its refusal to acknowledge harvest overestimation, even when it stared officials in the face. It was sensible in the main, arguing that the Voit standard invoked by Fröhlich was grossly exaggerated. Citing the nutritionist Hindhede, the officials argued that calories counted for more than protein; that fat, protein and carbohydrates were largely interchangeable; that higher yields, drying potatoes and preventing waste would close most of the nutrition gap; and for the rest, that in wartime one should tighten belts.[18]

Fröhlich regarded his granaries as cheap at the price, but they involved an addition of about 12 per cent to the national debt—not a light burden in times of fiscal stringency. One year later the Treasury rejected a plan for storing a mere 10,000 tons as being too costly.[19]

IV

Of all government organs, the Naval Office gave a great deal of impetus to the question of economic preparation in its early years, by placing blockade on the agenda and keeping it there. Its primary contribution was to collect information: apart from its two well-known surveys of Germany's overseas interests and occasional articles in its journal *Nauticus*, the Naval Office also carried out a unique survey of industrial raw materials which showed the low level of stocks held by industrial firms.[20] A paper completed in 1907 contains a shrewd assessment of the effects of blockade, and mirrors very closely the Campbell studies carried out at the Department of Naval Intelligence in Britain at approximately the same time. In this paper, the Naval Office highlights the importance of the Dutch and Belgian ports. Some three-quarters of Germany's imports (by value) came over the sea, directly and indirectly. If food and raw materials were declared contraband, then even access to a neutral Antwerp and Rotterdam could not prevent an effective blockade. Tirpitz stressed that a short war was not guaranteed, and that blockade would only begin to bite

---

[18] G. Fröhlich , 'Deutsche Volksernährung im Kriege', *Schmollers Jahrbücher*, vol. 36 (1912); C. von Delbrück to A. von Bethmann Hollweg (and enclosed memorandum), 30 Mar. 1912, Reichsarchiv, *Kriegsrüstung*, vol. 2, no. 79, pp. 239–47. My assessment of this episode differs from that of Burchardt, *Friedenswirtschaft*, pp. 127–8, 197–8, and J. Lee, 'Administrators and Agriculture: Aspects of German Agricultural Policy in the First World War', in J. M. Winter (ed.), *War and Economic Development* (Cambridge 1975).

[19] Burchardt, *Friedenswirtschaft*, p. 159; Reichsarchiv, *Kriegsrüstung*, vol. 2, no. 81, Delbrück and State Secretary Kühn of the Treasury to Bethmann Hollweg, 30 Mar. 1913, esp. Kühn, pp. 251–2.

[20] The two *Seeinteressen*, (ch. 22 n. 10, above); Burchardt, *Friedenswirtschaft*, pp. 92–3.

in the longer term (which he defined, correctly, as about one and a half years). He saw how much domestic agriculture depended heavily on fodder and fertilizer imports, and that demand would increase in wartime, while production would fall. He emphasized transport and distributional difficulties, showing that most grain was consumed where it was grown, and that the large deficit in the west of the country was filled from overseas, and not from the east. Although eastern Europe was the most important source of imported grain, the shipments arrived by sea through the western seaports. This led to the most important point. Tirpitz's conclusions were similar to Campbell's in Britain: Germany's railways did not have sufficient capacity to carry grain from the east to replace the grain imported by sea.[21]

Burchardt is carried away by his aversion to Tirpitz, and argues that the admiral's only purpose in fanning the fear of blockade was to accelerate naval construction.[22] That is misleading. In fact Tirpitz made sensible suggestions about the need to survey stocks, to set up an authority in advance to regulate prices, and to examine possible food substitutions. He referred to the English Royal Commission on Food Supply, the dangers of social unrest, and also commended, by implication, the idea of stockpiling. All in all, it was one of the most balanced and far-sighted analyses of the blockade danger.

The Hague conference and the Declaration of London gave the navy another opportunity to ponder the issues. Tirpitz opposed immunity for private property at sea, and for two reasons, both of them sound: he distrusted the British; and he wanted to keep the way clear for a *guerre de course* against British shipping in wartime. The navy carried out some tough bargaining at the London Naval Conference and extracted concessions for merchant raiding, in return for its agreement to Britain's contraband proposals.[23]

Practical preparations were the business of the Prussian War Ministry, the Imperial Ministry of the Interior, and the General Staff. From 1906 onwards the problems of preparation were almost constantly under discussion, with greater intensity after 1909, and once again after 1912. But the sum total of all this activity, which took place at the highest governmental and military levels, was almost nil. Little more need be said. Instead of following the chronicle of these futile discussions, it is better to ponder the reasons for their sterile outcome.

[21] Reichsarchiv, *Kriegsrüstung*, vol. 2, Tirpitz to the Minister of the Interior Posadowsky-Wehner, 28 Jan. 1907, and attached memorandum, pp. 218–23; also (for an earlier assessment of the limitation of railways) Tirpitz to Minister for War von Einem, 13 Mar. 1906, ibid. no. 70 , p. 206; Campbell: chs. 15 and 16 above.

[22] Burchardt, *Friedenswirtschaft*, pp. 72–3, 164, 170.

[23] Declaration of London: ch. 19 above; Burchardt, *Friedenswirtschaft*, pp. 64–5, 73, 185, 187; Tirpitz's opposition to immunity for private property at sea: his two memos to Bülow, 20 and 29 Apr. 1907, in Lepsius *et al.* (eds.), *Grosse Politik*, vol. 23, pt. 2, pp. 359–72.

The General Staff showed a good deal of concern for food supply in wartime. Moltke, who took over Schlieffen's position in 1905, was uneasy about his predecessor's strategy, but lacked the confidence and authority to give it an exhaustive review. Instead he fretted and tinkered. One source of disquiet was the food supply in wartime. In 1907 he stated that 'the interests of the people can no longer be separated from those of the army', and demanded a comprehensive investigation of economic preparation for war. From 1907 onwards the army reckoned on a total British blockade. In May 1914 Moltke expressed his worry about a long and difficult war. In such circumstances, economic collapse at home might undermine the front. But he failed to let these premonitions affect his plans. All the proposals were strictly limited to problems of mobilization and the earliest period of the war.[24]

Whatever the General Staff's concerns about war economy, it was not going to allow them to foreclose the option of war. In 1911 the General Staff produced a long memorandum on the shortfall of imports in wartime. The facts were roughly the same as those outlined in other studies. But the conclusion was a guarded optimism. As in the more careful naval studies, the key question was once again whether it was possible to carry the supplies into Germany by rail to replace the blockaded ports. Tirpitz, like his counterpart Campbell in Britain, had denied that this was possible. Both navies had a vested interest in showing that blockade was effective. The General Staff, like its British counterparts, could not afford to be pessimistic. It calculated the capacity required to ship the import deficit through Switzerland and Austria at fifty trains a day, each of one hundred railway cars (that makes almost three and a half cars every minute, day and night). With careful management, the staff officers said, it could be done. But they failed to ask whether supplies could actually be purchased anywhere. Both British and German General Staffs were keen to find that a continental war could not be stopped short by blockade. A similar comforting conclusion was published in the General Staff's journal in 1913 by one of the civilian warners, Arthur Dix. Dix found that a multi-front war was feasible, and preached the virtues of the offensive spirit.[25]

Since it would not accept that the problem of food supply in war was insoluble, the army tried to get something done. The first requirement was

[24] Moltke's disquiet: Burchardt, *Friedenswirtschaft*, pp. 6, 10, 25–6, 44–9, 56, 193–4; Moltke to the War Ministry, 12 Feb. 1907, Reichsarchiv, *Kriegsrüstung*, vol. 2, no. 76, p. 224; Moltke to the War Ministry, 1 Nov. 1912, in E. von Ludendorff, *The General Staff and its Problems* (New York n.d. ?1920), p. 18.; Moltke to Clemens von Delbrück (Minister of the Interior), 14 May 1914, Reichsarchiv, *Kriegsrüstung*, vol. 2, no. 85, pp. 287–91.

[25] Director of the army administrative department Generalmajor Staabs, to the War Minister von Heeringen, 4 Nov. 1911, Reichsarchiv, *Kriegsrüstung*, vol. 2, no. 78, esp. pp. 235–6; naval attitudes: n. 1 above; British attitudes: ch. 20 above; A. Dix, 'Volkswirtschaftliche Kriegsvorsorge', *Vierteljahrshefte für Truppenführung und Heereskunde*, vol. 10 (1913), esp. pp. 444 and 451.

a stocktaking of grain. This was achieved in 1910, and more comprehensively in 1914. The General Staff pressed vigorously for export prohibitions on grain on the outbreak of war, and for the purchase of emergency stocks. Its railway department, which prepared to assume control of the railways on mobilization, was aware (like its British counterparts at the CID) of the need to allocate some capacity for feeding the large towns. In 1913 the General Staff began to press for grain stockpiles for the big cities and for fortress towns; and by 1914, unsatisfied with existing provisions, it helped to set up a system for grain requisition, in co-operation with the civilian authorities at the local level. These preparations indicated the army's impatience with economic incentives and indirect methods of control, and foreshadowed its readiness to take food by force if necessary—an attitude that did a great deal to disenchant the farming community in the later stages of the war.[26]

In peacetime, however, the General Staff had no executive powers, but was merely a planning agency. It could afford to be extravagant. The Ministry of Interior was the focus for actual war preparation. With no responsibility for either foreign policy or war, the civilian administration did not feel the same urgency as the army. Its response was to procrastinate. It considered many schemes, convened many conferences, corresponded in volume and created a semblance of action. In 1910 it helped to launch the voluntary grain stocktaking; in 1912 it created a "Standing Commission for Economic Mobilization" made up of civilian and military bodies. This commission met many times and generated a good deal of paper. It assembled merchants, industrialists and landowners in advisory committees. One of its schemes provided for emergency purchases of grain in Rotterdam on the outbreak of war, and probed the use of Belgium as a wartime conduit of supplies. This shows how poorly informed the ministry was about the shape of the war to come. For all the appearance of action, the Ministry of the Interior was a delaying force. Even when it overcame its own reluctance to act, it could usually count on a veto from the Treasury.[27]

For all the bustle of discussion and debate, actual economic preparations for war amounted almost to nothing. What is more, they had far too little impact on economic management once the war broke out. Instead, resources were sunk in other forms of preparation. First they were used in building up the navy, which continued to absorb very large sums of money; that may be viewed, however, as a deterrent rather than a preparatory

---

[26] Burchardt, *Friedenswirtschaft*, pp. 222–4.

[27] Ibid., pp. 58, 158, 200 ff., 209–10, 238; also R. Zilch, 'Zur wirtschaftlichen Vorbereitung des deutschen Imperialismus auf den ersten Weltkrieg', *Zeitschrift für Geschichtswissenschaft*, vol. 24 (1976); C. von Delbruck, *Die wirtschaftliche Mobilmachung in Deutschland, 1914* (Munich 1924), pp. 61–92; Reichsarchiv, *Kriegsrüstung*, vol. 2, nos. 80–2.

measure. Additional resources helped to enlarge the army and improve its equipment; this was taken in hand in 1913, rather late in the day. For many years a "war chest" (*Kriegsschutz*) of 120 million marks in gold (about £6 million) was kept at the Juliusturm at Spandau, a relic of older and simpler economic times.

V

In his study of war preparation, Burchardt castigates the officials, and especially the Ministry of the Interior, for their ineffectiveness.[28] How far is this justified?

Most studies postulated a short war, defined as one of from six to ten months. A long war would last for two years.[29] For the military to contemplate and even to prepare for a long war, i.e. for failure, would itself smack of defeatism. The possibility of failure has no place in the military mind.

In hindsight, of all the proposals, the ones for dietary reform and for an Economic General Staff had the greatest relevance: the need for a dietary shift and for some sort of organized management appear in some nebulous form in most of the pre-war studies, naval and military, official and academic. Indeed, the two were closely related, since working out the requisite changes in consumption would have been one of the tasks of the staff. The failure to do anything arose, first, from a lack of any sense of real urgency (the military, who wanted the war most avidly, were the most complacent about economic difficulties). The Ministry of Interior's commission was little more than a talking shop. To have given it a permanent staff and some teeth would have cut across entrenched peacetime attitudes and lines of authority. This mental block is revealing, because no such block held up purely *military* preparations—for call-up, invasion and mass bloodshed, much more drastic in their implications, but less disturbing to the bureaucratic mind.

Of all the proposals, stockpiling is the one that had the most immediate appeal. It is the failure to create any stockpiles that Burchardt implicitly regrets. But for all its intuitive attraction, stockpiling was not an appropriate policy. For a short war, stockpiling was unnecessary. For a long one, it was impossible.

Most of the pre-war studies of food supply accepted that the critical period of shortfall would be in the last months of the harvest year, i.e. approximately from May to July. They differed on the size of the shortfall, and on the means to cover it. Export prohibitions, dietary substitutions, belt-tightening, agricultural development, good railway management as

---

[28] Burchardt, *Friedenswirtschaft*, pp. 242–4.
[29] For an excellent study of the war-duration question, ibid., ch. 1.

well as local and national stockpiles were all canvassed to bridge this gap. Hardly anyone (Tirpitz is one exception) saw beyond the first year.

Now the experience of 1914–15 shows that the optimists were justified. Despite fears to the contrary, the German economy passed through the first year of war without any serious shortfalls, and even the second year of the war, although it already exposed serious weaknesses in the food-supply system, did not reduce the standard of nutrition to a critical level. So the fears of the warners about the economic dangers of a short war were as exaggerated as the hopes of the British blockade theorists. The main benefit of a two-million-ton stockpile of wheat, as Fröhlich suggested, would not have been the grain itself, but the new storage facilities. In Germany, grain was stored on the farm until it was called for by the market. This left the farmer with a choice of how to use it: the most serious problem of wartime food administration was the excessive feeding of bread grain to animals. With central storage facilities, the authorities could have removed grain from the farms at an earlier stage and controlled its disposition better.[30]

More ambitious plans were rarely discussed, and this for good technical and financial reasons. Unlike gold, food is a flow, not a stock. It has to be coaxed out of the soil over again every year. In the Edwardian world, year-end surpluses of grain were small: the world's wheat stocks on 1 August (i.e. approximately the amount carried over from year to year in the northern hemisphere) were always less than a quarter of annual consumption and sometimes as little as one-ninth. [31] The amounts of grain required to make good a serious shortfall were simply not available: large purchases would push up the price. Furthermore, food does not store very well. Grain has considerable volume and in western Europe it requires sheltered storage. This storage, whether in elevators or sheds, was very expensive. Moreover, given the structure of the German grain market, these granaries had no economic justification. To make a real dent in the food shortfall of the last two years of the war, the peacetime expenditure would have had to be enormous. An additional 100 grams of wheat flour per person per day for two years (about 160 calories) would have required a stockpile of about six million tons of wheat grain. This was about twice Germany's annual wheat imports and the cost for purchase and storage (assuming prices remained unchanged) would have been about 1,800 billion marks—about the same as the ordinary imperial budget, and more than a third of the existing national debt. Such quantities were not available at short notice. Six million tons were about twice the North American stocks at the end of the harvest year, and about half the world's carry-over. In financial terms,

[30] Chs. 1, 4 above.
[31] H. Farnsworth, '"World" Wheat Stocks, 1890–1914 and 1922–39', *Wheat Studies*, vol. 16 (1939–40), esp. chart 7, p. 56.

such an outlay was well beyond the bounds of practical politics. Moreover, it would have been regarded internationally as a belligerent gesture on a par with the Tirpitz plan (to which it would have been a coherent complement). Stocks could be built up gradually from year to year (indeed, given their size and the need for storage, they could hardly have been laid down otherwise).[32] But time was another commodity in short supply. War did not wait for the granaries, and broke out in 1914. On the face of it, then, any plan for grain storage on this scale was an absurdity.

In terms of German realities, a more practical approach was to shift the cost on to the states and municipalities, which had a larger tax base than the Empire, and to concentrate stockpiles in the large towns. Placing the cost on the towns was also a regressive form of finance more in tune with Conservative preferences. This approach was actually mooted and was actively under discussion in 1913–14, but it came to nothing.[33] Conceivably a few more years of discussion would have brought some form of limited stockpiling—but time ran out.

The British grain market provides an insight into Germany's problems: and also of the opportunities later presented for a war against seaborne commerce. Despite having to import some four-fifths of its bread grains, Britain held a domestic stockpile that sometimes (especially towards the end of the harvest year) fell below seven weeks' supply. By drawing on the staggered harvests of its different suppliers, on the American, Indian and Russian winter- and spring-wheat harvests in one half of the year, and on Australian and Argentinian harvests during the second half, Britain simply kept much of her stocks on the grainfields themselves. Three to seven weeks' supplies were afloat on merchant ships bound for Britain, which served, in effect, as floating warehouses. The North American bulk grain-system, with its grain cars, country and terminal elevators and large fresh-water grain carriers, arose in order to beat the ice on the Great Lakes, but it also created a very large storage capacity in country and terminal elevators, as well as the trading and hedging facilities for the orderly release of these stocks. They were easier to control than Germany's millions of farms. Few of these regulatory mechanisms were available to Germany in case of war.[34]

---

[32] At 200 marks per ton. This is based on estimates by Fröhlich and the Treasury of a cost of about 200 marks per ton, and 100 marks for storage. This excludes administration, maintenance, insurance, wastage, etc.: Fröhlich, 'Volksernährung', p. 78, and 'Denkschrift des Geheimen Finanzrats D. Meydenbauer für den Preussischen Finanzminister Dr. Lenze vom 23. April 1914', Reichsarchiv, *Kriegsrüstung*, vol. 2, no. 84, pp. 283–5. American and world stocks: Farnsworth, '"World" Wheat Stocks', table 1, p. 63. One plan for storing a whole year's food supply at the cost of 3.3 billion marks was submitted to the government in 1914; it received no response: Burchardt, *Friedenswirtschaft*, pp. 128, 153.

[33] For attempts to devolve stockpiling to local authorities: Burchardt, *Friedenswirtschaft*, p. 218.

[34] Food Supply. Royal Commission. Report, pp. 6–17; A. Millar, *Wheat and its Products* (1916), pp. 1–15.

Burchardt gets somewhat carried away in his appreciation of the warners.[35] They identified the problems correctly, but the purpose of their proposals was to sustain the war economy of an expansionary Germany, and their horizon was limited to the short war envisaged by the General Staff. It is no accident that they were mostly National Liberals, nationalists of the forward variety, who anticipated war and strove to alarm the authorities and pressure them into active preparation. With a less bellicose attitude, the warners might have stressed how difficult it was to prepare for war for a country in Germany's position, and the great economic advantages of keeping the peace.

<h1 style="text-align:center">VI</h1>

The last question to consider is how economics affected Germany's strategy in the First World War. Economic preparation, military security and diplomacy were all intertwined, to say nothing of those domestic social pressures which Kehr, Wehler and Berghahn have written about.

The first thing to point out is that the question of the German economy's preparedness for war was not merely a matter for subordinates and experts, but one which claimed the attention of leaders at the highest levels. Moltke, Tirpitz and Bethmann Hollweg all circulated documents over their signatures that pondered the implications of Germany's supply weaknesses. It is a factor they took into account.

In the past, some leaders had been able to see the full implications more clearly. The elder Moltke's prophecy of 1890 was often quoted: if a war broke out, neither its duration nor its end could be foreseen; none of the Great Powers could be defeated in one or two campaigns; the war could last seven years, it could last thirty. Likewise, Caprivi had considered the requirements of a long defensive war, and strove for self-sufficiency. A number of writers foresaw that a coming war might take the form of a prolonged defensive stalemate.[36]

A maverick course, that might have prevailed by default, was espoused by Admiral Tirpitz. The navy only had a tenuous relation with the army. The navy alone, whatever its pretensions, could never start a war. That was the view of the naval staff in 1909. If Britain initiated a war, Tirpitz saw no prospect of success at sea, and recommended shifting it to land, by means of an attack on France, 'if we do not want to end up in a position of dependency on our unweakened neighbours through economic exhaustion resulting from a long naval war'. The navy had no practical operational plans to counter a British blockade, its combat readiness was limited for a

---

[35] Burchardt, *Friedenswirtschaft*, pp. 130–1.
[36] Ibid., pp. 21–4; echoed by Bernhardi, *Next War*, p. 13.

good part of the year, and this remained true up to the outbreak of the war.[37]

The navy's target of effective parity with the Royal Navy was very distant, its project designed to last a generation or longer. So long as the programme was incomplete, there was no question of war; indeed, there was no necessity for it even then. In Tirpitz's scheme, war was indefinitely postponed. He had nothing to gain and everything to lose. In consequence, the navy could make no contribution to the logistical problems of war: neither a short nor a prolonged one. It assumed that peace would prevail. In this respect, it had the most benign of the strategies contemplated by the German armed forces. It is curious that Burchardt should blame Tirpitz for the blockade danger, as if Germany without a navy or with only a small one (but still a great continental power) could remain immune to blockade.[38]

But the dominant strategy was different. It was foreshadowed in the writings of Clausewitz and in Bismarck's brilliant campaigns. From the 1890s onwards it was contained in the Schlieffen plan. For the military mind, seeking the most economic and rapid solution, this plan was attractive on military grounds alone.[39] Which is not to suggest it *was* a good plan; it manifestly led to disaster. If we assume that in July 1914 Germany could hope for a better October 1918 than she actually experienced, some other strategy would have been more appropriate. This is where economic factors come in. For those factors appeared to foreclose any other options.

A clear expression of this constraint comes in Schlieffen's own essay, 'War in the Present'. The army of millions, he says, cannot hold the field for long because it cost billions to support. No economy could sustain modern armies for any length of time. Like the British Admiralty at almost exactly the same time, Schlieffen foresaw domestic collapse if the war was protracted. Whatever his preference on other grounds, a rapid decision was the only choice on economic ones.[40]

In its effect, the Schlieffen plan was a strategic solution for an economic problem or, to be more precise, for an economic and a logistic problem. This applies not only to its governing principle, the need to obtain a rapid decision, but also to its operational details, which expressed economic and technological constraints. The most important constraints it addressed were (*a*) the staying power of the economy, (*b*) the massive firepower of defensive positions, and (*c*) the large manpower available to both sides. Firepower had become so intense that troops had to be dispersed much more thinly for their protection. Their massive numbers therefore allowed them to occupy very long fronts. A battlefield saturated with firepower,

[37] Lambi, *The Navy*, pp. 351, 383–4.
[38] Burchardt, *Friedenswirtschaft*, p. 73.
[39] Van Evera, 'The Cult of the Offensive'.
[40] A. von Schlieffen, 'Der Krieg in der Gegenwart', *Deutsche Revue*, vol. 34 (1909), p. 19.

and with manpower deployed in enormous breadth, offered little or no prospect of success for a frontal attack, and few opportunities for manœuvre. All this is clearly expressed in his essay of 1909. In order to escape these constraints. Schieffen designed the deep flanking movement through Belgium.

Outflanking the enemy front carried its own costs. Speed and precision were only achieved at the cost of inflexibility in command. Every step had to be laid down in advance and the plan had to be followed with unwavering fidelity. Once in motion it became a runaway steamroller, beyond the control of statesmen and soldiers. The field commanders were largely left to their own devices. Furthermore, the plan carried a heavy political cost of violating the peace and invading neutral Belgium. The onus of starting the war proved a tremendous liability.

But while sacrificing so much to evade the central economic constraints inherent in Germany's geopolitical position, the General Staff neglected others, and these other constraints proved fatal to its success. These constraints were mobility, communications and logistics.

Once beyond their own railheads, the mass armies slowed down to a foot-slogging pace while the opposing enemy, operating on internal lines, could move its own reserves into position more rapidly by rail. It gave the defence an advantage of mobility over the attack and, at the end, absorbed all offensives on the western front, and indeed on other fronts as well. It was fundamental to the technology of the time, and its disregard by Schieffen was a deep flaw in his concept, which (given the balance of forces) doomed it to failure, or at least made it a very risky enterprise. The second difficulty was the closely related one of logistics: a mass army marching beyond its railheads was very difficult to supply and this also acted to slow down and exhaust the flanking movement. The third problem was of control: once the forces had advanced beyond the rigid telegraph system (itself of low capacity and a cumbersome means of communication), they could no longer be commanded from a single centre. The attacking generals had insufficient information to respond to changing circumstances, while the defence, with its communications intact, maintained its flexibility. That also reduced the chances of a precise and surgical flanking movement.[41]

The technical conditions for overcoming these limitations were already germinating. Motorized transport, wireless communication, aerial reconnaissance were all in being, and in a few more years they restored mobility and control to the battlefield. As in economic preparations for war, the best strategy was the passive one of waiting.

If economics had an effect on the generals, it was through an incorrect,

[41] These points are convincingly argued in M. van Creveld's books, *Supplying War* (Cambridge 1977), ch. 4, and *Command in War* (Cambridge, Mass. 1985).

indeed almost perverse, reading of economic trends. On the one hand, the country's surge of growth in the late-Victorian period instilled confidence in the military leaders. On the other, it seemed to have imbued them with neo-mercantilist pessimism. Germany's economic performance was way ahead of its European rivals, and it had the resources in raw materials, innovation, enterprise and skill to continue its economic rise. And yet the generals refused to extrapolate this trend, but perversely anticipated its reversal. They firmly believed that time was working against Germany, not only politically, but also economically. 'Are we willing to recoil before the hostile forces, and sink step by step lower in our economic, political, and national importance?' asked General von Bernhardi in 1912?[42]

The sharp brains and proud personalities of the General Staff could not admit inaction as a possibility. For one thing, the clear economic difficulties of a passive defensive war seemed to rule it out. Furthermore, the necessary restraint on foreign policy was out of tune with the national mood in Germany at the time. Economics suggested inaction, but the leaders felt an imperative to act. That imperative itself cannot be seen as economic. But the channel it chose was determined by economic, technological and social constraints. The Schlieffen plan may be regarded (like the French ideology of attack and Joffre's Lorraine offensive of August 1914) as a wilful rejection of material constraints, in line with the belief, embraced by soldiers of all nations, in the dominance of the moral over the material—but a rejection nevertheless shaped by these very constraints. In brief, it showed the limitations of intuitive reasoning: unwillingness to revise preconceptions, the application of inappropriate doctrine and exaggerated self-confidence.

As the official German historians of the war put it at the end of a section on economics and demography, 'all competent authorities, also the economic ones, took the view that in the case of war the decision must be sought as quickly as possible. On economic grounds as well it was necessary to do everything to achieve a quick victory.'[43] Moltke was sufficiently impressed by the dangers of blockade to modify the Schlieffen plan to avoid a violation of Dutch territory in order to leave Holland as a "windpipe" for the supply of Germany.[44]

Many writers have pointed out the importance of the "short-war fallacy" in German plans, the gamble on a quick decision. But the deepest flaw in German military thinking was the limit of its geographical horizon. This was also a typical failure of intuitive reasoning: the preference for data that were close at hand. Unlike the navy, the army never grasped the significance of international economic specialization, and how it exposed

---

[42] Bernhardi, *Next War*, p. 104; Schlieffen, 'Krieg', p. 24.
[43] Reichsarchiv, *Der Weltkrieg*, vol. 1, p. 46.
[44] Ritter, *Sword and Scepter*, vol. 2, pp. 152, 218.

Germany to a world system that lay beyond its control. The military horizon was essentially European, and thus failed to perceive the forces that would eventually bring Germany down. In his revealing essay of 1909, Count Schlieffen lists all of Germany's enemies, encircling it with a "Chinese Wall" of fortifications. His only reference to overseas is the expectation that unrest in the British Empire would *draw off* the British Army and prevent it from intervening in Europe. It did not occur to him that the Empire could actually *reinforce* the metropolis. Likewise, in his chapter on the allied order of battle, Bernhardi dismissed the forces of the self-governing colonies as ineffective militias, and made no mention at all of those of the United States. Where he referred to the United States, he did so in the misguided belief that the United States had an irreconcilable economic and political conflict with the United Kingdom, and would not permit Britain to put down Germany.[45] This mental closure drove Germany into disaster three times running, in 1914, in 1917 and again in 1941. Transatlantic (and Pacific) economic and political power simply lay below the German mental horizons. That is also shown in the lack of interest in the strategic and tactical lessons of the American civil war, that more than any other (together with the Russo-Japanese war) formed the operational precedent to the First World War.[46]

VII

'What . . . is the real deterrent to Germany from attacking France, when she knows that England is behind the latter country,' asked Hankey in 1911. 'Is it the fear of four or six divisions of British troops, or is it the consciousness that the commercial prosperity which Germany has built up since 1870, and on which she has concentrated every effort, will be shattered? Surely the latter!'[47] But the deterrent failed to work. It is worth asking why.

The German game plan for 1914, as it unfolded after the murder in Sarajevo, entailed some very high risks: the risk that diplomacy would embroil Germany in war; and the risk that war, if it came, would have an adverse outcome. If the gamble turned out badly, the losses could be as massive as they actually turned out to be. This is where we take leave of conventional rationality. Rationality (e.g. in economics) has room for risk-taking, but hardly for risks on such a scale. Even Russian roulette is safer than deliberately entering a war with powers of equal or superior resources to one's own. A one-half probability of failure (surely it was no lower than that) is not a risk upon which any rational person would choose to wager

---

[45] Schlieffen, 'Krieg', p. 23; Bernhardi, *Next War*, pp. 99–100, 135.

[46] Burchardt, *Friedenswirtschaft*, pp. 30–7.

[47] M. Hankey, 'The Case against Sending the Expeditionary Force to France' (Nov. 1911), fo. 8, HP 7/3, fo. 20.

such colossal stakes. Yet the leaders of Germany placed the fate of their political system and the property, livelihoods and lives of millions of their countrymen on a bet of this magnitude. Not only that, they continued to do so repeatedly during the war: in starting the battle of Verdun in 1916, the unrestricted submarine campaign of 1917 and the spring offensives of 1918. How can such action be explained?

Certainly not in economic terms: they chose to fly in the face of economics, and economics, in the widest sense, brought them down—as the blockade strategists in Britain had predicted. General Bernhardi's *Germany and the Next War* provides an insight into the military mind on the eve of the war. He affected to despise economic motives and, in passing, the United States of America and its "plutocratic" values. The leaders of the American peace movement, he wrote,

appear to believe that public opinion must represent the view which the American plutocrats think most profitable to themselves. They have no notion that the widening development of mankind has quite other concerns than material prosperity, commerce and money-making.

A few pages later the General gives vent to the mystical and fatalistic dimension. Action is not to be judged by its consequences, but by the intentions that drive it.

For the moral justification of the political decision we must not look to its possible consequences, but to its aim and its motives, to the conditions assumed by the agent, and to the trustworthiness, honour, and sincerity of the considerations which led to action.

In another passage he wrote, 'Even defeat may bear a rich harvest.'

It is impossible to conclude this section without some speculation on the cast of mind that made this possible. The most striking feature about it is a fundamental incompetence: an unworthiness to manage the affairs of a great nation. This incompetence radiated from the very top downwards, and should provide a warning about the fitness of any group of persons, however capable, for handling the means of mass destruction. On 30 March 1911 Bethmann Hollweg spoke in the Reichstag, explaining his restraint in Morocco in terms of Bismarck's sagacious admonition, that,

Even victorious wars can only be justified when they are forced upon a nation, and we cannot see the cards held by Providence so closely as to anticipate the historical development by personal calculation.

Bernhardi quotes these words, but follows them with another epigram from Bismarck: 'Men Make History.' It was not calculation that finally drove the German leaders, but a reckless, fatalistic abandon.[48]

[48] Bernhardi, *Next War*, pp. 33, 40, 28, 38–40.

The passive defensive strategy had been ruled out. As we have seen, this option seemed to be expensive. This was visible to the leadership. For them, war was an *economizing* force, that would avert the need for massive stockpiling.

Nevertheless, in moments, hours and days of sobriety, the leaders could not ignore the possibility of losing. Moltke, on whose shoulders the responsibility lay, was especially prone to doubt, and indeed he collapsed at the same time as his strategy. He had no inner mental resources for the possibility of failure. As an intuitive reasoner, he blocked out the warning signals and refused to draw implications. He lacked the courage of his convictions and the ability to follow them to their logical conclusion. That is shown in his memorandum of May 1914.[49] Soldiers are trained and expected to take high risks, to lay their very life on the line. The requirements from the strategist and the statesman are quite different; self-immolation should not enter their range of possibilities. But Moltke failed to make the transition. Instead, he bridged the difference between his values and his responsibilities with a paralysing fatalism.

Finally, there is a glimmer of rationality even in this disastrous gamble. What seems hopelessly irrational for the nation, may still appear otherwise to the individual. If the decision had turned out well, the payout, in terms of reputation and reward, was bound to be great. Failure, even the worst possible case, would cost no more than position and prestige. Unlike the millions they consigned to suffering and death, their own lives and property (as actually turned out to be the case) were secure. It is one of the achievements of the Second World War that this outcome was not allowed to recur.

---

[49] Moltke to Clemens von Delbrück (Minister of the Interior), 14 May 1914, Reichsarchiv, *Kriegsrüstung*, vol. 2, no. 85, pp. 287–91.

24

'A SECOND DECISION FOR WAR': THE U-BOAT CAMPAIGN

THE decision to begin unrestricted submarine warfare on 1 February 1917 was Germany's most critical action during the course of the war. On the eve of the Russian revolution and of Britain's impending bankruptcy, it fortified the Allied side with all the wealth and power of the United States. In its consequences for Germany, it was rightly likened by the German Chancellor to 'a second decision for war'.[1] In the deliberations of July 1914 economic considerations had entered the calculations, but they were buried in the background. In 1916 economic considerations were no longer marginal: economic warfare was the decisive strategy. How did the Germans come to choose it?

I

Britain announced war zones in the Channel and North Sea in October and November 1914, and declared that large areas would be mined. While the German naval command pondered the situation, its U-boats sunk about ten British merchant ships between October and the end of January 1915. In November 1914 Tirpitz told an American journalist that Germany possessed the means to intercept the bulk of Britain's food imports. The German Press picked up this hint, and began to agitate for deploying the new weapon. Businessmen and academics also pressed the navy to use the submarine. Britain, two professors wrote, 'with brutal frankness, has established the starvation of our population as a war aim'. If German reprisals were going to violate international law, Britain had set the precedent. These thoughts, addressed to the commander of the fleet, were endorsed by some of the most distinguished professors at the University of Berlin. The scholars pointed out how much Britain depended on imports, and recommended a combined air and undersea attack, with U-boats to destroy shipping and Zeppelins to attack food warehouses in the ports. Among the signatures on this document were those of two leading

---

[1] K. Jarausch, *The Enigmatic Chancellor: Bethmann Hollweg and the Hubris of Imperial Germany* (New Haven 1973), p. 281. Britain was no longer able to finance its purchases in North America: K. Burk, 'The Mobilization of Anglo-American Finance during World War I', in N. F. Dreisziger (ed.), *Mobilization for Total War: The Canadian, American and British Experience, 1914–18, 1939–1945* (Waterloo, Ontario 1981), p. 36.

economists, Max Sering and Gustav von Schmoller. Professor Sering was certain that Britain would comply within a few weeks.[2]

In addition to international law (and the fear of American reactions), another German inhibition was the small number of boats. Submarines had a short range and limited endurance. At the end of January 1915 only twenty-one boats were available, eight of them obsolete. Raw numbers do not signify a great deal, since there were different classes of boats, with different capabilities, and all of them required long periods of maintenance in port. This was not sufficiently appreciated by the naval command.[3] The first submarine campaign of February 1915 began as a tactical rather than a strategic venture. Britain's trade was the target, but the economic effect was not worked out. The sinkings began as a reprisal against the blockade and as an experiment in the use of a new weapon. The success of the U-boats and the sinking of the *Lusitania* in May 1915 revealed their potential power and also the risks that their actions courted.

In Department B1 of the Admiralty staff, reserve Lieutenant Dr Richard Fuss (a bank manager in peacetime) began to collect data on British trade in March 1915. A second expert, whose role eventually came to match the one played by Fuss, was Dr Hermann Levy, a professor of economics at Heidelberg. Levy's modest reputation was based on a series of publications in the German tradition of historical economics: he wrote about the development of economic institutions and had no aptitude for quantitative or analytical work. Levy published a great deal; one of his works was a book on English agriculture. His energy also found an outlet in a number of novels, published under his own name and an assumed one. One of Levy's monographs was translated into English before the war, but that should not be taken as a measure of his authority. His study of English landownership was unfocused, lacking in rigour, thin on data and dubious in its judgements.[4]

Levy began his war work at the Imperial Grain Office, and edited a digest of economic news for the Admiralty. In January 1915 he wrote a short paper for the Admiralty which focused on Britain's policy of economic specialization. Using data from the British Royal Commission on Food Supply of 1905, he cited the high level of imports and the low level of stocks. England, for commercial reasons, preferred to supply itself 'from

[2] A collection of documents is in A. Spindler, *Der Handelskrieg mit U-Booten* (Berlin 1932), vol. 1, pp. 177 ff., in the series *Der Krieg zur See, 1914–1918*, ed. by the Marine-Archiv. The professors' memorandum is from 26 Jan. 1915 (doc. 24, ibid., pp. 234–42, quote on p. 241; 'a few weeks', p. 234). Also A. Spindler, *Wie es zu dem Entschluss zum uneingeschränkten U-Boots-Krieg 1917 gekommen ist* (Göttingen 1960), pp. 1–14; Ritter, *Sword and Scepter*, vol. 3, pp. 124–5; B. Stegemann, *Die Deutsche Marinepolitik, 1916–1918* (Berlin 1970), pp. 23–4.

[3] Spindler, *Wie es zum Entschluss*, pp. 5–7.

[4] As I found when I consulted it for my book on English landownership; H. Levy, *Large and Small Holdings: A Study of English Agricultural Economics* (1911). Levy's literary *nom de plume* was Hermann Lint.

hand to mouth'. In consequence, prices were already rising to record heights. A shortage of raw materials would also affect British manufacturing industry and give rise to unemployment; the English working classes would be badly affected.[5] In August 1915 he wrote another paper for the Admiralty staff, which examined the prospects of economic warfare against British trade. Levy divided the consequences into three: first, the direct effect of sinkings on reduction of tonnage, rise of prices, shortage of goods, contraction of trade, etc.; secondly, the indirect effects of disrupting the flow of trade, clogging up harbours, raising insurance and so on; and, thirdly, the impact on more vulnerable sectors of the economy.

In its quest to transform its U-boats into strategic weapons, the navy faced a problem: how to deliver a decisive blow with limited means. If the navy was to have a decisive impact on the war, it needed a sector that was both vital to the economy and exposed to attack. Levy found that sector: it was England's supply of wheat. Grain prices in Britain were already much higher than in Germany, proof of difficulties in sustaining the flow of imports. Here was a target small enough for the submarines to destroy, and yet critical for Britain's survival. By choosing a period when British stocks were low, the target could be made smaller still.[6]

Levy's views formed the core of economic reasoning that supported the submarine campaign. A more developed version of his ideas appeared in a published pamphlet.[7] As a writer on English agriculture, Levy was familiar with the decline of Britain's grain production and its reliance on wheat. Levy took his ideas directly out of the work of the Royal Commission on Food Supply of 1903–5, and indirectly from Captain Stewart Murray, who had brought that Commission into being.[8]

According to Levy, what made the British bread supply open to successful attack was the system of staggered importation of grain from all over the world. In Germany and other large grain producers, domestic stocks lasted for most of the year. Britain relied on an "uninterrupted stream" of grain, and did not hold much of it in storage. At their highest, stocks rose to seventeen weeks' supply; at their lowest, they would last only six and a half weeks.

The Royal Commission on Food Supply also provided Levy with a mechanism that converted grain shortage into political collapse. He quoted

---

[5] 'Ausarbeitung des Heidelberger Nationalökonomen Professors Dr. Levy für den Admiralstab über die wirtschaftliche lage Englands im Falle der Blockade' (10 Jan. 1915), in Spindler, *Handelskrieg*, doc. 19, pp. 225–8.

[6] Prof. Dr H. Levy, 'Wirtschaftliche Strategie in U-Bootkrieg' (19 Aug. 1915) [2 different copies], from microfilm of German naval archives (currently at Freiburg im Breisgau), USNA, Admiralstab, roll T1022/905 PG/75952, vol. 20.

[7] H. Levy, *Die neue Kontinentalsperre. Ist Grossbritannien wirtschaftlich bedroht?* (Berlin 1915).

[8] Ch. 15 above. Levy, with typical carelessness, repeatedly described it as a parliamentary committee.

a passage from the Commission's report: if wheat imports were cut off when domestic stocks were already exhausted, there would be a rise in prices, a dangerous panic, and a shortage so serious that the war could not be carried on. German Admiralty staff files contain a printed flow chart (from August 1915) which describes twenty-five different ways in which the U-Boat war would raise costs within the British economy. Its conception is reminiscent of the Campbell project of defeating Germany by means of bankruptcy. Levy also had a notion of the direct and indirect linkages of blockade, but for him the rising price of corn and meat was to be the crux. He expected this mechanism to drive Britain into defeat.[9]

On 30 August 1915 the Admiralty staff printed a memorandum which advocated just that: a submarine campaign not for limited objectives, but for a decisive one: to force Britain to sue for peace by means of economic warfare. To secure such a prize, submarines should disregard international law and sink without warning, even at the cost of bringing the United States into the war.[10]

II

August 1915 marks the start of the Admiralty staff's effort to promote economic warfare as a strategy to win the war. The case is expounded in full in the chief of the Admiralty staff's memorandum of 12 February 1916. This pamphlet of thirty-eight pages was circulated in more than five hundred copies in naval and military circles, and launched the "battle of memoranda" which continued until the end of the year. The papers were prepared by Dr Fuss, who was joined by Levy in July and was advised by the grain merchants Weil and Newman and by other experts from business, finance and agriculture. The sequence of naval papers (one in July, another in August) culminated in the chief of the Admiralty staff's memorandum of 22 December 1916. The case for economic warfare as a decisive weapon is best considered in this long tract, which crowned about sixteen months' work.[11]

The Admiralty's strategic problem was to identify a target that was critical, and also capable of destruction before the United States could place its full weight on the Allied side. The paper of 22 December identified two such targets: the British wheat supply and the merchant tonnage that carried it.

[9] 'Der U-Bootkrieg und die englische Volkswirtschaft (in graphischer Darstellung)', p. 3 (printed. Aug. 1915), USNA, Admiralstab, T1022/905 PG/75952, vol. 20; Campbell: chs. 14, 15 above; Levy, *Kontinentalsperre*, pp. 6, 38.

[10] Memorandum on economic warfare [untitled] (30 Aug. 1915), USNA, Admiralstab T1022/905 PG/75931.

[11] An account of the department's work: Stegemann, *Marinepolitik*, pp. 51–64. Some of the papers are printed in *Beilagen, Aktenstücke*; others (including the 12 Feb. 1916 memorandum), may be found in USNA, Admiralstab, T1022/905. I have not seen the originals in Freiburg.

One constraint on the project was the capacity of Germany's submarines to sink merchant ships. In the first few months of 1916 sinkings amounted to some 200,000 tons of shipping a month, and were still at this level in August. But in October and November they rose to 400,000 tons. These results were achieved with so-called "cruiser" warfare, which required the submarines to approach merchant vessels on the surface and allow their crews to lower the lifeboats. The Admiralty staff promised that, if restrictions were lifted, a monthly sinking rate of 600,000 tons could be achieved, coming down to 500,000 tons as the traffic became thinner. An oft-repeated figure was four million tons in six months, or 667,000 tons a month. The actual sinkings for the first six months of the unrestricted submarine campaign almost matched this forecast and reached an average of 643,000 tons.[12]

Unrestricted submarine warfare could raise the kill by 50 per cent;[13] but it introduced a time constraint. This question of time (the *Terminfrage* as it later became) arose out of several factors, some of them perhaps not entirely conscious to the planners. Few soldiers or statesmen in Germany had any doubt that unrestricted submarine warfare would bring the United States into the war. The U-boats had to finish their work before American intervention became decisive. That is why there was no room for half-measures. The navy had to promise victory, because, if it failed, the outcome was certain defeat.

When the proposal was put by the navy to the army in January 1916, the time scale for victory was given as two months. A few days later the time had risen to four months. In the navy's paper of 12 February 1916 it was six months. Thereafter, the figure fluctuated: six to eight months, then five months, four, and in December 1916 five to seven months.[14] This suggests that the time constraint was not entirely derived from economic calculations, but was a prior constraint on the plan.

There was a feeling that time was working against Germany. A note of desperation recurs in the battle of notes and memoranda. Up to August 1916 the argument was that Germany's allies, and possibly also the German people, could not survive another winter of war. In December 1916 it was the prospect of another *year* of war which could no longer be

[12] 'England und der U-Boot-Krieg', Lecture of Lt. d.L. Dr Richard Fuss, read on 31 Mar. 1917 at the Industry Club in Düsseldorf (printed, Berlin 1917), pp. 11–12, USNA, Admiralstab, T1022/905 PG/75931, vol. 1; Stegemann, *Marinepolitik*, p. 58; Holtzendorff memorandum of 22 Dec. 1916, *Beilagen, Aktenstücke*, p. 247; tonnage sunk Feb.–July 1917: M. Olson, Jr., *The Economics of the Wartime Shortage* (Durham, North Carolina 1963), p. 83.

[13] There is a little puzzle here: although unrestricted sinkings were meant to be 50 per cent higher, the navy asserted that they would be twice as effective. See the Admiralty memorandum of 22 Dec. 1916, *Beilagen, Aktenstücke*, pp. 240, 278.

[14] These estimates may all be found in *Beilagen, Aktenstücke*, pp. 143, 146, 165, 177, 204, 264.

faced. In a war of attrition an already exhausted Germany was bound to lose, because it had fewer resources. Both the Admiralty staff and the army High Command declared that submarine warfare was a desperate measure, the last remaining chance to snatch victory out of the jaws of defeat.[15]

Wheat was almost the sole ingredient of bread in Britain, and some 80 per cent was imported. Furthermore, the quantities imported (about six million tons a year) corresponded quite closely with the U-boats' sinking capacity. In the summer of 1916 a new factor emerged. Professor Levy reported that overseas harvests were poor.[16] North America, which had provided 90 per cent of British imports in 1915, would not have a surplus for export, and Britain would have to look to India, to South America and especially to Australia for the rest. A ton of shipping could carry five tons of grain from North America, but only half that amount from the southern hemisphere or India. It would take double the tonnage to import the same amount of grain, thus employing a much higher proportion of the merchant fleet. Out of this estimate there came a curious calculation, that every 100,000 tons of shipping destroyed signified a deficit of 240,000 tons of grain, or twelve days of English consumption. Curious, because not all shipping carried grain; because some grain would still come from North America; and because other things (e.g. counter-measures) would not remain equal. Even under the best possible assumptions the figures did not add up. It is difficult to pin down a single statement of the tonnage required to ship the grain, but one that comes closest puts it at 1.4 million tons, i.e. about one-seventh of the tonnage available to Britain for civilian purposes (including neutral ships).[17] Other cargoes were also vital: fats, pit-prop timber and ores from Spain and Scandinavia. The poor harvest overseas seemed to determine the critical period. Working backwards from the beginning of the new harvest in August, the campaign would have to begin no later than 1 February 1917.[18]

The cargo space available to Britain was a far more unwieldy target. It was estimated in December 1916 at some twenty million tons, about five times the six-month sinking capacity of the U-boats. So the primary task of Department B1 was to show how, by sinking some four million tons, a critical situation could be created, so difficult that Britain would be forced to sue for peace.

One step, as we have seen, was to inflate the tonnage required for carrying grain, by assuming supply from more distant producers. The second move was to lower the estimate of tonnage available to the allies, in

[15] Ibid., pp. 146, 155, 177, 241–2, 284–7.
[16] Stegemann, *Marinepolitik*, p. 56.
[17] Memorandum of 22 Dec. 1916, *Beilagen, Aktenstücke*, pp. 248–53, 261–2.
[18] Ibid., pp. 239–41, 264.

order to make it a more plausible target. In broad outline it was done this way. Out of twenty million tons of shipping available, some eight were committed to the supply and transport of troops and their equipment. Another four million were refitting, or carried the imports of Britain's Allies, or engaged in coastal shipping. That left some eight million tons of shipping.[19] Of three million tons of neutral shipping, 40 per cent would be scared away. Altogether the monthly traffic to England was 6.14 million tons. After six months of submarine warfare this trade would be cut by 39 per cent.[20] If 40 per cent of effective shipping capacity was sunk in six months, the paper implied, the grain supply would be cut in the same proportion. The rise in prices, and then the actual shortages of bread, would create such panic and outcry that Britain would not be able to continue the war. In its memorandum, the Admiralty staff stressed that compliance with international law should be suspended in order to bring about the terror and panic which were necessary for success.[21]

A good part of the December paper demonstrated that the process of collapse was already in progress: freight, insurance and commodity prices had risen enormously, with bread prices much higher than in Germany. Labour unrest was already spreading, together with anti-war agitation, demonstrations and other symptoms of panic.[22]

Another part dealt with possible British counter-measures and adaptations. For ships to sail in convoy would not provide a practical solution, since convoys took time to assemble, sailed at the speed of the slowest, and would also present a large target to submarines. Their irregular arrival would congest the harbours and the railways. It would not be easy to release ships from military duties or Allied support. The English lacked the aptitude to organize an efficient system of rationing and the fortitude to endure shortages. Some captured German ships might be pressed into service, but these would be more than offset by the desertion of the Dutch and Danish neutrals. American intervention could not make a critical difference within the time-span projected. American financial support could not increase the flow of goods to the Allies, who already used the whole of the United States' capacity. Time was too short for the United States to raise, train and dispatch a significant number of troops, whose quality was dubious anyway.[23]

From the very start, the naval programme encountered strong resistance, most effectively from the Chancellor Bethmann Hollweg and the Interior Minister Helfferich. Between them, they attacked its more obvious fallacies. What this came to, was a rejection of the Admiralty's time limit: of the idea that the war could be ended with a decisive blow in

---

[19] *Beilagen, Aktenstücke*, pp. 264–7.
[21] Ibid., pp. 278–9.
[23] Ibid., 275–6, 266–76, 279–83.
[20] Ibid., pp. 273–4.
[22] Ibid., 254–7.

the space of a few months. Indeed, Bethmann Hollweg regarded war weariness (on both sides) as the only chance of a peace settlement, and was certain that American entry would stiffen the Allies and make such a peace impossible.

England would be able to adapt. New construction and captured enemy tonnage would augment the fleet; naval counter-measures would reduce the sinkings; shipping would be shifted from military to civilian requirements—the "sideshow" expedition to Saloniki might be recalled. Rationing and other organizational measures would effect economies. As blockade could never be total, and the essential grain cargoes were quite small, it was not possible to starve Britain out. England had eighteen million tons of shipping. Who believed that it could no longer fight with fourteen million?[24]

In August 1916 Helfferich pointed out that Germany stood to lose a substantial overseas trade, which was vital to provision the army, the occupied territories (by means of the American relief commission) and the large towns. Furthermore, the tonnage figures were incorrect. With twelve million tons available for trade, the loss even of one-third would not compel England to surrender.[25]

Both the Chancellor and the Minister of the Interior warned very strongly of ignoring American political, financial, productive and military potential. German envoys in the United States agreed. The statesmen viewed the project as a dangerous gamble. Even within the navy the calculations were viewed with suspicion, and an army study produced a more pessimistic forecast.[26] Helfferich even argued (as proved to be the case) that the campaign would actually increase British food supplies. An allied United States would make sacrifices to provide for Britain that she would not make as a neutral.[27]

Other fallacies eluded the critics. The key to these errors is found in a phrase in the December 1916 memorandum. Admiral Holtzendorff, the chief of the Admiralty staff, wrote, 'The economy of a country resembles a masterpiece of precision mechanics; once it falls into disorder, interference, frictions and breakages continue incessantly.'[28]

A less appropriate metaphor is difficult to imagine. The war economy resembles a self-repairing organism and not a machine. Fuss and Levy simply assumed that very little could be done to counter the submarines. They made the most favourable assumptions, and refused to consider

---

[24] *Beilagen, Aktenstücke*, Bethmann Hollweg, docs. 149, 150, 152 (29 Feb., 5 Mar., 13 Mar. 1916).

[25] Ibid., docs. 157 (31 Aug.), 167 (6 Oct. 1916).

[26] Ibid.; also Stegemann, *Marinepolitik*, pp. 57, 74; L. Simon, 'Die Fiktion des Frachtraummangels' (1 Sept. 1916), USNA, Admiralstab, T1022/1019 PG/76094.

[27] *Beilagen, Aktenstücke*, p. 228.

[28] Ibid., p. 245.

British adaptations. They did not have the tools, the understanding, nor, probably, the will to undertake an analysis that took into account the British responses and adaptations. Their form of argument was essentially anecdotal and historical. For evidence of an economic crisis in Britain they used parliamentary speeches, newspaper cuttings and selected official statistics. Instead of probing the possible causes of price inflation, they simply took rising prices as evidence of material shortages, without ever considering the effect of monetary expansion and full employment of both labour and plant. There was no attempt to calculate real wages. Their blockade economics were intuitive, and show no grasp of how the price mechanism enables an economy to substitute commodities and factors for each other. Mancur Olson has described these adaptations concisely and well: as prices change, the economy adapts by substitutions among its inputs and output. Home production, which had not been profitable before, now became viable. As freights rose, many commodities could not be carried economically, thus freeing tonnage for other commodities—and so on.[29]

The largest single constraint was not the submarine, but congestion at the ports and on the railways. Decisive action could—and did—clear much of it away.[30] German blockade economics manifested the same lack of empathy with the price mechanism as did the rationing efforts within Germany; which in their turn had exacerbated the domestic food crisis.[31] The 1 February deadline was also misguided, since the six-month period ended with the English harvest and the prospect of the new harvest was likely to stiffen resistance. Other things being equal, an earlier date would have been a better time to begin.

Incidentally, this episode also throws a light on Britain's censorship policy. German planning depended on the statistics published in Britain, on parliamentary statements and on comments in the Press. Without this source of information the whole project would have drifted even further into the dark. The British authorities would have done better to keep their data under lock and key. That is what the Germans did, and it is difficult to establish the performance of their wartime economy even today.

The shortcomings of Levy and Fuss underline once again the desperate need for a competent "Economic General Staff" with conceptual and practical capacity to handle a problem of this kind. Once again it demonstrates the unsatisfactory nature of strategic–economic planning carried out by captive economists in military back rooms.

[29] Olson, *Wartime Shortage*, ch. 4.
[30] See M. Doughty, *Merchant Shipping and War: A Study in Defence Planning in Twentieth-century Britain* (1982), ch. 1.
[31] Ch. 4 above.

III

On the face of it, the decision to begin unrestricted submarine warfare was an economic one: it took the form of a rudimentary analysis of costs and benefits. The outcome was failure. With so much uncertainty, and with an intense personal commitment to the outcome, the economists and their masters were both walking into the pitfalls of "intuitive reasoning".[32]

One of the primary features of intuitive reasoning is the excessive confidence people have in their own prospects and judgement. Military men are especially prone to this kind of delusion. With egos already inflated by deference and flattery, where bluster is the norm, it is easy for soldiers to lose their sense of reality. Thus in February 1915, with only twenty-one submarines, the chief of the Admiralty staff Admiral Bachmann, after consulting with Tirpitz and his own officers, gave an assurance that Britain would come round within six weeks of opening the campaign if all restrictions were removed.[33]

The "theory" for the campaign came out of the work of the Royal Commission on Food Supply, as modified by the new capabilities of the U-boats. The German Admiralty went through the motions of normative reasoning: it took advice from experts, and collected statistics to build up its case. But the "experts" were actually selected for their bias. In the face of powerful objections, the Admiralty demonstrated a typical failing of intuitive reasoning. It clung to its preconceptions. The Admiralty had caught a glimpse of economic victory early in the war, and was extremely reluctant to give it up. Like scientists stuck in a "degenerating research programme", they could not be swayed by argument or evidence.[34] As "intuitive reasoners" Levy and Fuss blocked out evidence that would not fit the theory. The institutional paradigm of historical economics was unsuitable for the task of modelling the dynamic effects of blockade. But no elaborate analysis was required. After all, the civilian statesmen were able to present a counter-argument easily enough. It was not the method that was necessarily defective, but those who applied it. "Availability" was another pitfall not avoided—the preference for evidence that was close at hand simply because it was more readily available. America was far away, and its intervention in the war a remote prospect, so the admirals gave it insufficient weight in their reasoning. Pride was also implicated. Both the experts and the admirals had staked their egos on the submarine plan.

---

[32] Introduction, sec. III.

[33] W. Hubatsch, *Die Ära Tirpitz: Studien zur deutschen Marinepolitik, 1890–1918* (Berlin and Frankfurt 1955), pp. 129–30.

[34] The point is that scientists do not readily abandon a position even in the face of disconfirming evidence and more powerful theory: I. Lakatos, *The Methodology of Scientific Research Programmes* (Cambridge 1978), pp. 113, 116–17.

There was a strong undercurrent of impotent anger, a quest for an effective reprisal for the deepening material deprivation in Germany.

It is tempting to ascribe behaviour to dispositions rather than situations. But the admirals, and the generals who supported them, were not stupid. They were competent men at the top of their professions. Rather, they acted like typical intuitive reasoners, in seeking guidance from a doctrine they knew and understood. They preferred the familiar doctrine of military leadership to the alien one of economic analysis. Now the military code is appropriate in its own sphere, and it diverges from economic egotism for excellent reasons.[35] The commander of a destroyer or an infantry battalion must be prepared for sacrifice, even self-sacrifice, as part of a larger design. A naval or military officer is trained to run much greater risks, even with his own life, than those that are acceptable in peacetime. Action in war is surrounded by imponderables and, other things being equal, victory goes to the stronger will. Will-power and an unshakeable belief in ultimate victory are themselves weapons. A soldier is trained to go on fighting in the hope that something will turn up—and to accept fate if it does not. This often goes with a bias towards military action, whatever the nature of the problem: political, economic or diplomatic. This can become the worship of force for force's sake, and a fatalistic attitude to defeat. There was also a technical reason: English merchant ships were increasingly armed, and the "cruiser" tactics of surface approach were becoming more dangerous to the U-boats.

The officer's code is well-suited to the needs of military command. But, as intuitive reasoners, the German commanders applied it to problems that this code could not resolve. The proper frame of reference was a political and economic assessment of benefits and costs. Bethmann Hollweg was far from a model of normative thinking: his role in the war decisions of July and August 1914 shows that he was capable of making wild leaps in the dark. But in this case his reasoning was much more "rational". Not that he was any "softer" than his military protagonists. He simply had a clearer view of the balance of risks and opportunities. This comes out in his attitude to international law. Although he stressed the danger of breaking international law, he did not regard it as a matter of principle. Legal proprieties would not be a consideration if there was a prospect of success. What he would not support was a gamble.[36]

In the language of political science, the submarine campaign was an "expressive" and not an "instrumental" course of action. Action itself became the end. More was at stake for the soldiers than for civilians. War is a professional undertaking, and professional competence and pride were

[35] Brennan and Tullock, 'Economic Theory of Military Tactics'.

[36] Bethmann Hollweg's regret that a total blockade was impossible: *Beilagen, Aktenstücke*, doc. 152, p. 171; doc. 158, p. 182; gamble: ibid., doc. 149, p. 161.

implicated. The soldiers' self-perception as the élite of an expanding empire required territorial gains in the west. Bethmann Hollweg regarded these acquisitions in Belgium and France as desirable, but not vital.[37] Since naval inaction was bound to result in their loss anyway, the admirals and generals regarded a short, decisive campaign (with a chance of success) as the lesser evil. Their civilian supporters expressed this preference for action when they said, 'Rather war with America than starvation'.[38] After the war, Bethmann Hollweg explained why he did not resign:

To my mind, the technical point of the calculations with regard to economics could not of itself be conclusive. . . . To sit absolutely passive, staring into the future, and to endure that defeat in war which lay before us, according to the judgement of the military branch, and, at the same time, to have in one's hand an instrument of warfare which had not been tried out, and which, when all was said and done, held out certain prospects of success—well, we had to make use of this instrument; it was not to be avoided.[39]

As Ritter has written, the submarine campaign was a victory for the military over civilians. This priority was personified in the vulgar and often neurotic militarism of the Kaiser, the man who made the final decision. But both kinds of rationality, the military and the economic one, were functional and designed to optimize the use of resources. The problem of wartime leadership was to know, in a situation fraught with uncertainty and stress, which one to heed.

The submarine campaign falls into a pattern with other great decisions of the war: with August 1914, with Verdun (1916) and with Ludendorff's spring offensives in 1918. In all three cases Germany embarked on an offensive against overwhelming material odds, almost, it seems, for the sake of the struggle itself. It attempted to break a political impasse with a military gamble, with little regard for the odds. It pitched professional zeal and the intensity of desperation against superior material forces.

The dominance of this mindset was confirmed when the naval campaign failed to achieve its goals. Sinkings continued in 1918, although it was no longer clear what they could achieve. The success rate declined steeply. More than six million tons were sunk in 1917, and only two million in 1918. The Admiralty staff was even prepared to jeopardize the peace negotiations in October and November 1918 in order to continue the anti-shipping campaign. Naval fatalism was expressed in the High Seas Fleet's intention

---

[37] Jarausch, *Enigmatic Chancellor*, ch. 7.

[38] Ibid., p. 287.

[39] Evidence of Bethmann Hollweg, Verfassunggebende Deutsche Nationalversammlung, *Stenographischer Berichten über die offentlichen Verhandlungen des Untersuchungsausschusses* (Berlin, 1920), 5 Nov. 1919, pp. 294, 295; translation from Carnegie Endowment for International Peace, *Official German Documents Relating to the World War* (New York 1923), p. 472.

of sailing out for battle on the very point of Germany's collapse, in late-October 1918.[40]

IV

The U-boat captains did not disappoint. Sinkings matched the forecast in the first six months, and continued to be a serious drain on the British war economy until the very end of the war. In the spring of 1917 and several times later they gave British leaders a great deal of anxiety.[41] Adaptations and counter-measures saw Britain through. German naval planners failed to appreciate the decisive importance of American financial support for a Britain that was almost bankrupt. They underestimated British organizational capacity. Tonnage losses were not an appropriate measure of success. The real target was the grain supply, and here the U-boats never even remotely approached their target. At the end of November 1916 the British wheat stock stood at less than sixteen weeks' supply. In government hands there was only an eleven days' supply.[42] The food controller demanded a six months' reserve, and the Royal Commission on Wheat Supply (the official supply agency) took this requirement into account, and also allowed for a 10 per cent loss to the submarines. The average losses of the Commission up to August 1917 only amounted to 6 per cent.[43] This fell far short of the 40 per cent or so implied by German expectations. Only once, in March 1917, did the monthly losses exceed 10 per cent, and in 1918 they rose only once above 2 per cent.[44] During the "decisive" first six months of the campaign British grain reserves more than doubled. By giving grain cargoes higher priority, government and millers' stocks (excluding bakers' and retailers') increased from five and a half weeks' supply at the end of March to fourteen weeks' supply at the end of July.[45]

The decision to launch unrestricted submarine warfare deprived Germany of any hope of avoiding defeat. It brought to bear the resources of all the Atlantic and Pacific English-speaking economies on the restricted

[40] J. A. Salter, *Allied Shipping Control: An Experiment in International Administration* (Oxford 1921), pp. 356–7; Rudin, *Armistice*, pp. 244–9.

[41] C. E. Fayle, *History of the Great War: Seaborne Trade*, vol. 3 (1924), chs. 6, 11.

[42] Total stocks: 'Wheat Supplies—Importing Countries' (?Jan. 1917), Anderson Papers PRO 30/68/7, fos. 15–16; government stocks: Wheat Supplies. Royal Commission. First Report with Appendices, PP 1921 Cmd. 1544 XVIII, App. 13, p. 40.

[43] J. F. Beale, 'Memorandum by the Wheat Commissioner for Consideration by the Food Controller', no. 9 (March 1917), Anderson Papers, PRO 30/68/8, fo. 91.

[44] Ibid., no. 23 (18 Sept. 1917), fo. 9; Wheat Supplies. Royal Commission. Report, App. 10, p. 37, for monthly losses through enemy action. Average losses for Feb.–Dec. 1917 were 6.73 per cent.

[45] Wheat Supplies. Royal Commission. Report, App. 13, p. 40. Retail and bakers' stocks (another 10–17 days' supply) bring the figure up to sixteen weeks, comparable to November 1916.

continental resources of Germany. It effected this result in two ways, by depriving Germany of a substantial indirect trade with the United States and by opening for the Allies much better access to North American resources. It confirmed the intuitions of Britain's pre-war naval planners, that the international system of maritime trade and naval power would prove decisive in the war.

SHAPING THE PEACE: THE ROLE OF THE HINTERLANDS

I

The international food economy had the same decisive impact on the outcome of the war as it had on its origins. As Geoffrey Blainey puts it, 'the transition from war to peace is essentially the reverse of the transition from peace to war. What causes nations to cease fighting one another must be relevant in explaining what causes nations to begin fighting one another.'[1] The peripheral economies of Australia, Canada and the United States made a decisive contribution to victory. They also made a claim to shape the peace.

Britain derived value from its satellite economies twice over. First, in securing a reliable (and for some commodities, like Australian wool and Canadian wheat and timber, an exclusive or unique) source of vital raw materials. Secondly, the proceeds of Britain's purchases financed an independent war effort by the Dominions. William Hughes, the Australian Prime Minister, wrote from London to his Governor-General: 'I pass laborious and fretful days, going round and round like a clockwork mouse. However I'll sell the wheat, copper, lead, butter, tallow hides etc. I must do so for without money we cannot finance the war.'[2]

The military effort of the Dominions was formidable. Canada, Australia and New Zealand mobilized 1.2 million men, almost one-fifth of the numbers enlisted in the British Isles. Australia and New Zealand lost proportionately many more men (from those mobilized) than the United Kingdom, and overall the Dominion losses were comparable with the British.[3] Even more decisive was the Dominion contribution in terms of the *quality* of fighting men. A disproportionate share of the Royal Flying Corps pilots came from the Dominions, and towards the end of the war about one-third of new pilots came from Canada alone. On the western front in 1918 the British army was largely exhausted. Australian and Canadian divisions formed the shock troops of the great attacks that broke German resistance. On the German army's "Black Day" of 8 August 1918

---

[1] Blainey, *Causes of War*, p. viii.

[2] Novar Papers, Australian National Library MS 696, Hughes to R. C. Munro-Ferguson, Sept. 1918, fo. 2738.

[3] Excluding South Africa, whose contingent suffered small losses: Winter, *The Great War and the British People*, table 3.4, p. 75. Australian dead were 14.5 per cent of the men mobilized, British dead were 11.8 per cent.

the attacking armies were made up of five Australian divisions, four Canadian, four British and nine French. Dominion troops bore the brunt of the offensives of August and September 1918. In General Monash the Australian army produced a highly competent manager of trench-war offensive, in a trade where competence was not abundant. By the summer of 1918 Monash's corps consisted of seven divisions, effectively more than an army. On another decisive front, in Palestine, Australian formations also formed the backbone of a decisive offensive.[4] By the end of the war Britain depended on her "colonies" to keep up the impetus in the field, to feed it and to clothe it. In return, Britain was compelled to admit the colonies into its highest counsels. The Premiers of the Dominions and some of their senior ministers came to Britain in the spring of 1918: Botha and Smuts from Africa, Massey from New Zealand, Hughes from Australia and Borden from Canada. They met frequently, sometimes two or three times a week. The Imperial War Cabinet discussed the conduct of the war and, more imortantly, the emerging form of the peace.

The peacemaking roles of Canada, Australia and the United States were all affected by the role their agrarian economies had played in the war. Although Canada loomed large in both combat and supply, it did not assert itself in making the peace. In contrast, the clash of statesmen from Australia and the United States had a great influence on the shape and the spirit of the peace treaty.

II

Canada

Canada had a somewhat "better" war than the South Pacific Dominions. Canada may have mobilized a slightly smaller proportion of its men (27 per cent) than Australia and New Zealand.[5] Its pre-war investment in wheat paid off. The U-boats forced Britain to bring as much as possible over the short passage from North America, and Canada's wheatfields became critical to British survival. In 1917, the most dangerous year of the submarine campaign, the American harvest was short. In that year Canada exported more than 70 per cent of its harvest, and its 4.6 million tons of wheat exports were almost 50 per cent more than the United States were able to send out (table 25.1). Canada's wheat economy prospered as never

---

[4] D. Winter, *The First of the Few: Fighter Pilots of the First World War* (1982), pp. 20–1; C. E. W. Bean, *The Australian Imperial Force in France during the Allied Offensive, 1918*, (Official History of Australia in the War of 1914–18, vol. 6, Sydney 1942), pp. 483 ff.; General Monash to William Morris Hughes, 16 Aug. 1918, Hughes Papers, NLA 1583/23/1/2, fo. 203.

[5] Australia mobilized 30 per cent, the United Kingdom 52 per cent. Given the different methods of estimation, this difference does not appear to be significant; various estimates: Sharpe, 'Enlistment in the Canadian Expeditionary Force', pp. 16–20.

TABLE 25.1. *North American Wheat production and exports, 1913–1919 (millions of metric tons; 60 lb. bushels)*

Year	USA Production	Exports	% exported	Canada Production	Exports	% exported
1913	20.4	4.5	22	6.3	3.7	58
1914	24.4	8.7	35	4.4	2.3	53
1915	27.4	6.6	24	10.7	7.3	68
1916	17.3	4.9	28	7.2	4.7	66
1917	16.9	3.1	18	6.4	4.6	72
1918	24.6	7.8	32	5.1	2.6	51

Note: North America provided about two-thirds of the Allies' wheat requirements in 1917 and 1918, but much of the Canadian export was routed through the United States: F. M. Surface, *The Grain Trade duing the World War* (New York 1928), pp. 21–7, 274–86.

Source: M. K. Bennett, 'Wheat and War, 1914–18 and Now', *Wheat Studies*, vol. 16 (Nov. 1939), pp. 109–10.

before, although it also felt serious growth pains, in the form of labour shortage and rising costs and debt.[6]

Manufacturing industry received an uplift from British contracts for shells, ships, explosives and aeroplanes. 'Canada found itself a new staple—artillery shells.' In 1917 the Dominion produced between one-quarter and one-third of all the ammunition used by British artillery in France.[7] Canada not only delivered the goods, but also lent the money to buy them. Britain's quartermasters found it a more friendly environment than the United States, and were able to purchase substantial amounts of grain and munitions with credit from private Canadian banks. About 17 per cent of British government wartime grain purchases were financed this way, and by the end of the war Canadian government loans covered most of the British munitions purchases in Canada.[8] Canada emerged from the war in a better financial shape than either Australia or the United Kingdom, because of its smaller commitment and its large sales of munitions and food. In both Britain and Australia the public debt rose more than tenfold, while Canada's central government debt increased about eight and a half times.[9] Canada did not emerge from the war with

[6] J. H. Thompson, *The Harvests of War: The Prairie West, 1914–1918* (Toronto 1978), pp. 59–66.
[7] M. Bliss, 'War Business as Usual: Canadian Munitions Production, 1914–1918', in N. F. Dreisziger (ed.), *Mobilization for Total War: The Canadian, American and British Experience, 1914–1918, 1939–1945* (Waterloo, Ontario 1981); Naylor, 'Great War', *Journal of Canadian Studies*, vol. 16 (1981), p. 34.
[8] Wheat Supplies. Royal Commission. Report, p. 33; Bliss, 'War Business', p. 47; D. Carnegie, *The History of Munitions Supply in Canada, 1914–1918* (1925), ch. 27.
[9] Canadian federal public debt increased from Can$294m. in 1913 to Can$2532 in 1919.

any anxieties about security. At the Imperial War Conference of 1918 the Dominions' resolution to have no truck with Asian migrants was affirmed once again.[10]

Sir Robert Borden, the Canadian Prime Minister, who had long hankered for a supporting role on the world stage, did not seek any spoils. All he wanted was a proper recognition for Canada's contribution to the war and a position at the Peace Conference that befitted his country's dignity. The war had created deep divisions in Canada: between French- and English-speakers, between farmers and town dwellers, between employers and labour. None of these could be healed in Paris, and Borden sensibly restricted his ambitions there. Rather than procrastinate, it was more important for Canada to see the war ended conclusively with a clear verdict.[11]

III

Australia

At the highest levels of making war and peace no rulebooks existed to guide the statesman. In such circumstances, personalities prevailed. Both the Imperial War Cabinet and the Peace Conference contained powerful egos, whose style was often a calculated element of their policy. No such guile can be attributed to the Prime Minister of Canada. He was a competent, lacklustre provincial Conservative lawyer, who lacked the globe-girdling imagination and ambition of some of his protagonists. 'From the first to the very last days of the war Borden never wavered in his conviction that Canada's contribution to the Great War was disinterested and highly principled.'[12] Since no vital Canadian interest depended on the peace treaty, it was both a noble and a sensible position to take.

William Morris Hughes, Borden's Australian counterpart, was his opposite in almost everything. A short man of large abilities, he had hacked his way from a life of casual labour in the outback and the Sydney waterfront into trade union leadership, a law degree, labour politics and

The UK debt rose 10.5 times; the Australian by 11.1 from 1915 (the Commonwealth had only some £7m. debt in 1913): Leacy (ed.), *Historical Statistics of Canada*, Table H31–51; M&D, 'Public Finance 5', p. 403; A. Barnard, 'Commonwealth Government Finances, 1901–82: A Handy Compendium', *Source Papers in Economic History*, no. 17 (Canberra 1986), table 1, p. 16.

[10] Imperial War Conference 1918. Extracts from Minutes of Proceedings and Papers Laid before the Conference, PP 1918 Cd. 9177, XVI, pp. 195–201, 245–8; Minutes of Proceedings and Papers Laid before the Conference (other than those published in Cd. 9177), printed, Nov. 1918, p. xvi, Hughes Papers 1538 23/4, NLA.

[11] R. C. Brown, 'Sir Robert Borden and Canada's War Aims', in B. Hunt and A. Preston (eds.), *War Aims and Strategic Policy in the Great War, 1914–1918* (1977).

[12] Ibid., p. 56.

finally a seat in cabinet. Never a man to shirk a scrap, Hughes jumped into the fray with a sharp tongue and a vile temper: as a swayer of men, he was second only to Lloyd George. Like Lloyd George he had risen to the top by pushing aside a weaker leader, and had split his party in order to manage the war more decisively. The great issue was conscription. In a referendum, the people of Australia rejected Hughes's call for compulsory service, and left him at the head of a government, but with no party to call his own.

Hughes had a positive disdain for the idealism of North American statesmen. He was as cynical and vigilant as a street-fighter, and made a virtue of unenlightened self-interest. Australia's position was not based on morality: 'We were going to say to thousands of millions of people', he told the Imperial War Cabinet, 'that no one else should come into Australia—which we had no moral right to do.'[13]

Hughes's task was more difficult than Borden's. Australian primary commodities were just as vital as Canada's. European armies were clad in wool and there was no substitute for the quantity and quality of Australia's product. Australia was by far the leading exporter. The British army preferred Australian meat over all others, while in the critical autumn of 1916 Australian wheat seemed to be the only source to fill in the gap left by the poor harvest in North America.[14] But the shortage of shipping cut the island continent off from its markets. At the same time, Australia mounted a large military effort, which could only be paid for out of its export earnings or by borrowing. Hughes pitted his energy against these heavy odds. From 1916 onwards he was constantly engaged in difficult and sometimes acrimonious negotiations with Britain over the allocation of shipping, the price of Australia's commodities, and the terms of payment.[15]

Unlike Canada's Borden, Hughes would not remain on the sidelines. If Australia's fate was to be decided in Europe, it was his duty to be there. He spent long periods in Britain during the war. In 1916 he came for a visit of three months and energetically promoted his view of the war as a struggle for economic survival. Speaking three or four times a week, he enjoined his audiences to destroy Germany, not merely on the field of battle but in the fields of commerce and industry. He demanded 'the extirpation, root,

[13] Minutes of Imperial War Cabinet, no. 38, 26 Nov. 1918, p. 5, Hughes Papers 23/1/8, NLA.
[14] Australian wool: Yates, *Forty Years*, p. 109; meat: Scott, *Australia during the War*, pp. 518, 523–5; wheat: ibid., ch. 17, and Royal Commission on Wheat Supplies, 'Wheat Requirements, 1st Nov. 1916–31st August 1917' (25 Nov. 1916), fo. 4, Alan Anderson Papers, PRO 30/68/7.
[15] Sketched out in Scott, *Australia during the War*, ch. 17; also Anderson Papers, PRO 30/68/1 (Australian–British cable correspondence re wheat purchases), and the Hughes Papers 1538/17 and 23, NLA; K. Tsokhas, 'W. M. Hughes, the Imperial Wool Purchase and the Pastoral Lobby, 1914–1920', *A. N. U. Working Papers in Economic History*, no. 106 (1988).

branch and seed of German control and influence in British commerce and industry'.[16]

In Britain Hughes made a line to a neo-mercantilist group of business MPs around W. A. S. Hewins, who regarded the war as an opportunity to set up the Empire economic bloc that British electors had thrice rejected before the war. In those circles he was sometimes promoted as a potential Prime Minister in place of the faltering Asquith. Pressure from the right and from the jingo Press secured him a place on the British delegation to the Inter-Allied Economic Conference in Paris, where he helped to secure resolutions for the economic punishment of Germany after the war.[17]

The Paris conference also agreed that Germany would have to restore the material damage it had caused. "Loser pays" was an established principle of international relations, and the question of reparations had been probed in three British government reports in 1916 and 1917. Public discussions and government studies established a rough consensus: reparation for material damages was more just and more likely to be realized than a punitive indemnity. Payments in kind were preferable to cash. Britain's principal claim would be for shipping losses, and that payment would have to be spread over many years.[18] In the United States, President Wilson advised moderation; in Britain Lloyd George warned, 'We must not arm Germany with a real wrong.' In a Treasury paper, John Maynard Keynes estimated the total Allied war bill at about £24 billion, and German capacity to pay at £2–3 billion. The Board of Trade placed a realistic payment even lower. American calculations were similar.[19]

This reasonable consensus was rudely upset by the Australian Hughes. In public speeches and in cabinet Hughes insisted that Germany be presented with the whole bill, no matter how large it turned out to be. On 26 November 1918 Hughes raised the question at the Imperial War Cabinet. Lloyd George attempted to make him see reason. An indemnity on the scale imagined by Hughes, he said, would make the German workmen 'our slaves' for two generations. In order to pay, Germany would have to sell goods, and no nation would willingly provide a dumping ground. Hughes dug in his heels, and the Prime Minister proposed a committee. Hughes could not be kept off the committee, which included his friend Hewins and other strong protectionists. From here on, Hughes made the running. The committee recommended an Allied claim for the

---

[16] See speech of 20 Mar. 1916, in W. M. Hughes, *"The Day"—And After* (n.d. [1916]), pp. 40–1.

[17] By excluding it from export markets and sources of raw material. See Fitzhardinge, *Hughes*, vol. 2, chs. 4–6; R. Bunselmeyer, *The Cost of the War, 1914–1919: British Economic War Aims and the Origins of Reparations* (Hamden, Conn. 1975), chs. 2–3.

[18] Bunselmeyer, *Origins of Reparations*, pp. 59–71.

[19] Lloyd George, *The Times*, 13 Sept. 1918, pp. 7–8; Bunselmeyer, *Origins of Reparations*, pp. 77–87.

whole cost of the war, more than ten times the Treasury estimates, at approximately £24 billion, to be discharged by means of 5 per cent bonds at a rate of £1.2 billion a year.[20]

Hughes's committee also appointed the British delegation to the Allied Commission on Reparation and Damage in Paris. Hughes was the leading delegate, and the two others, the banker Lord Cunliffe and the jurist Lord Sumner, were securely in his pocket. At Paris, Hughes persisted in his massive demands. He made a common cause with France, but encountered stiff resistance from the United States and became a thorn in the flesh of Lloyd George and Wilson alike. By colluding with the French, Hughes almost single-handedly shifted the balance of the Allies towards a stern reparations policy. The French eventually toned down their demands, but Hughes and his henchmen persisted. In April 1919, when his basic point had been accepted, Hughes still protested that £10 billion was too low, and that it was wrong to limit German liability to less than the whole cost of the war. In the end it was British intransigence that kept reparations demands at once indeterminate and very high.[21] The "war guilt" clause (231) of the Peace Treaty, which was drafted to justify massive and indeterminate reparations, did more than any other factor to poison international relations between the wars. For this Hughes must bear a considerable part of the blame.

What was the reason for this pig-headed rigidity? Hughes had come up in life as an unscrupulous negotiator, sharp, shrewd and single-minded. How Germany, and indeed Europe, would manage was none of his business. He represented Australia. He rejected any priority for the physical damage in Belgium and France: 'Australia would get no reparation for damage incurred during the war,' he told the Imperial War Cabinet. Australia's loss, at £75 for every man, woman and child, was just as real as the houses destroyed in Belgium. 'Speaking for Australia, he wanted to know what Australia was to get for the sacrifices she had made.' Borden, in contrast, was appalled at Hughes's proposals, and doubted whether Canada could have carried one-tenth of the burden that he wanted to impose on Germany. Hughes repeated these arguments at the Peace Conference, and they contained (as his arch-rival John Foster Dulles independently acknowledged) an element of frontier radicalism: a demand that the loss of lives should have an equal claim with the destruction of property.[22]

[20] Minutes of Imperial War Cabinet, no. 38, 26 Nov. 1918, pp. 5–6, Hughes Papers 23/1/8, NLA; Bunselmeyer, *Origins of Reparations*, ch. 6, esp. p. 99.

[21] Hughes to Lloyd George (11 Apr. 1919; draft), Hughes Papers 24/1, NLA; M. Trachtenberg, 'Reparations at the Paris Peace Conference', *Journal of Modern History*, vol. 51 (1979).

[22] Minutes of Imperial War Cabinet, no. 38, 26 Nov. 1918, p. 5; no. 47, 30 Dec. 1918, pp. 5–6; no. 46, 24 Dec. 1918, p. 16; Hughes Papers 23/1/8, NLA; Hughes at the Peace

Hughes cared little for the post-war settlement in Europe. His interests were primarily Australian. His position on reparation was designed to secure a share of the spoils for his country. It also underscored a reputation for toughness. Hughes's other targets were also intensely parochial, even if the parish happened to cover a good part of the Pacific. As an economic warrior, he was keen to retain control of the German mineral enterprises which he had confiscated for the Commonwealth at the beginning of the war.

Another motive was his objectives as salesman-in-chief for Australian primary commodities. Hughes took up this role in 1916, when the shortage of shipping threatened to deprive Australia of its export markets. He entered the fray with gusto, and his tough style of negotiation brought some remarkable successes. When shipping was short, he purchased a small fleet of merchant vessels for the Commonwealth. The whole of the country's wool clip was sold to the British government for the duration of the war and one year after, together with 3.5 million tons of wheat, although there was no tonnage to carry the grain. He also worked to sell Australia's other commodities, agricultural and mineral. Hughes conducted the negotiations in person and played his cards close to his chest. Peace brought new difficulties: the British cabinet's Australian Purchasing Committee offered him an unacceptable contract for wheat and dismissed his demand for a ten-year commitment to Australian minerals. A tough attitude on reparations gave him some leverage in commodity negotiations. Although he failed to guarantee Australia's mineral markets, in July 1919 he concluded the last of the great government-to-government wheat sales, at a higher price than ever before. In another economic coup, Hughes managed to secure a half-share in the Pacific phosphate island of Nauru, which became a rich source of revenue for the Commonwealth. [23]

His remaining objectives were all to do with upholding the "White Australia" policy against the imagined threat of Japan. These goals embroiled him in some bitter quarrels during the Peace Conference. The first was to ensure Australian control of the German Pacific islands captured during the war, and especially of New Guinea, and to retain control of immigration into these islands. The second was to block Japan's demand for a racial equality clause in the Covenant of the League of

Conference: P. M. Burnett (ed.), *Reparation at the Paris Peace Conference from the Standpoint of the American Delegation* (New York 1940), vol. 1, doc. 110; John Foster Dulles, 'Observations on Memorandum by Mr. Cravath . . .' *Foreign Relations of the United States*, The Paris Peace Conference, vol. 2 (Washington DC 1942), p. 620.

[23] War Cabinet, 'Report of the Australian Purchases Committee' (6 Nov. 1918), Hughes Papers, 23/3/26, fo. 2475 ff., NLA; Hughes to Bonar Law, 21 Nov. 1918, ibid., 23/1/3, fos. 257 *et seq.* (and following docs. re minerals and metals): Nauru e.g. Scott, *Australia in the War*, pp. 797–801; Hudson, *Hughes in Paris*, pp. 29–31, 99–101.

Nations, in order to prevent it from basing a right to immigration on the
Covenant of the League. After his return to Australia, he told Parliament
in Melbourne that Australia had gone to war 'to maintain those ideals
which we have nailed to the very topmost of our flagpole—White
Australia'.[24]

Without the force of his singular personality it is unlikely that Hughes,
the head of a small nation far from the world's cockpits, would have been
able to make an impact that shaped the inter-war world. But without
Australia's infantry and Australia's wool, meat and wheat it is unlikely that
even Hughes could have single-handedly thwarted Germany, Japan and
the United States. Britain relied on the Dominions for help in holding on
to its post-war empire.[25] The war marked the coming of age of the staple
economies and it earned them a voice in the world's councils. In the person
of Hughes, that voice found an extraordinary amplifier.

IV

The United States

The United States was the greatest of the staple economies. It supplied
Britain with more than half of its bread and flour, and some 80 per cent of
its meat and fats in the last two years of the war. After its entry into the
war, the United States also lent the money to buy the food. No other
American asset was more valuable to the Allies: neither men, munitions
nor ships. This hold over Allied stomachs enabled the United States to
follow its own foreign policy, which culminated in President Wilson's
independent armistice negotiations with Germany.[26]

The United States' food power was concentrated in the hands of Herbert
Hoover. He had an extraordinary career as a mining engineer, manager
and entrepreneur, in which he accumulated a comfortable fortune before
the war.[27] In August 1914 he came forward to help the American embassy
in London to organize the homeward movement of 200,000 American
travellers from Europe. This led into food relief for Belgium and northern
France, which grew into the Commission for the Relief of Belgium.
Hoover shipped and distributed large quantities of food in Belgium and
northern France. He dealt with statesmen as an equal, borrowed millions
from Allied governments and ran ships under his commission's flag.
Hoover earned a world-wide reputation as a capable and humane

---

[24] Hudson, *Hughes in Paris*, chs. 2, 5; Fitzhardinge, *Hughes*, vol. 2, ch. 16; Hughes,
Commonwealth Parl. debs. 10 Sept. 1919, pp. 12164–79; quoted in Booker, *The Great
Professional*, p. 224
[25] K. Jefferey, *The British Army and the Crisis of Empire, 1918–22* (Manchester 1984).
[26] L. M. Barnard, *British Food Policy during the First World War* (1985), p. 165 ff.
[27] G. H. Nash, *The Life of Herbert Hoover: The Engineer, 1874–1914* (New York 1983).

administrator. In May 1917, shortly after the United States entered the war, President Wilson designated him as United States Food Administrator. In November 1918, when the war ended, Hoover returned to Europe to take charge of American relief efforts.

Hoover was a shrewd, broad-minded and generous person, with a great deal of drive, whose personality earned him the loyalty and devotion of subordinates. The eloquence, moderation and intelligence of his memoirs are striking. That is one of the difficulties of studying his work: so much of the story comes from the man himself. Hoover respected the verdict of history, and acted as his own advocate. He wrote four volumes of memoirs and history covering the war period, and his associate Frank Surface wrote three official histories of the war food organizations. Other volumes of documents and narrative came from The Hoover Institution at Stanford University.

Hoover became United States Food Administrator on 10 August 1917. In the years of Belgian relief he had learned a great deal about food in wartime and had acquired a band of able lieutenants. Their attitude was systematic and thorough. The physiologist Alonzo Taylor described it in a telling phrase as 'social science engineering'.[28]

Hoover's "engineers" made up a body of experts, the Advisory Committee on Alimentation, which included some of the leading American physiological nutritionists, together with a prominent statistician and Food Administration officials, themselves academic scientists.[29]

These advisers set out a bold policy of economies and substitutions, of which the most daring was the prohibition of distilling and brewing. In their enthusiasm, some of the experts saw their role as more than merely technical. Professor Chittenden of Yale, whom we have met before, regarded the war 'as the opportunity for the people of the world to gain a just appreciation of the real importance of an understanding of the laws of nutrition and the laws of dietetics', or, in other words, to propagate his doctrine of the parsimonious diet.[30]

One side of Hoover's work was to curtail consumption. The Food Administration undertook a great economy campaign with the slogan "Food will win the War". Posters, leaflets, circulars and the Press urged everyone along the food chain, from wholesalers to housekeepers, to cut their intake or to substitute some commodities for others. The Administration declared two wheatless days a week and one wheatless meal a day and raised the flour extraction ratio from 71 to 74 per cent. The methods were quite drastic. Fortunately Americans were used to eating maize and

---

[28] [Alonzo E. Taylor], 'Memorandum' (11 June 1917), fo. 1, Lusk Papers 1/1, HIA.

[29] 'Advisory Committee on Alimentation' (membership list, n.d. 1917), USFA 36, HIA.

[30] Chittenden, in 'Report of conference held September 20, 1917 . . . to consider questions relating to the subsistence of the Army', fo. 28; USFA 36, HIA.

oat products for breakfast, while the south had long subsisted on maize bread. The response was good, and the economies significant. In 1917, when the harvest fell below pre-war domestic requirements, 3.1 million tons of wheat exports were found out of savings.[31]

Grain and pork dominated the war effort. Grain had the highest priority. Hoover's task was relatively simple. Congress provided funds to maintain a minimum price for wheat, at two dollars a bushel for the standard grade. Hoover set up a Grain Corporation, to control the purchase and disposition of wheat. The price was high enough to induce a large increase in acreage in both 1918 and 1919, and delivered record harvests, which put an end to any fear of supply shortages.

Pig meat and its products presented Hoover with a more difficult problem. Congress did not allocate funds to support a minimum price, but Hoover still contrived to create one. It took 12 bushels of maize to produce 100 lbs. of the average hog. Hoover consulted the Allies about the quantities they required. As Food Administrator, Hoover controlled their access to American meat. This gave him control of their buying power. Armed with this power, Hoover persuaded the meat-packing firms to promise the growers a minimum price that represented a corn/hog price ratio of 13 to 1, or about 11 per cent above the farmers' break-even. Fifteen million farmers made their plans accordingly.[32] This promise was based on more than a handshake. Its real foundation was the credits that Washington gave the Allies. In effect, Washington supported hog prices indirectly, by means of its loans to the Allies. This arrangement eventually gave rise to serious complications.

In the autumn of 1917 the food prospect looked grim. The American harvest barely covered domestic requirements, and German submarines made it hard to carry overseas. Come winter, the prospect became even darker. America's rail system was ill-equipped for massive exports and in January a series of blizzards caused congestion on the railroads and in the ports. In addition to economies at home, Hoover looked for savings overseas. His associate Alonzo Taylor sailed to Europe and persuaded the Allies to take large cuts in their grain imports.[33]

But this was not enough. In February 1918 Hoover sent Professor Chittenden and another leading physiologist, Graham Lusk, to try and convince the Allies once again to cut down their consumption of grain. Chittenden's classical "diet squad" experiments of 1904 were replicated in

[31] Surface, *Grain Trade*, pp. 20, 228; [Alonzo E. Taylor], 'Memorandum' (11 June 1917), fo. 14, Lusk Papers, HIA.

[32] Frank M. Surface, *American Pork Production in the World War* (New York 1926), chs. 3–4.

[33] Surface, *Grain Trade*, pp. 187–201; A. E. Taylor, 'Report of the Representative of the United States Food Administration as a Member of the House Mission to Europe, November and December 1917' (n.d. 1918), Hoover Papers, Pre-Commerce 41, HPL.

the winter of 1917–18 by another scientist, Francis Benedict. Equipped with these new data, Chittenden and Lusk entered a series of confrontations with the food scientists of Britain, France and Italy.[34]

The issue was the different role that wheat played in the European, and especially the British, diet. The United States had an abundance of maize and no shortage of meat and fats. Consequently, Hoover attempted to economize in wheat. It was difficult for Hoover to advocate economy of grain at home when the British allowed unlimited consumption.[35] In Britain, however, livestock products were in short supply, so the Food Ministry rationed them, but kept bread unrestricted and cheap, and used it as the elastic element in the diet.

Chittenden and Lusk wanted the Europeans to reduce their bread ration by about one-quarter, from 415 grams a day (about twice the German ration). The saving would amount to 4.6 million tons.[36] Chittenden's point was blunt:

the allies are trying to maintain a per capita diet of from 2700 calories. The German industrial classes have worked and supported their army effectively for nearly two years on 2000 calories . . . the allied nations were attempting a cereal program, not only difficult from the standpoint of tonnage, but unnecessary from the standpoint of physiological requirements . . .'[37]

Lusk told the British that the Germans had lost weight. 'They are trained down hard like athletes,' he said, but there was no evidence that health had suffered.[38]

British scientists summarized the American argument: 'by gradually reducing the intake of Calories (say over a month) the body weight is lowered and with it basal metabolism; there is thus attained a more economical working of the body . . . without loss of efficiency or injury to health.' But they questioned whether the results of one experiment could be made the basis of a national policy. 'The issue of the present conflict', they wrote, 'will be determined by industrial efficiency and political stability. The policy advocated would risk both.'[39] Informally, the British

[34] Francis G. Benedict to Graham Lusk, 25 Feb., and 25 Apr. 1918, Lusk Papers 1/2, HIA; F. G. Benedict *et al.*, 'Tentative Conclusions with regard to War-ration Research Conducted on Twenty-five Young Men . . .' (2 Feb. 1918), Lusk Papers 1/4, HIA; Chittenden, 'Sixty Years', chs. 10–11.

[35] [Alonzo Taylor], 'Appendix: Remarks Submitted to the Inter-Allied Conference in Paris' [Nov.–Dec. 1917], fo. 5, Hoover Papers, Pre-Commerce 15, "Alonzo Taylor" file, HPL.

[36] 'A Calculation Showing the Influence upon the Ration of Reducing the Quantity of Bread by One Hundred Grams' (London, 2 Mar. 1918), Lusk Papers 1/2, HIA.

[37] R. Chittenden, 'Memorandum', fos. 2–3, enclosed with letter from Chittenden to Lusk, 29 Jan. 1918, Lusk Papers 1/2, HIA.

[38] 'Prepared for the Royal Society by Graham Lusk', Lusk Papers 1/2, HIA.

[39] W. B.H[ardy], 'Prepared by the Royal Society and submitted to Chittenden and Lusk' (n.d. March 1918), fo. 1, Lusk Papers 1/2, HIA.

scientists made the point even more strongly. As the Americans reported, 'they evidently feared that too many obstacles placed in the way of the workers obtaining their usual supplies of food and drink might result in a social upheaval. They seemed to think that some form of socialism would ultimately result, but they hoped that nothing would happen at present to compel a premature peace.'[40]

British food scientists were not nutritional radicals, and the Food Minister took little notice of them anyway.[41] Rather like the Germans, they believed that a war to defend civilization was no time to experiment with new diets. Towards the end of March the conflict shifted over to Paris, where an Inter-Allied Scientific Commission for Nutrition had been established in response to American demands.[42] Lusk and Chittenden failed to convince the physiologists of Europe. But the Americans' case did not rest on argument alone. They also held the keys to the granaries. The Commission agreed that the ration could be lowered temporarily by 10 per cent without any permanent damage to health.[43]

Although Hoover strove for complete authority over American food, 'from the soil to the stomach', his instincts were with the market system and with price incentives.[44] In contrast to the German food policy, Hoover gave first priority to the needs of producers, not to those of consumers. The guaranteed price was high in historical terms. What is more, producer prices kept well ahead of other prices in wartime. Both wheat and hog prices exceeded an index of other commodities.[45] In other words, the terms of trade between town and country rose sharply in favour of the country. They had been high and rising for a more than a decade before the war. This is a measure of the high priority that the United States gave to food production—ahead of other commodities and therefore, in terms of the price system, at their expense. With the money lent by the United States, Britain purchased about three times as much food and cotton as she did munitions.[46] The shift of prices in favour of food establishes Hoover's effectiveness much better than words. In the hog market, the price level was a direct outcome of his efforts. These efforts soon became all too successful. The high price of hogs gave rise to a surplus of pork products.

The disposal of the pork surplus became one of Hoover's chief

---

[40] Chittenden and Lusk to Hoover, 25 Mar. 1918; also (in almost same words), 5 Apr. 1918, fo. 8, both in Lusk Papers 1/2, HIA.

[41] Chittenden and Lusk to Hoover, 16 Mar. 1918, Lusk Papers 1/2, HIA.

[42] 'Statement of Results and Recommendations of the American Special War Mission to Europe, November–December 1917' (4 Jan. 1918), fo. 9, Hoover Papers, Pre-Commerce 41, HPL.

[43] Chittenden and Lusk to Hoover, 5 Apr. 1918, Lusk Papers 1/2, HIA.

[44] Barnard, *British Food Policy*, p. 172, quoting Hoover's *Memoirs*.

[45] Surface, *Pork Production*, pp. 199–202; *Grain Trade*, p. 335.

[46] K. Burk, *Britain, America and the Sinews of War, 1914–1918* (1985), App. 4, p. 266.

preoccupations in the last year of the war. Even as Chittenden was preaching the gospel of the low protein diet in Europe, Hoover was pressing pork on the Allies. The logic was simple: meat occupied much less cargo space than grain of equivalent value and 'food is food'. The British, however, for their own reasons, gave priority to grain (which is a more efficient food) and also wanted some fodder for their animals, so as not to become entirely dependent on imports.[47]

As the war approached its end and the pork surpluses mounted, Hoover pressed more and more of it on the reluctant Allies. He was bound by the prices promised to the growers, and preferred a surplus to a shortage.

V

Although Hoover preferred price incentives to decrees, the whole purpose of his organization was to curb the normal forces of supply and demand and create a *regulated* market: 'Government control, pursuing the rule of supply and need, has checked, if it has not defeated, the hitherto inevitable sequence of war prices.'[48]

He stressed this several times: the wartime economy would be a moral economy. Hoover himself and his high officials, who came from business, took no salary. A legitimate profit was necessary, but profiteering was out. As stated to the Press, 'I do not believe that extortionate profits are necessary to secure the maximum effort on the part of the American people in this war. If we are going to adopt that theory, we have admitted everything that has been charged against us of being the most materialistic, the most avaricious, and the most venal of people in this world.'[49] The ethos he wished to impart is expressed on a card printed in gothic lettering and designed for mass circulation, which reads:

Go back to the simple life, be contented with simple food, simple pleasures, simple clothes. Work hard, pray hard, play hard. Work, eat, recreate and sleep. Do it all courageously. We have a victory to win.

HOOVER.[50]

This was the sod-house ethos, which Hoover had imbibed as a child. In his mining career Hoover acted as a risk-taking innovator. But his conception of capitalism had been formed as a boy on the farming frontier; it was an ethical capitalism, where a fair profit, no more, was earned by hard work, and speculative, even mercantile profit was suspect. His commitment to

[47] Barnard, *British Food Policy*, pp. 177–87.

[48] *The Standard Loaf*, USFA Bulletin no. 11 (Washington DC, Dec. 1917), p. 11.

[49] Address to the Pittsburgh press club, 18 Apr. 1918, in *Food Control a War Measure*, USFA Bulletin no. 15 (Washington 1918), p. 11.

[50] Hoover Papers, Pre-Commerce 67, HPL.

the hog farmers was much more than a calculated policy. Hoover was born in the heart of the corn belt, in the hamlet of West Branch, Iowa, to pioneering farming settlers. In a memoir he wrote,

Every fall, the cellar was filled with bins and jars and barrels. That was social security itself. The farm families were their own lawyers, labor leaders, engineers, doctors, tailors, dressmakers, and beauty parlor artists. . . . I know that my clothes, partly homespun and dyed with butternuts, showed no influence of Paris and London . . . That economic system avoided strikes, lockouts, class conflicts, labor boards and arbitration. It absolutely denied collective bargaining to small boys. The prevailing rate for picking potato bugs was one cent a hundred and if you wanted firecrackers on the Fourth of July you took it or left it.

These farm families consumed perhaps eighty percent of the product of their land. The remaining twenty percent was exchanged for the few outside essentials and to pay interest on the mortgage. When prices rose and fell on the Chicago market, they affected only twenty percent of the income of the family. Today . . . eighty percent of the product of the farm must go to the market. When the prices of these things wobble in Chicago, it has four times the effect on the family income that it did in those days . . .[51]

His mission, he explained to his staff, was not merely to manage an emergency but also to redress an historical wrong to America's farmers. The war economy was a scheme of social reform: 'if we do that duty it will represent the honest and fair treatment of the farmer, the lifting of his level of life, the abolition of speculation, the honest and economic distribution of our daily bread.' Sailing to Europe in July 1918 on the *Olympic*, with seven thousand doughboys on board, Hoover said in a talk to the troops, 'My father and your own, side by side, redeemed the West from the Wilderness . . .'[52]

This attachment to his roots gave rise to a serious crisis. First-year economists are taught how hog prices rising above equilibrium will stimulate over-production. In the autumn of 1918 the hog cycle was moving towards a new peak. Hoover sold large quantities of pork products to the reluctant Allies, who purchased much more than they needed. On 30 December 1918 the Allies, especially Britain and France, refused to buy any more, and cancelled their outstanding contracts. Hoover was in a quandary: pork is perishable and large shipments had been cut to British specifications. Hoover had to find an outlet overseas for some 400 million pounds of pork every month.

The British wanted no more American pork. They could meet any shortage with Australian mutton and Argentinian beef, on easier terms. Within weeks of the end of the war, the United States began to stop

[51] Hoover, *Memoirs*, vol. 1, p. 6 (written in 1915–16—see ibid., p. v).
[52] Nov. 1918, quoted in his *Memoirs*, vol. 1, p. 280; diary of Lewis L. Strauss, 15 July 1918, HIA.

credits for Allied purchases. This gave the Allies an excuse to stop buying pork. When Hoover complained, the American Treasury pointed out that the Allies no longer asked for loans to buy food, and that Britain was welcome to borrow as much as she wished in the private market. The Treasury had another motive. Its loans had supported a high price for pork at home. Consumers, labour and business all clamoured for prices to come down. When the prop of Allied purchases fell away, Hoover was left with a liability. The hog agreement was voluntary, and Congress was not inclined to vote funds to maintain the prices at their high levels. Between December 1918 and March 1919 disposing of hogs was Hoover's constant and uppermost preoccupation. He tried every form of cajoling and persuasion, pointing out that both the Allies and the US government had incurred a moral obligation towards the producers and the packers.

'The Allies and the United States contemplate the provisioning of Germany during the Armistice as shall be found necessary,' stated Clause 26 of the Armistice agreement with Germany. Hoover's official historian claimed it had been included on Hoover's suggestion. As soon as the war ended, Hoover began to wind down his activities in the United States and shifted the headquarters of the Food Administration to Paris. His mission there was twofold. First, to look after food relief in post-war Europe; second, to find an outlet for the surpluses piling up in Chicago.[53]

Hoover soon came into conflict with his Allies. Ever since the Paris Economic Conference of 1916 they regarded control of the world's raw materials as one of the fruits of victory, and they proposed to allocate food resources by means of the inter-allied machinery. Hoover would have none of that. Together with Wilson, he regarded American food resources as a lever of diplomacy and international power, and insisted on retaining control over American supplies, much to the chagrin of the British and especially the French.[54]

The Germans soon began to clamour for food, but the Allies were in no hurry to redeem their promise. Blockade was the only lever left to force the Germans to abide by the eventual peace settlement.[55] After the armistice, the blockade was actually tightened considerably, as the Allies entered the Baltic and put an end to trading with Scandinavia. In mid-February

---

[53] Surface, *Pork Production*, p. 84.

[54] The British: Minutes of the Imperial War Cabinet, 'Notes of an Allied Conversation', 3 Dec. 1918, p. 4, Hughes Papers 23/1/8, NLA; the French: M. Trachtenberg, *Reparation in World Politics: France and European Economic Diplomacy, 1916–1923* (New York 1980), ch. 1; Hoover: his letters to Wilson, quoted in H. Hoover, *An American Epic*, vol. 2 (Chicago 1960), pp. 253, 255.

[55] David Lloyd George, speaking to Hughes, Imperial War Cabinet minutes, 35th meeting (11 Oct. 1918), p. 3. The German Foreign Minister Dr Solf appealed for food several times in the first week of the armistice: Herbert Hoover, 'Why We Are Feeding Germany' (n.d. 1919), ARA, vol. 20, fo. 96, HPL; Major A. M. Bertie, '. . . A Visit to Berlin, East and West Prussia and Courland, 17th March–9th April 1919, Further Reports p. 17.

French destroyers sailed into the Baltic and stopped all coastal trade, provoking a coal crisis in Prussia and Northern Germany. They also ordered the German fishing fleet back into port and deprived Germany of a small but important source of protein.

By November 1918 Hoover's physiologists Alonzo Taylor and Vernon Kellogg were busy collecting evidence on the food situation in Germany. Their first report was dire. Hoover searched for ways to open the German market. On 22 December 1918 he asked the Allies to allow the neutrals to purchase food above their requirements, which they could re-export to Germany. The Allies agreed on Christmas Day, but reversed their decision on New Year's Eve.[56]

By then the issue had moved to the Armistice Commission. When the armistice terms were drafted, they overlooked the disposal of the German merchant fleet. When the armistice came up for renewal in December 1918, the Allies insisted on taking over the ships as a condition of sending food to Germany. The Germans actually agreed to this, but now a new obstacle arose. How was Germany going to pay for the food? The Germans wanted to pay with their gold reserves and also asked to begin to export once again. This demand opened up a fissure between the United States and the Allies. The French delegates insisted that German gold should be earmarked for reparations. They did not care how the Germans paid for their food, and indeed if they got any food at all. The French hoped that the United States might finance the food with a loan, but Hoover needed cash.[57]

In January, the controversy focused on the use of the German merchant fleet. The Allies demanded its unconditional surrender. The Germans answered that this went beyond the terms of the armistice, and that they would only turn over the fleet against a guarantee of food deliveries. This impasse lasted throughout January and February, and in the meantime the food situation in Germany deteriorated.

Hoover's stratagem of selling to Germany through the neutrals was rejected within a day of the Allies' cancellation of their pork contracts. It was a second slap in the face, and he took the matter up with Wilson. Germany had to be fed:

It becomes necessary, therefore, to at once consider some modification of the present blockade measures that will establish production and exports with which to pay for food and some other imports at as early a date as possible. . . . A relaxation of commodity, finance, shipping and correspondence blockade is the only measure that will protect the situation against the evils which may arise from actual hunger.

---

[56] Surface, *Pork Production* (1926), pp. 84–5.
[57] Draft letter from Hoover to L. Snyder, 14 Jan. 1918, Hoover Papers, Pre-Commerce 40, HPL.

Even a partial revival of the ordinary activities of life within enemy territories will tend powerfully towards the end of Bolshevism and the stabilising of governments.

Wilson annotated this letter with the words: 'To these conclusions I entirely agree.'[58]

Wilson had always opposed a punitive indemnity, and had no sympathy for French demands. On 13 January 1919 the question came before the "Big Four", and the French Finance Minister Klotz insisted that German liquid assets be held over for reparations. Wilson (with Hoover at his elbow) declared that 'so long as hunger gnaws, foundations of governments crumble'. He pressed for a decision. During January and February the American representative John Foster Dulles conducted a prolonged duel with Hughes and Klotz over the extent of the reparation demands. Hughes would not budge an inch, and at the reparations commission he carried the authority of the British Empire. Eventually Hughes had to be restrained by the British government.[59] These exchanges generated a great deal of animosity.

While the Allies bickered over the division of Germany's gold reserves, the internal situation in Germany went from bad to worse.

[58] Herbert Hoover, 'Memorandum on Blockade Submitted to the President by Mr. Hoover' (1 Jan. 1919), Hoover–Wilson Correspondence, box 8, Hoover Papers, HIA.

[59] Notes on the Meeting of the Supreme War Council, 13 Jan. 1919, *Foreign Relations of the United States*, Paris Peace Conference, vol. 3, p. 528; Hughes: Balfour to Hughes, Sumner and Cunliffe, 19 Feb. 1919, Hughes Papers 24/1, NLA; the statements of Hughes and Dulles at the Peace Conference: Fitzhardinge, *Hughes*, vol. 2, pp. 383–4; Burnett, *Reparation* (1940), vol. 1, docs. 110, 113, 115, 116.

NEITHER DOMINION NOR PEACE: GERMANY AFTER THE ARMISTICE

I

When the armistice failed to lift the blockade, Germany faced another winter of hunger and cold. As long as food was short, the war economy continued. There was one difference. The government no longer carried the blame. The onus had shifted to the Allies. From the start the coalition of Majority Socialists and the bourgeois democratic bloc faced a threat from both political extremes: from disaffected conservatives on the right, and from revolutionary socialists on the left.

Combat had ended, but the war continued. On the Allied side, blockade became the prime weapon. A renewal of fighting became increasingly unlikely. The blockade allowed the Germans to bend to the Allies' will, while rejecting its legitimacy. The food shortage became a pawn, not only in Germany's contest with the Allies but in domestic struggles as well. On the one hand, the Spartacist radicals hoped that hunger would pave the way for a coup, while the right regarded it as a vindication of the war and a demonstration of Allied perfidy. The domestic crisis of coup and blockade pushed the government back into the arms of the army. While the majority wanted no part in a Communist revolution, blockade provided a moral foundation for the Ebert–Noske regime. Hunger brought together the forces of democracy and repression, and gave them a strong card to bargain with. Once the French, British and American forces had begun to demobilize and the war could not be easily restarted, it was a good card to play. So long as supplies were withheld, the German government could threaten to give in to the radical left and open the country to Bolshevism. It was important, therefore, that the imminence of starvation should be credible.

The War Food Office was actually optimistic in September 1918, and believed that domestic production could maintain the existing ration for eleven months, with the last month's supplies coming from the occupied areas.[1] Soon after the armistice the German Foreign Secretary Dr Solf appealed to the United States' humanitarian instincts to save thousands of women and children from death by starvation.[2] The British Press and

---

[1] Vernon Kellogg and Alonzo Taylor to Hoover, 22 Feb. 1919, printed in Taylor and Kellogg, *German Food and Trade Conditions*, p. 3.

[2] *Daily Telegraph*, 18 Nov. 1918, quoted in S. L. Bane and R. H. Lutz (eds.), *The Blockade of Germany after the Armistice, 1918–1919* (Stanford, California 1942), pp. 632–3.

British officials were inclined to be sceptical about these German alarms.[3] Despite a good deal of vindictive feeling in the United States its Food Administrators took a different view. Hoover's envoy Alonzo Taylor sent a detailed questionnaire to the German food authorities and urged them to set up the "Free Scientific Commission", which produced, within a fortnight, those quantitative data on the medical and demographic effects of the blockade discussed in Chapter 1.[4]

On the eve of the New Year, Hoover received the following picture of conditions in Germany:

The special privations suffered by the great mass of the people and particularly by the dwellers in large cities have been more terrible than any foreigner realized and more terrible even than most people themselves realized for they were deliberately deceived by the authorities as to the food situation. This physical deterioration has destroyed not only the people's physical power of resistance but has had profound psychological results. The Germans and especially those of Northern Germany have lost their spirit, their patriotism and their national pride. They have sunk into an apathy which is almost incredible. They have been morally shattered by the revelation that they have been deceived by their leaders. They are helpless and almost hopeless.[5]

From late December onwards the British government sent small teams of German-speaking officers and civilian experts on missions of inquiry into the different parts of Germany and their reports provide continuity with those of the German regional commanders cited in Chapter 5. Reports also came from American envoys. These documents reflect the Allied view of the German food situation throughout that winter of 1918–19.[6] They are not unbiased. Increasingly they advocate the supply of food to Germany, to enable the Ebert—Noske government to resist Bolshevism and save it from collapse. Indeed, they were eventually published in blue books in order to justify just that policy. There is also an undercurrent of humanitarian empathy, stronger in some reports than in others, and none is vindictive.

The tone was factual and dire. The itineraries were stereotyped. The officers met local officials, heard about hunger and low stocks and entered the figures in their notebooks. They were impressed by the rationing system and disgusted by the soup they sampled at the public kitchens. The

---

[3] *The Times*, 2 Dec. 1918, p. 2; Great Britain, Ministry of Labour, 'Food Situation in Germany' (28 Nov. 1918), Hughes Papers 23/27, fo. 2505, NLA.

[4] Ch. 1, sec. I, above. Alonzo E. Taylor, 'On Nutritional Conditions in Germany' (15 Dec. 1918), ARA, vol. 20, HPL; the German responses, containing a mass of data on German nutritional experiences and requirements, are in ARA, box 64, HIA.

[5] 'A French Picture of Post Armistice Germany', Morris to Hoover, (telegram), 31 Dec. 1918, ARA, vol. 20, fo. 153, HPL.

[6] The British reports were published and are bound in one volume, PP 1919 LIII. American data may be found in the records of the ARA, HIA; and in United States Department of State, *Foreign Relations of the United States*, The Paris Peace Conference, vols. 2 and 12 (Washington DC 1942, 1947).

officers had a standard list of questions to be answered. The most important was how long the stocks of food could be expected to last. Throughout the winter the estimate was always approximately the same: existing food stocks will last another month or six weeks. Only the actual deadline shifted: from February, to March, April and then May.[7]

How much room for manœuvre did the German authorities really have? For how long could they hold out? One key to this question was the size of the military food reserves. The end of fighting in the west removed a great burden from the German food economy. Numbers in uniform fell and those who remained did not need to eat so well. Army stocks had been replenished from the harvest of 1918. The good faith of German negotiators was partly measured by the amounts of food held back for the use of the military. When pressed on this point, officials insisted that most of the stocks had been looted, destroyed or abandoned in the first weeks after the armistice, or handed over to civilians.[8]

The evidence seems to point to a different conclusion. One British military mission to Hamburg late in January 1919 discovered a large army stockpile of foods stored in warehouses in the port. It contained some 50,000 tons, including concentrated food of high quality and an abundance of wine.[9] In almost every area that the missions visited, soldiers were on higher rations than civilians. Quartermasters everywhere said they were scraping the bottom of the barrel, but the army maintained upwards of 500,000 men on a good ration. In Leipzig the British officers surmised that this was why so many soldiers chose to remain in uniform.[10] When volunteers were needed for the *Freikorps* on the Eastern frontiers, one of the main incentives was better food. In March 1919, during the uprising of workers in the Soviet republic of Munich, the rebels were desperately hungry. In contrast, the troops sent by Gustav Noske to crush the revolution were hearty and well fed.[11] Under British pressure, the military administrators admitted that their stocks were sufficient to last until the next harvest. In February the army still had upwards of 340,000 tons of food, or not far short of Germany's monthly request for external relief— and more than half the quantities eventually sent in by the Allies.[12]

[7] February: ARA, vol. 20, fo. 245, HPL; May: ibid., p. 262; Taylor and Kellogg, *German Food and Trade Conditions*, p. 3; British sources: February: Cornwall and Hinchley-Cooke, Leipzig visit, Officers' Reports, p. 12; February, March, mid-April: Somerville, Broad and Pease, Munich visit, p. 19; Seddon, Henwood and Rose, Hamburg visit, pp. 29, 40–1; May: Trafford and Christie-Miller, Hanover visit, p. 58.

[8] Leipzig visit, 12–15 Jan. 1919; Berlin visit, 2–11 Feb. 1919; Officers' Reports, pp. 12, 61.

[9] Hamburg visit, 28 Jan.—8 Feb. 1919, Officers' Reports, pp. 37, 49.

[10] Leipzig visit, Officers' Reports, p. 12

[11] Frankfurt an der Oder, Officers' Reports, p. 88; Silesia, Pomerania, Further Reports, pp. 11, 16; H. N. Brailsford, *Across the Blockade: A Record of Travels in Enemy Europe* (1919), p. 136.

[12] Germany, Ministry of War, 'Memorandum of Food Supplies of the German Army' (7 Feb. 1919), Officers' Reports, App. 4, pp. 78–9.

Noske's war ministry kept a sufficient reserve of food to resist the military and ideological menace in the East and in the large cities at home. These stockpiles were one of the main props of the Socialist-military government of Ebert, Groener and Noske. The Allies did not make an issue of these hoards, since they relied on Noske to maintain order and ward off the Bolsheviks.

As the months rolled on the deadlines receded and disaster failed to materialize. On the contrary, the visitors were often perplexed by their failure to find evidence of hardship. In the countryside there were signs of apparent plenty. In Hamburg early in February, 'the adult population does not, to the lay eye, show very obvious signs of under-nutrition. Plumpness, however, is certainly no longer common, and some faces are drawn and sallow.' In Berlin at the same time, 'people in the streets seemed well-clothed and looked well-nourished', while 'we were surprised by the amount of food in evidence'. [13] Official rations did not fall. When they varied, it was no more than in previous years. The Bonn ration in the last months of 1918 was not very different from what it had been a year before. In three towns in Bavaria (Würzburg, Nürenberg and Regensburg) the rations in April 1919 were similar to those of November 1918, with seasonal declines in the potato ration made up with more bread in two of the three towns. Prices remained approximately the same.[14] An American who visited Berlin between mid-April and early May 1919 reported that 'the most striking external feature of Germany at the present moment is the apparently almost complete normality of the life of the population'. He was told that the food situation was gradually improving, and saw no outward appearance of malnutrition (though he avoided the poorer quarters).[15] The Cambridge economist C. W. Guillebaud observed a few days later that

I was surprised by the good external appearance of the vast majority of the persons whom I met about the streets. There are very few fat people in Berlin to-day, but equally there is no obvious expression of hunger and exhaustion on the faces of the people. The bulk of the middle and upper classes looked in quite normal health, and their faces did not appear sunken or pinched. The poor certainly showed the influence of privation to a greater extent, but although lack of food and the depressing influence of defeat have taken the desire and the capacity to work hard from the majority of the people, the bulk of the adults are, in appearance at least, a long way from actual starvation. The food of the poor is monotonous and

---

[13] Officers' Reports, pp. 27, 38, 59–60, 62; also Leipzig visit, 13–14 Feb. 1919, ibid., p. 83.
[14] Further Reports, pp. 31–2.
[15] E. L. Dresel and L. Osborne, Report of a journey to Germany, 16 April to 5 May 1919, *Foreign Relations of the United States*, Paris Peace Conference vol. 12, pp. 114–15. Compare the unsigned report (23 Mar. 1919) in Further Reports, p. 8.

unpalatable to a high degree, but it is at least sufficient to maintain life for the healthy adult who is neither old nor constitutionally liable to disease.[16]

A shrewd estimate of the German food situation came from Ernest Starling, the British nutrition expert, who gave a very accurate assessment of the wartime food equilibrium in Germany, including the size of the black market.[17] It appears therefore that conditions in Germany after the armistice were bad, but not really worse than in previous wartime years.[18] Despite the clamour, the German food economy does not seem to have fallen markedly below its wartime equilibrium. As in wartime, there was a great deal of anxiety. But this fell short of real desperation. Part of the German posture was bluff, and it worked. John Maynard Keynes, who was one of the Allied armistice negotiators, thought that they had 'rather overestimated, I think, the urgency at that date (January–February) of [the German] request for imported cereals. Even then, I fancy, they had rather more up their sleeves than we had credited them with.'[19]

Which is not to say that the suffering was unreal. The shortage was as great as in the previous year. And suffering had lost its point. Towards the end of the war, this equilibrium was sufficient to maintain bodily health, but not morale and sense of purpose. Now deprivation combined a sense of futility with the hope of early relief. Society had lost its direction and, while the radicals nurtured violent fantasies, the affluent plunged into hedonistic pleasure. Early in February two British officers reported from Berlin, 'Every dancing hall is filled to overflowing and, almost within sound of their orchestras, Spartacists and Government troops shoot each other dead every other day.'[20] Late in March another officer wrote,

The apathy of all classes at present is combined with a high degree of nervous excitability. The combination is perhaps significant of the main cause—the undernourishment. I cannot better describe the dominant psychical note than by calling it a sort of mental slow-fever. One of its results is the desire for distraction at any cost. The anomalous outburst of dancing and reckless extravagance in other amusements is connected with this.[21]

This atmosphere of listlessness and sensuality, of dancing and despair, is captured in the work of German artists of the time, of Otto Dix, Max

---

[16] C. W. Guillebaud, 'Report of a Visit to Berlin, May 2nd to May 8th, 1919' (printed), p. 9, ADM 137/2853.

[17] Starling, 'Report on Food Conditions in Germany', pp. 5–7.

[18] Only one family in the Leipzig nutrition survey was followed through early 1919. The calorie intake of this family during January–April 1919 (as a percentage of the norm) was 119, 111, 112 and 97 respectively. In November 1919 it was 108: Kruse and Hintze, *Sparsame Ernährung*, p. 158.

[19] J. M. Keynes, 'Melchior: A Defeated Enemy' (first published 1949), in *The Collected Writings of John Maynard Keynes*, vol. 10. Essays in Biography (1972), p. 401.

[20] Officers' Reports, p. 75; also p. 67.

[21] Unsigned report (23 Mar. 1919), Further Reports, p. 8.

Beckmann and Georg Grosz. Futility and disgust dominates their savage parodies of middle-class pleasures, which (in their depiction of prostitution and jazz) project the earnest outrage of a populist morality. War profiteers fondle the prostitutes while disfigured veterans hobble along the pavements. The same gruesome style spilled over into the lurid posters which plastered the walls. Some are merely brutal fear-mongering. Others harness an avant-garde graphical sophistication to broadcast alarm (fig. 26.1). A sample of Anglo-Saxon attitudes of those winter days in Berlin is given by Taylor and Kellogg, who were among the most acute of observers of wartime Germany.

The people are underfed, under weight, disillusioned, apathetic, embittered; and there is profound moral degeneration. There is little civic conscience. Idle women go to prostitution; idle men agitate or drift into crime. Men have lost the sense of responsibility for their families, their trade or for the state; the whole situation represents a storm-and-stress period, the immediate or ultimate outcome of which no one can venture to predict.[22]

FIG. 26.1. 'To the Lampposts': government scaremongering, winter 1918–19; a poster by Max Pechstein (see his *Errinerungen* (Wiesbaden 1960), p. 104). Courtesy of the Hoover Institution Archives, Stanford University

[22] Taylor and Kellogg, *German Food and Trade Conditions*, p. 7.

By February this atmosphere of permanent crisis suited both the Germans and the Americans: the Americans, with their neéd to offload unsaleable surpluses; the Germans, with their craving for imports. For lack of raw materials, industry was standing idle. Unemployment was on the rise, and fed unrest. Throughout their encounters with Allied representatives, the successor regime did its best to capitalize on the threat of revolution. The visitors saw through the ruse and resented it, but went along, because (even when highly exaggerated) it suited their needs. The threat of Bolshevism was their only means to persuade the Allies to treat the defeated Germany with more consideration.

British and American officials negotiating the economic aspects of the peace began to lean towards the German point of view. A groundswell of sympathy and indignation began to rise. Many of the people in the field— the German-speaking officers, the doctors and nutrition experts, the economists—felt that the withholding of food was both inhumane and inexpedient. The blockade's legality was dubious, its morality repugnant, its political implications dangerous. It threatened to deliver the country into the hands of the Reds; it created a hotbed of resentment and a desire for revenge. For British officials in contact with Germany, this became the conventional wisdom. They went out with this expectation in mind, and that was how they reported. A section of the Press also began to swing towards this view.[23]

John Maynard Keynes, acting as one of the economic negotiators, fought to open Germany to food.[24] He was present at the "Big Four" council on 13 January, when Wilson pleaded 'in lofty strains' for the relief of Germany. He accurately noted that the real mover was Hoover, and reported that day to Britain,

the underlying motive of the whole thing is Mr. Hoover's abundant stocks of low-grade pig products at high prices which must at all costs be unloaded on someone, enemies failing Allies. When Mr. Hoover sleeps at night visions of pigs float across his bedclothes and he frankly admits that at all hazards the nightmare must be dissipated.[25]

The Germans, Keynes said, held back their ships as a bargaining counter in the peace negotiations, and hoped for an American loan to pay for the food.

---

[23] This is the dominant sentiment in the British reports (which were published precisely with this effect in mind). American responses: see General T. H. Bliss to Hoover, 30 Dec. 1918, printed in Hoover, *American Epic*, vol. 2, p. 321; 'Note by Mr. Wise on Food Supplies for the Left Bank of the Rhine' (3 Jan. 1919), ARA, vol. 20, fos. 160–2, HPL (especially regarding food supply in the occupied territories); Press comments: the selection in Bane and Lutz, *Blockade of Germany*, pp. 678 ff.

[24] Keynes, 'Melchior', pp. 397–8, 401–2, 413.

[25] Ibid., pp. 398–9.

Preoccupation with these two ideas prevented the Germans from seeing the real situation, which was that England and the United States really desired and intended to facilitate the food supply of Germany, that the game we had to play with the French prevented our saying so too openly or making categorical promises, that we could not, for domestic political reasons, lend them money, but were willing to allow them to use, for the purchase of food, assets which otherwise would certainly be pinched for reparation a little later on, and that they (the Germans) had nothing to gain by hanging on to the ships or gold which at this juncture they would be allowed to use for food, but which under the Treaty would be taken for reparation.[26]

In order to get temporary relief from the pressure of pork, Hoover took a large personal risk. He instructed the Grain Corporation and the Commission for the Relief of Belgium to purchase large quantities of pork as a holding operation, until he could find new markets in Europe. Hoover staked his reputation and public standing on this gambit. In the meantime, the American Treasury, as an interim solution, agreed to support the price of hogs for a few months. This took some of the pressure off the farmers and the packers, but not off Hoover, who still had to conjure a market for their products. His promise was due to expire in April 1918 but a moral commitment remained. For his own part, Hoover was (rightly) convinced that the overall position was one not of surplus but of shortage. Events and his own work proved him right. When the guarantee was removed, prices moved up, and not down, in the false expectation of large orders from a hungry but insolvent Europe.

During January and February he worked relentlessly to open the gates of Germany to American food, fighting the French all the way and having to overcome the expectations that Hughes had created at the Reparations Committee. American Treasury support for pig prices was to lapse on 6 March. As this deadline approached, some drastic action was required. It was taken. On 7 March the question of food for Germany came up before the Supreme Economic Council, where Britain and the United States overrode French objections. The next day it came up before the Council of Four, and, with Hoover present, Lloyd George made a powerful speech which outlined the dire consequences for peace and stability if the food was withheld. France could not go on resisting alone, and the question of payment was soon settled. The first shipments arrived in Hamburg on 25 March 1919, and the sales were handled by Hoover's agencies. The total delivered until shipments ceased was only 622,000 tons, less than 1.5 times the amount the Germans specified as their monthly requirement (in crude terms). Germany did not buy as much as she said she needed, only as much as she could afford—perhaps more than she could afford. By spending the last of their gold on Hoover's food, the government helped to precipitate

[26] Ibid., p. 401.

the great inflation that followed. There was no more talk of impending famine.[27]

It was easy for Keynes to scoff at Hoover and his hogs. And Hoover's philanthropy was hedged with so many qualifications and special interests that few were willing to accept it at face value. It has attracted some scorching criticism.[28] The generosity and goodwill of the man himself is not in question, but it has to be seen in a broader historical context. Along with the urge to help, Hoover also had an urge to power. The moral mission overseas may be seen as a typical and appropriate expression of American power.[29] There was a tradition of promoting American values overseas by means of philanthropy. This tradition goes back a long way and includes the Peabody 5 per cent housing schemes in London, American missionary work in China, as well as Andrew Carnegie's public libraries, swimming baths and the endowment for international peace. The Rockefeller Foundation is another example, with its anti-hookworm campaign, its International Health Commission and its support for the social sciences and medical education overseas between the wars. Hoover's work on the Commission for the Relief of Belgium and the American Relief Administration fits into a tradition that also embraces Wilson's "Fourteen Points", the Marshall Plan and "Point 4" assistance programmes, a tradition that comes right up to the present with American support for "green revolution" agricultural aid in the 1960s and 1970s.

What do all these enterprises have in common? It is not necessary to question the benign impulse, the simple belief of businessmen in their values. There is something in them of Rotary writ large. The underlying purpose may be summed up in one phrase: "Making the world safe for capitalism." They were all measures of social reform designed to pre-empt a radical or socialist challenge. That is the link between the domestic and international action which some of the foundations promoted; which marks the efforts of Hoover as well. Its essence is expressed in Mackenzie King's search for a common ground between capital and labour, in Hoover's inter-war work for promoting child health, and in Roosevelt's New Deal. This is a key to understanding why such obviously self-serving

---

[27] The story is told in several places: Surface, *Pork Products*; F. M. Surface and R. L. Bland, *American Food in the World War and Reconstruction Period* (Stanford 1931), pp. 25–51; 'Why and How Germany was Fed', ARA, vol. 20, fos. 73–93, HPL; Hoover, *American Epic*, vol. 2, chs. 34–6; Bane and Lutz, *Blockade of Germany*; E. F. Willis, 'Herbert Hoover and the Blockade of Germany, 1918–1919', in F. J. Cox *et al.* (eds.), *Studies in Modern European History in Honor of Franklin Charles Palm* (New York 1956). See also C. P. Vincent, *The Politics of Hunger: The Allied Blockade of Germany, 1915–1919* (Athens, Ohio 1985), ch. 4.

[28] M. N. Rothbard, 'Hoover's 1919 Food Diplomacy in Retrospect', in L. E. Gelfand (ed.), *Herbert Hoover: The Great War and its Aftermath 1914–23* (Iowa City, Iowa 1979).

[29] D. A. Baldwin, *Economic Statecraft* (Princeton 1985), ch. 6.

slogans as "the Open Door" and "The Freedom of the Seas" should carry strong moral overtones in the United States.

At the end of the First World War the engine behind this impulse was the abundance of the United States' primary production. Hoover aligned the interests of his constituents with those of humanity and progress. Germany paid with gold and securities for its food. Out of a total of approximately $231 million in gold paid by the Germans for food during 1919, some $160 million was paid to Hoover (the rest went to Britain). Australia received £5.5 million in reparations (about $26.5 million).[30] In the long run, however, Hoover's enlightened self-interest was not sufficient to undo the damage done by the single-minded mercantilism of the British, under Hughes's guidance, in league with the French. The Peace Treaty, with its open-ended reparation demands, established a peace that most Germans, and many liberals in Britain and the United States, regarded as unjust. The blockade after the armistice, with all its sufferings, both imagined and real, allowed the Germans to reject the role that Billy Hughes had prepared for them, and to nurture a self-righteous dream of revenge. That is how the agrarian outcomes of one great war became the origins of the next.

II

Before we conclude, it is time to think again about the legal and moral aspects of the blockade. Up to 1914 Asquith's government had never given up its commitment to the Declaration of London. The Liberal commitment to the Declaration of London did not matter too much. Without a tribunal the Declaration was as putty in the hands of the lawyers.

A few weeks after the war began the British government began to ignore the Declaration, seized cargoes consigned to Germany regardless of the flag that carried them, and treated food as "absolute contraband". American protest was insincere and ineffectual. But when the Germans began their submarine campaign, the United States responded with great indignation. President Wilson turned a blind eye, for example, to the mining of international waters by Britain, but invoked international law to enter the war against Germany, first as an active supplier of the Allied war economy, and later as a belligerent.[31]

How then was the law utilized by Britain and the United States? To the legal positivist, the law is merely what it is, and not what it perhaps ought to be; the validity of international law can only be established empirically. The record of international law in the First World War, and of maritime

---

[30] Gold payments: 'Why and How Germany was Fed', ARA, vol. 20, fos. 85–6, HPL; Australian reparations: Scott, *Australia during the War*, p. 808.
[31] This interpretation follows Coogan, *End of Neutrality*, chs. 8–11.

law in particular, suggests its primary function: this was to provide a *casus belli*. No infringement of the law could actually force a nation into war against its better judgement. But if statesmen wanted to fight, then international law provided the justification. It allowed belligerents to don the cloak of legality. Bertrand Russell has put this well. Municipal (i.e. national) law is designed to suppress violence, but the main purpose of international law 'is in actual fact to afford the sort of pretext which is considered respectable for engaging in war with another Power. A Great Power is considered unscrupulous when it goes to war without previously providing itself with such a pretext . . .'[32] This pretext is primarily needed to justify war *at home*, and is based on the false analogy between domestic and international law. Domestically, the law compels obedience, and carries a connotation of justice. No compulsion exists in international law. No one compelled Britain to intervene when Belgium was invaded. When it chose to intervene, Britain did so on a point of law. Likewise, as Lord Devlin put it, 'When in April 1917 the United States went to war she did so on a point of law.'[33]

Admiral Fisher in his simplicity could only see that international law had no teeth. McKenna was more sophisticated, and realized the value of legality. He understood that the law is a mercenary profession, and that a formula would always be found. Indeed, when the time came, McKenna ably provided the formula himself. The German government, he said, had centralized and nationalized all food production, and therefore all food sent to Germany was contraband of war.[34]

Beyond its uses to statesmen as a prop of the *casus belli*, international law has a second function which takes us from positive law to natural law, from legality to morality. Law is not only a matter of international treaties but also the repository of past and current standards of justice and morality; a matter not only for experts, but also for the laity. In the common law tradition the arbiters of justice are ordinary people, sitting as a jury. In the pre-war law of the sea the crucial distinction between combatants and civilians centred on two principles: (*a*) that non-combatants should not be deprived of food, and (*b*) that unarmed vessels should not be attacked without providing for the safety of passengers and crew. Both these principles helped to draw the United States into the war, and to justify this intervention to the American people.

Do such principles have a universal validity? Michael Walzer has contended that they do. This would be easier to endorse if non-combatants were held to be entirely blameless. Rousseau asserted that individuals are foreign to a war. This appealing and influential doctrine reflected the

[32] Bertrand Russell, *Justice in War-time* (Chicago 1916), p. 22.
[33] Lord Devlin, *Naval Prize Bill*, p. 11.
[34] Coogan, *End of Neutrality*, p. 160. That was still untrue at the time.

dynastic wars of Rousseau's time. But does it apply to societies which are founded on popular sovereignty rather than divine right? When citizens have political rights, they also acquire responsibilities and may suffer for their folly. As the jurist John Westlake put it in 1909,

since 1815 there have been no wars in Europe which were merely those of ruling persons or families, and not those of the respective combatant nations. The wars have not necessarily been approved of by the numerical majority, though this has often been the case, but always they have been approved by such a part of the population in each combatant State as, by its numbers and influences combined, must for all practical purposes, external as well as internal, be regarded as representing the nation.[35]

Even without this proviso, most writers on international law stop short of Walzer's position, and agree with Bismarck that necessity or self-defence can override the principle of "humanity in warfare". It is not forbidden to cause suffering, only *unnecessary* suffering. As Bismarck argued in 1885, starving civilians was justified, if it shortened the war.

The argument from necessity raises questions about what constitutes necessity. Sinking of merchant ships without warning may be necessary for tactical or strategic advantage. But is a particular war *itself* necessary? This leads from the problem of "humanity in warfare", from *jus in bello*, to the question of the "just war", the *jus ad bellum*. German violations of the law of nations were held to justify American intervention in the war. In other words, German violations of "humanity in warfare" provided America with grounds for waging a "just war".

In retrospect, the project of blockade as a decisive strategy gives rise to unease. No doubt Hankey would have answered, and rightly, that it was merely a contingency plan, and that it was left to Germany to start the war. This act placed a large credit in the moral balance of the Allies, and, despite their early violation of maritime law, they remained in moral credit at the end of the war. Their economic blockade against the German home economy made no distinction between combatants and non-combatants. German officials made a point of attributing 'excess' wartime civilian deaths to the 'enemy's commerce blockade, contravening the law of nations'.[36] Be that as it may (and the numbers were certainly exaggerated), these figures were balanced in western public opinion by the more visible work of German submarines. Germans knew how to ridicule and ride roughshod over moral scruples, but embraced them again when it suited them.

---

[35] M. Walzer, *Just and Unjust Wars: A Moral Argument with Historical Illustrations* (1978), p. 174; Best, *Humanity in Warfare*, p. 56; J. Westlake, 'Note on Belligerent Rights at Sea', in A. Latifi, *Effects of War on Property* (1909), p. 150.
[36] 'Schädigung', p. 398 (ch. 1 n.3, above).

The Germans refused to regard themselves as culpable for their plight. The continuing blockade, the Allied demands for ships and their procrastination over food encouraged this attitude. A Canadian graduate student (who had spent the war in German internment and had many German friends) wrote in a paper circulated to the Imperial War Cabinet that the German people as a whole had not the slightest idea of the real popular feeling in other lands towards them.

The impression has been carefully fostered and supported by all sorts of arguments in the press that the Blockade of Germany justified everything that occurred in the case of submarine warfare. . . . As a result the ordinary German is quite incapable of appreciating why the new Germany, which he believes the Revolution to have assured, has not been immediately acclaimed by the popular sentiment of the Western nations.[37]

The same attitude was discovered by the British officers who visited Berlin in February:

Practically the only "inhumanity" which is spoken of is that of the blockade, and it will probably be found, when claims for indemnification for lives and property are presented to Germany, that these will be met by a counterclaim, based on the loss of life among the civil population, the loss of enterprise, &c., which they maintain can be traced to the internal conditions arising from the blockade.[38]

This sense of maltreatment and injustice hardened in Germany as the months of hunger wore on. A *Simplicissimus* supplement of 4 February 1919 showed an anguished Germania crucified on its cover, while Allied torturers standing around say: 'One more armistice extension and she will be ready for the Peace' (fig. 26.2). A more down-to-earth and chilling note was sounded by the proprietor of a pub where three British officers had an expensive black-market meal. He was a discharged *Unteroffizier*, who had volunteered for a Guard Regiment at the beginning of the war, had been four times wounded, and had now volunteered for a *Freikorps* regiment. 'He did not appear to bear the slightest hostility, but remarked that of course Germany would have to have another war as soon as possible, probably within 20 years, as the present situation was unbearable.'[39]

It suited the Germans to take this line during the armistice because their defeat was not final and clear-cut. Fighting had stopped short of Germany's total overthrow; her sovereignty remained intact; most of her territory remained unoccupied, and the Allies flinched from a military occupation to

[37] Winthrop Bell [Memorandum on Internal Conditions in Germany] (circulated to Imperial War Cabinet by R. L. Borden, 11 Dec. 1919), Hughes Papers 23/3/29, fo. 2606, pp. 14–15, NLA.

[38] Officers' Reports, pp. 74–5; also pp. 42, 65, 86; Further Reports, pp. 7–8. The document in question was 'Schädigung'(ch. 1, n. 3 above). For a different (but later and not unbiased) impression: Brailsford, *Blockade*, p. 107.

[39] Officers' Reports, p. 64.

(Zeichnung von E. Schilling)

„Noch eine Waffenstillstandsverlängerung und sie wird reif sein für den Frieden!"

FIG. 26.2 The Tortured Germania. 'One more armistice extension and she will be ready for the Peace!', *Simplicissimus*, 4 Feb. 1919

impose their will. In this respect, Ludendorff's obstinacy at the end had served a purpose; military resistance managed to salvage something out of defeat. After the armistice, moral argument (and the threat of Bolshevism) were the main weapons still available to Germany. But if the Allies failed to muster the will to drive Germany to a total military defeat, the German military regime stood peculiarly discredited. Germany became a moral void that the Allies, with their rhetoric of virtue and their large reserves of food, were well placed to fill.

Those who invoke the law of nations must also be ready to live by its precepts. Clause 26 of the armistice said that the existing blockade would remain in force, but the Allies would 'contemplate the provisioning of Germany as shall be found necessary'. As A. J. Balfour said a few months later, 'almost a promise had been made'.[40] In fact, the armistice turned the screw even tighter, as the blockade extended into the Baltic.

The Allies could only impose final justice on Germany by resorting to measures that the Declaration of London had proscribed before the war. In doing so, they could no longer plead *necessity*. That is the key point. The legal position is debatable (legal positions always are), but the moral aspect was clear. As the blockade continued to inflict hunger rations on Germany into the winter of 1918–19, the Allies rapidly exhausted their moral credit. In depriving the Germans of food, the Allies applied military power for political and economic ends, in a way that increasingly sapped the resolve of their own officials and officers. On 8 March 1919, at the Supreme War Council called to resolve Hoover's pork crisis, Lloyd George uttered some prophetic words:

he wished to urge with all his might that steps be taken to revictual Germany. The honour of the Allies was involved. Under the terms of the Armistice the Allies did imply that they meant to let food into Germany. . . . But so far, not a single ton of food had been sent into Germany. The fishing fleet had even been prevented from going out to catch a few herrings. The Allies were now on top, but the memories of starvation might one day turn against them. The Germans were being allowed to starve whilst at the same time hundreds of thousands of tons of food were lying at Rotterdam. . . . these incidents constituted far more formidable weapons for use against the Allies than any of the armaments it was sought to limit. The Allies were sowing hatred for the future: they were piling up agony, not for the Germans, but for themselves . . .[41]

By then the damage was done. It took another fortnight for the first food to arrive. By the end of May Germany had received less than a month's

---

[40] Minutes of the Supreme War Council, 17th Session, 3rd meeting, 7 Mar. 1919, in *Foreign Relations of the United States*, Paris Peace Conference, 1919, vol. 4 (Washington, DC 1943), p. 281.

[41] Ibid., p. 280.

recommended supplies.[42] Moreover, the Allies threatened to renew the blockade if Germany refused to sign. This weighed heavily with the Social Democrats in Germany when they decided to sign the treaty.[43] In his reply to the Allied terms, which was addressed to his compatriots as much as to the Allies, the German delegate Brockdorff-Rantzau made a bid for moral equality:

Crimes in war may not be excusable, but they are committed in the struggle for victory, when we think only of maintaining our national existence, and are in such passion as makes the conscience of peoples blunt. The hundreds of thousands of noncombatants who have perished since November 11, because of the blockade, were destroyed coolly and deliberately after our opponents had won a certain and assured victory. Remember that when you speak of guilt and atonement.[44]

And this brings up one final function of international law. It helps to reconcile the loser to his defeat, to accept its legitimacy and to acquiesce in his own punishment. That was clearly shown in the aftermath of the Second World War. The blockade policy after the armistice deprived the Allies of such legitimacy. It transformed a "just war" against the Kaiser to an unjust one against civilians, a war in which the means no longer matched the ends. The blockade scrambled the moral verdict of the war and planted the seeds of a new *casus belli*. The appeal to justice mobilized peoples for war. When the Allies failed to sustain their moral supremacy in Germany, their war effort fell short of its reward, and could not establish either dominion or peace.

---

[42] A. J. Mayer, *Politics and Diplomacy of Peacemaking* (1967), compare pp. 502 and 514.
[43] V. Schiff, *The Germans at Versailles, 1919* (1930), pp. 144, 153; Brailsford, *Blockade*, pp. 115–16.
[44] Speech of Count Brockdorff-Rantzau on 7 May 1919 at Versailles, trans. in A. Luckau, *The German Delegation at the Paris Peace Conference* (New York 1941), p. 221.

CONCLUSION

FOR Britain, the Edwardian naval arms race and the Great War that followed formed a crisis of its system of economic specialization and free trade. Free markets cannot exist without superior authority, since traders might be tempted to grab each other's goods instead of paying for them. Markets require a policeman, and the policeman of nineteenth-century free trade was the Royal Navy. When no single power dominates, free trade no longer resembles the perfect competition of Chicago economics, but the armed vigilance of Chicago's gangsters. The growth of competing industrial powers was not merely a challenge to Britain's economy, it was also a serious danger to its national security.

This problem had to be faced by Britain's leaders. In 1902 the Colonial Secretary Joseph Chamberlain launched his tariff reform campaign, which was designed to bind the settler societies closer to Britain by means of an imperial free trade zone, protected by tariff barriers. It was an attempt to add Britain's overseas resources to its assets as a Great Power. In the language of the day, he sought to create a *Zollverein*, a tariff union, to underpin a *Kriegsverein*, a military union. Chamberlain's plan was thrice rejected by British voters before the First World War. With food prices rising and real incomes falling, the Edwardian period was not a good time to tax imported food. The "Atlantic orientation" of Fisher and Hankey was an alternative to the Chamberlain plan, another attempt to harness the same resources for similar ends.

If the process of international specialization created instability, it also boosted Britain's power to wage war. During the First World War it was said that the admiral who commanded the British Grand Fleet was the only person who could lose the war in an afternoon. That this dictum contains a great deal of truth is a measure of the value of the navy for Britain's war effort. This is not to say that land forces were not vital. But the transport and supply of land forces, even across the Channel, to say nothing of the long hauls across the Atlantic and Indian oceans, depended on the Royal Navy's capacity to secure them. The Royal Navy was a machine for converting Britain's resources into the sinews of war.

Britain's free trade policy made it a wealthier country than a policy of protection might have done. That at any rate was the justification for free trade, even if there are theoretical grounds for doubt, and no one has yet attempted to measure the benefit of free trade for British Gross National Product. Did this amount to 5 per cent of the national product? 10 per cent? nothing? Let us assume that free trade did invigorate the British economy.[1]

[1] D. McCloskey, 'Magnanimous Albion: Free Trade and British National Income, 1841–1881', in his *Enterprise and Trade in Victorian Britain* (1981).

International specialization had a powerful stimulating effect on the development of the peripheral economies. An increasing part of their output was taken up by domestic consumption and investment; but the political, financial, commercial and ethnic ties with Britain were strong enough to add their economic power to that of Britain in a crisis. The combined domestic product of Canada, Australia and New Zealand in 1913 was almost 40 per cent of Britain's, and amplified its war-making power correspondingly. Overseas settler populations added about one-third to the British demographic pool. The economic resources of the United States were committed to Britain from an early stage of the war, and almost unreservedly from 1917 onwards.

The development of the transoceanic economies made them the object of aspiration for migrants from Britain. We have no accurate measures of well-being, but the large flows of emigrants from Britain to the Dominions and the United States suggest that overseas destinations offered better lives. Emigration is at once an index of dissatisfaction with the "old country" and a measure of the opportunities that allowed millions of discontented people to take control of their own lives, for better or worse, and mostly it seems for the better. Change itself, the ability to move in the desired direction, is a form of fulfilment. Having escaped the constraints of British society, many of these people were able to view Britain without resentment, and recent migrants provided a disproportionate share of the first volunteers in the Dominions. The opportunities for emigration made the British Empire a better place to live in. On the prairies, social radicalism and economic success were combined with imperial loyalty. Among the native-born populations which already formed large majorities in the Dominion countries, the ease of movement enhanced a feeling of belonging to a just and benevolent entity, one they could identify with and one they were willing to fight for. This identification helped to form that sense of righteousness which was so prominent in the public discourse of the time, though such sentiments had other sources as well.

If one questions the importance of a perception of justice, observe the experience of Ireland. Many Irish joined the British Army, but Britain did not dare conscript them, and their alienation helped to prevent conscription in Australia and delay it in Canada. Racial solidarity was another cement of the imperial bond. On the Pacific rim Asian exclusion was both a social and an economic imperative which reinforced the imperial connection over and above the ties of language, culture, shared values, traditions and institutions, and the millions of threads of personal kinship that extended across the oceans to Britain. These factors translated into a political commitment to Britain that was almost unconditional in the case of the Dominions, and which was strong and eventually decisive in the case of the United States.

All these assets extended British power on the eve of the First World

War beyond the magnitudes suggested by the size of Britain's population and its Gross National Product. These assets disposed Britain to intervene in the war. It was a *permissive* factor rather than a direct causal one, a necessary condition rather than a sufficient one, but this permissive factor underpinned the strategy of the "Atlantic orientation". For Britain, economic power was an *enabling* factor, a reason to intervene in the war.

For Germany the economics of specialization were *disabling*. German reliance on overseas imports and markets made the prospect of blockade attractive to Britain. In London it inclined some staff officers and statesmen to project a war of economic attrition against Germany. In Berlin it helped to narrow down the operational options to a single one, the Schlieffen plan for a Blitzkrieg on Paris.

The prospect of blockade did not close off the option of war altogether. Why? The British Atlantic orientation was premised on deterrence as much as it was a plan for war. It failed in this respect because it was not visible enough. None of the German generals and statesmen, neither Schlieffen, Bernhardi, Moltke nor Bethmann Hollweg, made sufficient allowance for the economic potential of the English-speaking economies; it was the overwhelming material and demographic preponderance of these economies that defeated Germany in the end. The Germans were victims of "intuitive reasoning", preferring the near, the available, the familiar, the vivid—and refusing to peer below the horizons of Europe.

Was it necessary to stop the Germans? I have not formed a definite opinion. But I lean towards the view that the economic preponderance of its adversaries should have been a sufficient constraint on Germany if it had been more properly communicated. Perhaps the real failure was not to inform the Germans in good time of the risks they were taking. Lloyd George did so successfully in his Mansion House speech of 1911, and created alarm in the Berlin bourses. In 1912 Fisher wrote to Churchill, 'I do earnestly pray that the Government will not allow the Navy trumpet to give an uncertain sound, and the German will then not prepare himself for the battle.'[2] But British statesmen themselves were not entirely conscious of the elements of their power.

A little *more* British bellicosity, combined with an awareness of the economic resources of the English-speaking peoples, might have inclined the Germans towards a strategy that was more adapted to their interests. That strategy was simply to do nothing. In the contemporary state of military arts they could have held out indefinitely against the Russians acting alone. France on her own, to say nothing of Britain, was very unlikely to attack. With its superior rate of economic growth, Germany could have consolidated its power and influence on the Continent much

---

[2] Fisher to Churchill, 5 Mar. 1912, *FG*, vol. 2, p. 436.

more effectively without war. It is a tragedy that the Atlantic orientation was strong enough to win the war, but not strong enough to prevent it.

The inclination to use power is proportional to that power. If Ireland had been the only island off the coast of Europe, it is unlikely that the invasion of Belgium would have induced it to declare war on Germany. There are some disadvantages to size, and survival is possible in the shadow of the giants. To say that Britain had to act because naval supremacy was vital to its existence is not convincing. Britain acted because it felt strong enough to act. At the Washington Conference of 1922 Britain conceded naval parity to the United States, and today Britain manages without naval primacy, with an economy as fully committed to overseas trade as during the Edwardian period. Rather, naval primacy was vital to maintain the kind of imperial posture, both formal and informal, both political and commercial, that Britain had built up in the nineteenth century, a posture that could no longer be sustained in the long run even *after* a British victory.

The German challenge was not the only one that Britain faced in the Edwardian period. Britain's naval supremacy was also challenged by Japan in the Far East, by France, Italy, Austria and Russia in the Mediterranean, and potentially, at least, by the United States, which had the capacity to outbuild Britain, and also to move its fleet from the Pacific into the Atlantic once the Panama Canal was completed. Military power is inversely related to the distance it has to be projected, so Britain surrendered traditional spheres of influence in the Far East, the Mediterranean and the North Atlantic and forged understandings and alliances with the newly dominant powers in those regions. With all her naval power concentrated in the North Sea, Britain was able to contemplate a military response to the German challenge.

Britain decided several years in advance that it had to intervene in a European war. It was not attacked or invaded. The threat that Britain moved to counter was not an immediate one. If the Germans occupied the Channel ports, it would still take them years to mount an effective threat to Britain. Germany's war of 1914 was described at the time, and is often considered today, as a preventive war, mounted to pre-empt a Russian build-up that would culminate in 1916.[3] Britain's declaration of war in 1914 was a preventive war of a similar kind, mounted to pre-empt a threat that could not materialize in less than two years. A battleship normally took as long or longer to build.

Britain was the wealthiest, per head, of the European nations, with a bias towards industrial, maritime and financial assets. The Atlantic

[3] e.g. in E. Zechlin, 'Cabinet versus Economic Warfare in Germany: Policy and Strategy during the Early Months of the First World War', in H. W. Koch (ed.), *The Origins of the First World War: Great Power Rivalry and German War Aims* (2nd edn. 1984), pp. 192–4.

orientation, therefore, sought to utilize Britain's capital assets by means of a capital-intensive strategy. In contrast, Germany's power was labour-intensive, and depended on an abundance of infantry. Russia and France together had even more infantry, so Germany fell back on "enterprise"— on surprise, manœuvre and mobility. The Allies had an advantage in both *matériel* and manpower. The first line of Britain's capital assets was its navy, the largest array of battleships in the world, an expression of British metallurgy and mechanical engineering. The second line was its mercantile shipping, comprising about 40 per cent of the world's tonnage. The third was its export industries, which paid for a good part of its trade with the English-speaking suppliers. The fourth asset was Britain's large investments overseas, with all the commercial and political goodwill they had created. It was rational for the planners to make use of Britain's comparative advantage, its abundance of capital.

The problem was to find a suitable target for Britain's economic weapons. That could only be the enemy's economy, centring on the civilian population, whose endurance became the ultimate target. Economic warfare attempted to destroy the resolve of German civilians. Now the correlation between moral and material resources in wartime is a loose one. Napoleon is supposed to have said 'in war the moral to the material is as three to one'. In economic warfare the role of social cohesion was critical. The blockade strategy was successful in this respect: the social damage it inflicted on Germany seems to have exceeded the material deprivation. Germany had sufficient food to maintain a reasonable level of physical efficiency, but failed to prevent social disintegration.

The alignment that was prefigured in the Atlantic orientation is the distant root of the North Atlantic Treaty Organization Alliance of today, and remains the foundation of British security. The apparent success of this strategy made it attractive between the wars. In the 1930s, when Britain began to face the same strategic dilemma, Hankey promoted a blockade strategy once again from his influential position as the cabinet secretary, and secretary of the Committee of Imperial Defence. Aerial attack on civilian populations was a more violent version of the same strategy, and between the wars it became axiomatic that "the bomber would always get through". The British bombardment of German cities during the Second World War once again attempted to use Britain's comparative advantage in capital, with American help, to subdue the civilian population without having to take on the German infantry. Germany, however, had learnt the lesson, and it appears that the food supply was much better organized in the Second World War.[4]

On the whole, German civilian morale did not crack under the impact of bombing. Social cohesion, the forces of approbation, yielded more to

[4] Burchardt, 'Kriegswirtschaft', pp. 76–82.

hunger than to bombs. Indeed, it seems that bombing actually *reinforced* the social bond.

Nuclear deterrence takes the idea of social destruction to its ultimate conclusion. As Ivan Bloch foresaw, where the threat was credible, it had the power to remove the option of war from serious consideration. Perhaps it is also important that nuclear power no longer insulates leaders from the consequences of their decisions. Fatalism is no longer sufficient to launch into war: it requires a personal death-wish.

Was it necessary to enter the war? Trevor Wilson says that the devoted prosecution of the war by vast numbers of Britons does not reveal them as deluded, irrational and manipulated. The same, however, could be said for the Germans. According to Wilson, the war was waged to preserve Britain as a major, independent power, and in order to vindicate parliamentary democracy against military autocracy. Even Wilson is not willing to say outright that the benefits outweighed the cost, though he comes very close to doing so.[5] This is to place a very high value on national self-esteem, to say nothing about other difficulties, such as the state of democracy in large parts of the Empire, among Britain's allies, and indeed in Britain itself. What *was* the cost of the war? The rough outline of economic damage is clear. It was made up of the economic growth forgone, the loss of financial assets, the sacrifice of skills and abilities (human capital). On the consumption side, the cost was of lives not lived, or lives disfigured by physical and emotional trauma. But does that provide a real measure of the cost? Is it possible to weigh the losses to the individuals who were killed, or to those whose well-being was dented by injury or bereavement, against the benefits to an abstract "community"? Even if the sums of this utilitarian calculus add up, they still make an immense imposition on those who bear the cost. It could be argued that "the community" willingly accepted the risks in advance, from "behind a veil of ignorance". But Britain's young manhood would have been astonished to learn in June 1914 that more than one in ten would be dead in four years, one in four among Oxbridge students. Still, there is some truth in this approach, especially under conditions of voluntary enlistment, but the risks were not equally distributed and not equally assumed. If we accept the utilitarian approach, then war elicits (as its advocates have always argued) extraordinary acts of altruism. But it is not altruism, or not entirely. The sacrifice was not voluntary, but largely induced by the forces of social approbation (in the case of voluntary enlistment), or coerced by the state.

The benefits are also not easily measurable. How can we estimate such intangibles as Great Power status, national pride, liberal democracy (if indeed these were the issues at stake), except perhaps in terms of the cost

[5] T. Wilson, *The Myriad Faces of War: Britain and the Great War, 1914–1918* (1986), pp. 2, 850–3.

of what it took to uphold them? The point is that these measures are again intangible and affect individual self-esteem. It is easy to paint the horrors of non-participation, and even defeat, but Germany in wartime was not all that different from Britain in wartime. Both had a good deal of public discussion and dissent. Both were capable of considerable brutality. For those who invoke Brest-Litovsk it is possible to counter with the Easter Rising. Political subordination does not imply economic inferiority. Both Germany and Japan have done well out of defeat. East Germany today is economically more successful than the Soviet Union. Our conventional guides to well-being, which measure economic values and entitlements, are seriously deficient as measures of cost and benefit in war. It requires a new branch of social accounting.

Yet some sort of estimate of cost and benefit must take place when soldiers and statesmen decide for war. The concept of intuitive reasoning provides a clue. These informal cost-benefit analyses do not measure what we *need* to know in order to make an intelligent decision—not the potential costs, the potential benefits, and the risks attached to them, but a crude proxy, some rudimentary game of simple outcomes, that are labelled "victory" or "defeat".

Was there any other choice? The question has to be asked, even if it cannot be answered, if only to show how difficult it is to answer. It highlights the First World War as a failure of politics, economics and society and reminds us that war is a trap which we have not yet achieved the insight and institutions to avoid.

LIST OF SOURCES CITED

A. ARCHIVAL SOURCES

Admiralty, Public Record Office, London.
American Relief Adminstration, Hoover Institution Archives, Stanford University.
Anderson, Alan, Public Record Office, London, PRO 30/68/7.
Armistice Commission, United States National Archives, Washington DC.
Asquith, Herbert H., Bodleian Library, Oxford.
Board of Trade, Public Record Office, London.
Borden, Robert Laird, Public Archives of Canada, Ottawa.
Cabinet, Public Record Office, London.
Chittenden, Russell H., Yale University Library.
Corbett, Julian S., National Maritime Museum, Greenwich.
Esher, Second Viscount, Churchill College, Cambridge.
Fisher, Irving, Yale University Library.
Fisher, John A., Churchill College, Cambridge.
Foreign Office, Public Record Office, London.
Germany, Admiralstab der Marine, Akten betreffend Handelskrieg mit U-Booten, United States National Archives, Washington DC.
Grant Duff, Adrian, Churchill College, Cambridge.
Haig, Douglas (Earl Haig) War Diaries, Public Record Office, London, WO 256/34.
Hankey, Maurice, Churchill College, Cambridge.
Harcourt, Lewis, Bodleian Library, Oxford.
Hawtrey, Ralph, Churchill College, Cambridge.
Hoover, Herbert, Hoover Presidential Library, West Branch, Iowa, and Hoover Institution Archives, Stanford University.
Hughes, William Morris, National Library of Australia, Canberra.
International Armistice Commission, United States National Archives, Washington DC.
King, William Lyon Mackenzie, Public Archives of Canada, Ottawa.
Laurier, Wilfrid, Public Archives of Canada, Ottawa.
Lemieux, Rodolphe, Public Archives of Canada, Ottawa.
Lloyd George, David, House of Lords Record Office, London.
Lusk, Graham, Hoover Institution Archives, Stanford University.
McKenna, Reginald, Churchill College, Cambridge.
Monats-Berichte der Stellvetreter Generalkommandos, Bayerische Hauptstaatsarchiv, Dept. IV. Kriegsarchiv, Munich.
Mountbatten (Battenberg), Prince Louis, Broadlands, Hampshire.
Müller and Gräf Poster Collection, Hoover Institution Archives, Stanford University.
Novar, Viscount (R. C. Munro-Ferguson), National Library of Australia, Canberra.
Slade, Edmond, Rear Admiral, National Maritime Museum, Greenwich.

Strauss, Lewis S., Hoover Institution Archives, Stanford University.
United States Food Administration, Hoover Institution Archives, Stanford University and United States National Archives, Washington DC.
War Office, Public Record Office, London.
World War One Subject Collection, Hoover Institution Archives, Stanford University.

B. UNPUBLISHED PAPERS AND DISSERTATIONS

Bott, J. P., 'The German Food Crisis of World War I: The Cases of Coblenz and Cologne' (University of Missouri Ph.D. thesis, 1981)
Burgmann, V., 'Revolutionaries and Racists: Australian Socialism and the Problem of Racism, 1887–1917' (Australian National University Ph.D. thesis, 1980).
Chittenden, R. H., 'Sixty Years in the Service of Science' (typescript, 1936, Yale University Library).
Ekins, A., 'Taming the Diggers: The Other Face of the Anzac Legend' (paper presented at the Australian Historical Association Conference, Sydney 1988).
Ermini, L., 'A Survey of Recent Contributions to the Criticism of Classical Rationality' (unpublished paper, University of California at San Diego 1986).
Fisher, F. J., 'Public Opinion and Agriculture, 1875–1900' (Hull University Ph.D. thesis, 1972).
Gandar, J. M., 'Economic Causation and British Emigration in the Late Nineteenth Century' (University of Missouri Ph.D. thesis, 1982).
Green, E., 'Bimetallism' (unpublished paper, 1985).
Henning, H., 'Die Situation der deutschen Kriegswirtschaft im Sommer 1918 und ihre Beurteilung durch Heeresleitung, Reichsführung und Bevölkerung' (Hamburg University Ph.D. thesis, 1957).
Johanesson, J. E., 'The Food Problem in Germany', (paper read at the Swedish Medical Society, Stockholm 28 Jan. 1919).
Martin, G. W., 'Financial and Manpower Aspects of the Dominions' and India's Contribution to Britain's War Effort, 1914–19' (Cambridge University Ph.D. thesis, 1986).
McQuilton, J., 'The Home Front in a Local Government Area: The Case of Yackandandah 1914–18' (paper presented at the Australian National University, 1987).
Mein Smith, P., 'Infant Survival in Australia, 1900–45: Mortality, Rules and Practice' (Australian National University Ph. D. thesis in progress).
Morris, P. A., 'Conditioning Factors Molding Public Opinion in British Columbia Hostile to Japanese Immigration into Canada' (University of Oregon MA thesis, 1963).
Murayama, Yuzo, 'The Economic History of Japanese Immigration to the Pacific Northwest 1890–1920' (University of Washington Ph.D. thesis, Seattle 1982).
Mutch, A., 'Rural Society in Lancaster, 1840–1914', (Manchester University Ph.D. thesis, 1980).
Osborne, J. W. M., 'The Voluntary Recruiting Movement in Britain, 1914–1916' (Stanford University Ph.D. thesis, 1979).

Patterson, G., 'Life and Death at Sea, 1850–1900' (paper read at the Social History Society Conference, University of Lancaster, Jan. 1983).

Ranft, B. M., 'The Naval Defence of British Sea-Borne Trade, 1860–1905' (Oxford University D.Phil. thesis, 1967).

Rosenhaft, E., 'A World Upside-down: Delinquency, Family and Work in the Lives of German Working-Class Youth, 1914–18' (unpublished paper, Liverpool University, ?1984).

Rothstein, M., 'American Wheat and the British Market, 1860–1905' (Cornell University Ph.D. thesis, 1960).

Sissons, D. C. S., 'The Immigration Question in Australian Diplomatic Relations with Japan' (unpublished paper, Canberra 1971).

Sumida, J. T., 'Financial Limitation, Technological Innovation, and British Naval Policy, 1904–1910' (University of Chicago Ph.D. thesis, 1982).

Swanson, M. R., 'The American Country Life Movement, 1900–1940' (University of Minnesota Ph.D. thesis, 1972).

Takeda, Isami, 'Australia–Japan Relations in the Era of the Anglo-Japanese Alliance, 1896–1911' (Sydney University Ph.D. thesis, 1984).

Twigg, J., 'The Vegetarian Movement in England, 1847–1981: With Particular Reference to its Ideology' (London University Ph.D. thesis, 1982).

C. OFFICIAL PAPERS

(In chronological order)

1. Australia

Australian Commonwealth Parliamentary Debates.

Official Year Book of NSW.

Victoria Year-Book.

New South Wales, *Decline of the Birth Rate and the Mortality of Infants in New South Wales. Royal Commission Report*, vol. 1 (Sydney 1904).

Coghlan, T. A., *Report on Immigration with Special Reference to Canada*, Intelligence Dept. New South Wales, Bulletin no. 3 (Sydney 1905).

Navigation Conference—Merchant Shipping Legislation—Report of a Conference between Representatives of the UK, Australia and NZ; Australia, Commonwealth PP no. 15, vol. III (1907–8).

2. Canada

Annual Report of the Department of the Interior.

Census and Statistics Monthly.

Lemieux, R., *Report of the Minister of Labor of his Mission to Japan on the Subject of the Influx of Oriental Laborers in the Province of British Columbia* (Ottawa, January 1908).

King, W.L., *Report of W.L. Mackenzie King . . . into the Methods by which Oriental Laborers have been Induced to Come to Canada* (Ottawa 1908).

3. France

Annuaire statistique (Paris 1913), vol. 33.

4. Germany

Statistisches Jahrbuch für das Deutsche Reich.

[Reichsmarineamt], *Die Seeinteressen des Deutschen Reiches. Zusammmengestellt auf Veranlassung des Reichsmarineamtes* (Berlin 1898).

Reichsmarineamt, *Die Entwicklung der deutschen Seeinteressen in dem letzten Jahrzehnt* (Berlin 1905).

'Schädigung der deutschen Volkskraft durch die völkerrechtswidrige feindliche Handelsblockade', Denkschrift des Reichsgesundheitsamts vom 16. Dez. 1918, in *Das Werk des Untersuchungsausschusses der Verfassunggebenden Deutschen Nationalversammlung und des Deutschen Reichstages, 1919–1928*, 4th ser., vol. 6 (Berlin 1928).

Verfassunggebende deutsche Nationalversammlung, Beilagen zu der Stenograph- ischen Berichten über die öffentlichen Verhandlungen des Untersuchungs- ausschusses, 2. Unterausschuss. Acktenstücke zur Friedensaktion Wilsons 1916/17 (Berlin 1920).

Das Werk des Untersuchungsausschusses der Verfassunggebenden Deutschen Nationalversammlung und des Deutschen Reichstages, 1919–1930, 4th ser. (Berlin 1925 ff.), 12 vols.

Deutsche Waffenstillstandkommission, *Der Waffenstillstand, 1918–1919* (Berlin 1928), 3 vols.

Hobohm, M., 'Soziale Heermissstände als Teilursache des deutschen Zusammen- bruchs von 1918', *Untersuchung*, 4th ser., vol. 11.

Lepsius, J., *et al.* (eds.), *Die Grosse Politik der europäischen Kabinette, 1871–1914* (Berlin 1924, 1925), vols. 15, 23.

Reichsarchiv, *Kriegsrüstung und Kriegswirtschaft* (Berlin 1930), 2 vols., in Reichsarchiv, *Der Weltkrieg, 1914 bis 1918* (Berlin 1925–1942), 14 vols.

5. Great Britain

Agricultural Returns for Great Britain.

House of Commons Debates.

Statistical Abstract for the United Kingdom.

Little, W. C., 'The Agricultural Labourer: Review of the Inquiry . . .' Labour. Royal Commission. Fifth and Final Report. Pt. 1, PP 1894 C. 7421 XXXV.

Board of Agriculture. Returns as to the Number and Size of Agricultural Holdings in Great Britain in the year 1895, PP 1896 C. 8243 LXVII.

Agricultural Depression. Royal Commission. Final Report, PP 1897 C. 8540 XV.

Fox, A. W., 'Wages and Earnings of Agricultural Labourers in the United King- dom. Report', PP 1900 Cd. 346 LXXXII.

Supply of Food and Raw Material in Time of War. Royal Commission. Minutes of Evidence, PP 1905 Cd. 2644 XXXIX.

Rew, R. H., 'Report on the Decline in the Agricultural Population of Great Britain, 1881–1906', PP 1906 Cd. 3273 XCVI.

Correspondence Respecting the Declaration of London, FO Miscellaneous no. 4 (1910), PP 1910 Cd. 5418 LXXIV.

Imperial Conference 1911. Minutes, PP 1911 Cd. 5745 LIV.

Imperial Conference 1911. Papers Laid Before the Conference, PP 1911 Cd. 5746–1 LIV.

Acreage and Livestock Returns for England and Wales, PP 1914–16 Cd. 7926 LXXIX.

Middleton, T. H.,'The Recent Development of German Agriculture', PP 1916 Cd. 8305 IV.

A Committee of the Royal Society, 'The Food Supply of the United Kingdom', PP 1916 Cd. 8421 IX.

Natural Resources . . . of HM's Dominions. Royal Commission. Memoranda and Tables. Trade Statistics and Trade of the Self-governing Dominions, PP 1914–16 Cd. 8156 XIV.

Natural Resources, Trade and Legislation of Certain Portions of HM's Dominions. Royal Commission, Final Report, PP 1917–18 Cd. 8462 X.

Imperial War Conference 1918. Extracts from Minutes of Proceedings and Papers Laid before the Conference, PP 1918 Cd. 9177 XVI.

Reports by British Officers on the Economic Conditions Prevailing in Germany, Dec. 1918–Mar. 1919, PP 1919 Cmd 52 LIII.

Further Reports by British Officers on the Economic Conditions Prevailing in Germany, Mar. and Apr. 1919, PP 1919 Cmd. 208 LIII.

Starling, E.H., 'Report on Food Conditions in Germany', PP 1919 Cmd. 280 LIII.

Wheat Supplies. Royal Commission. First Report with Appendices, PP 1921 Cmd. 1544 XVIII.

Public Record Office, *List of the Papers of the Committee of Imperial Defence to 1914* (1964).

Ministry of Agriculture, Fisheries and Food, *A Century of Agricultural Statistics: Great Britain, 1866–1966* (1968).

6. *The United States*

Yearbook of the United States Department of Agriculture.

Report of the Industrial Commission on Agriculture and Agricultural Labor, US 57 Congress, 1 Sess., house doc. 179, Industrial Commission, vol. 10 (Washington DC 1901).

Commissioner of Labor, Eleventh Special Report, *Regulation and Restriction of Output* (Washington DC 1904).

Fisher, I., 'National Vitality', *Report of the National Conservation Commission*, US 60 Congress, 2 Sess. 1989, sen. doc. 676, vol. 3.

'Special Message from the President . . . Transmitting the Report of the Country Life Commission', US 60 Congress, 2 Sess. 1909, sen. doc. 705, ser. 5408, Country Life Commission.

United States Department of Agriculture, *Crop Reporter* (1910–11).

Herrick, M. T., *Preliminary Report on Land and Agricultural Credit in Europe*, US 62 Congress, 3 Sess. sen. doc. 967, ser. 6364 (Washington DC 1912–13).

The Standard Loaf, USFA Bulletin no. 11 (Washington DC, Dec. 1917).

Food Control a War Measure, USFA Bulletin no. 15 (Washington DC 1918).

United States Department of State, *Foreign Relations of the United States*, The Paris Peace Conference (Washington DC 1942–47), 13 vols.

United States Department of Agriculture, *Wheat. Acreage, Yield and Production, by States, 1866–1943*, Agricultural Marketing Service, Bulletin no. 158 (Washington DC 1955).

United States Bureau of Census, *The Statistical History of the United States from Colonial Times to the Present* (New York 1976).

D. Books and Articles.

(Books published in London unless indicated otherwise.)

Adachi, K., *The Enemy that Never Was: A History of the Japanese Canadians* (Toronto 1976).

Adams, R. J. Q., and Poirier, P. P., *The Conscription Controversy in Great Britain, 1900–18* (1987).

Aereboe, F., *Der Einfluss des Krieges auf die landwirtschaftliche Produktion in Deutschland* (Stuttgart 1927).

—— and Warmbold, H., *Preisverhältnisse landwirtschaftlicher Erzeugnisse im Kriege*, Beiträge zur Kriegswirtschaft, no. 6 (Berlin 1917).

Agricultural Committee on National Wheat Stores Report (1897–8).

Alford, K., and McLean, M., 'Partners or Parasites of Men? Women's Economic Status in Australia, Britain and Canada, 1850–1900', *ANU Working Papers in Economic History*, no. 66 (Apr. 1986).

Allen, R. C., 'The Price of Freehold Land and the Interest Rate in the Seventeenth and Eighteenth Centuries', *Economic History Review*, vol. 41 (1988).

Anderson, G., *Victorian Clerks* (Manchester 1976).

Andrews, F., 'Freight Costs and Market Values', *USDA Yearbook 1906* (Washington, DC 1906).

Angell, N., *The Great Illusion* (1910).

Ankli, R. E., 'The Growth of the Canadian Economy, 1876–1920: Export-led and/ or Neoclassical Growth', *Explorations in Economic History*, vol. 17 (July 1980).

Anon., 'British Naval Policy and German Aspirations', *Fortnightly Review* (Sept. 1905).

Armstrong, W. A., 'The Workfolk', in Mingay, G. (ed.), *The Victorian Countryside* (1981), vol. 2.

Asquith, H. H., *The Genesis of the War*(1923).

—— *Letters to Venetia Stanley*, ed. Brock, M. and E. (Oxford 1982).

Atack, J., 'Farm and Farm-making Costs Revisited', *Agricultural History*, vol. 56 (1982).

Atwater, W. O., *Principles of Nutrition and Nutritive Value of Food*, USDA Farmers' Bulletin no. 147 (Washington DC 1902).

Avery, D., and Neary, P., 'Laurier, Borden and a White British Columbia', *Journal of Canadian Studies*, vol. 12 (1977).

Axelrod, R., *The Evolution of Co-operation* (New York 1984).

Ay, K. L., *Die Entstehung einer Revolution. Die Volksstimmung in Bayern während des Ersten Weltkrieges* (Berlin 1968).

Babington, A., *For the Sake of Example* (1983).

Bach, F. W., *Untersuchungen über die Lebensmittelrationierung im Kriege und ihre physiologisch-hygienische Bedeutung* (Munich 1919).

Bacon, R. H., *The Life of Lord Fisher of Kilverstone* (1929), 2 vols.

—— *From 1900 Onwards* (1940).

Bailey, L. H., *The Country Life Movement* (New York 1911).

Baines, D., *Migration in a Mature Economy: Emigration and Internal Migration in England and Wales, 1861–1900* (Cambridge 1986).

Baldwin, D. A., *Economic Statecraft* (Princeton 1985).

Ball, C. R., *et al.*, 'Wheat Production and Marketing', *USDA Yearbook 1921* (Washington DC 1922).

Ball, F. C., *One of the Damned: The Life and Times of Robert Tressell, Author of the Ragged Trousered Philanthropists* (1973).

Ballod, C., 'Güterbedarf und Konsumtion', in Zahn, F. (ed.), *Die Statistik in Deutschland nach ihrem heutigen Stand* (Munich and Berlin 1911).

—— 'Die Volksernährung in Krieg und Frieden', *Schmollers Jahrbücher*, vol. 39 (1915).

Bane, S. L., and Lutz, R. H. (eds.), *The Blockade of Germany after the Armistice 1918–1919* (Stanford 1942).

Barkin, K., *The Controversy over German Industrialization 1890–1902* (Chicago 1970).

Barnard, A., 'Commonwealth Government Finances, 1901–82: A Handy Compendium', *Source Papers in Economic History*, no. 17 (Canberra 1986).

Barnard, L. M., *British Food Policy during the First World War* (1985).

Barnes, D. G., *A History of the English Corn Laws* (1930).

Barrett, J., *Falling in: Australians and "Boy Conscription", 1911–1915* (Sydney 1979).

Batocki, H. C. von, *Warenpreis und Geldwert im Kriege* (Königsberg 1919).

—— 'Umstellung der Landwirtschaft', in Anschütz, G., *et al.*, *Handbuch der Politik* (3rd edn. Berlin and Leipzig 1920), vol. 2.

—— 'Rationierung der Lebensmittel', in Anschütz, G., *et al.*, *Handbuch der Politik* (3rd edn. Berlin and Leipzig 1920), vol. 2.

Baturinskii, D. A., *Agrarnaya politika Tsarskogo pravitel'stva i krest'yanskii pozemel'nyi bank* (Moscow 1925).

Beale, H. K., *Theodore Roosevelt and the Rise of America to World Power* (Baltimore 1956).

Beames, J., *Army without Banners* (1931).

Bean, C. E. W., *The Australian Imperial Force in France during the Allied Offensive, 1918* (Official History of Australia in the War of 1914–18, vol. 6; Sydney 1942).

—— *Anzac to Amiens. A Shorter History of the Australian Fighting Services in the First World War* (Canberra 1948).

Bedford, Duke of, *A Great Agricultural Estate* (1897).

Beechert, E., 'Labour Relations in the Hawaiian Sugar Industry, 1850–1937', in Albert, B., and Graves, A. (eds.), *Crisis and Change in the International Sugar Economy, 1860–1914* (Norwich and Edinburgh 1984).

Behrend, W., 'Die Kartoffel im Kriege', *Preussische Jahrbücher*, no. 134 (1908).

Bell, A. C., *A History of the Blockade of Germany . . . 1914–1918* (1937).

—— *Die englische Hungerblockade im Weltkrieg, 1914–15*, ed. Böhmert, V. (Essen 1943).

Bellerby, J. R., *Agriculture and Industry Relative Income* (1956).

—— and Taylor, F. D. W., 'Aggregate Tithe Rent charge on farm Land in the United Kingdom, 1867–1938', *Journal of Agricultural Economics*, vol. 11 (1955).

Beninde, M., and Rubner, M., 'Welchen Einfluss hat die Kriegsernährung auf die Volksgesundheit ausgeübt und übt sie noch aus?', Gutachten der Wissenschaftlichen Deputation für das Medizinalwesen vom 18. Juli 1917, in Beninde, M., *Hungerblockade und Volksgesundheit*, Veröffentlichungen aus dem Gebiete der Medizinalverwaltung, vol. 10, pt. 3 (Berlin 1920).

Bennett, M. K., 'Average Pre-War and Post-War Farm Costs of Wheat Production in the North American Spring-Wheat Belt,' *Wheat Studies*, vol. 1 (1925).

—— *Farm Cost Studies in the United States* (Stanford 1928).

—— 'World Wheat Crops, 1885–1932: New Series, with Areas and Yields, by Countries', *Wheat Studies*, vol. 9 (1933).

—— 'Per Capita Wheat Consumption in Western Europe, I. Measurement , from 1885–86', *Wheat Studies*, vol. 11 (1935).

—— 'Wheat and War, 1914–18 and Now', *Wheat Studies*, vol. 16 (Nov. 1939).

Berghahn, V. R., *Der Tirpitz-Plan. Genesis und Verfall einer innenpolitischen Krisenstrategie unter Wilhelm II.* (Düsseldorf 1970).

—— *Germany and the Approach of War in 1914* (1973).

Bernhardi, F. von, *Germany and the Next War* (1912, English trans. 1914).

Berthold, R., 'Zur Entwicklung der deutschen Agrarproduktion und der Ernährungswirtschaft zwischen 1907 und 1925', *Jahrbuch der Wirtschaftsgeschichte*, vol. 4 (1974).

Best, G., *Humanity in Warfare* (1980).

Bicha, K. D., 'The Plains Farmer and the Prairie Province Frontier, 1897–1914', *Journal of Economic History*, vol. 25 (1965).

—— 'Prairie Radicals: A Common Pietism', *Journal of Church and State*, vol. 18 (1976).

Bickersteth, J. B., *The Land of Open Doors, being Letters from Western Canada* (1914).

Bidwell, S., and Graham, D., *Fire-power: British Army Weapons and Theories of War, 1904–1945* (1982).

Binnie-Clark, G., *Wheat and Woman* (Toronto 1914, new edn. 1979).

Blainey, G., *The Causes of War* (Melbourne 1977).

—— *All for Australia* (Sydney 1984).

Blaustein, A., 'Versuch einer Bibliographie zur Kriegswirtschaftslehre', *Weltwirtschaftliches Archiv*, vol. 3 (1914).

Bliss, M., 'War Business as Usual: Canadian Munitions Production, 1914–1918', in Dreisziger, N. F. (ed.), *Mobilization for Total War: The Canadian, American and British Experience, 1914–1918, 1939–1945* (Waterloo, Ontario 1981).

Bloch, I. S., *Is War Now Impossible?*, being an abridgement of *The War of the Future in its Technical, Economic and Political Relationships* (1899).

Blücher, Princess Evelyn, *An English Wife in Berlin* (1920).

Bogue, A. G., *From Prairie to Corn Belt* (Chicago 1963).

Böhm, O., *Die Kornhäuser* (Stuttgart 1898).

Booker, M., *The Great Professional: A Study of W. M. Hughes* (Sydney 1980).

Robert Laird Borden: His Memoirs, ed. Borden, H. (abridged edn. Toronto 1969), 2 vols.

Borowsky, P., *Deutsche Ukrainepolitik, 1918* (Lübeck and Hamburg 1970).

Bowen, J. C., *Wheat and Flour Prices from Farmer to Consumer*, United States Department of Labor, Bureau of Labor Statistics, Bulletin no. 130 (Washington DC 1913).

Bowles, T. G., *The Declaration of Paris of 1856* (1900).

—— *Sea Law and Sea Power* (1909).

Bowley, A. L., 'Rural Population in England and Wales: A Study of Changes of Density, Occupations and Ages', *Journal of the Royal Statistical Society*, vol. 77 (May 1914).

—— and Burnett-Hurst, A. R., *Livelihood and Poverty* (1913).

Brailsford, H. N., *The War of Steel and Gold* (1914).

—— *Across the Blockade: A Record of Travels in Enemy Europe* (1919).

Brennan, G., and Tullock, G., 'An Economic Theory of Military Tactics: Methodological Individualism at War', *Journal of Economic Behavior and Organization*, vol. 3 (1983).

Brex, Twells (ed.), *"Scare Mongerings" from the Daily Mail, 1896–1914* (1914).

Brown, R. C., *Robert Laird Borden: A Biography* (Toronto 1975), vol. 1.

—— 'Sir Robert Borden and Canada's War Aims', in Hunt, B., and Preston, A. (eds.), *War Aims and Strategic Policy in the Great War, 1914–1918* (1977).

Buchheim, C., 'Aspects of XIXth Century Anglo-German Trade Rivalry Reconsidered', *Journal of European Economic History*, vol. 10 (1981).

Bueno de Mesquita, B., *The War Trap* (New Haven 1981).

Bumm, F. (ed.), *Deutschlands Gesundheitsverhältnisse unter dem Einfluss des Weltkrieges* (Stuttgart 1928).

Bunselmeyer, R., *The Cost of the War, 1914–1919: British Economic War Aims and the Origins of Reparations* (Hamden, Conn. 1975).

Burchardt, L., *Friedenswirtschaft und Kriegsvorsorge: Deutschlands wirtschaftliche Rüstungsbestrebungen vor 1914* (Boppard am Rhein 1968)

—— 'Die Auswirkung der Kriegswirtschaft auf die deutsche Zivilbevölkerung im ersten und im zweiten Weltkrieg', *Militärgeschichtliche Mitteilungen*, no. 1 (1974).

Burk, K., 'The Mobilization of Anglo-American Finance during World War I', in Dreisziger, N. F. (ed.), *Mobilization for Total War: The Canadian, American and British Experience', 1914–18, 1939–1945* (Waterloo, Ontario 1981).

Burk, K., *Britain, America and the Sinews of War, 1914–1918* (1985).

Burnett, J., *Plenty and Want* (1979 edn.).

—— Vincent, D., and Mayall, D., *The Autobiography of the Working Class: An Annotated, Critical Bibliography* (Brighton 1984, 1987), 2 vols.

Burnett, P. M. (ed.), *Reparation at the Paris Peace Conference from the Standpoint of the American Delegation* (New York 1940), 2 vols.

Butlin, N. G., 'Colonial Socialism in Australia, 1860–1900' in Aitken, H. G. J. (ed.), *The State and Economic Growth* (New York 1959).

—— *Investment in Australian Economic Development, 1861–1900* (Cambridge 1964).

—— 'The Australian Economy Heavily Disguised', *Business Archives and History*, vol. 4 (1964).

—— 'Australian National Accounts, 1788–1983', *Source Papers in Economic History*, no. 6 (Canberra 1985).

—— *Bicentennial Diary* (Brisbane 1988).

Caird, J., *The Landed Interest and the Supply of Food* (4th edn. 1880).

Cairncross, A., *Home and Foreign Investment, 1870–1913: Studies in Capital Accumulation* (1953).

Callwell, C. E., *Field Marshall Henry Wilson: His Life and Diaries* (1927), 2 vols.

Calvert, H., *The Wealth and Welfare of the Punjab being Some Studies in Punjab Rural Economics* (Lahore 1922).

Campbell-Bannerman, H. 'The Hague Conference and the Limitation of Armaments', *The Nation*, 2 Mar. 1907.

Carnegie, A., 'The Reunion of Britain and America—A Look Ahead', *North American Review*, vol. 156 (1893).

Carnegie, D., *The History of Munitions Supply in Canada, 1914–1918* (1925).

Carnegie Endowment for International Peace (trans.), *Official German Documents Relating to the World War* (New York 1923).

Caron, F., *An Economic History of Modern France* (1979).

Carrier, N. H., and Jeffery, J. H., *External Migration: A Study of the Available Statistics, 1815–1950* (1953).

Carson, G., *Cornflake Crusade* (1959).

Challener, R. D., *Admirals, Generals, and American Foreign Policy, 1898–1914* (Princeton 1973).

Channon, G., *The Politics of Food* (1987).

Chatfield, Admiral of the Fleet, Lord, *The Navy and Defence* (1942).

[Chipman, G. F.], *The Siege of Ottawa* (Winnipeg 1910).

Chittenden, R. H., *Physiological Economy in Nutrition* (New York 1904).

—— *The Nutrition of Man* (New York 1907).

Chomley, C. H., *Protection in Canada and Australia* (1904).

Choucri, N., and North, R. C., *Nations in Conflict: National Growth and International Violence* (San Francisco 1975).

Churchill, R. S., *Winston S. Churchill*, vol. 2, Companion vol., Pt. 2 (1969).

Clark, L., *Alfred Williams: His Life and Work* (1945, Newton Abbott 1969).

Clarke, G. S. [Lord Sydenham of Combe], 'A Naval Union with Great Britain: A Reply to Mr. Andrew Carnegie', *North American Review*, vol. 158 (1894).

Clarke, I. F., *Voices Prophesying War, 1763–1984* (1966).

Clausewitz, Carl von, *On War*, ed. and trans. Howard, M., and Paret, P. (Princeton 1976).

Cole, G. D. H., *Labour in Wartime* (1915).

Collins, E. J. T., 'Agriculture in a Free Trade Economy: Great Britain, 1870–1930', in Villani, P. (ed.), *Trasformazioni delle società rurali nei aesi dell'Europa occidentale e mediterranea* (Naples 1986).

—— 'The Rationality of "Surplus" Agricultural Labour: Mechanization in English Agriculture in the Nineteenth Century', *Agricultural History Review*, vol. 35 (1987).

Coogan, J. W., *The End of Neutrality: The United States, Britain and Maritime Rights, 1899–1915* (Ithaca, NY 1981).

Cooper, C. E., *Behind the Lines: One Woman's War, 1914–18*, ed. Denholm, D. (1982).

Copp, T., *The Anatomy of Poverty: The Conditions of the Working Class in Montreal, 1897–1921* (Toronto 1974).

Corbett, J. S., *Some Principles of Maritime Strategy* (1911).

Creveld, M. van, *Supplying War* (Cambridge 1977).

—— *Fighting Power* (1983).

—— *Command in War* (Cambridge, Mass. 1985).

Crichton-Browne, Sir James, *Parcimony in Nutrition* (1909)

Cronin, K., *Colonial Casualties: Chinese in Early Victoria* (Melbourne 1982).

Crookes, Sir William, *The Wheat Problem* (2nd edn. 1917).

Crowl, P. A., 'Alfred Thayer Mahan: The Naval Historian', in Paret, P., *et al.* (eds.), *Makers of Modern Strategy* (Princeton 1986).

Daniels, R., *The Politics of Prejudice: The Anti-Japanese Movement in California and the Struggle for Japanese Exclusion*, University of California Publications in History, vol. 71 (Berkeley, Calif. 1962).

Davenport-Hines, R. P. T., *Dudley Docker: The Life and Times of a Trade Warrior* (Cambridge 1984).

David, P.,'The Landscape and the Machine', in his *Technical Choice, Innovation and Economic Growth* (Cambridge 1975).

Davis, L. E., and Huttenback, R. E., *Mammon and Empire* (Cambridge 1986).

Davison, G., 'Sydney and the Bush: An Urban Context for the Australian Legend', *Historical Studies*, vol. 18 (1978).

Dawson, R. M., *William Lyon Mackenzie King. A Political Biography, 1. 1874–1923* (Toronto 1958).

Dawson, W. H., *The Evolution of Modern Germany* (1908).

Decker, L. E., 'The Great Speculation: An Interpretation of Mid-continent Pioneering', in Ellis, D. M. (ed.), *The Frontier in American Development: Essays in Honor of Paul Wallace Gates* (Ithaca, NY 1969).

Deist, W., *Flottenpolitik und Flottenpropaganda* (Stuttgart 1976).

—— (ed.), *Militär und Innenpolitik im Weltkrieg, 1914–1918* (Düsseldorf 1970), 2 vols.

Delbrück, C. von, *Die wirtschaftliche Mobilmachung in Deutschland, 1914* (Munich 1924).

Denoon, D., *Settler Capitalism* (Oxford 1983).

Desai, A. V., *Real Wages in Germany, 1871–1913* (Oxford 1968).

Devlin, Lord, *The House of Lords and the Naval Prize Bill, 1911* (1968).

Dickmann, F., *Die Kriegsschuldfrage auf der Friedenskonferenz von Paris 1919* (Munich 1964).

Digby, A., *Pauper Palaces* (1978).

Dix, A., 'Volkswirtschaftliche Kriegsvorsorge', *Vierteljahrshefte für Truppenführung und Heereskunde*, vol. 10 (1913).

Dixon, N., *The Psychology of Military Incompetence* (1976).

—— *Our Own Worst Enemy* (1987).

Dohrn, S., *Die Entstehung weiblicher Büroarbeit in England 1860 bis 1914* (Frankfurt 1986).

Doughty, M., *Merchant Shipping and War: A Study in Defence Planning in Twentieth-century Britain* (1982).

Dovring, F., *Land and Labour in Europe, 1900–1950* (1956).

Drache, H. M., *The Day of the Bonanza: A History of Bonanza Farming in the Red River Valley of the North* (Fargo, N. Dakota 1964).

—— 'Midwest Agriculture: Changing with Technology', *Agricultural History*, vol. 50 (Jan. 1976).

—— 'Thomas D. Campbell—The Plower of the Plains', in Wessel, T. R. (ed.), *Agriculture in the Great Plains, 1897–1936, Agricultural History*, vol. 51 (1977).

Dunae, P., *Gentlemen Emigrants: From the British Public Schools to the Canadian Frontier* (Vancouver 1981).

Dunbabin, J. P. D., *Rural Discontent in Nineteenth-century Britain* (1974).

Dunluce, Viscount, and Greenwood, M., *An Inquiry into the Composition of Dietaries, with Special Reference to the Dietaries of Munitions Workers* (1918).

Dunsdorfs, E., *The Australian Wheat Growing Industry, 1788–1948* (Melbourne 1956).

Easterbrook, W. T., and Watkins M. H. (eds.), *Approaches to Canadian Economic History* (Toronto 1967).

Elbaum, B., and Wilkinson, F., 'Industrial Relations and Uneven Development: A Comparative Study of the American and British Steel Industries', *Cambridge Journal of Economics*, vol. 3 (1979).

Elsner, L., 'Foreign Workers and Forced Labor in Germany during the First World War', in Hoerder, D. (ed.), *Labor Migration in the Atlantic Economies* (Westport, Connecticut 1985).

Eltzbacher, P. (ed.), *Germany's Food. Can it Last?* (1915).

Esher, Lord, 'Modern War and Peace', in his *King Edward VII and Other Essays* (1915).

—— 'The Naval and Military Situation', in his *King Edward VII and Other Essays* (1915).

—— *The Tragedy of Lord Kitchener* (1921).

Esthus, R. A., *Theodore Roosevelt and Japan* (Seattle 1966).

Eulenberg, F., 'Bedeutung der Lebensmittelpreise für die Ernährung', *Handbuch der Hygiene* (2nd edn. Leipzig 1913), vol. 3, pt. 1.

Evans, E., *The Contentious Tithe* (1976).

Fairlie, S., 'The Corn Laws and British Wheat Production, 1829–76', *Economic History Review*, vol. 22 (1969).

Farnsworth, H. C., 'Decline and Recovery of Wheat Prices in the "Nineties" ', *Wheat Studies*, vol. 10 (1934).

—— ' "World" Wheat Stocks, 1890–1914 and 1922–39', *Wheat Studies*, vol. 16 (1939–40).

—— 'Wheat in the Post-Surplus Period, with Recent Analogies and Contrasts, 1900–1909', *Wheat Studies*, vol. 17 (1941).

Fay, C. R., *Co-Operation at Home and Abroad* (5th edn. 1948).

Fayle, C. E., *History of the Great War: Seaborne Trade* (1924), 3 vols.

Feinstein, C. H., *National Income, Expenditure and Output of the United Kingdom, 1855–1965* (Cambridge 1972).
—— and Pollard, S. (eds.), *Studies in Capital Formation in the United Kingdom, 1750–1920* (Oxford 1988).
Feldman, G., *Army, Industry and Labor in Germany, 1914–1918* (Princeton 1966).
Field, F. W., *Capital Investments in Canada* (Montreal 1914).
Fischer, A., 'Volksernährung', in *Handwörterbuch der Staatswissenschaften*, ed. Elster, L. and Weber, A. (4th edn. Jena 1929), supplementary volume.
Fischer, F., *The War of Illusions: German Policies from 1911 to 1914* (1975).
Fisher, F. M., and Temin, P., 'Regional Specialization and the Supply of Wheat in the United States, 1867–1914', *Review of Economics and Statistics*, vol. 52 (1970).
Fisher, I., and Fiske, E. L., *How to Live: Rules for Healthful Living Based on Modern Science* (15th edn. New York 1919).
Fisher, I.N., *My Father Irving Fisher* (New York 1956).
Fisher, J. A., *Memories* (1919).
—— *Records* (1919).
—— *Fear God and Dread Nought: The Correspondence of Admiral of the Fleet Lord Fisher of Kilverstone*, ed. Marder, A. J. (1952–9), 3 vols.
Fite, G. C., *The Farmer's Frontier, 1865–1900* (New York 1966).
Fitzhardinge, L. F., *That Fiery Particle: A Political Biography of William Morris Hughes, 1862–1914*, vol. 1 (Sydney 1964).
—— *The Little Digger, 1914–1952. William Morris Hughes: A Political Biography*, vol. 2 (Sydney 1979).
Fitzpatrick, S., *Rising Damp: Sydney, 1870–90* (Melbourne 1987).
Flemming, J., *Landwirtschaftliche Interessen und Demokratie* (Bonn 1978).
Fletcher, C. R. L., and Kipling, R., *A School History of England* (Oxford 1911).
Fletcher, T. W., 'The Great Depression of British Agriculture, 1873–1896', *Economic History Review*, vol. 13 (1960–1).
—— 'Lancashire Livestock Farming during the Great Depression', *Agricultural History Review*, vol. 9 (1961).
Fogarty, J., and Duncan, T., *Australia and Argentina: On Parallel Paths* (Sydney 1984).
Fowke, V. C., *The National Policy and the Wheat Economy* (Toronto 1957).
Fraser, P., *Lord Esher: A Political Biography* (1973).
Fraser, T. G., 'Imperial Policy and Indian Minorities Overseas, 1905–23', in Hepburn, A. C. (ed.), *Minorities in History* (1978).
—— 'The Sikh Problem in Canada and its Political Consequences, 1905–1921', *Journal of Imperial and Commonwealth History*, vol. 7 (1978).
French, D., *British Economic and Strategic Planning, 1905–1915* (1982).
—— *British Strategy and War Aims, 1914–1916* (1986).
Friedensburg, F., *Kohl und Eisen im Weltkriege und in den Friedensschlüssen* (Munich and Berlin 1934).
Friesen, G., *The Canadian Prairies: A History* (Toronto 1984).
Frisch, R. E., 'Fatness and Fertility', *Scientific American*, vol. 258 (Mar. 1988).
Fröhlich, G., 'Deutsche Volksernährung im Kriege', *Schmollers Jahrbücher*, vol. 36 (1912).

Fry, M. G., *Lloyd George and Foreign Policy* (Montreal 1977).

Galbraith, J. K., *Economics and the Public Purpose* (paperback edn. 1975).

Geiss, I., 'Die manipulierte Kriegsschuldfrage', *Militärgeschichtliche Mitteilungen*, no. 2 (1983).

Gelder, W. de, *A Dutch Homesteader on the Prairies*, intr. and trans. Ganzervoort, H. (Toronto 1973).

Gellner, E., 'Nationalism', in his *Thought and Change* (1964).

Gilbert, A. D., 'The Land and the Church', in Mingay, G. (ed.), *The Victorian Countryside*, (1981) vol. 1.

Goleman, D., *Vital Lies, Simple Truths: The Psychology of Self-deception* (New York 1985).

Gordon, D. C., *The Dominion Partnership in Imperial Defence, 1870–1914* (Baltimore 1965).

Gospel, H. F., and Littler, C. R. (eds.), *Managerial Strategies and Industrial Relations* (1983).

Grain Growers' Guide (Winnipeg).

Gratz, G., and Schüller, R., *Der wirtschaftliche Zusammenbruch Österreich-Ungarns* (Vienna 1930).

Gray, J. H., *Boomtime: Peopleing the Canadian Prairies* (Saskatoon, Saskatchewan 1979).

Groves, F. R., *Settlers of the Marsh* (Toronto 1925, paperback edn. 1966).

Haggard, H. R., *Rural England: Being an Account of Agricultural and Social Researches Carried Out in the Years 1901 & 1902* (new edn. 1906), 2 vols.

—— *Rural Denmark and its Lessons* (1911).

Haig, D., *The Private Papers of Douglas Haig, 1914–1919*, ed. Blake, R. (1952).

Hall, A. D., *The Book of the Rothamsted Experiments* (1905).

Hall, B. T., 'Our Food Supply in Time of War and Imperial Defence', *Journal of the Royal United Services Institution*, vol. 45 (1901).

Hallett, M. E., 'A Governor-General's Views on Oriental Immigration to British Columbia, 1904–1911', *BC Studies*, vol. 14 (summer 1972).

Hallmann, H., *Der Weg zum deutschen Schlachtflottenbau* (Stuttgart 1933).

Hammerton, A. J., *Emigrant Gentlewomen: Genteel Poverty and Female Emigration, 1830–1914* (1979).

Hankey, Lord, *The Supreme Command, 1914–1918* (1961), 2 vols.

Hardach, G., *The First World War, 1914–1918* (1977).

Hardinge of Penshurst, Lord, *Old Diplomacy* (1947).

Hargreaves, M. W. M., 'The Dry Farming Movement in Retrospect', in Wessel, T. R. (ed.), *Agriculture in the Great Plains, 1897–1936, Agricultural History*, vol. 51 (1977).

Harley, C. K., 'Skilled Labour and the Choice of Technique in Edwardian Industry', *Explorations in Economic History*, vol. 11 (1974).

—— 'Western Settlement and the Price of Wheat, 1872–1913', *Journal of Economic History*, vol. 38 (Dec. 1978).

—— 'Transportation, the World Wheat Trade, and the Kuznets Cycle, 1850–1913', *Explorations in Economic History*, vol. 17 (1980).

Harrison, R., 'The War Emergency Workers' National Committee, 1914–1920', in Briggs, A., and Saville, J. (eds.), *Essays in Labour History*, vol. 2 (1971).

Hart, R. A., *The Great White Fleet: Its Voyage around the World, 1907–1909* (Boston 1965).

Hazlehurst, C., *Politicians at War, July 1914 to May 1915* (1971).

Heinemann, U., *Die verdrängte Niederlage. Politische Öffentlichkeit und Kriegschuldfrage in der Weimarer Republik* (Göttingen 1983).

Hertel, H., *Co-operation in Danish Agriculture* (1918).

Herwig, H., *"Luxury" Fleet: The Imperial German Navy, 1888–1918* (1980).

Hibbard, B. H., *Effects of the Great War upon Agriculture in the United States and Great Britain* (New York 1919).

Hicks, N., *This Sin and Scandal: Australia's Population Debate, 1891–1911* (Canberra 1978).

Hilton, B., *Corn, Cash and Commerce* (1977).

Hindhede, M., *What to Eat and Why* (1914).

Hirschfeld, E., 'Die Ernährung in ihrem Einfluss auf Krankheit und Sterblichkeit', in Mosse, M., and Tugendreich, G. (eds.), *Krankheit und soziale Lage* (Munich 1913).

Hirschmann, A. O., *Exit, Voice and Loyalty* (Cambridge, Mass. 1970).

Hobsbawm, E. J., 'Artisan or Labour Aristocrat?', *Economic History Review*, vol. 37 (1984).

—— and Rudé, G., *Captain Swing* (1969).

Hobson, J. A., *Imperialism: A Study* (1902).

—— *An Economic Interpretation of Investment* (1911).

Hoffman, R. J. S., *Great Britain and the German Trade Rivalry, 1875–1914* (Philadelphia 1933).

Hoffmann, W. G., *Das Wachstum der deutschen Wirtschaft seit der Mitte des 19. Jahrhunderts* (Berlin 1965).

Hoover, H., *The Memoirs of Herbert Hoover* (1952), vol. 1.

—— *An American Epic* (Chicago 1960), 3 vols.

Hopkins, M. [pseud. of H. Joseph], *Deep Furrows* (Toronto 1918).

Horn, D., *The German Naval Mutinies of World War I* (New Brunswick, New Jersey 1969).

Howard, M., 'The Armed Forces', *New Cambridge Modern History*, vol. 11 (1962).

—— *The Continental Commitment* (1972).

—— 'Men against Fire: Expectations of War in 1914', *International Security*, vol. 9 (1984).

Howe, G. M., *Man, Environment and Disease in Britain* (1972).

Hubatsch, W., *Die Ära Tirpitz: Studien zur deutschen Marinepolitik 1890–1918* (Berlin and Frankfurt 1955).

Hudson, W. J., *Billy Hughes in Paris: The Birth of Australian Diplomacy* (Melbourne 1978).

Hughes, W. M., *"The Day"—And After* (n. d. [1916]).

Hunt, E., 'Labour Productivity in English Agriculture, 1850–1914', *Economic History Review*, vol. 20 (1967).

Hurd, W. B., *Racial Origins and Nativity of the Canadian People*, Census Monograph no. 4 (Ottawa 1937).

Huttenback, R. A., *Racism and Empire: White Settlers and Colored Immigrants in the British Self-governing Colonies, 1830–1910* (Ithaca, NY 1976).

Jackson, R. V., 'Owner-occupation of Houses in Sydney, 1871 to 1891', *Australian Economic History Review*, vol. 10 (1970).

Jarausch, K., *The Enigmatic Chancellor: Bethmann Hollweg and the Hubris of Imperial Germany* (New Haven 1973).

Jebb, R., 'The Imperial Problem of Asiatic Immigration', *Journal of the Royal Society of Arts*, vol. 56 (1908).

Jefferey, K., *The British Army and the Crisis of Empire, 1918–22* (Manchester 1984).

Jefferies, R., *Hodge and his Masters* (1880).

Johanson, D., 'History of the White Australia Policy', in Rivett, K. (ed.), *Immigration: Control or Colour Bar?* (Melbourne, rev. edn. 1962).

Johnson, P., *Saving and Spending: The Working-class Economy in Britain, 1870–1939* (Oxford 1985).

Johnston, H., *The Voyage of the Komagata Maru: The Sikh Challenge to Canada's Colour Bar* (Delhi 1979).

Johnston, R., and Percy, M., 'Reciprocity, Imperial Sentiment and Party Politics in the 1911 Election', *Canadian Journal of Political Science*, vol. 13 (1980).

—— Percy, M., and Norrie, K. H., 'Reciprocity and the Canadian General Election of 1911', *Explorations in Economic History*, vol. 19 (1982).

Joll, J., *The Origins of the First World War* (1984).

Jones, G., and Barnes, M., *Britain on Borrowed Time* (1967).

Kahneman, D., Slovik, P., and Tversky, A. (eds.), *Judgement under Uncertainty: Heuristics and Biases* (Cambridge 1982).

Kain, R. J. P., and Prince, H. C., *The Tithe Surveys of England and Wales* (Cambridge 1985).

Kaiser, D., 'Germany and the Origins of the First World War', *Journal of Modern History*, vol. 55 (1983).

Kehr, E., *Battleship Building and Party Politics in Germany, 1894–1901* (1930; ed. and trans. Anderson, P. R. and E. N., Chicago 1973).

—— *Economic Interest, Militarism and Foreign Policy*, ed. Craig, G. A. (Berkeley 1977).

Kemp, P. (ed.), *The Fisher Papers* (1964), Navy Records Society vol. 106, 2 vols.

Kendle, J., *The Colonial and Imperial Conferences, 1887–1911: A Study in Imperial Organization* (1967).

—— *The Round Table Movement and Imperial Union* (Toronto 1975).

Kendrick, J. W., *Productivity Trends in the United States* (Princeton 1961).

Kennedy, P. M., *The Rise and Fall of British Naval Mastery* (1976).

—— *The Rise of the Anglo-German Antagonism, 1860–1914* (1980).

—— 'The First World War and the International Power System', *International Security*, vol. 9 (1984).

Keynes, J. M., 'Melchior: A Defeated Enemy' (first published 1949), in *The Collected Writings of John Maynard Keynes*, 10. *Essays in Biography* (1972).

Kindleberger, C. P., *Economic Growth in France and Britain, 1851–1950* (Cambridge, Mass. 1964).

Kleine-Natrop, H., *Devisenpolitik in Deutschland vor dem Kriege und in der Kriegs- und Nachkriegszeit* (Berlin 1922).

Knee, F., *The Diary of Fred Knee*, ed. Englander, D. (Coventry 1977).

Kocka, J., *Facing Total War: German Society, 1914–1918* (Leamington Spa 1984).

Kruse, W., and Hintze, K., *Sparsame Ernährung. Nach Erhebungen im Krieg und Frieden* (Dresden 1922).

Ladurie, E. Le Roy, 'L'Aménorrhée de famine (XVIIe-XXe siècles)', *Annales*, vol. 24 (1969).

Lakatos, I., *The Methodology of Scientific Research Programmes* (Cambridge 1978).

Lambi, I. N., *The Navy and German Power Politics, 1862–1914* (1984).

Langworthy, C. F., *Food Customs and Diet in American Homes*, USDA Office of Experimental Stations, Circular 110 (Washington DC 1911).

Larmour, R., *Canada's Opportunity* (Toronto 1907).

Larson, H. M., *The Wheat Market and the Farmer in Minnesota, 1858–1900* (New York 1926).

Lau, K., 'Die Heeresverpflegung', in Schwarte, M. (ed.), *Der grosse Krieg, 1914–1918* (Leipzig 1923), vol. 9, pt. 2.

Laut, A., *The Canadian Commonwealth* (Indianapolis 1915).

Lawrence, D. H., 'You Touched Me', *The Complete Short Stories of D. H. Lawrence*, vol. 2 (1955).

Lawson, W. R., *British Railways: A Financial and Commercial Survey* (New York 1914).

Lazonick, W., 'Industrial Organization and Technological Change: The Decline of the British Cotton Industry', *Business History Review*, vol. 57 (1983).

Lea, Homer, *The Valor of Ignorance* (New York 1909).

Leacy, F. H. (ed.), *Historical Statistics of Canada* (2nd edn. Ottawa 1983).

Lee, J., 'Administrators and Agriculture: Aspects of German Agricultural Policy in the First World War', in Winter, J. M. (ed.), *War and Economic Development* (Cambridge 1975).

Lee, Jenny, and Fahey, C., 'A Boom for Whom? Some Developments in the Australian Labour Market, 1870–91', *Labour History*, no. 50 (May 1981).

Leed, E. J., *No Man's Land: Combat and Identity in World War I* (Cambridge 1979).

Lees-Milne, J., *The Enigmatic Edwardian: The Life of Reginald, 2nd Viscount Esher* (1986).

Lenin, V. I., *Imperialism, the Highest Stage of Capitalism* (1917), English trans. in *Selected Works in Three Volumes* (Moscow 1975), vol. 1.

Levy, H., *Large and Small Holdings: A Study of English Agricultural Economics* (1911).

—— *Die neue Kontinentalsperre. Ist Grossbritannien wirtschaftlich bedroht?* (Berlin 1915).

Lewis, W. A., *Growth and Fluctuations, 1870–1913* (1978).

Leyen, R. von, 'Die englische Hungerblockade in ihren Wirkungen auf die Kriminalität und Verwahrlesung der Jugendlichen', in Rubmann, M. (ed.), *Hunger! Wirkungen moderner Kriegsmethoden* (Berlin 1919).

Liberal Land Enquiry, *The Land*, 1. Rural (1913).

Liebknecht, K., *Militarism and Anti-Militarism* (1906, English trans. Glasgow 1917).

Loewy, A., 'Über Kriegskost', *Deutsche medizinische Wochenschrift*, vol. 43 (8 Feb. and 15 Feb. 1917).

—— 'Unternährung', *Realencyklopädie der gesamten Heilkunde*, ed. Eulenburg, A., *Ergebnisse der gesamten Medizin*, vol. 2 (Berlin and Vienna 1922).

Loreburn, Lord, *Capture at Sea* (1913).

Luckau, A., *The German Delegation at the Paris Peace Conference* (New York 1941).

Ludendorff, E. von, *My War Memories, 1914–1918* (2nd edn. 1920).

—— *The General Staff and its Problems* (New York n.d. ?1920).

Lutz, R. H. (ed.), *Documents of the German Revolution: Fall of the German Empire, 1914–1918* (Stanford 1932).

Macarthy, P. G., 'Wages in Australia, 1891 to 1914', *Australian Economic History Review*, vol. 10 (1970).

MacDougall, J., *Rural Life in Canada* (Toronto 1913).

Mackay, R. F., *Fisher of Kilverstone* (Oxford 1973).

Mackinder, H. J., *Britain and the British Seas* (Oxford 1906).

Mackintosh, J. P., 'The Role of the Committee of Imperial Defence before 1914', *English Historical Review*, vol. 77 (1962).

Mackintosh, W. A., *The Economic Background of Dominion—Provincial Relations* (Toronto 1964).

Mahan, A. T., *The Influence of Sea Power upon History, 1660–1783* (1890, Sagamore Press edn. New York 1957).

—— *The Problem of Asia and its Effect upon International Policies* (1900).

—— *Some Neglected Aspects of War* (1907).

—— and Beresford, Lord Charles, 'Possibilities of an Anglo-American Reunion', *North American Review*, vol. 159 (1894).

Mai, G., *Kriegswirtschaft und Arbeiterbewegung in Württemberg, 1914–1918* (Stuttgart 1983).

Malich, U., 'Zur Entwicklung des Reallohns im ersten Weltkrieg', *Jahrbuch für Wirtschaftsgeschichte* (1980).

Mallaby, G., 'Maurice Hankey', *The Dictionary of National Biography 1961–1970* (Oxford 1981).

Mallet, B., *British Budgets, 1887–88 to 1912–13* (1913).

Mann, T., *Tom Mann's Memoirs* (1923, Fitzroy edn. 1967).

Marder, A. J., *British Naval Policy, 1880–1905: The Anatomy of British Sea-power* (1940).

—— *From The Dreadnought to Scapa Flow* (1961–70), 5 vols.

Markham, V., *Return Passage* (1953).

Markus, A., *Fear and Hatred: Purifying Australia and California, 1850–1901* (Sydney 1979).

—— and Ricklefs, M. C. (eds.), *Surrender Australia? Essays in the Study and Uses of History. Geoffrey Blainey and Asian Immigration* (Sydney 1985).

Marr, W. L., and Paterson, D. G., *Canada: An Economic History* (Toronto 1980).

Marston, R. B., *War, Famine and our Food Supply* (1897).

Martins, S. W., *A Great Estate at Work* (Cambridge 1980).

Marx, K., *Capital* (Moscow 1954).

Matthews, A. H. H., *Fifty Years of Agricultural Politics, being the History of the Central Chamber of Agriculture* (1915).

Matthews, R. C. O., Feinstein, C. H., and Odling-Smee, J. C., *British Economic Growth, 1856–1973* (Oxford 1982).

Maxse, J. L., *"Germany on the Brain" or, The Obsession of "A Crank": Gleanings from the National Review, 1899–1914* (1915).

May, R. E., *Die deutsche Volksernährung. Gemessen am tatsächlichen Konsum grosser Konsumentenkreise*, offprint from *Schmollers Jahrbücher*, vol. 41, nos. 1 and 2 (Munich and Leipzig 1917).

Mayer, A. J., *Politics and Diplomacy of Peacemaking* (1967).

—— *The Persistence of the Old Regime: Europe to the Great War* (1981).

McCloskey, D., 'Magnanimous Albion: Free Trade and British National Income, 1841–1881', in his *Enterprise and Trade in Victorian Britain* (1981).

McDermott, J., 'Sir Francis Oppenheimer: "Stranger Within" the Foreign Office', *History*, vol. 66 (June 1981).

McQueen, H., *A New Brittania* (rev. edn. 1976, 3rd edn. Ringwood, Victoria 1986).

McQuillan, D. A., 'The Mobility of Immigrants and Americans: A Comparison of Farmers on the Kansas Frontier', *Agricultural History*, vol. 53 (1979).

Meacham, S., *A Life Apart: The English Working Class, 1890–1914* (1977).

Meaney, N., *The Search for Security in the Pacific, 1901–14* (Sydney 1976).

Meerwarth, R., Günther, A., and Zimmerman,W., *Die Einwirkung des Krieges auf Bevölkerungsbewegung, Einkommen und Lebenshaltung in Deutschland* (Stuttgart 1932).

Meitzen, A., and Grossmann, F., *Der Boden und die landwirtschaftlichen Verhältnisse des preussischen Staates* (Berlin 1906), vol. 6.

Mendel, A., 'The Debate between Prussian Junkerdom and the Forces of Urban Industry, 1897–1902', *Jahrbuch des Instituts für deutsche Geschichte*, vol. 4 (1975).

Merton, R., *Erinnernswertes aus meinem Leben* (Frankfurt 1955).

Millar, A., *Wheat and its Products* (1916).

Mitchell, B. R., *European Historical Statistics, 1750–1970* (abridged edn. 1978).

—— and Deane, P., *Abstract of British Historical Statistics* (Cambridge 1971).

Mitchell, E., *In Western Canada before the War* (1915).

Mock, W., *Imperiale Herrschaft und nationales Interesse: "Constructive Imperialism" oder Freihandel in Grossbritannien vor dem Ersten Weltkrieg* (Stuttgart 1982).

Moeller, R. G., 'Dimensions of Social Conflict in the Great War: The View from the German Countryside', *Central European History*, vol. 14 (1981).

Moltke, O. von, 'Noch ein Wort über Krieg und Volksernährung', *Preussische Jahrbücher*, vol. 155 (1914).

Moon, P. T., *Imperialism and World Politics* (New York 1927).

More, C., *Skill and the English Working Class, 1870–1914* (1980).

Morgan, D. H., *Harvesters and Harvesting, 1840–1900* (1982).

Morison, E. E., *Admiral Sims and the Modern American Navy* (Boston 1942).

Morison, S. E. (ed.), *The Letters of Theodore Roosevelt* (Cambridge, Mass. 1952), vol. 6.

Morley, J., *Memorandum on Resignation* (1914, publ. 1928).

Morris, A. J. A., *The Scaremongers: The Advocacy of War and Rearmament, 1896–1914* (1984).

Mosely Industrial Commission to the United States of America, Oct.-Dec. 1902, *Reports of the Delegates* (1903).

Moses, J. A., *The Politics of Illusion: The Fischer Controversy in German Historiography* (1975).

Müller, A., *The Kaiser and his Court*, ed. Görlitz, W. (1961).

Murray, S. L., *Our Food Supply in Time of War* (1900).

—— *The Electors of Great Britain and the Defence of the Country* (1900).

—— 'Our Food Supply in Time of War and Imperial Defence', *Journal of the Royal United Services Institution*, vol. 45 (1901).

—— *The Future Peace of the Anglo-Saxons: Addressed to the Working Men and their Representatives* (1905).

—— 'The Internal Condition of Great Britain during a Great War', *Journal of the Royal United Services Institution*, vol. 57 (1913).

Musgrove, F., 'Middle-class Education and Employment in the Nineteenth Century', *Economic History Review*, vol. 12 (1959).

Mutch, A., Mechanization of the Harvest in South-west Lancashire, 1850–1914', *Agricultural History Review*, vol. 29 (1981).

Mutch, A., 'The Mechanization of the Harvest in South-west Lancashire, 1850–1914', *Agricultural History Review*, vol. 29 (1981).

—— 'Farmers' Organizations and Agricultural Depression in Lancashire, 1890–1900', *Agricultural History Review*, vol. 31 (1983).

Naylor, J. F., *A Man and an Institution: Sir Maurice Hankey, the Cabinet Secretariat and the Custody of Cabinet Secrecy* (Cambridge 1984).

Naylor, R. T., 'The Canadian State, the Accumulation of Capital and the Great War', *Journal of Canadian Studies*, vol. 16 (1981).

Nisbett, R., and Ross, L., *Human Inference: Strategies and Shortcomings of Social Judgement* (Englewood Cliffs, NJ 1980).

Norton, Trist & Gilbert, 'A Century of Land Values', *Journal of the Royal Statistical Society*, vol. 54 (1891).

Notestein, W., *The Future Population of Europe and the Soviet Union* (Geneva 1944).

O'Grada, C., 'The Beginnings of the Irish Creamery System, 1880–1914', *Economic History Review*, vol. 30 (1977).

—— 'The Landlord and Agricultural Transformation, 1870–1900: A Comment on Richard Perren's Hypothesis', *Agricultural History Review*, vol. 27 (1979).

—— 'Agricultural Decline, 1860–1914' in Floud, R., and McCloskey, D. (eds.), *The Economic History of Britain since 1700* (Cambridge 1981), vol. 2.

Obelkevich, J., *Religion and Rural Society: South Lindsey, 1825–1875* (Oxford 1976).

Oddy, D. J., 'A Nutritional Analysis of Historical Evidence: The Working-Class Diet, 1880–1914', in Oddy, D., and Miller, D. (eds.), *The Making of the Modern British Diet* (1976).

Offer, A., 'Ricardo's Paradox and the Movement of Rents in Britain, c.1870–1910', *Economic History Review*, vol. 30 (1980).

—— *Property and Politics, 1870–1914* (Cambridge 1981).

—— 'Using the Past in Britain: Retrospect and Prospect', *The Public Historian*, vol. 6 (1984).

Ojala, E. M., *Agriculture and Economic Progress* (Oxford 1952).

Olmstead, V., 'Annual Report of the Bureau of Statistics for the Fiscal Year 1909–10', USDA *Crop Reporter* (Jan. 1911).

Olney, R. J., *Lincolnshire Politics, 1832–1885* (Oxford 1973).

Olson, M., Jr., *The Economics of the Wartime Shortage* (Durham, North Carolina 1963).

—— 'The United Kingdom and the World Market in Wheat and Other Primary Products, 1870–1914', *Explorations in Economic History*, vol. 11 (1974).

—— and Harris, C. C., Jr., 'Free Trade in "Corn": A Statistical Study of the Prices and Production of Wheat in Great Britain from 1873 to 1914', *Quarterly Journal of Economics*, vol. 73 (1959).

d'Ombrain, N., *War Machinery and High Policy* (1973).

Oppenheimer, F., *Stranger Within: Autobiographical Pages* (1960).

Orwin, C. S., 'III. A Specialist in Arable Farming', *Progress in English Farming Systems* (Oxford 1930).

—— Whetham, E., *History of British Agriculture, 1846–1914* (1964).

Parker, W. F., *Mackinder: Geography as Statecraft* (Oxford 1982).

Parker, W. N., 'Productivity Growth in American Grain Farming: An Analysis of its Nineteenth Century Sources' in Fogel, R. W., and Engerman, S. L. (eds.), *The Reinterpretation of American Economic History* (New York 1971).

Parkinson, R., *Tormented Warrior: Ludendorff and the Supreme Command* (1978).

Parry, C., 'Foreign Policy and International Law', in Hinsely, F. H. (ed.), *British Foreign Policy under Sir Edward Grey* (Cambridge 1977).

Partridge, E. A., *A War on Poverty* (Winnipeg 1925).

Paterson, D. G., *British Direct Investment in Canada, 1890–1914* (Toronto 1976).

Patterson, G. D., *The Tariff in the Australian Colonies, 1856–1900* (Melbourne 1968).

Paul, R. W., 'The Wheat Trade between California and the United Kingdom', *Mississippi Valley Historical Review*, vol. 45 (1958–9).

Pavlovsky, G., *Agricultural Russia on the Eve of the Revolution* (1930).

Pearson, C. H., *National Life and Character: A Forecast* (2nd edn. 1894).

Pechstein, M., *Errinerungen* (Wiesbaden 1960).

Peebles, J. M., *Death Defeated or the Psychic Secret of How to Keep Young* (Battle Creek, Michigan 1908).

Perkin, H., 'Middle-Class and Employment in the Nineteenth Century: A Critical Note', *Economic History Review*, vol. 14 (1961).

Perkins, J. A., 'The Agricultural Revolution in Germany, 1850–1914', *Journal of European Economic History*, vol. 10 (1981).

Perren, R., 'The Landlord and Agricultural Transformation 1870–1900', in Perry, P. J. (ed.), *British Agriculture, 1875–1914* (1973).

Peterson, R. F., *Wheat: Botany, Cultivation and Utilization* (1965).

Phelps Brown, E. H., and Browne, M. H., *A Century of Pay* (1968).

Phillips, J., *A Man's Country? The Image of the Pakeha Male: A History* (Auckland 1987).

Piva, M. J., *The Condition of the Working Class in Toronto, 1900–1921* (Ottawa 1979).

Playne, C. E., *The Neuroses of Nations* (New York 1925).

Plunkett, H., *The Rural Life Problem in the United States* (New York 1912).

Pomfret, R., 'The Staple Theory as an Approach to Canadian and Australian Economic Development', *Australian Economic History Review*, vol. 21 (1981).

Porritt, E., *The Revolt in Canada against the New Feudalism* (1911).

Prais, S. J., *Productivity and Industrial Structure* (Cambridge 1981).

Pratt, E. A., *The Transition in Agriculture* (1906).

Preston, R. A., *Canada and "Imperial Defense": A Study of the Origins of the British Commonwealth's Defense Organization, 1867–1919* (Durham, NC 1967).

Price, C. A., *The Great White Walls Are Built: Restrictive Immigration to North America and Australasia, 1836–1888* (Canberra 1974).

Pyke, E. L., *Desperate Germany* (1918).

Ranft, B., 'The Protection of British Seaborne Trade and the Development of Systematic Planning for War, 1860–1906', in Ranft, B. (ed.), *Technical Change and British Naval Policy, 1860–1939* (1977).

—— 'Restraints on War at Sea before 1945', in Howard, M. (ed.), *Restraints on War* (Oxford 1979).

—— 'The Royal Navy and the Mercantile Marine, 1860–1914: Partners in Ignorance', in Palmer, S., and Williams, G. (eds.), *Charted and Uncharted Waters* (1981).

Rasmussen, L., *et al.* (eds.), *A Harvest Yet to Reap: A History of Prairie Women* (Toronto 1976).

Rathbone, H. R., 'The Wheat Supplies of the British Isles', in Newton, A. P. (ed.), *The Staple Trades of the Empire* (1917).

Rausser, G. C., 'New Conceptual Developments and Measurements for Modeling the US Agricultural Sector', in Rausser, G. C. (ed.), *New Directions in Econometric Modeling and Forecasting in US Agriculture* (New York 1982).

Read, D. (ed.), *The Great War and Canadian Society: An Oral History* (Toronto 1978).

Reid, R. T. [later Lord Loreburn], 'Capture of Private Property at Sea', *The Times*, 14 Oct. 1905.

Rew, R. H., 'The Nation's Food Supply', *Journal of the Royal Statistical Society*, vol. 76, pt. 1 (Dec. 1912).

—— *Food Supplies in Peace and War* (1920).

Rhee, H. A., *The Rent of Agricultural Land in England and Wales, 1870–1946* (Oxford 1949).

Richardson, L. F., *Statistics of Deadly Quarrels* (1960).

Richter, L., *Family Life in Germany under the Blockade* (1919).

"A Rifleman", *The Struggle for Bread* (1913).

Ritter, G., *The Sword and the Scepter* (Coral Gables, Florida 1970, 1972), vols. 2, 3.

Robertson, H., *Salt of the Earth* (Toronto 1974).

Robson, L. L., *The First A.I.F.: A Study of its Recruitment, 1914–1918* (Melbourne 1970).

—— 'The Origin and Character of the First A.I.F., 1914–18: Some Statistical Evidence', *Historical Studies*, vol. 15 (1975).

Roesle, E. E., 'Die Geburts- und Sterblichkeitsverhältnisse', in Bumm, F. (ed.), *Deutschlands Gesundheitsverhältnisse unter dem Einfluss der Weltkrieges* (Stuttgart 1928).

Roesler, K., *Die Finanzpolitik des Deutschen Reiches im Ersten Weltkrieg* (Berlin 1977).

Röhl, J., 'Admiral von Müller and the Approach of War, 1911–1914', *Historical Journal*, vol. 12 (1969).

Rolfes, M., 'Landwirtschaft, 1850–1914', in Aubin, H., and Zorn, W. (eds.), *Handbuch der deutschen Wirtschafts- und Sozialgeschichte*, vol. 2 (Stuttgart 1976).

Rosenberg, N., *Inside the Black Box* (Cambridge 1982).

Roskill, S., *Hankey: Man of Secrets* (1974), vol. 1.

Rothbard, M. N., 'Hoover's 1919 Food Diplomacy in Retrospect', in Gelfand, L. E. (ed.), *Herbert Hoover: The Great War and its Aftermath, 1914–23* (Iowa City, Iowa 1979).

Rothstein, M., 'Frank Norris and Popular Perceptions of the Market', *Agricultural History*, vol. 56 (1982).

Rowntree, B. S., *Poverty. A Study of Town Life* (4th edn. 1902).

—— *Land and Labour: Lessons from Belgium* (1910).

—— and Kendall, M., *How the Labourer Lives: A Study of the Rural Labour Problem* (1913, repr. 1918).

Rubinow, I. M., *Russia's Wheat Surplus: The Conditions under which it is Produced*, USDA Bureau of Statistics, Bulletin no. 42 (Washington DC 1906).

Rubinstein, W. D., 'British Radicalism and the "Dark Side" of Populism', in his *Élites and the Wealthy in Modern British History* (Brighton 1987).

Rubmann, M., (ed.), *Hunger! Wirkungen moderner Kriegsmethoden* (Berlin 1919).

Rubner, M., *Volksernährungsfragen* (Leipzig 1908).

—— *Wandlungen in der Volksernährung* (Leipzig 1913).

—— 'Über Moderne Ernährungsreformen', *Archiv für Hygiene*, vol. 81 (1913).

—— 'Über Nährwert einiger wichtiger Gemüsearten und deren Preiswert', offprint from *Berliner Klinische Wochenschrift*, no. 15 (Berlin 1916).

—— 'Das Ernährungswesen im Allgemeinen', in Bumm, F. (ed.), *Deutschlands Gesundheitsverhältnisse unter dem Einfluss des Weltkrieges* (Stuttgart 1928).

—— 'Der Gesundheitszustand im Allgemeinen', in Bumm (ed.), *Gesundheitsverhältnisse*.

—— *Deutschlands Volksernährung. Zeitgemässe Betrachtungen* (Berlin 1930).

Rudin, H., *Armistice 1918* (New Haven 1944).

Russell, B., *Justice in War-time* (Chicago 1916).

Russell, E. J., *A History of Agricultural Science in Great Britain* (1966).

Salter, J. A., *Allied Shipping Control: An Experiment in International Administration* (Oxford 1921).

Saul, S. B., 'The American Impact upon British Industry', *Business History*, vol. 3 (1960).

Schiff, V., *The Germans at Versailles, 1919* (1930).

Schlieffen, A. von, 'Der Krieg in der Gegenwart', *Deutsche Revue*, vol. 34 (1909).

Schmidt, L. B., 'The Westward Movement of Wheat', in Schmidt, L. B., and Ross, E. D. (eds.), *Readings in the Economic History of American Agriculture* (New York 1925).

Schmoller, G., Sering M., and Wagner A. (eds.), *Handels- und Machtpolitik* (Stuttgart 1900).

Schulze, K., and Otto, W., 'Das Militärveterinärwesen', in Schwarte, M. (ed.), *Der grosse Krieg, 1914–1918* (Leipzig 1923), vol. 9, pt. 2.

Schumacher, M., *Land und Politik* (Düsseldorf 1978).

Schumpeter, J., *Imperialism and Social Classes* (New York 1951).

Schurman, D. M., *Julian S. Corbett, 1854–1922* (1981).

Schwartz, R. W., *John Harvey Kellogg, M. D.* (Nashville, Tenessee 1970).

Schwarz, K.-D., *Weltkrieg und Revolution in Nürnberg* (Stuttgart 1971).

Scitovsky, T., *The Joyless Economy* (New York 1976).

Scobie, J. R., *Revolution on the Pampas: A Social History of Argentine Wheat, 1860–1910* (Austin, Texas 1964).

Scott, E., *Australia during the War* (Official History of Australia in the War of 1914–1918, vol. 11; Sydney 1936).

Scott, J. B., (ed.), *The Declaration of London, February 26, 1909* (New York 1919).

Scott, P., *Fifty Years in the Royal Navy* (1919).

Searle, G., 'The "Revolt from the Right" in Edwardian Britain', in Kennedy, P., and Nicholls, A. (eds.), *Nationalist and Racialist Movements in Britain and Germany before 1914* (1981).

Sellheim, H., 'Frauenkrankheiten und Geburtshilfe', in Bumm, F. (ed.), *Deutschlands Gesundheitsverhältnisse unter dem Einfluss des Weltkrieges* (Stuttgart 1928).

Semmel, B., *Liberalism and Naval Strategy: Ideology, Interest, and Sea Power during the Pax Britannica* (Boston 1986).

Sen, A., *On Ethics and Economics* (Oxford 1987).

[Shadwell, A.], 'Labour and Industry, VI. Prospects and the Part of the Employers', *The Times*, 28 Feb. 1913.

Shanin, T., *The Awkward Class* (Oxford 1972).

Shannon, F. A., *The Farmer's Last Frontier: Agriculture, 1860–1897* (New York 1945).

Sharp, P. F., *The Agrarian Revolt in Western Canada: A Survey Showing American Parallels* (Minneapolis 1948).

Sharpe, C. A., 'Enlistment in the Canadian Expeditionary Force, 1914–1918: A Regional Analysis', *Journal of Canadian Studies*, vol.18 (1983–4).

Shergold, R. R., *Working-class Life: The "American Standard" in Comparative Perspective, 1899–1913* (Pittsburgh 1982).

Simon, H. A., 'Rational Decision Making in Business Organizations', in his *Models of Bounded Rationality* (Cambridge, Mass. 1982), vol. 2.

Simplicissimus (Munich).

Skalweit, A., 'The Maintenance of the Agricultural Labour Supply during the War', *International Review of Agricultural Economics*, vol. 13 (1922).

Skalweit, E., *Die deutsche Kriegsernährungswirtschaft* (Stuttgart 1927).

Skelton, O. D., *Life and Letters of Sir Wilfrid Laurier* (Toronto 1921; abridged edn. 1965), vol. 2.

Smith, Adam, *An Inquiry into the Nature and Causes of the Wealth of Nations*, ed. Cannan, E. (New York 1937).

—— *A Theory of Moral Sentiments*, ed. Raphael, D. D., and Macfie, A. L. (Oxford 1976).

Smith, E. L., *Go East for a Farm: A Study of Rural Migration* (Oxford 1932).

Smith, F. B., 'Health', in Benson, J. (ed.), *The Working Class in England 1875–1914* (1985).

Smith, R. E., *Wheat Fields and Markets of the World* (St Louis 1908).

Solberg, C. E., 'Land Tenure and Land Settlement: Policy and Patterns in the Canadian Prairies and the Argentine Pampas, 1880–1930', in Platt, D. C. M., and di Tella, G. (eds.), *Argentina, Australia and Canada: Studies in Comparative Development, 1870–1965* (1985).

Spindler, A., *Der Handelskrieg mit U-Booten* (Berlin 1932), vol. 1.

—— *Wie es zu dem Entschluss zum uneingeschränkten U-Boots-Krieg 1917 gekommen ist* (Göttingen 1960).

Stacey, C. P., *Canada and the Age of Conflict* (Toronto 1977).

Staley, E., *War and the Private Investor* (Chicago 1935).

Stamp, J., *British Incomes and Property* (1916).

Starling, E. H., 'The Significance of Fats in the Diet', *British Medical Journal* (3 Aug. 1918).

—— 'The Food Supply of Germany during the War', *Journal of the Royal Statistical Society*, vol. 83 (1920).

The Starving of Germany, papers read at an Extraordinary Meeting of United Medical Societies held at Headquarters of Berlin Medical Society, 18 Dec. 1918 (Berlin 1919).

Stead, W. T., 'Character Sketch—Admiral Fisher', *Review of Reviews* (Feb. 1910).

Stearns, P. N., *Lives of Labour: Work in a Maturing Industrial Society* (1975).

Stegemann, B., *Die Deutsche Marinepolitik, 1916–1918* (Berlin 1970).

Stein, H. von, *Erlebnisse und Betrachtungen aus der Zeit des Weltkrieges* (Leipzig 1919).

Steinberg, J., *Yesterday's Deterrent* (1965).

—— 'The Copenhagen Complex', *Journal of Contemporary History*, vol. 1 (1966).

Stephens, H., *Book of the Farm* (2nd edn., Edinburgh 1851).

Stewart, B., *No English Need Apply, or Canada as a Field for the Emigrant* (1909).

Stovin, C., *Journals of a Methodist Farmer*, ed. Stovin, J. (1982).

Street, A. G., *Farmer's Glory* (1932).

Stromberg, R. N., *Redemption by War: The Intellectuals and 1914* (Lawrence, Kansas 1982).

Strutt, E. G., 'Presidential Address', *Transactions of the Surveyors' Institution*, vol. 45 (1912–13).

Stumpf, R., *The Private War of Richard Stumpf*, ed. Horn, D. (1969).

Sturmey, S. G., *British Shipping and World Competition* (1962).

Sugimoto, H. N., 'The Vancouver Riots of 1907: A Canadian Episode', in Conroy, H., and Myakawa, T. S. (eds.), *East Across the Pacific* (Santa Barbara, California 1972).

Summers, A., 'The Character of Edwardian Nationalism: Three Popular Leagues', in Kennedy, P., and Nicholls, A. (eds.), *Nationalist and Racialist Movements in Britain and Germany before 1914* (1981).

Surface, F. M., *American Pork Production in the World War* (New York 1926).

—— *The Grain Trade during the World War* (New York 1928).

—— and Bland, R. L., *American Food in the World War and Reconstruction Period* (Stanford 1931).

Sydenham of Combe, Lord (Clarke, G. S.), *My Working Life* (1927).

Sykes, A., *Tariff Reform in British Politics, 1903–1913* (Oxford 1979).

Tanner, T. W., *Compulsory Citizen Soldiers* (? Sydney 1980).

Taussig, F. W. (ed.), *Selected Readings in International Trade and Tariff Problems* (Boston 1921).

Taylor, A. E., and Kellogg, V. L., *German Food and Trade Conditions*, American Relief Administration, Bulletin no. 1 (New York 1919).

Taylor, A. J. P., *The Struggle for Mastery in Europe, 1848–1918* (Oxford 1971).

Taylor, F. W. D., 'United Kingdom: Numbers in Agriculture', *The Farm Economist*, vol. 8 (1955).

Terraine, J., *Douglas Haig, The Educated Soldier* (1963).

—— *The Western Front, 1914–1918* (1970).

Teuteberg, H. J., and Wiegelmann, G., *Der Wandel der Nahrungsgewohnheiten unter dem Einfluss der Industrialisierung* (Göttingen 1972).

Thomas, B., *Migration and Economic Growth* (2nd edn. Cambridge 1973).

Thompson, F. M. L., *English Landed Society in the Nineteenth Century* (1963).

—— 'The Second Agricultural Revolution, 1815–1880', *Economic History Review*, vol. 21 (1968).

Thompson, J. J., *The Harvests of War: The Prairie West, 1914–1918* (Toronto 1978).

Thompson, R. J., 'An Inquiry into the Rent of Agricultural Land in England and Wales during the Nineteenth Century', *Journal of the Royal Statistical Society*, vol. 70 (1907).

Timlin, M. F., 'Canada's Immigration Policy, 1896–1910', *Canadian Journal of Economics and Political Science*, vol. 26 (1960).

Tirpitz, A. von, *My Memoirs* (1919), 2 vols.

Tobin, E. H., 'War and the Working Class: The Case of Düsseldorf, 1914–1918', *Central European History*, vol. 28 (1985).

Trachtenberg, M., 'Reparations at the Paris Peace Conference', *Journal of Modern History*, vol. 51 (1979).

—— *Reparation in World Politics: France and European Economic Diplomacy, 1916–1923* (New York 1980).

Tracy, M., *Agriculture in Western Europe: Crisis and Adaptation since 1880* (2nd edn. 1982).

Travers, T., *The Killing Ground: The British Army, the Western Front and the Emergence of Modern Warfare, 1900–1918* (1987).

Tressell, R., *The Ragged-trousered Philanthropists* (abridged edn. 1915, complete edn. 1955).

Triebel, A., 'Variations in Patterns of Consumption in Germany in the Period of the First World War', in Wall, R., and Winter, J. M. (eds.), *The Upheaval of War* (forthcoming).

Tsokhas, K., 'W. M. Hughes, The Imperial Wool Purchase and the Pastoral Lobby, 1914–1920', *A.N.U. Working Papers in Economic History*, no. 106 (1988).

Tuchman, B., *The March of Folly* (1984).

Tucker, G. N., *The Naval Service of Canada* (Ottawa 1952), vol. 1.

Turner, I., *Room for Manœuvre* (Melbourne 1982).

Twopeny, R. E. N., *Town Life in Australia* (1883).

Ullrich, V., *Kriegsalltag. Hamburg im ersten Weltkrieg* (Cologne 1982).

Urquhart, M. C., 'New Estimates of Gross National Product, Canada, 1870–1926: Some Implications for Canadian Development', in Engerman, S. L., and Gallman, R. E. (eds.), *Long-term Factors in American Economic Growth* (Chicago 1986).

Van Evera, S., 'The Cult of the Offensive and the Origins of the First World War', *International Security*, vol. 9 (1984).

Vickery, H. B., 'Biographical Memoir of Russell Henry Chittenden, 1856–1943', *National Academy of Science Biographical Memoirs*, vol. 24, 2nd memoir (Washington 1944).

Vincent, C. P., *The Politics of Hunger: The Allied Blockade of Germany, 1915–1919* (Athens, Ohio 1985).

Viner, J., 'Power versus Plenty as Objectives of Foreign Policy in the Seventeenth and Eighteenth Centuries', in his *The Long View and the Short* (Glencoe, Illinois 1958).

Voelcker, J. A., 'The Woburn Experimental Farm and its Work (1876–1921)', *Journal of the Royal Society of Agriculture*, vol. 84 (1923).

Voit, C. von, *Physiologie des allgemeinen Stoffwechsels und der Ernährung* (L. Herman (ed.), Handbuch der Physiologie, vol. 6; Leipzig 1881).

Wakefield, E. G., *A View of the Art of Colonization* (1849).

Wall, J. F., *The World of Andrew Carnegie* (New York 1970).

Walzer, M., *Just and Unjust Wars: A Moral Argument with Historical Illustrations* (1978).

Ward, P., *White Canada Forever* (Montreal 1978).

Ward, R., *The Australian Legend* (Melbourne 1958).

Ward, W. P., *White Canada Forever: Popular Attitudes and Public Policy toward Orientals in British Columbia* (Montreal 1978).

Watkins, M. H., 'The Staple Theory Revisited', *Journal of Canadian Studies*, vol. 12, no. 5 (winter 1977).

Watson, W. F., *Machines and Men: An Autobiography of an Itinerant Mechanic* (1935).

Webb, S. B., 'Agricultural Protection in Wilhelmian Germany: Forging an Empire with Pork and Rye', *Journal of Economic History*, vol. 42 (June 1982).

Weir, G. R., 'Tirpitz, Technology and Building U-Boats, 1897–1916', *International History Review*, vol. 6 (May 1984).

Welker, G., *Die Münchener Erhebung über den Lebensmittelverbrauch im Februar 1915* (Munich, Berlin and Leipzig 1915).

Westergaard, H. L., *Economic Development in Denmark before and during the World War* (1922).

Westlake, J., 'Note on Belligerent Rights at Sea', in Latifi, A., *Effects of War on Property* (1909).

White, R., *Inventing Australia* (Sydney 1981).

Wilding, M., 'Introduction' to 'John Miller' (William Lane), *The Workingman's Paradise: An Australian Labour Novel* (repr. Sydney 1980).

Williams, A., *Life in a Railway Factory* (1915).

Williams, W. A., *The Roots of the Modern American Empire* (New York 1969).

Williamson, J. G., 'Greasing the Wheels of Spluttering Export Engines: Midwestern Grains and American Growth', *Explorations in Economic History*, vol. 17 (July 1980).

Williamson, S. R., *The Politics of Grand Strategy: Britain and France Prepare for War, 1904–1914* (Cambridge, Mass. 1969).

Willis, E. F., 'Herbert Hoover and the Blockade of Germany, 1918–1919', in Cox, F. J., *et al.* (eds.), *Studies in Modern European History in Honor of Franklin Charles Palm* (New York 1956).

Wilson, T., *The Myriad Faces of War: Britain and the Great War, 1914–1918* (1986).

Wilson, W., *A History of the American People*, vol. 5 (New York 1902).

Winter, D., *The First of the Few: Fighter Pilots of the First World War* (1982).

Winter, J. M., *Socialism and the Challenge of War* (1974).

—— 'Britain's "Lost Generation" of the First World War', *Population Studies*, vol. 31 (1977).

—— *The Great War and the British People* (1985).

Witt, P.-C., 'Reichsfinanzen und Rüstungspolitik, 1898–1914', in Schottelius, H., and Deist, W. (eds.), *Marine und Marinepolitik im kaiserlichen Deutschland, 1871–1914* (Düsseldorf 1972).

Wood, J. C., *British Economists and the Empire* (1983).

Wood, L. A., *A History of the Farmers' Movement in Canada* (Toronto 1924).

Woodsworth, J. S., *Strangers within our Gates or Coming Canadians* (Toronto 1909, new edn. 1972).

Woodward, E. L., *Great Britain and the German Navy* (Oxford 1935).

Woytinsky, W. S. and E. S., *World Commerce and Governments: Trends and Outlook* (New York 1955).

Wright, C. P., and Davis, J. S., 'India as a Producer and Exporter of Wheat', *Wheat Studies*, vol. 3 (July 1927).

Wright, G., 'Comment', in Engerman, S. L., and Gallman, R. E. (eds.), *Long-term Factors in American Economic Growth* (Chicago 1986).

Wright, Q., *A Study of War* (Chicago 1942), 2 vols.

Yates, P. L., *Forty Years of Foreign Trade* (1959).

Zechlin, E., 'Cabinet versus Economic Warfare in Germany: Policy and Strategy during the Early Months of the First World War', in Koch, H. W. (ed.), *The Origins of the First World War: Great Power Rivalry and German War Aims* (2nd edn. 1984).

Zilch, R., 'Zur wirtschaftlichen Vorbereitung des deutschen Imperialismus auf den ersten Weltkrieg', *Zeitschrift für Geschichtswissenschaft*, vol. 24 (1976).

Zimmermann, W., 'Die Veränderungen der Einkommens- und Lebensverhältnisse der deutschen Arbeiter durch den Krieg', in Meerwarth, R., *et al.*, *Einwirkung*.

INDEX